THE CAMBRIDGE COMPANION TO
GALEN

Galen of Pergamum (AD 129–c.216) was the most influential doctor of later antiquity, whose work was to influence medical theory and practice for more than 1,500 years. He was a prolific writer on anatomy, physiology, diagnosis and prognosis, pulse-doctrine, pharmacology, therapeutics and the theory of medicine; but he also wrote extensively on philosophical topics, making original contributions to logic and the philosophy of science, and outlining a scientific epistemology which married a deep respect for empirical adequacy with a commitment to rigorous rational exposition and demonstration. He was also a vigorous polemicist, deeply involved in the doctrinal disputes among the medical schools of his day. This volume offers an introduction to and overview of Galen's achievement in all these fields, while seeking also to evaluate that achievement in the light of the advances made in Galen scholarship over the past thirty years.

R. J. HANKINSON is Professor of Philosophy at the University of Texas at Austin. He is editor of *Galen: On Antecedent Causes* (1998, 2004) in the Cambridge Classical Texts and Commentaries series.

OTHER VOLUMES IN THE SERIES OF CAMBRIDGE COMPANIONS

ABELARD *Edited by* JEFFREY E. BROWER *and* KEVIN
GUILFOY

ADORNO *Edited by* THOMAS HUHN

ANSELM *Edited by* BRIAN DAVIES *and* BRIAN LEFTOW

AQUINAS *Edited by* NORMAN KRETZMANN *and*
ELEONORE STUMP

ARABIC PHILOSOPHY *Edited by* PETER ADAMSON
and RICHARD C. TAYLOR

HANNAH ARENDT *Edited by* DANA VILLA

ARISTOTLE *Edited by* JONATHAN BARNES

ATHEISM *Edited by* MICHAEL MARTIN

AUGUSTINE *Edited by* ELEONORE STUMP *and*
NORMAN KRETZMANN

BACON *Edited by* MARKKU PELTONEN

BERKELEY *Edited by* KENNETH P. WINKLER

BRENTANO *Edited by* DALE JACQUETTE

CARNAP *Edited by* MICHAEL FRIEDMAN

CRITICAL THEORY *Edited by* FRED RUSH

DARWIN *Edited by* JONATHAN HODGE *and* GREGORY
RADICK

SIMONE DE BEAUVOIR *Edited by* CLAUDIA CARD

DESCARTES *Edited by* JOHN COTTINGHAM

DUNS SCOTUS *Edited by* THOMAS WILLIAMS

EARLY GREEK PHILOSOPHY *Edited by* A. A. LONG

EARLY MODERN PHILOSOPHY *Edited by*
MICHAEL RUTHERFORD

FEMINISM IN PHILOSOPHY *Edited by* MIRANDA
FRICKER *and* JENNIFER HORNSBY

FOUCAULT 2nd edition *Edited by* GARY GUTTING

FREUD *Edited by* JEROME NEU

GADAMER *Edited by* ROBERT J. DOSTAL

GALILEO *Edited by* PETER MACHAMER

GERMAN IDEALISM *Edited by* KARL AMERIKS

GREEK AND ROMAN PHILOSOPHY *Edited by*
DAVID SEDLEY

HABERMAS *Edited by* STEPHEN K. WHITE

HAYEK *Edited by* EDWARD FESER

HEGEL *Edited by* FREDERICK BEISER

HEIDEGGER 2nd edition *Edited by* CHARLES GUIGNON

HOBBES *Edited by* TOM SORELL
HOBBES' 'LEVIATHAN' *Edited by* PATRICIA
SPRINGBORG
HUME *Edited by* DAVID FATE NORTON
HUSSERL *Edited by* BARRY SMITH *and* DAVID
WOODRUFF SMITH
WILLIAM JAMES *Edited by* RUTH ANNA PUTNAM
KANT *Edited by* PAUL GUYER
KANT AND MODERN PHILOSOPHY *Edited by*
PAUL GUYER
KEYNES ROGER E. BACKHOUSE *and* BRADLEY W.
BATEMAN
KIERKEGAARD *Edited by* ALASTAIR HANNAY *and*
GORDON MARINO
LEIBNIZ *Edited by* NICHOLAS JOLLEY
LEVINAS *Edited by* SIMON CRITCHLEY *and* ROBERT
BERNASCONI
LOCKE *Edited by* VERE CHAPPELL
LOCKE'S 'ESSAY CONCERNING HUMAN
UNDERSTANDING' *Edited by* LEX NEWMAN
LOGICAL EMPIRICISM *Edited by* ALAN
RICHARDSON *and* THOMAS UEBEL
MAIMONIDES *Edited by* KENNETH SEESKIN
MALEBRANCHE *Edited by* STEVEN NADLER
MARX *Edited by* TERRELL CARVER
MEDIEVAL JEWISH PHILOSOPHY *Edited by*
DANIEL H. FRANK *and* OLIVER LEAMAN
MEDIEVAL PHILOSOPHY *Edited by* A. S. MCGRADE
MERLEAU-PONTY *Edited by* TAYLOR CARMAN *and*
MARK B. N. HANSEN
MILL *Edited by* JOHN SKORUPSKI
MONTAIGNE *Edited by* ULLRICH LANGER
NEWTON *Edited by* I. BERNARD COHEN *and* GEORGE E.
SMITH
NIETZSCHE *Edited by* BERND MAGNUS *and* KATHLEEN
HIGGINS
OCKHAM *Edited by* PAUL VINCENT SPADE
PASCAL *Edited by* NICHOLAS HAMMOND
PEIRCE *Edited by* CHERYL MISAK

THE PHILOSOPHY OF BIOLOGY *Edited by* DAVID
L. HULL *and* MICHAEL RUSE
PICO DELLA MIRANDOLA: NEW ESSAYS
Edited by M. V. DOUGHERTY
PLATO *Edited by* RICHARD KRAUT
PLATO'S 'REPUBLIC' *Edited by* G. R. F. FERRARI
PLOTINUS *Edited by* LLOYD P. GERSON
QUINE *Edited by* ROGER F. GIBSON JR.
RAWLS *Edited by* SAMUEL FREEMAN
THOMAS REID *Edited by* TERENCE CUNEO *and* RENE
VAN WOUDENBERG
RENAISSANCE PHILOSOPHY *Edited by* JAMES
HANKINS
ROUSSEAU *Edited by* PATRICK RILEY
BERTRAND RUSSELL *Edited by* NICHOLAS GRIFFIN
SARTRE *Edited by* CHRISTINA HOWELLS
SCHOPENHAUER *Edited by* CHRISTOPHER JANAWAY
THE SCOTTISH ENLIGHTENMENT *Edited by*
ALEXANDER BROADIE
ADAM SMITH *Edited by* KNUD HAAKONSSEN
SPINOZA *Edited by* DON GARRETT
THE STOICS *Edited by* BRAD INWOOD
TOCQUEVILLE *Edited by* CHERYL B. WELCH
WITTGENSTEIN *Edited by* HANS SLUGA *and* DAVID
STERN

The Cambridge Companion to
GALEN

Edited by

R. J. Hankinson
University of Texas at Austin

CAMBRIDGE
UNIVERSITY PRESS

CAMBRIDGE
UNIVERSITY PRESS

University Printing House, Cambridge CB2 8BS, United Kingdom

One Liberty Plaza, 20th Floor, New York, NY 10006, USA

477 Williamstown Road, Port Melbourne, VIC 3207, Australia

4843/24, 2nd Floor, Ansari Road, Daryaganj, Delhi - 110002, India

79 Anson Road, #06-04/06, Singapore 079906

Cambridge University Press is part of the University of Cambridge.

It furthers the University's mission by disseminating knowledge in the pursuit of education, learning and research at the highest international levels of excellence.

www.cambridge.org
Information on this title: www.cambridge.org/9780521525589

First published 2008

A catalogue record for this publication is available from the British Library

Library of Congress Cataloging in Publication data
The Cambridge companion to Galen / edited by R. J. Hankinson.
    p.   cm. – (Series of Cambridge companions)
Includes bibliographical references and index.
ISBN 978-0-521-81954-1 (hardback) – ISBN 978-0-521-52558-9 (pbk.)
1. Galen.   I. Hankinson, R.J.   II. Title.   III. Series.
B577.G24C36   2007
610.92 – dc22

                                    2007045731

ISBN 978-0-521-81954-1 Hardback
ISBN 978-0-521-52558-9 Paperback

CONTENTS

Notes on contributors   *page* xi
Preface   xv
Note on citations and abbreviations   xix

1   The man and his work   1
     R. J. HANKINSON

2   Galen and his contemporaries   34
     G. E. R. LLOYD

3   Methodology   49
     TEUN TIELEMAN

4   Logic   66
     BEN MORISON

5   Language   116
     BEN MORISON

6   Epistemology   157
     R. J. HANKINSON

7   Psychology   184
     PIERLUIGI DONINI

8   Philosophy of nature   210
     R. J. HANKINSON

9   Anatomy   242
     JULIUS ROCCA

10 Physiology   263
    ARMELLE DEBRU

11 Therapeutics   283
    PHILIP J. VAN DER EIJK

12 Drugs and pharmacology   304
    SABINE VOGT

13 Commentary   323
    REBECCA FLEMMING

14 The fortunes of Galen   355
    VIVIAN NUTTON

    Appendix 1: A guide to the editions and
    abbreviations of the Galenic corpus   391
    Appendix 2: English titles and modern
    translations   399
    Bibliography   405
    Index   435

NOTES ON CONTRIBUTORS

ARMELLE DEBRU, former Professor of Classics at the University of Lille, is currently Professor of History of Medicine in the University of Paris Descartes. She is the author of *Le corps respirant: la pensée physiologique chez Galien* (1996), editor of *Galen on Pharmacology* (1997), and has published extensively on the history of physiology, experimentation and other aspects of medical thought in Greek and Latin medical texts.

PIERLUIGI DONINI is Professor of the History of Ancient Philosophy at the State University of Milan. His research is principally concerned with Aristotle and the history of Aristotelianism, Stoic ethics and the question of determinism, and the history of Platonism in the Roman period.

PHILIP J. VAN DER EIJK is Professor of Greek at Newcastle University. He has published widely on ancient philosophy, medicine and science, comparative literature and patristics. He is the author of *Medicine and Philosophy in Classical Antiquity* (2005), of *Diocles of Carystus* (2000–1), of *Philoponus: On Aristotle On the Soul 1* (2005–6), and of *Aristoteles; De insomniis. De divinatione per somnum* (1994). He has edited and co-authored *Ancient Histories of Medicine* (1999) and co-edited *Ancient Medicine in its Socio-Cultural Context* (1995).

REBECCA FLEMMING is Lecturer in Classics (Ancient History) in the University of Cambridge. She is the author of *Medicine and the Making of Roman Women: Gender, Nature, and Authority from Celsus to Galen* (2000) and a range of essays and articles on other aspects

xi

of classical medicine and society, and on Roman women. She is currently writing a book on medicine and empire in the Roman world.

R. J. HANKINSON is Professor of Philosophy and Classics at the University of Texas at Austin. He has published numerous articles on many aspects of ancient philosophy and science; his books include *The Sceptics* (1995), *Cause and Explanation in the Ancient Greek World* (1998) and *Galen on Antecedent Causes* (1998).

G. E. R. LLOYD retired from his Personal Chair in Ancient Philosophy and Science at Cambridge and from the Mastership of Darwin College in 2000; he is currently Senior Scholar in Residence at the Needham Research Institute. His two most recent books are *The Delusions of Invulnerability* (2005) and *Principles and Practices in Ancient Greek and Chinese Science* (2006).

BEN MORISON is Michael Cohen Fellow in Philosophy at Exeter College, Oxford. He has also held visiting appointments at Princeton University. He has published a monograph on Aristotle's treatment of place in *Physics IV* (*On Location: Aristotle's Concept of Place*: 2004). His current projects include work on ancient logic, and a commentary on Aristotle's *Physics VI*.

VIVIAN NUTTON is Professor of the History of Medicine at the Wellcome Trust Centre for the History of Medicine at UCL, University of London. He has published extensively on the history of medicine from Antiquity to the nineteenth century, including editions of Galen and a major survey of medicine from Homer to Late Antiquity, *Ancient Medicine* (2004).

JULIUS ROCCA, a former Wellcome Trust Research Fellow at the Faculty of Classics, Cambridge, and recently a Fellow at the Center for Hellenic Studies, Washington, DC, holds a Wellcome Trust Award at the Department of Classics and Ancient History, University of Exeter. His publications include *Galen on the Brain* (2003). Among other projects, he is currently working on a history of anatomy in *Antiquity*.

TEUN TIELEMAN is Senior Lecturer in Ancient Philosophy at the University of Utrecht. His publications include *Galen and Chrysippus on the Soul: Argument and Refutation in the De Placitis II-III* (1996) and *Chrysippus' On Affections: Reconstruction and*

Interpretation (2003). He is currently co-directing with Annette Merz (New Testament Studies, Utrecht) an interdisciplinary research programme entitled *Habent Sua Fata Libelli: 'Text Processing' in the Philosophical and Religious Movements of the Roman Empire.*

SABINE VOGT is Acquisitions Editor for Classical Studies at Walter de Gruyter Publishers. She is author of *Aristoteles: Physiognomonika* (Aristoteles: Werke in deutscher Übersetzung, Bd. 18.VI) (Berlin, 1999). She is currently preparing an edition with commentary of the fragments of Servilius Damokrates, and occasionally teaches at the Humboldt University of Berlin.

PREFACE

Galen was one of the most successful men of Antiquity. Having grown up and studied in the provinces, he came to Rome at the age of thirty-three, at the height of the Empire's prosperity, and quickly made a name for himself as a theorist and practitioner of medicine, as a philosopher, and as a public controversialist. As a result of his meteoric rise, he gained an *entrée* into the Imperial circle, becoming one of the philosopher–emperor Marcus Aurelius' personal physicians, indeed the one entrusted with the medical care of the imperial prince Commodus in the emperor's absence. In the course of a long life, he wrote voluminously on an impressive variety of subjects, ranging from medicine through philosophy and linguistics to grammar and literary criticism; and although only a fraction of his vast output survives, it still constitutes, by some distance, the largest surviving *oeuvre* of any ancient author. His synthesis and systematization of medicine, which included a good deal of personal discovery and innovation, was to achieve canonical status already in antiquity; the great medical encyclopaedia of Oribasius in the fourth century was founded directly on Galen's work. With the rise of Arabic learning in Baghdad, and subsequently throughout the Islamic world, Galen's treatises were translated, first into Syriac and then into Arabic, where they also formed the basis of Arab medicine, and were extensively excerpted and commented upon in the succeeding centuries.

When the flame of learning was finally rekindled in the West, Galen was among the first of the classical authors to be translated into Latin, originally from the Arabic, and then later directly from Greek manuscripts. His *Ars Medica* was read in Paris and Oxford in the thirteenth century. By the fourteenth century he had become a canonical figure in Europe as well. Dante places him with the virtuous pagans in a relatively comfortable antechamber to the inferno; Chaucer mentions him along with Hippocrates as the model of the figure of the physician. For several centuries, European learned medicine was basically Galenic; medical students from Salerno to Salamanca, Padua to Paris, learned therapeutics at least indirectly from Galen's *On the Therapeutic Method*, diagnosis and prognosis from his works on the pulse, and anatomy from his anatomical texts, as faithfully demonstrated by professors in the theatres.

Although the first cracks in the façade of his pre-eminence date from 1543 and the publication of Vesalius' *de Fabrica*, his influence continued to be enormous. As late as the seventeenth century, avatars of the new science such as Descartes and Galileo still talk respectfully of Galen and Galenism, even if they sometimes take issue with it, and Galen's demonstration of the cerebral origin of the nerves is still being repeated in the anatomical schools. If Vesalius, and later Harvey, rendered Galen's account of human anatomy and physiology largely obsolescent, his influence continued to be felt in clinical medicine, even as a revival of Hippocratism sought to re-inject a certain empiricism and distrust of systematicity into medical practice. As late as the nineteenth century at the University of Würzburg, the medical student's oral exam consisted in being asked to comment on a passage of Galen chosen at random; the much-maligned edition of Kühn, comprising twenty-two large volumes appearing between 1819 and 1833, and still our best text for much of Galen, was produced with the interests of practising doctors rather than scholars in mind. And some typically Galenic forms of treatment, notably bloodletting, persisted even into the twentieth century. Ninety years ago the physician–scholar Arthur Brock, writing from a wartime military hospital in the introduction to his translation of Galen's *On the Natural Faculties*, could seriously, if somewhat forlornly, advocate a return to some aspects of Galenic practice. It is only in the last hundred years or so that Galen has suffered a final eclipse as a medical authority; although I am told that in parts of rural Spain a doctor may still be familiarly referred to as '*un galeno*'.

But for a while at least that eclipse seemed total; and only a few scholars continued the slow and demanding work of producing proper critical editions of his works that had begun in Germany in the latter part of the nineteenth century. After the First World

War, the stream dwindled and then virtually dried up. It was not until the 1970s that there began to appear signs of a revival of scholarly interest in the man who, along with Ptolemy, and arguably also Archimedes, has the right to claim to have been the most influential of all Greek scientists, and rivalling even Plato and Aristotle in the depth and continuity of his intellectual impact on succeeding centuries. At least now Galen is receiving renewed and vigorous attention from classicists and philosophers as well as historians of culture and medicine.

But of those five giants, Galen is nowadays by far the least well known, even among the generally educated, who will usually know at least the names of others as well as that of Hippocrates, Galen's acknowledged master in matters medical, as well. This *Companion* has been undertaken in the conviction that this state of affairs needs to be remedied, and in the hope of contributing something to that remedy. As such, contributors were asked to make their articles as accessible as possible to the non-specialist, at least the non-specialist in medical history; and they were also asked to make their contributions as representative as possible of Galen's importance in the wide variety of fields surveyed. For obvious reasons, they were not asked to aim at comprehensiveness of treatment; nor did I insist on respect for any orthodoxy (or for any unorthodoxy, for that matter). How far we have succeeded in this aim is obviously for others to decide. But I hope that this brief survey will at least have indicated the worthiness of the enterprise.

To present a rounded picture of Galen's importance and achievements, contributions were solicited from historians of philosophy as well as of medicine; and I have tried to strike a balance in the presentation of the various facets of Galen's intellectual persona. I had hoped to cover more areas, but at various stages four people who had originally agreed to participate in the project withdrew from it for various reasons (and none). In particular, it is a great loss not to have been able to publish the promised article concerning Galen's work on diagnostics and the theory of the pulse, one of his most important contributions to medical theory and practice; I have tried, inadequately, partially to remedy this deficiency in the introductory chapter on Galen's life and work. In addition, it will be apparent that different chapters sometimes range over the same territory, sometimes even quoting the same texts. In almost all cases, these are approached from different angles, and with the aim of illuminating distinct features of Galen's multi-faceted intellectual personality. But some reduplication has been inevitable, and here again I have not sought to intervene with too heavy an editorial hand; here, too, we would crave the reader's indulgence. These problems have also drawn out the gestation period of this volume to more than usually elephantine proportions; I would like to record my gratitude to the surviving contributors for their cheerfulness in the face of delay, and their conscientiousness in responding to my often hasty and frequently importunate questions.

NOTE ON CITATIONS AND ABBREVIATIONS

It is not easy to impose order and orthodoxy of citation on Galen's sprawling corpus; and within this *Companion* I have tolerated slight variations in referential style in line with the preferences of the various contributors. But I hope – and trust – that none of these variations will cause confusion. Ever since the late medieval period, when Galen's writings began to exercise their extraordinary, resurgent grip on Western medical theory and practice by way of Latin translations, it has been customary to refer to his multifarious texts by way of their Latin titles. For this book, I have insisted on their being assigned English titles, although the preferred abbreviations for them will usually reflect their Latin originals (this is to maintain some degree of consistency with the usual manner of citation elsewhere – although, as I noted above, this too is various). As an aid to cross-reference, two appendixes have been provided. Appendix 1 lists the texts, with their Latin names and abbreviations, as they appear in the massive Kühn edition of 1819–33, as well as listing other, later, critical editions where they exist. Appendix 2 relates the preferred English titles to the Latin abbreviations in the case of the bulk of the texts (and all of those cited in this *Companion*), as well as indicating where translations exist into modern languages. Every treatise will be cited on its first appearance in each chapter by way of English title followed by standard Latin abbreviation; thereafter it will (typically) be referred to by that abbreviation. In the case of reference to particular passages of text, I have also permitted some variability in citation convention. But I have insisted that every text which appears in Kühn (*Galeni Opera Omnia*, 20 vols. in 22, Leipzig, 1819–33) should be referred to by way of volume (in Roman) and page (in Arabic) number in that edition, even in cases where the Kühn text has been superseded by later critical editions, the reason for this being that such later texts generally (and translations usually) contain marginal references to it, and so Kühn references may be used to navigate other editions. Thus a typical minimal reference might read: '*Aff.Dig.* V 40–1', indicating a reference to the text *The Passions of the Soul* located at pages 40–1 of Kühn volume V. On occasion, line numbers have been added for further precision, even though Kühn's text does not print marginal line-numbers. However, contributors have sometimes preferred to cite the later editions too, in particular when they appear either in the three-volume collection *Galeni Scripta Minora* which appeared in Leipzig in 1884, 1891 and 1893 (edited by Marquardt, Müller and Helmreich, respectively), abbreviated '*SM*', or in the *Corpus Medicorum Graecorum* series begun by the Berlin Academy at the end of the nineteenth century, and which still continues its monumental task of producing proper critical editions of the entire Greek medical corpus, abbreviated '*CMG*'. Thus, since *Aff.Dig.* is also edited in *SM* I, a fuller reference might read '*Aff.Dig.* V 40–1, = *SM* I, 31,9–14', further citing page 31, lines 9–14 of *Galeni Scripta Minora* I. Finally, this text is also edited in the *CMG* (by de Boer, 1937), and consequently a complete reference would read '*Aff.Dig.* V 40–1, = *SM* I, 31,9–14, = *CMG* V 4,1,1, 27, 21–3', additionally citing page 27, lines 21–3 of *CMG* volume V (which is the Galen section), sub-volume 4,1,1 (the 1937 edition of the text in question by Wilko de Boer). But in general, we have not thought it worthwhile to cite more than two different editions. Finally, Galen himself divided his longer works into books; later editors divided these into chapters (often arbitrarily, not to say perversely); and some modern editions break the text down into smaller sections still. Some have preferred on occasion also to cite using these further tools, and I have not stood in their way. Book (Roman) and chapter (Arabic) numbers appear immediately after the title abbreviation, and are separated from the remainder of the reference by a colon (in the case of single-book treatises, no book number will be cited: '*Aff.Dig.* 8: V 40–1, = *SM* I, 31,9–14', a reference to chapter 8 of *Aff.Dig.*). Thus, *On the Doctrines of Hippocrates and Plato* (*PHP*), a major treatise in nine books, occupies the bulk of Kühn volume V; it has also been edited in recent times, with English translation and commentary, by Phillip De Lacy as *CMG* V 4,1,2 (3 vols., Berlin, 1978–83). So a (very) full reference to a particular passage might read as follows: '*PHP* II 2:

V 212–13, = *CMG* V 4,1,2, 102,18–24'. Here, the page and line numbers refer to the Greek text, and not to the facing English translation; and this convention has been adhered to in other similar cases. In addition, some contributors have preferred to indicate the later editions (*SM*, *CMG*, or others) by citing page number plus the name of the editor; in this manner the last reference would read '*PHP* II 2: V 212–13, = 102,18–24 De Lacy'; in such cases, however, the edition will have been fully referenced at the first mention of the text in the chapter. All of this may seem excessively complex and unwieldy, and perhaps it is. But it should at least be relatively unambiguous.

1 The man and his work

Galen was born in September AD 129, in Pergamum on the Ionian seaboard of Asia Minor. He died sometime in the second decade of the third century, probably in Rome.[1] He lived, and worked, until well into his eighties; and over the course of that long and productive life wrote (or rather dictated, sometimes more than one treatise at a time, to relays of slaves)[2] a vast number of works on a wide variety of topics, ranging from medicine, through logic and philosophy, to philology and literary criticism. Many – indeed most – of these books are lost; but we are fortunate to possess two short texts from Galen's own hand that deal with his output: *On My Own Books* (*Lib.Prop.*) XIX 8–48, = *SM* 2, 91–14,[3] and *The Order of My Own Books* (*Ord.Lib.Prop.*) XIX 49–61, = *SM* 2, 80–90;[4] the latter deals with the order in which an aspirant doctor should read them, while the former was written in order, he says, to help people determine which of the many works circulating under his name was genuine. These lists are not exhaustive: several indisputably genuine texts fail to appear in them, either because they were written later, or because for whatever reason Galen chose to disown them; moreover the Greek text suffers from several *lacunae* (although some of these have been filled from Arabic sources and by way of a newly recovered Greek manuscript in Véronique Boudon's recent edition).[5] But a fair proportion, particularly of the medical output, does survive (in fact it constitutes the most extensive surviving corpus of any ancient author, accounting for about 10 per cent of what we possess of Greek prior to AD 350);[6] and this, along with the bibliographical information supplied by the two texts just mentioned, allows us to form a three-dimensional picture of Galen, the man and his achievement.

Second-century Pergamum was a great and thriving city, one of the largest of Asia Minor;[7] and Galen was born into a good family in it. His father, Nicon, whom he revered, was an architect (a profession that encompassed that of engineer), and he ensured that Galen received the best possible liberal education, as well as providing him with an exemplar of the life well lived, both morally and intellectually (*The Passions of the Soul* [*Aff.Dig.*] V 40, = *SM* 1 31,9–12). His mother, by contrast was a bad-tempered shrew, prone to biting her servants, as well as screaming at and attacking her husband (40–1, = *SM* 1 31, 12–14). Galen apparently never married (nor do we hear of any brothers or sisters); and, while he treats women patients, and will listen to advice from midwives, his world as he portrays it is almost exclusively a masculine one, and he frequently seems to find female company irritating. When the wife of Boethus, whom he was treating, faints in the bath, Galen berates her maidservants for standing around screaming and wailing, and doing nothing to help (*Praen.* XIV 643–4, = 112,12–114,2), although a little earlier he has described her chief nurse as 'a most excellent woman'. An exception is his attitude to the female Platonist Arria whom, at the very end of his life, he describes as 'dearest of all to me, and most highly praised by all on account of her rigorous philosophising and her great appreciation for Plato's writings' (*On Theriac to Piso* [*Ther.Pis.*] XIV 218); but this is indeed exceptional. And while he allows that 'women are similar to men in that they are rational animals, that is capable of acquiring knowledge'[8] (in apparent contrast with Aristotle), he still thinks (in common with most ancient theorists) that women are in general markedly inferior to men, on account of their being adapted for childbearing (see, e.g., *On the Utility of the Parts* [*UP*] IV 145–58, = ii 286,13–296,7 Helmreich).

Moreover, he evinces an ascetic distaste for sexual excess in general, and homosexuality in particular (homosexuals are derided as 'woolworkers': *On the Therapeutic Method* [*MM*] X 10–11; cf. *On Affected Parts* [*Loc.Aff.*] VIII 225–6), and his attitude to such practices as fellatio and cunnilingus is equally puritanical (*On the Powers* [*and Mixtures*] *of Simple Drugs* [*SMT*] XII 248–50). He understands that sex is extremely pleasurable (indeed, a providential Nature has made it so in order to ensure the continuation of species: *UP* IV 144, 181–2, = ii 285,27–286,12, 314,19–315,4); and Galen expresses his deep admiration at the marvellous skill of the Creator in constructing the functional architecture of the penis (*UP* IV 211–19, = ii 337,3–342,20).[9] But he still thinks that a preoccupation with sex is bestial, and incompatible with the highest human life (*The Best Doctor is also a Philosopher* [*Opt.Med.*] I 59, = *SM* 2, 6,3–9). His treatise *On Moral Character* (*Mor.*), which survives only in an Arabic epitome,[10] takes the fact that people tend to satisfy their appetites (particularly their sexual ones) in private as a sign that they are aware of their shameful and unworthy nature: 'the rational soul behaves like this when the appetitive soul attempts to win it over to desiring sexual intercourse, since it sees that this is harmful both to the body and to the soul' (*Mor.* 2, 245–6 Mattock). In fact, it is not even true to say that 'pleasure is the goal of the appetitive soul . . . The goal of the appetitive soul is the [preservation of the] life of the body, and the pleasures of food and sexual intercourse are like the bait that is placed in the trap in order to snare the animal' (*ibid.*, 249). Finally, in *On Affected Parts* (*Loc.Aff.*) VIII 417–21, he notes that, while the retention of semen and menstrual fluid, even in small amounts, can have serious pathological effects, and hence that regular sexual release is a good idea for purposes of regimen, this doesn't mean one should do it for fun. Indeed, he praises the example of Diogenes the Cynic for relying on masturbation rather than loose women for such purposes 'as all moderate men should'. It is hard to resist the temptation of essaying a Freudian 'explanation' for all of this.

At all events, from his father's example (and in horrified reaction against that of his mother), he learned to despise the siren lures of wealth and reputation, and to treat the slings and arrows of fortune with indifference (*ibid.* 42–5, = 32,11–35,3). Nicon also looked after his son's physical health, prescribing him a regimen that kept him free of the sort of illness that attacked his more acratic friends (*On Good and Bad Humours* [*Bon.Mal.Suc.*] VI 755–6, = *CMG* V 4,2, 392,21–393,11). At *Ord.Lib.Prop.* XIX 59, = *SM* 2, 88,7–15, Galen praises his father for having given him an excellent grounding in grammar and mathematics, and he says that he began to study logic at fourteen. He learned philosophy from leading adherents of the major schools, Platonic, Aristotelian, Stoic and Epicurean, carefully selected by his father for their moral and intellectual virtues (cf. *Aff.Dig.* V 41–2, = *SM* I 31,23–32,11), although as he later tells us he was less than impressed with some of their arguments. Indeed he seemed well on his way to a career as a philosopher when his father, moved by a dream, decided that he should take up medical studies as well (*Ord.Lib.Prop.* XIX 59, = *SM* 2, 88,13–17).[11]

This he did with equal determination and drive, seeking out instruction from a variety of different doctors. At Pergamum he studied with Satyrus (whom he accuses of peddling misleading interpretations of Hippocrates: *Ord. Lib.Prop.* XIX 57–8, = *SM* 2, 87,8–19), but on his father's death in AD 149, at which he no doubt came into a considerable fortune (notwithstanding his protestations of asceticism and indifference to money; his father had been a landowner: *On the Properties of Foodstuffs* [*Alim.Fac.*] VI 552–53, = *CMG* V 4,2, 261, 6–24; *Bon.Mal.Suc.* VI 755, = *CMG* V 4, 2, 393, 1), he travelled first to Smyrna to study with Pelops, a leading Rationalist physician[12] (he wrote some early works here, two of which survive: *On the Anatomy of the Uterus* [*Ut.Diss.*] II 887–908, = *CMG* V 2,1], and *On Medical Experience* [*Med.Exp.*, = Walzer, 1944]: *Lib.Prop.* XIX 16–17, = *SM* 2, 97,6–23) where he also attended lectures by the Platonist Albinus (*Lib.Prop.* XIX 16–7, = *SM* 2, 97,6–98,11; cf. *On Hippocrates' 'Nature of Man'* [*HNH*] V 136, = *CMG* V 9,1, 70,8–15), and then to Corinth and finally Alexandria and elsewhere in search of the leading anatomist of the day, Numisianus (*On Anatomical Procedures* [*AA*] II 217–8;[13] cf. *On Black Bile* [*At.Bil.*] V 112, = *CMG* V 4,1,1, 75,17).

He returned to Pergamum in AD 157 where he was offered the job of physician at the gladiatorial school 'even though I was young, only 28', a job which naturally afforded him the best possible on-the-job training in orthopaedic surgery, and in which, by his own account, he was unprecedentedly successful: although many had died under his predecessors, he hardly lost a single patient. Thus his initial contract was renewed four successive times, and he held the post for four years, until the autumn of 161.[14]

Shortly thereafter, he left Pergamum to seek his fortune in Rome, motivated in part apparently by the political unrest which had broken out there (which he characterizes with the loaded, Thucydidean term 'stasis': *Praen.* XIV 622–3, = *CMG* V 8,1, 92,6–10; cf. 648, = 116,27; this is one of several episodes that reveal Galen to be of a somewhat timid disposition, at least as far as his own physical safety was concerned). But before arriving in Rome he travelled extensively around the eastern Mediterranean to investigate local herbal and mineral remedies, and he frequently reports on what he observed.[15] He recorded the local names for grain-plants in Thrace and Macedonia (*Alim.Fac.* VI 513–14, = *CMG* V 4,2, 236,13–27). He visited Cyprus in search of useful minerals (*SMT* XII 171, 227, 229, 231–8, etc.), even going down a copper mine in search of ore (*On Antidotes* [*Ant.*] XIV 6); and he ventured as far as Palestine in search of bitumen and other medicinally useful substances to be found around the Dead Sea (*SMT* XII 171, 203).

In Rome, at any rate by his own account, his rise, both social and professional, was meteoric and, again by his own account, entirely due to his own brilliance. The various cases recounted in *Praen.* afford our most important, if evidently partial (in both senses of the word) evidence for this; but I begin with a tale told in the relatively late *On Affected Parts* (*Loc.Aff.*) VIII 361–6. At the very beginning of his first Roman sojourn, he tells us, his superior knowledge and ability at differential diagnosis won him the admiration and support of the philosopher Glaucon, whom (or so at least he says) he came upon by chance in the street, and who asked him to visit a patient who was suffering from a diarrhoea of the sort often, apparently, mischaracterized by incompetent doctors as dysentery. Glaucon, as a philosopher, is keen to test whether Galen really can perform correct diagnoses and prognoses 'which seem more akin to divination than medicine'. Galen duly obliges, and makes several crucial observations, including that of bloody serum in the stool which is, he says, a clear sign of liver disease, a diagnosis he verifies by palpation of the patient's abdomen, and which is confirmed by observation of the pulse and other signs which lead him to conclude that the liver is not merely weakened but actually inflamed. In this case the patient was also a doctor; and Galen infers from a preparation of hyssop and honeywater that he sees by the window that he had diagnosed himself as suffering from pleurisy. This good fortune allows him to impress Glaucon all the more, as he is now able to tell the patient where he is feeling pain; Glaucon, wrongly supposing that Galen has made this determination from the pulse alone, is all the more astonished, an astonishment compounded when Galen is able to predict that he will feel the desire to cough, and will in fact cough at very long intervals. Again by chance this prediction is vindicated almost immediately. Next he is able to make further predictions and retrodictions of the course of the illness which are also, as he admits, partly due to good fortune (although these are not simply lucky guesses), which the patient confirms. Finally, he is able to reveal the patient's own mistaken diagnosis, much to the latter's surprise:

And from this time onwards, Glaucon held both myself and the entire medical art in the highest regard, whereas previously he had not esteemed it highly, simply because he had never come across men worthy of respect who were versed in it. (Loc.Aff. VIII 366)

The moral of the story, Galen tells his readers, is that doctors need to remember how important it is to know which symptoms are proper to particular diseases and which common to several, which are always associated with a particular ailment, which for the most part, which half of the time, and which rarely.[16] But they also need to be able to grasp opportunities offered by good fortune, such as happened in this case: 'for while good fortune often provides many opportunities for achieving a great reputation, still most people are unable to avail themselves of them on account of their ignorance' (ibid.).

That story exemplifies in a particularly clear manner several features of Galen's autobiographical style. Most obviously, Galen was able to move with relative ease in the highest social circles almost as soon as he arrived in Rome. Although he invariably portrays his success as the result of his own ability, integrity and industry, as well as his talent for unmasking the baseless pretensions of his rivals, it is evident that he availed himself of both his own social standing and of various connections with his family at Pergamum.[17] The first case he recounts in Praen. was the cure of a fellow Pergamene living in Rome, the Peripatetic philosopher Eudemus, who had apparently known Galen's father: at any rate he knew of the dreams that had made Nicon turn him towards medicine, although apparently he also thought that for Galen this was merely a sideline, considering him rather to be a philosopher like himself (Praen. XIV 608, = 76,26–78,2 Nutton).[18]

But while it was important for Galen that philosophers should accept him as one of their own, he was equally concerned to be taken seriously as a doctor, in both theory and practice. This accounts for the centrality of a philosopher, Glaucon, in the story from Loc.Aff. Glaucon is evidently already known to him, but in what circles and for what reasons it is not clear – in any event, he is at least presented as not yet having first-hand knowledge of Galen's clinical prowess.

Philosophers might be expected to understand the true reasons for successes of this sort, and not to dismiss them as mere divination, or, worse, as witchcraft. In the characteristic polemic against the degeneracy of the times with which he begins *Praen.*,[19] Galen rails at the pseudo-doctors who make their way by flattery and insinuation, who gain pupils by making the art out to be easy (XIV 599–601, = 68,3–70,1 Nutton).[20] But worst of all, when a good man makes a sound prediction on the basis of methodical understanding, proper training, long experience, precise observation and rational deduction, far from receiving the acclaim he deserves he is suspected of sorcery (which is a good deal worse than the mere slur that scientific prognosis is nothing but fortune-telling),[21] and will incur the malicious enmity of the others, who will conspire against him, as they did against Quintus ('the best doctor of his generation') and force him either into silence or exile on trumped-up charges (*Praen.* XIV 601–3, = 70,1–72,12 Nutton). Good men are compelled to abandon the fray, 'leaving it to the scoundrels to obtain a reputation'; this is caused by the materialism and hedonism of their rich clients who value nothing unless it leads to pleasure ('geometry and arithmetic they need only in calculating expenses and improving their mansions'); worst of all, they abandon philosophy for sophistry; 'at any rate, as Plato says somewhere, in a contest between a doctor and a cook before a jury of children or fools, the cook would win by a wide margin' (*Praen.* XIV 603–5, = 72,13–74,11 Nutton).[22]

All of this is couched in lurid and at times barely coherent terms; Galen was never one to pull his polemical punches. But it betrays a depth of feeling which is hard to gainsay; and it is, as I said, entirely characteristic of the man and his work (although one may discern a certain mellowing in his attitude that comes with increasing age and security). It comes as no surprise to discover that another work of autobiography (and no doubt of self-promotion, not to say autohagiography, as well as moral philosophy) was entitled *On Slander*.[23]

At any event, Galen presents the cure of Eudemus, which was certainly not his first clinical essay in Rome, and perhaps post-dated the Glaucon episode (*Praen.* XIV 605, = 74,12–15 Nutton), as a turning-point in his career, but also in his worldly education.[24] Having no idea, as a naive provincial, of the wickedness of the big city, he simply went about his business, oblivious of the malicious gossip he was incurring. The case is described in unusually precise detail, even for Galen (it occupies *Praen.* XIV 605–19, = 74,12–88,13 Nutton). The details are designed to emphasize the complexity of the case, and also how the other doctors involved failed to measure up to them. It is a feature of medicine as it was practised at the time (at least the medicine of the elite) that several doctors were often summoned to the patient's bedside, where they made competing diagnoses and prognoses, leaving the patient, or his representatives, to choose among them.[25]

As Galen presents the case, he was regularly at odds with the advice of the other doctors; and he was regularly proved right. He suspects that the illness is more serious than the others (and indeed the patient himself) suppose: it may be an incipient quartan fever (XIV 606–7, = 74,17–76,8).[26] In due course, Galen's forebodings are borne out; and Eudemus comes to rely upon him, particularly as 'fortuitously, at the same time' Galen was able to make a similarly successful prognosis (XIV 607–9, = 76,8–78,10). Even so, the other doctors demur, prescribing a strong drug (theriac),[27] which Galen says will be worse than useless (XIV 609–11, = 78,10–80,1). And so indeed it proves, particularly when the other doctors administer a second dose (XIV 611, = 80,1–5). Galen makes further predictions on the basis of the pulse and examination of urine (XIV 611, = 80,5–15). Eudemus is then joined by Sergius Paulus, shortly to become the prefect of the city, and Flavius Boethus, an ex-consul and future governor of Palestine, who will subsequently help Galen in his ascent, both of whom happen to be students of Aristotelian philosophy, and he tells them too of Galen's past successes and latest prognostics. When these, too, are vindicated, 'Eudemus was amazed, and revealed my predictions to all his visitors, who included almost all of the social and intellectual leaders of Rome' (XIV 611–12, = 80,15–25). Boethus, it turns out, had heard of Galen, and had invited him 'to give a demonstration of how speech and breath are produced and by what organs' (XIV 612, = 80,25–7); of which more later. At this point, things begin to get ugly; Galen now says that he will be able to cure Eudemus, a position ridiculed by the other doctors, who now accept that their patient has been stricken three times with quartan fever (and hence suppose the case to be hopeless). Here for the first time, Galen says, he becomes aware that his enemies are motivated by jealousy, and that they seek to win over the lay-people present (XIV 613–14, = 82,8–31). Of course, his opponents' slanders are exposed for what

they are, even though they continue to accuse him of practising divination (XIV 614–15, = 84,1–10); and Galen triumphantly predicts the
successful outcome of the disease, much to their discomfiture (XIV
615–17, = 84,10–86,7). Eudemus, being a philosopher, asks for a complete account of how Galen arrived at his opinion, which Galen duly
does; and Eudemus, confident now in the final result, says: 'you have
reasoned out your discovery of what is to come as a logician should'
(XIV 617–28, = 86,7–30): high praise indeed from a philosopher.

It is worth briefly relating this case, and Galen's presentation of
it, to the previous one. Here again a philosopher figures, although
in this case one with excellent social and political connections. He
is thus disposed to appreciate the rigour of Galen's methods, and to
see through the sophistry of the other quacks. As Galen presents
it, it is this fact, allied to Galen's evident practical success, which
tips the balance. Galen not only gets things right; he can explain
how it is that he does so, at least in general terms and at least
to the logically literate. The logically illiterate, of course, hate him
all the more for that. There is, however, one obvious difference
between the two cases. In the first, Galen emphasizes how good luck
helped him make a good impression; and he conceals, at least for a
time, the basis for some of his predictions. In the second, everything
is presented as being above board. It is not that Galen exactly engages
in sharp practice in the first; but his *modus operandi* at least seems
somewhat at odds with the persona of openness adopted in the second. All of which should put us on our guard when faced with Galen's
very considerable rhetorical and persuasive skills. He is invariably
the hero in his own drama; but just what kind of hero – a cunning
Odysseus, a frank Achilles – varies from drama to drama. For all that,
we should not allow such observations to take us too far into cyni-
cism. Galen's extraordinary industry is irrefutable. He did make a big
splash, if not perhaps invariably for precisely the virtuous reasons he
would have us believe; and there is no evidence to suppose that he
was a mere charlatan.

We have looked at length at two cases from the beginning of
Galen's Roman career. *Praen.* lists several more striking successes
that took place over the next few years. They are carefully chosen
(confected?) to illustrate different aspects of Galen's expertise, as
well as different stages in his social ascent; and they differ widely in
tone. Two of them illustrate Galen's ability to diagnose psychological

causes of distress, and one involves inference from psychological disturbance to a diagnosis. In the best known, Galen recounts how he diagnosed love-sickness in the wife of Justus.[28] He was called in to see the woman, who was suffering from insomnia and despondency, although without other physical symptoms (Praen. XIV 630–1, = 100,7–22). Galen's preliminary diagnosis is that she is suffering either from a physiologically based depression caused by black bile,[29] or some more directly psychological malaise (XIV 631, = 100,22–102,2). He visits her on successive days, but finds her unwilling to receive him or talk about her complaint (a fact which is in itself diagnostically relevant), but by interrogating her maid he reinforces his provisional conclusion that she is suffering from a kind of grief (XIV 631–2, = 102,2–9), the source of which he discovered 'by chance', when someone happened to enter while he was consulting with the patient, and mention that he had just seen Pylades dancing in the theatre. The woman evinced signs of distress, and Galen immediately took her pulse and found it 'irregular in several ways', a sure sign of mental disturbance. Galen then contrived to check his diagnosis (the woman is hopelessly in love with a dancer) by having the names of other dancers mentioned apparently at random (they produce no effect) and then finally having Pylades' name brought up again, with the same discombobulating results. The diagnosis (although presumably not the cure, which Galen does not mention) is now secure (Praen. XIV 632–3, = 102,9–28).

Galen again relies upon a variety of diagnostic observations, and his ability to profit from a lucky chance; also noticeable is his attempt to confirm the initial diagnosis by an empirical test.[30] The case is, as Galen admits here and elsewhere, very similar to a celebrated diagnosis made by the third-century BC Alexandrian doctor Erasistratus (and the story falls squarely within a clear romantic tradition).[31] Galen does not seek to take credit for originality where none is deserved. Indeed, he sees himself as championing (and reviving) the great tradition of medical and scientific explanation that stretches back to Hippocrates, Plato and Aristotle.[32] As noted earlier, his association with Peripatetics (although how seriously these upper-class thinkers took their philosophy is another matter) is hardly adventitious, since he himself adopts a version of the Aristotelian account of method and science.[33] Indeed part of what he thinks responsible for the degeneracy of contemporary medicine is its cavalier disregard for the careful and methodical determination of the essential natures of things on the basis of which (and only on the basis of which) can a secure, explanatory scientific practice be erected,[34] and only thus can the sorts of diagnosis and prognosis which Galen recounts in *Praen.*, and to which he attributes his great success, be achieved.

The events just related may all be dated to Galen's first year in Rome,[35] as may also his public debate with leading Stoic and Peripatetic philosophers in the course of making good on his promise to Boethus to demonstrate 'how speech and breath are produced and by what organs' (XIV 612, = 80,25–7). Public demonstration, or demonstration before an influential invited audience, of either scientific or argumentative skill (or, as in this case, both) was a standard feature of the intellectual life of the times (it also served as a rather cruder form of entertainment, at any rate in the case of the vivisectional demonstrations).[36] Boethus was to become a major patron for Galen; and Galen dedicated the first six books of *On the Doctrines of Hippocrates and Plato* (*PHP*), his major exploration of the relations between philosophy and medicine, and his attack upon the Stoics' unitary psychology, to him, as well as the first book of *On the Utility of the Parts* (*UP*), his great work of functional anatomy: 'Boethus left Rome . . . with these works in his possession. His destination was Syria Palestina where he was to serve as governor [in AD 165], where too he died [in AD 169]' (*Lib.Prop.* XIX 16, = *SM* 2, 96,19–24).[37] Galen also dedicated to him *On the Causes of Breathing* (*Caus.Resp.*),[38] the lost *On the Voice*, all of which are obviously relevant to the topic of his demonstration, as well as six books on *On the Anatomy of Hippocrates* and three on *On the Anatomy of Erasistratus*, both composed 'in a rather combative vein', in response to the aging but cantankerous anatomist Martialius, with whom Galen has several public confrontations (*Lib.Prop.* XIX 12–14, = *SM* 2, 94,16–96,1).[39] In addition, we learn from *AA* II 215–18 that he also dedicated the lost texts *On Vivisection* and *On Dissection of Dead Bodies* to him, as well as a short set of anatomical notes. Moreover, he says that he sent the rest of *UP* to him when it was completed. He made 'many anatomical demonstrations' for him (*AA* II 218). Boethus was clearly the most important figure in Galen's early career.

The public disputation described in *Praen.*[40] also took place in the first year of Galen's first stay in Rome, although as I said it was only one of many; in fact, Galen was making public demonstrations almost on a daily basis (*On Bloodletting Against the Erasistrateans at Rome* [*Ven.Sect.Er.Rom.*] XI 194).[41] Boethus was taking tutorials in Aristotelian philosophy from one Alexander of Damascus 'who was expert too in the doctrines of Plato, but inclined more to those of Aristotle' (*Praen.* XIV 627, = 96.6–9 Nutton).[42] The idea was for Galen to make his demonstrations of the sources of the voice on his usual live subjects (in this case kids and pigs): 'before dissecting, I said that would show what was revealed by dissection, and that I rather hoped that Alexander could be my guide, indeed the guide of all us, in drawing the logical conclusions from what transpired' (*Praen.* XIV 627–8, = 96,19–23). Before the demonstration can even begin, however, Alexander questions whether we should accept the evidence of the senses. Galen walks out, saying that he doesn't wish to associate with rustic Pyrrhonists (*Praen.* XIV 628, = 96,27–98,8).[43] Not an auspicious start; but Galen is persuaded to return at a later date and make the promised demonstration, which he does to great acclaim (XIV 629–30, = 98,9–100,6).

This demonstration, which he repeated many times, was a theatrical *tour de force*; it also served to demonstrate Galen's greatest anatomical discovery, that of the function of the intercostal muscles in breathing and voice-production. Galen is scrupulous about indicating what he himself had discovered as opposed to what he has learned (and confirmed) from others. On his return to Rome in 169, he discovered some juvenilia of his in circulation, including *The Movement of the Chest and Lungs*, which he had

written as a favour to a fellow student . . . The books remained in the possession of certain other individuals . . . Then someone added his own preface and tried to pass it off as his own; but was found out. I added a passage to the end of the third book, advertising my own subsequent discoveries; for what I had written in the three books were the doctrines of my teacher Pelops. (*Lib.Prop.* XIX 17, = *SM* 2, 97,23–98,10)[44]

Galen devotes most of Book 8 of *AA* (II 661–90) to describe an exhaustive series of experiments and observations regarding the effects of ligature and section of a wide variety of nerves in the thoracic region, as well as to the effects of various spinal chord sections.[45] In chapter 4 (II 667–75) Galen describes a sequence of experiments on live animals involving isolating and ligating key nerves:

For a demonstration, it is better to put the threads under all the nerves without tying them. Then you can show that the animal cries out when struck, but that it suddenly becomes silent after the nerves have been tied. The spectators are astonished. They think it wonderful that voice is destroyed when small nerves in the back are tied. Have several assistants to help you in such demonstrations so that the loops may be put round all the nerves quickly. If you do not want to loosen them, it does not matter how you bind, but if you want to loosen them again to show that the animal recovers its voice – for this surprises the spectators even more – do not bind the loops too tightly so that it is easy to loosen them quickly. (*AA* II 669; trans. after Singer, 1956)

The theatricality of the spectacle is apparent. Galen's aim is to astonish – but it is also to teach and to demonstrate, and he is rightly proud both of his practical skill in isolating the structures, and in the theoretical conclusions, regarding the nature and function of the nervous system, that he can draw from them. Observation alone is not enough: science requires that the observations be systematized and structured into a properly explanatory system; and only someone gifted and practised in logic can do that.

All of this took place in Galen's evidently hectic first year in Rome. His success was immediate, as was the enmity of his inferior opponents. Things reached such a pitch that within a couple of years Galen gave up public performances in order 'to concentrate on healing the sick', and letting his therapeutic achievements speak for themselves (*Lib.Prop.* XIX 15, *SM* 2, 96,7–16).[46] Shortly thereafter, he left Rome and returned to Pergamum, under somewhat peculiar circumstances. He had told Eudemus that he intended to return as soon as he could, disgusted as he was with the degeneracy of Rome (*Praen.* XIV 622–3, = 92,6–10). Moreover, after another spectacular cure (this time of Boethus' wife), he says both that the malice of his enemies had increased (it was not helped by a gift of 400 gold sesterces from the grateful husband), while he also feared that the praise of his friends would lead to his being drawn into the imperial circle (*Praen.* XIV 647, = 116,16–23). As he tells the story, it seems as though he almost immediately made to leave, and in secret, fearful of being detained by 'one of the influential men in Rome, or even by the emperor himself . . . like a runaway slave' (*Praen.* XIV 648–9, = 116,24–118,8). And yet his departure took place in the summer of 166, while the cure of Boethus' wife must have occurred at least one, and probably two, years earlier.[47] Whatever we are to make of this (and it does not reflect well on Galen's candour), he escaped Rome by pretending to go for a country holiday, then slipping off to Brindisi, across the Adriatic to Corinth, and thence by sea again to Asia Minor. Perhaps he genuinely feared for his life. Perhaps he was, as he claims, averse to a high-profile public career in imperial service. Perhaps. The brief mention in *Lib.Prop.* notes that his departure happened shortly after an outbreak of plague (XIX 15, = *SM* 2, 96, 17–19).

The next couple of years are veiled in obscurity. Galen merely says that on his return home 'I did what I usually did' (*Lib.Prop.* XIX 17, = *SM* 2, 98,11–12), which presumably means treating patients, writing and research, although he does not explicitly date any of his texts to this period. It is conceivable that he also visited Lycia and Cyprus in search of medicinal plants (*SMT* XII 203, 220, 226–7).[48] About two and a half years later, Galen received a summons to join the Emperors (Lucius Verus and Marcus Aurelius) in their camp at Aquileia, where they were preparing to campaign against the German tribes on the Danube, his name having been mentioned in the course of 'a discussion about those who had demonstrated medicine and philosophy by deeds as well as words' (*Praen.* XIV 649, = 118,18–19). This self-characterization (adroitly placed in the mouths of others) is pointed: for Galen frequently castigates his medical opponents for their reliance on book-learning and lack of serious clinical practice (he calls them '*logiatroi*', word-doctors; *On Hippocrates' 'Nature of Man'* [HNH] XV, = *CMG* V 9,1, 81,23–4) and he also takes philosophers to task for failing to live up to their precepts, and preferring the appearance of wisdom to its reality ('we have not found even five people who actually want to be wise instead of merely appearing to be so': *On the Therapeutic Method* [MM] X 114). At *Praen.* XIV 655–6, = 124,14–22 he lumps them both together, and charges them with having brought both disciplines into disrepute by their malice, incompetence and moral laxity. He is particularly scornful of Methodist doctors and Cynic philosophers, both of whom he abominates as offering a fraudulent simulacrum of the truth, and for neglecting, indeed despising, the proper training in logical and analytical methods (*On the Diagnosis and Cure of the Errors of the Soul* [Pecc.Dig.] V 69–72, = *SM* 1, 53, 23–56,9).[49]

At all events, Galen travelled up the Ionian seaboard to the Troad,
where he found a ship bound for Thessalonika. He persuaded the
captain to make a stop in Lemnos, where he was hoping to procure
a supply of the famous branded medicinal earth, the terra sigillata.
Unfortunately they landed at the wrong port on the wrong side of the
island; being unable to persuade the captain to wait, he was unable
to make his purchase. Some twenty years later, he succeeded in buy-
ing 20,000 stamped cakes, which he used for a variety of conditions;
Galen was not a man to do things by halves (the whole story is told at
SMT XII 169–75). Next he crossed to Thrace and travelled to Macedonia on foot (*SMT* XII 171), arriving at Aquileia in the winter of 168–9,
just in time for an outbreak of the plague, 'which caused destruction
on a scale previously unknown'. The emperors both rapidly set off
for Rome (although Lucius Verus died suddenly on the way), leaving
Galen and other doctors to cope as best they could with the disease
and the rough winter weather (*Lib.Prop.* XIX 18, = *SM* 2, 98,23–
99,3). Some time in the spring, Galen rejoined the surviving emperor
Marcus Aurelius in Rome; and from now on, in spite of his earlier
reservations, his professional life was intimately linked with that of
the Imperial family. It may have been at this time that he treated the
boy Sextus Quintilius, an associate of the young prince Commodus
(*Praen.* XIV 651–7, = 120,16–126,15); although this may have taken
place later, during Marcus' absence on the prolonged German wars, or
even after his return in 176. Marcus asked Galen to accompany him
on the campaign; no doubt still scarred by his experience of military
life the previous winter, Galen contrived politely to avoid the invi-
tation by letting it be known that he had received instructions from
the god Asclepius not to go (*Lib.Prop.* XIX 18–19, = *SM* 2, 99,6–13);
this was a clever move, since Asclepius was Marcus' patron deity,
and as such he could hardly go against his wishes.[50] Once again, there
is a suggestion that Galen, for all his vaunted concern with virtue,
lacked a certain amount of physical courage.[51]

Galen says that Marcus at least believed that the campaign would
not be a long one (*Lib.Prop.* XIX 19, = *SM* 2, 99,13–14; cf. *Praen.* XIV
650, = 118,27); but in the event he was away from Rome for seven
years, during which time Galen attended to the medical needs of the
young Commodus, curing him of a fever and tonsilitis in less than
three days, in a manner utterly contrary to that recommended by the

Methodist doctors in the entourage of the Emperor's cousin, Annia Faustina,[52] who had visited the boy out of concern for his welfare.[53] Once again, Galen remarks that his diagnosis and cure caused great wonderment, although it was in reality nothing exceptional, at least for anyone who knew what they were doing (*Praen*. XIV 661, = 130, 11–12). As he explains to Commodus' tutor Peitholaus, all one needs to know about diagnosis and prognosis is contained in three treatises he had recently written, *On the Differences of Fevers* (*Diff.Feb.*), *On Crises* (*Cris.*) and *On Critical Days* (*Di.Dec.*), which demonstrate that almost all the basic information was already to be found in the works of Hippocrates:

I only added the theory of pulses, which was all that he had not worked out, just as his successors . . . have made various additions . . . Indeed, a knowledge of the dispositions (*diatheseis*) of the body depends on this theory, just as in turn the prognosis of future events depends upon accurate knowledge of these dispositions.[54] (*Praen*. XIV 665, = 134,38)

Galen did indeed consider his development of pulse doctrine his greatest contribution to diagnostic medicine, and his sphygmological skill is emphasized both in these case-histories and throughout his clinical works, and given detailed exposition in a series of treatises dedicated to the subject. But even in this field he does not claim complete originality, acknowledging the pioneering role of the great third-century BC Alexandrian Herophilus (*Diagnosis by Pulses* [*Dig.Puls.*] VIII 911, 956; *Causes of Pulses* [*Caus.Puls.*] IX 22; *Prognosis by Pulses* [*Praes.Puls.*] IX 278), and recognizing, albeit sometimes somewhat backhandedly, the contributions of later theorists.[55] All these texts, along with *Differences of Pulses* (*Diff.Puls.*), were probably written at around this period (although *Diff.Puls.* may be earlier), and together they constitute a formidable body of text,[56] not much less than 1,000 pages of the Kühn edition (although this includes the Latin translation).[57] His approach consisted of a rigorous classification of pulse-types, according to their size (the extent of the dilatation of the vessel, specified in each of the three dimensions of length, breadth and depth), their speed (how rapidly the diastole is accomplished), their strength, the hardness or softness of the vessels themselves, frequency (interval between pulses), and whether the pulse is consistent or not, and if not whether even in its inconsistency it exhibits some regularity (*On the Pulse for Beginners* [*Puls.*]

VIII 455–8); moreover, recurrent types of pulse are given evocative names: the 'gazelle-like', the 'ant-like', the 'worm-like' and suchlike (*Puls.* VIII 459–60).[58] Evidently, there is a very large number of possible permutations among these variables, although not all of them are diagnostically and therapeutically relevant. But, Galen thinks, it is possible with long practice (which is necessary in order to hone one's sense of touch to detect minute variations: Galen tells us how he trained himself to be able to perceive the faint trace of the arterial systole, which others had said was indiscernible: *Diagnosis by Pulses* [*Dig.Puls.*] VIII 786–806) and experience to discern which particular pulses are associated with what physical conditions, how they vary with age, gender, physical condition and season, how they are affected by emotional states and how various environmental and ingestive factors typically affected them[59] (*Puls.* VIII 462–77), which in turn leads to being able to use them as early warning signs of determinate unhealthy states (*Puls.* VIII 477–92).

But, as his diagnostic practice as already exhibited in some of the histories we have been looking at would indicate, this on its own is not enough: for different patients have different natural constitutions, and hence different healthy states; and in order to make the best possible diagnosis and prognosis in a case of illness, it helps enormously to know what the individual's diagnostic signs looked like when in health. But of course that is not always possible; and in those cases the doctor must fall back on what he can infer about the patient's constitution on the basis of age, gender, general state of health, mode of life and so on (*Puls.* VIII 462–3). There is a good deal of common sense in all of this; and some of Galen's observations are valid enough (indeed his general diagnostic categories in regard to the pulse are by and large compatible with modern clinical practice, even if the baroque complexities of the theory are largely fantastical); on the other hand, they are underpinned by, and taken by Galen to stand in relations of mutual support with, an utterly exploded set of physical and physiological theories.[60]

Some time after the winter of 169, and probably after the emperor's return to Rome in 176,[61] Galen performed a cure on the imperial person which he describes as 'truly remarkable' (*Praen.* XIV 657, = 126,16). His regular doctors, and indeed Marcus himself, all believed a paroxysm[62] had begun, but none such transpired over the succeeding two days. Galen is then called in:

Three doctors had already examined him at dawn and at the eighth hour [i.e. early afternoon]; they had taken his pulse; and they agreed that this was apparently the beginning of an attack of illness. When I stood by in silence, the emperor looked at me and asked why, when the others had taken his pulse, I alone had not done so. I replied that since they had already done so twice and the peculiarities of the pulse were probably known to them through their experience on their travels abroad with him, I expected they could obtain a better diagnosis of his present condition than I. On hearing this, he commanded me to take his pulse. It seemed to me that his pulse, compared with the general norm for each age and constitution, was far from showing the beginning of an attack, and so I said that there was no attack of fever but his stomach was overloaded with the food he had taken, which had turned to phlegm before excretion, and then manifested itself. (*Praen.* XIV 658–9, = 128,1–13)

The emperor immediately recognizes the plausibility of Galen's diagnosis, and asks for advice. Galen is a little reticent to prescribe his usual treatment of peppered wine, 'since doctors should employ the safest remedies in the case of kings', and so Galen prescribes instead a woollen pad for the stomach impregnated with nard. It turns out that the emperor had been wont to use this very remedy himself in similar circumstances. He then had his feet massaged, and ordered the peppered wine (a heating and drying agent to counteract the cold moisture of the phlegm) in any case (*Praen.* XIV 659–60, = 128,13–25). 'As you well know', Galen says, 'he was always speaking of me as the first among physicians and unique among philosophers', in sharp contrast to 'the many avaricious, quarrelsome, proud, jealous and spiteful he had already experienced' (*Praen.* XIV 660, = 128,27–30). This cure was remarkable, in Galen's view, because he was able to determine that the specific sign[63] of the onset of an illness was not present in this case, a specific sign which it was notoriously difficult to perceive. Galen, on his own account was going out on something of a limb here:

Having tested my own diagnosis of the beginning of a paroxysm long and carefully, I dared tell the emperor, a little rashly perhaps, but still I insisted on telling him, as soon as I had touched his pulse, an opinion contrary to what he had conjectured himself and had been told by his doctors. (*Praen.* XIV 661, = 130,7–10)

Here again we may see signs of a certain timidity of disposition lurking behind the bluster and the self-confidence, which sometimes appear, to Galen's admirers as well as to his detractors, as vainglorious arrogance. For contrary to the rather unattractive image he often seems to be consciously trying to project, Galen was capable of intellectual modesty, of avowing frankly areas of his own ignorance (even if he was still excessively confident in some domains where that confidence was less than fully justified); and he was also capable of changing his mind.[64] But Galen must have felt that everything was going his way: to secure the patronage of the wise and humane philosopher–emperor by means of a brilliant piece of rational diagnosis. And while his autobiographical self-presentation is no doubt both romanticized and self-serving, as autobiographies generally are, there is no reason to doubt that the account has a firm basis in fact. Galen did enter the imperial orbit; and he was indeed a star.[65]

During the emperor's absence, and when he was seeing to the health of Commodus with a success for which history may perhaps not judge him kindly, Galen continued to produce writing at a prodigious rate. In this time, in addition to the works already mentioned, he finished his great work of functional anatomy, *On the Utility of the Parts* (*UP*),[66] as well as completing his major work of medicophilosophical doxology, *On the Doctrines of Hippocrates and Plato* (*PHP*).[67] In this period, too, he wrote *On Anatomical Procedures* (*AA*),[68] and probably the first six books of his therapeutic masterpiece *On the Therapeutic Method* (*MM*)[69] as well, along with several shorter works. In fact this may have been the most productive period of his life (*Lib.Prop.* XIX 19–20, = *SM* 2, 99,25–100,18). Indeed it was the success of *UP*, and the consequent envious slander it aroused among his unworthy opponents, that eventually induced him (at the urging of his friends, he says) briefly to come out of performing retirement and undertake a last series of public demonstrations (*Lib.Prop.* XIX 20–2, = *SM* 2, 100,18–102,10).

Hereafter, our evidence for his life becomes a lot sparser. *Praen.* was probably published in 178; his other (partially) biographical writing, *On slander*, has not survived. Marcus Aurelius died in 180, and the purple was taken by his son Commodus, whose capricious, cruel and deranged reign lasted until his assassination in 192. The empire was then offered to Pertinax, a self-made man who had risen to senatorial rank, and who had a distinguished record of public service. He tried to undo the harm wrought by his predecessor, as well as offering clemency to his own enemies; and sought to restore public finances by, among other things, selling off the luxury goods acquired by Commodus, and attempting to undo the web of corruption which had stifled trade and ruined the economy. He lasted eighty-six days before the Pretorian Guard, seeing their power threatened, marched to the palace and killed him. Gibbon paints an affecting portrait of his futile appeal to their better nature and his courageous death. Galen wrote a book *Public Pronouncements in the Presence of*[70] *Pertinax* (*Lib.Prop.* XIX 46, = *SM* 2, 122,4), listed among his works relevant to moral philosophy. We know nothing of its content; but it is a safe bet that he honoured the memory of the murdered emperor, the only one named in the title of any of his books.

There followed a period of chaos, with the Pretorian guard first auctioning off the empire to the highest bidder, one Didius Julianus (his principate lasted sixty-six days), which precipitated the three-way civil war from which Septimius Severus would eventually emerge victorious and restore a certain measure of order and dignity to the empire (Galen uncharacteristically flatters him, and his co-emperor, the unworthy Caracalla, in a late work as 'the greatest of emperors': *On Theriac to Piso* [*Ther.Pis.*] XIV 217). Galen was presumably in Rome for most if not all of this period, although he seems to have made a trip back to Pergamum at some time, probably in the 190s, stopping again at Lemnos to replenish his supplies (*SMT* XII 171).[71] He may also have had his library finally brought back with him at this time; at any rate he says that when he started to write commentaries on Hippocrates' texts (probably in the 170s; the task occupied him, on and off, for at least twenty years),[72] he had to reconstruct the errors of the other exegetes from memory, since he did not have his books with him in Rome (*Lib.Prop.* XIX 34, = *SM* 2, 112,5–7). At all events, Galen certainly spent his first period at Rome without his own library, a fact which lends credence to his claims that he had not intended to settle permanently there, even if that was precisely what he did, although always conscious of his status as an exile, albeit one of a large and privileged expatriate population.[73] He writes 'for Greeks and for those who aspire to Greek pursuits even though barbarian by birth' (*On the Preservation of Health* [*San.Tu.*] VI 51, = *CMG* V 4,2, 24,22–5); and while the context concerns the inadequacies of German child-rearing, 'barbarian' is still traditionally, and pointedly, contrasted with 'Greek' and with Greek alone.

At all events, the mature (if that is the right word) Commodus hardly figures in Galen's extant writings; and it seems reasonable to suppose that Galen either distanced himself as far as possible from him as the emperor's excesses and paranoia became more and more apparent, or that at least he later had the grace to elide any such connection. He does mention treating members of the terrorized senatorial class for anxiety induced by their (justified) fear of being poisoned (*On Hippocrates' 'Epidemics'* [*Hipp.Epid. VI comm.VIII*], = *CMG* V 10,2,2, 494,2–25). It may perhaps be not too fanciful to see a veiled reference to him in his contention in later works that all people are not born equally gifted with basic virtue, and then made or unmade by their upbringing: rather, some are naturally so virtuous as to be able to resist corrupting influences, while others are so vicious by nature that no amount of decent moral education and example can make them good (cf. e.g. *The Faculties of the Soul Follow the Mixtures of the Body* [*QAM*] IV 768–9, 814–21, = *SM* 2, 32,14–33,16, 73,3–79,9).[74] Furthermore, his admiration for the fortitude of the slaves of Perennis[75] under judicial torture may also contain a coded expression of distaste for the tyrant, as well as giving a brief taste of Galen's moral and political views.[76] The story is preserved in the Arabic epitome of *On Moral Character* [*Mor*]:

this [sc. courage under torture] was observed in the case of the slaves of Perennis and their attitude to their late master; although they had not been educated, they acted like freeborn men, since they were free by nature. This indicates that love of nobility exists in some people by nature. (reported by Walzer, 1947, = 1962, 158 n. 2)[77]

One further reference to Commodus is to be found in *On Antidotes* (*Ant.*)[78] XIV 65: when he became emperor, he saw no use for theriac and cinnamon, and had all the precious store of *materia medica*, laid up since the time of Hadrian, destroyed, so that when Galen was asked by the emperor Severus (193–211) to prepare his imperial theriac again, he had to go back to materials stored in the time of Hadrian and Trajan (cf. 64: Galen discovered these stores when preparing theriac for Marcus).[79] This passage, if genuine (see n. 78), shows that Galen continued to serve in the imperial orbit.

Immediately prior to the assassination of Commodus, Galen suffered a serious personal loss. In 192, a great fire burned down the Temple of Peace and many other buildings in the neighbourhood. The temple was a meeting place for intellectuals, and also served as a book repository and store. Galen lost all his copies of his own books in it, some of them irretrievably. He refers to the fire in several places. At the beginning of *On the Composition of Drugs according to Kind* (*Comp.Med.Gen.*) XIII 362–3, he says that the two first books of the treatise had been published and deposited there when the fire destroyed them; and as none of his friends had copies, he was forced to rewrite them. But he thought he should point this out in case anyone later should happen to come across a copy of the earlier version and wonder why it had been written twice. At *Hipp.Epid. VI comm. VIII*, = *CMG* V 10,2,2, 495,2–12, he says that *On Prognosis* 'along with many other books' had been lost, and while he still hoped one would turn up, he had not yet found any other copy in existence. He also lost a valuable store of medicaments, made in part from precious materials from the imperial stores, which he deposited there in wooden boxes (*Ant.* XIV 65). Indeed, much of the fruits of his period of intensive research and writing while Marcus was on campaign were also lost (*Lib.Prop.* XIX 19, = *SM* 2, 99,23–5). Some texts were recovered in other copies (some of them after Galen's death: he never knew that *Praen.* had survived); others he rewrote. But it is remarkable that he never seems to treat this as a great personal disaster (unlike the grammarian Callistus, who also lost his books in the fire, and died of a fever brought on by grief and insomnia: *Hipp.Epid. VI comm.VIII*, = *CMG* V 10,2,2, 486,19–24). If, as seems likely, *Aff.Dig.* was written after this episode,[80] it is striking that no mention is made of it in the passage (43–5, = 33,11–35,3) where he discusses equanimity in the face of loss (although this is a record of a much earlier exhortation, to a rich man in Pergamum). Perhaps Galen really was able in the face of adversity to cultivate the philosophical calm he sought to induce in others.

The last years of Galen's life are shrouded in obscurity. We do not even know when he died, although it now appears overwhelmingly likely that he lived well into the third century. *On Antidotes* must have been written in the third century, and *On Theriac to Piso*, which Nutton argues to be genuine,[81] no earlier than 204 (it reports an equestrian accident that befell Piso's favourite son at the Secular Games of that year), and probably later than 207.[82] We do know that Galen carried on writing and working almost until the end, finishing the treatises on drugs and remedies, among others, and completing his therapeutic masterpiece *MM*, as well as the *Ars Medica*, his compendium of diagnostics and therapeutics which was to become the fundamental medical text of the late Middle Ages and

Renaissance, and his treatment of differential diagnosis, *On Affected Parts* (*Loc.Aff.*). If *Prop.Plac.* was not quite written on his death bed, as Nutton romantically suggests (1999, 217–18), it cannot have pre-dated it by much.

Galen, as we have seen, sets great store by moral virtue, believing (or at any rate professing to believe) that it is only by systematically curing oneself of the tendency towards luxury and vice that we have any prospect of doing anything worthwhile in life (*Opt.Med.* I 59–61, = *SM* 2, 6,4–7,24); and *Aff.Dig.* is almost entirely devoted to laying out and exhorting us to follow a plan of constant moral self-improvement. But it has long been noted that Galen seems in certain very obvious respects to fail to live up to his own ideals – and, worse, he seems altogether unaware of these failings. Was he in need of what he recommends to others (*Aff.Dig.* V 8–14, = *SM* 1, 5,24–11,2), friends of unimpeachable candour to point out his faults? He prescribes mildness of demeanour and imperviousness to the slanders of others, and yet he attacks those he perceives as his enemies with relentless ferocity, even while praising his own calmness. He censures others for contentiousness and squabbling, but his texts are packed with polemic; he attacks other doctors for being *arrivistes*, seeking to flatter their way into the best society, yet he too was an immigrant from the provinces with an eye for making a name for himself in the best society; he scorns the money-grubbing greed of others as being unworthy of a liberal mind, and yet he flaunts the gift of 40,000 sesterces he receives from his consular friend Boethus for curing his wife (*Praen.* XIV 647, = Nutton 116,16–19). Nutton (1979, 180) refers to 'Galen's inconsistency'; Ilberg (1897, 617) is particularly upset by his contentiousness, describing him as 'a low character'.

Is this fair? Is Galen nothing more than a bullying hypocrite, a perfect example of the type he regularly and mercilessly excoriates? I think a less negative assessment is in order. If he came from the provinces, that does not show that he was motivated by the desire for wealth (which in any case he had no need of), and neither does his acceptance of gifts from grateful patients. Moreover, if he is contentious, it is in pursuit of the truth, rather than of spurious fame or gain. At the beginning of *MM*, in the course of one of his finest excoriations of the degeneracy of the times, (X 1–10), Galen distinguishes between two sorts of competition (or rather strife: *eris*): the healthy type between colleagues genuinely desirous of the truth (X 5–7) and its degenerate modern sibling (X 7–9), as exemplified by Thessalus, the upstart doctor from a family of wool-carders, uncouth and uneducated, who dares to profane the sacred art by saying that it can be taught in six months and 'has no need of geometry, astronomy, logic, music, or any of the other noble disciplines' (X 5).

Abstracting (if we can) from the snobbish tone,[83] and making allowances for the fact that Galen is evidently a partisan here, there is still no reason to doubt the fundamental sincerity of his belief that truth can only be won by the sort of diligent application allied to natural talent developed by a liberal education that he himself exemplifies, nor about his belief that many, perhaps most, of his opponents are quacks and charlatans, who are not really concerned with the truth. If nothing else, Galen's vast literary output, over a period of perhaps seventy years, when he was constantly engaged in other activities, is testament to his prodigious energy and industry; while his undoubted rhetorical excessiveness, so grating to many modern ears, is none the less characteristic of its times. There is no doubt that Galen's texts are rhetorical; no doubt that he is the hero of his own story; and no doubt that Galen sometimes misrepresents the positions of his opponents in order to sharpen his critique and to emphasize his differences from them. But rhetorical extravagance does not imply falsehood, as some apparently suppose; nor is exaggeration invariably a cardinal sin. Galen saw himself, no doubt in self-aggrandizing terms, as a man on a heroic mission to rescue medicine, and science in general, from their degenerate decrepitude. Desperate times called for desperate measures. And if he was often mistaken, and in general unjustifiably over-confident of the truth of his position and the security of his first principles,[84] he was not incapable of changing his mind, and of learning from his errors, when he cared to admit to them.

Indeed, one can detect a softening of his doctrinaire and polemical tone in later works such as *On the Formation of the Foetus* (*Foet.Form.*), *The Powers of the Soul Follow the Mixtures of the Body* (*QAM*) and *On His Own Opinions* (*Prop.Plac.*). Alexander of Aphrodisias, who was no great fan of Galen's philosophy, was yet moved to call him '*endoxos*', a man of justifiable standing (*in Arist.Top. CIAG* II 2, 549,23–4); and his jibe that Galen had spent eighty years coming to the conclusion that he knew nothing is surely an unfair spin on the agnosticism regarding some issues in philosophy and cosmology

which Galen calmly avows in *On His Own Opinions*,[85] his last work
and one which Nutton nicely characterizes as 'Galen's philosophical
testament'.[86]

NOTES

1. Galen's dates have been established by Nutton (1972a, 1973; cf. 1979,
   210), although that of his death is vaguer: somewhere between AD
   210 and 217 is probable, and later rather than earlier in that span
   seems likelier to me: see p. 22. At any event, Nutton has con-
   clusively proved that the (very late) tradition which places Galen's
   death in 199, a date still regularly asserted in numerous contexts, is
   utterly without credibility, while an Arabic tradition has him working until well into his eighties; see further Strohmeier (2006) and
   forthcoming. There is no adequate full-length biography of Galen;
   García Ballester (1972b) is no more than serviceable, while Sarton
   (1954) pre-dates the recent explosion of Galen scholarship, and is
   in any case very unreliable. The best short account is to be found
   in Nutton (2004, ch. 15); also useful is the Introduction to Singer
   (1997).
2. His patron Boethus supplied him with expert shorthand takers: *On Prognosis* (*Praen.*) XIV 630, = *CMG* V 8,1, 98,27–100,1 (Nutton, 1979).
3. For the style of referencing throughout this volume, see *Note on
   Citations*.
4. See further chs. 2 and 13 (Lloyd, Flemming) both in this volume.
5. For a preliminary account, see Boudon (2002).
6. Nutton (2004, 390 n. 22); and about a third as much again survives in
   translations into other languages (Arabic, Hebrew, Latin). Moreover, a
   great deal, perhaps half his total output, has been lost. For some idea of
   its extent, in two circumscribed areas, see the lists at the beginning of
   chs. 4 and 5 (Morison) in this volume.
7. Galen estimates its population, *exempli gratia*, as being 40,000 male
   citizens, rising to 120,000 if you included wives and slaves (*Aff.Dig.* V
   49, = *SM* 1, 38,17–21); but it is not clear how accurate this is supposed to
   be, nor upon what evidence (if any) it is based. But if it is even remotely
   accurate, Pergamum was a big town.
8. *On the Doctrines of Hippocrates and Plato* [*PHP*] V 742, = *CMG* V 4,1,2,
   556,28–30 De Lacy. The compliment is somewhat backhanded, since he
   immediately remarks (following Plato) that 'men are superior in every
   employment and discipline'.
9. See further Frede (2003, 78–9).

10. Translated in Mattock (1972).

11. Cf. *On Prognosis* (*Praen.*) XIV 608, = *CMG* V 8,1, 76,28–78,2 (Nutton, 1979); his father had originally intended him to become a philosopher.

12. The Rationalists (or Dogmatists) were one of the three general 'sects' or schools (*haireseis*) into which medical practitioners of the time were grouped, the others being Empiricists and Methodists. The distinction is already found in the first-century BC medical encyclopaedist Celsus (*de Medicina* Proem. 13–67), although its canonization owes much to Galen himself (see ch. 2 [Lloyd] in this volume, pp. 35, 41–2). Although there are many distinct types of Rationalist, they are linked by their common commitment to finding the internal causal bases of diseases, and hence of therapy. By contrast, Empiricists content themselves with observing regular conjunctions of events and devising therapies accordingly; while Methodists rely on a single, extremely general typology of diseases into 'relaxed', 'constricted' and 'mixed', and hold that which of these categories an ailment falls under is immediately obvious, at least to the trained eye. Galen himself agreed with the Rationalists about the importance of inferring to the hidden, causal structure of things; but he also allowed that experience was absolutely necessary in order to confirm what reason suggests (see ch. 6 [Hankinson] in this volume); and as such he claims to be an adherent of no school (indeed he thinks that uncritical party allegiance is responsible for serious medical malpractice: *Ord.Lib.Prop.* XIX 50–5, = *SM* 2, 80,11–83.23). But he has no time at all for the Methodists: see p. 14. Galen treated of the differences among them in *On Sects for Beginners* [*SI*]: I 64–105, = *SM* 3, 1–32. On the schools, see Frede (1985 introduction; 1982, 1987b, 1988, 1990); Edelstein (1967a, 1967b); Hankinson (1987b, 1995); and see ch. 6 (Hankinson) in this volume, pp. 171–5.

13. 'Later I went to Corinth to hear Numisianus, the most famous pupil of Quintus; then I visited Alexandria and several other places where I heard that he was living.' For more on Galen's anatomical education, see ch. 9 (Rocca) in this volume. For Galen's Egyptian experience, see Nutton (1993c).

14. See *On the Composition of Drugs according to Kind* (*Comp.Med.Gen.*) XIII 599–601; his reputation for surgical excellence had preceded him, he says; but he also impressed the authorities with a public display of his skills on an ape (*On Recognizing the Best Physician* [*Opt.Med.Cogn.*] 9 4–7, = *CMG* Suppl.Or. IV, 103,10–105,19 Iskandar: this may have been one of Galen's earliest public demonstrations; see further pp. 11–13); see also Scarborough (1971). Galen mentions that his first appointment lasted only seven and a half months, which some have interpreted to be the normal length of the priesthood (and so Galen's service under five priests would only last a little over three years); but Nutton (1973, 163–4)

convincingly argues that the first priesthood was artificially cut short, presumably by the official's death, and that an interim appointment was made to finish out the normal year.

15. E.g., at *On the Properties of Foodstuffs* (*Alim.Fac.*) VI 507, = *CMG* V 4,2, 232,11–12, he notes that he has seen peasants of Cyprus make a type of bread with barley-groats; and he also noticed that a tree which is poisonous in Persia produces edible fruit in Alexandria (*ibid.* 617, = 303,5–9). In Alexandria, too, he observed how rapid were the deaths caused by vipers; so much so that they were used as a 'humane' method of execution: *Ther.Pis.* XIV 236–7 (this follows his account of the death of Cleopatra: 235–6).

16. This is actually a classificatory scheme borrowed from Empiricist medicine (*Outline of Empiricism* [*Subf.Emp.*] 6, Fr 10b 56 Deichgraber); Galen is not himself an Empiricist, but he is by no means universally hostile to their practice. See n. 12 above.

17. As Nutton (1979, 158) notes, 'Galen's early career was a paradigm of successful social mobility, yet only J.Ilberg . . . has noted the importance of his friends from Pergamum in assisting his rise. It was not only his medical and philosophical ability . . . but also his family connections, made among the leading citizens of Pergamum and Asia, that enabled him to make his mark almost at once in Rome. When he arrived . . . he came not as an impoverished and friendless provincial, but as a man of means whose school friends and associates were already there: Teuthras, Apellas, Eudemus, Epigenes and possibly even Glaucon.' On the social make-up of Galen's clientele, see Horstmanshoff (1995); on the social status of doctors, see Pleket (1995).

18. Nutton (1979, 157) suggests that he may be 'the unnamed pupil of Aspasius who on his return to his native Pergamum after a long absence' taught Galen (*Aff.Dig.* 8: 41–2, = *SM* 1, 32,5–7). It is possible (and Galen does refer to him as 'my teacher' at *Praen.* XIV 613, = 82,11–13 Nutton); but there is no other evidence in favour of this view, and we might perhaps have expected Galen to mention it in the context of his celebrated cure. But on the other hand, Galen is seeking in *Praen.* to emphasize his credentials as a self-made man, and might thus suppress such information to that very end.

19. Equally characteristic is the exordium to *MM*: X 1–8; see Hankinson (1991b).

20. A particular bugbear of Galen's: he is constantly berating the Methodists for their claim to be able to teach the whole of medicine in a single six-month course: see e.g. *On Sects for Beginners* (*SI*) I 82–3, = *SM* 1, 14,22–15,7; *MM* X 781, 927.

21. Charges of sorcery were not to be taken lightly, being capital offences: cf. Nutton (1979, 150). It is not at all clear, however, whether any such

charges were laid against doctors; cf. also *Praen.* XIV 655, = 124,17 Nutton. In *The Best Doctor is also a Philosopher* (*Opt.Med.*), a short but important exposition of Galen's belief that the proper physician must have a thorough grounding in all aspects of the philosophical curriculum, logic, physics and ethics, Galen repeats the claim that prognostic excellence invites the charge of recourse to the supernatural: *Opt.Med.* I 54–5, = *SM* 2, 2, 9–11.

22. The reference is to Plato's *Gorgias* 464d–e.

23. It is lost, but Galen refers to it at *Lib.Prop.* XIX 46, = *SM* 2, 122,2, as 'containing material concerning my own life'; *Lib.Prop.* XIX 15, = *SM* 2, 96,5–16.

24. This case is also discussed in ch. 2 (Lloyd) in this volume, pp. 38, 44.

25. On the practice of 'multiple consultations', see Nutton (1979, 160).

26. A fever with a periodicity of seventy-two hours; usually now identified as a species of recurrent malaria.

27. A generic term covering drugs composed of a wide variety of ingredients including animal venoms, used as a prophylactic as well as a panacea: see Nutton (1979, 160–1). Two treatises on the subject are ascribed to Galen, although only one of them is probably authentic – see p. 22; *On Antidotes* (*Ant.*), also now generally thought to be genuine, also deals with the subject. See further ch. 13 (Flemming) in this volume.

28. Curiously not named as such in the course of the actual clinical discussion, but only in an earlier anticipation of it: *Praen.* XIV 626, = 94,22 Nutton. The identity of this Justus is disputed (see Nutton, 1979, 186–7), but he will have been someone of social standing and importance in order for the case to fulfil its rhetorical purpose here.

29. On the theory of depression and 'black bile', which had an extremely long medical history (and traces of which still survive in our vocabulary of melancholy), see Jackson (1986, esp. 41–5); on Galen and mental illness, see Jackson (1969); on Galen's psychophysical account of human functioning, see Hankinson (1993), and ch. 7 (Donini) in this volume.

30. On the importance of such testing for Galen, see chs. 3 and 6 (Tieleman and Hankinson) in this volume.

31. On this, see Nutton (1979, 194–6).

32. See further Hankinson (1992b); and ch. 8 in this volume.

33. See ch. 3 (Tieleman) in this volume; Galen wrote, initially for his own benefit, extensive commentaries on the *Analytics* of both Aristotle and Theophrastus: *Lib.Prop.* XIX 41–2, = *SM* 2, 117,20–118,12.

34. See Hankinson (1991a, 1994d).

35. For chronological details, see Nutton (1979, 217–18).

36. On Galen and the 'Second Sophistic', with its culture of display and disputation, see Kollesch (1981); Brunt (1994); von Staden (1997a); and

ch. 2 (Lloyd) in this volume. On the anatomical demonstrations, see Hankinson (1994e); and ch. 9 (Rocca) in this volume.

37. On Boethus' life and career, see Nutton (1979, 164); all of our evidence derives from Galen.

38. *Lib.Prop.* (XIX 12, = *SM* 2, 94,18) refers to two books: perhaps *On the Function of Breathing* (*Ut.Resp.*) is also meant (both are edited in Furley and Wilkie, 1984); but the *On the Causes of Breathing* (*Caus.Resp.*) we possess is only four pages long, and may well be an abridgement of the original.

39. On the disputes with Martialius, and the question of his name (he is apparently the same man elsewhere referred to as Martianius) see ch. 2 (Lloyd) in this volume, p. 36.

40. It is also treated in (Lloyd) ch. 2 in this volume, p. 38.

41. *Ven.Sect.Er.Rom.*, along with two other treatises on venesection, is translated with notes and essays by Brain (1986).

42. This Alexander, who is described in *AA* II 218 as 'the official exponent of the Peripatetic doctrines in Athens', is often identified with Alexander of Aphrodisias, holder of the Athenian chair some time after 198. Nutton, who favours the identification, notes that 'the Arabic biographers, who had much more of Galen to hand than we have . . . regarded the identification as certain'. But *AA* was written in the 170s, twenty years at least before Alexander of Aphrodisias was appointed. It is possible that this is a later insertion, but even so it would be surprising in a description of events that occurred at least thirty-five years earlier without more explicit signposting. And the description of this Alexander's philosophical allegiance hardly suits the better-known commentator on Aristotle, whose Aristotle is much less Platonic than that of some others. Moreover, the existence of two different toponymics is peculiar. That Alexander of Aphrodisias did at least know of Galen's work is, however, certain: see p. 24.

43. On his contempt for Pyrrhonian scepticism, see ch. 6 (Hankinson) in this volume. On the case, see ch. 2 (Lloyd) in this volume, p. 44.

44. Elsewhere he says that he outlined his own discoveries in *Caus.Resp.* (*AA* II 660); they are sketched in the *Caus.Resp.* we possess; but see n. 38 above.

45. Some of these are described in more detail in ch. 9 (Rocca) in this volume; see also Rocca (2003).

46. At least, this seems the likely date of his abandonment of public demonstration; but as Lloyd (ch. 2 in this volume, p. 37) says, the text is unclear, and it might refer to a somewhat later date, after his return to Rome in 169. At all events, some time after that he did briefly come out of retirement: p. 19.

47. See Nutton (1979, 202–3, 210, 217–18).

48. See Nutton (1979, 210).

49. A blackly humorous anecdote recounted in *MM* X 909–14 underlines the connection. Galen is attending the bedside of an ailing Cynic philosopher Theagenes, and offers detailed advice on treatment. But Theagenes' primary physician, the Methodist Attalus, rejects this, saying 'leave Theagenes in my care for three days and you will se him completely recovered' (X 912). Galen demurs: 'what if small, sticky beads of sweat suddenly appear, and then he dies?' Attalus merely laughs at him, and cuts Galen's lengthy disquisition short by walking out. Galen leaves too, washing his hands of the matter, and Attalus persists in his treatment, telling everyone that Theagenes is well on the way to recovery. Of course Galen is right: the patient suddenly dies. Not knowing this, Attalus arrives with his retinue, fully expecting to be able to display a restored Theagenes to all of them. He marches into the bedchamber, where he finds Theagenes' servants washing the corpse; and since, as befits the household of a philosopher, they are uttering no lamentations, he fails to realize what has happened until the last possible moment. Galen revels in his discomfiture with typical *Schadenfreude*: 'Attalus distinguished himself in front of a large crowd by showing off his patient relieved of his inflammation within four days, just as he had promised he would' (X 915).

50. Galen does not specify how these instructions were supposed to have reached him – and perhaps he declined to specify. But no doubt it would have been assumed that they arrived in a dream; as we have seen already, even the educated and sophisticated, like Galen's father, placed implicit trust in prophetic dreams (cf. *On His Own Opinions* [*Prop.Plac.*] 2.2, = *CMG* V 3,1, 58,7–16 Nutton [1999]); see also Nutton, 1979, 135–40; cf. *UP* X 12: III 812–13, = ii 93,5–10 Helmreich [1909]). Elsewhere Galen records having been directed to therapies by divine dream injunction (*On Treatment by Bloodletting* [*Cur.Rat.Ven.Sect.*] XI 314–15; *MM* X 971–2).

51. However, see Walsh (1931) for a more sympathetic view.

52. On the identification of this particular Annia, see Nutton (1979, 222–3) (it was first suggested by Ilberg, 1905, 206). Galen apparently does not like her – her attitude is superior and sarcastic, snotty even – but he does not have much time for women in general: see above, p. 2.

53. The Methodists adopted the *diatritos*, a period of forty-eight hours' fasting before applying treatment in the case of fevers, an approach that Galen considered misguided to the point of criminality: see e.g. *On Antecedent Causes* (*CP*) iii–iv 22–9, 76,10–78,23 Hankinson (1998a); see also Hankinson (1998a, 173–4).

54. On the importance of the determination of the *diatheseis* in medical practice, see ch. 8 (Hankinson) in this volume, pp. 230-1.

55. See von Staden (1991) for Galen's debts, both acknowledged and elided, to his predecessors on this score.

56. And stigmatized, not without some justice, as 'the most uncongenial of all to read': Nutton (1979, 221).

57. For the editions of Galen, see Note on citations and abbreviations.

58. Dalrymple (1993) describes doctors from the old Muslim quarter of New Delhi still using a similar classification, with much of the same terminology, which they acknowledge as being Galenic (for the persistence of such Galenic debts, see ch. 14 [Nutton] in this volume, n. 2).

59. Such as bathing, exercise, food, wine and water: VIII 467-70.

60. For more on which see ch. 6 (Hankinson) and ch. 10 (Debru) both in this volume.

61. Nutton (1979, 217) accepts both dates as possible; I incline to the latter on the grounds that Galen suggests that the other doctors had a great deal of experience of the Emperor's condition while abroad, which seems to suit the period 169-76 better than the brief campaign of 168.

62. A technical term for the rapid worsening of a disease to the point of crisis, which would be followed either by recovery (whether temporary or permanent) or death: see in particular *Opportune Moments in Diseases as a Whole* (*Tot.Morb.Temp.*) VII 440-62, esp. 440; and *Opportune Moments in Diseases* (*Morb.Temp.*) VII 46-39; the subject is also of great importance in *On Crises* (*Cris.*) IX 550-760.

63. This is also a technical diagnostic term in which a relatively precisely defined outcome is indicated, contrasted with general signs, which only show that a result of certain type is to be expected: see e.g. *Prognosis by Pulses* (*Praes.Puls.*) IX 421-30; *Cris.* IX 763-8. On medical indications, see ch. 11 (van der Eijk) in this volume, pp. 292-5.

64. See ch. 6 (Hankinson) in this volume.

65. See ch. 2 (Lloyd) in this volume and Nutton (1984a), for an assessment of Galen's fame in his own time and shortly thereafter.

66. See ch. 8 (Hankinson), ch. 9 (Rocca) and ch. 10 (Debru) all in this volume. *UP* is edited in Helmreich (1907/1909), and translated in May (1967).

67. Edition, translation and commentary in De Lacy (1978-83). See ch. 3 (Tieleman), ch. 4 (Morison), ch. 6 (Hankinson) and ch. 9 (Rocca) all in this volume, for discussions on various important passages.

68. See Garofalo (1986), for a partial edition of the surviving Greek; Simon (1906), for an edition of the books only preserved in Arabic. The Greek text is translated in Singer (1956); the Arabic in Duckworth *et al.* (1962). See Rocca, ch. 9 in this volume.

69. Books I and II translated with commentary in Hankinson (1991b): for the dating, see xxxiii–xxxiv. See also ch. 11 (van der Eijk) in this volume.
70. Or possibly 'in the Reign of': but other similar titles show that the pronouncements in question are Galen's – and it is hard to think that he is simply dating them thereby.
71. For this hypothesis, see Greenhill (1854, 208); Nutton (1979, 209).
72. See ch. 13 (Flemming) in this volume.
73. Nutton (1979, 177) points out that for Galen 'home' always refers to Pergamum (cf. *Praen.* XIV 620, = 90,8–9; *SMT* XII 272), 'our king' to Attalus (*SMT* XII 251: not to be confused with the doctor of the same name: above n. 49.); etc.; see also Nutton (2004, 227).
74. See further Hankinson (1993). Although Galen's view owes something to both Aristotelian and Platonic ethics, and is aimed squarely against that of the Stoics, it seems to be more uncompromising than any of them. Walzer (1949b, 1954) over-estimates the extent of Galen's debt to the Platonizing Stoic Posidonius in this context, and consequently under-estimates his originality (Posidonius, whom Galen does indeed cite with approval, is often credited by modern scholars with being the source of Galen's views, sometimes on the flimsiest of grounds).
75. One of Commodus' shady 'advisors', turned conspirator against him.
76. Nutton (1999, 140) remarks that 'a positive reference to the behaviour of [the] slaves . . . is hardly likely to have been made public until after the death of . . . Commodus in 192'; that may be right, although Galen might have thought even Commodus able to distinguish between approval for their comportment in their predicament and support for the revolt that landed them there.
77. It appears in curiously abridged form in the translation of Mattock (1972, 243) with no reference to Perennis. I have no idea why.
78. *Ant.* is now generally thought genuine: see Nutton (1997c).
79. The story is pointed: if anyone had need of theriac, it was Commodus, who would eventually be drugged and assassinated.
80. As is likely, on the assumption that *Mor.* was published after 192 (n. 76 above), since it is referred to at *Aff.Dig.* V 27, = *SM* I, 20,21.
81. Nutton (1995, 1997c).
82. See Nutton (1997c); see also Swain (1996, 430–2).
83. Frede (1985, xxx–xxxi), notes that the emergence of 'low' medicines such as Methodism could be, and evidently was, perceived as a social threat; cf. Hankinson (1991b, 84–5).
84. Although see ch. 6 (Hankinson) in this volume, for a more nuanced assessment of this charge (forcefully made in Lloyd, 1996a).

85. As argued by Nutton (1999, 38–9); the 'agnostic' passages are *Prop.Plac.*
2.1–3.2, 4.1, 7.1–5, 11.1, 14.1–15.2, = 56,12–60,11, 62,18–19,76,25–
80,13, 90,18–20, 110,4–118,10; see also ch. 6 (Hankinson) in this volume,
and Hankinson (forthcoming (1)).
86. See Nutton (1987d); for a positive assessment of Galen's importance as
a philosopher, see Frede (1981); for a slightly less complimentary view,
see Donini (1980).

2   Galen and his contemporaries

A considerable portion of Galen's massive literary output is devoted to commenting on and criticizing other theorists, his own contemporaries as well as figures from the past, both doctors and philosophers, individuals and groups, some of whom he praises but most of whom attract his disapproval. One could touch on almost every aspect of Galen's work, in logic, moral philosophy, psychology, physiology, anatomy, pathology, pharmacology and therapeutics by way of an analysis of his reaction to others. So the potential field suggested by the title of this chapter is vast. I shall adopt what may at first sight seem an unusual tactic in order to focus on the topic that will form the core of my discussion, namely Galen's use of his contemporaries and predecessors as foils in constructing his own position by way of contrasting it with theirs. The first section of this chapter will be devoted to Galen and his medical colleagues, before I turn in the second, but shorter section, to his relationship with his philosophical ones.

My starting-point will be the contrast that Galen himself sometimes draws between situations of overt polemic and other contexts, whether of medical practice or of instruction. Of course it is a well-known ploy to disclaim arguing rhetorically when doing precisely that, and there are plenty of occasions where Galen offers such token disclaimers in the heat of sustained polemic. But there are also contexts where his overt aim – as he describes it – is not to win a debate, but to instruct.

This might make it seem that Galen's oeuvre can be divided into (at least) two broad groups, which to some extent might be seen as mirroring the contrast we find, within the Hippocratic Corpus, between technical writings on the one hand, and polemical works

34

dealing with issues of theory or methodology on the other.[1] The *Epidemics* would come in the first category, while such works as *On Ancient Medicine, On the Nature of Man* and *On the Art* would come in the other, though of course plenty of other works do not fit neatly into just those two groups. However, the question we have to press where Galen is concerned is whether or how far such a division can be applied to his own works.

In his autobiobibliographical work *On My Own Books* (*Lib.Prop.*) XIX 10,2ff., = *SM* 2, 92,11ff., he describes how he composed some of his works, particularly in the early stages of his career when he says he had no thought of publication. He wrote some at the request of friends, to whom he gave them without even keeping a copy himself. Some of these works, as he explains, then fell into the hands of unscrupulous individuals who passed them off as their own, in, however, often severely mutilated versions, with additions and alterations that Galen discovered in his second period in Rome from 169. At that point, he set out to revise those early works and in some cases he specifically added to the title that they were addressed 'to Beginners'.[2]

That clearly suggests a pedagogic function. But it is equally obvious from those works 'to Beginners' that have survived that pedagogy did not exclude polemic. The work *On Sects for Beginners* (*SI*) shows that among the subjects on which Galen thought tyros should be instructed were the strengths and weaknesses of competing methodologies or 'schools' of medicine. But it is far from being the case that Galen presents the positions of the 'Dogmatists', the 'Empiricists' and the 'Methodists' as they themselves might have represented them. Even though the three-fold classification of medical sects had already been anticipated, in a sense, by Celsus,[3] Galen's account – of the Methodists especially – betrays the influence of his own evaluations. He does not offer as neutral a version of their views as possible and then allow the students to make up their own minds on the subject. Rather, his analysis is influenced at every stage by his own ideas about the correct method.

Yet some works addressed 'for Beginners' are relatively free from controversy (cf. Boudon 1994). The introductory work *On the Pulse for Beginners* (*Puls.*) concentrates on giving a brief summary of the signs to be looked for in the pulse without entering into such debates as those about the contents of the arteries (where the Erasistrateans of course maintained that naturally they contain air, not blood) or about the causes of their dilatation. Similarly his elementary work *On Bones for Beginners* (*Oss.*) is an unvarnished introduction to that aspect of anatomy.

Further passages in *Lib.Prop.* and elsewhere provide a glimpse of Galen's modes of operation, and the goals he set himself, at different times in his career. Several refer to the circumstances in which he gave public lectures. Thus at one point[4] he refers to a lecture in which he attacked a man called Martialius, whom he describes as a 'remarkably malicious and adversarial personality'. He had asked Galen's friends to what sect he belonged, only to be told that he considered those who termed themselves Hippocrateans, Praxagoreans and so on as slaves – the implication being that Galen belonged to no sect. Martialius, by contrast, 'declared the superiority of Erasistratus in all areas of the art and especially in anatomy'. That provoked Galen, so he tells us, to compose the six books on *Hippocrates' Anatomy* and the three on *Erasistratus' Anatomy* in what he himself describes as 'a rather combative vein'.[5]

But Galen did not just write books to refute Erasistratus' views. He deliberately used the forum of a public lecture to discomfit the unfortunate Martialius. Galen was lecturing on the books of the ancient doctors and the topic chosen for discussion was Erasistratus' work *On the Bringing Up of Blood*, in particular the text in which he rejected venesection. At that point Galen chose to elaborate his refutation of that view specifically in order to 'cause grief to'[6] Martialius. His speech – so Galen himself tells us – was well received, and a friend of his who was hostile to Martialius asked him to dictate the lecture to a shorthand scribe so that he could use it against Martialius during his examination of patients.

I shall be returning to several aspects of this story later, but for now want to concentrate on Galen's own admission of the polemical character of some of his work. Some of his anatomical treatises were written, on his own account, in a controversial vein, and he was not above deliberate attempts to cause his opponents embarrassment. Yet, as is well known, he also tells us that he was on the receiving end of a fair amount of gossip and slander. His anatomical discoveries, his skill as a practitioner, his general fame and success, provoked a good deal of jealousy among rivals, and he expresses himself disgusted at the malicious backbiting to which he was subjected.

Just after the Martialius story he says that he decided to give no more public lectures or demonstrations but to dedicate himself 'to the greater cause of the healing of the sick'.[7]

Quite when that conversion took place is not as clear as it might be, for it might be after the work he wrote in his thirty-fourth year (i.e. 163 or so)[8] or more loosely after his return to Rome when summoned by the emperor in 169. Yet that does not make a substantial difference. The important point is that we have Galen's word for it that there was a change in what I have called his modes of operation. At a certain stage he turned away from public demonstrations and lectures before large crowds and devoted himself more particularly (if no doubt not exclusively) on the one hand to his medical practice, and on the other to his substantial literary output, most notably, of course, the major commentaries on the Hippocratic Corpus.

Yet that did not mean an end to polemic. It was certainly not the case that he ever gave up refuting rival views on every aspect of medical theory and practice. His own commentaries on Hippocratic treatises were among the writings he worked on during the last period of his long life. But they contain extensive passages devoted to the demolition of competing interpretations, not just of particular Hippocratic texts, but of what Hippocrates himself stood for. The unfortunate Lycus' misreading of one particular Aphorism, and Julian's criticisms of the *Aphorisms* as a whole, were each the subject of a work by Galen aiming to correct the error of their ways.[9]

If we piece together the evidence from a number of treatises, we can build up a picture of the various types of exchanges in which Galen was involved with colleagues, friends and rivals. First there is the public lecture of the type already mentioned where, for instance, Galen was challenged to speak on the works of the ancients. In the Martialius episode it appears that the treatise of Erasistratus on which Galen was asked to comment was not his choice, but suggested to him. Moreover the particular text in that treatise on which he was to speak was picked at random. We are told that a stylus was inserted into the book 'as is the custom' and it was taken to indicate the text for Galen's lecture.[10] Again later in *Lib.Prop.*[11] Galen refers to another occasion when he invited anyone in his audience to choose a subject from the works of earlier anatomists on which he should discourse – whereupon someone called upon him to talk about the chest. Galen was about to undertake a thorough examination of what

had been said on this previously, when he was interrupted by someone who said that Lycus had written down all the discoveries down
to his time, so Galen could ignore the rest and concentrate on him.
That did not satisfy Galen in the demonstrations that he then undertook, lasting over several days.

Sometimes the public occasion involved not just a lecture, with
question and answer session, or a debate, but also an actual anatomical dissection. Two very famous examples are cited in *On Anatomical Procedures* (*AA*), one occasion when Galen challenged the Erasistrateans to show him an artery that is empty of blood,[12] and another
when competing experts predicted, or rather guessed, what they
would find when they carried out the dissection of an elephant.[13]
On both those occasions the audience was made up partly of rival
supporters, who are said to have laid bets on the outcome.

Those types of context appear to be rather formal occasions.
Lib.Prop. speaks of the large auditoria in which lectures were sometimes held.[14] But there were other less formal discussions that could
be just as polemical in tone. One place in Rome which served as a
meeting place was the Temple of Peace (the building where Galen
deposited many of his writings – only for them to be destroyed when
the temple was burned down in 192).[15] It was evidently not necessary to wait for a grand public occasion to enter into discussion or
dispute – whether on anatomy or any other of the gamut of topics
that divided the medical sects. We hear of a group of Galen's enemies
who met on a regular basis at the Temple of Peace, devoting most of
their time and energy – on his account – to denigrating him.

Finally it is probably more surprising to us, in the twenty-first
century, that clinical practice offered yet another context for debate
and dispute on a wide range of questions, including some that went
well beyond the particular issues of the diagnosis and treatment of
the patient at whose bedside these discussions took place.[16] Here
On Prognosis (*Praen.*) provides some of our most detailed evidence.
In one case after another Galen is called in to comment on patients
who were already in the care of other doctors. Time and again Galen
exposes the errors of their diagnoses, prognoses and treatments. Thus
Eudemus, in ch. 2,[17] whom Galen had diagnosed as suffering from
an incipient quartan fever, was thought by his regular doctors to be
affected merely by the wine he had drunk the day before. On another

occasion,[18] Eudemus collects all the best doctors to deal with a young man seized with an acute disease at the end of autumn. The best reputed among them prescribe theriac,[19] but Galen, who had initially stayed aloof 'as he did not wish to engage in a battle of words with them', pronounces that that treatment will simply exacerbate the case.

With several of his most illustrious patients,[20] the doctors whose treatment Galen criticizes are represented as praying that his prognoses will prove wrong. We can credit Galen's own remark that he came to be hated by them when, on his own account of these cases at least, he always turned out to have got it right, winning praise from his patients from the Emperor downwards. Evidently, in this type of situation, there was no solidarity among the elite doctors. One might have thought that, out of caution and a due sense of the difficulties of diagnosis and the risks of treatment, they would have closed ranks and presented a united front when dealing with members of the imperial household or other important personages. Yet the insecurities of medical practice at the time played rather into the hands of the ambitious, who were quite prepared to chance their arm with diagnoses and therapies, even when the former were largely guesswork and the latter of doubtful efficacy. It is true that Galen presents himself as more hesitant initially than some of his rivals – needing more time to arrive at a firm diagnosis or saying that the success of his treatment could be judged only after a number of days. Yet once he has made his mind up, he is supremely confident, flatly contradicting alternative views and providing Eudemus (among others) with explanations for his own judgements – often in that context claiming[21] that he was doing no more than follow Hippocrates or implement his own teaching as set out in one or other of his treatises.

Thus by his own account the relationships that Galen entertained with his medical colleagues were generally marked by bitter rivalry. Face to face disputes were frequent: gossip and slander were rife behind his back, and that is before we come to the circulation of writings designed to expose the shortcomings of others' views. He does not have many friends among the doctors at Rome. Up to a point he respects his teacher, Pelops, but even he is not immune to criticism.[22] On occasion he commends Numisianus, Rufus of Ephesus and one or two others.[23] But most of those he names and most he

leaves unnamed seem to have been on the look-out to do him down, interpreting his diagnostic successes as divination and his success in clinical practice as due to magic or sorcery.[24]
While he has a sustained interest in the history of medical theory, his reconstruction of the views of his predecessors is a weapon in his polemic with his contemporaries. Both ideals and counter-ideals serve such a purpose. On the one hand, he constructs an account of Hippocrates that provides him with his 'guide to all that is good'. Yet to find authority for his own physiological and pathological views in Hippocrates involves him in a massive reinterpretation of texts in the Corpus, notably *On the Nature of Man*.[25] While his interpretation turned out to be massively influential, we have to remember that other alternative pictures of Hippocrates were current in Galen's own day, not just the views of self-styled Hippocrateans, but also those of Empiricists and others who saw Hippocrates as a forerunner of their own methodologies.

On the other hand, Galen describes a whole series of counter-ideals. The Methodists were his chief bogey men, in part no doubt because of their claim that the whole of medicine could be learned in a mere six months (where Galen himself insists that it takes a lifetime of training – including, of course, deep study of the treatises he wrote for his pupils' instruction). But many other figures from the past are also criticized. As Lonie showed in a pioneering article in 1964 (and cf. now Vegetti, 1999b), Galen uses Erasistratus as a means of attack on contemporary Erasistrateans, and conversely those contemporaries as a way of criticizing Erasistratus himself. It is true that he is not always critical of Erasistratus, Herophilus, Praxagoras, Diocles and so on: sometimes they are adduced on his side of an argument with others, notably when he is attacking Methodists or Sceptics of various persuasions. But he repeatedly uses them as foils, to present his own more accurate, more complete, more perfect, anatomical, physiological, pathological and therapeutic theories. While Hippocratic commentary occupies a dominant place in his writing, polemical writings aimed at Erasistratus, the Empiricists, the Methodists and a number of other writers on the pulse and on anatomy, bulk large in his oeuvre even if many of these are no longer extant.[26]

Yet on occasion we can see that Galen actually owes a good deal more to the figures he treats negatively than that treatment might lead us to expect. His diagnosis, in *Praen.*,[27] that a young woman was not sick, but in love, mirrors a famous and much-reported episode where Erasistratus similarly recognized a young man's passion. Galen mentions that case but says that he does not know how Erasistratus did it. His own discovery stemmed from spotting irregularities in the pulse.

On pulse lore itself several of his remarks about Archigenes are critical in tone, though we cannot judge how far this was true of his eight-book commentary on his work in that area, since that has not survived. However as von Staden showed,[28] Galen may well have been more heavily indebted to Archigenes, particularly as a source for Herophilus' ideas, than he lets on.

A third example may be anatomy, even though the originality of many of his contributions there is certain. Yet among his important predecessors were not just Herophilus and Erasistratus, but more recent figures, notably Marinus and Quintus. Marinus composed a work in twenty books on anatomy that Galen took sufficiently seriously to epitomize in four books of his own. While again these are not extant, we have an extensive summary of Marinus' magnum opus in *Lib.Prop.* ch. 3.[29] From this it is clear first that Galen's own *AA* did not use the same structure as Marinus' discussion, and secondly that that work certainly anticipated Galen's own treatise in attempting a comprehensive survey of the entire body, down to such details as the musculature of the cheek.

I may conclude this section by turning back to the question of the medical sects. Galen, we said, inherited a taxonomy on the subject and yet he puts in a considerable effort to defining the three main positions. Although he refers to groups such as the Herophileans, Erasistrateans, Asclepiadeans, Praxagoreans and others, they tend to be subsumed under one or other of the three groups around which the analysis in *SI* revolves – namely, Dogmatists, Empiricists and Methodists. All three of those groups are, however, mistaken, in Galen's view. To put the matter in the crudest possible terms, this is because the Dogmatists pay insufficient attention to experience, the Empiricists under-estimate the role of theory and argument and the Methodists abandoned pretty well the whole of the framework within which, traditionally, elite Greek medicine had been practised. But we can see how important and how useful it is, to Galen, to be able to corral as many medical theorists as he can into these three sects. Insofar as he can label his predecessors and contemporaries Dogmatists, Empiricists, or Methodists, the job of dismissing their views is to that extent made easier. They must be wrong, since their underlying methodology is fundamentally flawed.

The analysis I would give of the relationship between Galen and his medical colleagues places the emphasis on rivalry and polemic. True, there are exceptions to the general rule and large stretches of Galen's work, in his pharmacological writings for instance, where he does not engage in criticism of those who had discussed the subjects before him. Yet his concern to see off the opposition often appears an over-riding one, not just when he discusses the status and methods of medicine in general, but in his major works on anatomy, physiology and therapeutics.

Yet among the colleagues with whom he interacted there were, of course, not just medical practitioners, but also (among others) philosophers. So I turn now, in the second section of this chapter, to review the situation there.[30] Two preliminary points may be made that both serve to generate the expectation that his reaction to philosophers would be very similar to the one I have described with regard to his medical colleagues – though we shall see that that conclusion needs to be qualified.

The first such point is the observation that philosophers always and everywhere have tended to use their predecessors' ideas as the starting-point for their own contributions to the field. They may or may not cite earlier philosophers in the spirit of attempting as accurate a historical reconstruction of their thought as they can manage. Their interpretations may, to the contrary, be largely geared to their own constructive purposes. Yet just as ancient Greek philosophers used the great names in their own tradition to suggest new ideas of their own, whether in elaboration or in criticism, so too in the last two centuries the major European philosophers have done the same. Even Wittgenstein cites Augustine.

But then the second preliminary remark that also tends to point in the same direction is that the distance that Galen observed between philosophy and medicine is appreciably less than we would recognize today. His little treatise entitled *The Best Doctor is also a Philosopher* (*Opt.Med.*) argues the case for that thesis on three main grounds. First the doctor will need logic and should be trained in demonstrative reasoning. Secondly he needs physics, that is natural philosophy, to provide him with the answers to such questions as the fundamental constituents of physical objects.[31] Thirdly he needs ethics, not just to be knowledgeable about what goodness and virtue consist in, but to *be* good. His patients should know that he is devoted to the art and practises it out of benevolence for humankind, not just to make money.

In keeping with the overlap between the concerns of medical practitioners on the one hand, and natural philosophers on the other, Galen often tackles the views of earlier and contemporary philosophers on such matters as the seat of the ruling principle and the nature of the physical elements. The former takes him into a sustained discussion of Stoic positions, that of Chrysippus especially, in *On the Doctrines of Hippocrates and Plato (PHP)* (cf. Vegetti, 1999a).[32] On element theory, Galen argues that it was Hippocrates himself who first propounded the correct solution, in terms of the four simple bodies and their basic qualities,[33] but he marshals Plato also on Hippocrates' side, on the basis, one might say, of a rather simplistic reading of the *Timaeus*. Although Plato is never said to be Galen's 'guide in all that is good' (as Hippocrates is) and is occasionally criticized, for example for his views on blood and the humours in general,[34] it is clear that on major issues, such as teleology, Galen is prepared to make the most of the authority of Plato's name to support the positions he himself advocates. The case is similar with Aristotle, though he attracts more criticism on such questions as his mistaken view that the heart is the control centre of the body.

Conversely, Galen evidently has his philosophical bogey men who are cited merely to be refuted. Atomists of various persuasions, Epicureans especially, are usually attacked whenever they are mentioned. But his chief philosophical enemies, ranking close to the Methodists as the butts of Galen's mockery and disapproval, are the Sceptics, both the Academics and the Pyrrhonists. He several times mentions[35] the threat that Scepticism posed and relates how he was saved from falling into such negative attitudes largely by his recognition of the value and certainty of geometrical reasoning.

Thus far the patterns of his interactions with philosophers follow those we have described with doctors. He can be just as polemical in refuting natural philosophical, psychological and indeed moral positions he dissents from as in dismissing medical theories and practices.[36] His debates with contemporary Stoics, Aristotelians and even Platonists can be almost as acrimonious as his arguments with Martialius or Lycus. In one respect, however, his attitudes to philosophers do differ from those we have so far discussed.

This is when he is dealing with real or potential patrons or clients. Two remarkable examples figure in the accounts he gives of his clinical practice in *Praen.* One is Eudemus, described as a Peripatetic philosopher,[37] the other Boethus, a man of consular rank, destined to be governor of Syria Palaestina, an important patron of Galen's, who is described as a student of Aristotle's philosophy.[38] Eudemus is one of the cases where Galen, when consulted, contradicts the opinion of his regular doctors with a successful diagnosis that leads Eudemus to recommend him in turn in other cases, indeed to commend him to 'almost all those who were preeminent in Rome in honour and education'.[39]

This brings Galen to the notice of Boethus, who is intrigued by the reports of Galen's skill in dissection, and asks him to demonstrate how speech and breath are produced in front of an audience that includes a number of philosophers and prominent people.[40] This turns acrimonious when the philosopher Alexander Damascius intervenes just when Galen had undertaken to demonstrate the nerves implanted in the larynx. Alexander suggests that they should first agree that they accept the evidence of the senses – a remark that Galen takes to be indicative of a preoccupation with Sceptical doubts, whereupon he leaves in a huff.[41] Galen's behaviour on that occasion does not deter Boethus, who becomes convinced of Galen's superior skills in diagnosis and cure by a series of episodes that Galen duly recounts. Yet the point of interest in the debate about the nerves that control speech is that Galen does not there, as he does elsewhere, embark on a series of criticisms of Aristotle for his failures to recognize such and indeed his errors regarding the control centre of the body.[42] We may take it that he was too tactful to launch into attacks on Aristotle in the presence of a patron who had some allegiance to Aristotelian philosophy.

The disputes among the philosophers that Galen records share some of the characteristics of those among medical practitioners. Reputations were similarly at stake, and they could be important also for livelihood, insofar as philosophers, like doctors, were paid to teach their pupils. The ambitious in both types of case went all out for victory.

Yet certain differences may be remarked. First – notwithstanding certain Stoic claims – victory in philosophy was never a matter of achieving a cure (however difficult it may have been to say whether a patient had indeed been cured). Nor was it ever a matter of predicting what would be found in a dissection (however hard it was to interpret what precisely that had revealed). Galen was certainly as concerned for his own reputation as a philosopher as he was for his fame as a doctor. He could be as aggressive in debate with philosophers as he could with medical rivals. Yet with some of his elite patients and patrons he holds back. The importance of maintaining and developing relations with the rich and powerful in those instances acted as a restraining influence, where otherwise he seldom missed an opportunity to demonstrate the superiority of his own views and practices.

Galen reports a highly developed contentiousness among his contemporaries, both his medical colleagues and his philosophical ones – and that is a characteristic he exhibits in ample measure himself. Quintus, he tells us in a rare moment of generosity in *Praen.*,[43] was the best doctor of his generation: yet he was hounded from Rome on a charge of murdering his patients that his envious rivals trumped up against him. As for any properly trained doctor, he says (with obvious relevance to himself) his correct predictions do not gain him admiration, but rather a reputation as a sorcerer. Galen himself, as we saw, gave up public lecturing and devoted himself to practice and to writing because of similar pressures. That certainly marked a shift in his modes of operation, as he developed his skills as a commentator and as an educator. But that did not mean an end to his readiness to take on and defeat whatever rivals stood in his way – the quality you evidently needed to make your way as an elite doctor in the society in which he lived.

NOTES

1. This does not coincide exactly with the distinction that Galen himself draws between *sungrammata* and *hupomnêmata*, where the former term refers to systematic treatises, the latter to clinical notes, e.g. *On Hippocrates' 'Prorrhetics'* (*Hipp.Prorrh.*) XVI 532,8f., 542,18f., = *CMG* V 9,2, 24,9f., 29,20f. See also ch. 13 (Flemming) in this volume.
2. See ch. 13 (Flemming) in this volume.

3. Celsus' terms were *rationales, empirici* and *methodici* (*On Medicine* I Proem para 13ff., *CML* I, 19,11ff.). At *Lib.Prop.* 1: XIX 12,7ff., = *SM* 2, 94,4ff., Galen says that the names of the three main sects are well known. But we have to be particularly wary of the term 'dogmatist' or 'rationalist', for those labelled such (by their opponents, generally) may have agreed on the possibility and the need to investigate the hidden causes of diseases (for instance) but did not share concrete solutions to such problems. In that connection, terms such as 'Herophilean' 'Erasistratean' and 'Praxagorean' are more informative, though they, too, could be used quite loosely.

4. *Lib.Prop.* 1: XIX 13,11ff., = *SM* 2, 94,26–95,2.

5. *philotimôteron, Lib.Prop.* 1: XIX 14,3–4, = *SM* 2, 95.12–14.

6. *hopôs lupêsaimi, Lib.Prop.* 1: XIX 14,10–11, = *SM* 2, 95,20.

7. *Lib.Prop.* 1: XIX 15,4–7, = *SM* 2, 96,6–9.

8. On Galen's chronology, see ch. 1 (Hankinson) in this volume; and Nutton (1972a, 1973).

9. *Against Lycus* (*Adv. Lyc.*) XVIIIA 196–245, = *CMG* V 10,3; *Against Julian* (*Adv. Jul.*) XVIIIA 246–199, = *CMG* V 10,3.

10. See *Lib.Prop.* 1: XIX 14,8ff., = *SM* 2, 95,17. A similar technique of choosing a passage at random in the Corpus of Galenic work continued to be used in much later European medical education, as the Statutes of the University of Würzburg of the year 1713 show, see Lloyd (1981, 292ff.).

11. See *Lib.Prop.* 2: XIX 21,16ff., 22,9ff., = *SM* 2, 101,14ff., 26ff.

12. *AA* VII 10: II 619,16ff. On Galen's demonstrations, see Debru (1995).

13. *AA* VII 16: II 642,3ff.

14. See *Lib.Prop.* 2: XIX 21,7–8, = *SM* 2,101,4ff.

15. See *Lib.Prop.* 2: XIX 21,13–16, = *SM* 2,101,10–14; see also ch. 1 (Hankinson) in this volume, pp. 21–2.

16. Such discussions go back to the classical period, as is clear from the Hippocratic *On Diseases* I ch. 1, see Lloyd (1979, 91ff.). On Galen as a diagnostician, see García Ballester (1994).

17. *Praen.* 1: XIV 608,3ff., = *CMG* V.8.1, 76,19ff. Eudemus' own view was that the wine was to blame.

18. *Praen.* 2: XIV 609,12ff., = *CMG* V 8,1, 78,13ff.

19. 'Theriac' is the generic term covering a wide variety of complex drugs composed primarily of venoms derived from various poisonous creatures, which were widely prescribed both therapeutically, and as antidotes, prophylactics and tonics. See ch. 12 (Vogt) in this volume, pp. 312–13.

20. *Praen.* 3: XIV 616,14ff.; 10: 656,6ff., = *CMG* V 8,1, 84,20ff., 124,23ff.

21. See, for example, *Praen.* 10: XIV 656,15–657,14, = *CMG* V 8,1, 124,31–126,15.

22. Thus Pelops erroneously argued that the brain is the source not just of the nerves but also of the blood vessels, see *On the Doctrines of Hippocrates and Plato* (*PHP*) V 543,16ff., = *CMG* V 4,1,2, 392,10ff.; Lloyd (1991a, 402, n. 14).

23. See, for example, *The Order of his Own Books* (*Ord.Lib.Prop.*) 3: XIX 58,4ff., = *SM* 2, 87,19ff.

24. See e.g. *Praen.* 10: XIV 601-2, 614-15, 626, = *CMG* V 8,1, 70,1-21, 84,2-10, 94,12-19, etc.

25. I surveyed the factors that led to Galen's presentation of the views of Hippocrates in Lloyd (1991a, ch. 17). On Galen as commentator, see Manetti and Roselli (1994), Roselli (1999) and, on his use of the 'ancients' more generally, Smith (1979); Vegetti (2001).

26. See ch. 13 (Flemming) in this volume.

27. The Erasistratus story is mentioned briefly by Galen at *Praen.* 6: XIV 630,17-631,5, = *CMG* V 8,1, 100,9-14.

28. Galen refers to his commentary on Archigenes' eight-book work on the pulse at *Lib.Prop.* 5: XIX 33,19ff., = *SM* 2, 111,5ff. On Galen's possible use of Archigenes as a source for the work of Herophilus on pulses, see von Staden (1991, 207ff.).

29. Galen refers to his summary of Marinus' work at *Lib.Prop.* 3: XIX 25,11-30,4, = *SM* 2,104,12-108,14. The subjects of Marinus' seventh book are described by Galen as follows (in Peter Singer's translation): 'The subjects of the seventh book are: the connection of the skull with the dura mater and other membranes; the nerves in the whole of the face; the muscles of the temples, the chewing muscles, the muscles leading from the sockets to the jaws and lips; the muscles in the jaws; then, the muscles within the lower jaw, as well as those on the outside of it; the nostrils, the parts about the membrane-like outgrowths and those in the tongue; then the tongue and its muscles, and the muscles related to the eye.' On Galen's use of Marinus, Quintus and Numesianus, see Grmek and Gourevitch (1994).

30. On Galen's attitudes towards philosophers of different persuasions, see Nutton (1984a), Donini (1992), Hankinson (1992b) and, on his complex relations with 'sophists' of various types, see von Staden (1997a).

31. See ch. 8 (Hankinson) in this volume.

32. See ch. 7 (Donini) in this volume.

33. See ch. 8 (Hankinson) in this volume.

34. Thus at *PHP* VIII 5: V 680,12ff., = *CMG* V 4,1,2, 506,14ff., Plato is said to be mistaken in including blood, along with bone and flesh and so on, as a secondary formation. In Galen's view, Plato did not appreciate that all four humours exist naturally in the body.

35. Galen refers to how the certainty of geometrical reasoning saved him from radical skeptical doubts at *Lib.Prop.* 11: XIX 39,14ff., 40,3ff., = *SM* 2,116,12ff., 20ff. Cf. Hankinson (1991a, pp. 93f.). On Galen's own epistemology more generally, see Frede (1981); Vegetti (1994); and ch. 6 (Hankinson) in this volume.

36. His works *The Passions of the Soul* (*Aff.Dig.*), *On the Diagnosis and Cure of the Errors of the Soul* (*Pecc.Dig.*) and *The Faculties of the Soul Follow the Mixtures of the Body* (*QAM*) set out a number of theses in moral philosophy where Galen dissents from the teachings of the major Hellenistic philosophers. His physiologically based psychology involves him in sustained debate with the Stoics especially in *PHP*.

37. Eudemus is described as a Peripatetic philosopher from Galen's own hometown of Pergamum at *Praen.* 2: XIV 605,18f., = *CMG* V.8.1, 74,16f.

38. See *Praen.* 2: XIV 612,10ff., = *CMG* V.8.1, 80,22ff.

39. Boethus is said to philosophize according to the Aristotelian sect at *Lib.Prop.* 1: XIX 13,5ff., = *SM* 2, 94,20f., and to be a keen adherent of Aristotle's views at *Praen.* 2: XIV 612,3ff., = *CMG* V.8.1, 80,18. Another Roman of consular rank who was an Aristotelian was Severus, with whom Galen was also associated: see *Praen.* 2: XIV 613,4ff., = *CMG* V.8.1, 82,6f.

40. This demonstration is mentioned at *Praen.* 2: XIV 612,12ff., = *CMG* V.8.1, 80,25ff., and described at some length in ch. 5, XIV 626,17–628, 18, = *CMG* V.8.1, 96.5–98.8.

41. Galen describes his leaving abruptly at his disgust with the remark of Alexander at *Praen.* 5: XIV 628,16ff., *CMG* V.8.1, 98,6ff. At XIV 629,4ff., *CMG* V.8.1,98,11ff., however, he explains that he later returned to perform the dissections in question, over the course of several days, before an audience that included those reputed in both medicine and philosophy. The background to the epistemological debates on the validity of dissection is discussed in Lloyd (1987, 163–7) and Hankinson (1994e).

42. For Galen, Aristotle's principal mistake, as I noted, was to consider the heart the control centre of the body and to fail to recognize the brain as the source of the nerves.

43. *Praen.* 1: XIV 602,12ff., *CMG* V.8.1, 70,23ff.

3   Methodology

INTRODUCTION

Galen's concern with methodology – i.e. the theoretical reflection upon scientific and/or philosophical method – leaps from almost every page of his extant work. Time and again he stresses the need to proceed in methodical fashion, attributing the mistakes of others to their lack of training in what he calls the rational or demonstrative method.[1] Demonstration (or proof, *apodeixis*) is his key term: the ideal physician will accept nothing on authority but waits for the proof or finds it himself if needed. If you expect others to accept your assertions without proof, you behave like a tyrant ordering people about.[2]

Galen devoted several separate treatises to the subject of method. At an early stage in his career (around 160 CE) he composed his methodological *chef d'oeuvre On demonstration* (hereafter, *Dem.*) in no less than fifteen books. Regrettably, it has not been preserved, although we can form an overall picture of its contents from references scattered throughout the extant corpus.[3] Of particular relevance are his great works *On the Doctrines of Hippocrates and Plato* (*PHP*) and *On the Therapeutic Method* (*MM*). *PHP* books I–VI (composed during Galen's first stay in Rome, 162–6 CE) can be read as an extended demonstration of scientific procedure as applied to issues concerning the soul.[4] Book IX (written after 176) includes a discussion of method, most notably division (*diaeresis*). *MM* (in fourteen books), as its title indicates, discusses the method to be used in clinical medicine. Its first two books (written around 175) are more theoretical than the others and based on the methodology advocated in *Dem.* as well.[5] Related to *MM* are a few smaller tracts concerned with

49

the medical schools and their respective methodologies: the *Outline of Empiricism* (*Subf.Emp.*), *On Medical Experience* (*Med.Exp.*) and *On Sects for Beginners* (*SI*).[6] In *MM* I–II Galen presents his version of the 'rational' (or 'logical') method as his alternative to the Empiricist and Methodist methods expounded in these three tracts.[7] A further treatise of immediate methodological relevance is *On Antecedent Causes* (*CP*).[8] To be sure, more treatises and numerous passages are involved in any reconstruction of Galen's methodology that aims at completeness if only because of his habit of making relevant points throughout his work. Moreover, it is insufficient to collect and systematize theoretical passages. One should also study the way Galen actually goes about his researches. Then we may expect to find not only applied method (as opposed to methodology) but, more specifically, the tensions resulting from the application of what are often philosophical concepts to the practice of empirical research.

Michael Frede, in his pioneering study of Galen's philosophical position,[9] has shown the fundamental importance of methodology for understanding his attitude to philosophical issues – a methodology that, Frede plausibly argued, represents Galen's response to, and compromise between, the medical schools of his day, especially the so-called Dogmatists (or Rationalists) and Empiricists. Conversely, as I hope to show, Galen implemented his version of the rational method by drawing on the philosophical tradition. It is precisely this confrontation between philosophical concepts and scientific (i.e. medical) problems which makes this physician-cum-philosopher such a remarkable and at times original figure on the intellectual stage of the second century CE.

In what follows I shall first take a look at the intellectual backdrop of Galen's methodology – the philosophical and the medical tradition. Next I shall illustrate Galen's methodology by reference to *PHP* I–III and VI and *MM* I–II for the reasons indicated above. Finally I shall present a few concluding remarks.

GALEN'S PHILOSOPHICAL EDUCATION

Many of Galen's philosophical works, including those concerned with method, were not included in the philosophical curriculum of Late Antiquity and disappeared for ever into the mists of history. Still it remains worth looking up the relevant pages of his *On My*

Own Books (*Lib.Prop.*), a comparatively long section entitled 'On the books useful for demonstrations' (ch. XI). What Galen says here may tell us more about his motivation and orientation in dealing with the subject of the proper scientific method.

Seeing that people try to prove themselves correct and refute their opponents on controversial issues, Galen turned to the philosophers to learn from them the theory of demonstration (*apodeiktikē theoria*), i.e. the method (*methodos*) with which to assess the proofs offered by others or, if these fail to pass the test, to find the truth himself (*Lib.Prop.* XIX 39, = *SM* 2, 115,19–116,12). He studied logic with respectable Stoics and Peripatetics. After some time, however, he found what they taught useless for demonstration, while they were divided over the little that did seem to be of use. He would have turned into a Sceptic (indeed one of the cruder, Pyrrhonist variety) were it not for the training in geometry and arithmetic he had received from his own father (who was a respected architect in his native Pergamum). These disciplines yielded true predictions of solar eclipses and proved successful in the construction of artifacts such as water-clocks and other feats of engineering. He therefore decided to adopt 'geometrical demonstrations' as his model (*Lib.Prop.* XIX 39–40, = *SM* 2, 116,12–117,4).[10]

Galen, then, presents the philosophers of his day as hopelessly divided on many issues for lack of a firm and shared methodological foundation. He contrasts them unfavourably with the technicians who apply their mathematical tools to good use. But Galen does not dismiss philosophy without qualification: the philosophers, too, despite their differences commend 'geometrical demonstrations'. As it is, the Peripatetics have achieved the greatest degree of unanimity – thanks to the geometrical model, we are given to understand (we are no doubt invited to think of the axiomatic–deductive model of science as expounded in the Aristotelian *Analytics*). So what one should do is to train oneself in the geometrical mode of demonstration and then read Galen's treatise *On Demonstration* (*Lib.Prop.* XIX 40–1, = *SM* 2, 117.4–20). The treatises preparatory to this great work Galen goes on to mention consist of collections of notes or commentaries (*hypomnēmata*)[11] concerned with the tracts of the Aristotelian *Organon*. At the request of friends he also wrote a tract on the *Categories* which appears to have been more demanding since he recommends it only to people who have previously studied this Aristotelian tract under the direction of a teacher or with the aid of the commentaries of Adrastus and Aspasius (*Lib.Prop.* XIX 41–2, = *SM* 2,117.20–119.2; cf.123.1–2).[12]

Although Galen's interest in logic also extended to Stoic propositional logic (*Lib.Prop.* XIX 42–3, = *SM* 2, 119.2–9), his main inspiration clearly came from the relevant Aristotelian works and the exegetical tradition connected with it, in line with his observation that the Aristotelians of his day were most nearly unanimous thanks to their appreciation of 'geometrical' demonstration. This Peripatetic background is further borne out by statements in other works. Galen calls Aristotle and Theophrastus the best authorities on demonstration,[13] even though he adds with characteristic self-confidence that in his *Dem.* he has explicated their unclear and concise pronouncements.[14] But if Aristotle and his school stood in need of explication, the substance of their doctrine apparently remained much the same in Galen's hands.

At all times it should be kept in mind that the appeal to past masters such as Aristotle involves the ancient exegetical tradition connected with the relevant Aristotelian works (references to more or less contemporary sources were often as a matter of convention suppressed). This is why the above passage from *Lib.Prop.* where he presents himself as building on the work of such commentators as Adrastus and Aspasius is as rare as it is revealing. Another glimpse of the scholastic background is provided by a remark made by Galen at the end of *MM* book II, that what he has been explaining is just basic textbook material.[15] I do not wish to argue that we should see Galen as a mere transcriber of the manuals of his day. But it does stand as a reminder of the traditional element involved in his project of making philosophical concepts operative for empirical research – which represents a considerable achievement in itself.

From a historical point of view there is no conflict between Galen's use of Peripatetic logic and methodology and his well-known admiration for Plato. By his time Peripatetic logic had become fully absorbed in Platonism, as is witnessed by Platonist manuals from the Imperial period.[16] Aristotle was taken to have further developed certain ideas which, in an embryonic form, were contained in the Platonic dialogues – an assumption that fits in well with Galen's vision of a tradition of good philosophy-cum-medicine with Plato and Hippocrates as its fountain-heads (which, of course, is his personal version of the prevalent syncretism of his day). He could find the method of division (*diaeresis*) more fully developed already in Plato (*PHP* IX) – a method he could connect with the Aristotelian method of definition (see p. 61 below) as well as with that of the revered Hippocrates. Indeed, Plato himself had recommended the legendary physician for his method (*Phaedrus* 270c–d). Here then his two heroes were most gratifyingly united with respect to one of his most central concerns.[17]

GALEN AND THE MEDICAL SCHOOLS[18]

Other sections of Galen's biobibliographical survey in *Lib.Prop.* concern his relation to the medical schools of his day, most notably the Rationalists, the Empiricists and the Methodists. Galen has no sympathy whatsoever for the new Methodist school, 'that mad, unmethodical sect' (*MM* X 51) – founded by Thessalus in the first century CE – whose therapeutic method was based on the assumption of only three types of disease (the fluid, the constipated and the mixed). Galen also heaps scorn on Thessalus' view that one could learn to become a doctor within six months. But his persistent concern with this school actually shows that he took it seriously as a threat to medical science and the medical profession. His attitude to the other two main schools was more positive – or, at any rate, more nuanced and discriminating. The experience (*empeiria*) of the Empiricists consists of the accumulation of observations of diseases and their therapy. One could also speak of the memory of such observations, memory being more or less equivalent to (medical) knowledge. In addition to one's own observations, one can also avail oneself of the reported observations of others, i.e. the recorded experience called *historia* in Greek. What the Empiricist practitioner does is to apply proven remedies to the same or similar illnesses and injuries. The similarity between diseases, or bodily parts, justifies the use of a particular treatment in regard to new cases (the so-called 'transition to what is similar', *metabasis tou homoiou*). Galen, for his part, thinks that an exclusive appeal to experience (or, to be more precise, experience thus delineated) is unduly restrictive; it stands in the way of the development of a complete art of medicine. One cannot dispense with logical (or 'rational') methods such as definition-cum-division and sign-inference (*endeixis*) from phenomena to hidden causes. It also includes dissection – whereas true-blue Empiricists considered anatomical knowledge useless for healing patients. Seen in this light, Galen can surely be characterized as a Rationalist, or Dogmatist. But his is a particular version of rationalism that is enriched with several distinctively Empiricist ideas; in fact, he more or less presents a compromise between the two positions.

In typical fashion Galen observes that Rationalists and Empiricists often concur in their choice of medical treatment (SI I 72, $= SM$ 3, 7,12). Indeed one can be a perfectly respectable medical practitioner while adhering to Empiricist principles. Dogmatist physicians are often prone to unfounded speculation and irresponsible, indeed dangerous, therapies. Many of them are insufficiently aware that logical methods require extensive training. Moreover, logical procedures should at all times be checked by experience. Both reason and experience are instruments of discovery and means of testing what has been discovered. The method envisaged by Galen can roughly be characterized as comprising a stage of discovery steered by reason (i.e. rational methods) followed by one of confirmation or otherwise by means of experience. For Galen, experience means not merely the accumulation of data involving no particular expertise. Galen's version of 'technical experience', as opposed to the Empiricist concept, involves techniques requiring skill and expertise such as anatomy and experimentation (see n. 36). The experience propounded by the Empiricists left room for a degree of improvisation[19] but this remained confined to the sphere of therapy. Galen engaged in the style of anatomical experimentation instigated by the Hellenistic medical scientists Herophilus and Erasistratus (first half of the third century BCE).[20] But in this context he retained the Empiricist requirement of a large number of identical observations, thereby foreshadowing the modern requirement of the repeatability of experimental observations.[21]

Regarding experimentation, another source of influence should be mentioned. There is an important analogy drawn by Galen between his concept of medical experience and so-called 'geometrical disciplines' such as engineering: the technician's computations are proved correct only when his instruments or machines (e.g. a clock) are seen to function in practice. Here too then a 'logical' stage (i.e. the calculations) is standardly followed by one of testing in practice. In addition, we may note the two directions involved in this model: the specialist moves away from common experience,[22] but having found the abstract proof and first principles, he returns again to the sphere of common observation so that his results can be judged by specialist and layman alike. Connected to this idea is Galen's requirement of usefulness and his concomitant rejection of speculation for its own sake. Medicine, like the other arts, remains wedded to its useful purpose – the physical well-being of humankind.[23]

THE THEORY IN PRACTICE: PHP II–III (AND VI)

In his great work, On the Doctrines of Hippocrates and Plato (PHP), Galen sets out to prove that the two past masters of its title were both in harmony and correct about the main issues of philosophy and medicine. The issue which takes up most of its nine books (I–VI) is that of the structure and location of the soul. Here Galen to his own satisfaction vindicates the well-known Platonic theory of the tripartition-cum-trilocation of the soul; reason in the brain, anger (or 'spirit') in the heart and appetite in the liver.[24] Given Galen's purpose, he also attempts to show through quotations that Hippocrates, i.e. the tracts he takes as genuinely Hippocratic, subscribed to this position as well. More interesting though is his use of post-Platonic medical science to show that Plato and Hippocrates had been on the right track, in particular his effective appeal to the anatomy and physiology of the nervous system in establishing the brain as the centre of the psychic functions of sensation and volition (and hence reason). Meanwhile, as we have noted, a prominent role is given to methodological issues with the lost Dem. looming in the background (see p. 49).

Galen first establishes common ground as to the sense of the governing or commanding part of the soul, i.e. the intellect or reason, as the principle of perception and voluntary motion, in order to formulate a definition of the term central to the inquiry to which one should stick throughout the subsequent demonstration.[25] From this initial definition Galen infers that this function requires the existence of bodily tissues (which we may dub 'nerves', neura) that transmit the sensory and motor stimuli from and to the central organ in which the commanding part is located. This inference is expressed in the following general principle or axiom: 'Where the centre of the nerves is, there is the seat of the commanding part.' So far the argument is abstract, or 'logical'. Empirical research, that is to say, dissection, is needed for the following step: to establish which bodily organ satisfies this principle. This shows that the brain is the centre of the nervous system both structurally and functionally and hence the seat of the commanding part of the soul.[26] In fact, we are dealing with a syllogistic proof that can be stated as follows:

(1)   Where the centre of the nerves is, there is the commanding part.

(2)   The centre of the nerves is the brain.

so

(3)   The brain is the seat of the commanding part.[27]

Plato, then, was right in locating his rational part in the brain. But this axiomatic–deductive proof is the summary conclusion of a far more extensive procedure that starts from the assumption 'The brain is the seat of the commanding part', i.e. the conclusion of the above syllogism, in search of those features that indicate its essential function to be that of the seat of the intellect. The rival assumption 'The heart is the seat of the commanding part' is subjected to the same procedure. Galen starts from the distinction (i.e. *diaeresis*) between a number of perceptible features of either organ – that is to say, features made perceptible by scientific research, skilful dissection of the body. This is how the inquiry into the function of the heart starts:

We must begin, then, with all the properties of the heart; and we must mention them all in turn, first by main heads and genera, then also by parts and species. Now the heart has position, size, texture, form, state and motion. (*PHP* V 228, = *CMG* V 4,1,2, 116.32–5)

The features in question are successively tested as to their indicative value. For example, the central location of the heart had often been taken (e.g. by authorities no less than Aristotle) to be significant; but on closer analysis this supposition turns out to be based on the axiom 'All things active have their source (or: principle) nearby'. This axiom, Galen shows through a few counter-examples, is neither logically obvious nor cogent. But he is fair enough to point out that the same objection can be levelled against Plato's appeal to the anatomically elevated position of the head, which does not indicate that it is the seat of the highest psychic function, i.e. reason, either.[28]

Indicative of the organ's essence are other features that can be shown to belong to it alone: the heart's throbbing during particular emotions such as anger and fear, or the fact that the heart and the brain are each the centre of a particular system of vessels, i.e. the arterial and nervous systems, respectively. Given Galen's teleology – encapsulated in the axiom 'Nature does nothing for no reason' – such proper characteristics provide an indication (*endeixis*) as to the function of an organ. Function then is identified with essence or being (*ousia*) – another Aristotelian feature.[29] But strictly speaking it is not sufficient to establish the brain as the structural centre of the nervous system: its corresponding *function* should be demonstrated on the basis of the structural data. Here Galen's sophisticated vivisective experiments enter the picture: by carefully intercepting the nerves at certain spots or cutting through the spinal cord of living animals he succeeds in showing the working of the nervous system and the central function of the brain.[30] Analogous experiments are designed and performed on the heart and the arterial system.

Interestingly enough, Galen admits that this type of experiment is not possible, or at least does not produce equally clear results, in the case of the liver as the (structural) centre of the venous system. Here, then, his demonstration does not go beyond the stage of identifying significant structural features.[31] Although Galen expects himself no less than others to satisfy strict criteria for his method of experimentation, he shows little doubt that he has established the liver as the seat of the Platonic appetitive part, thus completing his vindication of the tripartite theory of the soul. Still his view of the ideal proof as being completed by a final experimental test recalls his appeal to the model provided by the so-called 'geometrical' disciplines (see p. 54).

What Galen has done is to follow an inverse procedure *vis-à-vis* the syllogistic proof stated at the outset. Its conclusion ('The brain is the seat of the commanding part') has in fact been taken as a question ('Is the brain the seat of the commanding part?'), motivating an inquiry aimed at finding the middle term connecting the two terms involved. Thus the syllogistic proof can be stated only when this enquiry has been successfully completed, i.e. when the middle term has been found, in this particular case 'being the centre (functional as well as structural) of the nervous system'. From a methodological point of view the argument moves from (perceptible) phenomena (the features of the brain) to the hidden cause (and back again), or – to use Aristotle's distinction, which fully applies here – from 'what is more obvious to us' to 'what is more obvious in itself' (or 'by nature').[32] In sum, we are dealing with a particular version of the Aristotelian theory of science including the dialectical method. The same holds for his use of logical principles such as definitions and axioms. Galen's distinction – an instance of *diaeresis* – between essence and accidental features, which recalls the Aristotelian *Categories*, features as a very similar principle of method in contemporary Platonist literature.[33]

A few further peculiarities should be noted. Galen's selection of distinctive or peculiar features that justify the inference to hidden principles recalls 'Rationalist' indication (*endeixis*, see p. 53). Further, Galen lays great stress on perceptible phenomena as distinct from opinions. Strikingly, he demotes the appeal to authorities, whether people in general or experts, i.e. Aristotelian *endoxa*, to the class of rhetoric, whereas Aristotle had designated the *endoxa* as the material of dialectical argument.[34] Galen for his part confines dialectic to the perceptible phenomena.[35] Whereas rhetorical arguments do not belong in scientific discourse at all, dialectical ones pertain to perceptible features that provide the raw material for scientific or demonstrative arguments. These are drawn from four different sources: the logically obvious, simple perception and common or technical experience.[36] The fourth and most disreputable class of arguments distinguished by Galen are the sophistical premises or arguments which typically make use of ambiguities of speech.[37] As such, they mark a failure in the initial stage of the procedure advocated by Galen, that of establishing the sense of the terms to be used in the course of the following argument.

Galen's adjustment of Aristotle's position as to the dialectical class is striking. It suits his well-known aversion to authority and sectarianism.[38] But his position on this particular point was not unprecedented. The great Alexandrian scientist Herophilus had likewise designated observable phenomena as the starting point for scientific research as opposed to (common) opinions, in which he did not put his trust.[39] We need not doubt that Galen had been influenced by Herophilus on this score. At *MM* X 107 he cites the latter's dictum that we should 'start from primary things even if they are not primary' (Fr. 50a–b von Staden). This clearly refers to the Aristotelian distinction[40] – accepted by both Herophilus and Galen – that the perceptible phenomena come first from the viewpoint of method, although they are not primary from the viewpoint of logic (cf. the analogous distinction between 'what is obvious to us' and 'what is obvious absolutely' or 'by nature', see e.g. Arist. *APo* 77b33ff. *Top.* 141b15ff.).

GALEN *ON THE THERAPEUTIC METHOD* (*MM* I–II)[41]

The subject-matter of *PHP* I–VI is physiological, dealing as it does with the respective functions of the main organs in the body. It is worth comparing Galen's method in these books with that recommended for the diagnosis and therapeutic treatment of illnesses in *MM* books I–II. As we shall see, the two works present essentially the same methodology as applied in two different contexts. As such, the two expositions can be used to supplement one another. In what follows I shall be highlighting those elements which further illustrate our findings from *PHP*.

The first book opens with a long tirade against the founder of the Methodist School, Thessalus, who dared to oppose the entire tradition of Hippocratic medicine and introduced his own distinction between three main types of illness (see p. 53). Galen regards this distinction as resulting from a failure to apply one of the logical methods, division (*diaeresis*). Plato in the *Philebus, Sophist* and *Politicus* and Aristotle in the *On the Parts of Animals* wrote about this method, showing how difficult it is to apply it properly (*MM* I 3: X 25–6). The trouble with Thessalus is his lack of training in this (or any other) method:

Yet the outrageous Thessalus thinks he is worthy of credence when he simply asserts that there are only two kinds of disease (at any rate which are simple . . . for another third type arises from them, which is composite in formula, made up from both of them). And if you have discovered these things by some method, as you boast, why don't you reveal it to us? (*MM* I 3: X 27; trans. Hankinson)

In spite of the name he chose for his school Thessalus is unmethodical. So it falls to Galen to explain how one discovers the number of diseases and their differences. Method follows a certain route in an orderly way: first this, then that (*MM* I 3: X 31). The very first thing to do in any method, not just division, is to define your subject (*MM* I 3: X 27). In this particular case then we should first 'define what disease, symptom and affection are', so that we may see both differences and resemblances between these three concepts. Next we may proceed to cut each of them into their proper *differentiae* according to the method the philosophers have taught, i.e. *diaeresis* (*MM* I 3: X 13).

Definition is one of the kinds of principles distinguished by Galen. At *MM* I 3: X 34 he adds indemonstrable propositions, or axioms, to the starting points of medicine or any other science. So having invoked the methodology of *Dem.* (X 39), he first establishes the common conception that must be agreed upon and without which it is impossible to discover the essence of disease. Disease is taken by all Greek-speaking people to involve an impairment of some natural *activity* or *function*, e.g. loss of vision when the eye is diseased (*MM* I 3: X 41). Galen stresses that only his use of *terms* conforms to ordinary Greek usage; the discovery of the actual *essence* of the matter is drawn not from common opinion but from scientific assumptions (*MM* I 3: X 42).[42]

The next step consists of selecting an appropriate axiom, 'Nothing occurs without a cause'. Its axiomatic status means that it is indemonstrable and agreed upon by all because it is obvious to the mind.[43] So if a natural activity such as vision is damaged or impeded, one should look for the cause, i.e. a particular disposition of the body. Whether one gives the name 'disease' to the cause or to the damaged activity is inessential provided one does so consistently. The doctor, at any rate, directs his therapy at the disposition being the cause of the impairment.

But not only does Galen distinguish between bodily disposition (or the body disposed in a certain way) and activity. One should further take care to distinguish between the actual damage to the activity ('"peculiar" or "proper" symptoms') and other, 'adventitious' symptoms (*MM* I 3: X 65). Likewise the features of the body-part at issue divide into essential and incidental ones (*MM* I 3: X 99–101), depending on whether or not they are directly causally related to its natural activity. For example, in the case of digestive failure, the stomach's colour is inessential: it does not cause the natural activity and so cannot be responsible for its impairment either (*MM* I 3: X 98–9). Hence one should know which features of the stomach are essential and which are not. Thus he fires the following questions at an Empiricist:

And [that] which you are aware of, is it the cause of the activity, or is it something that simply happens in the stomach for some other reason? What indeed do you know? Its position, clearly, and its size, and its texture, and its configuration: but none of these things is a cause of an activity. (*MM* I 3: X 100; trans. Hankinson)

Of course, the Empiricist does not engage in (systematic) anatomy so will never know the true essential features of hidden organs such as the stomach – which knowledge he considers unnecessary for therapy. The four elementary qualities – the Hot, the Cold, the Wet and the Dry – are essential to the natural disposition of each organ (that is to say, on the level of the tissues constituting the organ; there are also diseases of the organ as a whole: *MM* I 3: X 125). 'Each body derives its activity from a blend of the four qualities' (*MM* I 3: X 105). If one knows the natural blend of a particular organ (i.e. its natural disposition), one will recognize its disturbance also, i.e. the symptoms essential to the impaired activity. Therapy, then, is aimed at restoring the natural balance between the qualities. The good Galenic doctor, for his part, having identified the essential symptoms, will derive his therapeutic *indication* therefrom (*MM* I 3: X 101) in the light of the medical axiom 'Opposites are cured by opposites' so as to restore the natural balance of the diseased organ (*MM* I 3: X 102–4). A stomach that has been morbidly chilled is cured by a 'hot' drug, etc.

At this point we may present a few conclusions as to the nature of the method set out here. It is typical of Rationalist medicine in its stress on the need to know the nature of the body[44] and its reference to the hidden causes of disease. The specific version of the rational or logical method we find here is clearly Aristotelian in inspiration: the movement is from the common conception to the statement of essence, i.e. what is also described as 'substituting the name for the definition', with definition in the sense of 'proper scientific account'.[45] Other features are the distinction between essential and accidental attributes familiar from the Aristotelian *Categories* and the employment of definition and axiom (both general and peculiar to the science of medicine) as logical principles.[46] Furthermore, the argument moves from the observed damaged activity to its hidden cause and back again: after the cause (i.e. the disposition at issue) has been discovered, the therapeutic indication derived from it is directed at curing the impaired activity. A successful cure confirms that the train of reasoning has been correct. The movement from phenomenon to principle and back is of course of Aristotelian provenance as well. The element of practical confirmation involved in the backward movement seems peculiar of Galen who, as we have noticed, models it on the so-called geometrical disciplines. What is more, most, if not all, characteristics of this method find their parallel in *PHP* I–VI. We are dealing with essentially the same coherent method, which must be the same as the one that he had expounded more fully still in the *Dem*.

EPILOGUE

Galen's philosophical education had familiarized him with the tracts of the Aristotelian *Organon* as well as the Platonic dialogues. Their influence is palpable in such methodological passages as we find scattered throughout the extant Galenic corpus. From Aristotle, he took the axiomatic–deductive ('geometrical') model of science and such principles as taking one's starting point from the phenomena when inquiring about causes. His use of the logical method of division (*diaresis*) was inspired by Plato in particular. But Galen did not converse with Aristotle, Plato and other great minds of the classical past in an intellectual vacuum; his relations with them were not unmediated. His reading of their works was coloured by the relevant exegetical and scholastic traditions, most notably those of Aristotelianism and Platonism. In addition, his version of the 'geometrical' method bears the stamp of his concern with practical utility and effectiveness for which he looked to the model provided by 'geometrical' arts such as engineering, where calculation is standardly followed by construction and testing in practice. The bid to combine logical and experimental methods is also typical of Galen's response to the medical schools of his day. He adopted Rational methods such as anatomy (including anatomical experimentation) so as to theorize about the functioning of our body. But he was receptive to Empiricist ideas and procedures also and persistently stressed the need for empirical corroboration. In synthesizing these various traditions he elaborated a powerful and in many respects original concept of medical procedure, powerful enough to put an end to the disagreement between the medical schools of his day and to pave the way for the modern concept of a unitary science.

NOTES

1. For a few typical examples see *MM* X 38, 61–2, *PHP* V 220, = *CMG* V4,1,2, 110,15–19 De Lacy.
2. *MM* X 20, 29, 105.
3. Usefully collected and discussed by von Müller (1897), whose view on the overall arrangement of subject-matter in the lost original is open to criticism, however: see Barnes, 1993, 69, n. 61. Since the appearance of von Müller's compilation a little additional evidence has surfaced, e.g. the reflections of *Dem.* in the *Doubts About Galen* by the Medieval Persian scientist Rhazes (865–925), on which now see Strohmeier (1998, esp. 267 ff.).
4. That Galen employs the methodology of *Dem.* is clear, e.g. from *PHP* V 213, 29, = *CMG* V4,1,2, 102.25–8, 108.21–5. For a study of Galen's procedure in *PHP* I–III and VI, see Tieleman (1996, part I).
5. *MM* X 38, 40.
6. See the translations with introduction by Frede (1985).
7. *Subf.Emp.* 12, p. 89 Deichgräber; *MM* X 123–4.
8. See Hankinson (1998a).
9. Frede (1981).
10. On these issues see also ch. 4 (Morison) and ch. 6 (Hankinson) both in this volume.
11. Galen makes it clear here that these *hypomnêmata* were intended for interested friends and acquaintances only. However, some of these writings came into the hands of others and were published (*ekdothenta, Lib.Prop.* XIX 41, = *SM* 2,118.2) without his consent. Galen then was more or less forced to re-assert his authorship, presenting a list of these *hypomnêmata* in ch. XIV (*Lib.Prop.* XIX 47, =122.19–123.9). The sense of *hypomnêma* is flexible; it may also indicate a draft version of a work that was intended for publication, or even a treatise that was published in an unpolished form: see, e.g., Dorandi (2000).
12. On these commentaries see Moraux (1984, 226–8, 294, 317). On Galen's knowledge of Aristotle's logical works see further Moraux (1984, 687 ff.), Tieleman (1996, 106 ff.).
13. *PHP* V 213, = *CMG* V 4,1,2, 104.3–5, *MM* X 118; for more on Galen's views on and contributions to logic, see ch. 4 (Morison) in this volume.
14. *PHP* V 219, = *CMG* V 4,1,2, 108.21–5.
15. *MM* X 145.

16. See e.g. Whitaker (1987).
17. Galen cites this Platonic passage at *MM* X 13–14.
18. For what follows see, in addition to the Galenic works *SI, Subf.Emp.* and *Med.Exp.* (on which see also p. 50) the studies by Frede (1981, 1985, ix–xxxiv), and Hankinson (1991b, xxvi–xxxiii).
19. For this so-called 'extemporary' kind of experience see *SI* I 66–7, = *SM* 3, 2,13–3,4; *Subf.Emp.* 2, p. 44 Deichgräber.
20. On Galen's experiments see Tieleman (2002), and further p. 57.
21. See *PHP* V 604, = *CMG* V 4,1,2, 442, 13–18, *On the Function of the Pulse* (*Us.Puls.*) V 165, and for the Empiricist provenance of this requirement, see e.g. *Subf.Emp.* 2, pp. 45–6 Deichgräber, *Med.Exp.* 7, 18, pp. 94, 119–21 Walzer; cf. Deichgräber (1930/65, 97–118).
22. This part of his procedure ('reason') is stressed by Galen at *Cur.Rat.Ven.Sect.* XI 255–6, but at the same time it is clear that the practising technician is considered to use both experience and reason as instruments of discovery. See also ch. 6 (Hankinson) in this volume, pp. 159–62.
23. For the complex of ideas in this paragraph see esp. *Pecc.Dig.* V 80–6, = *CMG* V 4,1,1, 53.9–59.8 with Tieleman (1996, 34 f.).
24. The placement of the Platonic appetitive part in the liver is not warranted by the Platonic *Timaeus* where it is assigned to the belly in general, with the liver fulfilling a different, though related, function. That the liver is central to digestion is an insight that post-dates Plato: see e.g. Tieleman (1996, xxx–xxxi).
25. *PHP* V 219, 274, = *CMG* V 4,1,2, 110.1–2, 156.13–19.
26. *PHP* V 219–20, = *CMG* V 4,1,2, 110.2–14.
27. Cf. *PHP* V 649, = *CMG* V 4,1,2, 480.19–22.
28. *PHP* V 228–231, = *CMG* V 4,1,2, 116.35–120.10.
29. *PHP* V 201–3, = *CMG* V 4,1,2, 92.7–94.10.
30. See ch. 9 (Rocca) in this volume for further discussion of these experiments.
31. *PHP* V 519–21, = *CMG* V 4,1,2, 372.16 ff.
32. On this distinction in Galen cf. Hankinson (1991b, 24).
33. See Alcinous *Did.* ch. 5, p. 156 Hermann (and see Dillon, 1993, 8–10, 72–7); Clem. Alex. *Strom.* VIII 9–15. Further affinities can be traced in what is left of the ancient exegetical tradition concerned with the Aristotelian *Topics* (*Top.*), i.e. with Aristotelian dialectic as the art of discovering arguments (division and definition being among the means of finding argument), see Tieleman (1996, 110 ff.).
34. Aristotle *Top.* I 1,100b20. Galen refers to this passage at *Puls.* VIII 579, turning it against the Pneumatist physician Archigenes who gave no demonstration but appealed to 'prominent men' on a particular issue.

Galen demands to learn their identity to decide whether or not Archigenes' reference to their view can be accepted as a 'respectable assumption' (*endoxon lemma*) according to Aristotle (who spoke of 'wise men'). The point here is the polemical one that Archigenes' language is so untechnical and vague that it remains unclear whether he means his statement to qualify as endoxic in the technical Aristotelian sense; it does not imply any willingness on Galen's part to accept undemonstrated appeal to authority. Cf. *Diff.Puls.* VIII 579.

35. *PHP* V 220–2, 226–7, = *CMG* V 4,1,2, 110.15–112.2, 116.19–31.
36. *PHP* V 357–8, = *CMG* V 4,1,2, 232.6–12.
37. *PHP* V 220–2, 226–7, = *CMG* V 4,1,2, 110.15–112.2, 116.19–31.
38. Still worth reading on this facet of Galen's attitude is Walzer (1949a, 48 ff.).
39. Herophilus Fr. 54, 203; cf. 204 von Staden (1989).
40. See Aristotle, *Parts of Animals* I 1, 639b7–11, 640a13–17.
41. For what follows cf. Hankinson (1991a).
42. Wrong beliefs may also arise from names (cf. e.g. 'hysteria'): see *MM* I 3: X 84.
43. Galen at *PHP* V 389–90, = *CMG* V 4,1,2, 258.8–18 is more precise in saying that 'almost all' philosophers subscribe to this principle, Epicurus being a notable exception. On the problem arising here in view of the obviousness claimed by Galen in passages such as *MM* X 49–50 see the discussion by Lloyd (1996a, 266 ff.).
44. Cf. *MM* I 3: X 17.
45. *MM* I 3: X 141.
46. *MM* I 3: X 146, 148 ('The distinction of categories is the foundation of logical theory').

4 Logic

WORKS OF GALEN CONCERNING LOGIC (LOST UNLESS
OTHERWISE INDICATED)

Under the heading 'books useful for demonstrations' (*On My Own
Books* [*Lib.Prop.*] XIX 39):

> *On demonstration,*[1] in fifteen books (*ibid.* 41)
> *On things necessary for demonstrations,* in one book (*ibid.*
> 43)
> *On propositions missed out in the expression of demonstra-
> tions,* in one book
> *On propositions with the same meaning,* in one book
> *On proofs with 'because',* in one book
> *On the number of syllogisms,* in one book
> *On example,* in two books
> *On induction,* in one book
> *On simile,* in one book
> *On similarity,* in three books
> *On hypothetical principles,* in one book
> *On what we mean in natural language by 'genus' and
> 'species' and words allied to them,* in one book
> *On the possible,*[2] in one book (*ibid.* 44)
> *On things said in many ways,* in three books
> *On what's common and particular in the arts,* in one book
> *On arguments which refute themselves,* in one book
> *On possible propositions,* in one book

I have been particularly helped by the writings of Jonathan Barnes, Susanne Bobzien
and Jim Hankinson.

66

On syllogisms from mixed propositions, in one book
How one should distinguish an enquiry into things from one
    into word and meaning, in one book
On Cleitomachus and his solutions to demonstrations
On common reason, in two books
To Favorinus on the best method of teaching (*Opt.Doct.*)
To Favorinus concerning Epictetus, in one book
On the use of syllogisms
On the best sect,[3] in one book
On the correctness of names,[4] in three books
On each thing's being both one and many
On the claim that it is impossible for one and the same thing
    to follow from contradictory propositions, in one book
On demonstrative discovery, in one book
Dialogues with a philosopher on common notions[5]
Against those who interpret words abusively, in one book
On the constitution of the arts,[6] in three books (*ibid.* 45)
On the meaning of the words 'species' and 'genus' and the
    words associated with them
Summary of the theory of demonstration,[7] in one book
On the judgment of disagreements in doctrines
The quantity of the first substance is inseparable, in one
    book
On demonstration 'per impossibile', in one book
On things which happen for the sake of something, in one
    book
On the enquiry into word and meaning

Under the heading 'Works concerning the philosophy of Plato' (*ibid.*
46):

On Plato's logical theory
On analogies in the Philebus, in one book

Under the heading 'Works concerning the philosophy of Aristotle'
(*ibid.* 47)

Commentary on *De Interpretatione,* in three books
Commentary on book I of *Prior Analytics,* in four books
Commentary on book II of *Prior Analytics,* in four books
Commentary on book I of *Posterior Analytics,* in six books

Commentary on book II of *Posterior Analytics*, in five books
Commentary on *The ten categories*, in four books
Commentary on Theophrastus' *On affirmation and denial*,
in six books
Commentary on *On the number of ways*, in three books
Commentary on Eudemus' *Speech*, in three books
Commentary on *Proofs with 'because'*, in one book
Commentary on *Syllogisms with mixed premisses*, in one
book
On linguistic sophisms (*Soph.*)[8]

Under the heading 'Differences with Stoic Philosophy' (*ibid.* 47)

On Chrysippus' logical theory, in three books
Commentary on Chrysippus' *First syllogistic*, in three books
Commentary on Chrysippus' *Second syllogistic*, in one book
On logical power and theory, in seven books
First and second book on *The use of theorems to do with
syllogisms*
That analytical geometry is better than that of the Stoics, in
one book

INTRODUCTION: THE IMPORTANCE OF LOGIC[9]

A cursory glance at the list of Galen's writings to do with logic reveals
that Galen took the study of logic very seriously. We know that Galen
started learning logic at a relatively young age. In *On the Order of
My Own Books* (*Ord.Lib.Prop.*) XIX 59, he says:[10]

My father was himself competent in the fields of mathematics, arithmetic,
and grammar, and reared me in these as well as the other subjects necessary
to the training of the young. In my fifteenth year he steered me towards
dialectic, with a view to my concentrating entirely on philosophy.

Doubtless, this early introduction to logic contributed to Galen's
feeling totally at ease with the subject. But it is not just familiarity with logic which is responsible for his obvious interest in the
subject. Galen holds that a proper grasp of logic is essential for
anyone engaged in the acquisition of knowledge of any kind. In
Ord.Lib.Prop., he says:[11]

If someone not only learns the methods [laid out in *On demonstration*] but also becomes practised in them, he will find the truth in every matter of fact.

This is not a one-off remark. At *CAM* I 245, Galen describes the logical method as one 'by which truth is discerned from falsehood' (cf. *On the Therapeutic Method* [*MM*] X 9; X 18; *Ord.Lib.Prop.* XIX 50; etc.). This claim is applied more specifically to medicine and philosophy, in *The Best Doctor is also a Philosopher* (*Opt.Med.*), where Galen says of the doctor:[12]

He must study logical method to know how many diseases there are, by species and by genus, and how, in each case, one is to find out what kind of treatment is indicated. The same method also tells us what the very nature of the body is.

When Galen refers to the 'logical method' here, what he has in mind is the theory of demonstration. A demonstration is an argument which takes first principles or generally accepted truths as its premises, and yields by deductive principles a conclusion, which then counts as having been proven. Galen's whole attitude to logical theory is dictated by his insistence that logic is to be studied only insofar as it contributes to the construction of demonstrations. Indeed, the very heading in *Lib.Prop.* under which he catalogues the majority of his works on logic is 'works useful for demonstrations' (*Lib.Prop.* XIX 39). We shall see later that this accounts for many of the differences between Galen and other philosophers, and also accounts for Galen's innovations in logic.

Doctors and philosophers attempt to find things out, and to find things out they must work things out from first principles. Galen does not just mean that doctors should employ common sense when diagnosing their patients' conditions or administering medicines to them, to avoid medical mishaps. Rather, he thinks that reasoning logically from first principles in medicine is required to merit being considered a doctor, properly speaking. This position, very roughly, distinguishes Galen from those in the Methodist and Empiricist sects of medicine, and puts him among the Rationalists,[13] so his attitude to logic is actually fundamental to marking out the kind of doctor he was. Given this, it is no surprise that Galen suggests in *Ord.Lib.Prop.* that someone who wants to become a doctor, after reading *On the Best Sect* (*Opt. Sect.*), which gave information about the various medical sects, should read his massive treatise on logical theory *On demonstration*.

The fact that this work has been lost, along with the vast majority of the treatises mentioned above, deals a severe blow to our ability to reconstruct all of Galen's views on logic. One complete, or nearly complete, logical treatise has come down to us under Galen's name, namely the *Institutio Logica*, or *Introduction to Logic* (*Inst. Log.*). It is not mentioned in the list above – at least, not under that title – and is an introductory work, which in no way gives a comprehensive picture of Galen's attitude to logic (although it contains much of interest, and will be discussed in detail later in this chapter). Nonetheless, Galen speaks so often of logic and the demonstrative method that we are in a position to reconstruct what he thought a demonstration is.

What is a demonstration?[14]

There are two main features of demonstrations. (i) They are valid arguments, and (ii) they are valid arguments whose premises must meet certain conditions.

(i) A valid argument is one whose conclusion follows by deductive principles from its premises. Two schools of Philosophy had contributed to the study of deductive principles, namely the Peripatetics and the Stoics. The Peripatetics had constructed a theory of argument based on Aristotle's categorical syllogistic, studying the connection between propositions stated using words such as 'all' and 'some', and Galen is enthusiastic about their system. Broadly speaking, however, he was hostile to the logic developed by the Stoics, which studied the logical connections between propositions expressed using words such as 'if' and 'or'. Instead, he employed a version of hypothetical syllogistic which owes something to the Stoics, but is markedly different in spirit (more on this below).

Galen realized that certain obviously valid arguments cannot have their validity accounted for by either the Peripatetic or Stoic accounts, namely ones he called 'relational'. Moreover, he thought that arguments of this type are very common, particularly in that paradigm science, geometry, as well as in astronomy and medicine. One way of thinking about Galen's claim is as follows: the Stoics were interested in propositional logic, and Aristotelians in a certain fragment of monadic predicate logic, but Galen saw that there were plenty of arguments useful for medical and mathematical demonstrations which depended upon a certain fragment of dyadic predicate logic. In fact, things aren't as simple as this because what Galen calls a 'relational syllogism' covers a puzzlingly disparate range of arguments, and it is far from clear that Galen had a syntactical characterization of relational arguments in mind – the only kind of characterization which we would these days accept as purely logical. But in any case, Galen was absolutely right that Aristotelian and Stoic syllogistic were unable to cope with the central cases of 'relational' syllogisms, and this is an unassailable logical insight. Relational syllogisms will also be discussed more below.

(ii) The premisses of a demonstration must meet certain further conditions (other than just being such as to entail the conclusion). Demonstrations must proceed from premisses which are not only true, but 'agreed by everybody' (*MM* X 32; cf. X 40; 50; etc.). The idea is that if everybody agrees to the basic premisses of an argument, and only logical deduction is employed to arrive at conclusions, then everybody will be forced to agree to the conclusions too. Galen doesn't mean that literally *everybody* agrees on them, that is, believes them. Rather, he probably has in mind that everybody from a certain restricted group of people (presumably rational, educated people) *should* agree on them. Propositions which are candidates for this are (a) first principles (or axioms), and (b) those which are evident to the senses. (Propositions which are proven on the basis of these two types of premiss are also allowed, but in what follows I leave them out for ease of exposition.)

(a) First principles, or axioms, must be clear and not in need of further proof. So, for instance, if we are to try to establish what the cause of damage to an eye might be, we will proceed 'from an indemonstrable axiom, agreed by all because it is plain to the intellect' (*MM* X 50; all translations from Hankinson, 1991b). These first principles or axioms 'derive their justification neither from others, nor from demonstration, but from themselves' (X 33). Or again, they belong to 'that subclass of things grasped by the intellect on their first appearance and which are indemonstrable' (X 36), of which the following are examples, attributed to previous philosophers (X 36–7):

That two quantities equal to a given quantity are equal to each other, and that equals added to equals yield equals, and that when equals are subtracted from equals the remainders are equal. And they say that 'nothing occurs cause-lessly' is of this type, and similarly 'everything comes to be from something existent', and that nothing comes to be from the absolutely non-existent. Equally, that nothing is annihilated into the absolutely non-existent and that it is necessary that everything must be either affirmed or denied.

Care needs to be taken when constructing a demonstration, to ensure that the premisses you believe to be axioms really are. Galen iden-tifies four types of premiss that might be used in an attempted scientific demonstration: (1) scientific premisses, which 'refer back to the essence of the matter under investigation and have it as their guide' (On the Doctrines of Hippocrates and Plato [PHP] V 221); (2) dialectical premisses – also called 'gymnastic' or 'topical' – which are used by dialecticians in the course of their refutations, or when training others (ibid.); (3) plausible or rhetorical premisses, which are derived 'from generally accepted and every-day examples and from certain inductions of the same sort or from witnesses' (ibid.); (4) sophistical premisses, which 'fraudulently exploit certain homonyms or forms of expression' (V 271). Obviously, of these four types of premiss, only those of the first sort have a place in a properly demonstrative argument. (But presumably the first sort of premiss is not the only sort – the axioms mentioned at MM X 36–7 do not fit the description of the first class.)

(b) Apart from first principles or axioms, any premiss which is 'evident to sense-perception, so that it needs no proof itself' (PHP V 256) is also allowed. Such premisses might include 'Speech is sent out through the windpipe' (ibid.), or even more complex ones such as 'unforced inhalation is produced by a different set of organs and muscles and nerves from those which produce forced inhalation' (V 234).[15] Now, facts such as these can perhaps be perceived, in some sense (by observation of many instances, and then a simple piece of induction). But presumably Galen did not think that the only way to come to know them is on the basis of perception. For such facts usually admit of a deeper explanation, which would be furnished by another demonstration. In fact, sometimes Galen denies that facts such as those expressed by universal statements can be grasped by perception (On the Powers [and Mixtures] of Simple Drugs [SMT] XI 499): to avoid outright inconsistency, it may be best to interpret him as meaning that although they can be entertained and believed on the basis of perception, and known in that sense, they nonetheless admit of explanation, and a full and proper demonstration would employ them only in conjunction with some such explanation. I suspect that Galen allows such propositions to be furnished by perception in a scientific *debate* – the participants can all agree on them because they can all tell that they are true (this is the context in *PHP*, in which Galen is arguing with the Stoics). If the science were to be laid out properly, however, these propositions would be proven on the basis of further axioms.

In addition to premisses such as these, perception can also furnish particular (as opposed to universal) facts, and this marks one important point of departure on Galen's part from Aristotelian theory. For instance, Galen refers to the following argument as a demonstration, right at the start of the *Institutio Logica* (i 3):

> Theo is equal to Dio;
> Philo is equal to the same Dio;
> Two things equal to the same are equal to one other;
> Therefore, Theo is equal to Dio.

Now, the third premiss here is recognizable as one of the axioms mentioned above at *MM* X 36. But the first and second premisses are particular facts, not general or universal truths. Something similar can be seen in the following argument at *Inst.Log.* xiv 4:

> It is not the case that Dio is both in Athens and at the Isthmus;
> But Dio is in Athens;
> Therefore, Dio is not at the Isthmus.

Whatever one makes of the first premiss, the second is presumably intended to be a particular proposition whose truth will be typically furnished by perception. Galen comments about this argument that demonstrations of its type are useful in the law courts. This gives some clue as to why Galen is prepared to include particular propositions in demonstrations. Aristotle had insisted that demonstrations not include particular propositions, because *science* is not concerned with particulars. But for Galen, demonstrations are not just used in laying out a science; they can be used in law courts, where reference to particular people is inevitable, and, of course, they can be used in medicine, where doctors are treating particular patients.

So a demonstration is a valid argument, starting from true premisses, such that the premisses are either the appropriate first principles or propositions furnished by perception, including particular propositions (or propositions which follow from such first principles and propositions furnished by perception). Mastering the demonstrative method – i.e. being able reliably to come up with demonstrative proofs – will therefore involve the ability to choose the correct first principles and the ability to recognize them as first principles, as well as the ability to construct arguments correctly. Small wonder, then, that Galen should claim that the demonstrative method is a tool for discerning truth from falsity, and small wonder, also, that the treatise *On demonstration* ran to fifteen books. The thirteenth book, for instance, dealt with the elements of the body (*Ord.Lib.Prop.* XIX 55; cf. *Opt.Med.* I 60, quoted above), showing that it did not just discuss logical theory in the narrow sense of how to construct deductions, but rather discussed which axioms are the correct ones for science. Being adept at the demonstrative method amounts to knowing the core of everything that is amenable to being treated scientifically.

Because Galen put heavy emphasis on the use of logic in demonstrating medical truths, he had much to criticize in the way other ancient logicians operated. Galen thought that logic is primarily a tool for extending our knowledge of medicine, geometry, etc. As is clear from the titles of the works above, Galen wrote polemical works discussing and attacking other philosophers' writings on logic, particularly the Stoics, whom he liked to accuse of having an interest in logical results which are of no use in actual day-to-day medical reasoning, and possessing an inability in logic leading to their being convinced by bad arguments into views which are false (I give a typical example below, where Galen berates the Stoics for propounding an argument which arrives fallaciously at the view that the heart, and not the brain, is the source of thought).

But the worst result of not being adequately trained in logic is that you fail to upgrade your mere beliefs about medical matters into knowledge – and thus fail to attain expertise in the medical art. For someone who has not had the good luck that Galen had in getting an early start in logical training, might well choose instead to trust what Galen says in his medical works, and not go through the hard work of deriving the facts he lays out from first principles; such a person will still get some benefit from reading Galen:[16]

This person will be able to benefit from my writings without the logical method, not in virtue of acquiring accurate knowledge of the facts (for that is reserved for those who have mastered the logical method), but rather in virtue of acquiring true opinion.

Although Galen doesn't say it, it is clear that if you want to be a proper doctor, you need to have knowledge – i.e. medical expertise – and not just mere medical opinion. The best doctor must also be a logician.

A CASE STUDY: PHP *II* 5 (V 240–62)[17]

After all these claims made on behalf of logic, let us see one example of how Galen thinks mastery of logic will enable us to discern the true from the false. In *PHP* V 227–284, Galen investigates the difficult question of where the ruling part of the soul resides, in order to show that it is in the head, and not in the heart, as for instance the Stoics had thought. Throughout, familiar Galenic themes emerge: he exhorts philosophers to use the correct kind of premiss – i.e. ones with axioms or premisses suitable for scientific demonstration – and not premisses whose apparent truth is owed, say, to etymology (see chapter 5 on language in this volume, pp. 116–56, for more on this). We must avoid premisses suffering from ambiguity, and therefore use language precisely, and yet also not get too stuck on using particular words, and therefore use language freely. The passage contains digressions, enraged outbursts, and ruthlessly precise logic chopping.

I am going to consider in some detail a part of the argument (*PHP* V 240–262), in which Galen considers an argument given by the Stoics purporting to prove that speech and respiration come about through the agency of the heart and not the brain. He supposes that the Stoics have been misled by – among other things – the proximity of the heart to the windpipe. As Galen puts it, 'they were misled by position, or rather, not by position, but their opinion about position' (V 240): they correctly observed the proximity of the heart to the windpipe, but incorrectly attached a certain significance to this, namely that the heart is the *source* of the windpipe's activity, apparently believing that 'all things that are active have their source nearby' (*ibid.*). Even if the Stoics were *quite generally* misled by proximity of position, they also made other mistakes along the way, as Galen takes pleasure in showing.

Galen gives three different versions of the argument, one from each of Zeno of Citium, Diogenes of Babylon and Chrysippus. This is Zeno's:[18]

Speech passes through the windpipe. If it were passing from the brain, it would not pass through the windpipe. Speech passes from the same region as discourse. Discourse passes from the mind. Therefore, the mind is not in the brain.

(Here, discourse is speech informed by reason.) The version given by Diogenes is rather more complicated (or long-winded, according to Galen), and concludes in addition that the mind is lower down the body than the brain. The version propounded by Chrysippus is slightly different again, and it seeks to show that speech, meaningful speech and thought all in fact come from the heart.

Galen is concerned to find fault with all three versions, but he concentrates his fire on Zeno's. Galen has two main complaints about the argument. He thinks that it contains ambiguous premisses, and he thinks that one of its premisses, even suitably disambiguated, lacks the necessary epistemic justification to allow the whole argument to count as a demonstration.

Galen's first worry concerns ambiguity, and the possibility that the argument relies on premisses of the fourth class of premiss which people use in attempted demonstrations (see p. 72), i.e. sophistical premisses. He starts by asking himself one important question: what does the word 'passes' (*chôrei*) mean in the very first premiss of Zeno's argument? Galen claims that the premiss should be reformulated as 'speech goes out (*exerchetai*) through the windpipe', or, even better, 'speech is sent out (*ekpempetai*) through the windpipe'. He justifies this by pointing out that Chrysippus' and Diogenes' versions of the argument use the latter expression (V 244). Changing the premiss in this way will involve changing the other premisses, too, because the same verb must appear in all of them. So now take the second premiss: 'If speech were passing from the brain, it would not pass through the windpipe.' This becomes: 'If speech were sent out from the brain, it would not be sent out through the windpipe'.

It is this premiss which really interests Galen. He points out that the proposition 'If speech were sent out from the brain, it would not be sent out through the windpipe' contains an ambiguity: the preposition 'from' (*apo*) could mean either 'by the agency of' (*hupo*) or 'out of' (*ex*), both of which are unambiguous (*sapheis*) (V 245). In other words, the proposition contains a homonym, one word with two meanings, namely the preposition 'from'. Thus, there are two different disambiguations of the second premiss: 'If speech were sent *out of* the brain, it would not be sent out through the windpipe' and 'If speech were sent out *by the agency of* the brain, it would not be sent out through the windpipe'. Galen thinks that the verb 'is sent out' (favoured by Chrysippus and Diogenes) is actually clearer than the verb 'passes' within this argument (V 244), presumably because the possible meaning of the preposition 'from' where it means 'by the agency of' is made more apparent with the passive verb of action. Formulated with the verb 'passes', the premiss is downright unclear. Formulated with the verb 'is sent out of', the premiss wears its ambiguity on its sleeve, but it still 'belongs to the fourth class, the sophistical premisses, since it hides behind a verbal form that has been given a fraudulent and sophistical ambiguity in the hope of thereby escaping refutation' (V 245).

Just what is the disastrous effect of the ambiguity? The crucial observation that Galen makes is that the first disambiguation – 'If speech were sent out of the brain, it would not be sent out through the windpipe' – is *true* (V 246), whereas the second, 'If speech were sent out by the agency of the brain, it would not be sent out through the windpipe', he thinks is *false* (*ibid.*). To show the falsity of the second reading, Galen musters an array of scatological counter-examples, pointing out that urine (V 245; 246; 253) is expelled by the agency of the mind (i.e. through choice). Not even the Stoics (who locate the mind in the heart) think that the mind must be located in a part continuous with the genitals, says Galen, so Galen imagines confronting them with the following piece of reasoning: 'Urine passes through the genitals; if it were sent out by the heart it would not go out through the genitals; but it is in fact sent out by our choice; choice, therefore, is not in the heart' (V 246). Galen does not stop there. 'A syllogism about excrement may also be constructed in the same way', he proclaims, in De Lacy's marvellous translation (*ibid.*). As if that wasn't enough, he even adds saliva and nasal mucus to a later list of counter-examples (V 253).

So the ambiguity in the premiss 'If speech were sent out from the brain, it would not be sent out through the windpipe' is rather important in this sense: it makes the difference between the proposition's being true or false. But so what if this premiss is ambiguous? Maybe if it is disambiguated in one way or the other, the argument can still go through. Galen will be keen to show that, on either reading, the argument will not go through. But before he shows this, he turns to a second problem with the argument, namely that it has missing premisses. Consider the following version of Zeno's argument:

(1) Speech is sent out through the windpipe.
(2) If speech were sent out of the brain, it would not be sent out through the windpipe.
(3) But speech is sent out of the same region as *logos*.
(4) *logos* is sent out of the mind.

So

(5) The mind is not in the brain.

This employs the preposition 'out of' in place of 'from' – it is the interpretation of premiss (2) according to which the premiss comes out true. Galen claims that the premiss is now 'dialectical' (V 250). What does this mean? Galen does not think the premiss is false – he has deliberately chosen the interpretation of the preposition 'from' according to which the proposition comes out true. Rather, his quarrel is with its epistemic status. He thinks it has not been argued for. The presence in an argument of premisses which have a justification, but whose justification has not been given in the argument, leads to the argument not being a proper demonstration. (Recall that a demonstration must proceed from premisses which have been 'agreed'; cf. p. 71.) This means that we need to add the justification of the second premiss into the argument, in order to stand a chance of transforming it into a demonstration. Galen's first shot is the following complex two-part argument (V 256–7), which I shall call argument 2:

(1′) Speech is sent out through the windpipe.
(2′) All that is sent out through something is sent out of parts continuous with it.
(3′) The brain is not continuous with the windpipe.

So

(4′) Speech is not sent out of the brain.

But

(5′)   From the region from which speech is sent out, *logos* is sent
       out.
(6a′) *logos* is sent out of the mind.
(6b′) *logos* is not sent out of the brain.

So

(7′)   The mind is not in the brain [conclusion from (6a′); (6b′)].

Premiss (1′) is a fact evident to sense-perception (V 256). It was also
premiss (1) in the original argument. Premiss (2′) is (by implication)
one of the first axioms (*ibid.*) and is a scientific premiss (*ibid.*); it did
not feature in the original argument. Premiss (3′) did not feature in the
original argument either, and is presumably equally supposed to be
an observed fact. From (1′), (2′) and (3′), we conclude (4′), which again
did not feature in the original argument. Premiss (5′) is presumably
meant to be an axiom, and was present in the original argument as
premiss (3). Premiss (6a′) is also presumably meant to be an axiom,
and was original premiss (4). (6b′) follows from (4′) and (5′), and did
not appear in argument (1), but is needed because (7′), the conclusion,
follows from it and (6a′). All the original premisses of argument (1),
with the exception of premiss (2), are included in this version of the
argument, and all three of these premisses are treated as self-standing
observations or axioms. Premisses (2′) and (3′) have been added to do
the logical work of the original premiss (2).

What is the alleged advantage of this formulation of the argument
over Zeno's? Of course, Galen thinks that he has disambiguated the
preposition 'from', and that is one advantage. But more importantly
in this context, he has added missing premisses from the original
argument to improve its chances of being a genuine demonstration.

It is worth dwelling on the question of missing premisses, because
it offers us an important insight into Galen's attitude to logic. We
know Galen wrote a book called *On propositions missed out in
the expression of demonstrations*, so we know that this was not
an idle interest of Galen's. But what exactly is the issue? Obviously,
being *invalid* is a disaster for an argument's status as a demonstration, as is having *false* premisses. But Galen does not think that
being valid and having true premisses are jointly sufficient for an

argument's being a successful demonstration. He thinks that a valid argument with true premisses might need some premisses added, to upgrade it into a demonstration. Now, these days we normally suppose that missing premisses are needed precisely in order to turn an invalid argument into a valid one. In fact, any invalid argument can be turned into a valid one by adding a premiss which is a conditional consisting of the conjunction of all the premisses as antecedent, and the conclusion as consequent. Consider the following argument:

(A)   Socrates walks; therefore Socrates moves.

This argument is not formally valid. (In fact, no ancient philosopher except the Stoic philosopher Antipater thought that single-premissed argument could be valid.)[19] But it can be made into a valid argument by adding a premiss following the recipe I have just given:

(B)   If Socrates walks, then Socrates moves; but Socrates walks; therefore Socrates moves.

This argument is valid. But it seems to me that Galen would not count it as a demonstration, even though it is valid. For his treatment of the very argument under examination from *PHP* suggests that he would not think that the added premiss 'If Socrates walks, then Socrates moves' is a first principle or axiom; rather, he would think of it as being dialectical. The following argument, though, *would* count as a demonstration:

(C)   Anything that walks moves; but Socrates walks; therefore Socrates moves.

Between (B) and (C) there is nothing to choose as far as validity is concerned – they are both valid arguments. But (C) contains a premiss which explains *why* Socrates counts as moving if he is walking: it is because *anything* that walks moves. Similarly in the argument from *PHP*, although it is *true* that if speech were sent out of the brain, it would not be sent out through the windpipe (the premiss which Galen rejected as 'dialectical'), this premiss states a fact which itself has an explanation, namely the explanation given in the extra premisses of argument 2:

(2′)   All that is sent out through something is sent out of parts continuous with it.

(3′)   The brain is not continuous with the windpipe.

I shall be returning to the question of missing premisses later (in the section on relational arguments; see pp. 105–13). But for now, what is important for us to see is that Galen thinks that Zeno's argument is unsatisfactory as it stands, and so he makes some 'friendly' adjustments, to turn argument 1 into argument 2. But despite these additions, Galen seems still to be dissatisfied with argument 2. He offers a 'more concise' (V 257) version of the argument as follows (argument 3):

(1″)   *logos* is sent out through the windpipe.
(2″)   All that is sent out through something is sent out of parts continuous with it.

So

(3″)   *logos* is sent out of the parts continuous with the windpipe.

But

(4″)   The brain is not continuous with the windpipe.

So

(5″)   *logos* is not sent out of the brain.

But

(6″)   *logos* is sent out of the mind.

So

(7″)   The mind is not in the brain.

The main difference between this argument and the previous ones is that it eschews any mention of speech at all, and so cannot really be viewed as an alternative *version* of Zeno's original argument (having the same conclusion is not a sufficient condition for two arguments being different versions of the same argument). It is hard to see why not mentioning speech makes this argument preferable to Galen's expanded version (argument 2) of Zeno's original argument 1. Nonetheless, argument 3 is the one Galen focuses on when he is discussing the significance of the ambiguity of the word 'from'.

Galen argues as follows. We have two options. We either interpret the word 'from' as meaning 'out of' (as has been done in the version of the argument given above), or we interpret it as meaning 'by the agency of'. What Galen states at V 259 is that *either* Zeno's argument is valid but unsound (because if you maintain uniformity of preposition for validity, at least one of the premisses is false on each reading of the preposition) *or* the argument is invalid (if you vary the prepositions in the premisses to make them true).

Here is the reasoning behind Galen's claim. Take premiss (6″), '*logos* is sent out of the mind'. In (6″), we have interpreted the preposition '*apo*' as meaning 'out of'. But as Galen says, (6″) is false. Rather, discourse is sent out *by the agency of* the mind. So then we need to change that premiss to make it true. However, if we do that, the argument will become invalid, because we need uniformity of preposition throughout: 'the reasoning [is] inconclusive, for all the premisses would no longer be formulated in the same way' (V 258-9). The only option to preserve validity would be to change *every* occurrence of 'out of' to 'by the agency of'. But in that case premiss (2″) becomes 'All that is sent out through something is sent out by the agency of parts continuous with it', which is false, and premiss 3″ would become '*logos* is sent out by the agency of the parts continuous with the windpipe', which is also false. In order to obtain true readings of each premiss, the preposition chosen would have to be 'out of' in premiss (2″) (and therefore in (3″) and (5″)), and 'by the agency of' in premiss (6″), meaning that premisses (5″) and (6″) read respectively: '*logos* is not sent out of the brain' and '*logos* is sent out by the agency of the mind', from which we cannot conclude that the mind is not in the brain, as Zeno wished. Galen is absolutely clear about the logical problems which arise from the ambiguity of the premiss, and his treatment of the argument is a nice example of his firm grasp of logical distinctions in the service of analysis.

Interestingly, Galen views these two points, the one about ambiguity, the other about the epistemic status of premiss (2) of Zeno's original argument, as connected. Galen could have made the point about ambiguity by focusing on Zeno's original formulation of the argument. But it is important to him to show that by not realizing that the original premiss (2) of his argument was epistemically unwarranted, Zeno had made it difficult for himself to realize that the argument committed a fallacy due to the preposition 'from' (V 258). This is because the original hypothetical premiss 'If it were coming from the brain, it would not come through the windpipe', taken on its own, 'has a semblance of truth' (V 259). Had Zeno put in the extra premiss (2') (along with the extra premiss (3')), then he would have realized that the original premiss 'If speech were sent out from the brain, it would not be sent out through the windpipe' had merely a semblance of truth, which he failed to see because he asserted it without thinking about *why* it was true. Had he reflected on why it is true, he would have seen that the axiom which underpins it very obviously relies on a *topological* or *locative* understanding of the preposition 'from'.

Galen's two criticisms of the argument do not seem by any means to exhaust the problems with Zeno's original argument. It is a striking fact that in the original argument every time, the conclusion is 'the mind is not *in* the brain', where you might have expected 'the mind is not the brain'. After all, if you have shown that *logos* is sent out of the mind and that *logos* is not sent out of the brain, then an application of Leibniz's law will show that the mind is not the brain. Yet, Galen's conclusion is firmly that the mind is not *in* the brain. It is intriguing that Galen should be so clear about the ambiguity of the meaning of the preposition 'from', and build his criticism of the argument around that fact, and yet say nothing about the wording of the *conclusion*, especially as he has insisted that the premisses need to be formulated in a uniform way in order to ensure validity. I do not know what the reason for this is, but one possibility is that Galen understood the word 'mind' in the premisses as referring to the 'ruling part' of the soul, but then in the conclusion switches to thinking of the word 'mind' as meaning 'the faculty of thought' in the conclusion, so that the conclusion means something like 'the faculty of thought is not situated in the brain' – i.e. the brain is not the ruling part of the soul. This would make the conclusion, to all intents and purposes, an identity statement after all.

THE *INSTITUTIO LOGICA*

Although just an introductory handbook of logic, the *Institutio Logica* is an important work in the history of logic. It and Apuleius' *De Interpretatione*[20] are the next books of logical theory to survive after Aristotle, and they contain valuable testimony concerning the logical theories of post-Aristotelian philosophers. *Inst.Log.* is unusual because it does not feature in Kühn's edition of Galen's works, published in 1821–33. The reason for this is that it was discovered in the winter of 1841–2 by the Franco-Greek adventurer Minoïdes Mynas, during one of his several forays into Greece, to all intents and purposes as a spy acting on the orders of the French Minister of Education. Mynas' instructions were to bring back manuscripts of unknown works, statues, etc.; among the other manuscripts that he succeeded in taking is the most important manuscript of Babrius' fables. This latter discovery seems particularly to have inspired Mynas. After one of his later journeys, he returned with what appeared to be a copy he had made of yet another manuscript of Babrius, containing several hitherto unknown fables. Mynas claimed that he had to make do with a copy, since he had been unable to persuade the monks of Mount Athos to part with the original – a cleverly plausible story. But Mynas had made it all up. There was no such manuscript, and he had simply invented some new fables, passing them off as copies of a non-existent original. This emerged only after scholarly editions and translations of the new fables had been published[21] – and after Mynas himself, with notable guile, had managed to persuade the British Museum to buy the 'copy' from him.

Under such circumstances, one might well start to have suspicions as to the authenticity of the *Institutio Logica*. But the work was not a fabrication by Mynas – it is in a twelfth-century hand.[22] What *is* in doubt is whether the work was actually written by Galen himself, or was an ancient forgery. These doubts come from two directions: the very next work in the manuscript is certainly a spurious work of Galen, and there is no mention of the *Institutio* in either of Galen's lists of his writings (*Lib.Prop.* and *Ord.Lib.Prop.*), at least, not under the transmitted title *Galenou eisagôgê dialektikou*.[23]

The first fact is not decisive, and several explanations could account for the second, if the work is in fact genuine. Perhaps Galen wrote the *Institutio Logica* after the catalogues. Alternatively, perhaps the *Institutio Logica* is one of the works which Galen describes in detail at the beginning of *Lib.Prop.*, which[24]

were given without inscription to friends or pupils, having been written with no thought for publication, but simply at the request of those individuals, who had desired a written record of lectures they had attended.

We know that these works included logical ones (*Lib.Prop.* XIX 41), and certainly the tone of the work befits a pedagogical, rather than a philosophical, treatise.

If the work was indeed one of those that Galen wrote for his friends, then an intriguing hypothesis suggests itself. Galen tells us at *Lib.Prop.* XIX 11 that his untitled introductory works were often given titles by others. So perhaps the work we have is in fact the *sunopsis tês apodeiktikês theôrias*, in one book, mentioned at *Lib.Prop.* XIX 45 (cf. Galen's own reference to *Inst.Log.* at xi 1, as *hupographê tês logikês theôrias*). Galen would in the catalogue be *de*scribing it as a *sunopsis*, or summary, of the theory of demonstration, whereas it was *in*scribed *eisagôgê dialektikê* by someone else. We know that the list of works in *Lib.Prop.* under the title 'books useful for demonstrations' contains some of those works he gave to friends, since it contains the commentaries on Aristotle mentioned at XIX 41–2, written at the request of friends.

In fact, the *Institutio Logica* is now accepted by all scholars as genuine, and it certainly reads as pure Galen; it is intemperate, filled with digressions, targets characteristic opponents, and refers to other works of Galen. It covers roughly the following ground: (i) the Aristotelian theory of the categories, (ii) Aristotelian or categorical syllogistic, (iii) hypothetical logic (including some aspects of Stoic hypothetical logic) and (iv) the logic of relations.

The discussion of the categories is relatively straightforward, although Galen trumpets his own discovery of an eleventh category (Aristotle had ten), namely the category of composition:[25]

Someone enquiring how someone wove a cloak or put together a net or box or a bed is inquiring into composition – something omitted by Aristotle in his book on the ten predicates, as I have shown in my commentaries on that book.

The remaining three subjects call for rather more discussion, and form the focus of the remainder of this chapter. Let us start with Galen's presentation of Aristotelian syllogistic. It is quite straightforward, but this fact in itself calls for some comment, because of the controversy surrounding Galen's alleged discovery of the fourth figure.

THE FOURTH FIGURE[26]

There is some evidence that Galen thought that the standard three figures of Aristotelian syllogistic were not sufficient for capturing all the various syllogistic forms. The three main pieces of evidence for this are as follows:

1. Various Arabic logicians attributed the fourth figure to Galen, including Avicenna (980–1037)[27] and Averroes (d. 1198).[28] The logician Ibn al-Salah (c. 1090–1153) wrote a treatise *On the Fourth Figure of the Categorical Syllogism Attributed to Galen* which survives,[29] and in which he enumerates a number of other Arabic logicians who made the attribution.

2. An anonymous Greek author says that some 'recent' philosophers grouped together some of the extra moods added by Theophrastus and Eudemus, to make a fourth figure, 'referring to Galen as the father of the doctrine'.[30] The text is first cited by Mynas in his edition of *Inst.Log.*, at page νσ'. Unfortunately, it is unclear from when or where this fragment originates, since Mynas simply says that this remark occurs in a commentary on Aristotle's *Prior Analytics* (*ibid.*).

3. There is a Greek fragment found by Carl Prantl in about 1858, in a logical work of Ioannes Italus (eleventh century) which runs as follows:

> These are the figures of syllogisms: But Galen said that there was also a fourth one in addition, in opposition to the Stagirite, and, thinking that he would appear brighter than the ancient commentators on the logical treatise, fell straightway as far below them as was possible.

Equally, however, there is plenty of evidence to suggest that Galen did *not* discover the fourth figure. For a start, Ibn al-Salah himself, in the very same work on the fourth figure mentioned in (1), says that in *On demonstration* and *On the number of syllogisms* – to both of which he apparently had access – Galen 'divided the assertoric (or: categorical) figures into three only and concluded with the statement that they have no fourth' (122b19; Rescher, 1966, 53). This tells us that Galen must have discovered the fourth figure relatively late in his life – if at all. But there is no work of Galen's called *On the fourth figure of the syllogism* in *Lib.Prop.* or *Ord.Lib.Prop.*, and indeed there is no mention of the fourth figure in *any* of Galen's extant writings. In fact, in *Inst.Log.* not only is there no mention of the fourth figure, but also it would be impossible for there to be one, given the way Galen sets up Aristotelian syllogistic in that work.

This needs some explanation. An Aristotelian syllogism of the kind discussed in *Prior Analytics* I 4–6 is an argument consisting of two premisses and a conclusion. The two premisses are in subject–predicate form, and (ignoring syllogisms with 'indeterminate' premisses) take one of four forms: universal affirmative ('P is said of all S', usually written 'PaS'); particular affirmative ('P is said of some S', written 'PiS'); universal negative ('P is said of no S', written 'PeS'); particular negative ('P is not said of some S', written 'PoS'). The way Galen presents Aristotelian syllogistic is as follows. At *Inst.Log.* vii 7, he defines a first-figure syllogism as one whose premisses are such that the middle term is subject in one premiss and predicate in the other, a second-figure syllogism as one where the middle term is predicate in both premisses, and a third-figure syllogism as one where the middle is subject in both. So defined, there is no scope for a fourth figure to exist, as Galen states at *Inst.Log.* xii 1. Symbolically, we get the following patterns for the premisses (where 'x' denotes any of 'a', 'e', 'i', 'o'):

1st figure	2nd figure	3rd figure
AxB	BxA	AxB
BxC	BxC	CxB

How, then, is it that some people thought there was a *fourth* figure? The answer is that we have here defined what figure a syllogism belongs to by adverting to the form of the *premisses*. But in the first figure, there are two possibilities for the form of the *conclusion*. Since the conclusion consists of the two terms which are not the middle term, the conclusion could either be of the form AxC, or of the form CxA. These possibilities yield distinct patterns for the syllogisms:

(i)	AxB	(ii)	AxB
	BxC		BxC
	AxC		CxA

Rather than treating these two forms as possible forms for first-figure syllogisms, some ancient logicians treated form (i) as that of first-figure syllogisms, and form (ii) as that of fourth-figure syllogisms.[31] As can be seen from this brief exposition, the issue is whether or not the form of the *conclusion* is included in the specification of the form of the first figure. If you insist that the conclusion of a first-figure syllogism must have as its predicate the term which is predicate for the middle term in the premisses, and as its subject the term which is subject for the middle term in the premisses, then you open up the possibility for a further figure (the fourth figure). If, however, you do as Galen did in the *Inst. Log.*, and in *On demonstration* and *On the number of syllogisms* (according to Ibn al-Salah), and define the first figure of syllogisms as those whose premisses are such that the middle term is predicate in one premiss and subject in the other, then there is no possibility of having a fourth figure.

In truth, the issue is of no logical significance. But the existence of the historical evidence attributing the discovery of the fourth figure to Galen must be assessed. If one believes that Galen did indeed discover the fourth figure, then there are two attitudes to take to all this evidence. First, one could argue that that *Inst.Log.* is simply not by Galen at all and that Ibn al-Salah is mistaken in his report of the other works of Galen, and that Galen never mentioned his discovery in any of his surviving works because he did not consider it important enough. Second, one could imagine that Galen discovered the fourth figure *after* he wrote *Inst.Log.* (which in turn was written after *On demonstration* and *On the number of syllogisms*, since both are mentioned in *Inst.Log.*), and *after* he wrote *Lib.Prop.* and *Ord.Lib.Prop.* (which is why there is no work mentioned in those books concerning the fourth figure). According to this hypothesis, no extant work of Galen's mentions the fourth figure because he discovered it relatively late in his life – or, again, because he did not think it merited mention.

Neither hypothesis is particularly attractive, especially given Galen's propensity for praising his own discoveries. And in fact, there is a better hypothesis to hand, namely that the later attributions to Galen of the discovery of the fourth figure are mistaken, and are founded on a misunderstanding of Galen's discovery of a rather different logical fact.[32] The evidence for this comes from a scholium, published in 1899 by Wallies in the preface (pp. ix–xii) of his edition of Ammonius' commentary on Aristotle's *Prior Analytics*. This

scholium states that there are three figures of 'simple' categorical syllogisms according to Aristotle, and that Galen said in his *On demonstration* that there are four, 'focussing on compound syllogisms composed of four terms, of which he finds many in Plato's dialogues' (ix,
28–30). In other words, Galen seems to have discovered four figures
of a different type of syllogism – not the straightforward syllogisms
that I have just been discussing, but a different kind of syllogism,
so-called 'compound' syllogisms.

The scholiast is less than forthcoming about how these compound
syllogisms work. What is clear is that they exploit the chaining
together of two-premissed syllogisms to make three-premissed syllogisms. For example, take the following two syllogisms:

(i)	AaB	(ii)	AaC
	BaC		CaD
	AaC		AaD

These can be chained together to yield the following three-premissed
syllogism:

> AaB
> BaC
> CaD
> AaD

This is one of the valid three-premissed syllogisms. Galen apparently
claimed that all the three-premissed syllogisms could be grouped
into just four figures. What is obscure, however, is quite how the
figures are to be individuated. A diagram in the scholium lists the
four figures as follows:

First with first	First with second	First with third	Second with third
(First)	(Second)	(Third)	(Fourth)

Clearly, the example of a 'chained' syllogism above is an example of
chaining a (simple) first-figure syllogism with another (simple) first-
figure syllogism, and would therefore seem to be an example of a
first-figure compound syllogism.

The problem with this interpretation of Galen's claim is that the scholiast also attributes to him the view that there are *no* valid syllogisms which are examples of the (simple) second figure chained with the (simple) second figure, and *no* valid syllogisms which are examples of the (simple) third figure chained with the (simple) third figure. On the face of it, this would be plain false, if the suggested reconstruction is correct.[33] For the argument 'AaB, AeC, BaD, therefore CeD' certainly looks like a clear case of a second-figure deduction (Camestres) chained with another second-figure deduction (Cesare), and the argument 'AaB, CiB, DaC, therefore AiD' a case of chaining Datisi (third figure) with Disamis (third figure).

There is a way of avoiding this problem.[34] Galen's observation may not have been that there is *no* valid chained argument consisting of a (simple) second-figure syllogism with a (simple) second-figure syllogism, or a (simple) third-figure syllogism with a (simple) third-figure syllogism. Rather, he may have claimed that there is no such argument *which cannot be analysed as one of the other combinations involving the first figure.* For instance, the argument 'AaB, AeC, BaD, therefore CeD' (Camestres followed by Cesare) *can* be analysed as a first-figure syllogism (Barbara) 'AaB, BaD, therefore AaD', chained with the second-figure syllogism (Cesare) 'AeC, AaD, therefore CaD'. Equally, the argument 'AaB, CiB, DaC, therefore AiD' (Datisi followed by Disamis) *can* be analysed as a first-figure syllogism (Darii) 'DaC, CiB, therefore DiB', chained with the third-figure syllogism (Datisi) 'AaB, DiB, therefore AiD'.

The details of Galen's theory of compound syllogisms are tantalisingly difficult to pin down, and cannot detain us here. But a few points deserve mention. First, Galen gives examples of such chained syllogisms in his extant writings (there is a nice example of two hypothetical arguments spliced together at *On Semen* [*Sem.*] IV 610), which seems to show his awareness of the relevant underlying logical rule, namely the 'cut' rule:[35]

$$\frac{A, B \vdash C \qquad C, D \vdash E}{A, B, D \vdash E}$$

Second, it betrays a logician's instinct to wonder how to generalise Aristotle's results concerning arguments with *two* premises, to arguments of *three* premises. But most importantly, the theory of the compound syllogism was applied by Galen (so the scholiast

reports) to actual arguments, and in particular to arguments propounded by Plato, a couple from *Alcibiades* and one from *Republic*.
We have already seen that Galen employs logical theory to analyse
and understand the reasoning of other philosophers (that, after all,
was part of what was going on in the discussion of the argument in
PHP above). And it cannot be a coincidence that in *Inst.Log*. Galen
analyses arguments from the same two dialogues of Plato, *Alcibiades*
and *Republic*: at xv 10–11 Galen says that an argument in *Alcibiades*
makes use of a quasi-disjunctive syllogism, and at xviii 2–4 he analyses an argument in the *Republic* as using a relational syllogism. The
latter example is particularly telling: Galen introduces a new piece
of logical theory (the relational syllogism) to account for the way an
argument propounded by Plato works. This is exactly matched by
what is reported by the scholiast concerning compound syllogisms:
Galen applies a new piece of logical theory (this time dealing with
compound syllogisms) to Platonic arguments. Perhaps Galen's lost
work *On Plato's logical theory* involved yet more discussion of the
logical form of various arguments in Plato.[36]

The upshot is this: Galen didn't invent the fourth figure of simple
Aristotelian syllogistic. That dubious achievement must have been
due to a later logician. However, Galen does seem to have made a
good start on the theory of compound syllogisms, stating that there
are four figures and applying that theory to actual arguments propounded by Plato.

HYPOTHETICAL LOGIC[37]

Galen's treatment of hypothetical logic is obscure, and troubling.
At first sight, it even appears to suggest that, *au fond*, Galen didn't
really understand logic. In fact, it illustrates two important tenets
of Galen's attitude to logic – namely, that the logician must look to
things and not to expressions, and must develop only such logical
devices as are useful for demonstrations. Of course, these slogans
are somewhat vague, and could be made more precise in a variety
of ways, but Galen's treatment of hypothetical logic reveals what he
thought their significance was.

Before sketching the outlines of Galen's hypothetical logic, it is
worth dwelling for a moment on the slogan that says that the logician must look to things and not to expressions. This does not mean

that Galen is sloppy about how arguments are formulated. In the argument from *PHP* discussed in detail above, Galen insisted that the premisses of the argument be formulated *correctly*, that is, using the correct preposition. Failure to use the correct preposition would result in your thinking that you had constructed a valid argument with true premisses; in fact, when you formulate the argument paying attention to which preposition you use, you discover that you get either a valid argument with false premisses, or an invalid argument with true premisses, neither of which is what you wanted. Clearly then, Galen thinks that it matters how the premisses are formulated: they need to be formulated so as to be unambiguous and to say the right thing. In other words, Galen is concerned about the expression of the argument to the extent that this affects the *meaning* of the propositions involved.

It might seem trivial or obvious that a logician would pay attention to the way an argument is expressed in order that the propositions of the argument have the correct meaning. But Galen complains that some logicians, notably the Stoics, went further than this. The Stoics had apparently wanted to find logically important differences between arguments such as the following:

(A) It is day.	(B) It is day.
But if it is day, it is light.	But that it is light follows that it is day.
Therefore, it is light.	Therefore, it is light.

Argument (A) is a first indemonstrable argument, according to the Stoics, whereas argument (B) is known as a 'subsyllogistic' argument. The Stoics claimed that the second premisses of each argument express different 'lekta', and favoured argument (A) over argument (B), yet presumably they wished to explain the validity of argument (B) by reference to its close relation to argument (A). (There is seemingly a reference to this very example at *Inst.Log.* iv 7, where Galen roundly condemns those who 'invent' a difference between 'implying', 'following' and 'depending on'.) In *Inst.Log.* xix 6, Galen says that subsyllogistic arguments are useless for logic,[38] presumably because he thinks the distinction between a syllogistic and a subsyllogistic argument is just the sort of distinction the Stoics were enamoured of: one concerning words not things, and hence (according to

Galen) a distinction not worth making when doing logic (cf. *Inst.Log.*
iii 5). Alexander of Aphrodisias believes that Aristotle 'looked to the
meanings (when the same things are meant) rather than to the words
and says that the same syllogism is deduced when the expression
of the conclusion is transformed in this way' (*In.An.Pr.* 84, 16–19).
Galen, too, seems to have thought that the meaning was the only logically relevant aspect of expressions. It is not just that Galen thinks
that the Stoics were wrong to detect nuances of meaning between
'if P then Q' and 'Q follows from P'; he also thinks that the Stoics
were wrong to insist that a canonically formulated argument differs
in any logically interesting way from an argument which means the
same and yet is formulated differently.

It seems likely that Galen wrote an entire work devoted to this
subject, namely *On propositions with the same meaning* (the word
used for 'propositions' here is sometimes translated 'premisses'). It
probably treated just these kinds of argument, i.e. ones which differ
merely in virtue of expression, and not in meaning. A good example
is the argument given by Galen in *Inst.Log.* xvi 1 as an example of
his third kind of syllogism (the 'relational' syllogism):

> Theo has twice as much as Dio;
> But Philo has twice as much as Theo;
> Therefore Philo has four times as much as Dio.

Galen immediately says (xvi 2) that you can produce 'the same argument in force' by turning around the expressions used, to give the
argument:

> Dio has half what Theo has;
> But Theo has half what Philo has;
> Therefore Dio has a quarter of what Philo has.

The only place *On propositions with the same meaning* is mentioned
outside *Lib.Prop.* is at *Inst.Log.* xi 2, where Galen is discussing the
various syllogistic figures. He says:

In each figure there are sixteen pairings of propositions, because there are
four propositions in each figure, two universal and two particular, even if
in turn of expression they appear more. You must exercise in them and
recognize them, as I said in my work on propositions of equal force.

There appear to be more propositions than Aristotle's two universal and two particular ones because of the various ways of expressing them. You must therefore learn to identify which expressions go with which propositions. This might sound trivially easy, but the recognition that it might be hard to tell which sentences express universal and which ones express particular propositions is not peculiar to Galen. It goes back to Aristotle, who considers the meaning of propositions of the form 'The F is G' (indefinite propositions), and proposes to treat them as equivalent to particular propositions (i.e. as equivalent to a proposition of the form 'Some F is G'). Galen takes the opposite view in *Inst.Log.*, and wants to treat 'The F is G' as another way of saying 'all Fs are G' (xii 8).

We can thus see that Galen was exercised by the question of how to express a given proposition in an argument. However, subsyllogistic arguments are a relatively minor part of logical theory, and if Galen's insistence that a logician pay attention to things not words resulted only in his rejection of any logically interesting difference between syllogistic and subsyllogistic arguments, the slogan would be of merely passing interest. But in fact there is a far more important issue on the horizon, concerning hypothetical logic more generally. To see what this issue is, we need to look at some basic tenets of Stoic logical theory.

In the background to most of Galen's remarks concerning hypothetical syllogistic are the five Stoic indemonstrables. The forms of these are as follows:

(I1)   If the first, then the second;
        But the first;
        Therefore the second.

(I2)   If the first, then the second;
        But not the second;
        Therefore not the first.

(I3)   Not both (the first and the second);
        But the first;
        Therefore not the second.

(I4)   Either the first or the second;
        But the first;
        Therefore not the second.

(I5) Either the first or the second;
      But not the first;
      Therefore the second.

As can be seen from this, there are three types of proposition at issue
here, namely conditional ones (expressed canonically by sentences
of the form 'if the first, then the second'), disjunctive ones ('either
the first or the second'), and negated conjunctive ones ('not both (the
first and the second)'). There is 'one canonical formulation for each
type' of proposition.[39]

Take the form common to any Stoic first indemonstrable
argument:

(I1) If the first, then the second;
      But the first;
      Therefore, the second.

(Argument (A) above is an instance of this form.) We have already
seen that, according to the Stoics, if an argument has its first premiss
expressed as the sentence 'the second follows from the first' (or something similar), then that argument cannot be a first indemonstrable,
since such sentences express a different proposition from a sentence
such as 'If the first, then the second'. In other words, 'the second
follows from the first' is not a *conditional*, according to the Stoics. Galen supposes the difference between these formulations to be
minor. But, more importantly, he is not convinced that *every* statement using the word 'if' should be classed as a conditional, as the
Stoics do. He thinks there is an important difference between the
statements 'If it is day, the sun is over the earth' and 'If it is not
day, it is night'. He is happy to say that the sentence 'if it is day,
the sun is over the earth' is a conditional sentence, but he says of
'If it is not day, it is night' that 'in the form of its expression it is
said to be a conditional', and 'those who attend to words only call
it a conditional, whereas those who attend to the nature of things
call it disjunctive' (*Inst.Log.* iii 5). Thus we can see that not only
does Galen deny that the presence of the word 'if' is *necessary* for a
statement to be a conditional (because the expression 'follows from'
would do just as well), but also he denies it is *sufficient* (for some
statements formulated with 'if' do not qualify as conditionals).

Now, it is certainly the case that in English the presence of the word 'if' is not sufficient for a statement to be a genuine conditional statement. For instance, someone who asserts the English sentence 'If you really want to know, I'm hungry' actually asserts the consequent, as does someone who asserts 'If you're hungry, there's food in the fridge'. Conversely, someone who asserts 'If he can eat all the food in the fridge, I'll eat my hat' denies the antecedent. But Galen's example, 'If it is not day, it is night', is not like either of those: it is not that someone who says 'If it is not day, it is night' actually asserts that it is night (asserting the consequent), or asserts that it is day (denying the antecedent). So what then leads Galen to deny that this if-statement is a genuine conditional?

Before answering this, we have to consider the underlying metaphysical picture that Galen has of how states of affairs are related. Galen thinks that there are three ways in which a pair of states of affairs might be related (*Inst.Log.* xiv 7): they might be in conflict, in consequence, or in neither relation. To simplify, consider pairs of states of affairs. Two states of affairs are 'in conflict' just if it is impossible for them both to hold together. Two states of affairs are 'in consequence' just if they necessarily hold together. Two states of affairs are neither in conflict nor in consequence just if it is possible for them both to hold together, and possible for them both not to hold together. The first two types of relation can be further subdivided. There are two types of conflict, complete and incomplete. States of affairs are in 'complete' conflict just if they are in conflict, but furthermore it is impossible for them both to fail to hold. States of affairs are in 'incomplete' conflict just if they are in conflict, but furthermore it is possible for them both to fail to hold. The two types of consequence are also called 'complete' and 'incomplete' consequence. Two states of affairs are in 'complete' consequence just if when one holds, the other must hold, and vice versa. Two states of affairs are in 'incomplete' consequence just if when one holds, the other must hold, but not vice versa.

The following examples should help make this clearer. The two states of affairs expressed by 'It is day' and 'It is night' are in complete conflict (both cannot be true together, but both cannot be false together). 'Dio is at the Isthmus' and 'Dio is in Athens' are in incomplete conflict (both cannot be true together, but both could be false together – for instance, if Dio is in Delphi). 'Dio is alive' and 'Dio is breathing' are in complete consequence (if one holds, the other must, and vice versa). 'Dio is sleeping' and 'Dio is alive' are in incomplete consequence (if the first holds, the second holds, but not the other way around). 'Dio is walking' and 'Theo is talking' are in neither conflict nor consequence (since both could be true together, and both could be false together).

Now we are in a position to appreciate in outline why Galen thinks the Stoics are wrong to classify a statement such as 'If it is not day, it is night' as a conditional. Galen thinks that statements should be classed as 'conditional', 'disjunctive', or 'conjunctive' according as to whether the propositions express the relations just described as holding between the states of affairs referred to in them. So a statement is 'conditional' if the proposition expresses a consequence-relation; 'disjunctive' if it expresses a conflict-relation; 'conjunctive' if it gives the truth-value of states of affairs which are unrelated. Galen seems to think that under normal circumstances, someone who says 'if it is day, it is not night' does not mean to claim that its not being night is in the *consequence* relation to its being day. Rather, he thinks that the person who says it in fact means to claim that day and night are in *conflict*, namely, complete conflict (the same goes for 'if it is not night, it is day'). Likewise, someone who says 'if Dio is in Athens, he is not at the Isthmus' does not mean to claim that Dio's failing to be at the Isthmus is in the *consequence*-relation to his being at Athens. Rather, it is being claimed that Dio's being in Athens and Dio's being at the Isthmus are in *conflict*, but this time, in incomplete conflict. Galen also seems to think that, in normal circumstances, someone who says 'if it is day, the sun is over the earth' means to say that its being day and the sun's being over the earth are in complete consequence, whereas someone who says 'if Dio is sleeping, Dio is alive' means to say that Dio's sleeping and his being alive are in incomplete consequence. In other words, *one and the same expression*, in this case 'if', *can be used to express a multitude of different logical relations holding between states of affairs.*

This view is strikingly at odds with the Stoic view that the word 'if' is always used to express one particular logical relation, and moreover is the canonical way of expressing that relation. We are beginning to understand the force of Galen's adherence to the slogan 'pay attention to things not words'.

The converse of the above principle also holds. *One and the same logical relation holding between states of affairs can be expressed using different expressions*. For example, if you want to express that Dio's being at the Isthmus and Dio's being in Athens are in incomplete conflict, then you can do this in two ways: 'If Dio is at the Isthmus, then Dio is not in Athens', or 'It is not the case that Dio is both at the Isthmus and in Athens'.

The most obvious question to raise about this view of what is meant by hypothetical statements is this: how do you know which proposition is being expressed when someone makes a statement of the form 'if P, then Q'? If it is just a question of examining how P and Q are related, then we appear to be reduced to the absurd position that there are no false 'if'-statements which express (e.g.) complete conflict, because in order to see whether the 'if'-statement in front of you expresses complete conflict (between P and the contradictory of Q), you just have to see whether P and the contradictory of Q actually are in complete conflict. If they are in complete conflict, then the statement expressed that they are. Hence – it seems – there is no way to have a false statement of complete conflict, using the word 'if'.

The same goes for disjunctive statements. Whereas for the Stoics, any statement with the word 'or' as the principal connective expresses a disjunctive proposition, Galen holds a different view. Some statements using the word 'or' will express *complete* conflict between the states of affairs mentioned, whereas others will express *incomplete* conflict. Only those statements which express complete conflict will count as disjunctions; those that express incomplete conflict will be what Galen calls 'paradisjunctions'. What seems to determine this is what relation the states of affairs mentioned actually bear to one another; in other words, he seems to hold that if they are in complete conflict, then the statement with 'or' expressed that they are. Hence – it seems – there is no way to have a false statement of complete conflict, using the word 'or'. As Benson Mates dismissively comments: 'Since there is a serious confusion here between a disjunction and a true disjunction, probably nothing of great interest can be inferred from Galen's report'.[40]

To allay these worries, Susanne Bobzien[41] has suggested that we need not attribute to Galen the view that the *meaning* of the 'if'-statement or the 'or'-statement is fully determined by what the relation between the antecedent and consequent *actually* is. All sorts of contextual factors could help the listener realize that the speaker was intending to produce a statement expressing that two states of affairs are in complete conflict – for instance, if the speaker had been asked to produce such a statement. Part of the listener's job in determining what the speaker is saying may well involve looking at which states of affairs are mentioned and what their relation is, but this need not by itself be determinate of what proposition is expressed.

Although Bobzien does not draw the analogy explicitly, there is an obvious one to be made between Galen's view and those modern pragmatic theories of communication which rely on the difference between literal meaning and speaker meaning. According to such theories, sometimes the speaker of a statement such as 'he climbed the hill and took a rest' implies not merely that both states of affairs hold, but that the state of affairs mentioned in the second conjunct happened after, or even because of, the state of affairs mentioned in the first conjunct. This is explained by appealing to a complex theory of conversational cooperation, due to Grice,[42] where the listener works out the literal proposition expressed by the speaker, and then goes through a series of steps determining that if the speaker is being relevant and helpful, etc. then the speaker must also have meant something further. The details of the theory are not important here; what is important is that we recognize that the statement does indeed express (at the level of what is meant by the speaker) a causal relation between the two states of affairs. Part of the story as to how the speaker managed to express this is to do with the listener's recognition that the states of affairs mentioned in the statement are eligible candidates for being causally related – hence Galen's suggestion that we need to look at the states of affairs mentioned in statements and what the relation between them is, rather than just at the words used.

What I want to underline is that there is a way of describing what is going on in the case of the causal statement expressed with 'and' which preserves all the main features of Galen's account of disjunctive and conditional statements. Here is how one could put it. (i) 'Causal' propositions are ones where one state of affairs is said to cause another; (ii) such statements are sometimes expressed using the word 'and', but also sometimes with the word 'because', and with many other words too; (iii) the statement expressed by 'he climbed the hill and took a rest' is one such causal statement (because the speaker succeeds in communicating that one state of affairs is caused by another); (iv) 'conjunctive' propositions are ones where two states of affairs are said to hold without any causal connection being imputed; (v) the statement under discussion is therefore not a conjunctive proposition. I see nothing objectionable in such a description, and therefore do not think that Galen's theory of disjunctive and conditional statements should be dismissed out of hand. What is going on is that Galen, as we might put it, goes straight for the speaker's meaning, not the literal meaning.

When someone says 'if it is day, it is not night', their *grounds* for saying this, usually, will be that day and night are in complete conflict (to use Galen's terminology). It is not absurd to think that the proposition meant by the speaker is that very fact: that day and night are in complete conflict. Equally, when someone says 'if Dio is at the Isthmus then he is not in Athens', their *grounds* for saying this will presumably be that Dio's being at the Isthmus and Dio's being in Athens are incomplete conflict (you can't be in two places at once), and so maybe, on some occasions, this is exactly what they mean to say.

There is not space here to deal with all the complexities and difficulties of Galen's sketchy account, how to cash out all its details and make it plausible and what its historical background is.[43] But what is very clear from Galen's discussion is that his favoured theory of disjunctive, conditional, and conjunctive propositions differs wildly from that of the Stoics, despite the fact that he nods in their general direction, and runs through the five standard Stoic indemonstrables at *Inst.Log.* vi 6. There are counterparts, so to speak, of most of the indemonstrables in Galen's system, but he does not think, as the Stoics did, that the relevant arguments have to be expressed *canonically*, nor does he think that in fact all the arguments expressed in the way the Stoics want will on closer inspection turn out to be the indemonstrable they appear to be.

But one thing we are in position to do now is understand Galen's discussion of the third indemonstrable. It reveals neatly how Galen builds his logic around the twin slogans: 'Pay attention to things not words', and 'logical theory must be useful for demonstrations'.

The third indemonstrable

Galen gives the standard form of the third indemonstrable at *Inst.Log.* vi 6:

(I3) Not both the first and the second;
      But the first;
      Therefore not the second.

In *Inst.Log.* xiv 4, Galen returns to it, and describes it, rather more
accurately this time, as an argument which 'from a negative conjunction and one of its elements concludes the contradictory of the
remaining one' (this time allowing that the minor premiss could be
either of the two embedded statements in the major premiss, not
just the first – if it is the second, then the conclusion would obviously be the contradictory of the first). Galen comments that this
indemonstrable is 'useful for many demonstrations in ordinary life,
and in the law courts', and gives as an example arguments starting
from the major premiss 'It is not the case that Dio is both in Athens
and at the Isthmus'. The two arguments you could construct on the
basis of this statement are as follows:

(D1) It is not the case that Dio is both in Athens and at the
      Isthmus;
      But Dio is in Athens;
      Therefore Dio is not at the Isthmus.

Or alternatively:

(D2) It is not the case that Dio is both in Athens and at the
      Isthmus;
      But Dio is at the Isthmus;
      Therefore Dio is not in Athens.

Take (D1). If someone were to accuse poor old Dio of some misde-
meanour committed at the Isthmus, it would be a fine defence to
point out that he was in Athens at the time (and produce witnesses
to that effect), and that he can't have been both in Athens and at
the Isthmus. Galen is surely right that such arguments abound in
courtrooms.

But Galen hedges his remark about the usefulness of such arguments. For he says that it is in fact only in cases where the states
of affairs referred to in the major premiss are in complete or incomplete conflict that 'the sort of argument I have mentioned is useful'
(xiv 6). In (D1) and (D2), the major premiss is 'It is not the case that
Dio is both in Athens and at the Isthmus'. Clearly, the two states of

affairs mentioned in this premiss, namely Dio's being in Athens and Dio's being at the Isthmus, are in incomplete conflict. So the argument just given does indeed meet one of the conditions for being useful, according to Galen. However, Galen thinks that the usefulness of such instances of the third indemonstrable is precisely due to the fact that the major premisses actually express complete or incomplete conflict between the mentioned states of affairs. Moreover, in such cases, the major premisses will in fact express *disjunctions*, and so the Stoics have been misled by the form of expression, namely the expression 'not both . . . and . . .', into thinking that the statements made are negated conjunctions (as opposed to disjunctions).

Galen allows, then, that there are third indemonstrables which are useful – that is, if you individuate third indemonstrables by means of the linguistic expression used, rather than by what the premisses actually mean or express (namely, disjunctive statements). But, as Galen puts it, such arguments are really constructed 'through conflicting things' (xiv 6). So what, then, of the instances of the third indemonstrable which are alleged to be useless for demonstrations? According to Galen, not every statement formed using the expression 'Not both . . . and . . .' will express that the relation of incomplete conflict actually holds between the two states of affairs mentioned in it. Sometimes, someone might use the expression 'Not both . . . and . . .' just in order to express that two states of affairs, even though they do not stand in a relation of consequence or of conflict, do not, as a matter of fact, currently hold together. It is precisely such instances of the third indemonstrable, involving a major premiss of this kind, which Galen thinks are useless for demonstration.

Helpfully, Galen gives us an example of such an argument. Take the statement 'it is not the case that both Dio walks and Theo talks' (iv 4; xiv 7). Such a statement (according to Galen) does not attribute incomplete conflict to the states of affairs of Dio walking and Theo talking. Rather, it states that the two states of affairs are neither in conflict nor in consequence, and simply denies that both states of affairs currently hold. As Galen says, we can construct a third indemonstrable argument using it, with either 'Dio walks' or 'Theo talks' as minor premisses (xiv 8). So let us take one of those arguments:

(DT1)   It is not the case that both Dio walks and Theo talks;
        But Dio walks;
        Therefore Theo doesn't talk.

Galen is distinctly unimpressed by such an argument. He comments:
'I have shown that material of this sort is utterly useless for demonstrations' (xiv 8). The reference is to one of Galen's lost works (cf.
also xix 6), but it would be good nonetheless to supply a reason as to
why Galen thinks that this argument is useless.

The reason seems to be something like the following. In (DT1), we
are dealing with states of affairs which are unrelated. The major premiss of (DT1) actually states (according to Galen) that the two states
of affairs are unrelated, and that they do not both obtain. Suppose
now that we put this argument forward as a demonstration. For the
argument to count as a demonstration, the premisses must be true,
but also, crucially, known to be true (either by perception or by logical argument). But as Bobzien puts it: 'when one has come to know
on its own the truth of one premiss, then *either* one has come to
know the truth of the conclusion, *or* it has become impossible to get
a sound argument' (2004, 91). If the two states of affairs are unconnected, then the only way of coming to know the truth of the first
premiss is to know the truth-values of the constituent statements
'Dio walks' and 'Theo talks' individually, and then note that they
are not both true.[44] But if you know that it is true that Dio walks
and false that Theo talks (and this is how you know the first premiss
to be true), then you already know the truth of the conclusion and
you do not need to engage in the demonstration to come to know it –
the demonstration is useless. If you know that it is false that Dio
walks and true that Theo talks (and this is how you come to know
the first premiss to be true), then you already know the falsity of the
second premiss, so you will not be able to construct a demonstration, for a demonstration must have true premisses. (Similarly if you
know the first premiss to be true because you know that it is false
that Dio walks and false that Theo talks.) Hence, the only condition
in which the demonstration is even possible is one where it is not
needed, because to know, in those circumstances, the truth of the
first premiss is already to know the truth of the conclusion.

This gives some flavour of Galen's insistence that the Stoics pay
too much attention to expressions not things, and that they end up,

because of that, spending time on parts of logical theory not useful for demonstrations.

When should hypothetical arguments be used in demonstrations? Galen suggests, in *Inst.Log.* xiv 1–2, that they are to be used primarily for establishing the existence of things which are not evident to the senses. There is something slightly odd about this, for sometimes Galen seems happy to produce proofs using hypothetical propositions without that aim, e.g. the following from *On whether Blood is Naturally Contained in the Arteries (Art.Sang.)* IV 704–5 (trans. Furley and Wilkie):

> If, when the arteries are wounded, blood is observed to be voided, then either it was contained in the arteries themselves, or it is transferred from elsewhere. But, when the arteries are wounded, blood is observed to be voided, and it is not transferred (as we shall demonstrate). Therefore it was contained in the arteries themselves.

However, in other places it is clear that Galen thinks that hypothetical propositions are not suitable for proofs. We have already seen an example from *PHP* above, where the proposition 'If speech were sent out of the brain, it would not be sent out through the windpipe' was dropped from a purported demonstration in favour of two other propositions, 'All that is sent out through something is sent out of parts continuous with it' and 'The brain is not continuous with the windpipe'. The thought seemed to be that the hypothetical statement stated a fact whose explanation lay in other, more general (and non-hypothetical) statements.

This feature of hypothetical statements, that their truth is often to be explained by non-hypothetical statements, is also alluded to at *SMT* XI 500, an admittedly difficult and possibly corrupt text. Galen points out that the statement 'if olive oil produces hoarseness, it is also pungent', which one would use in a first indemonstrable along with the proposition 'Olive oil produces hoarseness', follows from the general statement 'everything which produces hoarseness is pungent'. But if one were to use the proposition 'everything which produces hoarseness is pungent' in the proof, then one could combine it with the proposition 'every olive oil produces hoarseness' (*SMT* XI 498) and avoid the hypothetical turn of expression altogether, and conclude that every oil is pungent. As in the argument from *PHP*, the hypothetical statement could be eliminated in a fully expressed demonstration, in favour of a more explanatory general statement.

It is perhaps this that Galen has in mind when he says that hypothetical propositions are not suitable to serve in demonstrations, except to establish existence claims.

RELATIONAL SYLLOGISMS

Probably the most important part of the *Institutio Logica* is its introduction of 'relational syllogisms' in chapter xvi, which Galen claims to be the 'third species of syllogism' (the first two species consisting of the Aristotelian categorical syllogisms and the hypothetical ones which have just been discussed). On the basis of this discovery, Jonathan Barnes once praised Galen as 'the third great figure in ancient logic after Aristotle and Chrysippus'.[45] In later papers, Barnes' praise was first tempered somewhat: 'The third logician of antiquity was, in a sense, no logician at all',[46] and then withdrawn completely: 'Had Galen thought of uniting categorical and hypothetical syllogistic in some fashion, he would have been the third logician of history. Instead, he discovered a bogus third species of syllogism.'[47] What are relational syllogisms, and do they in fact form a species?

We are hampered in this investigation by the fact that chapters xvi–xviii of *Inst.Log.* are terribly corrupt. Perhaps this is not surprising, given the unfamiliarity of the material, although it is worth noting that scribes often have difficulties when copying logical texts, whether they contain familiar material or not. But some things get through loud and clear. At the opening of chapter xvi, after Galen has dealt with categorical and hypothetical syllogistic in the previous chapters, he says:

There is also another, third, kind of syllogism useful for demonstrations, which I call 'coming about through a relation', although Aristotelians are forced to number them with categorical syllogisms. There is no small use for them on the part of those who do arithmetic and calculations.

Immediately we can see the familiar Galenic theme of the usefulness of this new type of syllogism. Relational syllogisms are needed to account for logical practice in arithmetic and calculations. It is not far-fetched to link this to Galen's account of his early logical education at *Lib.Prop.* XIX 39 (trans. Singer):

So I applied myself to all the best-reputed Stoic and Peripatetic philosophers of the time; but while I learned many pieces of logical theory from them which in the fullness of time I found to be quite useless for establishing proofs, there were very few that they had researched in any useful manner likely to lead them to the goal set before them.

Galen signals his dissatisfaction with Aristotelian and Stoic logic, and in particular signals that he found much of what he had been taught insufficient for proof. A few lines later he states that he found intellectual solace in the practices of the geometers, mathematicians and arithmeticians, and observed that in fact all philosophers praised the manner in which geometers conducted their proofs.

It is thus clear that from the start, Galen was interested in proofs in geometry, mathematics and arithmetic. When we put this together with his statement in *Inst.Log.* xvi 1 that there is no small use for relational syllogisms (which are part neither of Aristotelian nor Stoic logic) in arithmetic and calculation, it is clear that at least part of his dissatisfaction with Aristotelian and Stoic logic was precisely their inability to account for the validity of relational arguments. So just as the theory of three-premissed syllogisms discussed above was introduced in part in order to account for certain arguments propounded by Plato, so the theory of relational syllogistic was introduced to account for certain arguments propounded by the arithmeticians and geometers.

Nor do we have to search far to find which arguments Galen has in mind. The very first argument mentioned in the *Inst.Log.* is the following argument (i 3):

> Theo is equal to Dio;
> Philo is equal to the same Dio;
> Two things equal to the same are equal to one other;
> Therefore, Theo is equal to Dio.

We don't know who – or what – Theo, Philo and Dio are; these names serve as 'dummy' names for Galen, and could refer to people, or pulses, or diseases, or indeed anything else.[48] But during his discussion of relational syllogisms in *Inst.Log.* xvi 6, Galen refers to arguments of this same form, and says that they will enable us

to argue and demonstrate in the same way that Euclid constructed his demonstration in his first theorem, demonstrating that the sides of a triangle are equal.

Galen is referring to the proof of the very first proposition of the first book of Euclid's *Elements*, the relevant part of which runs as follows:

Each of CA and CB is equal to AB. But things equal to one another are also equal to the same. Therefore CA is also equal to CB.

(CA, CB and AB are all sides of a triangle. The proposition 'things equal to one another are also equal to the same' is the first of Euclid's 'common notions'.)

Galen is claiming that Aristotelian and Stoic logics cannot account for the validity of this argument, and in this he is entirely right. The argument does not involve propositions expressed using the words 'if', 'or', or 'not both ... and ...', so it cannot be analysed by the Stoics. As for Aristotelian logic, the best it can offer is summed up by the following attempt by Alexander of Aphrodisias (*In.An.Pr.* 344, 13–20; trans. from Barnes, 1993a, 179):

It is not the case that, if a's being equal to c follows by necessity from the assumption that a is equal to b and b to c, then this is thereby a syllogism. It will be inferred syllogistically if we assume in addition the universal proposition which says 'things equal to the same are equal to one another' and if we condense what was assumed as two propositions into a single proposition which has the same force as the two (this is: 'a and c are equal to the same thing – for they are equal to b'). For in this way, it is inferred by a syllogism that a and c are equal to one another.

This attempt by Alexander to reduce the argument to something Aristotelian logic can cope with is a failure.[49] The only way in which Alexander's version of the argument can be straitjacketed into Aristotelian logic is to introduce talk of ordered pairs, as follows:

1. All pairs of things related such that each is equal to some third thing are a pair such that each is equal to the other.
2. <a, c> is a pair such that each is equal to some third thing.
3. Therefore, <a, c> is a pair such that each is equal to the other.

Galen's remark that the Aristotelians are 'forced' to put arguments such as Euclid's among categorical syllogisms is apt: this argument is indeed a product of force. For a start, we must assume that Aristotelian logic has been supplemented so as to cope with singular terms (because the expression '<a, c>' is treated as a singular term for a pair). But even if this is allowed, the argument is not a proper counterpart of Euclid's argument. As can be seen quite plainly, any mention of quantity b has to drop out in order that the second premiss attribute to the pair <a, c> exactly the same predicate which was the subject of the first premiss – the predicate 'being a pair such that each member of the pair is equal to some object'. This is cunningly concealed in Alexander's formulation, for he phrases premiss (2) as 'a and c are equal to the same thing – *for they are equal to b'*. But this expression 'for they are equal to b' (what Ryle would call a 'namely-rider') cannot actually appear as part of the content of the premiss. For if it did, the first premiss would have to be reformulated as 'All pairs of things related such that each is equal to some third thing, namely b, are a pair such that each is equal to the other'. This proposition – while doubtless *true* – is not the premiss Alexander wants, which is the perfectly general 'All pairs of things related such that each is equal to some third thing are a pair such that each is equal to the other' (the first Euclidean common notion), which contains no namely-riders.

This should suffice for us to see that Galen has correctly observed that neither Aristotelian nor Stoic logic can account for the validity of the argument embedded in the proof of the first theorem of the first book of Euclid's *Elements*. No wonder, then, that Galen's immersion in the practices of the geometers led him to be dissatisfied with the systems of the Peripatetics and the Stoics.

So far, Galen's insight that Aristotelian and Stoic logic is, in this sense, incomplete, stands as a correct and praiseworthy one. The trouble comes when we consider all the arguments that Galen puts forward as belonging to the 'third class' of syllogisms. On the one hand, it is difficult to be clear about what many of the arguments are (this may not be entirely Galen's fault – as has been said, the corrupt text bears some responsibility, too). In particular, it is difficult to tell whether the arguments contain *axioms* as extra premisses or not. On the other hand, even allowing for the indeterminacy of what the arguments are, it is far from clear what unites the arguments, other than the fact that they cannot be treated by Peripatetic or Stoic logic. But unless there is something to unite them, Galen's claim that they form a class will be idle. It is one thing to recognize that not every argument owes its validity to those logical devices isolated by the Peripatetics and the Stoics. It is another to find, describe and delineate a whole class of such arguments.

Let us take these two difficulties in turn: (i) what are the arguments that Galen has in mind (and what is the role of the axioms), and (ii) what do they have in common?

(i) When Galen opens his chapter on relational syllogisms, his first example of such a syllogism is the following argument (xvi 1):

> Theo has twice as many possessions as Dio;
> But Philo has twice as many possessions as Theo;
> Therefore, Philo has four times as many possessions as Dio.

This argument has just two premisses, unlike the argument from Euclid discussed above, which had three premisses. What is missing from this argument is a general premiss which would be the analogue of the common notion 'things equal to the same are equal to one another', namely a premiss such as 'twice as much as twice as much is four times as much'. The omission of the premiss is no mere slip on Galen's part. He immediately goes on (xvi 2) to give another version of the argument, rewording it using the expression 'half as many' in place of 'twice as many', but also missing out the general premiss. And in xvi 3 he refers to similar arguments using the expressions 'three times' and 'a third', still without mentioning the general premiss. And finally in xvi 4 he says:

Similarly too for additions and subtractions, for if the first number is equal to the second, and another equal number is added to each of them, then the whole will also be equal to the whole. And where there are two equal numbers, let two equal numbers be subtracted from each; the remainder will also be equal to the remainder.

Here too, Galen refers in general terms to two more types of relational arguments, but without mentioning the general premisses which would play the role in them that the first Euclidean common notion played in arguments of the sort found in i 3. This is particularly strange because those general principles would be 'if equals are added to equals, then the wholes too will be equal', and 'if equals are subtracted from equals, then the remainders too will be equal' – which are in fact the second and third of Euclid's common notions. Does Galen intend these general premisses to be part of the arguments, or not? In i 3, Galen had included the premiss 'things equal to the same are equal to one another' as a premiss in a relational argument, but in xvi 1–4 he does not include the analogous general propositions as premisses in the relational arguments which he uses to introduce the very notion of a relational argument.

The puzzling thing is that these general propositions are actually of crucial importance for Galen. He says that all relational arguments 'have the same construction from certain axioms' (xvi 5). Here, 'axiom' means something like 'first principle' (see p. 71), so immediately we can see that not just *any* general proposition must feature in or underlie a relational syllogism; it must be an *axiom*. But what does 'have the same construction from [an axiom]' mean? The other remarks Galen makes about the role of the axioms are no more revealing: 'the construction of the demonstrative syllogisms will be through the force of an axiom' (xvi 10); 'the syllogism holds in virtue of one of the axioms' (*ibid.*); 'syllogisms put forward according to any relation you like will have their construction and demonstrative force warranted through a general axiom' (xvi 12); relational syllogisms 'are constructed through the force of an axiom' (xviii 8).

Nor do the other *examples* Galen gives of relational syllogisms shed much more light on this question. They are:

(xvi 12) The excellence of the better thing is preferable;
    But the soul is better than the body;
    Therefore the excellence of the soul is preferable to that of the body.

(xvi 13) The good of the better thing is preferable;
    But the soul is better than the body;
    Therefore the good of the soul is preferable to that of the body.

(xviii 4) The city and the soul are said to be, and are, just in the same way;
    But the city is said to be just because its parts perform their own functions;
    Therefore the soul too is said to be just in that way.

(xviii 5) As the first is to the second, so the third is the fourth;
    The first is double the second;
    Therefore the third is double the fourth.

But it is unclear whether these arguments contain axioms or not. Perhaps the first premisses of the arguments from xvi 12 and xvi 13 are axioms. However, the argument from xviii 4 (the argument underpinning the city–soul analogy in Plato's *Republic*, familiar from 368e and 435a) seems, according to Galen, to involve or depend on the axiom 'the form of justice from which everything particular is said to be just is one single thing in all of them' (xvi 3), which is unstated in the argument as he gives it. Similarly, the first premiss in the argument from xviii 5 cannot be an axiom – its truth will depend on what the first, second, third and fourth items actually are. Rather, that argument depends on the axiom 'things which are in the same general ratio are also in all the same particular ratios', as Galen says in xvi 6.

The only conclusion one can come to is that sometimes Galen gives a relational argument with the relevant axiom, and sometimes without.

There are three interpretations one might adopt of how the axiom is related to the relational argument. Either (a) the axioms are essential premisses in the syllogisms, or (b) the axioms are rules of inference which 'underwrite' the inference (and are never premisses in the arguments), or (c) the arguments are valid with or without the axioms (so *stating* the axiom in a given argument makes no difference to its validity), but they need to be stated to turn mere arguments into demonstrations.

The difficulty with interpretations (a) and (b) is, quite simply, that sometimes Galen clearly makes the relevant axiom a premiss in the relational argument (i 3; xvi 12, 13) and sometimes clearly makes it not a premiss (xvi 1, 2, 3, 4; xviii 4, 5).[50] But is interpretation (c) a viable one? The view would be that Galen thinks that the arguments *without* the relevant axiom are still valid, but just not demonstrations. We have already seen (p. 80) that Galen is prepared to accept that arguments might be valid without being demonstrations, and might need extra premisses in order to be turned into demonstrations (and that this might even have been the subject of *On propositions missed out in the expression of demonstrations*). How well does interpretation (c) fit what Galen says?

The answer is that it *almost* fits. One problem is that in xvi 3 Galen says that one can propound *demonstratively*, using any numbers suitably related, an argument such as

> Theo has twice as many possessions as Dio;
> But Philo has twice as many possessions as Theo;
> Therefore, Philo has four times as many possessions as Dio.

But this argument lacks the relevant general premiss, and so, on the interpretation proposed, it should not count as a demonstration. Perhaps – somewhat hopefully – one could argue that Galen meant that one can propound such arguments demonstratively *when they are suitably reinforced by an axiom*. Another problem with the interpretation is that it does not do justice to Galen's remarks that the axiom is responsible for holding the syllogism together (xvi 10; xviii 8), but it does at least chime well with the remark in xvi 12 that the role of the axiom is to give demonstrative force or warrant to the syllogism. The truth seems to be that Galen is not terribly clear in his own mind about the role of the axiom.

One particularly difficult passage in chapter xvi is worth mentioning as a sort of test case for this interpretation. Galen is discussing what happens when you want to argue that Sophroniscus is father of Socrates, on the basis of the fact that Socrates is son of Sophroniscus (xvi 10).[51] Galen envisages in xvi 11 two ways of filling the argument out. One way would involve making the argument a hypothetical one by adding the premiss 'if Socrates is son of Sophroniscus, Sophroniscus is father of Socrates'. Another would involve (here the text is desperately corrupt) adding the categorical premiss 'whomever someone has a father, he is son of that person'. Galen is clearly in favour of the second addition, remarking that 'the construction of the argument would be more compelling'. If one added the straightforward conditional premiss 'if Socrates is son of Sophroniscus, Sophroniscus is father of Socrates', the argument is a simple Stoic first indemonstrable (or the Galenic equivalent). If one supplements the argument with a categorical premiss such as 'whomever someone has as a father, he is son of that person',[52] the argument is not a first indemonstrable, but rather a relational argument (or so Galen implicitly claims). Such arguments are said to be more compelling than their hypothetical counterparts, presumably because of the generality of the premiss. But now it is difficult to see what a relational argument is, according to Galen, because we are left trying to find what the following two arguments have in common (apart from lying outside of Aristotelian and Stoic logics):

(1)   Whomever someone has a father, he is son of that person;
        Socrates has Sophroniscus as father;
        Therefore, Socrates is son of Sophroniscus.

(2) Two things equal to the same are equal to one other;
     a is equal to c;
     b is equal to c;
     Therefore, a is equal to b.

It is hard to see what logical form arguments (1) and (2) share, if we think of logical form as being a matter of syntactical form. However, if there is one lesson that we have to absorb from Galen's attitude to logic, it is that one cannot determine logical properties by looking at syntactical form. So we should at least entertain the possibility that Galen didn't think that there is a common logical form (in that sense) to relational arguments.

One suggestion might be as follows. Galen was struck by the role of universal statements in demonstrations. In hypothetical demonstrations, there is no universal statement. In Aristotelian demonstrations, at least one premiss has to be universal, but it contributes essentially to the validity of the argument (the universal premisses cannot be missed out). In a relational argument, the universal premiss can be missed out without affecting the validity of the argument, but it must be there to turn the argument into a demonstration (it plays an epistemic role, and not a deductive role). This does not delimit a class of syllogisms via syntactic means, but we should never have expected a logician of Galen's type to do that.

Of course, some might say that this means Galen is not a logician at all. Frustration at Galen's lack of interest in syntactic form is part of what lies behind Jonathan Barnes' claims, quoted at the beginning of this section, that Galen wasn't really a logician, and that his third species of syllogism is 'bogus'. At least we know what Galen's reply would have been to these charges: we are quibbling over words, not things.

NOTES

1. Fragments and testimonia collected in Mueller (1897).
2. Fragment preserved in Arabic, trans. in Rescher (1967, appendix B).
3. Cf. I 106–223 for a spurious version of this work.
4. See ch. 5 (Morison) in this volume for a lengthy discussion of the possible content of this work.
5. Title uncertain.

6. Presumably including *To Patrophilus on the composition of the art of medicine* [*CAM*], I 224–304.

7. See p. 85, for a possible identification of this book.

8. XIV 582–98.

9. In this section I am particularly indebted to Barnes (1991) and Hankinson (1991b).

10. Trans. Singer (1997).

11. *Ord.Lib.Prop.* XIX 53.

12. *Opt.Med.* I 59–60, trans. Singer (1997) (adapted).

13. See Frede (1981, 286–7) for necessary qualifications to this. On the sects, see also ch. 6 (Hankinson) in this volume.

14. Cf. particularly Barnes (1991, 69–72).

15. Cf. Barnes (1991, 72).

16. *Ord.Lib.Prop.* XIX 54.

17. For other discussions shedding light on this important passage, see: Barnes (2003, 4–24); Hankinson (1991d, 211–17); Hankinson (1991c, 209–33); Ierodiakonou (2002, 108–9).

18. V 241, translation lightly adapted from De Lacy (1978). Note that 'mind' here refers to the organ of thought: this is not an argument concerning the mind–brain distinction in the modern sense, but rather an argument attempting to establish whether the organ of thought is (or is a part of) the organ known as the brain.

19. Although see below, n. 50.

20. Doubts about whether Apuleius really wrote *De Interpretatione* persist. For discussion and references, see Harrison (2000, 11–12).

21. Lewis (1859); Davies (1860).

22. See Wilson (1987, 56).

23. Relevant here also is the lack of discussion of the 'fourth figure' – for this, see p. 85.

24. *Lib.Prop.* XIX 10.

25. *Inst.Log.* xiii 11.

26. On this see in particular Rescher (1966) and Lukasiewicz (1951, 38–42).

27. In the section of the *Shifa* on the *Analytics*, according to Rescher (1966, 10).

28. *Middle Commentary on Prior Analytics*, i: 5, i: 8, i: 23. See Rescher (1966, 2).

29. Edited and translated in Rescher (1966, chs. IV and V).

30. Lukasiewicz (1951, 38).

31. Attempting to divide in a similar way the second and third figures yields no new forms, since you obtain only relettered versions of the original forms.

32. This is the view of Lukasiewicz (1951, 38–42).
33. On this, see Hankinson (1994b, 57, n. 1).
34. Here, I am indebted to discussion with Jacob Rosen.
35. See Bobzien (2004, 84).
36. We find something similar in Alcinous' *Didaskalikos*, ch. 6, where the author identifies Plato's use of various argument forms in *Alcibiades*, *Parmenides* and *Phaedo*.
37. My discussion is profoundly indebted to Susanne Bobzien's pioneering work (Bobzien, 2004).
38. See Barnes (1993b, 45–8).
39. Bobzien (2004, 65).
40. (1953, 53).
41. Bobzien (2004, 77–80).
42. See Grice (1989).
43. Bobzien thinks that Galen's hypothetical syllogistic is due to Middle Peripatetic philosophers.
44. Bobzien ignores – as do I – the possibility that you come to know the truth of such statements by testimony. When the child is told by its mother that there isn't an Easter egg in the kitchen *and* an Easter egg in the sitting room, it plausibly knows this, and can conduct a useful time-saving argument on the basis of it when it finds an Easter egg in the kitchen. Such cases are ignored by Galen, presumably because they would not count as proper demonstrations.
45. Barnes (1993a, 173).
46. Barnes (1993b, 51).
47. Barnes (2003, 24).
48. See ch. 5 (Morison) in this volume, p. 142, for more on these 'dummy' names.
49. Cf. Hankinson (1994b, 63–4).
50. Barnes has a slightly different reason for rejecting the thesis that the axioms are rules of inference (1993a, 185). He changes his mind by the time of writing his (2003), remarking that 'it must be admitted that some passages in *Inst.Log.* suggest that Galen . . . construed the axioms as supplementary premisses. But this cannot – or at any rate should not – have been Galen's considered view' (2003, 19, n. 26).
51. If Galen thinks that this little argument is valid *as it stands*, then he is showing yet more logical originality, since it seems as though no ancient logician, apart from the Stoic Antipater, considered that there could be any valid single-premissed arguments.
52. It is one of the puzzles of this text that Galen imagines a slightly different argument here, with the premiss 'Lamprocles has Socrates as father'.

5 Language

WORKS OF GALEN CONCERNING LANGUAGE (LOST
UNLESS OTHERWISE INDICATED)

Under the heading 'commentaries on Hippocrates' (*On My Own
Books* [*Lib.Prop.*] XIX 33):

> *An explanation of Hippocratic terminology*[1] (*ibid.* 37)

Under the heading 'books useful for demonstrations' (*ibid.* 39):

> *On propositions with the same meaning*, in one book (*ibid.*
> 43)
> *On things said in many ways*, in three books
> *How one should distinguish an enquiry into things from one
> into word and meaning*, in one book
> *On the correctness of names*, in three books
> *Against those who interpret words abusively*, in one book
> (*ibid.* 44)
> *On the enquiry into word and meaning* (*ibid.* 45)

Under the heading 'works concerning the philosophy of Aristotle'
(*ibid.* 47):

> Commentary on *On how many ways*, in three books
> Commentary on Eudemus' *Speech*, in three books
> *On linguistic sophisms* (*Soph.*)[2]

Under the heading 'works common to grammarians and orators'
(*ibid.* 48):

I have benefited enormously from the writings of Jonathan Barnes and Jim Hankinson.
Thanks also to Gregory Hutchinson, Hendrik Lorenz, Jonathan Barnes, and Nigel and
Hanneke Wilson.

Dictionary of words used by the Attic prose-writers, in forty-eight books

Ordinary terms in Eupolis, in three books

Ordinary terms in Aristophanes, in five books

Ordinary terms in Cratinus, in two books

Examples of words specific to the writers of comedy, in one book

Whether the texts of ancient comedy are a worthwhile part of the educational curriculum

To those who criticize linguistic solecisms, in six books

False Atticisms,[3] in one book

On clarity and unclarity

Whether the same person can be a literary critic and a grammarian, in one book

Mentioned in *The Order of my Own Books* (*Ord.Lib.Prop.*):

On Medical Names (*Med.Nam.*)[4] (XIX 55)

INTRODUCTION

In this chapter I shall be looking at Galen's remarks about language (his philosophy of language, if you like), but not his own use of it (the way he employs hiatus, word order, particles, etc.). As is clear from the list of works above, Galen was extremely interested in linguistic matters. Unfortunately, only two or three of those works have survived. Nevertheless, we can reconstruct many of Galen's views, since hardly a page goes by without him making some observation or other about language. We know that he was very interested in unusual or dialectal names for herbs and foods, in the recent vogue for 'atticizing', in the use of Greek by previous philosophers and doctors (in particular, Hippocrates), in the correctness of names and etymology, neologisms and metaphor, in abuse of language, etc. The aim of this chapter is to attribute to Galen a coherent view about language concerning what it is for, and how it should be used.

First, a note of caution. We know that Galen was interested in logic, and for some time now in philosophy, it has been natural to think of logic and language as intimately related. We are taught to use the resources of mathematical logic when testing whether a given natural-language argument is valid or not. Roughly speaking, we translate a given argument into logical symbols, and then see whether or not there is a derivation of the formula representing the conclusion from the formulae representing the premisses, using the rules of inference of a particular logical calculus. Again, philosophers and linguists have often drawn on logical resources in giving the semantics of natural language (there even exists a book called *Everything linguists have always wanted to know about logic, but were ashamed to ask*). For instance, according to some theories, the meaning of the word 'and' in English can be given by the truth-table for the sign '∧' in propositional logic.

As you might expect, Galen's remarks about language, even those made in discussions of logical matters, do not spell out connections such as these between logic and language. Galen was interested neither in translating arguments into the symbols of a formal language nor in rendering the meaning of natural language using the resources of logic. (In both these respects, he is no different from any other ancient logician.) Logic and language are indeed related for Galen, but not in these ways. In the passage from *PHP* analysed by Morison in chapter 4 in this volume (pp. 75–83), Galen accuses Chrysippus of not being careful enough in the formulation of the premisses of his argument concerning the location of the regent part of the soul. Effectively, Galen criticized Chrysippus for not paying enough attention to the meaning of the preposition '*apo*'. It is not that Galen wanted to formulate Chrysippus' argument in a formal language; rather, he wanted to ensure that the premisses of the argument did not harbour ambiguities, and did genuinely share terms (rather than being unconnected to one another). Perhaps the book *On things said in many ways* had something to say about such cases (among other things – see pp. 140–2 on words with more than one meaning). Galen's views on subsyllogistic arguments, and the various ways of expressing universal statements, are also examples of his preoccupation with language in logical contexts, and are discussed in chapter 4 (pp. 92–4). As far as Galen is concerned, when doing logic, one should look to things and not to words. As we shall see, however, Galen's interest in language goes far beyond the role of language in logic.

CORRECTNESS OF NAMES[5]

Many of the books above which are listed in *Lib.Prop.* as being useful for demonstrations seem not to have dealt directly with the question of how meaning affects an argument's validity, at least to judge from their titles: *How one should distinguish an enquiry into things from one into word and meaning, On the correctness of names, Against those who interpret words insolently, On the enquiry into word and meaning.* Of these treatises, *On the correctness of names* (now lost) is singled out as being of particular importance: at the very end of *Ord.Lib.Prop.* Galen makes the bold statement that it should be read before any of his other books (XIX 61).[6] Actually, in *Ord.Lib.Prop.* Galen makes many recommendations as to which book of his to read first – it all depends on what your aim is. Read *On the Best Sect Opt.Sec.* if you want to be a doctor, followed by *De Demonstratione* (XIX 52). Read the works for beginners (XIX 54) if you want to skip becoming an expert in the logical art and go straight into learning how to be a doctor. Read *De Demonstratione* (XIX 60) if you are thinking of embarking on reading the philosophical works. But Galen recommends starting with *On the correctness of names* whatever your intentions or ambitions might be. This gives us some indication of just how important Galen thought it was to have the right view of language.

But why should it be of such importance to have the right view of language? Galen tells us that *On the correctness of names* was written 'because of those who use words badly' (*dia tous kakôs chrômenous tois onomasin, Ord.Lib.Prop.* XIX 61). This on its own does not help us understand why the book should be read *first*, nor why the book is 'useful for demonstrations'. In fact, it isn't even of any help to us in determining what the content of the book was. The book may have been written *because of* the existence of bad name-users, but we can't tell from that or its title whether it attacked these people (cf. the title of *Against those who interpret words abusively*[7]), tried to reform them, or even mentioned them at all. And if it was in fact addressed to abusers of language, that still leaves the content of the book greatly underdetermined, since in his extant works Galen does not shy from criticizing those whom he thinks misuse language, levelling a bewildering variety of charges at them: they are unclear, they fall prey to ambiguity, they invent words where there are perfectly good words already in use, they find differences in meaning between two words where there are none, they use old Attic words instead of words currently in use, they make metaphors out of metaphors, they use metaphors in inappropriate contexts, etc. To know more precisely what *On the correctness of names* said, we have to look at evidence from other texts. But even before doing that, we need to know something of the philosophical background to the question of the correctness of names, for which the *locus classicus* is Plato's *Cratylus*, a dialogue to which Galen appeals often during his tirades about language.

PLATO[8]

The correctness of names[9] is the principal subject-matter of the *Cratylus*. Plato distinguishes two questions: (1) whether a name or word is the correct name or word for something according to whether the individual letters or phonemes of the word compose a description whose meaning (itself composed from the semantic properties of those letters or phonemes) is somehow fitting for the thing, and (2) whether a name or word in a language is correctly applied to a thing by someone given the conventional usage (*ethos*) of a word. Bernard Williams helpfully labels these two types of correctness 'external' and 'internal' correctness, respectively.[10] The question whether or not a word is correct in the first way is settled by making reference to facts external to how that name is actually used, whereas the question whether or not it is correct in the second way is settled by making reference to facts internal to the linguistic practices surrounding that name. (Fittingly enough, the terms 'internal' and 'external' here do not seem entirely appropriate, but I shall stick to Williams' usage in my discussion.)

An example of each will help clarify. In the first part of the dialogue, Socrates responds to Hermogenes' challenge that 'no one is able to persuade me that the correctness of names is determined by anything besides convention and agreement' (*Crat.* 384c10–d2). He offers Hermogenes an alternative account of how a word might be the appropriate or correct one for a given thing. In a famous example, Socrates claims at 399c5–6 that man alone of all beasts is correctly called '*anthrôpos*' in Greek because he is '*anathrôn ha opôpe*' ('observing closely what he has seen'). Dozens of other such etymologies are given in the first part of the dialogue. However elaborate or unconvincing we may find Socrates' attempts to show the appropriateness of this or that word, the idea is not unfamiliar. When we say that such and such a word or name is a *misnomer* – say, the name 'the United Nations' – we are employing this notion of correctness. We do not mean that it would be a linguistic mistake or slip of the tongue if someone were to use that name to refer to the successor institution of the League of Nations, or that this would demonstrate linguistic incompetence. Rather, we mean that the name is an inappropriate one, given its meaning or connotation, because it fails to reflect the nature of the thing named. Or again, to use an example discussed by Galen,[11] the 'carotid' artery is so called because it was supposed to induce stupor (*karon*) when ligatured. In fact, it doesn't. The name has stuck, despite being a misnomer – the name does not reflect the nature of, or encode correct information about, the relevant artery.

Cratylus is very much in favour of the kind of etymologies Socrates has been giving because he, too, has been arguing that the correctness of a name consists in its being able to be analysed as a disguised complex description whose meaning is appropriate in this kind of way. Cratylus also holds the thesis that if a word is not a correct name for a thing, it shouldn't count as a name for that thing at all.[12] In the second part of the dialogue, Socrates turns his guns on Cratylus, picking in particular on the word '*sklêron*', meaning 'hard'. Unfortunately for Cratylus, it contains the letter 'l', which is supposed to indicate softness. According to him, then, the word '*sklêron*' cannot be the correct name (and therefore not a name at all) for hardness. But, as Socrates points out, 'what about when someone says "sklêron", and pronounces it the way we do at present? Don't we understand him? Don't you yourself know what I mean by it?' (*Crat.* 434e1–3). Yes, admits Cratylus, 'because of usage' (434e4); Socrates then presses him into allowing for a kind of correctness which is determined by usage (435b8–c2). The good for which language exists is teaching or informing (435d4; e6–7), so language is used well when it is used to inform successfully – in effect, Cratylus is admitting that successful communication can come about through the use of internally correct words (rather than externally correct ones).

Much of the first part of the *Cratylus* is devoted to seeing whether an internally correct name, N, is actually the externally correct one for its *nominatum*, X – hence the enquiry into whether '*anthrôpos*' is the correct name for man. But there are two ways in which this kind of etymologizing can lead to error, both of which will help us understand Galen's later remarks about the correctness of names.

(1) Suppose that the account you offer of the meaning of N is
actually mistaken – in other words, your etymological analysis wrongly 'unpacks' the implicit meaning of N. An interesting example from the *Cratylus* is the name 'Apollo'. Socrates
points out that people are afraid of the name 'Apollo' – presumably because they think it is somehow connected to the
verb *'apollumi'*, meaning 'I destroy'. In fact, Socrates points
out, the name is 'most beautifully suited to the power of the
god' (404e5–6), because it can be linked to each of his four
powers, namely 'music, prophecy, medicine, and archery'
(405a3–4). (In other words, the name is genuinely the externally correct one for Apollo.) Ordinary people analyse the
word 'Apollo' wrongly – they analyse it as merely implying
destructiveness, but that is not all there is to it. But someone who made such an error might *thereby* misunderstand
what the nature of Apollo himself is, by assuming that they
have correctly analysed his name as meaning 'the destructive one', and further assuming that this name is actually
appropriate for him. To generalize: people might be misled
by their faulty analysis of N into a false understanding of X.
One might think that the meaning one has discerned in N is
suitable for X, when in fact one has discerned in N a meaning
which it does not have (or which is only partially correct).
Faulty etymology can lead to misunderstanding: Plato does
not explicitly point to this danger, but it is not hard to see.

(2) Alternatively, the person who initially conferred N on X,
thinking N's meaning to be appropriate for X, might actually have failed to understand the proper nature of X. In that
case, N might have passed into common usage, and now
be the (internally) correct one for X, despite being (externally) incorrect. For instance, Socrates points out at 437b4–7
that the words for error ('*hamartia*') and mishap ('*sumphora*')
seem to be decomposable into roughly the same meanings
as the words for comprehension ('*sunesis*') and knowledge
('*epistêmê*'). One member of each of these two pairs must
therefore have been named wrongly. But if something X can
receive the wrong name N – a name which encodes some
description which does not actually hold of X – then in
the course of an etymology, one might decompose N in the

appropriate way, not realize that it actually is an externally incorrect name, and thereby be misled into a false understanding of X. As Plato puts it, in a passage echoed often by Galen: 'if someone is investigating things and follows their names, enquiring into what each thing should be like, don't you think that there is no small danger that he would be deceived?' (*Crat.* 436a9–b3).[13]

In both these cases, you are led to a faulty conception of the *nominatum* – in the first case because you made a mistake in your analysis of N, and in the second case because N didn't reflect the nature of X in the first place (although this isn't, as it were, your fault). Plato does not dwell on or analyse these two potential errors. His concern is what the correctness of names consists in. Galen, on the other hand, is much more concerned by the ability of language to mislead, as we shall see.

THE CONTENT OF ON THE CORRECTNESS OF NAMES

The only explicit information we get in Galen's extant works as to the content of *On the correctness of names* comes in *On the Doctrines of Hippocrates and Plato* (*PHP*). There, we learn that the work discussed arguments from etymology, including how etymology can bear false witness – sometimes etymology can argue as well for the false view as for the true view, and sometimes it can even argue more forcefully for the false (*PHP* V 214; 218). In other words, Galen argued in that work that etymologizing about a word can lead to making mistakes about its referent. Galen tells us that in *On the correctness of names* he argued that Chrysippus 'gave a faulty etymology' (*etumologounta mochthêrôs*: V 214) of the word '*egô*' ('I'), in the course of an argument concerning the place of the regent part of the soul. He quotes the relevant words of Chrysippus:[14]

We also say '*egô*' (I) in this way, pointing to ourselves at that place in which thought appears to be, the gesture being carried there naturally and appropriately; and apart from such a gesture of the hand, we nod toward ourselves as we say '*egô*'; indeed the very word '*egô*' is of this description and its pronunciation is accompanied by the gesture next described. For as we pronounce '*egô*', at the first syllable we drop the lower lip in a way that points to ourselves, and in conformity with the movement of the chin, the nod toward the chest, and such gesturing, the next syllable is juxtaposed; and it gives no suggestion of distance, such as that produced by the second syllable of *'ekeinos'* (that person, he).

Here we seem to be in familiar territory – this splendid explanation of the word *'egô'* would be entirely at home in the *Cratylus*.[15] But Galen is not happy with it. He thinks that Chrysippus' attempt to analyse the word *'egô'* into its basic meaning fails. Chrysippus tried to explain how the words *'egô'* (meaning 'I') and *'ekeinos'* (meaning 'that man') mean what they do, in terms of the meanings of their syllables. Chrysippus claimed that the first syllable *'e'* means the same in both words (*PHP* V 217), and so had to explain how the words differ in meaning by referring to the differences between the second syllables, *'gô'* and *'kei'*, claiming that *'gô'* does not indicate distance, whereas *'kei'* does. And this, claims Galen, was left unsubstantiated by Chrysippus – 'This is mere assertion with no demonstration, much less a secure and scientific demonstration; indeed it does not even advance so far as rhetorical or sophistical plausibility' (*ibid.*) – hence, the etymology is found wanting. Moreover, slightly later in *PHP*, Galen tells us that the second book of *On the correctness of names* contained a discussion of what Chrysippus and his followers thought the role of the letter *'e'* was, and 'how absurd they are in their remarks' about it (V 225). (Although Galen does not say what this role was, we can guess from the passage quoted above that its role is to be deictic.[16]) Hence, in *On the correctness of names*, Galen criticized Chrysippus' etymology of *'egô'* in two ways: what it says about the letter *'e'* is absurd, and what it says about the syllable *'gô'* is implausible.

Galen also complains in *PHP* that Chrysippus attempts to demonstrate that the ruling part of the soul is in the heart by appealing to inappropriate premisses, including one 'from etymology' (V 215–16). Galen categorizes premisses into four types: scientific, dialectical, rhetorical (or persuasive) and sophistical. The scientific ones, which deal with the essence of a thing, are the most appropriate for use in a demonstration (V 219); the others are progressively less appropriate (V 221, 227, 273, etc.). Premisses which stem from etymology are considered 'rhetorical' premisses, and 'don't differ much from the sophistical' (V 228). But the premiss that in uttering the word *'egô'* 'we somehow draw the mouth and jaw downward as though toward the chest when we pronounce the first syllable *"e'"* comes from etymology (V 215). Hence Chrysippus' attempted demonstration makes use of an inappropriate premiss. Galen tells us that his *On demonstration* contained a discussion of all arguments from inappropriate or non-demonstrative premisses[17] and that *On the correctness of names* contained a discussion of a subclass of such arguments, namely those from etymological premisses (V 218).

Thus we learn from *PHP* that *On the correctness of names* outlined two quite different reasons for why Chrysippus' etymology of the word *'egô'* is problematic: (i) the etymology is faulty (in two ways), and anyway (ii) one shouldn't use arguments from etymological premisses to prove things about the nature of the soul – such premisses are inappropriate for demonstrations of the essence of something. These two problems are closely allied with the two types of error that etymology can give rise to, which I mentioned earlier. Let me take them in turn.

(1) In finding fault with Chrysippus' etymology, Galen attributes to Chrysippus the first kind of mistake discussed above. For Galen thinks Chrysippus was misled into attributing to the referent of the word *'egô'* properties it doesn't have, based on his faulty etymology of the word. That is, Galen claims Chrysippus was misled into thinking that the regent part of the soul (the referent of *'egô'*) is in the chest, since the word *'egô'* is the appropriate one for the regent part of the soul, and the word involves indicating the chest, hence the regent part must be situated there (otherwise *'egô'* would not be the appropriate word for it). This is akin to supposing that Apollo's nature is purely destructive, on the grounds that the name 'Apollo' is the appropriate one for him, and the word is derived from *'apollumi'*, meaning 'I destroy', hence Apollo's nature must be destructive. If you give a faulty etymology of the word *'egô'*, then – barring some happy accident – you are going to come to an incorrect view about the nature of its referent.

(2) In arguing that etymologies are not appropriate grounds for demonstrations, Galen seems to have in mind the fact that etymology is always vulnerable to the second kind of mistake mentioned above. For the danger with etymologies is that

even correct ones may fail to reveal the essence of the thing in question when the word was not an appropriate one in the first place. Etymologies cannot be guaranteed to reveal the essence of something – only, at best, the presuppositions of those who are responsible for the word being used in the way it is. And, indeed, the only way you can tell whether the etymology does in fact reveal the essence of the thing is to find out independently what the essence of that thing is by appropriate reasoning. Etymology is at best redundant, at worst misleading.

Despite his trenchant criticisms of Chrysippus' etymology, Galen does not seem to dismiss the very idea that there are such things as correct names. This is not as surprising as it might seem. After all, Galen's treatise is called *On the correctness of names*, and not – for instance – *Against those who say there is such a thing as the correctness of a name*. There is no need to suppose that Galen thinks that there is no such thing as the project of giving etymologies, i.e. justifications of external correctness. He claimed only that Chrysippus' attempted etymology rested on incorrect or implausible views about the letter '*e*' and the syllables '*gô*' and '*kei*', and that no attempt at etymology, not even a *successful* one, should be pressed into service as part of a demonstration.

In sum, what Galen tells us explicitly about the content of *On the correctness of names* is that in it, Galen lambasts Chrysippus' etymology of the word '*egô*' for being implausible and incorrect, and in any case irrelevant to any demonstration. This last point emerges particularly strongly from the passages in *PHP* I have referred to, and it explains why Galen listed *On the correctness of names* in *Lib.Prop.* under the heading 'works useful for demonstrations' (XIX 39). It also helps explain why he says in *Ord.Lib.Prop.* (XIX 61) that it would be good to read *On the correctness of names* before embarking on the reading of any other philosophical or medical work: he obviously thought that it was a common mistake among doctors or philosophers to try to work out how things are by looking at words and not the things themselves.

Galen is surely right about this. In a field such as medicine, there are many names in ordinary use which have not been coined by experts, and which could be very misleading (e.g. 'funny bone');

equally, there may be some names which were coined by previous doctors who were mistaken but which are still used by doctors (e.g. 'carotid'). The temptation for the student to try to remember which names go with which things by connecting the meaning or connotation of the name with the nature of the thing named is obvious, but, as Galen reminds us, it must be resisted. As we shall see, time and time again Galen levels against doctors and philosophers the charge of looking at the name not the thing.

OTHER REFERENCES IN GALEN TO THE CORRECTNESS
OF NAMES

No other extant work of Galen, so far as I know, refers explicitly to *On the correctness of names*. However, there are enough references elsewhere to words being correct, or appropriate, that we can confirm the picture that has emerged of Galen's view of the correctness of names, and add a few more details. Galen's view, in outline, is this: (i) There is such a thing as the external correctness of a name; (ii) Doctors and scientists should not give it any attention in their investigations; (iii) They might make mistakes by giving bad etymologies, e.g. Chrysippus ('1st mistake'); (iv) Or they might make mistakes because words are unreliable guides to the nature of things ('2nd mistake'). Let me take each of these claims in turn.

There is such a thing as the external correctness of a name

There are some places where Galen clearly does engage in something like the project of showing how a name is correct. It is true that these attempts to justify or explain the correctness of a name are not as outlandish as those in the *Cratylus*, or Chrysippus' attempted analysis of *'egô'*, but they are recognizable attempts to explain why a name is appropriate, i.e. why it is not a misnomer. For instance, in *PHP* Galen discusses the word *'asplanchnos'*. Literally, this word means 'having no internal organ', but it is used by ordinary people of 'those who pity no one, love no one, and pay no attention whatever to persons who praise, blame, injure, or help [them], but are as insensible as stones' (V 316). Galen argues that the word *'asplanchnos'* is a correct or appropriate name for such people,[18] because the liver (an internal organ) is indeed where the desiderative part of the soul is to be found. Equally, says Galen, the word *'megalosplanchnos'* ('large-organed') is correctly applied by Euripides to Medea, because she has intense desires and passions (V 317).[19] I take it that this constitutes a genuine attempt on Galen's part to explain the correctness of a term, by showing, roughly speaking, that its connotations are correct – the meaning of the word correctly corresponds to the nature of the thing, or reports that nature truly.

Galen doesn't claim, of course, that this counts as a *demonstration* that the appetitive part lies in one of the internal organs, because he does not allow arguments from etymology to form part of demonstrations. Nor does he claim that the argument has any *confirmatory* force (nor should he – otherwise, he could have allowed Chrysippus a similar use of the etymological argument concerning *'egô'*). Why, then, does Galen go to such lengths to inform us that ordinary Greek speakers and Euripides are in fact using the correct name? The answer is that Galen cannot resist another dig at Chrysippus. As he himself explains at V 318–19, *even if* one permits Chrysippus to use etymological arguments in his attempt to show that the soul is in the heart, one can see that Chrysippus went about it in the wrong way! He did not look to the writings of Plato, or Hippocrates, or Euripides, or anyone like that, in order to back up his claims but rather to those of ignorant people such as Tyrtaeus and Stesichorus (V 319). If you *are* going to appeal to authorities in your etymological arguments – not that this is the right way of going about things, implies Galen – you had better appeal to genuine and trustworthy authorities. For our purposes, the important point is that Galen has argued that insensitive people are correctly called *'asplanchnoi'*. This is not an assertion about how the word should be used. It is an assertion about the external correctness of the word. He is saying that it is not a misnomer. It is important to observe that Galen's explanation relies on the simplest of etymological decompositions of the word *'asplanchnos'* and *presupposes* that the alpha privative and the word *'splanchnos'* have a certain meaning (and remains neutral as to how they manage to mean what they do). In this respect, his explanation of the correctness of the word is of a slightly different character to (and a good deal more plausible than) the ones in the *Cratylus*. But it is still – for all that – an explanation of correctness.

Elsewhere in *PHP*, Galen also seems to argue that a word is etymologically appropriate. Chrysippus had argued that the heart (*'kardia'*) got its name from the fact that it has 'a certain power and sovereignty' ('*kratêsin kai kureian*'), and is more or less called '*kratia*' (V 328). Well, says Galen, maybe the heart does have a certain sovereignty when it comes to living, but that does not mean it has sovereignty over *all* aspects of living (328–9). Galen seems to say that the word '*kardia*' is etymologically appropriate for the heart, and that Chrysippus has failed to see exactly how.

More common than his explanations of correctness, however, are Galen's claims that a word is *not* a correct or appropriate one for an object, i.e. that it is a misnomer. For instance, the standard word for a membrane is '*chitôn*', which literally means 'tunic' (*On the Utility of the Parts* [*UP*] III 290–1). But at *UP* III 488 he explains that the pericardium is not 'rightly' (*dikaiôs*) called a *chitôn*, since tunics are usually in contact with what they enclose, whereas the pericardium does not actually touch the heart (except perhaps when the heart is fully expanded) – it is more like a housing or fence (*herkos*). Galen does not say that the word should not be used of the pericardium, and in fact he himself is perfectly happy to use it in this way (e.g. *On Anatomical Procedures* (*AA*) II 595). Once more, this is a point about *external* incorrectness. But, again, Galen's explanation of the incorrectness of the name is rather more sober than any in the *Cratylus*: Galen relies on the fact that the word *chitôn* already has a literal meaning (remaining silent on how it comes to mean that), and simply observes that, given this meaning, the word is inappropriate for the pericardium. Or again, at *UP* III 478, Galen points out that 'tricuspid' is not a correct name for the membranes at the opening of the venous artery, since there are only two of them.

It is impossible to avoid the conclusion that Galen accepts that there is such a thing as the correctness of a name – it is presupposed by his discussions of the correctness and incorrectness of these various names.

Doctors and scientists should not give it any attention in their investigations

However, even if it is true that there is such a thing as the correctness of a name, it need not be something that has a place in the investigations of doctors and philosophers. As Galen says, the fact that the pericardium is not really correctly called a 'tunic' is an issue 'for someone who cares about the correctness of names' (*hotôi phrontis onomatôn orthotêtos*: *UP* III 488); in truth, it does not matter what you call it – pericardium, tunic, membrane, housing – it's still 'a wondrous achievement of nature'. The name *chitôn* is not a correct name for the pericardium, for the name does not capture adequately what the pericardium is or does. But for these purposes, i.e. when writing about the usefulness of the pericardium, it doesn't matter what you call it. Settling the question of whether the standard word used of the pericardium is the correct or appropriate one is irrelevant to settling the question of what the function of the pericardium is. Galen implies that you may not come to see what the pericardium is really like if you limit yourself to that activity – but he falls short of suggesting that being interested in the correctness of the name is an illegitimate intellectual activity altogether.

Elsewhere, Galen is more explicit about who should be interested in the correctness of names. In *On Critical Days* (*Di.Dec.*) IX 788–9 Galen is considering the word '*krisis*', and admits that there has been some debate as to how to use it, but he says of the doctors who get caught up in that dispute that they

are involved in long disputes about meaning, without even being aware of this: that they have strayed from medical matters and are embarking on an enquiry suitable for dialecticians, grammarians, or orators. For it is the dialectician's task to investigate about the correctness of names, and the task of grammarians and orators to investigate whether the name is the customary one for the Greeks. And some doctors do this even though they have as much knowledge of dialectic, grammar, or oratory, as donkeys do of the lyre.

A division of labour is proposed according to the two types of linguistic appropriateness which Galen mentions: there is the correctness of a name ('external' correctness), which is a matter for the dialecticians, and the customary usage of the name ('internal' correctness), which is a matter for the grammarians and orators.[20] Doctors lack expertise in both areas, and so cannot decide matters of correctness or usage. Moreover, they need not decide them, because what the doctor has to do is get clear about the essence of the disease, or whatever, that he is investigating. Both tasks – settling external and internal correctness – are treated as clearly defined and acceptable tasks, albeit ones that need not concern the doctor in his role as doctor.

Here I depart slightly from the views of two influential commentators. Referring to this passage from *Di.Dec.*, Hankinson writes: '[Galen] strongly denounces what he considers to be merely terminological disputes, as being fit subject-matter for logicians, rhetoricians and grammarians, but not for practising doctors and natural scientists' (1994a, 171). But I don't think that Galen is denouncing these disputes, at least I don't think he is accusing them of being somehow *unworthy in themselves*, and *therefore* fit only for logicians, rhetoricians and grammarians (as if logic, rhetoric and grammar were worthless activities). Rather, Galen is denouncing the doctors and natural scientists who engage in these terminological disputes, because such disputes belong to a domain other than medicine – their mistake is to think that there is information relevant to their domain of enquiry to be gleaned from etymological matters. Barnes says that the word used of logicians in the *Di.Dec.* passage is pejorative (1991, 73, n. 76).[21] But again, the context seems to me to suggest otherwise. After all, Galen isn't denouncing or showing disdain for the orators and grammarians who are concerned with, and study, ordinary Greek usage, nor would one expect him to – Galen himself wrote plenty of books on rhetorical and grammatical themes (*Lib.Prop.* XIX 48). So I see no reason to think he is denouncing the practice of discussing the correctness of names, or the dialecticians who engage in such discussions. What Galen is doing is denouncing those philosophers or doctors who think that it is by engaging in such discussions that they will achieve knowledge about the nature of things.

More evidence for this comes from *On Recognizing the Best Physician* (*Opt.Med.Cogn.*), *CMG* Suppl. Or. IV, 129.21–131.1, where Galen attacks wealthy people who 'investigate the etymology of words, and how these were used in the past. They neglect the most useful, the best and greatest of all sciences, medicine and philosophy.' His complaint about investigations into etymology and previous usage is that they are conducted *at the expense of* medicine and philosophy, not that they are conducted *tout court*.

Of course, there is in all this a clear implication that the study of etymology is *inferior* to medicine, because, unlike medicine, it will not result in conferring knowledge of how things are. This is certainly one reason for Galen's dismissive attitude towards disputes stemming from language, and why he is keen for such disputes not to interfere with medicine and philosophy. But he does not dismiss them out of hand. Doctors and philosophers should not get involved in disputes over the correctness of names, because they are not fit to settle them, they will get distracted from their central business, and they will be misled.

They might make mistakes by giving bad etymologies, e.g. Chrysippus ('1st mistake')

Scientists will be misled in at least two ways by etymology. Since they are not qualified to conduct linguistic investigations, being neither dialecticians, nor orators, nor grammarians, they are liable to make mistakes when they do engage in constructing etymologies. Such mistakes might lead to errors of the sort that Chrysippus made in his etymology of the word *'egô'*, which resulted in his having importantly mistaken views on the location of the soul.

Or they might make mistakes because words are unreliable guides to the nature of a thing ('2nd mistake')

Another potential error – and the more significant one – is that some philosophers or natural scientists think that the etymology of a word will in fact reveal the nature of the thing signified. Indeed, this is why they get seduced by etymology in the first place. Galen draws attention to this error many times. We have already seen one such example, where Galen says that the pericardium is sometimes called a *chitôn*. Galen implies that if the natural scientist or philosopher were distracted by the business of the correctness of names, he might end up not realizing how the pericardium actually relates to the heart, since he might assume that it is like a tunic (as the name suggests) and touches it.

Galen puts the matter succinctly at *On the Therapeutic Method* (*MM*) X 44:[22]

It is essential for anyone who wants to discover the truth in these matters to try and completely rid himself of all additional beliefs that arise as a result of the names, and to go straight for the actual substance of things.

A name sometimes 'encodes' a description which does not actually hold of the thing named, because those that originally coined the name were ignorant, so if you were to look at the names of those things, you will acquire additional – false – beliefs about the things named. Plato himself alluded to this kind of mistake at *Crat.* 436a9–b11, and Galen often refers to that passage: 'But, as Plato said, since the ancients were ignorant of most things, some things they failed to name at all, and others they named incorrectly. Therefore you must not be deceived[23] by names, but look to the very essence of things' (*Differences of Symptoms* [*Symp.Diff.*] VII 66; cf. also *Differences of Fevers* [*Diff.Feb.*] VII 354; *MM* X 772; *Outline of Empiricism* [*Subf.Emp.*] 59 Deichgräber; etc.).

Four examples.

(i) The word '*apepsia*' is used both for cases where some digestive process takes place such that the nature of the food is altered in some bad way, and for cases where there is no digestive process going at all – it would be better to reserve the word '*apepsia*' for those cases where there is nothing going on, and use the word '*duspepsia*' for the cases where there is a bad change (*Symp.Diff.* VII 66). Galen wants to avoid this kind of homonymy, and confer on each thing a single name to avoid unclarity and sophisms (*Symp.Diff.* VII 46; cf. *Difficulties in Breathing* [*Diff.Resp.*] VII 758; *MM* X 45). It's not hard to see what problems might arise: someone might well not understand that those cases correctly described in Greek as '*apepsia*' are actually of two different types, presumably needing two different treatments. Or there might be the following sophism in the offing: you point to someone who is alleged to suffer from '*apepsia*', and you show that there is in fact something going on in his gut, and then claim to have shown that he doesn't in fact suffer from '*apepsia*'. Galen's diagnosis of what is wrong is that the ancients who conferred that single name on the two conditions were ignorant of their subject matter, and this is reflected in their choice of name. If you want to understand the medical problems of someone with '*apepsia*', it is not enough to look to the name.

(ii) At *UP* III 626, Galen embarks on the difficult question of what to call the organ of perception and the source of voluntary movement – i.e. the brain. The difficulty is this. There is a word commonly used of the brain, namely *ho enkephalos*. This word literally means 'the thing in the head' (or 'the medulla in the head', if you assume ellipsis of the word *muelos*). But then what are we to do in the case of those animals which lack a head or have only a sketchy one (*hupographên*), e.g. crabs or moths? In these cases, Aristotle calls the organ 'the thing analogous to the brain' (626), but Aristotle 'is sometimes deceived by names' (627).[24] He has been deceived by the fact that in animals with a head, the brain has not been named according to its essence (i.e. being the organ of perception and voluntary motion), but rather according to its position. Galen continues (628–9):

> The enkephalos has above all got its name from its position (it has been named in this way because it lies in the head). But because in the case of those animals which don't have a head we find it in the chest area, we shall not say that in these cases it is something else and merely analogous to an enkephalos, but rather we shall say that it is itself an enkephalos, and that the old word does not become it.

Galen attacks Aristotle for having failed to understand the nature of the brain in animals which lack a head. In calling it 'that which is *analogous* to a brain', Aristotle presupposes that it isn't in fact a brain just like any other. But it *is* a brain like any other – it just doesn't happen to be in a head. Aristotle has failed to see that the word for 'brain', enkephalos, encodes false information about what a brain really is, and has thereby been fooled into thinking that animals which lack a head do not, strictly speaking, have a brain. The word 'does not become' the brain – i.e. it is a misnomer – because it suggests that the brain is always to be found in a head.

Galen observes that there is no word for the brain like the word 'eye' in the case of sight, or 'ear' in the case of hearing – that is, no self-standing word as opposed to a phrase (627). For this reason, Galen recommends those who are having trouble seeing his point to imagine that the relevant organ is called by the name the Romans use, i.e. 'cerebrum' (629, to kerebron), and then they will understand his claim easily: in crabs, the cerebrum is to be found in the chest. (His idea is that so formulated, the claim will not strike one as strange, unlike the claim: in crabs, the enkephalos is to be found in the chest.) Or even, says Galen, call it 'skindapsos' (in these contexts a nonsense word like 'blabla').[25] You won't say that the crabs have something *analogous* to a skindapsos; rather you will say that they have a skindapsos! Eyes and ears and hearts are not so-called with reference to their position, so when we call something an enkephalos, it shouldn't be assumed that we are trying to affirm something about its position.

Notice again that Galen accepts that *enkephalos* is the *right* word for the brain, at least in the sense that it is the word prescribed by correct usage. He is not suggesting eliminating that word from ordinary vocabulary, or from the vocabulary of philosophers. (He is certainly not recommending that we actually call it '*skindapsos*'!) He is merely warning us against thinking that an animal without a head cannot have an *enkephalos*, as Aristotle allegedly did. That would be to look to the word, not the thing. It is a clear case of the men of old having misnamed something ('the old word does not become it'), in this case because they were looking to some accidental feature of the thing (its position), not its essence or function.

(iii) In *PHP*, Galen discusses what the role of the heart is in perception and choice, and whether in fact the heart might be the seat of the regent part of the soul. He suggests, as a method of settling this question, that one look at 'the structures that connect the heart with the brain' (V 263) – the jugular veins, the carotid arteries and the nerves by those arteries – and that one cut or otherwise impair these connections, to see what the effect is on the animal. Some had thought that when you cut or tie the arteries connecting the heart to the brain, the animal becomes stupefied (*karôdes*). But 'when the arteries have been intercepted by ligatures or cut in the manner described, the animal will not be voiceless or stupefied, as the majority of Hippocrates' successors have written because of their faulty dissection, but all the arteries above the injury will become completely pulseless' (264). In fact, what had happened was that Hippocrates' successors were clumsy in their dissection, and had intercepted the nerves along with the arteries when they cut them (267), and the interception of the nerves produced voicelessness. They then either called this voicelessness 'stupor' (*karon*), which would itself be an error in naming, or mistook the voicelessness for stupor, which would be an error of fact (*ibid.*).

The mistake which principally interests Galen in that particular part of *PHP* is the one made by the doctors who thought that the heart had some control of behaviour, on the basis of their faulty dissecting. But there is a point to be made concerning correctness. The arteries were named 'carotid' by those who thought that cutting or intercepting them would result in stupefaction (*karon*). Someone who knew what the word 'carotid' literally meant might easily reason as follows: blocking the channel of communication between the heart and the brain results in stupefaction, therefore the heart is responsible for sending messages to the brain. But this would be to fall victim to the fact that the name 'carotid' is a misnomer. Galen was not alone in thinking that the artery had been misnamed – Rufus of Ephesus even suggests that 'if you wanted to change this name, you wouldn't be wrong' (*On the naming of parts of the body* 210).

(iv) At the start of book IX of *MM* (X 599), Galen considers so-called 'ephemeral' fevers, i.e. fevers which typically last one day. They are the least serious kind of fever, but they can metamorphose into one of the other two more deadly types of fever, those arising from putre-faction of the humours, and those which take hold of the solid parts of the body, i.e. 'hectic' ones (600). Galen distinguishes two ways in which ephemeral fevers can arise – either from causes such as lack of sleep, indigestion, swellings, etc., or from causes such as being exposed to too much heat (e.g. through sunbathing), or too much cold (e.g. through bathing in excessively cold water). In the latter case, the pores of the skin get blocked (through contraction or with-ering) and the appropriate humours cannot escape in the way they normally do, and the body gets overheated – hence the fever (601–2). Sometimes, this latter type of fever can last beyond a day, and may even last for three days, simply because it takes time for the pores to unblock. But this is when there is the problem of the name (603):

How could a fever which is prolonged until a third day be called 'ephemeral'? Such a fever should stop on the second day, if you go by the name. (It has already been said before that the length of a day in this context is twenty-four hours, so the word 'day' includes the night too.) And if there is no rotting of the humours and the body itself has not received a feverish heat 'hectically', it would indeed fall outside these two types. Therefore either it is necessary to allow for yet another type of fever outside of the three mentioned in our primary division of fevers, or – paying no attention to the name – we shall call it 'ephemeral'. For the name 'ephemeral' is not right for the essence of such fevers.

Note several things about this. First, Galen is his usual careful self concerning the word '*ephêmeros*', noting that the word itself could mislead because of its etymological connection with the word for day, i.e. *hêmera*: we should understand the word 'day' here as referring to the full twenty-four hours, not just the period when it isn't night. But even if the word '*ephêmeros*' means 'lasting for twenty-four hours', it is not an appropriate name for some of the fevers that Galen wants to refer to as 'ephemeral'. He points out that if we continue to call them 'ephemeral', we must then no longer pay attention to the name, since 'the name "ephemeral" is not right for the essence of such fevers'. In fact, Galen decides not to do this, but rather calls them 'continuant' (603–4):

> But lacking its proper name, we give it its name from what often accompanies it, for the sake of clarity of exposition. So their nature is the same as ephemeral ones, but their name is not the same. [chapter 2] For in the case of fevers where there is just one paroxysm staying from the beginning throughout the whole, extended over several days, [604] they call them 'continuant', not using a Greek word, but choosing to commit a solecism rather than leave that kind [idea] of fever unnamed. But although all such fevers belong to a common kind [idea] from which they get their name, it is not correspondingly the case that their nature is simple and one. For whereas some of them indicate clearly signs of rotting, others do not at all, namely the ones which we say belong to the genus of ephemeral fevers. For since the cessation of the paroxysm usually comes about when the heated humours are transpired, whereas they are not transpired because of the blockage of the pores, the paroxysm has to go on for several days.

Fevers which do not come on intermittently (as quotidian or tertian fevers do) but whose paroxysm remains from start to finish already have the name of 'continuant' (sunochous).[26] Standard fevers of this type are serious fevers arising from putrefaction of the humours, so Galen is uneasy about using the term to cover prolonged fevers due to pore-blockage: not only is the word a solecism, but also it could result in confusion over what a 'continuant' fever is – two quite different types of fever will be labelled 'continuant', one of which is of the same type as an ephemeral fever. Thus, if you continue to call these fevers 'ephemeral', the name is liable to mislead because of its connotations; if you call these fevers 'continuant', then you end up using one word for two quite different kinds of condition. Both courses of action have their drawbacks.[27]

In sum: words are sometimes misleading – they can fail to reveal the essence of the thing they name. Once the doctor has learned that lesson, he need no longer worry about the correctness of names.

THE CORRECT USE OF LANGUAGE

We have now seen one reason why Galen thought that it was important to get clear about the issue of the correctness of names. Many doctors and philosophers make the mistake of thinking that they can get to the heart of some matter or other by looking to the words used, and making inferences on the basis of them. But this is not the end of the story concerning correctness. As often as Galen tells us we should not be concerned with the correctness of names, he will praise his own use of language as being correct, explain why it is correct and criticize others for not using language correctly. So for instance, at *Synopsis on Pulses* (*Syn.Puls.*) IX 446 he says: 'That we are using correctly the names for pulses, preserving here too as elsewhere the usage of the Greeks, has been shown in books II and III of *Differences of Pulses*.' Obviously, the type of correctness at issue here is internal correctness – the kind that is decided by usage or custom. So although he argues that doctors and philosophers should not give any thought to the *external* correctness of names, Galen himself thinks it important to use the *internally* correct names – and will often criticize others for not doing the same (as we shall see). Thus, we should not be puzzled by Galen's apparent inconsistency in exhorting us on the one hand not to worry about the correctness of names, but on the other to use the correct names for things. Once we remember the two different types of correctness, the illusion of contradiction falls away.

Galen wrote *On the correctness of names* 'because of those who use words badly' (*Lib.Prop.* XIX 61). We have seen that the book contained a warning to those engaged in the project of demonstrating things, that they should not be tempted into putting forward arguments on the basis of etymology. But this does not involve *using* words badly – at least not in the sense of misspeaking, or abusing language – so this leaves us needing an explanation of why Galen said that he wrote the book because of those who *abuse* language. The simple answer is that the book must also have dealt with the other kind of correctness which Plato recognised, namely correct *usage*. In *On the correctness of names*, Galen must have said something like the following: words cannot be relied on to reflect the essence of the things they name so you should not worry about (external) correctness, but you *should* endeavour to follow Greek usage and respect (internal) correctness.

THE FUNCTION OF LANGUAGE IS TO COMMUNICATE. It cannot be doubted that Galen's considered view was that the Greek language must be used properly, that is, according to the way Greeks ordinarily use it. But *why* should this be? After all, Galen does not think that the words the Greeks use reflect accurately the nature of the things they name – that is the whole point of the lesson we are supposed to learn about the (external) correctness of names. The proper explanation for why Galen thinks it is so important to observe correct usage lies in the fact that Galen identifies the role of language as being a tool for teaching and learning (i.e. communicating), just as Plato did in the *Cratylus* (435d4; e7). Consider the following passage from *Differences of Pulses* (*Diff.Puls.*) VIII 496:

> Words are of no help at all to us in gaining knowledge of things, but only in teaching, which can even be achieved by coming to agreements. For if someone gave absolutely no names to things, and was still able to know about those things and understand what [conditions] they naturally indicated, he would appear to be no less able to do this than those who gave things names – at least, not for that reason.

Don't look at words to discern the nature of things – investigate the things themselves. You could conduct this investigation without ever naming things, or knowing the names of things. Language serves a different purpose: 'We use names and linguistic communication generally in order to express the thoughts in our mind that we have gained from examining the nature of things' (*PHP* V 724–5; cf. *Diff.Puls.* VIII 567; *On Crises* [*Cris.*] IX 570; etc.; cf. e.g. Sextus Empiricus, *Against the Professors* (*M*) I 176). We express these thoughts when we wish to tell things to others, i.e. teach or inform them (*MM* X 81):[28]

> However, if you wish to teach someone else what you know, you will certainly need to use some names for things, and should have clarity as your aim in their usage. The best teacher is the one whose particular concern is to assign names in such a way that the pupil can learn in the clearest possible way. And since we are ourselves currently engaged in such an activity, it is essential that we assign names to things in some manner; that we do so clearly is now our concern.

So the idea is this. You find out what the nature of things is, and for this you do not even need to give things names. But then, if you want to communicate to others the thoughts that you have – the knowledge that you have gained – you have to use language, and in particular, give things names. Success in doing this involves having clarity as one of your aims, as Galen emphasizes in the passage above from *MM* 81, and at *Diff.Puls*. VIII 567: 'we always try to express our thoughts using the clearest words.' The emphasis on clarity as a linguistic virtue is a commonplace in Galen. For instance, in *On Linguistic Sophisms* (*Soph*.) XIV 585–9, Galen argues that the function of language is to signify, and so its virtue is signifying well, and its vice signifying badly, which he calls 'unclarity' (589).[29]

Galen doesn't just argue that the function of language is to communicate our thoughts to others; he even argues more strongly that it is part of *human nature* to share knowledge with others through language (*Med.Nam*. 9.12–16).[30] But Galen rues this fact with these 'heartfelt words':[31] 'I wish I could both learn and teach things without the names for them' (*Diff.Puls*. VIII 493). Why does Galen regret the fact that we have to use words to communicate? The answer is that as soon as you are engaged in communicating your thoughts to others, there is scope for doing so more or less successfully, and scope for miscommunication entirely. Language – even Galen's beloved Greek language – is not always a perfect tool for this. In order to communicate successfully, choices need to be made between names according to how clearly they indicate things – cf. *Differences of Fevers* (*Diff.Feb*.) VII 354; *On Tremor, Palpitation, Spasm and Rigor* (*Trem.Palp*.) VII 624; *On Unnatural Swellings* (*Tum.Pr.Nat*.) VII 716; etc. Names must have clear application conditions, and so we find countless Galenic discussions of both philosophical and medical matters beginning with the observation that terms need to be defined clearly – cf. *On Bones for Beginners* (*Oss*.) II 734; *UP* III 91; *PHP* V 506; *The Powers [and Mixtures] of Simple Drugs* (*SMT*) XI 379–80, 462–3, 542, 749; etc.

The principal way in which a word may fail to have clear application conditions is if it is ambiguous, that is, if it seems to cover two quite different kinds of thing (*Diff.Resp*. VII 758; cf. also *SMT* XI 462–3; etc.):

> Common words, which then signify no more one thing than the other, confuse and confound the hearer, so that he does not know what is being said, until the ambiguity has been distinguished.

In some cases, words actually in use in Greek suffer from this problem, for instance the example of *apepsia* which I discussed above, and any number of others.[32] How should you proceed if this happens? You need carefully to distinguish the various meanings – in some cases, presumably, this should be enough to keep a reader on their guard against fallacies. In other cases, it might be that there are unambiguous words that can be used instead of the homonymous one (I take it that the argument from *PHP* involving '*apo*', discussed in chapter 4, is one of these cases). Or, another word can be used to capture one of the meanings, as in the case of the ambiguous word '*apepsia*', where Galen suggested using the word '*duspepsia*' for bad digestion (as opposed to no digestion). Finally, one might insist that the word be used with just one of its senses. For instance, in *On the Preservation of Health* (*San.Tu.*), Galen wonders about the difference in meaning between *ponos* ('exertion'), *kinêsis* ('movement') and *gumnasion* ('exercise'), specifically 'whether exertion is the same thing as both movement and exercise, or whether exertion and movement are the same, and exercise something else, or whether movement is something else and exertion and exercise don't differ' (VI 85). Not every movement counts as exercise or exertion, thinks Galen. But what about the difference between exercise and exertion? 'Exercise' has a general sense (where it covers all vigorous movement), and a specific sense, where it covers wrestling or throwing the discus or other such activities. 'Exertion' seems to mean the same thing as 'exercise' in the wide sense. Galen continues (86):

Well, let this be stipulated by me concerning these terms, and let the whole of the rest of this treatise be understood according to these meanings. If someone wants to use them differently, I shall let them; after all, I have not come here to investigate the correctness of words, but how someone might be most healthy. I am forced to define the meanings of words for this purpose which is useful to me: to distinguish between exercise and exertion, on the one hand, and, speaking generally, any movement whatsoever.

Galen is not going to be concerned in this work with whether or not these distinctions in the senses of the words really correspond to what etymology dictates, or even – in this case – correct usage would predict. The idea seems to be that the usage of these words just isn't determinate enough to settle the question of how they should be used; instead, Galen is going to use the words '*ponos*' ('exertion') and '*gumnasion*' ('exercise') interchangeably, ignoring the specific sense of '*gumnasion*' where it refers to certain sports, and distinguishing them both from '*kinêsis*' ('movement'). Thus Galen is aware of the danger of ambiguity lurking in the use of words, and has various ways of avoiding or combating it.

However, ambiguity is not the only threat to successful communication. It is not enough that you discern the nature of things correctly and then apportion out words carefully and unambiguously yourself. Language is a joint venture: to succeed in communicating, the audience to whom you are trying to communicate your thoughts must go along with, or accept, how you are using words. How can one achieve this? Galen makes one suggestion in the *Diff.Puls.* passage quoted above: 'words are of no help at all to us in gaining knowledge of things, but only in teaching, which can even be achieved by coming to agreements'. So all you need do is secure agreement between you and your pupils as to how words are to be used, and then successful teaching should follow.[33] That suggests that any sounds would be able to serve as the relevant names, as long as they are agreed upon by both parties, and this is in fact what Galen seems to endorse (continuing his discussion at *Diff.Puls.* VIII 496):

> But if when he tried to teach he gave whatever names he saw fit, even then he would be no worse off. Even if someone wants to call a strong pulse 'Dio' or 'Theo', and makes no mistakes in teaching what causes give rise to it, and of what condition it is indicative, and to what it will lead – not even this person seems to me in any way to go amiss.

'Dio' and 'Theo' are Galen's standard 'dummy' names, comparable to 'Jane Doe' and 'Richard Roe' (and were also used as such by, among others, Stoic logicians). You might coin new words or use unorthodox existent ones ('Dio', 'Theo') for the various kinds of pulse, and achieve clarity that way – as long as you secure agreement between you and your pupils that this is what you are going to do. This is not an isolated text: one often finds Galen saying something similar, e.g. at *MM* X 70, 81; etc.[34]

In some cases, of course, it will in fact be necessary to give new words to things, for instance where there simply is no word in use for it. This is something that Galen acknowledges in a number of places, e.g. *Med.Nam.* 8.13–28; *Symp.Diff.* VII 46; etc. Galen even gives us some advice as to how one might do this, at *Opportune Moments in Diseases* (*Morb.Temp.*) VII 417–18:

It is common practice for all the Greeks, for those things of which we have names provided by those of old, to use those names, and for those things of which we do not have names, either to transfer the usage from those for which we do have names, or to make up names by some analogy from the already named things, or to make use of names given to other things.

But even though, in this text, Galen tells us how to proceed in giving new names, or using old words in a new way, it is clear that he thinks that we should do this only when there are no words available in language already. He does not, in *Diff.Puls.*, go on to use 'Dio' and 'Theo' of various kinds of pulse. Why is this, when it would apparently be so easy and convenient to adopt new words at will, and get your pupils to agree to it too?

TO COMMUNICATE WELL, FOLLOW THE USAGE OF THE GREEKS

The short answer is that Galen thinks we should follow Greek usage, when there is such a usage to follow.[35] Already we can see Galen's view in the continuation of the discussion in *Diff.Puls.* VIII 496-7:

It is sufficient for someone [497] who intends to teach any subject you like to legislate concerning words, but someone who refers back to earlier people must teach their usage, neither then nor now harping on as to whether they named something rightly or wrongly, or daring to correct them, or blaming them – which are things the sophists do. For these things are all superfluous and outside the scope of our art, because this branch of knowledge does not concern the correctness of names, but of things; that is, men do not send those who do not name things well to the doctor, but rather those who are sick. So this very treatise does not profess to teach more than the names to which we and other doctors are accustomed, but would be well content if it achieves this in due measure.

Galen accepts that he could *in principle* stipulate a new set of terms for pulses. This would, however, be misleading if you were concerned with trying to learn and teach what previous doctors and philosophers thought – in that case, you would do better to learn their use of words, and teach accordingly. So we find Galen himself, as is appropriate for a commentator, writing an explanation of Hippocratic terminology (*Lib.Prop.* XIX 37), and at *Thrasybulus* (*Thras.*) V 881 analysing the terminology of other doctors.

But *Diff.Puls.* (or, more accurately, the first book of *Diff.Puls.*, as Galen makes clear at VIII 499) is not concerned with the learning or understanding of what previous doctors said, and so Galen will not need to discuss or follow their usage. Rather, he says that he is going to teach the current word-using practice or, as he puts it, 'the names to which we and other doctors are accustomed' (497). He is not going to coin new words, or use pre-existent words in a new way. Even if one *could* use fresh names, it does not follow that one *should*. Where there is such a thing as Greek usage, one should stick to it.

WHAT IS THE USAGE OF THE GREEKS?

What does following the usage of the Greeks actually entail?[36] In *Thras.* V 868–9, Galen explains:

For those whose chief and primary concern is the knowledge of things, and whose efforts are directed towards this central aim, but who desire, purely for the purpose of communication with others, to learn the terms applied to those things, I shall offer an account of Greek usage, not the usage of all the Greeks, nor with respect to all words – this would be a matter of linguistic [869] or grammatical experience – but I admit that I have experience most of all of Attic words, and in second place both Ionic and Doric words, and similarly of Aeolic.

Galen is simply going to teach the normal Attic usage of Greek words, even though he has some knowledge of the other dialects. We must not confuse this with the vogue for 'atticization' which was rife during the Second Sophistic.[37] This was a movement which attempted to bring about a return, in 'literary' works, to the Greek of the classical period, complete with outdated and pretentious vocabulary. Galen was dead against it. 'I myself use the names that people use nowadays, since I think that it is better to teach things clearly than to atticize in the old-fashioned way' (*On the Powers of Foodstuffs* [*Alim.Fac.*] VI 579; trans. Powell). Or again:[38]

This is not written for those who prefer to Atticize in their speech (for perhaps someone who is disdainful of a healthy body, as also of a healthy soul, will not even want to read about it). Rather, it is written especially for physicians who are not greatly concerned with Attic style, and also for those others who live as rational beings, preferring to give heed to their body and soul ahead of reward, reputation, wealth and political power . . . Since it is likely that the clearer language will be of greater benefit to these people, I write names that they recognize, even if they were not usual among the Greeks of old.

The fact is that those who indulged in atticization were often not understood – this seems to be the point of the opening exchange of Lucian's *Lexiphanes*, for instance, where Lycinus misunderstands Lexiphanes' word *'neochmos'* ('recent'), confusing it with *'auchmos'* ('drought'). According to Galen, part of what makes usage correct is that it is widely understood, and this is one reason why he favours Aristophanes' usage as authoritative – it had to be understood by all those in the theatre (*Med.Nam.* 31.25–32.3; cf. *Differences of Diseases* [*Morb.Diff.*] VI 852; *Differences of Symptoms* [*Symp.Diff.*] VII 45; etc.).

FOLLOWING THE USAGE OF THE GREEKS REDUCES MISUNDERSTANDINGS

Whatever Galen's views about what counts as proper Greek usage might have been, we as yet lack a reason for why he insists that we follow Greek usage, rather than, for instance, adopt new ways of speaking. We know that his reason is not that Greek reflects accurately the nature of things – he has argued strongly against this in his remarks about external correctness. Nor is it mere snobbery about the Greek language that drives Galen – or so he would have us believe. As he explains near the beginning of book II of *Diff.Puls.* (VIII 567–8), talking about those who resolutely neglect to use the proper Greek words for things:

But if everyone were to agree to embark on one language, as if it were new currency, by decree, perhaps then we could try to forget [568] the language of the Greeks and master the one laid down by these people. Not even if the one they agreed to use was one of the foreign languages would we have hesitated to learn it, to please them in every way.

He would be quite happy to agree to use a *foreign* language, instead of ordinary Greek, if everyone followed suit. Snobbery does not seem to be the answer, therefore.

The true reason why Galen thinks that philosophical and medical writers should follow the usage of the Greeks must be this: successful communication involves clarity of expression, and clarity is achieved when people come to agreements as to how words are to be used. Since communicating is the point of using language in the first place, words should always be used as people have agreed they should be used. If you don't use words in the way those around you use them, you will fail to get your message across. Galen makes the connection between clarity and ordinary usage explicit at *Diff.Puls.* VIII 567: 'We follow the usage of the Greeks, because we have been brought up with it, and we try always to express our thoughts using the clearest words'. And at *On Hippocrates' 'Epidemics'* (*Hipp.Epid.*) XVIIA 678, Galen refers to the use of 'the most usual and, as a result, the clearest words, which it is the custom of orators to call "ordinary".'[39] Galen is by no means alone in recommending such usage: Sextus Empiricus, writing at roughly the same time as Galen, also urges one to communicate in ordinary Greek for the sake of clarity and precision (*M* I 176). Thus, we need to investigate how it is that failure to use customary or ordinary words might result in failure to communicate.

The first and most obvious way in which you might fail to get your message across is if you want something – e.g. a certain type of food or herb – but use the wrong name in asking for it. Clearly, using ordinary language correctly in these circumstances is important for straightforward prudential reasons. This explains why Galen goes to such trouble to spell out the different names for herbs and foods in *SMT* and *Alim.Fac.* Time and again in *Alim.Fac.* he favours the normal everyday word for various foods rather than the obsolete Attic one (VI 585, 591, 592, etc.), or simply lists the different words people currently use for something (e.g. apricots, at VI 594). You need to know the current words, especially when there are many of them, for food, so that you can communicate properly with people were you to need to ask them where to find them locally, or were you to prescribe a regime of apricots to them, or if someone serves you something and you want to know what it is. Obviously, the same goes for medicinal herbs, and so in *SMT* we find very many passages where Galen tells us the different names for various herbs – Barnes lists scores of them (1997, 8–9, esp. n. 12). As he puts it: 'If you need a particular plant when you're in the countryside, you need to know its rustic name; if you want to get hold of a particular sort of earth from Syria, it's a good idea to know what it's called in Syria' (1997, 9). Knowing the literary word for mulberries is of no help in ordinary communication. It is relatively easy to see why Galen would recommend knowing about and using current usage in such cases, and what the dangers are of not doing so.

But even in less potentially life-threatening situations, Galen is keen that one respects ordinary usage, because misunderstandings and errors are still liable to arise. There seem to be two main ways in which language might be abused.

Finding a difference in meaning between two words where there is none in ordinary usage

Galen often criticizes the Stoics for discerning differences in meaning in words which ordinarily mean the same thing. For instance, at *MM* X 44, he writes:

So if someone adheres to this conception, but chooses to call it a section but not a part (or alternatively a part but not a section), he would in no way impede the discovery of things for me; but he would show himself not to be a native Greek-speaker. Similarly, if someone makes a distinction between 'whole' and 'totality' he is ignorant of the Greek language.

Galen knew perfectly well that there *were* some philosophers who insisted on distinguishing between a part (*'meros'*) and a section (*'morion'*), and between a whole (*'holon'*) and a totality (*'pan'*), namely the Stoics (cf. Ammonius *In. An. Pr.* 8, 20–2 for the first distinction; Sextus *M* IX 332 for the second). This is not the only place where he criticizes the Stoics for making this kind of mistake: at *PHP* V 336 he reminds us that if we use words properly, there is no difference in meaning between the words *'odunê'* and *'algêdona'* which both mean 'pain', as there is no difference between the words 'column' and 'pillar' – even though Chrysippus appears to have distinguished *'odunê'* and *'algêdona'* by having one be a species of the other.

What is the danger in finding differences of meaning where there are none? After all, in the passage from *MM* just quoted, Galen explicitly says that this makes no difference to his discovery of the nature of things. And if one stipulates the different senses carefully enough, what harm could come of it? Well, the first thing to notice is that

Galen says that *his* understanding of the nature of things will not be impaired – it does not follow that *nobody's* understanding would be impaired. And it is not hard to see how someone might indeed fail to understand the nature of things as a result of this mangling of ordinary usage: if the words actually do mean the same thing in ordinary Greek, it is going to be difficult to remember that they are being used in different senses in the discussion. Force of habit will kick in, and the reader might well read the two words as having the same sense, in which case you will fail to communicate what you wanted to communicate.

In fact, Galen has a special tactic when there are many words meaning the same thing, namely using the various synonymous words indiscriminately, to underline the fact that there is no difference. He claims Plato adopted this tactic, too (*PHP* V 487–8; cf. *Symp.Diff.* VII 117–18), presumably referring to Plato's use of many different words for the Forms. So at *Symp.Diff.* VII 108 and 117–18, he tells us that he will not distinguish between different words for various conditions, and at *Morb.Temp.* VII 411, he tells us that he will use three words meaning 'growth' indiscriminately, since they all mean the same thing. There is a nice example of this laissez-faire attitude in *SMT*: the word for 'stone' in Greek can be either masculine or feminine, and Galen explicitly says that he is going to use both in his discussion, 'to show that in fact the clarity of the exposition is not adversely affected, whichever one you write' (XII 194).[40]

Using a word but not with its correct meaning

Galen is even clearer that one should not commit solecisms. 'Right from the start, therefore, you should avoid the kind of statement that makes it necessary for the hearer to give to each word a meaning other than the usual one' (*PHP* V 381). He explains in some detail what happens if you don't, focusing again on his favourite target, Chrysippus. The word 'irrational', Galen explains, can be used in two different senses: 'lacking reason' or 'reasoning badly'; it is ambiguous in just the same way as other adjectives starting with an alpha privative (V 383–5). But Chrysippus uses the word 'irrational' in a third sense, namely 'rejecting reason' (V 382, 386). Galen disapproves of this strongly, but why? Why, exactly, can't Chrysippus use the word that way, if he wants? Galen's answer is straightforward: something which ordinary users of Greek would not class as irrational (namely, the affections of the soul – the exact example isn't important for our purposes here), Chrysippus will class as irrational (in his sense). This hardly promotes clarity in the argument (V 383):

[Chrysippus] could have avoided all these ambiguities, fabricated so ineptly and so contrary to Greek usage, and made his argument exact and articulate by using words correctly and clearly.

Quite simply, ordinary Greek users are going to find Chrysippus' argument confusing. His argument will fail to be 'exact and articulate'. An argument which fails to be exact and articulate can hardly claim to succeed in its goal of demonstrating its conclusion.

Another example of the same phenomenon is found at *Diff.Resp.* VII 756–9. Galen is discussing difficulties in breathing. Breathing consists of four parts: an inhalation, a pause, an exhalation and then another pause. Inhalation and exhalation are movements, and so can be said to be quick or slow (according to how much time they take), or big or small (according to how great the dilation and contraction are). The intervening periods of rest can be long or short (according to how much time they take). So you can have problems in breathing due to the inhalations and exhalations being too quick or slow, or too big or small, and problems due to the intervening periods between inhalation and exhalation being too long or short. But consider those periods of rest between inhalations and exhalations. What should we say when those periods are long or short? Galen explains (757):

We call vines or olive trees or whatever else you can plant 'thick' whenever we want to indicate a very short gap between them; in the same way also we call them 'sparse' whenever there is a large space in between the planted bodies, and generally any things composed of several things which are separated one from another get these names.

So you could call breathing with short gaps between inhalations and exhalations 'thick', and breathing with longer gaps 'sparse'. (This kind of explication of the paradigmatic use of a word is common in Galen – for another example, see the explication below of the word 'full', at *Diff.Puls.* VIII 671.)

The problem is that 'some of the more recent doctors' (758) use a single pair of contrary predicates – either 'frequent'/'sparse', or 'quick'/'slow' – to cover both phenomena, namely 'quick'/'slow' breathing *and* 'frequent'/'sparse' breathing. These doctors use words 'neither according to the usage of Hippocrates, nor the other older doctors, nor in general other Greeks', and are actually courting obscurity (*ibid.*). Galen seems to think that a particularly bad result of this misuse is that they might use a word such as 'fast', which paradigmatically applies to *motions*, of frequent breathing, i.e. breathing characterized by short periods of *rest*: 'no one is ignorant of the fact that all men, both the ones alive now and the old ones, predicate slowness and swiftness of nothing other than things that are in motion' (759).[41] Galen ends his rant with the following observation: 'But if someone, as I have said, wants to name them not in this way but differently, following neither Hippocrates nor the other doctors nor the Greeks generally, and not caring for clear rendering into words, this man can be allowed to win only a Cadmeian victory' (*ibid.*). They may get their way and end up using the names however they like, but their victory will be Cadmeian since there will be a real risk that no one will understand them.

Yet another discussion of the misuse of words can be found at *Diff.Puls.* VIII 670–94, in which Galen embarks on a long discussion of the difference between a full pulse and a hard one.[42] (The proper meaning of 'hard' also occupies him at *SMT* XI 718.) He first of all gives some paradigmatic uses of the word 'full' (671):

We talk of a jug of wine being full, and a basket of barley being full. In the same way too, we say that theatres, or stadiums, or assembly rooms, are full of people, just as we say that they are empty too. And in the same way, we say that both the stomach and the mouth are sometimes full, sometimes empty.

To reinforce this point, he quotes a couple of lines from Theocritus in which the word 'full' is exactly used of a mouth (which is said to be full of honey and honeycomb). And then he gives a careful definition of the word 'full' (*ibid.*):

And in general every vessel containing space inside itself is either full or empty: whenever its interval is taken up by some other body, either one or many, it is full; whenever it contains only air, it is empty. All men call things full or empty strictly and primarily in this way.

What is noteworthy about this definition is that it specifies first of all what kind of thing might be full (or empty), and then says what conditions it needs to fulfil in order to count as full (or empty). Galen also points to extended uses of the word, for instance to characterize wool or wine (VIII 672). Galen has an interesting view about what constitutes an extended use; he says, for instance, that those who call someone 'empty of sense' are not using a metaphor, because 'they preserve the thought of a vessel and container' (*ibid.*).

Galen is building towards a criticism of those doctors who call a pulse 'full'. The problem is that when they do so, they do not use the word in either its literal sense, or in this extended sense. When they call a pulse 'full', they apply the word 'according to the body of the artery itself, i.e. its coverings' (675), and Galen points out that we would then be better off calling the pulse 'hard' and 'soft', not 'full' or 'empty' (*ibid.*). He is very clear about what should be done (*ibid.*):

> If we have the appropriate words, we should use them. Otherwise, it's better to put each thing into words using a phrase, and not to name it metaphorically, whenever someone wants to teach and not babble away (since it is permitted to single out the subject of the conversation using both metaphorical words and catachrestic ones, when you are doing so to someone who already knows about the thing, for the sake of brief communication). However, the initial teaching of all technical things needs the appropriate words in order to be clear and articulated.

The problem is, says Galen, that if you call a pulse 'full', that will lead people to think you mean that the artery is full of something – e.g. airy or watery stuff. But in fact, those who call pulses full don't mean this at all, but something else. They don't mean to talk about what's in the artery, but rather what the covering of the artery is like. Galen mocks them mercilessly for it. 'Look, they say, I'll show you a full pulse in those who are ill' (678) – rather than describe such a pulse, they resort to ostension. 'Well look', retorts Galen, 'I touch the artery, as you order, but not knowing which of its accidents you are calling the fullness in it, I don't understand from your ostension any more about the thing than before, when you weren't showing me' (679). Galen thinks that the doctors are extending the use of the word 'full' to pulses from its use of wine, which is already a metaphor. 'It is allowed for all men to make a metaphor from things properly so-called, but not to make again further metaphors out of things already metaphor-ed. This isn't even permitted to poets, let alone to those who are supposed to teach something technical or scientific' (681). Once Galen recovers his composure, he makes his point (683):

The qualities of the body itself, of the artery, as we were showing a little earlier, are not rightly named 'fullness' or 'emptiness', but 'hardness' or
'softness'; someone would correctly name the amount of the contained stuff
itself 'fullness' or 'emptiness'.

Galen implies that it is difficult for someone to understand what a
doctor who calls a pulse 'full' means by that: it doesn't mean what
you expect it to mean, and when they spell out what they do in fact
mean, it turns out that they have made a metaphor out of a metaphor.
They mean to pick out a certain kind of pulse, but the listener will
naturally assume they are attributing to it a certain property, which
is not in fact the property they are trying to single out.

The discussion of 'hard' takes a similar tack, and one finds similar discussions in other works (cf. the discussion of the proper use
of the word 'hot' in *SMT; On Mixtures [Temp.]* I 538; *Diagnosis
by Pulses [Dig.Puls.]* book II; etc.). But what these discussions all
have in common is this: those who misuse words which already
have an established meaning do so at their peril – interlocutors will
be puzzled and will misunderstand what they mean, whereas the
whole point of words is to enable communication to take place,
which is precisely why to achieve this goal there exist words whose
uses have been agreed upon.

CONCLUDING REMARKS

I have argued that we can find in Galen a coherent picture concerning the correctness of language. He thinks that etymology is of no
use in discerning the nature of the world, but that successful communication is threatened by the abuse of already existing linguistic
usage. He expresses these two views in a way which verges on the
inconsistent: he will say that we should not care about the correctness of words, but that we should use language correctly. Careful
attention to which type of correctness is at issue helps dissolve the
illusion of contradiction.

The view is, I take it, a satisfying and coherent one. But Galen
is not so easily pinned down. Even though we have seen that Galen
complains vociferously about those doctors who misuse language,
arguing that it becomes difficult to understand them, he also occasionally tells us that we *shouldn't* criticize those who engage in

solecisms. He is certainly prepared to be lenient with abuses of language in conversational contexts. In *PHP*, Galen writes (V 383):

Now if a person speaks to a problem from memory on the spur of the moment, the better course even for him is to give clear and distinct meanings to the words he uses; his errors, however, will be pardoned.

But immediately following this passage, Galen reverts to type, saying:

But to announce that one is writing a scientific and theoretical treatise and then to call a certain motion disobedient to reason yet demand that we take the motion to be rational, or to speak of it as rejecting reason yet demand that we take it to be nothing other than reason and judgment – I am inclined to think that such behaviour deserves the severest censure.

Nonetheless, the glimmer of charity here has echoes elsewhere. Galen did write a book called – surprisingly – *To those who criticize linguistic solecisms* (*Lib.Prop.* XIX 48), which was not a negligible work (it was in six books). The following passage, from *Morb.Temp.* VII 418, might well give us some indication of what that book said:[43]

But, if one wants, it is possible not to keep the usual words of the Greeks and (if it is necessary to invent words oneself) not to observe the rules that I have just laid down. In fact, this is what often happens in the case of modern doctors who haven't benefited like the ancients from a basic education. It is necessary to let them speak as they want (because they like to quarrel and they have no shame), and it is necessary to use language in their way in order to avoid lengthy verbal disputes – and in any case, no patient will have been hurt by their linguistic crimes.

The extraordinary thing about this passage is that immediately before it, Galen has been encouraging us to follow the usage of the Greeks, or create metaphors, etc. if there are no words already in existence (cf. p. 143). How, then, can he go on to say that it is fine for the recent doctors, who abuse language, to ignore the rules he lays down, and that one should make an effort to understand them? This is not apparent inconsistency across works – it is apparent inconsistency *from one sentence to another*. This is the final piece of the puzzle for us in understanding Galen's view on language.

Recall that we have already seen that Galen often points out that we can use any words we like for things. To give just one example, at *UP* III 866, Galen says that he doesn't care about words – you can *say* if you want that the workings of the various parts of the body associated with teeth have come about by chance, just as 'when you can see the sun above the earth you can call such a situation "night", and the sun itself not "light", but, if you want, "darkness".' In the passage from *Morb.Temp.*, we simply find this view taken to its logical conclusion. Of course, anyone *can* use language in whatever way they want. If you want to understand them, it is possible to do so – you need to immerse yourself in their usage of words, and try to work out what they mean. What they write will probably be understandable, with enough effort. But this does not mean that their abuse of language is to be encouraged, or even that it is somehow acceptable or excusable. Those who abuse language always run the risk that someone will not put in the hard work necessary for deciphering their words, and will give up, or misunderstand them. Language is not governed by external correctness, and so any word could have ended up being the conventional word for something, *if we had all agreed to it*. Those who use language in a way that we have not agreed to, exploiting the arbitrariness of language, should beware.

NOTES

1. Possibly to be identified with the treatise at XIX 62–157.
2. XIV 583–98; see Edlow (1977); Schiaparelli (2002); Ebbesen (1981).
3. Reading *parasêmôn* (cf. *Scripta Minora* II, XC–XCI).
4. Survives in Arabic (at any rate if the text is genuine); see Meyerhof and Schacht (1931).
5. See also Hankinson (1994a, 171–80).
6. It seems to have been a commonplace that philosophical enquiries should start with an investigation into the meaning of the terms to be employed in that enquiry (cf. Epictetus, *Diss.* I xvii 12, attributing the thought to both Antisthenes and Socrates). But Galen is recommending something slightly different. He is recommending that we start our entire philosophico-medical training by reading his treatise on the correctness of names, whereas the other philosophers encourage us to start each enquiry separately (not the whole business of philosophy) with an investigation into names (not necessarily into their correctness). I am grateful to Jonathan Barnes for help on this point.
7. *Pros tous epêreastikôs akouontas tôn onomatôn* (*Lib.Prop.* XIX 44).
8. References are to the OCT ed. Duke *et al.*

9. It has become customary to talk of the correctness of *names*, but in fact Plato and Galen between them discuss the correctness of common nouns, adjectives and adverbs – the correctness of words quite generally is at stake.

10. Williams (1994, 35).

11. And discussed in more detail on pp. 135–6.

12. This may sound like a strange view, but it seems to be implicit in the notion of a misnomer. If a word counts as a 'mis-nomer' by not reflecting the nature of its *nominatum*, a 'nomer' (or 'name') must be expected to reflect the nature of its *nominatum*.

13. See p. 133 for references to Galen.

14. V 215 (*SVF* II 895); De Lacy's translation. Cf. also V 216–18; 328.

15. 'The belief that words encode descriptive content that can be recovered by finding the words from which they are derived is the basis for Stoic etymology as it was for the etymologies proposed by Socrates in the *Cratylus*' (Allen, 2005, 14–15).

16. We shouldn't be surprised to find single letters being attributed a specific role, since this is characteristic of the *Cratylus*: '"*a*" often signifies togetherness' (405c7–8), or '"*r*" seems to me to be a tool for copying every sort of motion' (426c1–2).

17. *epicheirêmata*; cf. Aristotle *Top.* VII 11, 162a16.

18. *asplanchnos orthôs onomazomenos* (V 317).

19. Doubtless Galen would have something similar to say about the English words 'heartless' and 'big-hearted'.

20. Galen here uses the word 'correctness' to cover external correctness alone. In some passages he also uses the word 'correct' to refer to internal correctness (see for instance the passage from *Syn.Puls.* quoted on p. 138).

21. The word is '*dialektikou*'. Barnes refers to *Diff.Puls.* VIII 571 as another passage in which the word is used pejoratively. But there the full phrase in which it appears is '*tous d'ek tês dialektikês lêrous tous epitripsantas tên iatrikên*' – a pejorative reference, to be sure, to the trifles that dialecticians might engage in. But the pejorative force comes from the word '*lêrous*' not '*dialektikês*'.

22. The passage is discussed by Hankinson (1994a, 174); Barnes (1991, 75, noting its possible Epicurean origin, 1997, 20).

23. *exapatasthai* – cf. *Crat.* 436b3; 11.

24. *Exapatômenos estin hote tois onomasin* – the same verb as at *Crat.* 436b3; 11.

25. It literally refers to a type of stringed instrument.

26. Galen notes that '*sunochos*' is not a normal word of Greek – cf. also *De Nat.Hom.* XV 172–3, where once again Galen points out that it is a

word used by the more recent doctors, and not by older doctors such as Hippocrates.

27. Cf. the discussion of the same problem in *Med.Nam.*, where Galen says that either name will do – the important thing is to look at the nature of the fever, not the name (14.11–23).

28. Translation from Hankinson (1991b).

29. Cf. Barnes (1997, 24, n. 37) for more references.

30. Cf. von Staden (1995b, 499–500).

31. Hankinson's nice phrase (1994a, 173).

32. See Barnes (1997, 25–7), for examples such as the Greek word for dog (*kuôn*), and – a somewhat different case, and a favourite of Galen's – 'hot'.

33. The emphasis on agreement as an important part of language comes from the *Cratylus* again: cf. 435c1.

34. See Hankinson (1994a, 171, n. 16).

35. Cf. Barnes (1997, 15).

36. On this, see Barnes (1997, 13–16).

37. On 'atticizing', see Swain (1996, 56–63); Herbst (1911).

38. *Alim.Fac.* VI 584 (trans. Powell).

39. Cf. von Staden (1995b, 504 n. 15).

40. Cf. Barnes (1997, 12).

41. Of course, strictly speaking, the doctors are not applying the word 'fast' *to* a period of rest; rather, they are applying it to an episode of breathing *on the basis of* the shortness of periods of rest between inhalations and exhalations.

42. Cf. von Staden (1995b, 501–13).

43. Cf. Barnes (1997, 13).

6 Epistemology

If there's one thing that Galen thinks he knows, it is that human beings are capable of knowing things. Indeed, if they are intelligent, industrious and uncorrupted by base physical desires, then they are capable of knowing quite a lot. On the other hand, there are inherent limitations to what human beings can know; and speculative philosophy has tended to over-estimate its ability to discover truth, or even plausibility, in its more abstruse reaches. Galen, then, is no sceptic; indeed, his contempt for scepticism is boundless. But nor is he a hopeless epistemological optimist either. If human knowledge has its scope, it also has its limits. But those limits are broad enough to allow the diligent doctor room to discover, and establish, all that he needs to know.

THE FOUNDATIONS OF KNOWLEDGE

It was not always so, however. Galen benefited from a varied education with a variety of teachers, both philosophical and medical.[1] As a result, he was early introduced to the ubiquity and the virulence of the disputes between both doctors and philosophers, disputes which seemed to hold out no hope of rational, non-partisan resolution. Things were particularly bad in logic:

I applied myself to all the best-reputed Stoic and Peripatetic philosophers of the time; but while I learned many pieces of logical theory from them which in the fullness of time I found to be quite useless for establishing proofs, there were very few that they had researched in any useful manner likely to lead them to the goal set before them. I found too that these pieces of logical theory were in conflict with one another, and indeed sometimes opposed to our natural conceptions (*phusikai ennoiai*); and, by God, indeed as far as these teachers were concerned, I might even have fallen into a Pyrrhonian impasse (*aporia*) myself, if I had not clung firmly to the facts of geometry, arithmetic and calculation. (*On My Own Books* [*Lib.Prop.*] XIX 39–40, = SM 2, 116,12–23: trans. after Singer, 1997)

Certainty, it seemed, was available in the mathematical arts, both pure and applied. Galen talks of the conviction to be found in eclipse-predictions, and in such matters as the construction of water clocks: the accuracy of the mathematical theory applied receives direct and incontrovertible confirmation from the success of its outcomes (*ibid.*, 40, = 116,26–117,2). As a result of this he decided to concentrate on the 'linear demonstrations' of the geometers, since even the squabbling schools agreed as to their incontrovertibility (40–1, = 117,3–16). His practical concerns in all of this are evident: logical theory for its own sake is a pointless waste of time. Logic matters only insofar as it delivers useful demonstrative results.[2] But that it can do so, if properly cultivated, is for Galen an article of faith: it is only idleness, incompetence, greed, and a thirst for easy fame that makes the practitioners of his day for the most part so hopeless.

But if useful knowledge is to be won, then we (or, at any rate, the better among us) must be capable of coming to know things. Are we? And if so how? And how are we to know that we can? These questions matter. For Galen not only rejects 'rustic Pyrrhonism';[3] he also seeks to refute it – or, at any rate, to laugh it out of court. He bridles at any suggestion that the senses, subject to certain provisos, might not be criteria;[4] and indeed what is clearly evident (*enargôs phainomenon*) to the senses is the starting-point of all physical inquiry:

We should first discuss what is actually hot, cold, dry and wet . . . The identification of which is something accessible to everyone, since our sense of touch is naturally able to make these distinctions, teaching us that fire is hot and ice cold. If anyone has a conception of hot and cold derived from some other source, I should be glad to know of it. It is a very strange kind of wisdom – in fact if truth be told a stupidity – when people claim some other criterion of perceptible fact prior to that of perception. (*Temp.* I 588, = 50,9–21 Helmreich; trans. after Singer)

It is simply pointless sophistry to take issue with that, and to suppose that there should be some logical investigation of the truth of perceptible facts. Galen cites Anaxagoras' dictum, cited by Sceptics, that snow is really dark, since it is frozen water and water is dark, as an example of such 'Pyrrhonian idiocy'; and sarcastically wonders why we should stop with snow: why not question the colour of ravens and swans (*ibid.* 589, = 50,25–51,10)?

In fact, there are 'two proper starting-points for proof: things evident to the intellect and those to perception' (*ibid.* 590, 51,14–15). At *On the Therapeutic Method* (*MM*) X 36–7, Galen ascribes this distinction to 'the ancient philosophers',[5] who

> said that there were two classes of evident things, one of which . . . is discerned by the senses, such as pale and dark, hard and soft, hot and cold, and the like; the other being that subclass of things grasped by the intellect on their first appearance and which are indemonstrable, such as for example that two quantities equal to a given quantity are equal to each other, and that equals when added to equals yield equals, and that when equals are subtracted from equals the remainders are equal. And they say that 'nothing occurs without a cause' is of this type, as is 'everything comes to be from something existent', and that nothing comes to be from the absolutely non-existent, and equally that nothing is annihilated into the absolutely non-existent, and that it is necessary of everything that it be either affirmed or denied,[6]

along with much else, all of which Galen discussed at length in his early (and now lost) treatise *On demonstration.*[7] This second class of undeniable truths is something of a mixed bag, ranging from mathematical truths to propositions in metaphysics to logical laws; but they share the feature of being, at any rate in Galen's view, undeniable *a priori* truths; at *MM* X 49–50, he describes 'nothing occurs without a cause' as 'an indemonstrable axiom, agreed by all because it is plain to the intellect'. Scepticism about such things reveals either ignorance or perversity or both; and as such is not worth taking seriously.

But Galen is also perfectly well aware that no empirical science (indeed, no empirical knowledge of any kind) can rest solely on such foundations, no matter how unimpeachable they may be, which is of course why he insists on the incontrovertibility of certain kinds of perceptually based proposition as well. In the final book of *On the Doctrines of Hippocrates and Plato* (*PHP*), Galen considers the question of how we should go about distinguishing similar but non-identical things from one another. The issue is quite general, and one which Galen considers to be of enormous importance in several different ways. One way in which Sophistical medical theorists can bamboozle the unwary is by taking advantage of barely discernible ambiguities; equally, the unwary may be misled into confusing two distinct but barely discernible sets of symptoms (and hence issuing the wrong diagnosis and prescription); and in general, we may misidentify objects that actually belong to one class by supposing that they fall into a different, superficially similar one. So in certain cases, the appropriate degree of perceptual and intellectual discrimination may be hard to come by. But it is (at least in the case of objects that are readily observable) rarely impossible. And by starting on the basis of such initial successful discriminations, the diligent inquirer can proceed, by way of methodical further investigation, to construct an ever-more complete and better-founded picture of reality. This is just what it is, for Galen, to proceed methodically rather than haphazardly.[8] He puts the point generally as follows:

If we have no natural criterion, we will not be able to find a scientific criterion either; but if we possess natural criteria, we will be able to find some scientific criterion as well. Do we possess any natural criteria common to all men? – For we must not call things 'natural' if they are not common to all; indeed what is natural must not only be common to all, but also have a common nature. – I say you all do have natural criteria, and in saying this I am merely reminding you rather than teaching or demonstrating or making an assertion on my own authority. What are these criteria? Eyes in their natural state seeing what is visible; ears in their natural state hearing what is audible; the tongue sensing flavours, the nostrils odours, the whole skin objects of touch; and besides, thought or mind or whatever you wish to call it, by which we distinguish entailment and incompatibility and other things that pertain to them, such as division and collection, similarity and dissimilarity. (PHP V 722–3, = CMG V 4,1,2, 542,7–19 De Lacy; trans. after De Lacy)

Again Galen emphasizes that there are two distinct routes to criterial self-evidence: the senses and the mind. And working in concert, they can yield secure science. Or so Galen fervently believes. Moreover, if they would only look clearly and dispassionately and carefully at the issue, with eyes unblinded by sectarian controversy and partisan commitment, all men of good sense and good will would realize this. The last passage hints at another ubiquitous theme in Galen's writing – distaste for terminological disputes, and disdain for terminological niceties. This is borne out in a particularly striking manner in another passage later in the same book:

The judgement of these things is reduced to an impression (*phantasia*) which, as the philosophers from the New Academy say, is not only 'persua-sive' (*pithanê*), but 'tested' (*periôdeumenê*) and 'unshaken' (*aperispastos*); or which as Chrysippus and his followers put it is apprehensive (*kataléptikê*); or as all men believe in common, it is reduced to evident (*enargês*) perception (*aisthêsis*) and intellection (*noêsis*). These expressions are thought to differ in meaning from one another, but if one examines them more carefully they have the same import; just as, indeed, when someone says that they begin from common notions (*koinai ennoiai*),[9] and set them up as the primary cri-teria of all things which is trustworthy in itself (*ex heautou piston*). That the first criterion must be trustworthy without proof is admitted by everyone, although not everyone supposes that it must be natural and common to all men. (*PHP* V 778, = 586,16–25)

What Galen is apparently saying is that the disputes between the Stoics and the sceptical Academy of Carneades are simply matters of terminology; and while it is a commonplace in Galen (indeed, in phi-losophy in general) that many apparently substantial disagreements can be diagnosed as trading on simple terminological confusions, this is an extremely strong claim to make. After all, the Stoics and Academics fought for about 200 years over the issue – were they sim-ply quarrelling over words?[10] I shall not follow that issue in detail here, although it does seem to me that as far as the pragmatics of the matter are concerned, Galen has a reasonable case;[11] and Galen is concerned only with the pragmatics (this is precisely why he rejects as useless speculative philosophy: see further, pp. 178–80 and ch. 8, pp. 233–6). His more general point mirrors that of earlier passages: only if we can be sure of our foundational beliefs can what we build upon them be secure. So the story now is this: items of knowledge are divided into two general classes, those which are fundamental and those which are derivative, while the former class is itself bifurcated into truths self-evident to reason and those self-evident to the senses:

To achieve a precise discrimination of likes and unlikes one must begin the investigation from the natural criteria, which are sense perception and thought, and the latter as I have said many times . . . you may call intellect, mind, reason or whatever you like . . . We agree to whatever name anyone wants to call it, lest a side-issue overwhelm the main task . . . It is ridiculous to quarrel about names. (*PHP* V 724–5, = 542,27–544,7)

As he puts it: 'nature gave us a double gift: the criteria themselves and untaught trust in them' (725, 544,1–12); and this 'untaught trust' is common to animals, too.[12] Here, as elsewhere, Galen gestures towards a favourite Hippocratic maxim. In *On Affected Parts* (*Loc.Aff.*) VIII 442–4, Galen tells of how once, when dissecting a pregnant goat, he discovered a fully-formed foetus within the womb, and immediately removed it and separated it from the mother. He then placed various bowls in front of it containing wine, honey, oil, milk and various other things. He recalls how the goat first got to its feet 'as if it knew they were for walking', licked itself dry of amniotic fluid, scratched an itch on its side with a hoof, and then finally, having sniffed all the bowls, chose the milk, causing the assembled learned company spontaneously to quote Hippocrates: 'the natures of everything are untaught' (*Nutrition* 39).

THE REFUTATION OF SCEPTICISM

This emphasis on the adaptiveness of animals' instincts forms part of Galen's rejection of scepticism; but it also takes a more argumentative form. The following excerpt is taken from *On the Best Method of Teaching* (*Opt.Doct.*), his attack on the Academic scepticism of Favorinus:[13]

It is plainly evident to us that there is something securely known[14] even if the sophists try their hardest to make it untrustworthy, saying that there is no natural criterion: for the compass describes a circle, while the ruler distinguishes lengths and the balance weights.[15] Man has created these things on the basis of natural organs and criteria, beyond which we have no more venerable and honourable criterion. So if we must begin from there – for mind tells us once again that while we may believe or disbelieve our natural criterion, we cannot judge it by means of something else: for how could this thing, by which everything else is judged, be judged by something else? – will you wish to place your trust in eyes which are seeing clearly and a tongue which is tasting as to the fact that this is an apple and that a fig? If you don't, I will suffer what you want to do to us [?]; but if you do want to dispute <with me, then I am ready to do so provided that you do place your trust in them>;[16] but if you don't, then I will simply leave, since you are not in a natural condition. (*Opt.Doct.* I 48–9, = *CMG* V 1,1, 102,10–104,2)

Here we have argument (albeit flavoured with abuse), as opposed to mere assertion. For what could be better grounded than the natural criteria themselves? We can perhaps doubt them; but there is nothing by which they can be *judged*, since they are themselves the source of all judgment. This has a certain Moorean quality to it: no argument *against* the senses could be better grounded than the sensory deliverances it seeks to undermine. Moreover, the sceptic here undercuts his own right to be taken seriously as an interlocutor. And Galen also gestures towards another influential anti-sceptical argument, to be found in Cicero (*Academica* 2.22): there are evidently successful productive and practical arts (*technai*) which take their starting-point from facts evident to perception; but if perception were generally misleading, there would be no way to explain their success (cf. *PHP* V 725–6, = 544,17–21). The same thing applies in the case of scientific demonstrations:

If they [sc. sceptics] overturn what is plainly apparent through the senses, they will have no place from which to begin their demonstrations. And if they begin from premisses which carry conviction (*pista*), how can they reasonably disbelieve them later, given that the starting-points (*archai*) of demonstrations carry more conviction than the things demonstrated, which require the credibility derived from other premisses? The *archai* of demonstrations are not only convincing in regard to themselves, but also in relation to the discovery of what is sought. (*On the Powers [and Mixtures] of Simple Drugs [SMT]* XI 462)

And elsewhere, Galen is similarly dismissive of standard sceptical arguments (cf. e.g. Sextus Empiricus, *Outlines of Pyrrhonism* [PH] 1.104) which trade on the phenomena of dreaming and delusion:

there are some things which we think we see, hear, or in general perceive, such as in dreams or delusions, while there are other things which we not only think we see or in general perceive but actually do so; and in the case of the second class everybody other than the Academics and Pyrrhonists, thinks that they have arrived at secure knowledge, while they consider everything of which the soul produces images while asleep or delirious to be false. (*Opt.Doct.* I 42, = 94,14–18)

Galen here suggests not only that waking experiences are in general veridical, but also that they can be known to be so from the inside. This is of a piece with his robust remarks about the reliability of perceptual evidence in the case of apples and figs (*Opt.Doct.* I 49, quoted above). Thus, in the case of perceptually based beliefs, Galen's stance is apparently two-fold: first, he denies that there can be any argument sufficiently strong to discredit sense-perception in general; but secondly he holds that everyone as a matter of fact relies upon it, and reasonably so.[17]

This evident fact renders scepticism at best inert. In the course of a long passage on which he discusses how the sense of touch can be trained to make fine distinctions between various pulses (*Diagnosis by Pulses* [*Dig.Puls.*] VIII 776–806), Galen takes Empiricist doctors to task for claiming that all they can feel is the impact of the pulse on the finger, not the expansion of the artery, since the latter is 'non-apparent' (*Dig.Puls.* VIII 776); Galen objects that they should at least allow, in conformity with their general practice (or at any rate with Pyrrhonian general practice), that it *appears* that the artery expands, even if they refuse to say whether it does so as to its nature (780–2).[18] But then, Galen says, let us grant them this; let us allow that we don't know whether anything exists by nature: the sun, moon, land, sea, nor if we are really awake, or thinking, or even alive. All they have to do is to say whether they are also at a loss regarding the ordinary practices of everyday life,

And when the sun appears clearly to have risen we should not do what we habitually do, but lie around in bed, being unsure as to whether it is night or day; or when finding ourselves at sea in a ship, not act accordingly, but, not believing it, dare to walk into the sea, since perhaps it is the sea but perhaps it isn't; or when we arrive in the harbour and see everyone disembarking, not trust in our senses for practical purposes, but rather remain on shipboard inquiring and doubting and saying that while it appears to be land perhaps it isn't really. But according to what they themselves say, they do treat all of these things as trustworthy at least for practical purposes, and are in doubt only as to their real natures. But that is just what we do too, relying on these things as trustworthy; what goes behind practical purposes is superfluous. So if they allow us this, I don't see what any further dispute could be about. 'About the nature of things', they say. All right then: we will say no more about that if you wish … since I see that you yourselves set great store by not subverting anything which is accepted by all in the course of ordinary life.[19] So let us do just what you do in practical matters, and make no fuss about anything which is clearly apparent, but immediately trust and follow it; suppose someone announces that after the rain came, the river was swollen and destroyed the bridge: if one of you balks at saying it simply like that, 'after the rain came', preferring 'when it appeared to have come', and not the river, but the apparent and seeming river, and not having been swollen, but seeming to have been swollen, and not that the bridge was swept away, but that it appeared to be swept away, how could he not appear to be crazy? (*Dig.Puls.* VIII 782–4)

Galen's language is pointedly ironic (note that last 'appear'); but his basic point is clear enough. Reformulating everything in the sceptically appropriate garb of appearances is simply pointless wordplay unless it has some practical effect on behaviour (see n. 19); but if it does, it will render ordinary life completely impossible. Scepticism is either trivial or practically disastrous. Either way, it can be ignored.

DEMONSTRATION AND THE LOGICAL METHODS

So there can be no good reason for global distrust in the senses; and all reasonable belief about empirical matters is founded upon them. But for all that, reasonable belief, let alone knowledge, is not always easily to be won. The basic reason for this, in Galen's view, is that properly founded understanding requires a systematic and exhaustive application of rational methods to the materials supplied by the senses, in order to yield robust, explanatory accounts, which in turn need to be tested by further experience in order to confirm the reliability of the theoretical substructure. And all of this requires effort, diligence, ability and commitment, a combination of qualities which is, in Galen's view, in distressingly short supply. A constant theme of his writings is that of the shortcomings, moral and intellectual, of his medical opponents;[20] they are concerned with fame and fortune rather than the truth, and are prepared to cheat and dupe their way to achieve it. Crucially, they fail to understand the 'logical methods' by which empirical information is to be synthesized and properly demonstrative knowledge established. And it is indeed important for Galen that medical knowledge, of both a theoretical and a practical kind, is capable of being exhibited in demonstrative form – that is, as a deductive inference of a secure conclusion from properly founded first principles.

Which prompts the obvious questions: How are such principles to be established, particularly in an empirical science? And what is the warrant for their foundation? We know that we must start from the evidence of the senses; but that on its own is unsystematic. Moreover, even though it is possible to build up useful empirical generalizations on the basis of repeated experience, in the manner of the Empiricist doctors,[21] this is not enough to secure medical science in its fullest sense. Rather, proper science requires a causal understanding of the reasons why certain therapies should be expected to work in certain conditions (and not merely a determination that they do), and this depends upon a causal understanding of the basic facts of physics and physiology.[22] From starting-points which are (or at least ought to be) evident to anyone who bothers to look (the facts which are evident to perception), the scientist needs to be able to generate the firm, axiomatic foundations of the science:

The Empiricists are right when they assert that there is for them no necessary order, either of discovery or of instruction: experience is unsystematic and irrational, and requires good fortune to arrive at the discovery of what was sought. On the other hand, those who make reason and order the mothers of invention, and who hold that there is only one road that leads to the goal, must proceed from something agreed by everybody, and proceed from there to the discovery of the rest. None the less, most of them fail to do this, but rather adopt disputed starting points (*archai*) and instead of first demonstrating them and then proceeding to discover the rest according to the same method, they lay down the law in place of demonstration. (*MM* X 31–2)

This is a typical Galenic complaint: his (non-Empiricist) opponents pretend to argue methodically, but in fact fail to do so, simply begging the question in favour of their own views. Essentially, Galen holds that it is possible to work backwards, as it were, from relatively low-level empirical observations and generalizations to the discovery of the fundamental facts about the world in virtue of which those generalizations are true: and it is here that he invokes the geometrical method of analysis.[23] He gives an example, of showing that the area of a right triangle of base 12 and height 5 is 30: you start from

two propositions: the first states that the area enclosed by sides of 12 and 5 is 60, the second ... that the triangle is half of the given area. Each of these needs to be proved on the basis of further premises, which are themselves based on others still, until we arrive at the primary ones which derive their justification neither from others by way of demonstration, but from themselves. It is the same, in my view, with everything demonstrated by medical science: all must be reduced to certain primary indemonstrable propositions which are self-justifying. (*MM* X 33–4)

In the case of geometry, these will be stipulative (yet self-evident) definitions, plus *a priori* axioms such as those mentioned above. But how is the method to be applied in the case of an empirical science? First, Galen says, we should start with the common conceptions, as laid down in *On demonstration*: these are the agreed starting-points. In the case of therapeutics, one crucial common conception is that of illness as being an impairment to any one of the body's natural activities and functions (*MM* X 40–2:[24] another 'starting point agreed by all' is that 'it is the business of the therapeutic method to restore health in bodies that are diseased'). Then we need to determine what those activities and functions are, which is sometimes a matter of self-evidence, as for instance in the case of the eye that its function is to see (*MM* X 43), but sometimes a matter for detailed investigation.[25] Next one must isolate the physiological basis for the activity, and hence for any impediment to it; and thus infer the cause of the impediment. And this will involve both the deliverances of element-theory,[26] and the application of an *a priori* principle, 'an indemonstrable axiom, agreed by all because it is plain to the intellect: . . . nothing occurs without a cause' (*MM* X 50). So, if the impediment is caused, e.g., by an excess of heat and moisture, then it will be treated by cooling and drying remedies (cf. e.g. *MM* X 103–4); and this latter in virtue of another *a priori* principle, owed to Hippocrates, that 'opposites cure opposites' (*MM* X 178, 650, 739, etc.).

Evidently, definitions play an important role in this. 'We derive our interpretations of terms from ordinary Greek usage', he says; 'however discoveries, investigations, and demonstrations of the actual substance of the matter are not drawn from the opinions of the masses, but from scientific hypotheses' (*MM* X 42). The lexical meanings of terms in ordinary language are the point of departure: but what is required is a real definition of the essence of what it is that such terms refer to: 'in every inquiry into something, it is necessary to replace its name with a definition.' The importance of such definitions is stressed in *Thrasybulus: Whether healthiness is a branch of medicine or gymnastics* (*Thras.*) V 806–9, as is their

relation to ordinary conceptions: 'the starting point of our investigation must be an understanding of its subject; and this understanding
is of two kinds: we may merely have a conception of the thing, or
we may know its actual nature' (V 806–7, = SM 3, 33,7–11). In *Art
of Medicine* (*Ars Med.*), he writes:

> Everything that arises from the unpacking of the definition is easily suffi-
> ciently memorable, since the salient points of the whole subject (*technê*)
> are contained within the best definition, which some label 'substantial'
> (*ousiôdês*), distinguishing it from those called 'conceptual'; the latter are
> constructed from incidental features of the things defined, but the former
> from their actual substance (*ousia*). (*Ars Med.* I 306, = 275,8–15 Boudon)

The brevity and memorability of the former make them useful for
instruction; but they are no substitute for the latter as far as real
knowledge is concerned (*Differences of Pulses* [*Diff.Puls.*] VIII 717–
19; cf. 709–10). Moreover, this process, the isolation of the proper
definitional structure of things, will be expedited by the method of
division, as practised by Plato and Aristotle:

> We must first accurately define what disease, affection, and symptom are,
> and to distinguish the ways in which they both resemble and are different
> from one another, and then to try and cut them into their proper *differentiae*
> according to the method the philosophers have taught us. (*MM* X 27; cf. 20–7)

Accurate division will bring to light the proper articulation of the
subject-matter, as well as exposing fallacies of equivocation; and
this is just as true in medicine as it is elsewhere: Galen singles out
the fourth-century doctor Mnesitheus for particular skill in division
(*Therapeutics to Glaucon* [*MMG*] XI 3; cf. *Against Lycus* [*Adv.Lyc.*]
XVIIIA 209).[27]

This process is not, for Galen, an inductive one: we do not simply
infer general truths on the basis of a suitably long run of empirical
concatenations. Rather we infer, 'indicatively' as he puts it, to the
hidden hearts of things. Indeed, Galen regularly denigrates induction as a scientific tool: at *Thras.* V 812, = SM 3, 37,20–2, he writes:
'we have shown in *On demonstration* that inductions (*epagôgai*) are
useless for scientific demonstrations'; while at *On Semen* (*Sem.*) IV
581, = *CMG* V 3,1, 132,21–2, he remarks: 'where we cannot establish a scientific demonstration by induction, we can hardly do so by
way of examples.' A similar rejection of 'argument' from induction

and example is to be found at *SMT* XI 469–83, where Galen rejects the attempts of 'Sophists' to infer, for instance, that olive oil has a cold disposition because it is thick like phlegm (which is cold): you might as well say that it is hot because it is thick like birdlime (cf. *SMT* XI 459–61, quoted below); and analogical argument is just as demonstratively useless (*Thras.* V 812–13, = *SM* 3, 37,20–6).[28]

But the upshot is that evident facts of perception, suitably rationally organized and aided by evident *a priori* truths, will allow us to determine the proper structure of things, in virtue of which they exhibit the symptomatic behaviour that they do; and this, in concert with further *a priori* ratiocination directed towards making precise the therapeutic goal (just what does 'correcting the imbalance' mean in this case?), plus well-informed estimates of the *extent* to which the therapy should be administered, will enable us to infer and apply the appropriate therapy.[29]

REASON AND EXPERIENCE

But lest this seem absurdly over-optimistic (and, indeed, given the evident empirical inadequacy of Galen's physics, physiology and therapeutics, deludedly so), we need to turn to another aspect of Galen's epistemology in practice: his insistence on the need for empirical confirmation. After all, his insistence on the superiority of geometrical reasoning was founded on the fact that the rationality of the principles is subject to direct testing, both theoretically and in some cases practically. As a means of practising in the rational method, Galen advises his students to learn how to calibrate sun-dials and water-clocks. By applying geometrical theory they can produce the results; and so the efficacy of the theory is subject to direct empirical verification:[30]

When we find a demonstrative method which leads us to what we were looking for and is clearly confirmed by the facts of the matter themselves, this gives us no small test of its truth, so that we may risk applying it in cases where there is no clear confirmation. (*Pecc.Dig.* V 68, = *SM* 1, 52,23–53,6)

What is more, attention to empirical evidence will enable the theorist to avoid the more obvious pitfalls into which the 'Sophists' are prone to fall,

When, dishonouring the senses and embroiling themselves in philosophical disputes, they destroy things clearly understood along with what they
are ignorant of. And the majority of them do this in ignorance not only of
physical theory, but also of the logical methods which anyone who seeks to
demonstrate anything must employ, with the result that they understand
neither what has been correctly discovered by the physicists nor what has
been reasonably held by them to be doubtful, but in both cases frequently
dare to make contrary claims. But, by the gods, if I were to begin by saying
that there were four elements, air and earth, water and fire, and that a pale
and bright colour belonged to nothing naturally apart from light and fire, and
then . . . were to assert that all bright things were principally composed of
fire, without bothering to notice that snow and white lead and ice and innumerable other things were both very bright and very cold . . . and if I were
then to turn my back on the refutation [sc. of this position] by means of the
senses, and think it perfectly all right to turn to reason (logos) and investigate
by way of it the nature of things, setting no store whatever by unreasoned
perception, would not all reasonable people think me to be insane, in my
ignorance of where reason needs to start from? For it is from perception, I
believe, and by way of perception that we learn all of the following type of
propositions, that the sun is bright, flames orange, and coals for the most
part red. If we abandon the senses we shall have no sort of demonstration.
(On the Powers [and Mixtures] of Simple Drugs [SMT] XI 459–61)

Once again, Galen emphasizes the non-negotiability of a sound
empirical foundation for medical science; and, more importantly,
that the general propositions upon which it is founded must pass
empirical muster: if you suppose that all bright things are hot, you
will simply be in conflict with evident perceptual facts. But in order
to see this you need to make use of reason as well, to compare the
general truth with the particular items of perceptual data. Equally,
reason is involved, and critically so, in exposing and diagnosing fallacy and sophistry, which Galen defines as false statements or arguments which resemble true ones (PHP V 782, = 590,2–9; Pecc.Dig. V
72–5, = SM 1, 56,9–58,13; etc.). Indeed, reason is the faculty which all
men possess (albeit to differing degrees) of being able to distinguish
superficially similar things (e.g. PHP V 777–8, = SM 1 586,7–16; it
can still be a difficult task and beyond most people: Thras. V 877–
8, = SM 3, 85,18–21); and the process of division, accurately and
rigorously carried out, is one important way of achieving this goal
(PHP V 741–2, 743, 750, 763, 774–5, 802–5 = SM 1 556,25–7, 558,5–7,
564,2–9, 574,15–16, 584,11–20, 606,27–608,29).

But the most important feature to emerge here and elsewhere has to do with the relations between reason (*logos*) and experience (*empeiria*), or empirical testing (*peira*). The question of the role of experience in the development of medicine was central to the debates between Rationalist and Empiricist doctors, debates which Galen both reports and participates in. His early school-exercise, *On Medical Experience* (*Med.Exp.*),[31] presents an account of a disputation between an Empiricist and a Rationalist doctor based upon an actual confrontation he had witnessed as a student in Smyrna between his teacher, the Rationalist Pelops, and 'Philip the Empiricist' (*Lib.Prop.* XIX 16–17, = *SM* 2, 97,13–23). But it is clearly at least partly invented; and in any event it is supposed to characterize the competing attitudes quite generally (*Med.Exp.* 2, 87 Walzer). The Rationalist argues that experience unorganized by reason is simply too chaotic and too various to yield any useful understanding; in order to know what is relevant in a particular case, the practitioner needs a principled method of ruling out the irrelevant: but that requires theory; and we have no way of specifying how many observations are required before some supposed empirical connection acquires a significant status. Moreover, even if some useful items of information can indeed be discovered this way, much that is essential to any serious medical science cannot (*Med.Exp.* 3–7, 87–97 Walzer). The Empiricist replies that, with a sufficient body of evidence acquired either by personal observation (*autopsia*) or confirmed testimony (*historia*),[32] sufficiently robust concatenations of event-types will begin to emerge; and that in any case it is obvious that people *do* learn by experience uninformed by theory. What is more, no one can discover anything of any empirical consequence without practical experience; and in any case, experience is sufficient for discovering everything requisite to the art. Furthermore, the Rationalists disagree among themselves about what the proper theory is; and their vaunted inquiry into the causes of things is unconfirmable and in any case useless (*ibid.* 9–13, 98–110 Walzer).

Thus the Empiricists suppose, at least in their early, hard-line form, that experience, *empeiria*, suffices for all medical knowledge. *Empeiria* is a technical term of Empiricist medicine: it is 'the observation or memory of things which one has seen to happen often and in a similar way' (*Subf.Emp.* 4, 50–1 Deichgräber), a definition later expanded to allow for testimonial knowledge. But the term in this general sense goes back to Aristotle (*Metaphysics* A.1, 980b25–982a2), where he contrasts an organized empirically based competence with *technê* properly so called, which requires a knowledge of causal connections and real definitions. Indeed, the medical Empiricists of the third century BC can be seen as taking over that Aristotelian account of empirical practice, but insisting that it was sufficient for *technê*.

Rationalists, on the other hand, feel that they must talk about the natures of things – the human body in particular – in virtue of which events evolve in the way they do. They seek to infer to the particular internal states of the body as a result of which people are either healthy or sick, healthy if things are in the appropriate condition, unhealthy if they are not. Thus Galen (to this extent at least a Rationalist, although he rejects all sectarian affiliation)[33] thinks that the body and its organs exhibit mixtures of the four fundamental qualities, hot, cold, wet and dry; and that when these are in balance (for a particular organ or function) all is well; but when that balance is disturbed, the natural functions of the body are damaged, and the balance needs to be restored.[34] Most importantly, for our purposes, the properly trained physician will infer, from facts about the individual's history and regimen, as well as more general facts (age, sex, etc.), what their particular temperament ought to be; and then, on the basis of a consideration of recent pathologically relevant external circumstances (exposure to excessive heat or cold, fatigue, excesses of regimen and so on: the so-called 'antecedent causes'),[35] as well as evident signs and symptoms, he can infer the patient's current internal conditions, and their particular type and degree of imbalance, a determination which in turn yields the 'therapeutic indications' (*On Sects for Beginners [SI]* I 69–72, = SM 3, 4,17–6,26; *Med.Exp.* 29, 147–8 Walzer).[36]

Empiricists allow that external factors such as heat and cold are pathologically relevant; they form part of their 'syndromes', or collections of related empirical facts, that determine therapy. They will even consent to call them 'causes' (*Subf.Emp.* 7, 63–4 Deichgräber); but they do so with no theoretical commitments; and such 'causes' function, for the Empiricists, simply as signs, items which themselves, in suitable concatenations, yield therapeutic indications. This, however, is their great mistake, according to Galen (*MM* X 242–9); in by-passing the full Rationalist account by way of the body's

internal conditions, they compromise their abilities both to understand the nature of disease and to extend their treatments into unfamiliar areas. It is not that Empiricists cannot, up to a certain point,
be effective doctors; indeed the prescriptions of the best Rationalists and Empiricists often coincide (*SI* I 72–4, 79, = *SM* 3, 7,1–9,3,
12,5–8). But there are certain things that simply could not have been
discovered by mere repeated experience, such as the cupping-glass[37]
(*On Affected Parts* [*Loc.Aff.*] VIII 154–5), and compound drugs (*MM*
X 163–4).[38] The latter are drugs (in this case) each of whose ingredients have been seen to be effective on different people, and so the
pharmacologist reasons that, in the absence of further information
about individuals' idiosyncrasies and how these affect their efficacy,
he should mix a cocktail of all of them, thus increasing the likelihood
of successful treatment. Galen reasonably notes that the claim of the
hard-line Empiricist, that the effectiveness of the multiple drug was
just discovered by accident, is unconvincing.[39]

On the other hand, it is unclear whether the 'hard-line Empiricist'
is much more than a Galenic straw man, at any rate by Galen's own
time. Moderate Empiricists, as Galen himself acknowledges, were
happy to talk of using a sort of reasoning they call *epilogismos*, or
'reasoning in terms of what is apparent' (*SI* I 77–9, = *SM* 3, 10,19–12,4;
Subf.Emp. 7, 8, 63–4, 68–9 Deichgräber; *Med.Exp.* 24–5, 29, 135–8,
148–9 Walzer); what they reject is the Rationalist 'analogism', or
inference to unobservable theoretical hidden states.[40] Indeed, many
Empiricists went further, allowing a species of analogical reasoning, which they called 'transition to the similar', into their practice:
when faced with an unfamiliar condition, it is permissible to ask
whether it seems similar to something previously encountered, and
if it does to try the latter's therapy on it (*SI* I 68–9, = *SM* 3, 3,21–
4,17; *Subf.Emp.* 3–4, 9, 49–50, 69–74 Deichgräber),[41] although it was
a matter of (somewhat scholastic) dispute as to whether transition
formed an integral part of Empiricist practice, or simply described a
manner in which Empiricists were moved to come up with possible
therapies (*Subf.Emp.* 4, 49–50 Deichgräber). Finally, the Empiricists
allow a form of definition (or 'determination' as they prefer to call it:
Subf.Emp. 6–7, 58–65 Deichgräber), but this relies 'solely on what is
evident': that is, they correspond to Galen's 'conceptual' definitions:
for obvious reasons, Empiricists will not attempt to produce 'substantial' ones.

At all events, even if Galen finds Empiricist practice unnecessarily circumscribed, he thinks it neither unfounded nor deceitful (indeed, on occasion he will commend it over that of Dogmatists: *Loc.Aff.* VIII 142–3). The same cannot be said of his attitude to Methodism, the third of the major medical groupings. Methodism was first elaborated by Thessalus in the mid-first century AD; and it is against Thessalian Methodism that Galen, somewhat anachronistically, trains most of his fire (although contemporaries, such as Julian and Statilius Attalus, come under attack, too: *MM* X 53–8; 909–14; *Against Julian (Adv. Jul.)* XVIIIA 246–99, = *CMG* V 10,3).[42] As Galen at least presents it, Methodism pays no attention to the surrounding and antecedent circumstances of the patient's condition, but seeks to infer directly, by means of a sort of trained observation of signs, their so-called 'commonalities' (*koinotêtes*) whether the illness is 'constricted', 'relaxed', or a mixture of the two. In the first two books of *MM* (indeed intermittently throughout the rest of the work) he savages Methodism for its shortcomings, practical, methodological, epistemological, even moral. The 'commonalities' are supposed to be evident, yet Thessalus says that no one before him had recognized them, while no two Methodists agree on what they actually are; and they fail to say how they are supposed to be apparent, and whether to the senses or the intellect (*MM* X 35–8).

Moreover, Thessalus' account of the goals (*skopoi*) of medical practice is hopelessly jejune: 'the fact that a hollow wound needs filling with flesh, while a simple one needs binding together, is obvious to any layman; but no layman knows how one may find by method the medicines to fill hollow wounds and bind simple ones' (*MM* X 386). The important thing is to be able to replace these 'primary *skopoi*, which belong by nature to all men' with technical ones; and that is beyond the competence of both the lay public and Methodist doctors (387–91; cf. 158–9). In fact, Methodism is fatally compromised both by the imprecisions of its basic concepts, and the extremely vague and general form of its prescriptions; it can produce no just understanding of the complexities and idiosyncrasies of particular cases (cf. 204–11); and as a result its therapies are insufficiently sophisticated and frequently fatal (390).

That rather lengthy discursus on Galen's attitude to the rival schools may be justified for the light it throws on Galen's own epistemology, practical and theoretical. Let us remain with the issue of

curing wounds for a moment. Galen gives his first account of the
treatment for 'hollow wounds' (or ulcers) at *MM* X 173–86.[43] An
evident primary goal of medicine is to restore the affected body to
its healthy condition (this is the sort of thing that everyone, even
Methodists, can agree on), and in this case evidently that will involve
filling out the hollow lesion with flesh. In order to do that we need
to know what causes the growth of flesh (blood), and then how to
promote the maximum beneficial blood flow. But we will also need
to treat the attendant consequences of wounds (pus and other discharges) which require drying and cleansing medications, but properly proportioned in the case of the desiccating agent so as not to
interfere with the action of the blood. Thus the diagnosis and cure
involves a range of reasoning, some *a priori*, some with empirical content (173–9). By contrast, the Methodists simply invoke the 'primary
indication', that the wound should be filled, and suppose that that
alone, along with a smattering of experience, will indicate the appropriate therapy (180–2). Empiricists will rely on past syndromes; but
if this patient's idiosyncrasies are too great, they will be at a loss, and
forced either to throw the dice or rely on imprecise analogies (183–
4). Even most Rationalists, despising as they do detailed physics (cf.
170), will not know how to promote the generation of flesh, and will
be in no better case than the Empiricists (184–5).

So Galen's method involves detailed, internal knowledge of the
workings of things; and it is only with such knowledge, he thinks,
that medicine can be perfected. Not that it will ever get everything
right: there will always be imprecision and guesswork even in the
best doctor's practice. Medicine is, as Galen allows, a stochastic art,
that is to say one in which even the greatest conceivable competence will not invariably ensure a favourable outcome. But this is
not because of any imprecision in the principles themselves, but
is rather due to the difficulty in making the precise determinations
necessary for a truly accurate prescription (e.g. 181–2).[44] Galen sometimes talks of dealing with fifteen different degrees of qualitative
intensity (209–10), and while it is not clear that he endorses this,
he certainly recognizes four, which are to be determined partly by
experience and partly by reason (*SMT* XII 2–4). But in all cases, he
thinks, the appropriate procedure, both in general analysis and in the
application of it to particular cases, is to start from a conception of
what needs to be accomplished, and then to infer, on the basis of both

a priori and empirically based principles, how best to achieve it in the particular instance at hand. Such a process, properly carried out, will require a grounding in physics, the true element-theory, which is where many Rationalists fall down, and are no better (indeed, often worse) than Empiricists (*MM* X 170); equally, all of these theoretically based accounts need to be tested at the tribunal of experience, *peira*: and this is something which characteristically Rationalists fail to understand as well.

Indeed, throughout his work, Galen insists on the necessity of *logos* and *peira* working together to generate and ground the theory; and both Rationalists and Empiricists are guilty of underestimating, misunderstanding, or simply rejecting the importance of one or the other (of course, the Methodists just get it all completely wrong). First of all, *peira* confirms the deliverances of *logos*: 'none of the things I have mentioned, whether original discoveries or owed to Hippocrates, is untested and unconfirmed, but all are judged by *peira*' (*MM* X 375). In the same vein: 'I will now repeat what I'm always accustomed to say in regard to any part of medical science: reasoning (*logismos*) will discover what is sought most expeditiously, while experience (*peira*) will confirm its trustworthiness' (*On the Preservation of Health* [*San.Tu.*] VI 308, = *CMG* V 4 2, 162,16–18 Koch); and 'Experience confirms the reasoning' (*On the Thinning Diet* [*Vict.Att.*], *CMG* V 4,2, 434,7–8 Kalbfleisch). Indeed, it is *peira* which judges disputes in medicine (*On Hippocrates' 'Regimen in Acute Diseases'* [*HVA*] XV 446, 447, 451, = *CMG* V 9,1, 130,26–7, 131,13–14, 132,32, 133,9 Helmreich). In general, then, *peira* functions to verify what has already been arrived at by reason. In the case of compound drugs, *logos* discovers the appropriate composition, while *peira* tests it (*On the Composition of Drugs according to Kind* [*Comp.Med.Gen.*] XIII 376). Moreover

As I have often said, *peira* is the judge of what is plainly apparent (*enargôs phainomena*), not reason (*logos*), which anyone can plausibly twist for himself. Reason seeks and determines the explanation of what is agreed to have occurred (for it would be absurd to assign an explanation for something which had never occurred at all as if it had). . . I have frequently urged everyone to be mindful of this, particularly when things which have seemed plausible to them have turned out on examination to be false. (*On Hippocrates' 'Epidemics' VI* [*Hipp.Epid.*] XVIIB 61–2, = *CMG* V 10,2,2, 156,15–23)

And in particular cases, we need to be not only able to judge by experience whether the deliverance of the argument is true (by *peira*), but also to test the validity of the reasoning itself (and here, of course, training and native ability in logic is required):

Whether all of these things are true is to be tested partly by experience and partly by reason, by experience whether some patients are observed, in the absence of fever, either to spit up pus or to pass it in urine . . . by reason whether the explanation they have given for it is true or false. (*On Hippocrates' 'Nature of Man'* [*HNH*] XV 152, = *CMG* V 9,1, 78,8–15 Mewaldt)

In this latter case, the reasoning was faulty, while its conclusion was not confirmed by *peira*. In general, then, *peira* tests the explanations given by reason, but it does not supply them (cf., e.g., *SMT* XI 475). However, Galen will sometimes, in accordance with his own empiricist tendencies, allow *peira* a broader role, in the context of discovery as well as that of justification:

Since everything having to do with medical science is discovered and validated either through experience, through reason, or through both, let us try to confute what is erroneous, and to praise and promote what is correct, by way of both instruments. (*On Critical Days* [*Di.Dec.*] IX 841–2)

Peira is particularly useful in determining the actual properties of drugs: '*logos* teaches us the general goal of curing in the case of each illness, *peira* the properties of the material' (*On the Composition of Drugs according to Places* [*Comp.Med.Loc.*] XIII 501); and

It was shown how the general power (*dunamis*: sc. of a drug) can be discovered indicatively by a single experience (*peira*), although not any chance experience, but one which occurs in accordance with the previously mentioned qualifications. But when the general capacity has once been discovered, there is no need for any further experience regarding its particular activities, except in order to confirm what reason (*logos*) discovers. (*SMT* XII 246)

This last text is of some importance. For it suggests that in some cases a single, well-chosen empirical test will be enough to establish the nature of a drug's powers. This is the sort of 'qualified experience' Galen elsewhere refers to, a rationally determined, specific test to isolate and test for a particular property (cf. e.g. *SMT* XI 573, 685, 703, 800; XII 38; *On the Powers of Foodstuffs* [*Alim.Fac.*] VI 480, 508, = *CMG* V 4,2, 216,5, 233,2–3 [Helmreich, 1923]). This is Galen's epistemology at its most scientific, and where his notion of the role and function of *peira* is most at odds with that at least of the original Empiricists, who relied precisely on 'chance experience', the happy accident, to throw up, in a suitably long run, useful items of empirical knowledge.[45] Galen's experience is 'indicative': it shows what the underlying states must be. Obviously this characterization raises as many questions as it answers. Galen is surely too sanguine in his belief that single such experiences, no matter how well designed and carried out, can ever be conclusive; and of course the determinations of such tests are only as good as the theory which supplies the 'qualification'. I have no space to follow those thoughts further; but it is Galen's insistence on the necessity of having theory answer to experience, and in a controlled manner, that sets his scientific practice and its associated epistemology apart from those of most of the rest of his contemporaries,[46] as well as showing the way in which to integrate and synthesize the insights of both Rationalists and Empiricists into a robust and methodologically sophisticated scientific programme.[47]

CODA: THE LIMITATIONS OF KNOWLEDGE

For all that, Galen's position may still seem over-optimistic. It is certainly evident that he over-estimates the ability of empirical experience and testing to verify theories, since he falsely supposes that they have verified his own false theories. But for all that, he is certainly less epistemologically reckless than his opponents, at least as he presents them. And as Armelle Debru reminds us elsewhere in this volume (ch. 10, pp. 279–81) the image of the dogmatic, self-righteous Galen which does indeed emerge from both his own texts and from the tradition, needs to be tempered. For in spite of his apparent commitment to the view that certain theoretical knowledge of the physical and physiological world can be won by the correct and rigorous application of the method, there are many areas of philosophical speculation which he supposes to be beyond such treatment, and many questions of philosophy, cosmology and theology which can simply never be answered with any degree of certainty. These include: whether the universe was created, whether there is an extra-cosmic void, whether god is corporeal, whether the soul is (or is not) corporeal or mortal, and what its substance is (*On His Own Opinions* [*Prop.Plac.*][48] 2, 56,12–24, 3,58,22–60,6 Nutton; cf. 14–15, 110,4–18,10 Nutton). He offers a similar list in *PHP*:

That the majority of disagreements in philosophy have not been concluded is not surprising, since these issues are not susceptible of clear judgement by empirical test (*peira*); for this reason some assert that the universe is ungenerated, others that it had a beginning, just as some say there is nothing outside it enclosing it, while others say that there is, and of the latter some hold it to be void containing no substance in it while others say there are other universes uncountable in number, a multitude stretching to infinity. It is impossible to adjudicate such a disagreement on the basis of clear perception. (*PHP* V 766, = 576,27–578,2 De Lacy; cf. 779–82, 588, 7–590,11)

But this is not true in medical disputes, 'where the helpful and the harmful can be judged by *peira*' (767, = 578,3). Galen makes the same point elsewhere, with different examples: 'whether the universe is created or uncreated, finite or infinite, the number of waves in the sea: none of these questions can be settled on the basis of the evident nature of the fact investigated' (*Pecc.Dig.* V 67, = *SM* I, 52,13–18), as they can be in geometry. Galen recounts a dispute between three philosophers on such questions. The Peripatetic denies the existence of any kind of void, while holding the cosmos to be unique; the Stoic agrees that it is unique and continuous, but claims that a void exists outside it; while the Epicurean accepts both sorts of void, but asserts that the cosmos is only one of infinitely many. But these disputes are just idle, 'since I know for sure that none of them can produce true demonstrations, but only contingent and likely arguments, and sometimes not even that' (*Pecc.Dig.* V 101–2, 79,21–80,16); moreover, such disputes are evidently not susceptible of empirical decision (cf. *ibid.* 98–100, = 77,10–79,9).[49] If you could travel outside the boundaries of the cosmos you could check whether there was anything – even a void – there. But as it is you can't. Such disputes are idle, and belong to theoretical philosophy, a term perhaps already starting to develop derogatory overtones. A little later on in *PHP*, Galen remarks that such questions are irrelevant to ethics and politics: 'they contribute nothing to proper household management, or exercising proper forethought in political affairs, or treating kinsmen, citizens and foreigners with justice and kindliness.' Beginning from useful and determinable inquiries, people have insensibly drifted into useless and indeterminable ones: and it simply doesn't matter whether or not the universe had a beginning (*PHP* V 780, = 588,15–21).[50]

Here again Galen's concern with practicalities comes to the fore. It is fortunate (indeed perhaps a sign of divine providence) that we are able to acquire secure knowledge where we need to. Thus it is useful for the doctor to know the location of the soul's faculties (although it is of no import for the moral philosopher), since he will thereby be able to apply his remedies to the appropriate places (*PHP* V 779, = 586,33–588,6). But it doesn't matter what the soul actually *is* as long as you understand its functions; and the same is true with divinity. We can know that God and the soul both exist, since their activities are evident (or so Galen thinks: *Prop.Plac.* 2, 56,12–58,21 Nutton); what precisely they are, and whether they – or any parts of them – are immortal cannot be determined either by reason, or by experience, or even by the method that conjoins the two.[51] As practitioners, and as practical epistemologists, we need to know how things work; and knowing that will involve knowing a fair amount of relatively arcane (but still empirically and rationally establishable) physics. But impractical metaphysical questions can be safely left to impractical metaphysicians. Galen's epistemology is indeed that of the practising, and practical, scientist.[52]

NOTES

1. See ch. 1 (Hankinson) in this volume, pp. 3–4.
2. See ch. 3 (Tieleman) in this volume, pp. 51–2; and esp. ch. 4 (Morison) in this volume; Barnes (1993a, 1993b, 2003).
3. His regular derogatory term for extreme scepticism: at *Differences of Pulses* (*Diff.Puls.*) VIII 710–11, Galen contrasts 'Sceptics and Aporetics', who will speak only of 'their perception of the peculiar affections of touch, afraid to say something about anything external as though it existed' with 'those who are rightly called "rustic Pyrrhonists", who claim that they do not even know for certain their own experiences'. See *On whether Blood is Naturally Contained in the Arteries* (*Art.Sang.*) IV 727, = 172 Furley/Wilkie; and cf. *On Mixtures* (*Temp.*) I 589, = 51,9–120 Helmreich: 'is this not a Pyrrhonian confusion, that is to say infinite nonsense?' See also Ioppolo (1993, 193, n. 37).
4. Note here his angry reaction to Alexander of Damascus for suggesting, prior to an anatomical demonstration, that one might at least question the senses' general reliability: *On Prognosis* (*Praen.*) XIV 627–8, = 96,19–98,8 Nutton; see ch. 1 (Hankinson) in this volume, p. 12.
5. 'The ancients' (*hoi palaioi*) in both medical and philosophical contexts, is for Galen a term of commendation, contrasted with *hoi neôteroi*, the newer ones, the upstarts. In philosophy, Plato and Aristotle are

inevitably *palaioi*, as is Hippocrates in medicine; but who else gets included under which rubric depends upon the context.

6. See Hankinson (1991b).

7. For more on *On demonstration*, see Mueller (1897); Barnes (1991); and ch. 4 (Morison) in this volume.

8. See *MM* X 20–40; Hankinson (1991b); ch. 3 (Tieleman) in this volume.

9. *Koinai ennoiai* here in the Stoic sense of 'basic general concepts', as opposed to the Euclidian sense of 'general axiom' (for the difference between the former and *prolēpseis*, see Sandbach, 1930). Galen uses the term to refer to the pre-theoretical grasp of the meaning of a general term: *On the Therapeutic Method* (*MM*) X 40: see further Hankinson, (1991b). For the Peripatetic sense of *ennoia*, 'the summary of the particulars in a universal', see Sextus Empiricus, *Adversus Mathematicos* (*M*) 7 224. If there are any serious differences between these (non-Euclidian) senses, Galen seeks to elide them.

10. For the disputes between Stoics and Academics in epistemology, see Frede (1983, 1999); Hankinson (1995a, 1997a, 2003b, 2003c).

11. I make it out in Hankinson (1992a).

12. The idea that animals exhibit an innate orientation towards what is beneficial and away from what is harmful had a long philosophical history. The Stoics speak of *oikeiôsis*, an animal's natural proprioceptive awareness of its own structure and its requirements (e.g. Diogenes Laertius, *Lives of the Philosophers* 7 85–6; Seneca, *Letters* 121 6–15; Hierocles, *Ethical Outline*, col. 1 line 34–col. 2. line 9); the Epicureans locate the notion in the innate pursuit of pleasure and avoidance of pain (cf. Cicero, *On Ends*, 1 28–9). See further Brunschwig (1986).

13. For which see Ioppolo (1993); see also Hankinson (1992a).

14. Accepting the supplement of Barigazzi (1991) for Galen's evidently lacunose text: *CMG* V 1,1, 102.10.

15. This comparison of the natural criteria with the artificial or instrumental ones of the compass, etc., recalls the Epicurean notion of the criterion as a *kanôn*, or yardstick, and their characterization of epistemology as canonics (Diogenes Laertius 10 31; cf. Lucretius 4 513–21).

16. The text is very suspect here – I have followed, roughly, Barigazzi's suggestions, but I suspect more radical surgery may be needed.

17. I deal more fully with these issues in (1997a, §13).

18. For a brief discussion of this passage, see Allen (2001, 145–6).

19. The sceptics indeed do claim not to be subverters of ordinary life: cf. Sextus, *PH* 1.13, 17, 21–4. See Hankinson (1995b, chs. 17–18).

20. Cf. ch. 1 (Hankinson) in this volume, pp. 7–8, 10–11, 14.

21. On medical Empiricism, see pp. 171–5; and Edelstein (1967b); Frede (1985 Int., 1987b, 1988, 1990); Hankinson (1987b, 1995a).

22. See ch. 8 (Hankinson) and ch. 10 (Debru) both in this volume.

23. Analysis is the subject of controversy; see Robinson (1969b) and Hintikka and Remes (1974); for analysis in the case of Galen, see Hankinson (forthcoming (1)).

24. For this definition of disease, see also *Differences of Symptoms* (*Symp.Diff.*) VII 47–9; *Art of Medicine* (*Ars Med.*) I 379, = 359,13–14 Boudon (2000).

25. On the key notions of 'activity', 'power' and 'function' (or 'utility'), see ch. 8 (Hankinson) and ch. 10 (Debru) both in this volume; see also Furley and Wilkie (1984, 58–69); Hankinson (1988a).

26. See ch. 8 (Hankinson) in this volume, pp. 210–17.

27. See ch. 11 (van der Eijk) in this volume, p. 289. On Galen's deployment of the 'Logical Methods', see Barnes (1991); and ch. 3 (Tieleman) in this volume.

28. On these passages see further Hankinson (forthcoming (1)). Note also that Galen wrote treatises on *Induction* and *Example*: *Lib.Prop.* XIX 43, = *SM* 2, 119,17.

29. This is not a trivial issue for Galen, and he is well aware of the specific difficulties involved in making an accurate assessment of the degree of imbalance, and hence of the strength of the required therapy; see further Harig (1974); ch. 12 (Vogt) in this volume, pp. 309–10; every patient and every ailment is *sui generis*, and determination of their idiosyncrasies is extraordinarily difficult and plagued with imprecision: *MM* X 169, 181, 209–10.

30. He goes into this at length in *On the Diagnosis and Cure of the Errors of Soul* (*Pecc.Dig.*) V 66–88, = *SM* 1, 51,10–70,3.

31. *Med.Exp.* exists in an Arabic translation of a Syriac version of Galen's original; it is translated (apart from the fragments surviving in Greek) in Walzer (1944); this is reprinted, along with an English version of the Greek fragments, in Frede (1985), which also contains English translations of two other relevant texts: *On Sects for Beginners* (*SI*), and *Outline of Empiricism* (*Subf.Emp.*).

32. For the role of *historia* in Empiricist medicine, see *Subf.Emp.* 8, 65–9 Deichgräber; see also Frede (1987b, 249–50); Hankinson (1987b, 1995a, 68).

33. For Galen's rejection of sectarianism, see ch. 2 (Lloyd) in this volume, pp. 36–42.

34. See ch. 8 (Hankinson), pp. 219–23; and ch. 11 (van der Eijk), p. 296 both in this volume.

35. *Aitia prokatarktika*: Galen wrote a short treatise of the same name (*CP*), edited with commentary in Hankinson (1998a); for the Empiricist attitude to causes, see Hankinson (1987a); on the types of cause, see ch. 8 in this volume, pp. 229–30; Hankinson (1987a, 1987b, 1994c).

36. For more on this, see ch. 11 (van der Eijk) in this volume.
37. A device used in blood-letting.
38. See also *On the Composition of Drugs according to Kind* (*Comp. Med.Gen.*) XIII 366–7.
39. For a discussion of this issue, see Frede (1987b, 248–9).
40. These modes of inference correspond very closely to 'commemorative' and 'indicative' sign-inferences respectively, which were the source of dispute between sceptical and Dogmatic schools of philosophy: see e.g. Sextus, *PH* 2 97–133; on the issue in general, see Sedley (1982); Allen (2001). Whether the distinction arose in the philosophical or medical schools is a matter of dispute: see e.g. Ebert (2005); Pellegrin (2005).
41. On the development of Empiricism, see Frede (1987b); Hankinson (1995a).
42. For more on Methodism, and the question of the fairness of Galen's presentation of it, see Edelstein (1967a); Frede (1982); Lloyd (1983, part III); the fragments of the school are now collected in Tecusan (2004); the long passage from ps.-Galen *On the Best Sect* [*Opt.Sec.*] (I 162–223), published by Tecusan as Fr. 279, is particularly illuminating; see also ch. 2 (Lloyd) in this volume.
43. This is dealt with in Barnes (1991, 100–2).
44. Similar points are made in the spurious [*Opt.Sect.*] I 109–12; on practical imprecision, see Harig (1974); and ch. 8 (Hankinson) in this volume, pp. 221–2; on the notion of stochastic arts in antiquity, see Ierodiakonou (1995).
45. For an investigation of the notion of 'qualified experience' in Galen's pharmacology, see van der Eijk (1999a).
46. Although it bears comparison with that of his scientific near-contemporary Ptolemy: see Long (1988).
47. See Frede (1985, xxxi–xxxiv); and also Frede (1981).
48. Until recently. *Prop.Plac.* survived only in a macaronic mixture of Latin, Arabic and Hebrew, along with a few Greek fragments, edited with translation and commentary in Nutton (1999). But a recently discovered Greek manuscript of the entire work has been edited by Boudon-Millot and Pietrobelli (2005). It is probably Galen's last work.
49. I discuss these passages at greater length in Hankinson (forthcoming, (1)).
50. These issues are also dealt with in ch. 8 (Hankinson) in this volume.
51. For the case of the soul, see Hankinson (1991a, 1993, 2006 and forthcoming, (2)); Tieleman (2003); and ch. 7 (Donini) in this volume.
52. I should like to thank Lesley Dean-Jones and Jennifer Greene for several helpful suggestions.

7 Psychology

Galen does not trouble to *establish* the soul's existence;[1] rather, he simply takes it to be evident that it does,[2] and thus that man and living things are composed of a body and a soul. As far as its nature and essence are concerned, however, there appear to be waverings and differences, in particular between the two texts principally dedicated to pyschological themes: the great treatise *On the Doctrines of Hippocrates and Plato* (*PHP*),[3] which belongs to the writer's early mature period, and the late pamphlet *The Faculties of the Soul Follow the Mixtures of the Body* (*QAM*).

But it is not only this discrepancy between these major psychological works which poses problems for us. Remarks on the soul and its nature are scattered through several of his other works, and at first sight they seem to imply quite different conceptions of the soul, both in regard to its nature and concerning its relations with the body. Indeed, it has been supposed[4] that Galen's views about the soul underwent a considerable evolution over time. But the exact point from which this evolution might be thought to have begun is controversial.

It is true that in the first book of the other great work of the author's maturity, *On the Utility of the Parts* (*UP*), which is roughly contemporaneous with *PHP*, Galen apparently talks in terms quite different from those he habitually employs elsewhere, since he speaks of the body as an instrument (*organon*) which the soul makes use of,[5] which might seem starkly at odds with the other expressions he tends to use in this regard, and in particular with what he will say in *QAM*, where he posits a certain relation of dependence[6] of souls and their capacities on the temperaments (*kraseis*: mixtures) of the bodies in which they reside. But in the first place the two conceptions are not necessarily in contradiction: one can hold both that the capacities of the soul correspond in some manner to the mixtures of the primary physical constituents of the bodily organs and that the same capacities – insofar as they find expression in the body, or, better, in certain of its organs – make use in turn of the organs in order to carry out the various functions of the living thing.[7] Moreover, it seems reasonable also to keep in view the purpose and general thesis of *UP*: at the beginning of a work entirely devoted to celebrating the providential teleology which directs the constitution of living things,[8] it is perfectly understandable that Galen would have wanted to present the relationship between the soul and the body in such a way as to accentuate the subordination of the latter to the former.

Thus freed from the problem which *UP* threatened to pose for us in regard to the nature of the soul, and prescinding for the moment from the problematic conception expressed in *QAM*, we should first take note of the powerful and constant presence in Galen of declarations of agnosticism. From the time of *PHP* right up until the late work in which he gives a last accounting of his own convictions (*Prop.Plac.*), he declares over and over again that he has no knowledge of the nature (*phusis*) or of the essence (*ousia*) of the soul,[9] while contending that he does know other important facts about it, e.g. that it is tripartite (just as Hippocrates and Plato held it to be), and that there are particular bodily organs in which each of the three parts has its seat.[10] But this agnosticism sometimes assumes another somewhat peculiar form; for there are plenty of cases[11] in which Galen allows himself to say either (a) that the soul *is* the *pneuma* contained within the cerebral cavity, or (b) that this *pneuma* is the 'primary instrument' of the soul in its relations with the physical organism and its functions. In the latter case, the real nature and essence of the soul would remain unknown; yet there seem to be limits to this basic agnosticism; a solution to the problem of the soul's essence looks as though it might be available, yet it does not seem securely established, since the very item which would underwrite it (the *pneuma*, if it is in fact identical to the soul) seems to suggest another quite different account, one in which it would be merely instrumental, and which would as a result once again render the fundamental question of the soul's nature indeterminate. In any case, it is clear that in the case of the problem of the cerebral *pneuma* Galen considers option

(b) much more probable.[12] So this fundamental ignorance concerning the nature of the soul ought to persist.

This agnosticism is in fact forced upon Galen by the strict demands and stringent criteria which he lays down in order for his beliefs and those of others to attain to the level of the certainty and authority of science: the contentions that can be made regarding the soul's essence never achieve the demonstrative and scientific cogency which, according to him at least, the Hippocratic and Platonic tripartition of the parts of the soul possesses;[13] they remain, he says, confined to the domain of plausibility and likelihood, to which Plato himself had assigned them.[14] Moreover, a similar cautiousness is also evinced by the division of competences Galen establishes between the philosopher and the doctor: the problem of the soul's nature may well be of concern to the former, but it is not necessary that it be resolved by the latter; equally, and contrariwise, the question of the soul's physical location, or rather of its parts, is important for the doctor, who is called upon from time to time to treat psychic and mental disturbances, but not for the philosopher, whose primary concern is to inculcate virtue in souls as far as is possible. And one might further distinguish the tasks of the theoretical philosopher (who is the only one who can really seek to resolve the question) from those of one who concerns himself rather with the practical aspects of the discipline.[15]

The first part of the first book of *PHP* is lost, and as a result we do not know exactly how Galen introduced the thesis of the Platonic origin of the tripartition of the soul into the rational (*logistikon*: but Galen often also employs, in *PHP* and elsewhere, the Stoic term *hêgemonikon*, or ruling part), the spirited (*thumoeides*) and desiderative (*epithumêtikon*), a thesis which he also attributes to Hippocrates. In the course of the work, he treats tripartition as if it were an objectively established and indisputable fact; but towards the end of the final book, we come across an important claim:[16] Galen maintains that he has at his disposal true and appropriate scientific demonstrations in the case of the distinction between the three parts of the soul, just as he has for their physical location; moreover he believes that he can also show that Plato himself had already given them. Indeed, he appeals in this regard to book IV of the *Republic*, of which he cites and analyses certain passages.[17]

From his point of view, moreover, it is preferable at least in theory to adopt Plato's terminology[18] as well, and to talk of 'parts' (*merê* or *moria*) or 'forms' (*eidê*) of the soul, thus avoiding the usage of Aristotle and Posidonius, who spoke of its capacities or powers (*dunameis*). This preference is justified by the fact that each of the three parts has, as we shall see, its own distinct physical location, while the term 'capacity' would rather imply, in Galen's view, a radically different picture, that of a single physical substrate (for Aristotle and Posidonius, the heart) endowed with a variety of powers. For all that, Galen may still perfectly well continue to speak of psychic *dunameis*. But he can talk in this way of the diverse capacities which he attributes to each of the three parts of the soul, thus employing the notion of *dunamis* to refer in his usual manner to the particular cause which one posits to account for a specific activity exemplified by a subject, and not, conversely, as so many philosophers are wrongly (in Galen's view) inclined to, in order to talk of faculties 'as if they were particular things which inhabit substances'.[19] Thus one says, for example, that the aloe plant has one capacity which is purgative, another which is tonic, another which promotes healing, and so on, without in any way implying that it is something over and above the aloe which is the basis for these functions; and in just the same way one may say that the rational part of the soul has one faculty of sensation, another of memory, another of intelligence and so on.

As far as the assignment of the three parts to one physical location, i.e. to a specific organ, is concerned, there were certainly available to Galen sources which he could make use of; but even so he had to take up a position in the lively controversy, which had been going on for some time at this point,[20] in regard to the seat of the rational part in particular: this was the dispute between those who held that it was located in the heart and those who placed it in the region of the brain. This dispute had also left clear traces of itself in the doxographical tradition, some aspects of which must have been well known to Galen.[21] The Stoics' choice of the heart as the seat of their unified directing part, and the persistent fidelity of the Aristotelians to their master's cardiocentric thesis,[22] made the question even more pressing for someone like Galen, who was on his own account inclined towards the Platonic theory, but yet was also heavily indebted to Aristotle, at least in regard to his scientific methodology and his logical and demonstrative procedures.[23]

Galen thus maintains that the Platonic location of the three parts in three distinct organs (the rational part in the brain, spirited part in the heart and desiderative part in the liver), which is in his view the right one, had already been anticipated by Hippocrates. As for the Platonic sources, he discovers them in particular in the *Timaeus*,[24] albeit in a somewhat forced manner, since in reality Plato is reasonably explicit only in regard to the seat of the rational part; in contrast, as far as the other two parts are concerned, he confines himself to expressions which indicate only in a general sort of way the regions of the thorax and stomach.[25] Still, Galen's contention, at least as far as Plato is concerned, remains substantially reasonable. Rather more delicate is the case of Hippocrates, particularly in relation to the thorniest question, namely that of the seat of the rational part. For the other two parts of the soul, indeed, Galen can adduce some textual evidence from the Hippocratic corpus;[26] for the rational part, at least insofar as what we still possess of *PHP* is concerned, on the other hand, he makes no use of the (admittedly few) Hippocratic passages which he could have adduced.[27] One might perhaps suppose that he referred to them in the initial part of the first book, which is now lost; but it is none the less significant that the accord between Plato and Hippocrates regarding the cerebral location of the rational part had already been noted in the doxographical tradition, with which we have reason to believe Galen was reasonably well acquainted.[28]

The agreement between Hippocrates and Plato is thus established at the minimum in regard to the main point of their doctrine, the one which (one might reasonably say) it was most important for Galen to defend. Here indeed one must bear in mind that, because of the loss of the first part of the first book (amounting, one might estimate, to roughly two-thirds of its total length), it is not easy today to determine precisely the task which Galen set himself at the outset, whether it was to examine all the verifiable cases of agreement between his two great authorities, or to limit himself only to the most important ones. In the course of the argument of the books which do survive, however, Galen several times[29] summarizes the contents of the earlier parts of the work, and sometimes hints at its initial scope; from these hints one may conclude with some certainty at least that in each case he considered the questions concerning the parts of the soul and its physical location to be the most important, and to which the other specific questions would have had to be referred.[30] The expositional structure of *PHP* is further complicated by a change in the original plan which the author himself reveals as such;[31] the upshot of all of this, however, is a long treatise in which the question of the location of the three parts of the soul in the physical organism remains fundamental, and to which the themes introduced by the change of plan (essentially the problem of the passions and the long polemic against Chrysippus which occupies books III and IV and a part of book V) are also relatively clearly related.

Moreover, if agreement between Hippocrates and Plato cannot always be established, Galen can account for this in terms of the philosopher's limited experience or lack of information in matters which are of greater relevance to the doctor.[32] Galen also relies upon a similar explanation in the delicate case of Aristotle, whose status as the inventor and guarantor of the scientifically demonstrative method[33] he needs at the very least to honour, but whose capital error of having located the rational part (and, furthermore, the other faculties of the soul too) in the heart he must also account for: Aristotle reasons correctly, but at a certain point makes a false assumption on account of his incomplete knowledge of anatomy, in particular his failure to recognize that the origin of the nerves lies in the brain.[34] The list of authorities Galen uses in *PHP* would not be complete without mention of the Stoic Posidonius, who is regularly called upon to play a hostile role in the polemic against Chrysippus; it is a matter of considerable importance for Galen to be able to show that even in the enemy camp of the Stoics there was someone who was able to see through and to correct the theses (which Galen thinks absurd) of the master of the school.

So behind the theory of *PHP* there lies the not inconsiderable backdrop of the great medical and philosophical authorities of the past, thus exhibiting in this book a perfectly general characteristic of all the author's work. As has been well said,[35] Galen demonstrates 'an independence of mind within the limits of tradition, a somewhat backward-looking rather than a forward-looking independence, which tends to choose among the old rather than to create the new'. At any rate it would be mistaken and unjust to suppose that Galen upholds the tripartition of the soul only, or even mainly, because he discovers it in Plato and Hippocrates; he accepts the teachings of the great men of old because he believes them to be true, and judges them to be so when he thinks them to have been scientifically demonstrated. The attempt to provide a scientific demonstration of the truth of tripartition and of the distribution of the three parts

among the corresponding organs is in fact Galen's principal undertaking in *PHP*, and much more important than the actual content of
the psychological theory he upholds is the method with which it is
established.

This method purports to be simply an application of that which
Galen himself had laid out theoretically in his great work *On demonstration*, which has not come down to us, but to which he refers in
PHP on many occasions.[36] Quoting one of these passages may perhaps help to illustrate the typical procedure of *PHP* better than any
commentary: this is the passage which is to be found near the beginning of book II, in which Galen introduces his critical discussion of
the arguments adopted by the Stoics in favour of the heart as the seat
of the principal (namely the rational) part of the soul.[37] In book II of
PHP, Galen writes:

But what premises should one seek which are relevant and appropriate to
the matter in question? These have also been discussed at length in the works
on demonstration,[38] both by the ancients in a somewhat obscure and concise
manner and by myself when I expounded their writings clearly and fully. For
the moment it will be enough to recall from all of that only the main point,
making use of it as a guide for finding (premises) in particular cases. The
main point was that relevant and appropriate premises ought to be found in
the very essence of the thing which is the object of the investigation: so in
this particular case, in which Chrysippus is discussing the ruling part of the
soul, we ought to give the definition of the object of the investigation and
then make use of it as a standard and as a guide in all the particular cases.
The governing part (as even the Stoics themselves concede) is the source of
sensation and volition.[39] Therefore the demonstration that the heart contains within itself the ruling part should not begin from any premiss other
than this, namely that it is this that initiates every voluntary movement
in every other [part of the] animal, and that each sensation is referred to it.
Where will the proof of all of this come from? Where else other than from
dissections? Indeed, if the heart distributes to every part the capacity of sensation along with that of movement, there must be some vessel which has its
origin in it in order to render them this service. So it has become clear from
the demonstrative method that it would be more useful to dissect animals
and to observe what sorts and how many kinds of physical structure have
their origin in the heart and ramify to the other parts of the animal; and to
observe, given that there are these types and this number of these structures,
that one of them transmits sensation or movement or both, while another
does something else; and in this way one will discover which capacities of

animals have their source in the heart. Whatever falls outside this course is superfluous and irrelevant to the question; and in this way a scientific premiss of a demonstration is distinguished from a rhetorical one, one useful for training,[40] or even a sophistical one. But not even in the case of these sorts of premiss have Zeno and Chrysippus taught us a method or a form of training. (*PHP* V 219–20, = *CMG* V 4,1,2, 108,21–110,19)

Thus dissection can make evident to the senses[41] what would otherwise remain hidden both to them and to the mind; and Galen refers to observations, and especially to anatomical experiments, which can prove with absolute and immediate clarity that the vessels which originate in the heart have nothing whatever to do with the transmission of voluntary movement and sensation, which are rather to be assigned to nerves which have their origin in the brain (experiments involving ligature of the laryngeal nerves and of the arteries downstream of the heart).[42] The demonstration can in the end be boiled down to a single syllogism, which Galen presents in one of the fortunately many passages in which he summarizes the sense and content of his lengthy work. Both of the premisses derive from the very essence of the matter, and the first is (or so he says) agreed by every doctor and philosopher: 'where the source of the nerves is, there too is the ruling part of the soul.'[43] The second premiss ('the origin of the nerves is in the brain') has been demonstrated to be true at the expense of its competitor ('the origin of the nerves is in the heart') in the course of the long preceding discussion. The conclusion is now evident: the ruling part resides in the brain. Galen is also concerned with demolishing from a logical point of view the supposed 'proofs' the Stoics continued to adduce in favour of the heart as the seat of rationality and the ruling part of the soul, by pointing out their groundlessness or their formal invalidity.[44] Thus both directly and indirectly (by means of the refutation of the arguments in favour of the heart), the association of the rational part of the soul with the brain is scientifically demonstrated. In its combination of direct observation, experimental tests and logically rigorous argumentation, one might well say that from a modern standpoint this is one of the finest results obtained by Greek science.

As far as the spirited part (*thumoeides*) is concerned, Galen's task might seem in principle easier, given that its location in the heart, which Galen clearly attributes to Plato,[45] is also accepted by the Stoics, who also ascribe to the cardiac seat of their *hêgemonikon* the movements of the passions, such as anger and fear. Thus there might be agreement in principle between Plato and Chrysippus, and between Galen and the Stoics, at least on this issue, and in effect *PHP* sometimes does appear (perhaps in contradiction with some earlier pronouncements) to incline towards presenting matters in this way.[46] But on the other hand, from the Stoic point of view these passionate movements are just as much rational impulses, and so Galen must first of all demonstrate that rationality has nothing to do with them. And this is what he effectively seeks to show, but only at a later stage, namely in book IV. In book III the situation is a little more confused and the argument less effective. Initially, Galen seems content to prove the necessary existence of a spirited part distinct from the rational, recapitulating an argument[47] which belongs to the arsenal of Platonico-Aristotelian polemics against the Stoics current in the early Imperial period: the fact that reason seeks to resist both desires and the impulses of anger and fear, which is particularly obvious in the case of weakness of the will (*akrasia*), shows that there has to be a difference in nature between the rational and (at the very least) an irrational part of the soul, given that one and the same thing cannot be opposed to itself.

But throughout almost all of book III of *PHP*, Galen seems hardly to be aware of the fact that Chrysippus' demonstrations in favour of the cardiac location of the *hêgemonikon*, even if they are almost always based on cases involving the passions, could equally have demonstrated (and this was certainly one of the author's intentions) that reason itself had its seat in the heart; this result follows if one is also convinced, as the Stoics are, that the passions are nothing other than judgements issued by reason. What Galen should have done before anything else is thus exactly what he puts off until book IV, namely showing that the passions are not in fact judgements. But in book III, on the other hand, he appears to take this thesis for granted, and the result is that some of his disproofs of Chrysippus[48] could easily be adjudged by a Stoic to be inconclusive or beside the point. In any case, Galen must have realized the weakness of his argument, since almost at once[49] he turns to the crucial point, and sets the discussion going along the right path (the one he will follow in book IV), by asking whether reasoning, becoming angry and the desires for food, drink and sex, are really the business of the same psychic faculty. Thus, in conclusion, a full demonstration of the difference in nature between the spirited and rational souls requires a proper examination of the case of the passions, and this is exactly what Galen will do in book IV, which thus appears as an indispensable part of the argument in favour of the Platonic tripartition.

For the third part of the soul[50] which, located in the liver, must be the principle of nutrition and the desires, Galen must honestly admit that he does not have to hand demonstrations as strong as those which he was able to adduce in the case of the other two: one cannot obtain any evidence by way of ligation of the veins, while even assaults made directly upon the organ do not have the same sort of immediate consequences as those which, in the case of the heart and the brain, make immediately evident the connection between the organ which is damaged or impaired and the psychic activities which depend upon it.[51] Being unable to argue directly from the essence of the matter in question, he tries to keep his discussion within the limits of the method which he has adopted up to this point; he must for this reason retreat to the 'particular attributes'[52] of the thing in question, and he does so by insisting on the structural aspects of the organ and of the venous system, basing himself on an account of the relations between structure, function and essence which he supposes to be securely grounded, at least from within his general (Hippocratic, Platonic, Aristotelian) conceptual framework.

The obvious and major difficulty with *PHP's* treatment of the liver[53] in any case consists in the attribution to this organ not only of the nutritive faculty but also of the desiderative soul: and it is a difficulty of which, one might well say, Galen is hardly sensible at all when he presents Hippocrates the doctor's concentration upon the liver as the origin of the veins, and that of the philosopher Plato upon the same organ as the seat of the desires and of the desiderative soul, as the obvious result of a simple parcelling out of the discourse between their various competences and interests.[54] According to him, the demonstration of one of the two things implies in and of itself the demonstration of the other. Of course, his thesis can be explicated and defended;[55] but it is hard not to feel dissatisfied with the lack of discussion of a question which seems to us to be somewhat more complex.

Galen's adoption of the Platonic tripartition of the soul brings along with it further difficulties when he has to confront the question of the passions[56] (which, as we have seen, is unavoidable in *PHP*, but which also concerns him in other writings). At its most general level of definition, passion ought to be confined to the irrational part of the soul, and in fact it is usually defined by him as an irrational impulse or movement,[57] or rather something which arises in human beings 'as a result of some irrational faculty which is disobedient to reason'.[58] But given that in his originally Platonic psychological model the irrational parts are in reality two, the result is the distribution of one and the same psychic phenomenon between two parts or distinct forms of the soul; and there can be no doubt about the fact that especially in *PHP* Galen treats the *pathê* as an undifferentiated phenomenon, to be found equally in the spirited and the desiderative parts of the soul.[59] All the same, elsewhere he is in a certain sense obliged (clearly, as a result of following Plato's lead)[60] to introduce a substantial distinction among the *pathê*: in the small work dedicated to the diagnosis and treatment of the passions, and making reference to what he had said in a more extensive treatment of ethics which has not come down to us,[61] he writes as follows:

how one may improve that part [sc. the spirited] of the soul has been discussed more fully in the books *On characters*, as has the fact that it is not necessary to destroy its strength altogether – as indeed no-one does with that of horses and dogs which we intend to make use of – but rather we must habituate that part to obedience as well, just as in the case of those animals. And no less was it demonstrated for you in the same work in what way one may employ the strength of the spirited soul as an ally against the other [part], which the old philosophers used to call the desiderative, and which is drawn irrationally towards the pleasures of the body.[62]

The upshot is that it is not at all clear what position Galen takes on the dispute which, in his day,[63] opposed the ideal of the total eradication of the passions (*apatheia*), as recommended by the Stoics, to that of merely moderating them (*metriopatheia*), which was usually adopted by Platonists and Peripatetics. One might be tempted to say that he was inclined towards the Stoic ideal insofar as the desires were concerned, while accepting the Platonic–Peripatetic thesis in regard to the spirited part, were it not for the fact that it seems impossible to suppose that, from within his own unabashedly teleological general framework, even the desiderative part and its impulses should not have some basic positive function.[64] No clear answer to this problem is to be found anywhere in Galen's works.

It is however perfectly clear that he does not in any way accept the Stoics' reduction (or, better, that of Chrysippus, his principal target) of the passions to errors of judgement attributable directly to reason: indeed the whole of book IV of *PHP* may be read as a long and implacable polemic against this Chrysippean thesis. Galen sometimes homes in acutely on its weakest points; he points out, for example, Chrysippus' difficulties in accounting for the well known and evident phenomenon of the slackening of passion with time.[65] If the passions are really only judgements falsely issued by reason, how can one account for the fact that, with the passage of time, anger and its associated distress attenuate, while the individual's judgement of the facts which caused the triggering of the passion remains unchanged? Even Chrysippus has to allow that, after a certain time has elapsed, a grief does not afflict us any more in the same way as on the first day, even though we continue to think that the loss we have borne is an irreparable harm; and he has to admit that it is hard to explain the reason for this fact. This, of course, poses no problem for Galen, who amuses himself by contrasting Chrysippus' embarrassment with Posidonius' explanation, which is based on a model of the soul inspired by Plato's tripartition, a model in which the reality of the passion can be confined to an irrational part of the soul whose processes have an origin and development completely independent of the judgements of the rational part.[66]

Yet the distinction between passions and errors (*hamartēmata*), which already seems to be typically Galenic in *PHP* and finds its most obvious application in the opuscula on the passions and errors of the soul, is to a certain extent inspired by Chrysippus, even though Galen develops it in an original manner, and Galen credits him with having correctly seen it without having been able subsequently to stick to it.[67] From Galen's standpoint, while passion is a phenomenon strictly confined to the irrational part, error, on the other hand, is something which involves only the rational soul, since it consists in incorrect reasoning or intellectual calculation. On occasion, he allows that the disorderly movements and impulses of the irrational part can be a negative influence on the rational part, and so may induce it to issue incorrect judgements;[68] but in the two short works on the passions and the errors of the soul, the distinction is applied with a certain rigidity,[69] and this prevents Galen from taking seriously into consideration, and from providing a serious account of, those mechanisms of interaction between the different parts of the soul which, in principle, he ought to be perfectly happy to accept as existing.

But in contrast with all of this, it seems we should distinguish from *PHP* and the other works so far cited the late text *QAM* which, surprisingly, adopts a thesis regarding the soul which at first sight seems different, perhaps profoundly different, from anything found earlier.[70] After having said, in the preface to his exposition, that he has always been convinced that the capacities of the soul 'follow upon'[71] the temperaments (*krâseis*) of the body, a little later on[72] Galen goes so far as to affirm that soul and its parts actually *are* the temperaments of organs in which they reside; and on the basis of this he derives a further thesis,[73] apparently completely novel, namely that one should look to doctors rather than philosophers to see to the education or re-education of men with a view to leading them towards virtue: to doctors precisely insofar as they are in a position to ameliorate the moral and intellectual qualities of souls which, in view of their relation of dependence upon the temperaments of the bodily organs, will be responsive to the changes in the dietary regime, environment and tenor of life which medical science will ultimately impose. In assessing the novelty of this thesis, one should also note that Galen has nothing to say about these therapeutic and practical consequences in the two short works of moral philosophy which have come down to us, even though they are dedicated precisely to the treatment and correction of the passions and errors of the soul.[74] And since in the other late work *On His Own Opinions (Prop.Plac.)*, which is roughly contemporary with *QAM*, he repeats his usual professions of ignorance with regard to the nature of the soul[75] and does not prescribe the treatment of moral vice and intellectual deficiencies after the manner proposed in *QAM* at all, a certain perplexity in regard to the pamphlet on the faculties of the soul seems more than justified; indeed it seems legitimate to ask how it might fit in with all the rest of Galen's *oeuvre*.

To begin with, it does indeed cohere at least with *PHP*, where Galen has already said at any rate that 'the movements of the passions (*pathêtikai kinêseis*) are always consequent upon (*hepomenon*: see n. 71) the dispositions of the body' and that 'they are the product of temperaments of the body which are similar to them'.[76] And one might also regard certain pages of book V of *PHP*[77] as a kind of embryonic nucleus already capable of developing into the general theme of *QAM*: it is certainly no accident that, in the context of an explanation of the movements of the passions which seeks to connect them to the temperaments of the body, Galen makes reference to exactly the same authorities to which he will appeal in order to corroborate his thesis in *QAM* – namely, Plato, Aristotle and Posidonius. Moreover, the scandalous proposal of the later text, to entrust to the doctor the treatment both of moral deviancy and intellectual incapacity, is simply a coherent development of the recommendation already contained in *PHP* that the doctor should take care of the human embryo right from its very conception by controlling the diet, exercise, sleep, waking life and desires of its parents.[78] The comparison with *PHP* allows us also to grasp what must be the original conceptual nucleus (which is effectively present throughout Galen's thought) out of which grew the theme he develops with so much evidence in the late work. In fact, both *PHP* and *QAM* are based upon the natural differences of character present in even the smallest children from the moment of birth, differences which are thus independent of (since they are prior to) whatever influence one might be tempted to ascribe to the environment;[79] and both works also make reference in this context to the Stoic Posidonius,[80] praising him for having paid the proper attention to the case of children.

Evidently, the observation of diversity of the behaviour of neonates and infants to be found in two works written many years apart implies that Galen had always ascribed to the soul and to its parts the possession of a natural endowment, innate and strictly individual, capable of individually determining and differentiating the characters and behaviours consequent upon them. Since it is impossible to ascribe this differentiation of individual characters to environmental influences, given that they show themselves from the very outset, the only possible explanation[81] is that the natural gifts of the soul are to be traced back to differences which already exist in the bodily organs which remain linked (in precisely what manner it is not important to say) to the soul, or rather individually to its various parts.

But it is true that *QAM* (in contrast with the other works) offers a positive doctrine of the relations between soul and body, and the account which is advanced is of a frankly Aristotelian or Peripatetic nature and provenance;[82] the soul will actually be the form of the body, and its parts are understood by Galen as being the forms of the bodily organs in which each of them resides. But the form is identical with the temperament, i.e. with the mixture of elementary bodies or of the corresponding qualities which constitute the organ. Thus the desiderative soul will be the form and temperament of the liver, the spirited will be the form and temperament of the heart, while the rational soul must consequently be the form and temperament of the brain. But on this latter issue, as will soon become more apparent, Galen remains somewhat more prudent.[83] So Galen appears to abandon much of the Platonic and Hippocratic position to which he was fundamentally committed in *PHP*. But even in this case, where the prevalence of an Aristotelian–Peripatetic point of view is undeniable, it still does not seem to me right to speak either of a genuine change of perspective and inspiration or of an evolution.[84] As we have seen, on one page of *PHP* Aristotle was already cited as one of the trio of authorities who underwrite the connection between bodily temperament and the movements of the soul; furthermore, for a Platonizing writer of the second century, the substantial agreement between Plato's and Aristotle's philosophies, at least as regards the most important doctrines, was an accepted fact, unless one wanted to side with the rather restricted group of Platonists who obstinately rejected any sort of *rapprochement* with Aristotle; and this was certainly not the case with Galen, whose fundamental sympathy with Aristotle, albeit one which obviously allowed for severe criticisms of certain aspects of his teaching, can be denied only with enormous difficulty, even if it can be interpreted in different ways and by deploying different historiographical categories.[85]

Galen does not, then, completely abandon his principled agnosticism concerning the nature and essence of the soul, even in *QAM*. Rather, it is limited to the rational part, and linked to the question of its mortality or immortality, which Galen continued to regard as undecidable:[86] even in *QAM*, he affirms that he does not know 'what the essence of the soul might be if we suppose it to belong to the class of incorporeals'.[87] The argument as it unfolds in the treatise leads to the certain exclusion from this latter class of things of the desiderative and spirited soul,[88] which will thus certainly be mortal, since they are forms, respectively, of the liver and of the heart. But as far as the rational part is concerned, judgement seems still to be suspended, notwithstanding the weight of the arguments which Galen can mount to show the strict connection of even this part of the soul with the body and its temperaments;[89] and sometimes in so doing he even treats Plato with a certain unaccustomed irony.[90]

So one might get the impression in reading *QAM* of an almost total renunciation of his earlier declarations of ignorance on the nature of the soul; however the contemporaneous *Prop.Plac.*, without making any distinction between the three parts or forms of the soul, repeats his declaration that he does not know with certainty 'whether the soul is immortal and governs animals by being mixed with the substance of the body, or whether the substance of the soul has no existence per se',[91] adding however immediately afterwards, consistently with the general tenor of *QAM*, 'but it seems[92] clear to me that, even if the soul [merely] takes up residence in bodies, it is subservient to their natures'. It is hard to believe that Galen would really contradict himself on a question to which he attributed such importance within such a short space of time; consequently, the emphatic insistence of *QAM* on the identification of the nature and *ousia* of the soul with the temperament demands its own particular explanation. One might be suggested if we accord more consideration to the fundamental thesis of the work[93] and to the contention that it is the doctor's business to concern himself with moral and intellectual education as well as with the possible correction of deviant humanity.

If indeed *QAM* was written mainly from the standpoint of the doctor who claims for himself and for his colleagues the ability to intervene in order to remedy human moral and intellectual deficiencies, the fact that the idea (which, as we have seen, Galen has accepted for a long time) of there being a physical basis for psychic qualities transforms itself immediately into the thesis of the corporeal nature of the soul itself (or at least of the majority of its parts) becomes more understandable. Indeed it is the doctor – and not the philosopher, who is adjudged incapable of altering souls – who is the one who can operate on the composition of the psychic temperaments. But if this is the case, Galen will also need to be able to tell him what these temperaments are which correspond, somehow or other, to the essence of the soul. One might say, in sum, that in *QAM* Galen makes a somewhat paradoxical use of his customary distinction between the different perspectives from which doctors and philosophers can approach the same questions. If it is a matter of operating on the soul with dietetic, pharmacological, or climatic therapies, it would be good for the doctor to be sure of proceeding on the basis of already acquired truths, truths which would not yet have been effectively acquired in the realm of theoretical philosophy. If we agree to consider *QAM* as being a more or less propagandizing manifesto, devoted principally to promoting the image and the office of the doctor, and not a work of an exclusively theoretical bent, the threatened contradictions with respect to Galen's other works disappear, and by contrast the vigorous persistence of some of the author's fundamental convictions is brought into relief.

There are some other fairly powerful considerations which bolster this way of reading a work of Galen's which remains none the less problematic and worrying. In contrast with *PHP*, Galen does not really insist in *QAM* either on the scientific nature of the argument or on the presence within it and the importance of the demonstrative method which would be employed to give it structure; appeals to science and to demonstration are indeed rare,[94] and in fact *QAM* relies much more on appeals to authority, to Hippocrates, Plato, Aristotle and Posidonius,[95] than on the direct experience or intellectual evidentness of some indemonstrable first principle, which would have been the starting-points of demonstrative scientific argument on the model proposed and adhered to in *PHP*. Of course, not every appeal to the authority of some great doctor or philosopher of the past would be enough in itself to reduce an argument from the level of science to that of dialectic or even of rhetoric pure and simple; but in *QAM* it is a matter both of the quantity and of the style of arguments deployed. From the point of view of the first, the recourse to authoritative testimony clearly predominates over the logical and demonstrative commitment of the argument,[96] and as far as the style is concerned, it has not escaped the notice of attentive readers of the treatise[97] that the thesis that Galen maintains suffers from some serious ambiguities. The exact nature of the dependence of the capacities and operations of the soul on the body is never made clear; the formulations Galen employs vary and are subject to different interpretations. Sometimes he says, indeed, that the capacities 'follow upon' the temperaments, or 'accompany' them (*hepesthai*), a formulation which seems to involve the positing of a fairly weak causal relation between the two related terms, or perhaps even the absence of a genuine causal relation, and the acknowledgement only of a conjunction, albeit a constant one;[98] but sometimes he has recourse to formulations which are apparently much stronger, saying that the soul is 'enslaved by and subjected to' (*douleuein*) the temperaments.[99] But in none of these cases is it ever made entirely clear what this means. All things considered, one might think that his very sparse appeals to science and demonstration in the course of the argument imply that Galen was fully conscious of the fact that in this treatise he was speaking at a different, indeed considerably lower, level than that of *PHP*.

So after all this discussion one may conclude that, while the discrepancy between *PHP* and *QAM* may be considerably reduced, it cannot be done away with altogether. In fact, *QAM* seems to represent starting-points already fully present in the earlier work pushed to their radical limits: but it is a development which seems to be informed primarily by contingent, particular motivations, having to do with the public promotion of the image and of the work of the doctor. The continuity of *QAM* with the conceptions maintained in the earlier works seems at the end of the day much more important than any radical novelties it might introduce. One last example of this: the idea which, as we have seen, Galen had at times propounded tentatively, namely that the soul might actually be identical with the cerebral *pneuma*, is also taken up again in a slightly reformulated form in *QAM*. Here, indeed, the theory upheld by the Stoics, namely that the soul just is *pneuma*, is also reduced to that of the identity of the soul and the *krasis* of the temperaments of the bodily elements, just as in the case of the theories of Aristotle and Plato.[100] In sum, whatever conception he had adopted previously in regard to the nature of the soul, for the Galen of *QAM* it would reduce to the theory of *krâsis*.

But to contend that in *QAM* Galen set out primarily to exalt the figure and the office of the doctor need not diminish the importance of the problems which the book raises. Galen and his pamphlet have at least the merit of bringing up for discussion serious issues and of giving them a precise response, albeit one which may be in the judgement of some an unacceptable one. The fact is that the thesis of *QAM* seems to imply, as is sometimes noted, 'a form of determinism of an almost positivist sort',[101] which may or may not be acceptable to modern tastes. Indeed, if it is true that the activities of the soul – and the qualities of these activities – depend upon physical and chemical composition of the organs; and if, moreover, this composition depends in turn in part on the original formation of the organs at the time of birth which is not in any way alterable by medical science (at any rate it wasn't in Galen's time), and also depends in part[102] on nutrition and in general on the manner and circumstances of life, which may be to a certain degree controllable and alterable, but essentially by the doctor as opposed to the philosopher; the consequence is that a man is genuinely the product of a series of factors in which his own free will and voluntary initiative may play a very minor or even non-existent part, while only the doctor's knowledge can have any influence over them, and a limited one at that. Clinical procedures and case-studies are substituted in place of the moral will of the Stoics, and of the decision and *prohairesis* of the Aristotelians and Epictetus. The prescriptions of the doctor, informed by an understanding of the social usefulness of certain behaviours, become the only possible criterion of reference. Galen is, in precisely this context, extremely lucid and coherent, since he sees the problem clearly,[103] sets it out explicitly and in a reasonably calm manner[104] resolves it with a peroration in favour of medical intervention and of the elimination from the body politic of incurable deviants.[105] The solution he envisions is thus clean and sharp and, as such, can even be praised.[106]

All the same, it can hardly be denied that from the time of Carneades until that of his near-contemporary Alexander, the despised philosophers whom Galen mocks in *QAM* had discussed the problems of responsibility and of human freedom of choice with some fairly subtle arguments, and with a theoretical thrust which in *QAM* Galen does not equal – indeed, with which he shows himself frankly unconcerned. The question which *QAM* sets out to discuss can hardly be resolved by the sword which cuts the Gordian knot. From Galen, who thought of himself (perfectly reasonably)[107] as a philosopher as well, we might have expected a greater respect, if not for the characters of his adversaries, at least for their arguments.

Translated from the Italian by the editor

NOTES

1. Here I disagree with Vivian Nutton's explanation in his edition of *On His Own Opinions* (*Prop.Plac.*: *CMG* V 3,2; Nutton (1999, 204, and 110,4–5)), according to which this text offers proofs in favour of the existence

of the soul. In my view (and all the more so if one posits a lacuna at the beginning of the passage, as Nutton does, correctly as I believe) Galen's reasoning concerns the existence of the capacities (dunameis); he turns to the soul only at 112,13 (note the second kai: 'also').

2. Tieleman (1996, 8–9), and note 6.

3. For the chronology of PHP, see the introduction to De Lacy (1978, 46–8).

4. See in particular Moraux (1984, 778–9). More cautious in this regard is Tieleman (1996, 9–10).

5. UP III 1–2 (i, 1,1–14 Helmreich). Moraux (1984, 778), speaks for this reason of 'Instrumentalismus' (cf. n. 4 above).

6. For now, provisionally, I use perfectly general terms for the relation between body and soul according to QAM; greater precision will follow.

7. Indeed, both of these conceptions are implicit in On Semen (Sem.) IV 611 (= CMG V 3.1, 162,6–19), on which see Accattino (1994, 1875–6).

8. On the teleology of UP, see Moraux (1984, 762–3); and more generally Hankinson (1989, 1994c, esp. 1845–7 and 1851–3).

9. Cf. e.g. PHP V 791–3, = CMG V 4,1,2, 598,25–600,6; Prop.Plac. 14.4, 15.2, = CMG V 3,2, 114,5–20 and 116,20–6; On the Function of Breathing (Ut.Resp.) IV 472, 501. See also Tieleman (1996, 9, n. 7) and Hankinson (1991, 201–2).

10. PHP V 793–4, CMG V 4,1,2, 598,25–600,6; see further pp. 197ff.

11. Typical of this is Ut.Resp. IV 508–9. Cf. also PHP V 606, = CMG V 4,1,2, 444,1–11; On the Powers (and Mixtures) of Simple Drugs (SMT) XI 731; On Hippocrates' 'Epidemics' (Hipp.Epid.) XVIIB 247–8; Causes of Symptoms (Symp.Caus.) VII 191.

12. See the passage of PHP cited in n. 11.

13. PHP V 791–3, CMG V 4,1,2, pp. 598,26–600,6. However, see further p. 193.

14. PHP V 792, = CMG V 4,1,2, p. 598,7 ff.; cf. Hankinson (1991c, 201), and Prop.Plac. 13.7, 14.4, = CMG V 3.2, 108,26 ff., and 114,12.

15. See in particular PHP V 779, = CMG V 4,1,2, 586,34ff.

16. V 793, = CMG V 4,1,2, 598,29–600,3.

17. V 795, = CMG V 4,1,2, 600,21 and 30ff. The passages in question are taken from Rep. IV, 436a–438b.

18. See e.g. PHP V 514, = CMG V 4,1,2, 368,3ff. His refusal to talk in terms of dunamis is particularly evident at V 521, = CMG V 4,1,2, 374,11–12.

19. Following the formulation of QAM IV 769, = SM 2, 33,19, where Galen cites the example of aloe and its dunameis (see also ch. 12 (Vogt) in this volume). On the capacities of the soul – and on the notion of dunamis in general – cf. also Hankinson (1991c, 205).

20. Mansfeld (1990, 3213) and Tieleman (1996, xxiii, n. 38) rightly note that Aristotle was already aware of it.

21. Mansfeld (1990, 3141–3) and Tieleman (1996, xxiii–iv).

22. It suffices to note the final part of Alexander of Aphrodisias' *On the Soul*, which was presumably written only a few years after Galen's work (94,7–100,17 Bruns).

23. On Galen's methodological Aristotelianism, see ch. 3 (Tieleman) in this volume.

24. *Tim.* 44d, 65e, 67b, 69d-70a; also *Phaed.* 96b.

25. *Tim.* 70a-b.

26. E.g., *Epid.* II 5,16 (V 130 L) (the spirited part in the heart) and *Epid.* II 4,1 (V 120–4 L) (the desiderative part in the liver). For the difficulties which confront Galen in reconciling Hippocrates with Plato, see also Lloyd (1991, 409f.).

27. See the discussion of Tieleman (1996, xxxii–v), to which I am much indebted for all of this section. Cf. also Vegetti (1999, 344). For Galen's silence regarding *Sacred Disease*, see in particular Mansfeld (1991, 125).

28. See n. 21.

29. See the citations in *CMG* V 4,1,2, 64–6.

30. See in particular *CMG* V 4,1,2, p. 66,3–7, and the important observations thereon in Tieleman (1996, 8–9 and nn. 4–5).

31. At the beginning of the third book: *PHP* V 286–7 (*CMG* V 4,1,2, p. 168,26) and cf. also the preface in De Lacy (1978, 49).

32. Vegetti (1999, 344), with reference to *PHP* V 696–8 (*CMG* V 4,1,2 pp. 518–20).

33. A single citation from *PHP* may suffice to show this: 'the best accounts of scientific demonstration were written by the old philosophers, Aristotle and Theophrastus in their Second Analytics' (V 213, = *CMG* V 4,1,2, 104,3–5 trans. De Lacy). But the importance for Galen of Theophrastus should not be exaggerated, nor should it be held to be greater than that of Aristotle: Tieleman (1996), 5, and n. 16. For Galen's dependence on Aristotle and the Aristotelian tradition in general, see also *ibid.*, 106–29.

34. Cf. Vegetti (1999, 344), and the references he makes to V 206–7, = *CMG* V 4,1,2, 96,28–98,13.

35. By M. Frede (1985, xvii). On Galen's relations with his authorities, see in particular the studies of Lloyd (1988, 1991); and of Nutton (1990, esp. 246). At all events, Galen's high regard for the authorities of the past did not prevent him from believing also in the possibility of the advancement (albeit with difficulty) of knowledge: see Hankinson (1994a).

36. V 213, 218, 219, 226, = *CMG* V 4,1,2, 102,27, 108,17, 108,23, 116,3. See further ch. 3 (Tieleman) in this volume.

37. This text is frequently cited nowadays to illustrate the method followed in *PHP* in showing that the heart cannot be the seat of the governing part, since the loss of the bulk of book I leaves us without the positive

version of the argument, in which he would have shown directly that the rational part had its seat in the brain. All the same, it is worth noting that references to earlier passages which we no longer possess, such as that which we find near the beginning of the part of book I which is preserved (e.g. V 188, = CMG V 4,1,2, 80,30), indubitably show that Galen must also have based his positive proof of the location of the ruling part in the brain in the first instance on the perceptible evidence provided by dissections.

38. I depart significantly here from the translation of De Lacy, which in my view obscures the fact that Galen refers precisely to works entitled *peri apodeixeôs* (namely, apart from his own, certainly at least those of Aristotle and Theophrastus: cf. the passage at CMG V 4,1,2, 104,3–5, cited above, n. 33).

39. I fear this translation of the Greek *hormê* will be controversial. But it seems clear to me that the term cannot be meant here in the specific Stoic sense of 'impulse'. In my view, Galen is playing with the ambiguity of the definition, which could be understood by the Stoics in *their* sense of *hormê*, but which for him implies another sense of the term, in terms of which he can contend that it makes no difference whether one speaks in terms of movement *kata prohairesin* or *kath'hormên* when referring to autonomously caused (willed in the human case) movement of the agent. De Lacy translates *hormê* by 'conation', not unreasonably. On this question, see also Mansfeld (1991, 118, 131–3). One clear case of the equivalence of *hormê* and *prohairesis* occurs at *On the Movement of Muscles (Mot.Musc.)* IV 372–3, cited by Mansfeld (1991, 132, n. 56). In *PHP*, cf. e.g. V 649, = CMG V 4,1,2, 480,9–10.

40. I.e. dialectical. On dialectical premisses, see Hankinson (1991, 212, n. 4) and Tieleman (1996, 18–23). This four-fold division is ultimately Aristotelian in origin.

41. One of Galen's two criteria of truth: cf. Hankinson (1991c, 206–7) and Vegetti (1994, 1710) (the other is the mind, or reason). See further ch. 3 (Tieleman) and ch. 6 (Hankinson) both in this volume.

42. See in general book II chapter 4 of *PHP*, especially V 231–2 and 234–5, = CMG V 4,1,2, 120,11–28, 122,31–124,32; and also, in Book I, V 185–6, = CMG V 4,1,2, 78,32–3, 80,2–3. These are, from a modern animal-welfare perspective, cruel experiments, and I cannot fail to echo the comment of Mansfeld (1991, 131) (of course I also share his positive assessment: 'but from a purely scientific point of view his method is impeccable'). There is a more detailed analysis of these experiments in Hankinson (1991c, 219–20), Tieleman (1996, 43–4), and Debru (1994, in particular (in regard to *PHP*) 1723–4, 1731–4 and 1750–1).

43. See the beginning of book VIII, V 648–50, = *CMG* V 4,1,2, 480,4–26, especially 16–24. This argument is also discussed by Tieleman (ch. 3) in this volume.

44. One celebrated proof is that deduced from the location of the emission of the voice; on this and Galen's discussion of it, see the in-depth analysis in Hankinson (1991, 215–29 and 232–3).

45. Cf. p. 186.

46. Cf. Tieleman (1996, 54–5). The passages to which he refers are at V 290–3, *CMG* V 4,1,2, 172,16–174,24.

47. Cf. e.g. *PHP* V 305–6, = *CMG* V 4,1,2, 188,1–14, and in the lines immediately following, note the stock example of Medea, which also appears in Alcinous; cf. further Mansfeld (1991, 123, n. 31), which lists Alcinous, *Didaskalikos* 176,37 ff. Hermann, Plutarch, *de Virt.Mot.* 447c–448e and Alexander of Aphrodisias, *de An.* 27,6; *Mantissa* 118,5 ff. Bruns.

48. E.g. at V 332, = *CMG* V 4,1,2, 210,2, and even more clearly at V 343, = *CMG* V 4,1,2, 218,21–6.

49. At V 337–8, = *CMG* V 4,1,2, 214,1–10, to be exact.

50. On which in general see De Lacy (1988), Tieleman (1996, 55–60).

51. *PHP* V 519–21, = *CMG* V 4,1,2, 372,16–374,8.

52. *Ta sumbebêkota idia*, V 520, = *CMG* V 4,1,2, 372,21–2, and cf. Tieleman (1996, 56). But for what comes next in the text cf., in particular, Hankinson (1991c, 224–8).

53. Emphasized by several authors, e.g. Vegetti (1999, 345–6) and (1990, 21–2); Hankinson (1991c, 229–31) (who also offers the most developed attempt at a defence of Galen on this score).

54. *PHP* V 577, = *CMG* V 4,1,2, 418,29–35.

55. See the pages of Hankinson (1991), noted above, n. 53.

56. It is notoriously difficult both to render into a modern language and to interpret the term *pathos*: passion, emotion, or affection? I adhere to the simplest and least problematic translation, given that Galen himself never manages clearly to formulate the question of a possible distinction between different psychic phenomena.

57. 'Impulse' (*hormê*) is the Stoic term, used in *The Passions of the Soul* (*Aff.Dig.*) V 7, = *CMG* V 4,1,1, 6,26; for 'movement' (*kinêsis*) see e.g. *PHP* V 372, = *CMG* V 4,1,2, 242,36.

58. *Aff.Dig.* V 3, = *CMG* V 4,1,1, 4,4–5.

59. Cf. especially V 413 and 424, = *CMG* V 4,1,2, 278,9, 288,14–17. In the first, passion is described as that condition in which rationality, which should naturally rule, is in reality dominated and ruled by 'the irrational faculties of the soul'. What Galen must have intended by the plural 'faculties' is placed beyond all possible doubt by what one reads a few pages later in the second passage just mentioned, where he repeats the

same point, saying that 'nothing is so evident as that there are certain powers in our souls, one of which naturally pursues pleasure, the other mastery and victory' (trans. De Lacy) and that these two faculties were rightly recognized by Posidonius even in other animals; thus these are precisely the spirited and the desiderative parts: and both of them are seats of 'passions'.

60. E.g. *Rep.* 440a.
61. On this, and on the Arabic summary of it which has been preserved, see Walzer (1949); Mattock (1972).
62. *Aff.Dig.* V 27, = *CMG* V 4,1,1, 19,8–15.
63. On this see Hankinson (1991c, 202–4).
64. See again the analysis of Hankinson (1991) (n. 63 above), which seems to me to be plausible.
65. *PHP* V 419, = *CMG* V 4,1,2, 284,3 ff.
66. *PHP* V 420, = *CMG* V 4,1,2, 284,22 ff.
67. *PHP* V 371, = *CMG* V 4,1,2, 242,32. The Chrysippean inspiration becomes particularly apparent when Galen says that one must treat the passions first, and then the errors: *Aff.Dig.* V 7, = *CMG* V 4,1,1, 6,26 ff. This is exactly the method of Chrysippus: cf. Donini (1995).
68. *Aff.Dig.* V 7, = *CMG* V 4,1,1,7,1, is a case in point.
69. On this see Donini (1988, esp. 67–72).
70. Analysis of the work in Donini (1974); Lloyd (1988) is fundamental for its interpretation.
71. *hepesthai*, an ambiguous word, which appears in the first line of the text: IV 767, = *SM* 2, 32,1. But see further p. 200.
72. IV 774, = *SM* 2, 37,20–4, where he says explicitly that the *ousia* of the soul is its temperament; and see also IV 782, = *SM* 2, 44,6–12 *à propos* of the two 'mortal' parts: the fundamental tripartition of *PHP* is obviously retained.
73. IV 807–8, = *SM* 2, 67,2–16.
74. On this, see also Vegetti (1984, 139–40); Sorabji (2000, 250).
75. Cf. n. 9 above.
76. *PHP* V 464 (*CMG* V 4,1,2, p. 322,3–4 and 322,13).
77. V 464–6 (*CMG* V 4,1,2, p. 322,3 ff.).
78. *PHP* V 465–66, = *CMG* V 4,1,2, 322,27–32, a text which appears as the beginning of Posidonius fr. 31 in the collection of Edelstein-Kidd. Galen's dependence on Posidonius is effectively confirmed at 324,3–5; cf. also Sorabji (2000, 257).
79. *QAM* IV 768–9 and 820–1, = *SM* 2, 32,14–33,16 and 78–9: babies at 79,17. The manner in which Galen presents the matter in the first of the two passages shows it to be one of the author's basic convictions; and *PHP* is cited a little further on (IV 772, = *SM* 2, 36,10) in the same

context. *PHP* treats the same theme on several occasions: V 459, 461, 466, 500–1 (*CMG* V 4,1,2, 316,22 ff., 318,20 ff., 324,3 ff., 356,6 ff.). Cf. also *Aff.Dig.* V 37–8, = *CMG* V 4,1,1, 25,25.

80. *PHP* V 461, 466, = *CMG* V 4,1,2, 318,20 ff., 324,3 ff.; *QAM* IV 820, = *SM* 2, 78,8.

81. Only possible explanation, because the theory of threefold *oikeiôsis*, one for each part of the soul (cf. *PHP* V 460, = *CMG* V 4,1,2, 318,12 ff.) is invoked in order to explain the origin of moral evil only, and not the difference between individual characters, contrary to what might appear to be the case from Sorabji (2000, p. 257). Galen never makes any explicit connection between the two questions (of the origins of evil and of the differences of character).

82. Cf. *QAM* IV 773–4, 782, = *SM* 2, 37,5–24, 44,12–18. On the similarities with Peripatetic definitions of the soul, see Donini (1974,151–2); Moraux (1984, 780. ff.); Gottschalk (1987, 1167–8).

83. Liver and heart: IV 782, = *SM* 2, 44,9–12; for the brain, see IV 774–5, = 37,26–38,2.

84. Nor is it probably without significance that in his autobio- and autobibliography, Galen himself lists *QAM* among the works to do with Platonic philosophy: see *On My Own Books* (*Lib.Prop.*) XIX 46; thus he would never have thought of himself as abandoning Plato.

85. See in this case the two slightly different accounts of Hankinson (1992b) and Donini (1992) in *ANRW* II 36.5. For the distinctively syncretist nature of Middle Platonism, see Alcinous *Didaskalikos* (Dillon, 1993), and Dillon (1977).

86. IV 773, = *SM* 2, 36,12 ff.

87. IV 776, = *SM* 2, 38,21–3.

88. Cf. IV 782, = *SM* 2, 44,4–11.

89. See the whole development of the argument from IV 775–82, = *SM* 2, 38,1–44,4.

90. E.g. IV 775, = *SM* 2, 38,7–8.

91. *Prop.Plac.* 116,20–6, in Nutton's translation.

92. Here I print Nutton's translation of 116,26–118,2. But I would like to note that the translation 'seems' for the Greek *phainetai* seems a little weak: *phainetai* does not necessarily carry the sense of a subjective impression (cf. Galen's favorite expression, *to phainomenon enargôs kata tên aisthêsin*, what is clearly evident to the senses): all the more, when it is opposed (as it is here) to the absence of secure knowledge, it should rather indicate the manifest evidentness of the facts. One may note further that 'to take residence in the bodies', if said of the soul, means that it ought to possess its own substance – that is, in the Platonic manner, it should pre-exist and survive the body in which it resides only transiently during the course of its life.

93. Here I develop, with acknowledgement, the lines of inquiry opened up by the excellent study of Lloyd (1988).

94. One might list IV 775–6, 785, 787, 805, 817, = *SM* 2, 38,19, 47,1, 48,4, 64,11, 75,23; but not all of even these passages bear directly on the matter at issue.

95. See the fundamental study of Lloyd (1988 esp. 16, 32–3 and 38).

96. Lloyd (1988, 32).

97. Lloyd (1988, esp. 33–4); Hankinson (1991c, 204, n. 30).

98. For *hepesthai*, see, e.g., IV 767, 774, 775, 783, 787, 792, 802, 804, = *SM* 2, 32,1, 37,25, 38,3, 44,19, 48,2, 52,5, 62,6, 64,4; cf. also the usage of *akolouthein* in 791, 803, 821, = 51,13, 62,18, 79,4.

99. E.g. IV 779, 782, 787, = *SM* 2, 41,17, 44,5, 48,7: in the last case reinforced by *despozesthai*. One may also note that the term appears also in *Prop.Plac.* (*CMG* V 3,2, 118,2) always in connection with the relations between the soul and the temperaments.

100. IV 783, = *SM* 2, 45,4 ff.

101. Donini (1974). Lloyd (1988, 36–7), does not fully agree, but on this issue I believe that Hankinson sees the matter better: (1993, 218, n. 99).

102. The two types of cause are spelled out clearly by Galen at IV 821, = *SM* 2, 79,2–4: 'the temperaments . . . are consequent not only upon the original generation but also upon dietetic regimes which produce good humours, just as these latter factors reciprocally increase the effectiveness of the former.'

103. IV 784 and 814–15, = *SM* 2, 46,1–7, 73,13 ff.

104. Apart from the attempt in the last chapter of *QAM* (IV 814, = *SM* 2, 73,3 ff.) to make it clear that the argument is not intended to express hostility towards philosophy. On this point, see Sorabji (2000, 260).

105. IV 815–16, = *SM* 2, 73,16–74,21, on which see Hankinson (1993, 218–20).

106. See in particular Hankinson (1993, 212 ff., especially 214–15).

107. I share in this regard the conclusions of Frede (1981, 84): 'it would seem that Galen does have a philosophical position of his own which is by no means negligible.'

8 Philosophy of nature

I use the term 'philosophy of nature' in a broad sense, to include most of the topics which would have belonged in the Hellenistic category of physics;[1] because, although Galen was a physician rather than a physicist, he was far from being merely a doctor.[2] Indeed, he considered it to be impossible to be a successful doctor without a thorough grounding in all of the then canonical branches of philosophy, namely logic, physics and ethics (see *The Best Doctor is also a Philosopher* [*Opt.Med.*] I 53–63, = SM 2, 1–8).[3] And this was no mere genuflection towards philosophy: this commitment is repeated, and its genuineness exemplified, on countless occasions throughout his works.

ELEMENTS, QUALITIES AND BODIES

Galen attributes the notion that proper medical practice requires serious physical knowledge to Hippocrates:[4]

He thought that one should have a precise understanding of the nature of the body, saying that this was the source [or principle: *archê*] of the whole theory of medicine. (*Opt.Med.* I 54, = SM 2, 1,11–13)

By contrast, Galen's degenerate contemporaries are shamefully ignorant of human anatomy and physiology. But the requisite knowledge involves more than just this:

This same discipline teaches the very nature of the body, both that which derives from the primary elements, which are mixed among one another as a whole, but also that which derives from the secondary [substances], which are called 'uniform' (*homoiomerê*), and a third in addition to these, namely that from the organic parts. Moreover, one must determine what is the function (*chreia*) and the activity (*energeia*) of each of these for the animal, and not in an untested manner, but as confirmed by demonstration. (*Opt.Med.* I 60, = *SM* 2, 6,14–22)

And the other parts of philosophy, logic and ethics, are needed by the doctor to ensure that he has the intellectual equipment and the moral conscientiousness required to come to a proper understanding of the nature of things (57–63, = *SM* 2, 4,10–9,24).

He need not, however, know the nature of everything. Galen repeatedly admits that he has no understanding of the substance of the soul, but claims that such understanding is irrelevant for the doctor;[5] and the same holds for a wide range of physical and metaphysical questions: the nature of god, the eternity of the world, the possible existence of an extramundane void, for example, questions whose resolution, even if it were possible, is of no practical import.[6] Galen's natural philosophy, like his philosophical psychology, is framed with the needs of the medical practitioner in mind. But while Galen's physics is certainly limited in scope, Frede (1981, 2003) goes too far in suggesting that Galen does not really have a physics as such at all.

The invocation of Hippocrates in *Opt.Med.*, although tendentious,[7] is certainly not adventitious: for it was he who showed how medicine should be undertaken. The doctrine that 'all bodies . . . are composed of hot, cold, wet and dry' is 'common to virtually all the most reputable doctors as well as to the best philosophers[8] . . . but I call them "Hippocrates' elements" because I think it proper to bear witness to him who first propounded and demonstrated them' (*MM* X 462–3). And he wrote a work *On the Elements according to Hippocrates* (*Hipp.Elem.*: X 413–508, = *CMG* V 1,2, De Lacy, 1996) to prove it.

Galen's claim has two striking components to it. His fathering of element theory on Hippocrates (rather than, say, Empedocles or Heraclitus) is startling enough. But even more remarkable is the contention that Hippocrates had offered a demonstration of its truth; for Galen cleaves to a strong and uncompromising notion of demonstration, one which is ultimately derived from Aristotle's *Posterior Analytics* (upon which Galen wrote eleven books of notes for his own purposes: *On My Own Books* [*Lib.Prop.*] I 42, = *SM* 2, 118,7–12;

cf. 47, = 122,23–123,1).[9] To demonstrate a proposition is to show how it follows of necessity from incontrovertible first principles; and in the empirical sciences, that is a tall order.

Galen is well aware of this. Speculative metaphysics cannot yield certain knowledge, since it is unsusceptible of empirical testing, *peira* (cf. *On the Diagnosis and Cure of the Errors of the Soul* [*Pecc.Dig.*] V 98–9, = *SM* 1, 77,10–19 [Marquardt, 1884]),[10] and the inquirer must sometimes remain content with plausibility rather than proof.[11] Yet he expresses no such qualifications in the case of the elements, which can be known by inference to exist even though they cannot be directly perceived (*Hipp.Elem.* I 413–14, = 56,3–58,2 De Lacy). An element is 'the smallest part of that of which it is an element' (413, = 56,3); they are 'the parts which are primary and simplest by nature and which are no longer capable of being resolved into other parts' (414–15, = 58,2–3; cf. *PHP* IV 661, = 490,12–13 De Lacy), that is, into parts of a different *type* (Galen is a continuum-theorist: there is no smallest, atomic quantity of stuff). Hippocrates' legacy is 'the method of discovery' of these fundamental constituents: 'we must determine first whether the element is single in form or if [the elements] are varied and dissimilar, and then, if they are many, varied and dissimilar, how many they are, and of what sort, and what their relationship is with one another' (415, = 58,6–10 De Lacy).

This is what (he claims) Hippocrates did. At *Nature of Man* (*Nat.Hom.*) 2.3, *CMG* I 1,3, 168,4–9 (Jouanna, 2002), 'Hippocrates'[12] writes 'if man were one [i.e. composed of a single element] he would never feel pain', a view Galen endorses and explicates. The sense of 'one' here is 'one in form and power' (*Hipp.Elem.* I 416, = 58,16–21 De Lacy), rather than numerically one; this allows Galen to classify the atomists (of all stripes) as being (in the appropriate senses) monists: their atoms differ in shape and size, but are all the same type of stuff. Galen notes the atomist line on the emergence and 'non-reality' of such properties as colour and taste (cf. frs. 68 B 9, 117, 125 DK [Democritus]), which entails that the primary bodies themselves never really become hot, cold, wet, or dry, or indeed undergo any alteration (417–19, = 60,5–62,13 De Lacy); but if something is to feel pain it must be capable both of change and sensation (419, = 62,15–18).[13]

Imagine a pin pricking an animal's skin: if the atomists are right, it cannot divide atoms, but can only separate them from one another.

But separation is not alteration: the pin can do nothing either to the individual atoms or to their aggregate that could produce pain (420–3, = 64,5–66,15 De Lacy). The upshot is that for anything to feel pain it must be composed of elements that are affectible (423–6, = 66,16–68,24 De Lacy). But are the elements sensitive as well, or affectible only? In fact, both are possible (427, = 70,10–12 De Lacy): neither reason nor empirical testing, Galen's two criteria of scientific truth,[14] can pronounce unequivocally on the question, since it is possible that, if the elements are capable at least of alteration, then in the course of such alterations some new property, not prefigured at the elemental level, may come to supervene upon them (427–8, 70,12–23 De Lacy). What is ruled out, Galen argues, is what one might call the supervenience of generically different properties: any supervenient properties must be similar in general type to properties actually disposed of by the elements they supervene upon. Thus, since sentience is a type of alteration, the elements in the aggregate upon which sentience supervenes must be capable of alteration, although not necessarily of sentience itself, just as for an object (e.g. a house) to have a shape, it must be composed of things which have shape, albeit not necessarily the *same* shape: no part of a house need be house-shaped (428–32, = 70,24–74,18 De Lacy).[15]

So far, Galen has used 'Hippocrates' to argue for two theses: (i) the fundamental elements (whatever they are) must be subject to alteration; and (ii) no version of type-monism is acceptable. So far, we have concentrated on (i); but (ii) is more closely connected with the Hippocratic text. (i) essentially outlines the (very general) conditions under which something may be subject to pain; (ii) rather has to do with the circumstances which might cause something to undergo pain (or, indeed, alteration of any kind). Change can take place only if its cause is qualitatively different from the thing affected: the hot cannot affect the hot, nor fire fire (here we ignore differences of *degree* as well as the question of whether elements or qualities are primary): 'the single [element] cannot be affected if there is nothing to dispose it' (433, = 76,8–9 De Lacy; cf. HNH XV 36–7, = 21,1–24 Mewaldt). In other words, if all there is in the world is (say) fire, nothing could affect the fire in such a way as to produce different phase-states from it (HNH XV 37, = 21,17–24 Mewaldt). As far as Galen is concerned, 'Hippocrates'' argument is directed only against monists, not against element theorists as such (HNH XV 29–32, 17,16–18,29

Mewaldt; *Hipp.Elem*. I 438–9, 80,19–82,15 De Lacy), a reading which is difficult (although not impossible) to square with the text. This is also true, he thinks (more defensibly), of the humours (on which more below, pp. 217–23): the author explicitly argues that man could not be made *just* of blood (or either variety of bile, or phlegm: 439–42, = 82,15–86, 10 De Lacy). Finally, Galen thinks 'Hippocrates' has diagnosed an important confusion: those who suppose that there is a single basic thing (fire, say), from which everything else is produced by some set of physical processes (e.g. condensation, rarefaction), are mistaking the truth that everything has a single *substrate* (the view of Plato and Aristotle) with the quite distinct (and absurd) thesis that there is really only one *type* of stuff (442–8, = 87,11–92,14 De Lacy; *HNH* XV 28–37, = 17,5–21,24 Mewaldt).

Next, elements (defined as above) must be distinguished from principles, *archai*:

In addition to this there are four qualities, pure cold, dryness, heat and moisture. These are not *elements* either of man or anything else, but rather *principles*: but this was confused by the earlier thinkers, who failed to distinguish the concepts of principle and element, since the word 'element' may be used in the case of the principles as well. But the two things are evidently distinct from one another, the one [sc. 'element'] being the least part of the whole, the other [sc. 'principle'] being that into which this least is conceptually changeable. For fire cannot itself be divided into two bodies and show itself to be a mixture of them, and nor can earth, water or air. But one may distinguish conceptually between the substance of the thing which changes, and the change itself. For the changing body is not the same as change which takes place in it. The changing body is the substrate, while the change in it occurs because of the exchange of the qualities; when pure heat is generated in it, fire is created, and similarly air when it receives pure moisture; and in respect of the same things earth is generated when what underlies everything in respect of its own qualityless nature receives into itself dryness without heat, and water [when it receives] coldness. (*HNH* XV 30–1, = 17,28–18,15 Mewaldt; cf. *Hipp.Elem*. I 480, 126,7–12 De Lacy)

This passage summarizes Galen's basic physics. The elements are the most basic *stuffs*; but they are generated by predominances of the four qualities in the underlying material. The distinction between elements and principles is owed to Aristotle (*Gen.Corr*. 2.1, 329a27–33), although Aristotle is prepared to call the elements 'principles' 'in a tertiary sense'. The association of water with coldness and air with moisture is striking, running counter to the orthodox Stoic view (cf. Diogenes Laertius 7.136–7, = 47B LS), as well as common sense (surely water ought to be moist?). But it is confirmed by a later passage (51–2, = 28,20–3 Mewaldt); and Galen is not saying, as the Stoics did, that each element is associated with a single, unique quality. Rather the qualities are related pairwise with the elements, although in each element one of them predominates. Thus water is cold *and* moist, air moist *and* hot, fire hot *and* dry, earth dry *and* cold, although more the first than the second in each case. This, too, is securely Aristotelian (*Gen.Corr*, 2.3, 330a30–331a6, esp. 331a1–6). Galen explicitly endorses this view at *Hipp.Elem.* I 468–70, = 112,24–116,5 De Lacy (cf. *HNH* XV 94, = 49,26–9 Mewaldt; *PHP* V 676, = 502,23–5 De Lacy), while at *On the Powers [and Mixtures] of Simple Drugs* (*SMT*) XI 510, he notes that the Stoics differ from Aristotle in supposing that air is cold.

Thus Galen argues for his version of traditional, continuous element-physics. But while he is concerned to vindicate the tradition, his argument is striking, sophisticated even; and it seeks to establish element-theory on a firm, even indubitable basis. Galen's account of how we can know them is empirically based.

He begins by criticizing those who reject element-theory on the grounds that we never actually encounter bodies in their pure elemental states. This is true, but irrelevant: we still associate heat with fire, coldness, dryness and solidity with earth, and so on (452–4, = 96,7–98,19). Moreover, it is obvious that plants derive from earth and water (you plant them in earth, then water them); what distinguishes them from mere mud is that they also contain admixtures of air and water (455, = 98,20–100,2). Given this, it is equally absurd to suppose that animals, which are nourished by plants, are not equally composed of the same elements (455–7, = 100,3–24). Athenaeus[16] holds that the qualities are basic, and that they are directly empirically determinable (457–8, = 102,2–14); but he wavers between talking of qualities, powers and bodies, and while the substances themselves (bread, porridge and so on) may be perceptually evident, their powers as such are not; moreover, the serious doctor needs to know not just *that* certain foods and drugs in certain conditions work, but why they do: which brings us back to physics, and shows why we need to apply logical methods of analysis (458–60, = 102,14–104,23).

Athenaeus fails to distinguish between the qualities as predicates and the bodies they are (primarily) predicated of. For Galen, in this respect a good Aristotelian, qualities cannot subsist independently of substances for them to inhere in (although the elements exhibit certain qualities paradigmatically). So how can Athenaeus make the qualities basic, but deny that they reside in elements which primarily exemplify them? Here Galen recounts how he forced one of his teachers, a follower of Athenaeus, to concede that we call 'hot' *par excellence* that body in which heat most particularly resides (otherwise the number of 'elements' will be unlimited, corresponding to the unlimited possible degrees of heat: 460–2, = 104,24–106,22). But then, Galen forces him to admit, we might as well call this postulated bearer of the property 'fire' (462–5, = 106,22–110,10). The final pages of the passage generalize the argument: in order to think in a tractable manner of the composition of things, we must do so on the basis of postulated elements which are in some sense inferred entities. These are not identical with their ordinary-language counterparts, but neither are they simply so called stipulatively. In order to arrive at a general explanation, we must isolate conceptually the pure bearers of those properties which are instantiated in ways evident to perception: animals *feel* hot; thus it is reasonable to suppose that they contain some (considerable) portion of what it is that is essentially hot, which we might as well call 'fire' (465–8, = 110,10–114,4). We need to distinguish, again in a broadly Aristotelian, albeit Stoic-influenced fashion,[17] between composite substances, such as the element fire, and their metaphysical constituents, namely matter, 'which underlies all the elements and is without qualities (*apoios*),' and form, in this case 'the extreme heat which enters into it' (469–70, = 114,4–116,5). All of this theory, metaphysical and physical, is essential for any properly founded science. Thus Galen seeks to make good on the claims of *Opt.Med.*

Still, the question as to why there should be four elements, and if so why *these* four, remains; and Galen allows as much: 'if you should wish to name not four but two or three as elements, you might perhaps be able to find some good reason' (468–9, = 114,4–7); and elsewhere he admits that in *Hipp.Elem.* 'the actual demonstration regarding the elements does not appear in full' (*The Order of My Own Books* [*Ord.Lib.Prop.*] XIV 55), referring the reader to two lost works, *On demonstration* (*Dem.*)[18] and *Opinions of Asclepiades* for fuller treatment. But whatever those discussions may have contained, Galen clearly allows himself to go beyond what any reasonable inference from the phenomena should permit him to do.

The crucial considerations in favour of the primacy of the four qualities are causal. At *Hipp.Elem.* I 483–6, = 130,1–132,18, he claims that it is evident that bodies which possess the qualities of heat, cold, moisture and dryness directly affect those bodies which are adjacent to them, while 'no other quality besides the four mentioned is such as to alter things through and through' (487, = 134,12–13): proximity to heavy things does not make light things heavy, nor do rough things make smooth things rough. In contrast with both Aristotle and the Stoics, who treated hot and cold as active, wet and dry as passive powers (Aristotle, *GC* 2.2, 329b24–6; *Mete.* 4.1, 378b12–26; see also 47D-G LS), Galen makes all of them active, although he allows that the former are more so: *On the Natural Faculties* (*Nat.Fac.*) II 7–9, = *SM* 3, 106,4–107,6.[19]

The possibility of blending (*krasis*: temperament) among the four primary qualities, and the emergence of further derivative ones from them, is now taken to be established, although Galen characteristically stresses that the doctor need not determine whether Aristotle was right that the qualities alone were subject to total mixture, or if the Stoic notion of total substantial interpenetration is to be preferred (*Hipp.Elem.* I 489, = 136,15–18), although he favours the former, on the grounds that it is easier to understand, (489–91, = 136,23–138,14; *Prop.Plac.* 15.1, = 116,5–19 Nutton [1999]; cf. *Nat.Fac.* II 5–6, = *SM* 3, 104,2–20).

TEMPERAMENTS, IMBALANCES AND THE HUMOURS

The theory of the elements and qualities is only the first stage; but, in emphasizing the importance for the practising doctor of understanding the structure of things at this most basic of levels, Galen is distancing himself from most contemporary Rationalist[20] practitioners, who at best pay lip-service to the need for such understanding. Galen's Hippocrates is to a large extent a hagiographical fiction;[21] but *Nat.Hom.* does associate the four humours, the things which 'compose the nature of the human body, and as a result of which it both suffers and is healthy' (4.1, 172,13–15; cf. 5.1, 174,11–176,1), with the four qualities, and distinguishes the former in terms of the latter (5.2, 176,2–9).

Galen adopts all this with enthusiasm (*Hipp.Elem.* I 491–8, 138,15–146,7; cf. *HNH* XV 34–5, 51–2, = 20,4–24, 28,8–23 Mewaldt):

'blood, phlegm, yellow and black bile are the elements of the generation of all blooded animals, and not only of man' (Hipp.Elem. I 492, =
138,18–140,1). From these derive the structures which Galen, following Aristotle (cf. e.g. PA 2.1–2, 646a12–648a19), calls 'uniform', e.g.
flesh, ligament, vein, artery, nerve (Hipp.Elem. I 492–3, = 140,1–14).
Their material is furnished by the maternal menstrual blood, also
following Aristotle (GA 2.4, 737b8–739b33): 'all the parts of blooded
animals have been generated from the mother's blood, but . . . this
contains a portion of phlegm and the two biles' (Hipp.Elem. I 494,
141,15–17),[22] which accounts for its ability to be the matter for structures quite different in qualitative type: both flesh and nerve are uniform, but flesh is hot, soft and bloody, while nerves are the opposite
(although these characterizations are relative, not absolute: 494–5,
142,1–6).

Galen allows that his argument is not demonstrative here: 'it
seems more natural by far', he says, to suppose that the Demiurge[23]
generated the embryo by making use of different materials in the
blood mixture, rather than that 'they all came into being from the
same substance' (495, = 142,6–17). It is 'more natural' in the sense of
its being a more reasonable physical explanation. Given Galen's commitment to the physics of total elemental intertransmutability, the
Demiurge could have started with any material he wanted; but it is
more economical, to have him (or nature: cf. Nat.Fac. II 83–4 Kühn,
= SM 3, 161,1–23) work with proximate matter, 'the matter from
which a thing is primarily generated, without its requiring any preliminary change' (Hipp.Elem. I 493, = 140,12–14). Menstrual blood,
in spite of its uniform appearance, is composite, like milk (494–5,
= 142,17–25); it contains fibres which promote clotting, and differs
from sample to sample in consistency and colour (496–7, = 142,25–
144,18), facts which supply empirical confirmation of its composite
(and variable) nature.[24]

It is a sign of the fundamental humoral constitution of the body
that certain drugs purge it of specific humours (Hipp.Elem. I 497–
8, 502–3 = 144,18–146,7, 148,20–150,14; cf. Nat.Hom. 5.3, 176,10–
178,5 Jouanna; and HNH XV 72–3, = 38,23–39,18 Mewaldt), and they
function by having specific powers of attraction for whatever they
are purgative of (On the Power of Cleansing Drugs [Purg.Med.Fac.] XI
334–5). This is supposedly confirmed by the phenomenon of 'superpurgation', where a powerful purgative, having emptied the body of

its proprietary humour proceeds to evacuate the others as well, leaving blood until last 'since it is most appropriate to the nature [sc. of the body]' (*Hipp.Elem.* I 503–6, = 152,2–154,10; on superpurgation, see *SMT* XI 615–18).[25]

The humours are defined by their associated qualities: 'yellow bile is hot and dry in power, black bile dry and cold; blood is moist and hot, while phlegm is moist and cold' (*Causes of Diseases* [*Caus.Morb.*] VII 21–2). Thus they are assimilable to the elements, although they do not exhibit their qualities in so unadulterated a form: 'no animal is absolutely hot like fire or absolutely wet like water' (*On Mixtures* [*Temp.*] I 510, = 1,16–17 Helmreich, 1904). Blood is somehow the most natural, and it is associated with warmth and moisture, while the other humours more easily tend towards imbalance:

These men [sc. Hippocrates, Aristotle, Praxagoras, Phylotimus and 'many others'] demonstrated that when nutriment is altered in the veins by the innate heat, blood is produced by its proper proportion, and the other humours by its disproportion; (*Nat.Fac.* II 117, = *SM* 3, 186,10–18)

although small quantities of the other humours are also necessary for health, they more readily tend towards pathological excess.[26]

Bodies can exhibit excesses of single qualities (they can be too hot, for instance, or too wet); but they can also be unbalanced in respect of the four possible qualitative mixtures: hot/wet, hot/dry, cold/wet and cold/dry (*Temp.* I 510–18, = 2,4–7,2 Helmreich). Some deny that there can be hot and wet or cold and dry combinations, since heat naturally desiccates; while others hold that such combinations are inherently unstable. But in the view of the more reputable theorists,

There are four qualities with the capacity to act on and be acted upon by one another: heat, cold, dryness and moisture . . . But of the six logically possible pairings of four things, two are physically impossible: a body cannot be at once wet and dry, or hot and cold.[27] There thus remain four pairings of the mixtures (*krâseis*): two wet and two dry, distinguished in terms of heat and cold. (*Temp.* I 518, = 6,18–7,2 Helmreich)

Indeed, that such mixtures are generated in all bodies is one of the things he claims is securely known (*Prop.Plac.* 12.1, = 94,18–21 Nutton). But Galen goes on to castigate 'the most distinguished of our predecessors, both doctors and philosophers' for 'leaving out of account the well-balanced mixture' (*Temp.* I 518–19, = 7,3–8). He argues, in Aristotelian vein, that the very notions of excess and defect entail that there be some well-balanced mean between them; and in the case of the body, that mean state is going to correspond to physical health (519, = 7,9–18; cf. *Ars Medica* [*Ars Med.*] I 309–10, = 278,10–19 Boudon [2000a]).[28]

Thus it is an error to claim that the hot and moist condition represents health. Terms like 'hot', 'dry' and so on, can be used in different senses. In the case of proper balance, they are relative and normative: to describe a condition as hot and wet is to say that it is hotter and moister than it ought to be. The only alternative is to suppose (evidently falsely in Galen's view) that there are no hot and wet distempers. Death indeed involves drying out and cooling down: but (ideally at least) from the well-balanced state, which will be relatively warmer and moister, but not absolutely so (*Temp.* I 519–23, = 7,18–9,18). Contrary to what his opponents suppose spring is the well-balanced season not because it is (excessively) warm and moist (it is cooler than summer and drier than winter), but precisely because it does not exhibit excess of any kind (524–7, = 10,4–12,7). Real excesses of heat and moisture 'so far from being the characteristics of spring or good mixture in general, constitute the worst possible state of the ambient air' (529, = 13,20–24), one associated with putrefaction and epidemic disease (529–33, = 13,24–16,3). Galen concludes that they have gone wrong both empirically, in failing to recognize the essentially temperate nature of spring, and rationally, in making no room for the well-balanced mixture, and supposing that each season must be associated with one of the four pairings (533–4, = 16,4–23).[29]

These errors derive from failing to distinguish between the absolute and comparative usage of the key terms. All animals are hotter and wetter than inanimate bodies or plants (534–7, = 16,24–18,9); but animals differ both specifically, in regard to the disposition of the properties: dogs are drier and hotter than humans, but wetter than insects and colder than lions; but also individually: some dogs are drier and some wetter than others (537–8, = 18,9–19,9; cf. 573–5, = 40,11–31,23).[30] The quality terms apply in the absolute sense only to the elements; elsewhere their sense is comparative, and relative to the particular comparison-class at issue, which may be generic, specific, or intra-species (538–51, = 19,10–27,6). Moreover, care is needed in determining whether it is the qualities as such which are being referred to, or the bodies which exemplify them (551–4, = 27,7–29,2; above, pp. 214–16). Moreover, not all imbalances need come in pairs: a mixture may be neither too moist nor too dry, but still either too hot or too cold. Thus there are four simple, in addition to the four compound imbalances; while the well-balanced temperament is intermediate between all of them (554–9, = 29,3–32,4).

All of these are matters of degree, and it requires much empirical practice reliably to discriminate them. Moreover, 'we need to distinguish between the mixture which is actually hot, and that which is so only potentially'; we need to start from what is actually hot, and proceed therefrom to determine what is hot in potentiality (559–60, = 32,5–23). This last distinction, as Galen acknowledges, is Aristotelian in origin; and it is central to Galen's accounts of nutrition and pharmacology as well as general physics and physiology. We establish mean conditions in each case by mixing equal quantities of the extremes, and then learning by experience what they feel like (560–3, = 32,24–34,19); thus we can determine, by long practice, the particular temperaments of each of the organs (e.g. the skin is intermediate, the heart is hot, and the bones cold and dry: 563–71, 575–6, 599–604, = 34,20–39,8, 41,24–42,15, 57,5–60,5).

What is actually hot or cold is straightforwardly determinable by touch,[31] although again experience is needed to train the sense to make the requisite fine distinctions, which will then allow us to test the various theories regarding the connection between age, gender and heat (588–98, = 50,9–56,11). Galen reports two theoretical disagreements: one as to whether old age is naturally wet or dry (in fact it is fundamentally dry, but characterized by wet excretions: 577–82, = 43,10–46,14), and a more recalcitrant one concerning the question of whether children are hotter than those in their prime. There are arguments on both sides, Galen says (582–5), but none are conclusive, since they argue from disputed premises rather than first principles and assume the points at issue (586–7, = 48,27–49,21). As it turns out, neither party is correct: children exude more moist heat, while those in their prime exhibit less of a dry, sharp heat (591–8, = 52,3–56,11); and this can be determined only by long tactile practice.

Here Galen is groping towards two important distinctions: between temperature and quantity of heat, and between temperature and experienced heat. But he lacks the tools, both conceptual and physical, to make them properly rigorous.[32] Here, as elsewhere,

Galen must rely on qualitative distinctions refined as far as possible by practice. At *On the Composition of Drugs according to Places* (*Comp.Med.Loc.*) XII 2–4, Galen distinguishes four different, empirically determined degrees of qualitative power, in another domain where absolute precision is unobtainable: the determination of the powers of various drugs. Take heating: the first degree is discovered by reason alone, since it is by definition subperceptible; the second is when the heat is plain to the touch, the third what heats vigorously without burning, and finally there is the heat that actually burns; and the same goes, *mutatis mutandis*, for the other properties. Drugs and foodstuffs are categorized according to their potential causal powers rather than their actual tactile properties, just as wood, being inflammable, is potentially hot even when it is not burning (*Temp.* I 646–54, = 86,1–90,28).

Thus even chilled wine is naturally hot, since it has the power to heat, at least provided it is broken down in the body; but if the excessive quantity ingested prevents this from occurring, it can have the opposite effect, just as an excess of fuel may smother rather than feed a fire (658–61, 94,3–95,25; cf. *Caus.Morb.* VII 8–12). Similarly, opium, even if administered warm, is a refrigerant, just as hot water extinguishes fires (666–7, 98,16–99,5). We need to distinguish between natural and acquired properties; but this is easily done, since the acquired properties are quickly lost, and the substance soon reverts to type (668–70, 99,23–100,21; cf. 674–5, = 103,5–24). Thus, what determines 'whether olive oil is hot is not that it is thick or yellow or light, but whether it catches fire easily: the potentially hot is what changes quickly to a state of actual heat' (685, = 109,24–7).[33]

One last passage is worth quoting:

whatever is easily altered by heat, or is naturally hot, is heated first, just as whatever is easily affected by cold, or is naturally cold, is cooled first . . . Yellow bile is naturally hottest, phlegm coolest. Of the other humours, blood is the next hottest after yellow bile, black bile is next coolest after phlegm. So yellow bile is easily altered by whatever it comes into contact with, while black bile is altered with difficulty. In summary, everything composed of rarified parts is easily altered, while everything composed of densely packed parts is hard to alter. (*On Uneven Distemper* (*Inaeq.Int.*) VIII 740–1; trans. after Grant, 2000)

Galen's views on qualities, humours, mixtures, properties and their causal relations are complex and also to some extent, in spite of his aspirations to the creation of a comprehensive theory, ad hoc. But such theoretical untidinesses attest to Galen's fundamental concern with empirical adequacy. He often seeks to shoehorn empirical data into his theoretical categories; but more than most ancient theorists, he is aware of the strains involved, and will on occasion candidly admit them. He is no blinkered Dogmatist. The rest of this chapter will seek, among other things, to bear that assessment out.

THE 'NATURAL FACULTIES'

This topic can be dealt with rapidly, since it is discussed in more detail in Debru (ch. 10 in this volume, pp. 266–71). In his treatise of the same name, Galen distinguishes the various natural 'faculties' (*dunameis*: powers, capacities, potentialities) which both generate and maintain the human animal, namely those of generation, growth and nutrition (*On the Natural Faculties* [*Nat.Fac.*] II 10–20, = SM 3, 107,24–115,9); these in their turn are associated with (although not reduced to) other more basic powers, of specific attraction, retention, assimilation and expulsion:

Nature does everything artistically (*technikôs*) and equitably, possessing certain *dunameis* by virtue of which each of the parts attracts to itself its appropriate fluid, and having done so attaches it to every part of itself and completely assimilates it, while those parts which are not mastered and which are not capable of complete assimilation, alteration and reception by the nourished part are eliminated by another distinct expulsive faculty. (*Nat.Fac.* II 29–30, = SM 3, 122,9–16)[34]

The fundamental nature of these metabolic faculties is underscored elsewhere (e.g. at *Prop.Plac.* 9.3, 86,21–88,5: *Causes of Diseases* [*Caus.Morb.*] VII 24). Crucially, they cannot be reduced to simple mechanics. The great mistake of earlier physicians like Erasistratus and Asclepiades was to think that the fluid dynamics of the body can be reduced to principles like that of *horror vacui*. Galen does not reject the latter as such (he invokes it in accounting for the propulsion of blood by the dilation of the arterial coats).[35] But mechanical principles cannot by themselves account for the specificity of natural interactions in the body, which demand explanation in terms of specific attractive and eliminative capacities. Thus Asclepiades and Erasistratus cannot explain why the kidneys attract and concentrate *urine* from the bloodstream on such principles (*Nat.Fac.* II 56–60, 62–6, = *SM* 3, 142,14–145,6, 146,26–149,10).

Nor can they explain the filling of the bladder with the urine via the ureters, and its subsequent expulsion through the urethra (30–8, = 122,22–128,23). Such explanations are as inadequate as the Epicurean account of magnetism in terms of the outflow, intertwining and rebounding of particles[36] (44–51, = 133,16–138,14). Any dispassionate observer will agree that magnets exert an attractive power, and more importantly a selective one: they attract *iron*, just as particular drugs attract only (or primarily) specific humours (42–4, = *SM* 3, 131,15–133,10; cf. *Prop.Plac.* 9.3, 86,14–88,5). Vacuum suction, on the other hand, attracts what is lightest and closest first, and so cannot discriminate in favour of more distant or heavier substances (*Nat.Fac.* II 205–6, = *SM* 3, 250,5–26). Hence

All the phenomena attest that there must exist in practically every part of the animal some nisus towards, or as it were an appetite for its appropriate quality, and an aversion to, or as it were a hatred for the alien one . . . thus from these things it has been demonstrated that there exist attractive and expulsive faculties in all of them. (*Nat.Fac.* II 159–61, = *SM* 3, 216,17–24)

None the less, Galen is aware that this talk of faculties is in some ways unsatisfactory. At the beginning of *Nat.Fac.*, he acknowledges that

So long as we do not know the essence of the activating cause we call it a faculty: thus we say that there is in the veins a haematopoietic faculty, a digestive faculty in the stomach, a pulse-creating faculty in the heart, and in each of the other parts a specific faculty corresponding to its activity. So if we are to investigate methodically how many and what sorts of faculty there are, we need to start from their outcomes (*erga*), for each outcome derives from a specific activity (*energeia*), and each activity from a specific cause. (*Nat.Fac.* II 9–10, = *SM* 3, 107,15–22)[37]

In this context,[38] faculties are conceptualized as causes (cf. *SMT* XI 380: 'a faculty is an active cause'), but causes whose actual nature is not fully understood. Galen says the same at *Causes of Pulses* (*Caus.Puls.*) IX 4–5: 'we call the cause which constructs the pulses, whatever it may be and even if we are ignorant of its essence, a capacity (*dunamis*) because of its being capable of effecting the pulses' (*ibid.* 4–5). These are relational items,[39] powers to generate *energeiai*, the proper activities of an organ or system, which in turn produce some outcome, in terms of which we may understand the item's overall utility (*chreia*). The outcomes, as far as physiology is concerned, are the bodily parts, while the activities are generation, which develops the form of the part, growth, which maintains it while increasing it in size, and nutrition, which simply maintains it. All of these involve alteration and assimilation of raw material, while generation involves the actualization of a faculty of moulding (*diaplasis*) as well (10–11, = 107,24–108,20). But the basic causal powers are still the hot, the cold, the wet and the dry:

> If you want to know which of the alterative faculties are primary and elementary, they are moisture and dryness, cold and heat ... Nature constructs bone, cartilage, nerve, membrane, ligament, vein and so forth in the first phase of the animal's generation by making use of a faculty which is in general terms generative and alterative, but in particular heating, cooling, drying and moistening, and those [faculties] which derive from a mixture of them, which for the sake of clarity we must describe as the bone-producing, nerve-producing and cartilage-producing. (*Nat.Fac.* II 12–13, = *SM* 3, 109,13–110,6)

The primary elementary qualities combine initially to generate the uniform parts. Hot, cold, wet and dry are the primary causal powers; and so diseases that arise from fundamentally hot and dry causes need cold and wet therapies, and vice versa, according to the general allopathic principle that 'opposites cure opposites' (cf. e.g. *On the Therapeutic Method* [*MM*] X 50, 103–4, 178, 650, 739, etc.), while lesions to organs which naturally exhibit a particular temperament require remedies that foster the creation of material of that temperament (cf. e.g. *MM* X 173–86). But exactly how they do their work in particular cases is still mysterious; and something else is evidently required.

CAUSES AND TELEOLOGY

That 'something else' is supplied by teleological considerations. For Galen, even more than for Aristotle, no satisfactory explanation of the complexities of natural processes is to be found in reductive materialism. Material factors are important; and the nature of particular materials contributes importantly to the eventual outcomes. Efficient causes, too, have a crucial role to play: nothing will happen unless something makes it happen (this for Galen is an *a priori* axiom: *MM* X 36–7, 49–50).[40] But in biological contexts, things happen in order to bring certain results about: there are final causes for structures and their activities. That is, Galen follows the scheme of Aristotle (*Phys.* 2.3):

> The two primary and most important types of cause are these: the goal for the sake of which something is made, and the creator by whom it is made. Third and fourth in order of importance are the instruments with which and the material from which it is made. (*On Antecedent Causes* [*CP*] vi 67, = 92,17–21 Hankinson [1998a])

Galen goes on to suggest that in particular cases these causal factors are individually necessary and jointly sufficient for their outcomes (vii 68–70, = 92,21–94,5 Hankinson), although not all of them are always required: chance occurrences are those where there is no final cause (cf. Aristotle, *Phys.* 2.5–6), while sometimes there is no instrumental cause either (vii 71, = 92,5–9).[41]

The last text makes final and efficient causes the most important; and elsewhere Galen downgrades the instrumental cause even further. In his great work of teleological anatomy *On the Utility of the Parts* (*UP*), he castigates Asclepiades for saying that the pulmonary arteries are particularly thin because they work so hard. In fact, they are constructed this way in order to be able to fulfil their function of vigorous movement. Their thinness is thus an instrumental cause, contributory to their being able to do their job, and not simply a side-effect of something else (*UP* III 466–70, = i 340,5–343,1 Helmreich [1907]):

> Asclepiades omits two causes, the first deriving from the Demiurge's providence . . . and the second, the material cause . . . and fastens on the most insignificant cause . . . indeed not properly a cause at all.[42] (*UP* III 466, = i 340,5–9)

A little earlier, Galen had written:

> There are several types of cause, the first and most important that for the sake of which something is generated, second that by which it is generated, third that from which, the fourth that by which, and the fifth, if you wish, that in accordance with which. And we will expect all genuine natural scientists to mention each of them in their accounts of the parts of animals' bodies. (*UP* III 465, = i 339, 12–18)

These are, in order, final, efficient, material, instrumental and formal causes, all designated by the prepositional formulae which had by this time become canonical.[43] The coolness to the formal cause is notable (this is the only passage in the genuine works where Galen even adverts to it). Elsewhere, Galen writes:

What contributes of its own nature some share of the generation for the thing generated is said to be its cause. These are many in kind: for both the matter and the purpose (*chreia*) and the goal (*skopos*) and the instrument and that whence comes the source of the change are causes. Each of these contributes to the completion of the thing generated. But those which, while contributing nothing, are still not to be separated from the things which do contribute, have the status of prerequisites. (*Differences of Symptoms* [*Symp.Diff.*] VII 47–8)[44]

All of these causes, Galen says, are genuine because they 'contribute from their own nature' to what is produced (cf. *CP* vii 76–7, = 96,7–15), and this applies to the instrumental cause too: gimlets bore holes properly because of their structure (cf. vi 55-vii 75, = 88,9–96,7). Such genuine, *per se* causes are contrasted with what are mere prerequisites for causal action, such as location, and an unimpeded space between agent and patient, which Galen also calls 'incidental causes' (vii 78–89, 96,15–100,11).[45]

Galen never abandons the thought that purposive explanation is pre-eminent. He berates Erasistratus and Asclepiades in *Nat.Fac.* for their teleological shortcomings. Erasistratus claims to see purpose in nature (*Nat.Fac.* II 78, 81–2, = *SM* 3, 157,21–5, 160,1–10) and to follow Peripatetic doctrine, but he does so in word only (88–91, = 165,7–167,13): he has the temerity to say that the spleen fulfils no function, whereas in fact its job is to purge the system of excess black bile (91, 131–3, = 167,15, 196,15–198,8; cf. *UP* III 315–16, = i 231,19–232,18). Galen is not entirely fair to Erasistratus here. Galen's teleology is particularly uncompromising; where Aristotle will often describe a structure (or product) as a 'residue', useless in itself, but a necessary by-product of something which is teleologically explicable, Galen does so far more sparingly, preferring to discern actual functions in apparently purposeless parts. Thus at *UP* III 372, 374, = i 272,16–21, 274,1–8, he exalts the functional adaptiveness of the gall-bladder (it fulfils the same role for yellow bile as the spleen does for black), a part Aristotle considered to be a mere residue (*PA* 4.2, 677a12–19).

UP is dedicated to demonstrating the intelligence and providentiality of the artificing Demiurge. Book I is devoted to a detailed analysis of the structure of the hand, demonstrating not merely the purposiveness of the arrangement of all its component parts (nerves, tendons, muscles) but also its economy. It is the latter fact above all which argues for intelligence behind the design.[46] In a passage that Galen describes as a 'Hymn to Nature' (*UP* III 236–42, = i 173,11–177,14), he censures those who think that some of the design is sub-optimal (he lambasts those who would have preferred the anus to be placed in the foot, so that they could defecate without getting out of bed), as well as those who are unable to appreciate fully the beauty of the Demiurge's creation, and censure him for utilizing such unpromising material. What matters, Galen says, is the excellence of form, not that of the material in which it is realized.

This introduces a further important consideration. Galen's Demiurge, like Plato's, is limited in what he can construct by the constraints imposed by the nature of matter. He is not like 'the God of Moses', for whom everything is possible, 'even should he wish to make a horse or cow out of ashes' (906, = ii 158,24–6). The Demiurge rather chooses the best of the available (physical) possibilities. Galen's material cause is thus genuinely a cause, even for God. But even so, things are ordered for the best: 'if you placed the sun any lower, where the moon is, everything here would be consumed by fire, while if you placed it higher . . . no part of the earth would be habitable on account of the cold' (240, = i 176,17–21). A similar excellence of arrangement can be observed in the body, which is 'so to speak, a microcosm'. Everything within it (at least if it is in good condition) functions appropriately and in harmony, and is conducive to the animal's overall well-being. In order to see this, we need to distinguish again between faculties, activities and their products, as well as what Galen calls the '*chreia*' of the parts themselves.

The *chreia* (variously translated as 'need', 'purpose', 'use', 'usefulness', 'utility' and 'function', none of which gets it quite right) is what the part is for, in the sense of what it contributes to the animal's overall economy. And 'as I have shown, one cannot discover the *chreia* of any organ without knowing what its activities are' (*UP* IV 153, = ii 293,7–10). A few lines later, Galen writes: 'the *energeia* of a part differs from its *chreia* . . . in that an *energeia* is an active motion, whereas the *chreia* is what is commonly called utility (*euchrêstia*)' (IV 346–7, = ii 437,8–12). Moreover, he distinguishes between the *chreia* of the part itself and of its activity, where the latter is the more important (347, = ii 438,1–2). Thus the activity of the arterial coats (contraction and dilation) is to propel the blood and *pneuma*; its *chreia* is to maintain the body's innate heat, and to generate psychic *pneuma* (the instrument with which the soul effects purposive action)[47] out of the less concocted vital *pneuma* (a modification of inspired air), as well as to effect the expulsion of 'the smoky residues' (*Caus.Puls.* IX 5–6; *On the Function of the Pulse* [*Us.Puls.*] V 161; cf. *On the Function of Respiration* [*Ut.Resp.*] V 491–2).[48]

CAUSATION AND NECESSITY

So far, we have concentrated on Galen's appropriation of his Aristotelian and Platonic inheritance in the realm of explanation; but there are other important strands to the weave. For Galen, the natural faculties are active causes; but they are to be distinguished from the activities they condition, which can in turn function as causes in their own right. Moreover, we can distinguish between causal activity within the body and that which is external to it, as well as between causal factors that are merely contributing to an outcome and those which are sufficient for it. Here Galen draws on a long non-Aristotelian tradition, which owes much to the Stoics, but also to earlier medical theorists. The Stoics talked of *aitia sunektika*, containing causes,[49] causes which more or less literally 'hold together' what they are causes of. Galen wrote a short treatise, *On Containing Causes* (*CC*), in which he rejects the Stoic idea that objects require constant internal causes of their persistence (*CC* 6.1–6, *CMG* Suppl. Or. II, 137,3–138,2),[50] but allows that one may call causes of the production of things 'containing', provided they meet certain requirements:[51] they must be co-temporal with, sufficient in the circumstances for, and co-variant with their effects. Sextus (*PH* 3.15) instances the case of the noose's being responsible for strangulation; and in a similar vein Galen, discussing the causes of the pupil's contraction and dilation, writes:

We might call the tension of choroid membrane the containing cause of the generation of the dilation, and its relaxation that of its contraction. (*Symp.Diff.* VII 93; cf. VIII 132: heat is a containing cause of not feeling hungry, while cold is one of hunger)

Galen credits the development of this notion in medical contexts, along with the related concepts of antecedent (*prokatarktika*) and preceding (*proêgoumena*) causes, to the Pneumatist doctor Athenaeus of Attaleia (*CC* 2.1–6, 134,3–36). Antecedent causes
have their origins external to the affected body, and are present prior
to the emergence of the effect. They are such items as heat, cold,
fatigue, insomnia, excessive indulgence in food, drink and sex;[52] and
they operate by precipitating imbalances in the body's internal structures. Erasistratus, for one, refused to consider them causes because
they were not invariably followed by their supposed effect (*CP* viii
102-x 138, 104,18–118,24; cf. Celsus, *On Medicine* [*Med.*] Pr. 54),
and held that they were of no use for diagnosis either. Galen, on the
other hand, thinks them of great importance both theoretically and
practically. It is quite possible that, of a thousand spectators at the
theatre on a hot afternoon, only four suffer from over-heating, and
only one develops fever (*CP* ii 11, 72,17–19 cf. viii 100–1, 104,7–17;
cf. Celsus, *Med.* Pr. 58–61); this is not because the heating is irrelevant to the condition, but because of the particular susceptibility of
the individuals in question. If they are naturally of the hot and dry
temperament characterized by an excess of yellow bile, their system will be more prone to be affected by such externals, and all the
more so if they have recently engaged in other activities of a heating
nature, such as wrestling or sex (*CP* iii 22–5, 76,10,25; cf. x 126–8,
114,12–116,4). As Galen trenchantly puts it, Erasistratus would have
been right if he had said that if chilling were the *sole* cause of (a certain type of) fever, then all exposed to the same degree of cold would
develop fever; but it is precisely because chilling is not the sole cause
that this conditional is vacuous; while as Erasistratus propounds it,
without the 'sole', it is simply false (*CP* viii 102–114, 104,18–108,26;
cf. xiii 167–8, 130,20–132,5).

Thus there can be both internal and external causes of disease.
But what exactly is a disease?

A disease is a disposition of the body which is such as primarily to impede
one of its activities; those dispositions which precede it are not indeed diseases . . . So, on our account, not just anything which occurs in a body
contrary to nature should immediately be labelled a disease, but rather only
that which primarily harms an activity [should be called] a disease, while
what precedes it <should be called> a cause of the disease, but not indeed a
disease. (*Symp.Diff.* VII 50; cf. *MM* X 40–2, 78–81)[53]

The talk of 'dispositions' is significant. A disposition (*diathesis*) is non-permanent, but equally non-ephemeral, temperament of the body; and these dispositions are responsible for the well- or ill-functioning of its various systems.[54] Galen holds that any proper analysis of physical functioning involves four distinct features: (1) the dispositions of the physical parts; (2) their proper activities; (3) the causes of the dispositions; and finally (4) 'the symptoms which necessarily follow the various alterations in bodies, whether in a natural state or not', although they do not in themselves affect the performance of the activities (*MM* X 63–7; 78).[55] Only (1) and (2) are serious candidates for being labelled 'disease', and which we opt for makes no real difference, as long as the chosen terminology is consistently applied;[56] but since what require treatment are the deviant dispositions (79–81), and

> Since it is essential that we assign names . . . clearly . . .; let us call the disposition that impairs the activity the disease; whatever follows from it a symptom; and whatever is responsible for it a cause. (*MM* X 81; cf. 65; and *CC* 8.10–12, 139,22–35)[57]

These immediate deviant dispositions constitute the containing causes of the impediments, but they are themselves the product of prior causes, some internal and some (generally) external to the body, the preceding[58] and antecedent causes, respectively.

All this suggests that containing causes are a subclass of efficient causes. But this is only partially correct. One of Galen's most detailed causal analyses again involves the activity of the pulse:

> Of the causes which bring about changes in pulses, some are causes of the generation of them while others are causes only of their alteration. Causes of their generation are the function (*chreia*) for the sake of which they are generated, the capacity (*dunamis*) by which, and the instruments by means of which they are propagated, while all the rest are causes of their alteration, both those which are called preceding (*proēgoumena*) and those which are antecedent (*prokatarktika*) even to them . . . Speaking generally, things which are external to a body and alter it in some way are called antecedent causes, because they precede the dispositions of the body. Whenever these dispositions in turn condition containing causes, they are preceding causes of them. Suppose that external cold brings about constriction of the skin, as a result of which normal exhalations are checked; they then form a mass, causing a fever to take hold, which alters the function of the pulse, which in turn changes the pulse itself. In this case the antecedent cause is the

external cold, while all the rest up to the alteration of the function of the pulse are preceding causes. Through the mediation of the preceding causes, the antecedent cause alters the function of the pulse, which is one of the containing causes, while this in turn brings about a change in the pulses themselves, since it is not possible to bring about a change in some containing cause and for what is conditioned by it to remain unchanged. But unless an alteration is effected in one of the containing causes, it is impossible to bring about a change in the pulses. For this reason these are the most important and most particular and primary causes of the pulses, and all the others are [causes] by way of them. For it is on account of their effecting an externally generated alteration to the containing causes that they are called causes. (*Caus.Puls.* IX 1–3)

Two important features emerge from this. First, at least in this case, it is only the (conjunctive) containing causes which are really responsible for the activity itself – the other causes merely alter it in some way (and even then they do so by way of altering the containing cause): within the context of a properly functioning body, the complete causal account of each individual proper function is to be given in terms of the conjunctive containing cause. Which leads to the second feature: the category of the containing cause subsumes within itself elements of the final and instrumental, as well as efficient, causation (cf. *CC* 8.6, 139,4–10). How so? When external pathogenic factors produce alterations in the internal states of the body, the requirement for the pulse itself, its *chreia*, will also be altered. If the body produces more 'smoky residues', then it will need to expel more of them; and this in turn will require that the pulse operates more vigorously, which in turn requires changes in the efficacy of the (efficient) faculty responsible, and its (instrumental) means of transmission. Galen is groping towards the notion of a homeostatic system, one which self-regulates in order to maintain its output values within a particular critical range: this is just how the healthy body responds to external influences in order to maintain its equilibrium. Of course, if the pathogenic influences become too strong, a genuine crisis may be precipitated, one which counts as a disease on Galen's definition. In that case, the body may right itself as a result of its own resources, or it may do so as a result of the administration of the appropriate treatment (to counteract the pathogenic influences and to repair any damage caused by them); or, in the limit, such interventions may be useless. The details of the scheme are obscure, and the pathology superannuated. But the underlying analytical structure is both reasonably clear, and reasonably sophisticated.

GOD AND THE LIMITS OF NATURAL INQUIRY

Galen's views on God are similar in structure to his thoughts about the soul: we can know that it exists on the basis of its evident effects, even if we don't know *what* it is.[59] Galen expresses his attitude most clearly at *Prop.Plac.* 2.1–3.6, = 56,12–62,17 Nutton: some features of the world could have been produced only by an intelligent creator (2.1–2, = 56,21–58,16), 'and I do not see how it hurts people if they are ignorant of the substance of the deity' (2.3, = 58,16–17):

Some who hold that the end [of philosophy] is practical have arrived at the investigation of these [sc. speculative] matters by a gradual passage from useful inquiries . . . While it is useless to ask whether the universe had a beginning or not, this is not the case with the inquiry about providence. All of us should examine the statement that there is something in the universe superior to men in power and wisdom; but we need not determine what sort of substance the gods have, whether they are entirely bodiless or whether they have bodies as we do. These and many other questions are completely useless for ethical and political matters, and for curing the ills of the soul. (*PHP* X 780–1, = 588,18–27 De Lacy)

An appreciation of divine providence is necessary, Galen thinks, not only in order to understand biological functioning and to resist the siren song of materialism, but also to live the properly moral life. On the other hand, unsurprisingly given his views on the divine substance, there is little positive theology in Galen.[60] His Demiurge is evidently no mere metaphor;[61] but while it may be blasphemy to deny providential power and purpose, it is equally blasphemous to suppose, as 'one of my Platonist teachers did', that the divine World Soul[62] is responsible for all growth and development, since it would then be responsible for producing vicious creatures like scorpions and snakes (*On the Formation of the Foetus* [*Foet.Form.*] VI 700–1, = CMG X 3,3, 104,25–106,2 [Nickel, s2001]).

This last text, one of the last that Galen wrote, is instructive. He never wavers from the view that the complexity and intricacy of the processes involved in the genesis and growth of animals requires explanation in terms of design, and that no mechanistic account can hope to be remotely credible (*Foet.Form.* VI 693, = 98,4–6); but how the processes are accomplished is a mystery. Does an incorporeal soul mould the semen-like material? Is the semen an *instrument* of soul which works on the menses? Is it itself the artificer (699, = 104,2–8)? No argument can make any of these positions even plausible, much less demonstrative (700, = 104,12–14). Yet, the foetus is evidently constructed 'with the greatest wisdom and power', something hardly to be accomplished by Aristotle's vegetative soul, or the Stoics' Nature (700, = 104,15–24; cf. *Nat.Fac.* II 1–2, = *SM* 3, 101,1–15). God is involved somehow; but in the end Galen has no idea how the 'moulding faculty' actually undertakes its artistic task (*Nat.Fac.* II 80–88, = *SM* 3, 159,5–165,6).[63]

This uncertainty is typical of Galen's attitude to such questions, particularly in his later writings.[64] But that Nature (which just is the activity of the Demiurge) is supremely artistic is never in doubt. In the 'Epode' to *UP*, he avers that even a superficial acquaintance with animals' structures should be enough to convince anybody who is unblinded by materialism of this; but anyone with a detailed knowledge of anatomy cannot fail to recognize the supreme artistry at work in marrying structure to function, and producing no superfluities (IV 347–351, = ii 438,3–441,10).[65] Nature produces parts which are not only beautiful and symmetrically arranged, but optimally designed to fulfil their assigned tasks, and almost never generating monstrosities[66] (IV 351–8, = ii 441,10–446,3):

Who then, other than someone implacably hostile to Nature, could be so benighted as not . . . to recognize at once the skill of the Demiurge? Who would not at once understand that some intelligence possessed of wonderful power was walking the earth and extending into every part of it? . . . Even here there is manifestly some intelligence deriving from the celestial bodies, and whoever gazes upon them is drawn immediately to marvel at the beauty of their substance,[67] the sun most of all, then the moon and the stars. (IV 358–9, = ii 446,3–16)

This intelligence is manifest even in the meanest creatures engendered in mud and rotting matter,[68] more obviously in brilliant men like Plato, Aristotle, Hipparchus and Archimedes,[69] but pre-eminently in the celestial bodies (IV 359, = 446,16–447,8). Indeed, Galen is inclined to think that they propagate the divine intelligence down through the air to the earth like light (IV 359–60, ii 447,8–12),[70] even though the precise modality of that propagation is obscure. This exemplifies a general feature of Galen's style of physical theorizing, one manifest, for example, in his psychology: even where we cannot say *how* some influence is transmitted, or *what* the actual substance is of the power to effect it, we can still be sure *that* it so operates. Sometimes we just have to accept that power can be transmitted in exotic ways:

Some even think that some substances can alter things that are close to them just by contact and solely by the power of the transmitted quality. This can easily be seen in the marine torpedo-fish, which possesses a force so strong that by transmitting this alterative power through a fisherman's trident to his hand it can immediately induce total numbness in it. These are sufficient indications that a small substance can effect large alterations by contact alone.[71] (*Loc.Aff.* VIII 421–2)

This is true in the case of the transmission of voluntary motion and sensation via the nerves: we can establish by experiment that they are the vehicles for the appropriate information (*On Anatomical Procedures* [*AA*] II 651–98 Kühn; 9.11–13, 18–31 Simon [1906]), but how they do so is obscure. Does *pneuma* flow through them? But they seem (with the exception, Galen thinks, of the optic nerve: *UP* III 639, = 463,4–10)[72] to be solid, although perhaps they are perforated with invisible lumina. At all events, some influence travels through them somehow or other, and very rapidly: and that is all we can know (*PHP* X 611–12, = 448,4–24 De Lacy; cf. X 200–10, 519–21, = 90,26–100,7, 372,16–374,8). In *On Semen* (*Sem.*), he claims that it is impossible for poisons to act by material penetration,

Since it is not possible that such a small amount of fluid should in the briefest time fill the bulk of the body which is sometimes very great; but [they act] because the quality is distributed, just as we see in the outside world the distribution of the sunlight to the circumambient air, and within us that from heart to arteries and brain to nerves. (*Sem.* IV 584–5, = 134,23–136,9 De Lacy)

So it is reasonable to hypothesize that qualitative alterations may occur without actual material transfer; but more than that we cannot say.

Galen's interest in physical questions is, like his interest in philosophy in general, severely practical (see in particular *PHP* X 779–81,

= 588,7–33); and the realm of the practical is circumscribed by what can be determined on empirical grounds, which rules out the possibility of saying anything serious about large areas of traditional physics and cosmology (*PHP* X 791–2, = 598,5–19; *Pecc.Dig.* X 98–102, = *SM* I, 77,10–80,16). But that does not mean that he has no physics at all; and his epistemological caution, and his refusal to rule out of account the possibility of novel and unexpected modalities of causal transmission, bear equal testimony to his credentials as a respectable empirical scientist.

NOTES

1. Which includes topics that we might be more inclined to regard as metaphysical, such as theology and the theory of causation; for a sense of the ambit of the Hellenistic notion of *phusikê*, consult the section-headings in Long and Sedley (1987) [hereafter, 'LS'], especially 'Stoic Physics', §§43–55.
2. See chs. 9–12 in this volume.
3. See ch. 1 (Hankinson) in this volume, pp. 3, 7, 14, 23–4.
4. However, Galen's Hippocrates is his own intellectual construction: see Smith (1979, ch. 2); and ch. 13 (Flemming) in this volume.
5. *On the Doctrines of Hippocrates and Plato (PHP)* V 793–5 = *CMG* V 4,1,2, 598,26–600,30 (De Lacy, 1978); *On His Own Opinions (Prop.Plac.)* *CMG* V 3,2, 3.1–2, 58,22–60,11; 7.1, 76,25; 15,2, 116,19–118,10, 15.5, 120,4–14 (Nutton, 1999); see Frede (1981); Tieleman (2003); Hankinson (forthcoming (1) and (2)); and see ch. 6 (Hankinson), and ch. 7 (Donini) both in this volume.
6. See e.g. *PHP* V 766, = 576,27–578,2 De Lacy: such things cannot be settled by perception, or empirical testing (*peira*); see further ch. 6 (Hankinson) in this volume, p. 179.
7. See again Smith (1979); for a more favourable opinion of Galen's practice in this regard, see ch. 13 (Flemming) in this volume.
8. Diocles, Mnesitheus, Dieuches and Athenaeus among doctors, Chrysippus and Aristotle among philosophers.
9. For Galen's views on demonstration, see chs. 3 (Tieleman) and 4 (Morison both in this volume); and Barnes (1991).
10. *Pecc.Dig.* is also edited in *CMG* V 4,1,1 (De Boer, 1937).
11. See Debru (1991); and ch. 6 (Hankinson) in this volume.
12. Almost certainly not the historical Hippocrates, although Galen is convinced that most of this text is attributable to the great man: *On*

Hippocrates' 'Nature of Man' (*HNH*) XIV 9-13, = *CMG* V 9,1, 7,14-9,11 (Mewaldt, 1915); see ch. 13 (Flemming) in this volume, p. 341.

13. See also *HNH* XV 35-41, = 20,25-23,14 Mewaldt.
14. See Frede (1981); ch. 3 (Tieleman) in this volume, pp. 53-5; ch. 6 (Hankinson) in this volume.
15. The same also goes for colour: new colours may emerge in compositions, but only if what compose them are themselves coloured; this is another hit at the atomists. On the interpretation and plausibility of this thesis, see Hankinson (forthcoming (1)); see also Caston (1997, 350-7).
16. Athenaeus was the founder of the Pneumatist school of medicine in the first century BC; he held that disease was caused by imbalances in the *pneuma*, the subtle, modified air that permeated the body. See p. 230.
17. The Aristotelian provenance of the matter–form analysis is obvious; but Galen evidently invokes the dubiously Aristotelian prime matter, and does so using the Stoic term *apoios*.
18. For more on this text, see Barnes (1991).
19. Cf. *SMT* XI 470: hot and dry ailments are more easily cured, since these are the more active qualities.
20. Or 'Dogmatist': on the medical 'sects', see chs. 2 (Lloyd), 3 (Tieleman), 1 and 6 (Hankinson) all in this volume.
21. See again Smith (1979).
22. Galen later came to favour the un-Aristotelian idea that the semen, too, contributed material as well as form to the embryo: *On Semen* (*Sem.*) IV 527-34, = 78,24-84,14 De Lacy; *On the Formation of the Foetus* (*Foet.Form.*) IV 659, = 62,8-11 Nickel; and see Nickel (1989, 86, n. 1); De Lacy (1996, 201).
23. Here Plato's term for the Craftsman God turns up in Galen for the first, but by no means the last time: see further pp. 233-4.
24. Galen goes as far as to say that blood can be yellowish, white or 'almost black'; which are the colours of bile, phlegm and black bile, respectively, although he does not labour the point (I 496-7, = 144,2-7).
25. However, see ch. 12 (Vogt) in this volume for discussion of the tensions between Galen's theory and his practice in pharmacology.
26. For the internal difficulties that Galen's somewhat lopsided theory runs into here, see Brain (1986, 7-8); but it is not as incoherent as Brain thinks.
27. Of course, it can be hot and cold in respect of different parts; but this would not involve a *mixture* of the qualities.
28. The authenticity of *Ars Med.* as we possess it has been called into question (Kollesch, 1988); but scholarly opinion inclines still to regard it as genuine: see Boudon (1996, 2000a, 157-64).

29. This is an index of the extent to which Galen is resistant to mere apriorism: what matters is not the neatness of the typology, but whether it is true. Cf. Barnes (1991, 97): 'Galen's list [sc. of types of disease] lacks symmetry and elegance . . . But Galen is not interested in elegant symmetry: his concern is for the truth.'

30. Following an ancient orthodoxy, deriving ultimately from Plato, and further developed in Aristotle and Theophrastus, Galen accounts for the different 'functions' of different animal-species in terms of their fundamental constitutions: thus lions, being extremely hot, are also extremely brave: *On Mixtures* (*Temp.*) I 565–6, = 35,28–36,7; cf. *On Moral Character* (*Mor.*) 1, 236 Mattock (1972).

31. In the case of the wet and the dry, touch will sometimes not suffice on its own to determine the true nature of the mixture, 'but reason must be employed as well; if a body is dry, it must also be hard, and this hardness is perceptible by touch; but not every hard body is necessarily dry' (598, = 56,12–16). Ice for example is hard; but it is (obviously) also wet. In general, wet things can be made hard by freezing, and so it is only if something appears hard at a moderate temperature that we can infer that it is naturally dry.

32. Galen was himself aware of the problem: *MM* X 183, 650–1; *Temp.* I 606–9; this is one reason why it is a stochastic, i.e. approximative, art: *On Treatment by Bloodletting* [*Cur.Rat.Ven.Sect.*] XI 285–6; see Harig (1974).

33. Galen discusses the properties of oil, as well as the mistaken inferences people are inclined to make regarding its natural properties, at *SMT* XI 470–82; see further Hankinson (forthcoming (1)).

34. See also e.g. *ibid.* 28, 46, 80–1, 133, 143–6, 148–9, 177–8, 180–3, 196, 213, = 121,2–9, 134,20–135,3, 159,5–17, 198,3–8, 204,8–206,12, 208,2–24, 229,14–230,7, 231,19–233,26, 243,17–23, 256,7–11, etc.

35. Which is for him, rather than cardiac action, the cause of blood-flow (although the expansive power of the arterial coats is transmitted from the heart): see *On the Function of the Pulse* (*Us.Puls.*) V 149–80, esp. 162–4,168–9, 170–2; *On Whether Blood is Naturally Contained in the Arteries* (*Art.Sang.*) IV 725–7, 730, 732, 733–4; and see Amacher (1964).

36. Asclepiades was significantly influenced by atomism: see Vallance (1990).

37. See Debru, ch. 10 in this volume, pp. 268–9.

38. See van der Eijk (1997, 293–7), for a discussion of the differences between Galen's various understandings of the term *dunamis*.

39. Thus they are not entities 'which inhabit substances as we do houses': *The Faculties of the Soul Follow the Mixtures of the Body* (*QAM*) IV 769–70, = *SM* 2,33,17–34,14.

40. See ch. 6 (Hankinson) in this volume, p. 159; and Hankinson (1994c).
41. Although Aristotle refers to instruments, he does not make them into a separate causal category (*Phys* 2.3, 195a1–3); but instrumental causes became a standard feature of Neoplatonic causal schemata; see Hankinson (1998b, 342–3, 379–83, 444–5).
42. Galen invokes Plato in the *Phaedo* and *Timaeus*: see *Phaed.* 98b-99b, on the real reasons for Socrates' remaining in jail (that he has thought it best), and the distinction between the genuine cause of the Demiurge's design and the other, material 'contributory causes' (*Tim.* 46c-e).
43. See Dillon (1977, 138); Hankinson (1998b, 338, 342–3, 351, 354, 384–5).
44. This passage refers to two different types of final cause; elsewhere Galen sometimes distinguishes something's *telos* from its *skopos*: 'the *skopos* of medicine is health; its *telos* is the achievement of it' (*On Sects for Beginners* [*SI*] I 64, = *SM* 3, 1,1–2). The *telos* here is the actualized end, that which is aimed at, but not invariably achieved, by medical practice, since medicine is a *technê stochastikê*, a conjectural art, that is, it is one where successful practice consists in adopting the best possible means towards an end, and not necessarily in achieving it: see Ierodiakonou (1995); Hankinson (1998a, 179, 192–3). But Galen does not always observe any such distinction: 'it does not matter whether you wish to call it the *telos* or the *chreia* or the *skopos*' (*CP* vi 57, 88,18–20 Hankinson).
45. See Hankinson (1998a, 192–212) for full discussion of this passage; in another context (*Symp.Diff.* VII 47–8) he uses the language of *per se* and incidental to distinguish between proximate and remote causes of the same effect.
46. See further Hankinson (1988a, 1989).
47. See ch. 7 (Donini) in this volume; and Hankinson (2006).
48. Galen's conceptualization of the operation and function of the arteries is thus curiously analogous to that of the two-stroke internal combustion engine.
49. This term has also been rendered 'cohesive', 'sustaining'; none of these translations is altogether satisfactory, but I will continue to use the first.
50. For the Stoics, it was their *pneuma*, a dynamic volatile mixture of air and fire, that was responsible for binding together the heavier elements: §47F, G LS.
51. Cf. also *Against Julian* XVIIA 279–80, = *CMG* V 10,3, 58,1–4.
52. See e.g. *On Hippocrates' 'Nature of Man'* (*HNH*) XV 114, 162, = *CMG* V 9,1, 59,31–5, 82,23–30; *On the differences of Fevers* (*Diff.Feb.*) VII 279; *MM* X 667; *CP* xv 187, 142,3–10 Hankinson. The sense in which some of them are 'external' is not an obvious one: see Hankinson (1987a) for further discussion; and see also Hankinson (2003).

53. Sometimes Galen says that for something to count as a disease, the damage to the natural activities must be *perceptible* (e.g. *Ars Med.* I 379, = 359,13–361,4 Boudon); but here he notes that to define disease simply as functional damage leads to the doctrine of 'perpetual suffering' (i.e that everyone is always a bit sick), which may be logically unassailable but is no use from the point of view of practical therapy. He makes the same point at *Temp.* I 675-7, = 104,8–105,5; and cf. *On Affected Parts* (*Loc.Aff.*) VIII 25–30.

54. On the general medical concept, see Ackerknecht (1982).

55. There is a broader sense of 'symptom' which covers anything which occurs within the body contrary to its nature, and thus encompasses all of these categories, with the exception of external (antecedent) causes: *Symp.Diff.* VII 54–5.

56. A constant Galenic theme: see Hankinson (1994a); and ch. 5 (Morison) in this volume.

57. For further analysis, see Hankinson (1991b, 161–4).

58. Galen does not invariably talk of preceding causes, *aitia proêgoumena*, at any rate in the technical sense he ascribes to Athenaeus: 'whatever is thus produced in the body which belongs to the class of what causes disease, but has not yet actually given rise to a disease, is known as a preceding cause' (*CC* 2.3, 57,16–18 ≈ 134,14–15); and he sometimes uses the term in a looser sense to refer to any cause that precedes its effect (i.e. any non-containing cause).

59. For more on Galen on the soul, see ch. 7 (Donini) in this volume; and Hankinson (1993, 2006), and the articles collected in Manuli and Vegetti (1988).

60. Although as Michael Frede has shown (Frede, 2003), there is more to be said about Galen's religious attitude than is sometimes thought; cf. Kudlien (1981).

61. *Pace* Siegel (1968); see also Hankinson (1989). Thus Galen's teleology is in general outline authentically Platonic, even if its fine structure owes more to Aristotle.

62. Another Platonic borrowing: *Tim.* 34a-37c.

63. For more on the development of the argument in this text, see Hankinson (forthcoming (2) and (3)).

64. See ch. 6 (Hankinson) in this volume, pp. 178–80.

65. On this passage, see Hankinson (1988a).

66. Such as a superfluous sixth finger: Nature does this only once in every 10 million cases, he says: IV 355–6, = ii 444,2–22. The comparison with human artists (usually to the latter's detriment) is commonplace: III 238–40, = i 175,3–176,7; *Nat.Fac.* II 82–5 = *SM* 3, 160,14–162,14.

67. Note, however, that at *Prop.Plac.* 4.1, 62,18–19, he writes 'I claim no knowledge concerning the celestial bodies'; but his ignorance concerns their material constitution, not their activities.

68. Galen accepted the prevailing doctrine of spontaneous generation (cf. *CP* vii 82, 98,1–4 Hankinson; see Hankinson, 1998a, 208–9); later, he instances the flea as an example of the care bestowed by Nature on even insignificant creatures: 361–2, = ii 448,9–449,14.

69. Note Galen's choice of intellectual hero: two philosophers, an astronomer and a mathematician–engineer.

70. See Frede (2003, 111–23) for a detailed analysis of Galen's views on light, the sun and the propagation of divine power.

71. Contact of some sort does seem to be necessary for causal interaction, however: see his account of neural transmission at *PHP* V 567, = 410,24–5 De Lacy (cf. *Nat.Fac.* II 161, = *SM* 3, 217,18–25; *CAM* I 251, = 78,22–7 Fortuna). I discuss these issues in more detail in Hankinson (forthcoming (2)).

72. See May (1968, 399–400, n. 42).

9 Anatomy

It is with pleasure I hear GALEN reason concerning the
structure of the human body.
(Hume, *Dialogues Concerning Natural Religion*, xii)

INTRODUCTION

In seeking the best physician, the prospective patient is advised,
according to Galen, first to 'find out how wide his knowledge is and
how penetrative is his training in anatomy'.[1] For Galen, anatomy is
more than a system of knowledge for its own sake. It is also used
to demonstrate that Nature does nothing in vain. Further, it provides information in examining psychic or physical activities and
is a precision tool for the operative practitioner.[2] These respective
epistemic, teleological, empirical and practical ends underscore the
crucial place of anatomy for Galen in his medical and philosophical
world.[3] To an appreciable extent, all four cannot be entirely separated. An examination of Galen's employment of anatomy is reward-
ing not only because it informed his medical practice and defined
for him the true worth of a physician, but also because it offers a
window into his investigations into the nature of the living organism. This chapter will begin by underscoring Galen's indebtedness
to his predecessors and teachers. It will next examine Galen's public
anatomical demonstrations and why he felt them to be necessary.
Although Galen's physiology is examined elsewhere in this volume
(ch.10 (Debru)), anatomy and physiology cannot entirely be separated, and the two come together in Galen's study of the brain and

nerves. This chapter will therefore conclude by discussing Galen's handling of two structures of the brain, the ventricles and the retiform plexus. Both perfectly encapsulate Galen's anatomical technique and methodology, as well as inevitably illustrating their shortcomings. Nonetheless, they form the high water mark of anatomical investigation in antiquity.

I

The depth and range of Galen's anatomical works attest to the subject's importance for him.[4] Anatomy was a prominent part of Galen's medical education. His teachers are characterised by him on the basis of their anatomical knowledge as much as for their expertise in Hippocratic interpretation.[5] Galen's first anatomy teacher was Satyrus,[6] the author of an 'Anatomy', which, however, was 'neither exhaustive nor final'.[7] Satyrus was taught by Quintus, a noted physician in Hadrian's time, possessed of the 'greatest skill in anatomy',[8] but who left no anatomical writings. Galen's wealthy background allowed him to travel in search of the best education. In Smyrna, Galen had attended lectures by Pelops, who 'wrote some very valuable books, but after his death all were destroyed by fire before anyone had copied them.'[9] Pelops was the pupil of Numisianus, who in turn was the 'most renowned' pupil of Quintus. Numisianus is described as 'a man of profound learning, who had valuable ideas on the subject of anatomy. He wrote many books, although during his lifetime these did not reach a wide public.'[10] Galen visited Corinth and several other places to glean information from Numisianus' pupils.[11] Lycus the Macedonian, also a pupil of Quintus, is described as 'far inferior' to Pelops and Satyrus, and was the 'author of a book on anatomy which at the present time enjoys a wide circulation, although he is a man who, in his lifetime, had no great reputation amongst the Greeks'.[12] Lycus also seems to have written a history of anatomy.[13] Yet in spite of his criticism of Lycus, Galen wrote a two-volume abridgment of his anatomical works.[14]

The study and assimilation by Galen of the works of his predecessors and teachers was surely a factor in his long stay in Alexandria (AD 153–7), even though Galen is reticent as to exactly what he did there.[15] Since Herophilus and Erasistratus, students and teachers of medicine had either frequented Alexandria or had received instruction from those who had studied there, although it is obvious that the breadth and depth of teaching must have been quite varied. But given this history and Alexandria's role in the instruction of some of Galen's teachers such as Satyrus and Pelops, medical scholarship in Alexandria must have been sufficient to have held Galen's attention for four years. And the cachet of an Alexandrian education could only benefit his future career. According to Galen, the spur to anatomical knowledge originated in Alexandria, for it was Herophilus (and Eudemus the Herophilean) who 'increased anatomical theory most' until Marinus and Numisianus.[16] Galen describes Marinus as having 'accumulated no small experience in dissections, and it was he himself who had set his hand to and had observed everything that he explained in his writings . . . . although now and then we may discover him in error'.[17] Galen singles out Marinus of Alexandria for having recovered (*anaktêsamenos*) the study of anatomy after it had fallen into neglect.[18] Marinus, together with several anonymous doctors gave 'their whole life' to this enterprise.[19] Galen composed a four-book summary of Marinus' twenty-volume text on anatomy.[20] In *On My Own Books* (*Lib.Prop.*), a work meant, among other things, to showcase Galen's achievements, he devotes more space to Marinus than to any other physician or philosopher. Marinus also thought the question of the controlling centre or *hêgemonikon* of the body important enough to dedicate an entire volume to it.[21] As will be shown, this was a subject to which Galen devoted a great deal of time and effort.

II

Galen returned to Pergamum in 157 with sufficient skills to be appointed physician to the gladiatorial school for four years.[22] Galen reveals how he was chosen, illustrating that combination of technical dexterity, polemic, showmanship and flair for the dramatic which he would exercise in his public demonstrations in Rome:

Once I attended a public gathering where men had met to test the knowledge of physicians. I performed many anatomical demonstrations before the spectators: I made an incision in the abdomen of an ape and exposed its intestines: then I called upon the physicians who were present to replace them back (in position) and to make the necessary abdominal sutures – but

none of them dared to do this. We ourselves then treated the ape display-
ing our skill, manual training, and dexterity. Furthermore, we deliberately
severed many large veins, thus allowing the blood to run freely, and called
upon the Elders of the physicians to provide treatment, but they had nothing to offer. We then provided treatment, making it clear to the intellectuals who were present that (physicians) who possess skills like mine should
be in charge of the wounded. That man was delighted when he put me
in charge of the wounded – and he was the first to entrust me with their
care. (*Opt.Med.Cogn.* 105,4–15 Iskandar)

The gladiatorial school of Pergamum gave Galen further opportunity
to master a set of practical skills he would need in order to produce his
anatomical and physiological texts. It would also reinforce Galen's
confidence in the value of public display. Properly handled, therefore,
anatomy readily lent itself to such an exhibition, and the results
could be impressive and were designed to be persuasive.[23] These
ends are perfectly encapsulated by the following passage:

I know an intelligent and wise man who selected and honoured me when he
saw a single act of mine: I dissected an animal by which I demonstrated the
organs of the voice and the organs of locomotion. Two months earlier, that
man had happened to fall from a considerable height, thus rupturing many
organs in his body, and losing his voice altogether, so that his voice became
like a whisper. His organs were treated, became sound, and recovered after
several days: yet his voice did not return. When this man saw from me what
he saw, he gained confidence in me and entrusted himself to me. I cured
him in a few days because I knew where the affected part was and attended
to it. (*Opt.Med.Cogn.* 107,3–11 Iskandar)[24]

These exhibitions were carried out in Rome, where Galen took
full advantage of the atmosphere created by the Second Sophistic.[25]
Galen's public exhibitions, such as those demonstrating the nerves
of the voice, were more than a painstaking exercise in identifying and
isolating the nerves in question.[26] In these and other performances
such as that cited above, Galen knew that part of his audience would
be familiar with at least some of his experimental methodology and
could follow his reasoning.[27] Galen therefore appealed to the intellectual aspirations of his target audience, using in part the devices
and techniques which such a group, accustomed to public discourse
from philosophers, rhetors and sophists, could relate to and appreciate. It is clear that a well-executed demonstration concerning such

an important function as the power of speech could assist a potential client in choosing a physician. A prospective patient might also be impressed by a display of anatomical erudition, especially if such learning was directly applicable to his own illness. For Galen, the anatomical science displayed on such occasions underscores the fundamental importance of such knowledge for both patient and physician. Galen's statement that 'physicians need anatomy to the highest degree'[28] is not simply self-serving but an indication that in Rome there are not only patients to be persuaded, but also medical colleagues.

In Galen's view, two medical sects denied the value of anatomical investigation in everyday practice. These were the Empiricists and Methodists. Empiricists denied the epistemological validity of anatomical dissection and experimentation. They regarded them as unattainable investigations into hidden causes, instead basing their methodology on experience.[29] According to Celsus, the Empiricist argues that such knowledge is unnecessary since what is obtained from vivisection and dissection is not true understanding of the body under normal conditions, since the very act of dissection produces significant changes in the appearance of the structures under investigation.[30] The best way to obtain useful information relevant to treatment is to take advantage of examinations on living persons as may come one's way.[31] For Galen, this is simply 'adventitious anatomy' (epeisaktos anatomia).[32] The Methodists also saw no need for the researches of anatomy and physiology. Methodist medical epistemology employed reason, not for use in the search for hidden causes but in the acquisition of information about the body which is 'obvious' to any thinking person.[33] They claimed to teach the method of medicine (hence their name) in six months.[34] This standpoint alone is deeply inimical to Galen, whose own extraordinarily lengthy medical education is seen by him as the paradigm of a good doctor. Galen considers the Methodist approach to medical education 'belief without demonstration'.[35] However, like the Empiricists, the Methodists did not entirely dispute the acquisition of anatomical knowledge obtained through dissection.[36] But dissection for the sake of acquisition of new knowledge was not considered. Not all doctors, then, performed anatomy to Galen's standards, much less deemed such extensive knowledge relevant for daily practice. Their arguments could not always easily be dismissed and Galen's awesome anatomical erudition should not blind us to this fact.

III

One of the most impressive of Galen's contributions to anatomical science is his description of the ventricles of the brain. Their study encapsulates his expertise in anatomical investigation. For him, what makes us who we are – possessors of the *hêgemonikon* of the rational soul – is possible only because of four communicating cavities deep within the brain. By its action as the 'first instrument' (*prôton organon*) of the rational soul, psychic *pneuma* in the ventricles is made by Galen to account for sensation and voluntary motion.[37] Galen based his decision on empirical grounds: his knowledge of anatomy, his vivisectional experiments on animals and partly his observations of brain-injured patients. Although Herophilus and Erasistratus were the first to state formally the importance of the ventricles it is Galen who creates their detailed anatomical and physiological portrait. To comprehend ventricular internal anatomy requires from Galen anatomical precision and painstaking dissection. The complexity is such that Galen remarks that: 'Often, indeed, when I have wished to attain to a complete knowledge of the nature of this region, have I met with no slight uncertainty.'[38] Galen's method of building an image of the anatomy under examination through repeated dissection is meant to resolve such uncertainty. Moreover, Galen's handling of the ventricles also affords glimpses of other, anonymous anatomists also engaged in the investigation of the brain.

Galen describes two paired lateral ventricles – the anterior (or first) ventricles – deep within each cerebral hemisphere, which communicate with each other and with the third (or middle) ventricle across the midline via an interventricular foramen. The third ventricle also communicates with the fourth (posterior) ventricle via a passage (the aqueduct) which Galen says some anatomists have viewed as a ventricle.[39] The roof of the fourth ventricle is dominated by the mass of the cerebellum. The floor of the fourth ventricle narrows into the central canal of the spinal cord, which Galen interprets as a passage through which psychic *pneuma* gains access to the nerves. Galen's ventricular system is thus a continuous series of symmetrical chambers, linked by passages or canals, and communicating with the brain substance, the cranial nerves and the spinal cord.[40] The anterior ventricles contain a fine network of veins and arteries known as the choroid plexuses, which are responsible for the final elaboration of psychic *pneuma*. The anterior ventricles communicate directly with the optic nerves via 'perceptible pores'.[41] Galen claims priority for the discovery of this ventricular origin of the optic nerves.[42] He does so by implicitly drawing attention to his own skill in dissection by stating that other anatomists 'have not understood this marvellous work of Nature' and so failed to elucidate this fact.[43]

The anterior ventricles also communicate with the nasal passages.[44] The olfactory outlet is the only sense instrument created within the anterior ventricles of the brain.[45] For Galen, the anterior ventricles encompass four functions: they elaborate psychic *pneuma*, they ensure its passage to the eye via the optic tract; they are the instruments of olfaction; they discharge residues.[46] The middle or third ventricle, through its communication with the anterior ventricles, allows psychic *pneuma* to pass to the fourth ventricle and spinal cord. By its complex series of ducts which lead to the pharynx via the base of the brain, it is also responsible for the removal of the heavier waste-products of nutrition.[47] According to Galen, some anatomists regard the middle ventricle only as a communicating duct or else consider it part of the fourth ventricle.[48] Others are 'completely ignorant' of the presence of the middle ventricle.[49] The polemic thrust aside, that Galen sets down rival accounts – if only in passing – indicates anatomical complexity as well as anatomical disputation. According to Galen, one large passage (the aqueduct) connects the third and fourth ventricles. It lies between the cerebral hemispheres and the cerebellum and was first noticed by Erasistratus, who 'wrote accurately' about the four ventricles of the brain.[50] This aqueduct is covered by the 'worm-like outgrowth' (*skolêkoeidês epiphusis*), the vermiform epiphysis of the cerebellum, which sets the limits of the extent of the aqueduct and regulates the flow of psychic *pneuma* through it.[51] Galen states that the aqueduct has the length it possesses in order that the vermiform epiphysis may have as full a range of movement as possible.[52] For Galen this is further evidence of the 'most precise skill' (*akribestatê technê*) of Nature.[53] Galen describes the anatomy of the fourth ventricle in a way which clearly indicates that its most notable feature (the *kalamos* or *calamus scriptorius* at its base) was delineated by Herophilus.[54] But subsequently there have been mistakes among anatomists regarding its true location.[55] The distal portion of the fourth ventricle ends at the beginning of the spinal cord or spinal marrow.[56] Galen also fixes the end of the fourth ventricle to that part of the surface of the brain where Galen's seventh (and for him the last) cranial nerve pair arise. Since the termination of the ventricular system marks the end of the brain, the outgrowth of this cranial nerve establishes the brain's distal limits.[57] Galen also describes where other (unnamed) anatomists have placed the end of the fourth ventricle.[58] But in fixing the end of the fourth ventricle at the point where animals are slaughtered (the region of the upper vertebral bodies in the neck), Galen reinforces both its critical importance and the legitimacy of his interpretation. The reason the butcher's wound is fatal here, according to Galen, is that the fourth ventricle has been opened, *not* that the dura has been incised. Galen also observes that the distal part of the fourth ventricle, where it borders on the first part of the spinal marrow, is not covered by any other part of the brain except the dura.[59] If, however, the dura is damaged in any way, then this is interpreted by Galen as an injury to the fourth ventricle and its contents, not to any other part of the brain or its covering membranes. In this way, Galen refutes the notion first mooted by Erasistratus, that it is damage to the dura alone which is responsible for the lack of sensation and motion in an animal when this area is incised.[60] The spinal marrow arises from the brain, and Galen refers to it as an 'offshoot from the substance of the brain'.[61] Psychic *pneuma* in the ventricles must be able to pass into the spinal marrow and hence the nerves.[62] The spinal marrow is the source of all the hard nerves of the body, the nerves of motion.[63] Cranial nerves, some of which are sensory as well as motor, are derived from the base of the brain. All other nerves are derived from either the spinal cord or cerebellum.

Galen's ventricular experiments reflect the methodology that characterises his entire approach to the investigation of the brain and the nerves. These experiments were performed on a variety of animals, and required a large and reliable supply.[64] The effects of incising the ventricles in the living animal are noted as follows:

(Incising) the posterior (ventricle) harms the animal most, and next after that the middle (ventricle). (Incising) each of the anterior (ventricles) causes a less serious injury, but of a greater degree in older animals, a lesser degree in the young. (*PHP* V 605, = 442,30–2 De Lacy)

To these observations, Galen adds that pressure on the ventricles produces similar effects; for example, during trepanation.[65] The physiological agent affected by these various injuries is stated to be psychic *pneuma*:

From these phenomena you might assume either of two things about the pneuma in the ventricles of the brain: if the soul is without body, the pneuma is, as it were, its first home; or if the soul is embodied, then pneuma is the soul. But when after a short time, following the closure of the ventricle, the animal regains sensation and motion, it is no longer possible to accept either alternative concerning pneuma. It is better, then, to accept that the soul resides in the actual body of the brain, whatever its substance may be – for the examination has not yet arrived at this question – , and that the soul's first instrument for all the sensations of the animal and for its voluntary motions is this pneuma; and therefore, when the pneuma has escaped, and until it collects again, whilst it does not deprive the animal of life, it makes it incapable of sensation and motion. For indeed, if pneuma itself were the substance of the soul, the animal would instantly die along with the escape of the pneuma. (*PHP* V 605–6, = 442,36–444,11 De Lacy; cf. 609, = 446,11–17)

Galen limits himself to demonstrating not the actions of the rational or hegemonic soul, but only its governing agency which he fixes within the ventricular system of the brain.[66] Although Galen never formally articulates a doctrine of ventricular or brain localization, his observations that different physical actions may be elicited, depending on which ventricle is pressed or incised, laid the groundwork for later such concepts.[67]

Galen's description of his experiments performed on the exposed brain merits citing in its entirety:

Should the dissection be thus performed, then after you have laid open the brain, and divested it of the dura mater, you can first of all press down upon the brain on each of its four ventricles, and observe what derangements have afflicted the animal. I will describe to you what is always to be seen when you make this dissection, and also before it, where the skull has been perforated, as soon as one presses upon the brain with the instrument which the ancients call 'the protector of the dura mater'. Should the brain be compressed on both the two anterior ventricles, then the degree of stupor which overcomes the animal is slight. Should it be compressed on the middle ventricle, then the stupor of the animal is heavier. And when one presses down upon that ventricle which is found in the part of the brain lying at the nape of the neck, then the animal falls into a very heavy and pronounced stupor. This is what happens also when you cut into the cerebral ventricles, except that if you cut into these ventricles, the animal does not revert to its natural condition as it does when you press upon them. Nevertheless it does sometimes do this if the incision should become united. This return to the normal condition follows more easily and more quickly, should the incision be made upon the two anterior ventricles. But if the incision encounters the middle ventricle, then the return to the normal comes to pass less easily and speedily. And if the incision should have been imposed upon the fourth, that is, the posterior ventricle, then the animal seldom returns to its natural condition; although nevertheless if the incision should be made into this fourth ventricle, provided that you do not make the cut very extensive, that you proceed quickly, and that in the compression of the wound in some way or other you employ a certain amount of haste, the animal will revert to its normal state, since the pressure upon the wound is then temporary only – and indeed especially in those regions where no portion of the brain overlies this ventricle, but where the meninx only is found. You then see how the animal blinks with its eyes, especially when you bring some object near to the eyes, even when you have exposed to view the posterior ventricle. Should you go towards the animal while it is in this condition, and should you press upon some one part of the two anterior ventricles, no matter which part it may be, in the place where as I stated the root of the two optic nerves lies, thereupon the animal ceases to blink with its two eyes, even when you bring some object near to the pupils, and the whole appearance of the eye on the side on which lies the ventricle of the brain upon which you are pressing becomes like the eyes of blind men. (*AA* IX.12; 18–19 DLT)

This is the most impressive account of anatomical exegesis and physiological experimentation extant in Antiquity and Galen provides a formidable combination of factors to manipulate successfully.[68] The underlying message is that failure to observe what Galen has expounded means only that the procedure has been improperly carried out; not that the methodology or the results can be called into question. It should also be noted that Galen exploits what he maintains is the anatomically verifiable link between the anterior ventricle and the eye to affirm the importance of the anterior ventricles in motor and sensory activities. With the brain exposed, Galen notes that the animal continues to blink its eyes, 'even when you have exposed to view the posterior ventricle'. Galen cites the posterior ventricle in this way to emphasize that it has no effect on the physiology of the eye. But when pressure is placed upon the anterior ventricles then, as one approaches the animal, it ceases to blink, and the 'whole appearance of the eye on the side on which lies the ventricle of the brain upon which you are pressing becomes like the eyes of blind men.' Another text infers that the reason for this lack of reaction is that the flow of psychic *pneuma* from the eyes to the optic nerves is impeded.[69]

Observations on humans could also yield clues. Galen noted the effects on the ventricles of trepanation.[70] Trepanation afforded Galen opportunity for observing symptoms which, he maintained, ensued from the consequent ventricular disturbance. Galen provides an account of the effects of a head injury and its interpretation in ventricular terms.[71] There, a young man from Smyrna is recorded as having survived a wound to the ventricles. In mentioning what he has witnessed, Galen easily moves from discussing a clinical condition to a similar picture reproducible in an animal.[72] As noted in the above citation, pressure applied to both anterior ventricles results in stupor (*karos*) which Galen describes as 'slight'. Pressure on the middle ventricle produces a stupor that is 'heavier' in degree, and when the posterior ventricle is affected, the stupor is 'pronounced'. During trepanation, the tension (*tonos*) of the *pneuma* in the ventricle falls, which accounts, says Galen, for the pain experienced (apart from that caused by the procedure).[73] An alteration to the balance of *pneumatic* tension by pressure is deemed sufficient by Galen to result in a pathological condition. It is also used by him to interpret the experimental effects of pressure on the ventricles.

From the standpoint of the severity of symptoms, the posterior ventricle is the most important. Galen underlines this by stating that psychic *pneuma* is the 'first instrument' of the soul, especially the *pneuma* in the posterior ventricles.[74] Galen notes that an incision into the posterior ventricle harms the animal most, next affected is the middle ventricle, whilst each anterior ventricle is least harmed by incision. The effects are more severe in older animals.[75] For Galen, ventricular incision allows him to create the conditions for resealing the ventricle, allowing both the animal to recuperate, and the results to be interpreted in *pneumatic* terms. That the animal can recover is ascribed to the replenishment of *pneuma* following closure of the incised ventricle.[76] No other substance, according to Galen, is as capable of *emptying* or of *collecting* again so easily. *Pneuma* is capable of moving into the body *instantaneously* (*en akarei chronôi*).[77] Psychic *pneuma* therefore can on empirical grounds be placed within the ventricular system.[78] Psychic *pneuma* accounts for sensation and

voluntary motion, and, being the soul's 'first instrument', the actions
of the soul can be accounted for in pneumatic terms.[79] The ventricles, seen as focal points for the *hêgemonikon* of the rational soul,
therefore have a clearly defined status within Galen's system in that
their interruption at various points leads to empirically verifiable
disturbances. Yet Galen's argument of using psychic *pneuma* in this
way also allows his pneumatic physiology to carry a set of functional
differentiae that effectively excludes the localization of soul within
the ventricular system.[80]

For Galen, the ventricles qualitatively change vital *pneuma* to its
psychic form. This is accomplished by two vascular structures in
the brain. These consist of the *retiform plexus* (*diktuoeides plegma*)
the famous *rete mirabile*, a network of small arteries at the base of the
brain, and the *choroid plexuses* (*choroeidê plegmata*), appendages of
small arteries and veins within the anterior and middle ventricles.[81]
This account will conclude by examining the former structure.
Galen's depiction of the retiform plexus not only illustrates his conception of a purposeful Nature but is also an excellent example of
the strength of his anatomical discourse:

> The plexus known as retiform by anatomists, is the most marvellous of the
> structures in this area. It surrounds as a circle the gland itself, and for the
> most part extends as far as the rear, since this plexus is immediately under
> all but a little of the base of the brain. It is not merely a net-like structure
> but looks as if you had taken several fisherman's nets and stretched one out
> over the other. But it is characteristic of Nature's net that the meshwork of
> one layer is always attached to the other, thereby making it impossible to
> remove any one net by itself; for, one after the other, all the rest follow the
> one you remove, since they are all attached to each other. Naturally, because
> of the fineness of the members composing this network, and their intimate
> conjunction, you could neither compare this plexus to any man-made net,
> nor ascribe its formation to chance. On the contrary, Nature appropriated
> as the material for this marvellous network the greatest part of the [internal
> carotid] arteries that ascend from the heart to the head. (*UP* III 696–7, = ii
> 10,9–11,2 Helmreich; cf. *PHP* V 607–8, = 444,20–29 De Lacy)

The retiform plexus, then, is described as a structure whose existence is already known to other anatomists. Galen also states that
the retiform plexus was named either by Herophilus or by 'those
about Herophilus'.[82] In either case, Galen cites an existing anatomical tradition created by the authority of Herophilus. To expose the

plexus it is necessary, after removing the brain, to examine a discrete area within the base of the cranial cavity that, covered by the dura mater, is indistinguishable from the rest of the base of the skull. The plexus is present in animals such as the ox, goat, pig and sheep. In other words, in those animals Galen routinely employed for brain dissection. It does not exist in man or primate, but like Herophilus, Galen extrapolates it to the human brain.[83]

The physiological importance of the retiform plexus is remarked on as follows:

Accordingly the pneuma in relation to the arteries is called vital, and that in regard to the brain is psychic, not that it exists as the substance of the soul, but rather as the first instrument of the soul which resides in the brain, whatever may be its substance. And just as vital pneuma is generated in the arteries as well as the heart, obtaining the material for its generation from inhalation and the vaporization of the humours, so the psychic pneuma is generated by a further elaboration of the vital. For it was necessary that this pneuma, by all means be changed in precisely the correct fashion. If Nature, needing to fashion semen and milk with precision, even though they are far inferior in power to psychic pneuma, nevertheless arranged for each a lengthy period in the organs of coction and for that reason provided for semen the spiral vessels for the testes and for milk the length of the vessels that go to the breasts, so naturally also that when elaborating psychic from vital pneuma in the brain it constructed close to the brain a complex labyrinth, as it were, the retiform plexus. (*PHP* V 608–9, = 444,29–446,10 De Lacy)

This 'complex labyrinth' (*poikilos laburinthos*) is analogously related by Galen to the vasculature of the mammary gland and the testis. The arterial convolutions at the base of the brain, according to Galen, allow sufficient time to elapse to complete the final processing of psychic *pneuma* in the ventricular system by the choroid plexuses. The stages of *pneumatic* elaboration are summarized by Galen in these words:

From the outside air, pneuma is drawn in by the rough arteries and receives its first elaboration in the flesh of the lungs, its second in the heart and the arteries, especially those of the retiform plexus, and then a final elaboration in the ventricles of the brain, which completes its transformation into psychic pneuma. (*UP* III 541–2, = i 393,23–394,6 Helmreich)

Pneumatic elaboration consists of a series of analogous processes in separate organs. Galen compares the process with the coction of nutriment.[84] Coction (*pepsis*) is a familiar process and verifiable in terms of its end product. It is a process that is also seen to take time. Galen wishes to draw the comparison between the substrates used in both pneumatic elaboration and the process of coction by referring to 'material *pneuma*' being 'analogous to the dry and moist nutriment'.[85] The elaboration of nutriment also allows Galen to claim that both the means and method of pneumatic elaboration may also be said to occur within specified organs. When Galen says that outside air is prepared in the lungs, this change is made possible by the fundamental *power* (*dunamis*) of the lungs that determines their status as unique organs for this particular physiological elaboration.[86] The familiar effects of the processing of nutriment are extended analogously to make the relatively lesser-known elaborations of psychic *pneuma* more acceptable to Galen's audience. The intent of the analogy of coction is to render the account of *pneumatic* elaboration in easily understood terms and to promote it as the most likely explanation.

The second of Galen's two arguments from analogy is anatomically based, and depends on a specific comparison of the elaboration of psychic *pneuma* with that of semen in the testicular vessels, which possess a broadly similar retinacular form to that of the retiform plexus.[87] The testicular plexus is not precisely of the same configuration as the retiform (it is composed of veins as well as arteries).[88] However, its elaborative function is set out by Galen in such a way that a comparison with the working up of psychic *pneuma* by the retiform plexus may better be understood. That this vascular plexus is *convoluted* is necessary so that blood will spend sufficient time in it in order to be elaborated into semen.[89] The outcome of this process is semen that is of the 'purest quality' (*eilikrinestatê poiotês*).[90] Galen explicitly compares the retiform plexus to two other broadly similar vascular structures, one of which is the testicular plexus:

The fact that this marvellous plexus was placed by Nature, who does nothing in vain, in such a well-protected space, seemed to be an indication of some great use. Since we find the vessels like those of the spiral of the intestines and those that enter the testes made for the precise concoctions of the matter contained in them as well as for the abundant provisioning of their further activities, it seemed reasonable to suppose that Nature has devised this stratagem in order to elaborate for a long time the matter within the arteries, being hot and thin and air-like blood, as well as to provide abundant nourishment to the psychic pneuma in the brain. (*Us.Puls.* V, 155–6 200 Furley/Wilkie)

For Galen, all three vascular structures possess the right degree of anatomical complexity conferred on them by Nature in order to elaborate the appropriate *matter* they contain. However, the comparison between the testicular vessels with those of the retiform plexus cannot be exact since the retiform plexus is a more complex vascular structure. Galen utilizes this increased complexity in the following way:

But the retiform plexus is much more intricately coiled than the plexus with ivy-like tendrils, as the elaboration which the psychic pneuma undergoes in the brain has to be of a more precise nature than that required by semen. Thus I was correct when I demonstrated in the *Commentaries* (sc. *PHP* V 608–9, = 444,29–446,10 De Lacy) that the vital pneuma drawn up through the arteries is the fitting material for the creation of psychic pneuma in the brain. (*UP* III 700, = ii 12,20–13,2 Helmreich)

For Galen, vital *pneuma* is the best and most appropriate material for the physiological requirements of the retiform plexus. Galen holds that a qualitative change over time occurs in the substance presented to an organ. The concept of elapsed time does not have to be placed in a teleological context, but Galen nonetheless appeals to a teleological agency. Galen uses Nature to underwrite his notion that a certain period of time is required in each organ for elaboration to be performed correctly.[91] In linking time with elaboration to his teleological and epistemological agendas, Galen goes no further than saying that this form of elaboration is *reasonable* (*eulogon*).[92] This is all Galen can do, since he cannot visualize pneumatic elaboration in the retiform plexus but must infer a supposedly similar process elsewhere. In so doing, Galen has no choice but to subordinate the skills of dissection to a physiological need.

CONCLUSION

Galen claims that 'it is not here my purpose to derive the knowledge of the nature of the things which I wish to understand from analogy; for this is not the aim of anatomy. Rather I am simply trying to give an account of those things which manifest themselves to the eyesight.'[93] The reality, as Galen well knew, was more complex. In the second century AD several anatomists were retracing and expanding the researches of Herophilus and Erasistratus. Galen was not working alone in the wilderness. Lycus and Marinus, for example, attest that the first half of the century witnessed a great increase in anatomical knowledge.[94] Galen's teachers were also sources of information, even though the exact mechanism of acquisition, much less its transmission, is never revealed. The knowledge provided by anatomy enabled Galen to discriminate between other doctors, whether as individuals or as representatives of a particular group. It provided him with a gold standard for medical practice, and helped establish his authority as the inheritor of an anatomical legacy which, according to him, reached back to Hippocrates.

In Galen's hands anatomical science in Antiquity reached its apogee. Until the advent of Vesalius and Harvey, Galen was regarded as its most important exponent. For centuries, Galen's was the voice that mattered in anatomical discourse. He deftly combined and enhanced the Aristotelian method of investigation together with advances in anatomy made by Herophilus and Erasistratus. To this, Galen added his own relentlessly detailed and formidable researches, especially concerning the brain and nerves (where he was not eclipsed until Thomas Willis). Since human dissection and vivisection began and ended with Herophilus and Erasistratus, Galen offered a completely systematized approach to anatomy based on animal models. But Galen also used anatomical knowledge as the hallmark of the complete physician. That this was a controversial approach is illustrated by the vehemence of Galen's attacks on medical sects such as the Empiricists and Methodists, who regarded detailed anatomical knowledge as neither necessary nor relevant to daily medical practice. Despite Galen's assertion that anatomy could be traced to Hippocratic origins, knowledge of the body was a relatively late acquisition in classical times and its progression was neither steady nor unchallenged. For it is worth noting that, even at its peak, anatomy did not invariably lead either to a better understanding of the function of the body nor to improvements in medical practice. However, the study of anatomy gave Galen a deserved reputation as an expert in this field. That expertise is not only worthy of exploration but also merits consideration on its own terms.

NOTES

1. On Recognizing the Best Physician (Opt.Med.Cogn.) CMG Suppl. Or.
   IV, 115,24–5 Iskandar.
2. Anatomical Procedures (AA), II 286.
3. Cf. Hankinson (1994e). See also his ch. 8 in this volume.
4. Extant texts: On Anatomical Procedures (AA); On the Utility of the
   Parts (UP); On Bones (for Beginners) (Oss.); On the Cause of Breathing (Caus.Resp.); On the Movement of Muscles (Mot.Musc.); On the
   Dissection of Muscles (for Beginners) (Musc.Diss.); On the Anatomy
   of the Nerves (Nerv.Diss.); On the Anatomy of Veins and Arteries
   (Ven.Art.Diss.); On the Organ of Smell (Inst.Od.); On the Anatomy
   of the Uterus (Ut.Diss.). On the Formation of the Foetus (Foet.Form.),
   primarily a philosophical tract, and the physiological works On Sperm
   (Sem.) and On Unclear Movements (Mot.Dub., currently being edited
   from the Latin by Vivian Nutton), also contain significant anatomical
   information. Lost anatomical works, whose titles are given by Galen in
   On my Own Books (Lib.Prop.: XIX 8–48, = SM 2, 91,1–124,17 [Müller,
   1891]), include the following: The movement of the chest and lungs;
   On the voice; On the dissection of dead bodies; On vivisection; On
   disagreement in anatomy; On the anatomy of Hippocrates; On the
   anatomy of Erasistratus; On the science of anatomy; On the ignorance
   of Lycus in anatomy; On the anatomy of Lycus; On the anatomy of
   Marinus. Fragments of On the voice are collected by H. Baumgarten,
   Diss. Göttingen (1962). On the otherwise lost On the dissection of dead
   bodies, see Ormos (1993).
5. For Galen, it was important that anatomy, like other parts of medicine,
   be traced to its Hippocratic origins. Hence, apart from isolated anatomical exegetics in his Hippocratic Commentaries, there is the lost six-
   volume On the anatomy of Hippocrates. In keeping with his practice
   in other areas, it is likely that Galen would have taken the very general
   statements on anatomy in the Hippocratic Writings and supplied his
   own extensive commentaries and glosses.
6. AA II 224–5; cf. The Order of My Books (Ord.Lib.Prop.) XIX 57–8, = SM
   2, 87,8–19.
7. AA XIV 1; 184 DLT (AA IX, 6–XV are preserved only in Arabic; the
   translation cited is that of Duckworth et al., 1962 [hereafter, DLT]).
   Galen was confident enough of his own abilities by this time to have
   composed for a fellow-student the lost On the movement of the thorax
   and lungs. Cf. Lib.Prop. XIX 17, = SM 2, 97,23–98,2.
8. Lib. Prop. XIX 22, = SM 2, 102,4–5.
9. AA II 217–218, 225; AA XIV 1: 184 DLT.

10. *AA* II 217; XIV 1:183 DLT.
11. Cf. Nutton (1987c, 237–8).
12. *AA* XIV 1: 184–5 DLT. Lycus was also the author of a large work on the anatomy of the muscles, which Galen derides as riddled with errors (*AA* II 217).
13. *Lib.Prop* XIX 22, = *SM* 2, 102,4–6.
14. A. recently discovered Arabic ms. allows the book titles of Lycus' eighteen- or nineteen-book work to be read for the first time. Cf. Boudon (2002a, 15). I examine Galen's teachers and their putative influence in 'Teachers and tradition: Galen and a history of anatomy' (forthcoming).
15. Cf. Nutton (1993c, 16ff.). Alexandria was the best place to study *human* osteology (*AA* II 220–1).
16. Cf. *On Affected Parts (Loc.Aff.)* VIII 212; cf. von Staden (1989, 62–3).
17. *AA* XIV 1:184–5 DLT. Cf. *Lib.Prop.* XIX 25, = *SM* 2, 104,12–13.
18. *On the Doctrines of Hippocrates and Plato (PHP)* V 650 = *CMG* V 4,1,2, 480,28–30 De Lacy.
19. *AA* II 621.
20. *Lib.Prop.* XIX 25–30, = *SM* 2, 104,12–108,14.
21. *Lib.Prop.* XIX 29, = *SM* 2, 108,6–7; cf. Rocca (2003, 45–6).
22. Cf. Nutton (1972b, 170).
23. Cf. von Staden (1995a).
24. Two other cases follow, both dependent on Galen's knowledge of nerve distribution (107,12–109,19).
25. Cf. von Staden (1997).
26. On these experiments see *AA* II 651–706; XI.4, 11: 81–7, 104–7 DLT.
27. Indeed, some of these demonstrations formed what Galen referred to as 'set problem(s) in anatomy'. *Lib.Prop.* XIX 13, = *SM* 2, 95,3.
28. *Opt.Med.Cogn.* 109,18–19 Iskandar.
29. Cf. Hankinson (1998a, 37–43).
30. *Prooem.* 40–3; *CML* I, 23,28–24,14 Marx.
31. *Prooem.* 44; 24,21–23 Marx.
32. *On the Therapeutic Method (MM)* X 100. Although the term might be the Empiricists' own, and Galen is not adverse to it as such (cf. AA II 221, 288.90).
33. Cf. Frede (1982, 262, 265–6).
34. See *MM* X 781, 927.
35. *MM* X 76.
36. Cf. Soranus, *Gyn.* I.5, *CMG* IV, 8,4–11.
37. *PHP* V 648, = 480,7–9 De Lacy; cf. V 219, = 110,1–2.
38. *AA* IX 7; 4 DLT.
39. *On the Utility of the Parts (UP)* III 666–7, = i 483,12–484,6 Helmreich.

40. On the importance of the argument from symmetry for Galen see Rocca (2004).
41. *UP* III 639, = i 463,9–10 Helmreich.
42. *PHP* V 613, = i 448,29–450,3 De Lacy.
43. *UP* IV 275-6, = ii 384,21–385,7; IV. 275–276 Helmreich.
44. *AA* IX 9; 8 DLT.
45. *UP* III 647, = i 469,16–17 Helmreich.
46. *UP* III 663, = i 481,6–14 Helmreich; Cf. *PHP* V 614, = 450,10–13 De Lacy.
47. *UP* I 649–50, = i 471,4–26 Helmreich.
48. *UP* III 666–7, = i 483,12–484,6 Helmreich.
49. *AA* II 727. Cf. *AA* II 416, where his contemporaries are chided for their inability to make full use of their alleged anatomical training.
50. *PHP* V 604, = 442,11–12 De Lacy; cf. V 603, = 440,31–34.
51. The cerebellum is also a source of nerves and contains a 'very great amount' of psychic *pneuma*. This *pneuma* must have access to these nerves and so the nature of the substance of the cerebellum serves as 'paths for *pneuma*'. *UP* III 673, = i 488,6–14 Helmreich.
52. *UP* III 682, = i 494,24–26 Helmreich.
53. *UP* III 683, = i 496,2–9 Helmreich.
54. *AA* II 731.
55. *UP* III 667, = i 484,11–15 Helmreich.
56. *AA* XV 1; 223 DLT; cf. IX 6; 1–2.
57. *UP* III 731-2, = ii 36,1–9 Helmreich.
58. *AA* IX 10; 14 DLT.
59. *PHP* V 609, = 446,21–22 De Lacy.
60. *Ibid.* 609–10, = 446,20–27.
61. Dissection proves this but even butchers are aware of it (*PHP* V 645, = 476,15–17 De Lacy). In *UP* IV 11, = ii 189,18–19 Helmreich, the spinal cord is 'like the trunk of a large tree'. It flows from the fount of the brain 'like a river' *UP* IV 47, = ii 215,21–22 Helmreich.
62. *PHP* V 617, = 452,18 De Lacy (opening in the spinal cord compared to the foramen in the optic nerves); *AA* IX 7; 3 DLT (compared to the olfactory tract).
63. *UP* III 724–725, = ii 30,24–31,15 Helmreich.
64. Cf. Rocca (2002, 89–90).
65. *PHP* V 605, = 442,32–35 De Lacy.
66. Cf. Rocca (2003, 196–8). More generally, see Hankinson (1991c).
67. Cf. Rocca (2003, 249–53).
68. The passage is analysed in Rocca (2003, 179–92).
69. At *PHP* V 614–16, = 450,10–452.7 De Lacy, Galen argues that this *pneuma* is responsible for changes in the diameter of the pupil,

citing in part those who are blind. In these, when one eye is closed, the other pupil remains unchanged, as if the *'pneumatic substance'* is prevented from reaching the eye since the *passages* in the optic nerves are impacted or *blocked*. Cf. V 623, = 458,3.

70. *PHP* V 605, = 442,22–35 De Lacy; cf. *Loc.Aff.* VIII 128; *On the Organ of Smell* (*Inst.Od.*) II 886, = *CMG* Supp. V, 64,1–3 Kollesch.

71. *UP* III 664, = i 481,22–482,5 Helmreich.

72. *UP* III 663–4, = i 481,14–22 Helmreich.

73. *Loc.Aff.* VIII 232–233.

74. *Loc.Aff.* VIII 175.

75. *PHP* V 605, = 442,30–32 De Lacy.

76. *PHP* V 185–7, = 78,27–80,18 De Lacy.

77. *On Tremor, Palpitation, Convulsion and Rigor (Trem. Palp.)* VII 596–7; cf. Rocca (2003, 194–5).

78. Cf. *Loc.Aff.* VIII 174–175.

79. Cf. *PHP* V 609, = 446,11–15 De Lacy.

80. Cf. Rocca (2003, 196–8).

81. On the choroid plexus see Rocca (2003, 219–24).

82. *On the Function of the Pulse* (*Us.Puls.*) V 155, 200 Furley/Wilkie. Although this passage does not explicitly state that either Herophilus or his followers were the first to do so (and note that at *UP* III 696, = ii 10,9–10 Helmreich, Galen simply states that it is 'the plexus called retiform by anatomists'). Herophilus, with possibly a small number of human subjects available for dissections, relied upon animal subjects to correlate and augment his human findings. Content with the knowledge that the retiform plexus is found in some animals, Herophilus extrapolated this structure to man. See the discussion in Rocca (2003, 203–5).

83. For the subsequent history of the retiform plexus, see the summary by Rocca (2003, 249–53).

84. *PHP* V 565–6, = 408,34–410,2 De Lacy; cf. Lloyd (1996, 83–103).

85. *PHP* V 281, = 164,17–18 De Lacy.

86. Each organ is a 'distinct substance' carrying particular powers (*PHP* V 621, = 456,11–12 De Lacy).

87. Cf. *On Semen* (*Sem.*) IV 565, = *CMG* V 3,1, 116,14–17 De Lacy; IV. 565 K.

88. *Sem.* IV 555–6, = 106,20–108,3 De Lacy. Cf. 566–7, = 118,14–22.

89. *Sem.* IV 556, = 108,10–11 De Lacy; cf. 562–3, = 114,8–21.

90. *Sem.* IV 583, = 134,20–21 De Lacy.

91. *UP* III 699–700, = ii 12,5–23 Helmreich.

92. A key word which Galen uses to flag uncertainty regarding structure and function in the body (cf. Debru, 1996, 163). For example, in describing the initial preparation of blood in the liver and its final elaboration in the

heart, Galen says that it is a 'reasonable proposition that no perfect and great work can be done at once, or from a single natural organ receive all of its fitting elaboration', *PHP* V 550-1, = 398.7-10 De Lacy. And the production of psychic *pneuma* in the choroid plexus of the brain is similarly qualified as 'reasonable'. Cf. Rocca (2003, 223).

93. *AA* IX 7; 4 DLT.
94. Whether this recrudescence of anatomical knowledge (and possibly anatomical investigation) amounted to an anatomical 'sect' is debatable; but see Grmek and Gourevitch (1994).

10 Physiology

The study of the principal functions of living things, such as respiration, nutrition, reproduction, perception and so on, was a major preoccupation of many Greek philosophers, from Democritus, Empedocles and Plato to the fundamental contribution made by Aristotle in his biological works. Alexandrian medicine played its part, too, both by considerably deepening anatomical understanding and by developing new types of explanation. In addition to Herophilus' groundbreaking discoveries in anatomy, in particular those concerning the brain and the nervous system, Erasistratus had also developed general physiological principles, and Galen acknowledges his debts in this regard in numerous contexts. Nor did these researches come to an end after the Hellenistic period. During his medical training at Pergamum, and afterwards at Smyrna and Alexandria, Galen was taught by some remarkable anatomists, for whom the study of anatomy was always closely bound up with that of physiology. This tradition, in turn, was linked to the authority of Hippocrates, in whom Galen is sure that he finds a highly sophisticated anatomical understanding (he wrote a treatise on Hippocrates' anatomy), as well as a physiology which is founded upon principles which are also supposedly his own. For what Galen learns also from his masters is 'the demonstration and proof' of facts and their explanations by way of reasoning and anatomical demonstration, which in turn entails a systematic recourse to the dissection of dead animals as well as to the vivisection of living ones. Indeed, vivisection is in his view the most appropriate method for discovering animal functions.

Many of the experiments he performed had already been carried out by his predecessors: those on thoracic movement, on the foetus, on the brain, on the heart, the blood-vessels, the pulse and so on. But he quickly became a master of this particular approach, one which answered to his desire for certain knowledge; and he proceeded to carry it through on an exceptionally and unprecedentedly wide front. It was in his capacity as both philosopher and doctor that he sought throughout his long life to uncover the structures and functions of all parts of the body, and to supply demonstrations of them. This was no easy task since, in contrast with anatomy, nothing indicates unequivocally what the role is of certain organs, such as the liver and the kidneys, or how functions as complex as digestion and generation come to realize themselves, or above all what further function some of them, such as respiration, might fulfil. Moreover, the field was already full of his predecessors' speculations; thus providing an explanation involves refuting other people's opinions as well as defending his own positions and giving the most convincing possible demonstration of them. One needs to show how the thing comes about, what its cause is, and what it is for (this, of course, had already been Aristotle's method). None of this could be done without a rational method, one founded on a mastery of the theory of demonstration, something which required training in both philosophy and logic, and which was the only way of arriving at the truth, such as that which Galen had developed in his great lost work *On Demonstration*.

Starting from his earliest youth, Galen's productivity in this field was enormous. He listed his works in the bibliographical catalogues which he produced (*On My Own Books* [*Lib.Prop.*]; *The Order of My Own Books* [*Ord.Lib.Prop.*]). While many of the writings mentioned have perished, we are particularly fortunate to possess three great works in which physiological questions occupy a central place: *On the Doctrines of Hippocrates and Plato* (*PHP*), *On the Natural Faculties* (*Nat.Fac.*) and also *On the Utility of the Parts* (*UP*), even though physiology is treated in the last one as something already understood. Particular functions are dealt with both in the major works and in specific texts: while vision is essentially described in book VII of *PHP*, smell is treated in *On the Organ of Smell* (*Inst.Od.*) and the other sense modalities are also covered in *UP*. Respiration was dealt with in *On the Cause of Breathing* (of which the text we possess as *Caus.Resp.* is probably only a fragment or summary) and in two other lost works, *On the Movement of Thorax and Lung*, and *On the Voice*. Much is also to be found in books VI and VII of *UP*.

The purpose of respiration is also the subject of the surviving treatise *On the Use of Breathing* (*Ut.Resp.*), while its voluntary nature was dealt with in the treatise *On the Movement of Muscles* (*Mot.Musc.*), which is dedicated to the exposition of muscular structure and how voluntary movement is exercised by it. The purpose of the pulse, examined in a specific treatise (*On the Use of the Pulse* [*Us.Puls.*]), is also a component of respiratory physiology. Much to do with digestion, the production of urine and biliary excretion is to be found in *UP*, and more especially in *Nat.Fac*. We should also note, in the case of reproduction, the texts *On Semen* (*Sem.*) and *On the Formation of the Foetus* (*Foet.Form.*), as well as many other works, such as the various *Commentaries* on the Hippocratic writings,[1] whose pathological works offer the opportunity for dealing with physiological issues, such as that of innate heat, etc. For this reason it is no easy task to get to grips with Galen's physiology. The major functions are not treated in the course of a continuous exposition, but rather piecemeal, and often in disputatious and polemical contexts. My aim here is to outline the conceptual framework of his physiology, and to offer a few examples which illustrate them.

PRINCIPAL CONCEPTS

We need to take account first of some of the central concepts of Galen's physiological thought; these were not invented by Galen, but none the less he gave them clear definitions and organized them in a systematic fashion.

The concept of 'function' (from the Latin *functio*) does not occur in antiquity in the sense with which it has been used since the seventeenth century. Aristotle, even though he deals with physiological functions, has no fixed term to denote the concept. In the Alexandrian period the concept of an activity (*energeia*), drawn from the vocabulary of philosophy (and meaning 'capacity in action', as opposed to 'passive capacity'), makes its appearance in this context, and Galen makes regular use of it. For him, *energeia* is a subset of the broader concept of motion (*kinêsis*), to which, following Aristotle, he gives the sense both of local motion and of qualitative change (*alloiôsis*). Also of importance for the analysis of bodily activities is the distinction between active and passive movement: thus bones are passively moved by the muscles, which are active; and similarly food is passively transformed into blood by the action of specific organs. These bodily activities are conceived of as being multiple and complex. One and the same activity may be parcelled out among several organs, and each may have several activities. Thus the liver has an activity of formation (of veins), production (of blood) and transmission (of the nutritive faculty). As Galen says, 'nothing in an animal's body is useless or inactive' (*Us.Part.* III 268, = 196,19–20 Helmreich); and he designates the outcome of an activity by the term 'work' (*ergon: Nat.Fac.* II 6–7, = *SM* 3, 105,7–106,3).

Next comes the question of what is responsible for the activity, which Galen designates by the general term 'cause'. Galen, like Aristotle, avails himself of several categories of cause in his physiology, which are different from those which he makes use of in his pathology.[2] As an anatomist, he reposes particular importance in instrumental causes (*aitia organika*) – for example, the muscles in the case of movement. But for Galen, just as for Aristotle, the final cause, 'that for the sake of which', is pre-eminent. Implicitly contained in our notion of function, it is for him at the heart of his thorough-going teleological view of the world, which seeks to ascribe to the smallest part of the body both a role and a structure perfectly adapted to its function or functions. Presiding over this end is something which he sometimes refers to as the Creator or 'Demiurge', or even God, sometimes as a providential and benevolent Nature. It is in here where he finds himself in the most violent opposition to those who adopt a more flexible attitude towards final causation (such as Erasistratus), as well as to those who are utterly opposed to any sort of teleological explanation (for example, the Atomists).[3]

It is within this causal structure that the concept, long familiar from both philosophy and medicine, of faculties (*dunameis*: powers, properties, capacities, etc.) finds its place; it is also one which encompasses several other concepts. Galen adopts a general classification of these faculties into two groups, a taxonomy which was widely accepted in his era. The 'psychic' faculties, or those 'of the soul' (*psuchê*), take care of the physiological domain of sensation and voluntary movement, and are exercised by the brain through the mediation of the nervous system. The second group comprises the 'natural' faculties, or those 'of nature', with which the treatise *On the Natural*

Faculties is concerned. These are innate, and are responsible for generation, growth and nutrition in living things. They depend upon the
basic compositional form of the tissues, which in turn derive from
the elements and their mixtures, and they directly constitute the
active factors of the activities of the parts or tissues. These general
faculties are given particular forms, which are responsible for the
corresponding activities.[4] Thus the specific cause of the activity of
nutrition is the nutritive faculty (*Nat.Fac.* II 18–19, = *SM* 3, 114,6–
17), while that of the production of blood is that haematopoietic faculty which is proper to the parts which produce it. This functional
perspective explains why Galen assigns the faculties to the category
of 'relatives': they exist *for* something (*pros ti*).

   All the activities and their causes cooperate with a view to producing a single result, the maintenance of the functional unity which
is the living creature. This idea is developed at the beginning of *On
the Utility of the Parts (UP)*. From this point of view, all parts of the
body are instruments (*organa*) for various types of activity, arranged
hierarchically, but for all that in a cooperative manner. Galen likes
to quote an aphorism from the *De Alimento* of the Hippocratic
Corpus (which he thought authentic, in contrast to modern scholarly
opinion): 'everything is in sympathy in the ensemble of the parts, and
in the parts everything works together to produce the results of each
of them' (*Alim.* 23). For Galen, too, 'all the parts of the body are in
sympathy, that is to say all of them cooperate in producing one effect'
(*UP* III 18 = i 13,7–9 Helmreich). The whole is overseen by Nature
or Providence, which seeks to bring about its best possible realiza-
tion. Each part has a 'use' or a 'usefulness' which is the best possible:
this is the upshot of his great work *On the Utility of the Parts*. It
underpins his notion of the mutual exchanges of materials, and of the
stable equilibria in the body; but it also allows him to put forward in
the name of this mutual exchange hypotheses which are in conflict
with his own observations – as, for instance, when he supposes that
a part of the burnt residues in the left ventricle of the heart must
pass the wrong way through the mitral valve, even though this latter has as its function precisely the prevention of any such passage,
or when he hypothesizes that the blood must pass directly through
the interventricular septum of the heart (*UP* III 497, = i 362,19–123
Helmreich; more cautiously *AA* II 623,2–3).

TWO GREAT PHYSIOLOGICAL MODELS

The general organizing principles of Galen's physiology can be found in two great treatises, which lay out the models to which all functions are to be reduced.

The Model of the Source

Philosophers are familiar with the treatise *On the Doctrines of Hippocrates and Plato (PHP)* for two main reasons. The first is that in this text Galen adopts the Platonic conception of the three psychological centres (it makes little difference for him whether we call them 'parts of the soul' or 'souls'). They govern the activities of the living animal and, as for Plato, are located in different organs: the brain for the ruling part, the heart for the emotional part and the liver for the vegetative part. The second is that he devotes an extremely long section, occupying practically the whole of books IV and V, to discussing Chrysippus' doctrines regarding the soul and the passions. This makes the work a major source for Stoic doctrine. In fact, Galen's account of the tripartition of the soul is both philosophical and physiological. The two types of discourse are presented as being equivalent: 'doctors allow that the faculties of sense and movement flow from the brain towards all the parts of the animal; philosophers agree that the rational part of the soul is located there' (*PHP* V 587, = 428,24–5 De Lacy); moreover 'it makes no difference whether one says that the liver is the source of the veins, or of the blood, or of the desiderative part of the soul' since 'it is somehow more appropriate for a physician to present his teaching in terms of bodily organs, a philosopher in terms of the powers of the soul' (*PHP* V 577, = 418,29–31 De Lacy). Even so, the physiological type of discourse predominates, as may be seen from the method of proof, which is taken from anatomy, indeed as much as possible from actual experimentation.

In fact, Galen understands the parts of the soul as principles or sources (*archai*) of the psychic and physiological activities. He makes use of this idea especially in the case of the ruling part of the soul, which he locates, following the Alexandrians, in the brain: 'where the source of the nerves is to be found, there too is found the ruling part of the soul' (*PHP* V 588, = 428,24–5 De Lacy). The 'source' is the origin of anatomical structures, as the trunk of a tree is for its branches; and similarly in the case of the liver and the veins. But the functional sense of the term is even more important. The source is 'the origin that pertains to power (*tên kata dunamin archên*)' (*PHP* V 277, = 160,31 De Lacy); further on, he adds 'if, therefore we call that part which supplies the power, or at least the matter, to the parts that grow from it the origin (*archê*)' (*PHP* V 552, = 398,31–3 De Lacy). This power or substance 'flows', he says, from this origin to the other parts of the body. In this way, he explains not only the transmission of the directing faculty of the brain by way of the nerves to the muscles, but also the transmission of the faculty of pulsation from the heart to the arteries, as well as that of the nutritive faculty from the liver to the veins which grow out of it. The notion of a source also allows him to ascribe a plurality of functions to a single organ. Thus the heart is not only the source of the arteries, but also of innate heat, and of the faculty of the pulse which is transmitted to the arteries, while the liver is the origin of the veins, and the source of blood and of the nutritive faculty: 'it is reasonable that what provides the whole body with the matter suitable for nourishment is the source of the power of nutrition and growth' (*PHP* V 533, = 384,9–11 De Lacy).

However, Galen rejects the idea that two organs can share in the same function. In opposition to this theoretical division of labour which others had maintained, he seeks to establish experimentally that the brain has no need of the cooperation of the heart in order to receive psychic *pneuma* into its ventricles. The *pneuma*, a vaporous substance which fills the ventricles of the brain, certainly derives in part from the arterial blood; however, Galen insists that it only requires a very small quantity of it (*Ut.Resp.* IV 503–4, = 122 Furley/Wilkie).[5] Ligature of the carotid arteries of a dog shows that the interruption of blood in this way does no harm, or at least not much and only in the long run, to the consciousness or activities of the animal (*PHP* V 263–4, = 148,14–150,2 De Lacy; *Ut.Resp.* IV 502–3, = 122 Furley/Wilkie). In the same way, he rules out any possibility of a collaboration between the liver and the heart in the production of blood (*PHP* V 534, = 384,17–19 De Lacy). This division of labour is even more noticeable in his parcelling out of the psychic and moral life among several distinct centres (or souls), each capable both of cooperation (see p. 267 above) and of conflict, which is the burden of his works on moral philosophy.[6]

Since the model of transmission is that of a stream which flows out from the source towards the rest of the body, the decisive experiment needed to establish its existence consists in trying to intercept it. This fact accounts for all of the experiments having to do with the transmission of sensation and movement by way of the nerves, involving the progressive sectioning of the spinal cord, and the famous public experiments on respiration and the voice (*On Anatomical Procedures* [*AA*] II 677–706). These impressive demonstrations, which Galen himself tells us about, show him sectioning one by one on live animals the different nerves and muscles which are involved in the activity of the thorax, notably those to with the forcible exhalation which produces the voice.[7] In the same fashion, interception of faculty of pulsation which is propagated, in his view, from the heart into the arteries is accomplished by an experiment, which had already been carried out by Erasistratus, involving the insertion of a tube into the femoral artery, whose tunic had been ligatured. This proves to Galen the opposite of what it had done to his predecessor, that it is not the mass of blood itself coming from the heart which causes arterial dilation, but rather its own attractive capacity which is transmitted to them via the arterial tunics (*On whether Blood is Naturally Contained in the Arteries* [*Art.Sang.*] IV 733, = 178–89 Furley/Wilkie).[8] The only faculty transmitted from the liver as a 'source' is that of nutrition; and in this case Galen is forced to abandon experimental demonstration in favour of reasoning alone: 'in the case of the liver, we are unable to make any such demonstration, whether by exposing it and applying pressure, or by ligating the veins' (*PHP* V 520, = 372, 32–4,1 De Lacy). As he says, it is hard to see what sort of experiment could be relevant here.

The Local Model: The Natural Faculties

The natural (i.e. physical) faculties constitute the other model in terms of which Galen organizes his physiological vision. As he explains at the beginning of *On the Natural Faculties*, these are directly implanted into the parts of the body, and are not under the control of the ruling part of the soul: 'All the natural activities of the body and of its parts . . . each of these two coats has an alterative faculty peculiar to it, which has engendered it from the menstrual blood of the mother.' Thus the special alterative faculties in each animal are the same number as the elementary parts; and further the activities must necessarily correspond each to one special part, just as each part has its special use (*Nat.Fac.* II 13–14, = *SM* 3, 110,15–26).

For Galen, the most important capacity is the one which each part of the body possesses for attracting to itself what is particularly appropriate for it. This he calls 'attraction of the specific property', in contrast with the attractive power of the void (the replacement of what is evacuated) dear to Erasistratus. It remains for Galen to commend his own model against the more mechanical ones:

These are the people who think that Nature is not artistic, that she does not show forethought for the animal's welfare, and that she has absolutely no native powers whereby she alters some substances, attracts others and discharges others. (*Nat.Fac.* II 26–7, = *SM* 3, 120,2–6)

This remark is made in connection with urinary functioning, which gives Galen the opportunity to lay out the differences between the two great physiological 'schools of thought' (*Nat.Fac.* II 27–30, = *SM* 3, 120,7–122,16), the one teleological, the other 'mechanist', as well as specifically to attack the theory of the doctor Asclepiades. The latter claimed that the kidneys had no role to play in the process, the ureters fulfilled no function and that the moisture collected in the bladder as a result of being directly absorbed from the surrounding tissues. Galen methodically demonstrates the replenishing role played by the ureters, while other arguments allow him to prove the attractive role of the kidneys (*Nat.Fac.* II 34–8, = *SM* 3, 125,18–128,23). Many other phenomena are also to be explained by the attractive faculty – for example, conception, in which the semen, which in his view is supplied by both male and female, attracts to itself exactly the right amount of blood needed for its growth and the formation of the embryo (*Nat.Fac.* II 84–5, = *SM* 3, 162,11–24).

INSTRUMENTS: PNEUMA AND INNATE HEAT

To this picture we should add the role played by two entities which Galen inherits from a long philosophical and medical tradition, namely *pneuma* and innate heat. These are essential elements in Galen's physiology, although he is less interested in their nature than in what they do; one needs, he thinks, to concentrate on their functional aspect in order to avoid falling into error.

As for the *pneuma*, the vaporous substance which is formed, he thinks, in part by the inspired air and in part by the vaporization of the arterial blood, as suggested in his treatise *On the Use of Breathing* (*Ut.Resp.* IV 502, = 120-2 Furley/Wilkie), Galen constantly reaffirms its functional conception. He considers it to be an 'instrument' (*organon*), although he remains non-committal as to the number of types of *pneuma* there are and as to its nature, both subjects of some dispute in his time. There are two main domains in which its activity is central. It is 'the principal instrument of all the animal's sensation and voluntary movements', as well as being 'the primary instrument of the soul' (*PHP* V 609, 446,11–14 De Lacy). Its action is established by way of various interventional experiments, for example lesion of the ventricles of the brain by pressure and incision. When the *pneuma* is no longer present, neither are the specific activities associated with it: 'when the *pneuma* has escaped and until it is collected again, it does not deprive the animal of its life but renders it incapable of sensation and motion' (*PHP* V 603, = 444,8–10 De Lacy). The experiment works both ways: 'when the *pneuma* is let out through wounds, the animal immediately becomes like a corpse, but when it has collected again the animal revives' (*PHP* V 609, = 446,13–15 De Lacy). Yet its mode of action is mysterious, and Galen often compares it to the effect of light. Moreover, in visual perception, its action is qualitative rather than substantial: the *pneuma* contained in the optic nerve, which is the only sort which he can affirm positively passes *through* the nerve, 'when it strikes the surrounding air, produces by its first impact an alteration that is transmitted to the furthest distance' (*PHP* V 619, = 454,13–15 De Lacy). As far as the other nerves are concerned, Galen is uncertain as to how they function, and he proposes several different hypotheses, some of which imply and some of which fail to imply the presence of *pneuma* in the nerves (*PHP* V 611, = 448,4–24 De Lacy). In all these matters, Galen is generally cautious: 'it is reasonable to think', he says. Hence one should not represent Galen's *pneuma* doctrine in the form of a tripartite pneumatology, hierarchized and dogmatic, which was a doctrine of later Galenism, and not of Galen himself.[9] Undecided as regards questions of substance and quantity, he nevertheless never wavers as regards its functional aspect: *pneuma* is an instrument for the transmission of sensation and other psychological and physiological faculties.

Innate heat also plays a major role as a physiological tool. For Galen (who attributes the same view to Hippocrates and Plato), the innate heat, which is supplied to the living creature at the moment of conception by the uterine blood, is responsible for its formation, and for all its subsequent activities, until it loses strength and is finally gradually extinguished in the course of the animal's life. In order to best fulfil its functions it needs to maintain its equilibrium. Respiration allows it to do so by supplying it with a source of fresh air. As he explains in *The Use of Breathing*, the *summetria* of the heat is not only a necessary condition of the good functioning of the physiological activities but is actually their cause (*Nat.Fac.* II 121, = *SM* 3, 189,15–18). But this functioning is also disturbed by any *duskrasia*, or imbalance of the qualities.[10] The heart (which is itself the source of the innate heat), the blood (considered as the source for vaporization which nourishes the *pneuma*) and the other parts of the body, in particular the brain, can exercise their functions only with the help of a moderate heat, which is sustained by way of the 'ventilation' of the body due to the influx of the external air's refreshing quality throughout the body.

PARTICULAR FUNCTIONS

These tools of physiological thought are constantly put to work by Galen in order to account for the particular functions of the various parts of the body. Let us begin by considering the example of digestion.

Digestion

Various different theories regarding this subject were held in Galen's time. He himself conceived of digestion as the exercise of natural faculties residing in each of the different organs through which the food passes, and not as a mechanical process. It begins in the mouth where, after being ground up by the teeth, the food undergoes a preliminary qualitative alteration as a result of the action of the saliva and of contact with the lining of the mouth, whose flesh begins to assimilate the food to itself (*Nat.Fac.* II 163, = *SM* 3, 218,10–219,9). Throughout its course, the process of nutrition involves the complex action of faculties residing in the numerous organs which take

part in it. Their capacities of attraction, retention, alteration and
expulsion also serve to explain for Galen the progress of the food
through the oesophagus, and the action of the stomach and the other
organs involved: 'throughout the entire body of the animal there is no
part which remains idle or inactive, but all of them are endowed by
the Creator with divine powers' (UP III 268, = i 196,19–23 Helmreich). These functions, and the parts of the body which deliver them,
derive from a providential nature. Hence it is in fact only when the
food is ready that the pylorus opens and transmits this food, once
transformed into a thick, white liquid, the chyle, into the intestines.
Galen vehemently opposes the notion that it is the internal pressure
of the stomach alone which is responsible for the entire process,
drawing on proofs derived from observation and animal vivisection
(Nat.Fac. II 152–7, = SM 3, 211,11–215,5).

One problem which is difficult to resolve is that of the regulation
of nourishment. In fact, Galen thinks, the parts attract to themselves
the nutritious blood in the appropriate quantities. No internal part,
apart from the stomach, has sensation (UP IV 7:e III 275, = i 201,19–
202,2 Helmreich); but, almost as if they were animals, each part does
possess a sort of understanding of what is appropriate for it and what
ought to be eliminated from it:

All of this shows that there exists in nearly every part of the animal a sort
of impetus and as it were an appetite for its proper quality and an aversion
from the alien quality. (Nat.Fac. II 159–60, = SM 3, 216,17–22)

But the nature of this 'understanding', which he also refers to as
'soul', remains obscure for him. The natural faculties are operative
throughout the digestive process. A notion dear to Galen is that the
veins exercise an alterative action on their contents by virtue of their
being in contact with the walls of the veins, which in turn causes
the food to take on the nature of the blood. In fact, the veins are
themselves formed out of the liver, as Galen demonstrates in book
VI of PHP. Attraction and excretion are also involved in the activity of purifying the blood: the lighter waste-products pass into the
gall-bladder where they are turned into yellow bile, while the heavier ones are attracted into the spleen where they contribute to the
formation of black bile. Throughout this process, the organs attract
not only this blood, but also blood which is supplied to them by the
arteries, which is warmer and lighter on account of its being mixed

with *pneuma*. For Galen, it is ridiculous to suppose, as Erasistratus had done, that the arteries, at least in their normal condition, contained *pneuma* only. However, this refutation is by no means as straightforward as it might seem, which is why he dedicated to it an entire treatise, *Art.Sang.*, making use of observation, experiment and reasoning. Galen's thought is shot through with the notion that the general intercommunication within and synergy of actions in the organism creates from it a unity, which accounts for our being able to speak of it as a 'system'.

One particular case concerns the nourishment of the lungs. Starting from the liver, the basic organ of haematopoiesis, and to which Galen assigns an extremely important role, the blood flows out into the veins, attracted by the organs themselves, arriving at the various different parts of the body, where it nourishes them, by transforming itself into the substance of the different parts, before it is finally completely used up in fulfilment of this function. It is the need for the irrigation of the lungs which accounts for the particular disposition, indeed the inversion, of the pulmonary blood-vessels which link it with the heart in both directions: arteries on the right, veins on the left. But this takes place in the context of another function, one which is linked to the cardio-respiratory mechanism.

Respiration

One part of what we would call the respiratory function is in fact connected by Galen with nutrition, since the inspired air helps to furnish the *pneuma*, which in turn helps to form the arterial blood which contributes to the nourishment of the organs. And a part of this *pneuma* itself, in the course of refining itself in order to produce pure and light blood, exhales the psychic *pneuma* which is indispensable to the exercise of the higher functions, namely sensation and movement. Respiration also has a function in regard to the innate heat. But the fact which seems for Galen at once both one of the most important and one of the most mysterious is that respiration seems immediately essential for the preservation of the living creature. Indeed, prior to this, the actual mechanism of respiration raises the question, which Galen treats of at length in book II of the treatise *On the Movement of Muscles* (*Mot.Musc.*) (IV 435–64), as to whether it is voluntary or not, since empirical evidence seems inconclusive on this point. Resolution of this question requires an understanding of the instruments of thoracic movement, its anatomical 'causes'. In effect, if he can show that the thorax is dilated by muscles, then in view of the fact that the latter are organs of the 'voluntary faculty', he will also be able to maintain that the respiratory mechanism depends upon the will, in other words the ruling part of the soul. In the case of this thoracic movement Galen, as a committed partisan of anatomy, adopts Erasistratus' neuro-muscular theory, according to which the thorax is moved by the animal's will through the intermediary of the muscles. This voluntary dilatation of the thorax sucks in air as a result of the attractive force of the vacuum. Galen first confronted this question during his studies, and he wrote two early monographs on the subject, *On the movement of the thorax and the lung* and *The voice* (*Ord.Lib.Prop.* XIX 55, = *SM* 2, 84,22–4). Later he wrote another short treatise after his discovery that the voice is produced by the contraction of certain muscles, and not just by natural exhalation. The action of the muscles, which is determined by the nerves, depends upon the brain and hence upon the ruling part of the soul, according to the model already established of the source or origin. His experiments that seek to prove this rely on the principle of interfering with the 'causes' of respiration, and of the voice which he associates with it, either by ligature or section. The neuro-muscular mechanism of thoracic movement was a particular preoccupation of Galen's, and he devoted to it some celebrated anatomical demonstrations during his Roman period. In front of a knowledgeable and cultured citizen public, he carried out a series of methodical vivisections on animals, paralysing them selectively by means of ligature and section of the nerves involved with the muscles that are concerned with respiration. But the purpose of the demonstration shifts: what interests our anatomist and his public (which also contains philosophers) is not the defence of the mechanistic theory of an Erasistratus, a version of which he indeed adopts, but rather showing that respiration, in the form of the forced exhalation produced by certain specific muscles, is the basis of the voice and hence of language. By this means he is able to demonstrate scientifically that all those people who considered the heart to be the source of reason, as the Stoics did, were mistaken. But he was to find out that clear demonstration is sometimes of no avail against theory and reasoning. For a long time the two theories, labelled 'encephalocentric' and 'cardiocentric' were to remain in living competition with one another, as the history of Christian anthropology amply testifies.

For Galen, the fact that the muscles are involved makes this movement necessarily and exclusively a voluntary one, since it must derive from the ruling part of the soul. He responds to objections with his usual formidable argumentative energy: How can we breathe while asleep? In the same way, he replies, as we can walk in our sleep. We forget that we are breathing just as we can be oblivious of every other voluntary action which nevertheless we still manage to perform. This issue remained controverted until the discovery of reflex actions.

As for the question of the purpose of respiration, it allows us to understand why an animal prevented from breathing dies almost immediately, which is not the case when it is deprived of nourishment. Consideration of the way in which flames are extinguished through lack of air allows him to express his lack of certain knowledge in this context:

If it could be discovered what happens to flames in these circumstances [i.e. when deprived of air] to quench them, it would perhaps be discovered what that useful something is in breathing, from which the natural heat in the animal profits. (*Ut.Resp.* IV 487–8, = 104 Furley/Wilkie)

On the Use of Breathing also contains a teleological analysis. The inspired air serves first of all to nourish as a result of its own substance the necessary supply of air. And this supply itself contributes to that *pneuma* which is destined to become psychic *pneuma*, and which continually serves to refill the cerebral ventricles, albeit in minute quantities. Another function for the inspired air is to mix with pure blood in order to transform it into nourishment in the correct proportions for different parts of the body. But, most importantly of all, it serves to moderate the innate heat. According to Galen, there also exists a type of respiration specific to the brain (in spite of the fact that he had observed serious head-injuries, and had performed trepanations, he was no more inclined than his contemporaries to attribute any major function to the matter of the brain). Finally, the respiration of the body as a whole (perspiration) rounds out the general picture of respiratory functioning. Allowing what has been utilized in internal transformations to escape through the pores of the skin, while absorbing in exchange an extremely small quantity of air from the outside, serves to ensure an exchange with the ambient environment which is essential for the preservation of life. Every experiment in which one blocks the pores with some sort of sealing agent reinforces the idea that such impediments have pathological consequences. What was to become from this point on a basic notion of health thus has a physiological underpinning

Reproduction and Embryology

From the time of Hippocrates, embryology was one of the most mysterious and controverted fields in the whole of ancient medicine. Galen devoted two important surviving treatises to the subject, *On Semen* (*Sem.*), which was probably written in the 170s,[11] and *On the Formation of the Foetus* (*Foet.Form.*) written at least twenty years later, towards the end of his life.[12] And he returns to the issue in his very late work *On His Own Opinions* (*Prop.Plac.*). Galen is concerned with the nature of semen, which had been a central and traditional question, one which was dominated by Aristotle's thesis to the effect that the male semen possessed the power of initiating the creative process, while the female provided nothing more than suitable matter in the form of the menstrual blood. Against this thesis, and in accordance with Hippocratic doctrine, Galen believes, and seeks to establish by means of observations and dissections, that the uterus grasps and holds in the male semen while itself emitting a semen which mixes with it. This double origin of semen resolves several problems, in particular regarding the differentiation of the sexes and the explanation of inherited characteristics. In this area, too, Galen accords the highest importance to the natural faculties. For him, the semen itself, and subsequently the embryo generated from it, attract to themselves from the vessels of the uterus blood and *pneuma*, the two materials which are combined in arterial blood. Gradually, the organs come to be formed. Under the influence of a constructive (*diaplattousa*) power, the foetus is formed in four stages: a first in which it is still semen (as Hippocrates labelled it); a second in which it grows in size, but without visible internal differentiation; a third in which the three main organs, the brain, the heart and the liver, become visible and distinct; and a fourth in which all the parts become distinguished. In *Foet.Form.* he traces the development of the foetus from its very beginning, the formation of its first parts, right up to its fully developed state. He follows the development of the vessels, which derive from the mother's uterus and which develop in the membrane called the 'chorion', their differentiation into two arteries and two veins through which the nourishment is attracted; they derive from the substance of the semen both their initial constitution and their subsequent growth, and they increase in both length and width, just as we see in the case of trees (*Foet.Form.* 2: IV 658–60, = 62,7–24 Nickel).

Next, Galen sketches the probable course of the development of the vessels and organs. At each stage he comes up against the problem of the soul: 'whenever it is not the primary object of our discourse, we will label this soul with the term common to all substance and call it "nature"' (3: IV 665, = 68,12–14 Nickel). In his view, contrary to what he had thought at the outset, which was that the heart was formed first of all, the foetus has no need of the heart 'until the division of the veins from the liver is completed' (3: IV 667, = 70,17–19). He acknowledges having changed his mind on this issue, now supposing that the liver is the first organ to be generated, since it produces the blood and governs the living creature as if it were a plant. For a certain period of time, the embryo has no need of a heart, that period before the venous system, which begins with the generation of the umbilical vein, is completely developed. Finally, last of all, the brain is formed.

Galen's whole description of the development of the vessels (one which goes no further than plausibility in his view) is modelled on that of plants.[13] It is not until the end of the process that

the heart has two ventricles, and into the right flows blood from the liver, which is moderately hot, while into the left flows the arterial blood, which is much hotter than the first. Once it has acquired the ventricles and the material appropriate to each of them, the heart begins to beat, and makes the arteries move by imposing its own motion on them. (*Foet.Form.* 3: IV 670, = 74,8–13 Nickel)

At this moment, the foetus ceases to be organized like a plant and becomes an animal. But observation in such cases has its limitations, which is why Galen makes more use than usual in *On the Formation of the Foetus* and *On Semen* of metaphors and analogies, and of the categories of probability and plausibility. He starts out always with the observations derived from dissections, but in particular by the

end of the treatise his investigation leads him into profound questions, an attitude once again far removed from the dogmatism which
is often ascribed to him.

UNRESOLVED QUESTIONS

The field of physiology is full of uncertainty, and Galen often avows
the limits of his knowledge. It is not only that he makes use of expressions such as 'it is probable that', and 'it is reasonable to think that':
in certain cases, he goes even further. He gave a brief account of these
doubts in one of his last works, *On His Own Opinions*. In particular,
they concern everything which is beyond this world:

> I do not know whether the universe is created and whether there is any-
> thing outside it or not. . . I have no knowledge of the creator of every-
> thing in the universe, whether it is corporeal or incorporeal and where it is
> located. (*Prop.Plac.* 2, 56,12–20 Nutton)[14]

In the case of the soul, he is sure that it exists, since it is what makes
sensation and movement possible, but he has no understanding of its
'substance', whether it is mortal or immortal and so on.[15] Another
area of ignorance concerns the embryo: he does not know whether
the same faculty which forms the embryo continues to supply the
source of its activities throughout its life, in the manner of the operation of automata, or if each part of the body knows what it is supposed
to do as if it were an animal, or if some 'extremely intelligent and
powerful' artisan is responsible for it, and if so who he is (*Foet.Form.*
6: IV 687–96, = 90,27–100,13 Nickel). What worries him is that

> When, however, I see that it is a consequence of this that the soul in the
> leading part is a different entity from the souls in the parts of the body
> or alternatively that there is just one general soul which manages all the
> parts, I reach an impasse, unable to discover anything about the artificer
> who constructs us even in terms of a probable conception, let alone a firm
> understanding. (*Foet.Form* 6: IV 696. = 100,20–24 Nickel)

Galen takes up the same theme in *On His Own Opinions* and in
the treatise *On Problematic Movements* (*Mot.Dub.*). In the latter,
he expresses his certainties about the nature of some movements,
but also his questions concerning others, which seem to him not
to conform to his strict distinction between voluntary movements,

which are brought about by the muscles, and hence dependent upon the brain, and involuntary ones, which are caused by different structures. As in other late treatises, we see the extent to which observation can provoke further questions, and how Galen did not shrink from confronting and frankly admitting doubts and impasses both in medicine and philosophy, an aspect of his intellectual personality which only an actual reading of his texts can restore to us.

Taking sides in many of the hotly debated topics of his times, Galen defends and demonstrates his opinions over an impressive range of questions. The more that physiological explanation is founded on anatomy, the more secure he thinks it is; the further removed it gets from it, the greater becomes the role played by supposition. The accounts thus become nuanced, complex and plausible only, with shades of meaning which the subsequent tradition of a rigid, dogmatic Galenism has served to erase. This is what makes returning to the actual texts themselves a valuable and often surprising corrective exercise for those of us who may have forgotten those hesitations and doubts which exist alongside his certainties, and which, together with his profound faith in Nature and its Creator, lend his work, in particular in the last treatises, a rare intensity.

Translated from the French by the editor

NOTES

1. On which see Flemming, ch. 13 in this volume.
2. For Galen's treatment of causation in general, see Hankinson, ch. 8 in this volume.
3. See von Staden (2000, 111–14).
4. For more on the physical aspects of this, see ch. 8 (Hankinson) in this volume.
5. See Debru (1996, 148–54).
6. *The Passions of the Soul* (*Aff.Dig.*) and *The Faculties of the Soul Follow the Mixtures of the Body* (*QAM*).
7. See also ch. 7 (Donini) and ch. 9 (Rocca) both in this volume.
8. See Amacher (1964); and Wilkie, *Introduction*, in Furley and Wilkie (1984, 50–1).
9. See Temkin (1973, 107); Harris (1973, 349–54).

10. Of which there are eight basic types; see Hankinson, ch. 8 in this volume, pp. 220–1.
11. See De Lacy (1992, 47).
12. See Nickel (2001, 42–4).
13. See May (1968, Introduction, 59–60).
14. See further Hankinson, ch. 6 in this volume.
15. See further Donini, ch. 7 in this volume.

11 Therapeutics

INTRODUCTION

For all Galen's many faces – medical scientist, public dissector and demonstrator, psychologist and moral philosopher, logician, linguist, commentator, lexicographer and literary critic, pharmacologist, historian of thought and story-teller – we should not forget that he regarded himself primarily as an *iatros*, a healer of patients and a restorer and preserver of health. Indeed, the principal job (*ergon*) or aim (*skopos*) of the medical art, he repeatedly says, is the treatment of disease and the preservation of health;[1] and it is his primary responsibility as a doctor to carry out that job in an indefinite number of particular cases. For while most other areas of Galen's activity are of a theoretical nature and aimed at attaining knowledge and understanding of universal truths, healing is by definition a practical activity concerned with individual patients constituting particular cases of illness.

Yet in spite of its fundamental importance, Galen's therapeutics has, as far as I am aware, never received anything remotely aspiring to a comprehensive scholarly treatment. The reason for this is not difficult to see. Therapeutics is, in a way, the *summa* of all of Galen's other activities: it both presupposes them and is their culmination. In order to make sense of Galen's therapeutic theory and practice, and indeed in order to be a successful healer oneself, one needs to

I am deeply grateful to the editor, Jim Hankinson, for his many valuable suggestions for improvement of this chapter, to Thomas Rütten and to the members of the Galen workshop at Exeter University in July 2004, for their comments on an earlier version. I am further indebted to the Wellcome Trust for its financial support of the project from which this chapter has arisen.

have mastered – as he says himself – his general theory of medical
science, his views on the specific modes of therapeutic intervention –
dietetics, pharmacology, surgery and their subspecies[2] – and his
views on the specific diagnosis and treatment of particular pathological conditions.[3] In addition, one needs to have a solid grasp of
the rules of logic and scientific methodology, in particular such epistemological tools as division, the analysis of items into genus and
species relationships, and the use of definitions; and one needs to
have a fairly advanced understanding of *endeixis* (therapeutic 'indication') and of what Galen calls *diorismos*, 'specification' or 'qualification', i.e. the correct determination of the relevant conditions
under which a general therapeutic statement is true.[4] One further
needs to know how to apply all these abstract rules and principles to
individual cases, to recognize and identify individual cases correctly
and to relate them to a more generic pattern; and as a healer, one
should have the flexibility to adjust the treatment to the requirements and circumstances of the individual patient one is trying to
cure.

Hence a comprehensive account of Galen's therapeutics would
have to cover, albeit in varying degrees of detail, pretty much all
areas of Galen's work – as indicated by the numerous cross-references
Galen gives in his therapeutic writings to more specialized treatment of the topic in other works. Apart from his general discussions
of therapeutics as offered in the *On the Therapeutic Method* (*MM*,
which fills the whole of vol. 10 of Kühn's edition)[5] and in the shorter
Therapeutics to Glaucon (*MMG*: XI 1–146),[6] it would have to comprise his views on the more specific modes of treatment such as
pharmacology, dietetics and surgery, as expounded in his voluminous works on drugs and drug treatment (vols. XI–XIII of Kühn), in
his works on food and regimen (vols. VI–VII), his writings on surgery,
as well as his commentaries on the relevant works of Hippocrates
(vols. XV–XVIII); and this would include also the subspecies of these
modes of treatment such as venesection, to which he devoted several specialized treatises (vol. XI),[7] and various modes of plasters and
bandages, the uses of bathing, the medicinal uses of various types of
oil, purgatives and of course his well-known compound theriac, etc.
It would further have to cover his views on the normal functioning
of the body and its parts, and hence the whole of his anatomy and
physiology (vols. II–IV); and it would have to comprise his views on

the prognosis, diagnosis, understanding and treatment of a very large number of specific medical conditions (diseases, injuries, affections) and on the correct aetiology, symptomatology and classification of fevers and other pathological states (vols. VII–IX). It would further have to comprise Galen's views on the preservation of health and hygiene and the prevention of disease as expounded, e.g., in his substantial works *On the Preservation of Health* (*San. Tu.*)[8] and *On the Properties of Foodstuffs*[9] (*Alim.Fac.*) (vol. VI), and it would have to take account of his deontological views (scattered all over his writings) on therapeutic intervention or non-intervention, on the causes of therapeutic error, or on the role of the patient in the therapeutic process.

Moreover, in all this we would have to distinguish between Galen's theory of therapeutics and his practice as a healer in individual cases, of which he gives numerous examples, often in the form of case-histories and anecdotes with which he intersperses his theoretical discussions. This distinction is problematic, for in the absence of eye-witnesses' reports, Galen's therapeutic practice can never be fully recovered beyond what he himself tells us about it in his works;[10] and that story is bound to be coloured by Galen's own interpretation and presentation of the pathological phenomena he was confronted with and of the therapeutic measures he took on each and every occasion – quite apart from his own literary embellishment, his rhetorical tendency to self-presentation and indeed self-glorification and his biased presentation of the failures of other healers.

Within this large field, we would then have to focus on some of the more striking general aspects of his therapeutics, such as the question of his originality versus his dependence on earlier modes of treatment as found in the works of his predecessors. How innovative was Galen as a healer? What new remedies or therapies did he propose for the treatment of particular diseases? What changes or 'advances' – if that term does not sound too positivistic – did he initiate in the application of specific remedies?[11] In this connection, we would have to examine his relation to, and representation of the views of earlier medical authorities, such as 'Hippocrates' (as Galen constructed him), or Plato, Aristotle, Diocles, Herophilus and Erasistratus, as well as his polemics against rival medical schools such as the Methodists and the Empiricists, the 'sophists' or the unidentified 'doctors' (*iatroi*) of his own age; and we would have to consider whether his therapeutics are really so superior to those proposed by his competitors. We would also be interested to know more about the rationale underlying his therapeutics, both explicit – as given by Galen himself – and implicit – as it is to be inferred from his works, or the works of predecessors, or from what is generally known of ancient therapeutics. And a further point of interest would be the narrative character and anecdotal structure of much of Galen's accounts of therapeutic activity.

It will be obvious that within the scope of this chapter we can deal with only a small selection of all this material. Besides, some of the areas mentioned are covered elsewhere in this volume, while others – such as the assessment of the rationale and possible efficacy of Galen's therapies from a contemporary medical perspective – are beyond my competence. My purpose is to discuss Galen's general theory of therapeutics; and my discussion will largely be centred around Galen's own synopsis of therapeutics as expounded in his *Therapeutics to Glaucon*, a treatise which was written in the early 170s and which has the advantage of being short and reasonably systematic. In addition, I will refer to relevant remarks in Galen's *On the Therapeutic Method*, especially books I and II; other textual evidence will be cited as appropriate.[12]

THE UNIVERSAL AND THE PARTICULAR

Glaucon has requested that Galen provide 'an outline of a general method of treatments' (*iamatôn tina . . . katholou methodon hupotupôsasthai*), and this is what Galen sets out to do (*MMG* I.1: XI 1). The terminology is significant here. First, there is the notion of the 'general' or 'universal' (*katholou*). Right from the start, Galen realizes that there is a tension between the theory of therapeutics, which aims at universal knowledge, and the practice of therapy which is concerned with particulars. On the one hand, he argues, the treatment of each individual patient ought to be based on universally valid scientific medical knowledge, i.e. anatomy, physiology, pathology, diagnostics, dietetics, pharmacology and surgery, founded on secure theoretical principles and obeying the rigorous rules of logic. The reason is, Galen insists, that without such a theoretical basis, therapy will often not be successful and prone to error. Indeed, time and time again Galen stresses this crucial importance of universal scientific theory for therapeutic practice, and he goes out of his way to point out how fatal errors made by rival healers can be explained by reference to their lack of a proper theoretical grounding or their failure to apply the rules of logic and philosophy of science with sufficient rigour. In other words, medical science in its full universal, theoretical sense is not just an academic luxury: it is, or at least it can be, a matter of life and death.

At the same time, however, therapy is concerned with 'the individual', or 'the peculiar' (*to idion*), the particular individual case the doctor is confronted with and which is different every time. Galen refers here to Aristotle's notion of 'the particular' (*to kath' hekaston*), as set out in *Metaphysics* 1.1 and illustrated by Aristotle with examples derived from medicine: the doctor may know what drugs to administer in cases of a certain type, and the good doctor may even know, on what universal grounds, i.e. for what general reasons, these drugs are to be administered in these types of cases, but ultimately his job is to cure individual people like Callias or Socrates, not humans of a certain type or indeed humans in general – even though, according to Aristotle, science is not of the particular as such (*Posterior Analytics* 1.24). Likewise, Aristotle's discussions of ethics provide a useful model for Galen here: the science of ethics is a practical science, which is valuable only if it can be applied to individual circumstances.[13] No general theory can fully cover these; each case is unique and defies reduction to a general pattern. And this means, Galen interestingly notes, that it is impossible to arrive at a universal theory by induction from particulars, for each particular case will add new information and it will be a never-ending process.[14] Nevertheless, Galen goes on to argue, there is such a thing as a theory of 'the common human nature' (*koinê phusis anthrôpôn*), based on a combination of theory and experience in anatomy and physiology, and he is confident that this theory will be sufficiently accurate and detailed to provide at least a relevant framework in which individual therapeutic actions can successfully take place (I.1: XI 1–2.)

Secondly, there is the word 'method' (*methodos*), perhaps better, though somewhat clumsily, translated 'methodicity' or 'methodicalness', for it is the opposite of 'proceeding by chance' or 'luck'. This term is charged with meaning, for Galen uses it frequently in polemical discussion with his two most prominent rivals in medicine, the

Empiricists and the Methodists. The former are often criticized by Galen for their lack of any method at all, their uncontrolled and ad hoc 'trial-and-error' approach to therapeutics, and their tendency to improvising and experimenting with remedies without any clear theoretical knowledge of what they are doing.[15] With the latter, especially the Methodist Thessalus, Galen's battles are more vigorous and his polemics more venomous, possibly because the Methodists could claim considerable success in their treatment of disease. As their name suggests, they, too, had their *methodos*, indeed, being 'methodical' was precisely what they claimed their medicine was all about; and this method was so effective, they claimed, that one could acquire it within six months.[16] But Galen, who adopts the same term and includes it prominently in the title of his principal work on therapeutics, *On the Therapeutic Method*, insists on numerous occasions that they are in fact *amethodoi*, 'without method'. Their treatments, e.g. their characteristic *diatritos*, the 'three-days-period'[17] of starving a patient, are dismissed as erroneous, ill-founded, inconsistent, dangerous or even downright harmful; and the reasons for these defects vary from lack of logical rigour, lack of proper anatomical and physiological knowledge, lack of experience and knowledge of the relevant condition, erroneous starting-points, etc.[18]

SOME FUNDAMENTAL THERAPEUTIC PRINCIPLES

Galen next states what his 'method' of healing involves. The first requirement the healer has to meet is to have knowledge of 'the quality and quantity of the relevant remedies' (*poiotês kai posotês tôn boêthêmatôn*), the 'mode of their application' (*tropos tês chrêseôs autôn*) and the 'discernment of the right time of application' (*diagnôsis tou kairou*) (*MMG* 1.1: XI 1–2). The first two may be learned through courses in dietetics, pharmacology and surgery; but the latter is the most difficult of all, he says – which reminds one of the first Hippocratic *Aphorism*: 'opportunity is fleeting' (*kairos oxus*). It is impossible to state general rules here, Galen says: it is a matter of 'conjecture' (*stochasmos*),[19] based on the healer's professional judgement of the circumstances, which differ from one individual case to another. A further complication is that the healer often comes across a patient for the first time when (s)he is ill, without having been able to examine the patient in his/her healthy state. This is another reason why a general knowledge of pathological conditions is both insufficient and at the same time the only thing one has at one's disposal: the healer will never have full advance knowledge of the patient (s)he is treating, and this always carries an element of risk. The best one can do is to work on the basis of a combination of general theoretical knowledge and practical experience.

The above may seem pretty commonsensical, but Galen then moves on to put his peculiar stamp on things. The most important thing, he says, is that the healer makes the right 'divisions', for this is where many doctors go wrong and to which most therapeutic failure can be reduced.[20] 'Division' renders *diairesis*, and a related concept which Galen uses in this context is *diorismos*, which can be translated as 'qualification', or 'specification', or 'determination'. These concepts represent two major epistemological procedures which Galen adopts from earlier Greek philosophy and science – he refers in this context to Hippocrates, Plato and to the fourth-century medical writer Mnesitheus of Athens, of whom he has preserved an important fragment on the use of division in medicine – and which he applies throughout his massive work. 'Division' refers to analysis of general classes of items (things, objects, phenomena, entities, but also ideas) into more specific kinds; sometimes it refers in particular to the analysis into genus, species and differentia. In the area of therapeutics, it means that the pathological condition to be addressed is properly understood in its generic kind and its specific manifestation, so that treatment can be targeted at the right level. For example, if it is known that conditions of kind A can only be treated with remedy B, it is important that if a specific condition C is in fact a species of kind A, it is recognized as such, so that treatment B can be applied accordingly. It is therefore important that these divisions are done according to the correct and relevant differentia (*diaphora*), in other words that one applies the division at the right cutting point (*tomê*). Another important application of the principle of division in the area of therapeutics is the distinction between disease (*nosos, nosêma*) and symptom (*sumptôma*) as two different kinds of 'unnatural states',[21] or between different kinds of symptoms,[22] or between disease and 'affection' (*pathos*),[23] or between several different kinds of 'imbalances' (*duskrasiai*),[24] 'fevers' (*puretoi*) and 'inflammations' (*phlegmonai*).[25]

As for the other term, *diorismos* means that a generic therapeutic rule, e.g. that treatment B is an effective remedy against conditions of

type A, is considered, and if necessary refined and adjusted, according
to a number of criteria that determine the extent to which that rule
is valid in a particular case.[26] Some of these criteria have to do with
the body of the patient, e.g. age, gender, physiological constitution,
life-style or character, some with the environmental factors such as
climate or season, and yet others with the nature of the remedy or the
mode of its application, e.g. raw or cooked, pure or mixed, externally
or internally administered, etc. As Galen puts it:

> If someone uses this method [sc. of division] on everything that is normal
> and everything that is abnormal, and derives flawless indications (endeixis)
> from all that results from this division, he alone would be free from errors in
> healing as far as is humanly possible, he would deal with patients whom he
> knows better than others, and even patients he does not know he would heal
> to the best of his ability as well as those he does know. For if one divided
> first according to the difference in age, then according to the temperaments
> and capacities and all the other factors that pertain to human beings – I
> mean colour, heat, physical disposition, movement of the arteries, habit,
> profession, and the character of the soul – and if to these he were to add the
> difference of male and female and whatever else must be divided in terms of
> place and seasons of the year and the other conditions of the air surrounding
> us, he would come close to an idea of the nature of the patient. (MMG I 1:
> XI 4–6, trans. Dickson, 1998, 39–41)[27]

Basically, what Galen means is that both in the examination of the
case the healer is confronted with and in the planning and execution of the treatment, (s)he should identify, analyse, categorize and
classify the relevant information in the right way. 'The right way'
means that in the diagnostic picture that emerges and in the therapeutic strategy that follows from it, the phenomena, and the way
they are broken down in conceptual theoretical analysis, are classi-
fied according to the hierarchy in which they actually stand. Thus
in books 1 and 2 of the *On the Therapeutic Method* Galen points
out that disease (*nosêma*) should be defined as that which impedes
a bodily faculty (*dunamis*) from exercising its activity (*energeia*),
like blindness impeding the eye from seeing.[28] And he insists that
in each particular case of disease, four items should be identified
and distinguished: the impaired activity, the condition (*diathesis*)
that brings the impairment about, the cause(s) of this situation and
the consequences that follow from it (such as symptoms and other
accompanying phenomena).[29] The crucial therapeutic side to this is
that the object of treatment is the condition, the *diathesis*, and not

any of the other items; this is why he thinks it preferable to label this the disease,[30] even though terminology is itself unimportant.[31] And it is therefore of vital importance that the various constituents involved in the pathological situation are properly distinguished and viewed in their correct interrelationship. It is here, Galen argues, that many healers get confused and do not address the situation in the right way. For instance, they mix up the cause of the disease with the condition itself, or they confuse the condition with its consequences, and as a result of these confusions their therapeutic strategy is doomed to failure. They also confuse the conceptual relations between health and disease by putting one in one type of category, and the other in another which is not correlative to it;[32] and they interdefine 'health' and 'disease', allowing us no independent grip on either.[33]

It now becomes clear why Galen's ideal healer should have a thorough grounding in logical analysis. (S)he should of course also possess a solid theoretical knowledge of anatomy and physiology, especially the different types of 'mixture' or 'blending' (*krasis*) that may occur in the body, and of pathology, especially concerning the division and classification of diseases (including fevers) and other nosological states[34] into different genera and species and the correct determination of the relevant physiological 'imbalance' (*duskrasia*). Furthermore, (s)he should have a firm grasp of the correct 'starting-points' or principles (*archai*). Examples of such correct starting-points are the principle that healing takes place by opposites, or the principle that nothing happens without a cause.[35] An example of a false starting point is the Methodists' notion of 'generality' or 'common condition' (*koinotês*), which according to Galen cannot empirically be observed and whose existence is uncertain. More in general, his criticism of 'Dogmatists' – i.e. any medical thinker who uses speculative knowledge – is that they adopt starting-points that are not secure and that are disputed.[36]

The healer should further have a thorough knowledge of causes, and a proper understanding of the different types of causes. Galen was strongly interested in causal analysis, and he wrote separate treatises on 'antecedent' and 'synectic' causes, adopting terminology from earlier, possibly Stoic or Pneumatist, origin.[37] Moreover, he was engaged in polemical discussion with a number of rival groups about the therapeutic relevance of antecedent causes: with the Methodists, who rejected causal explanation as irrelevant and misguided, with the Empiricists, who did recognize antecedent causes but refused to speculate on their causal significance and made the error of deriving therapeutic indications *directly* from antecedent causes, rather than using them (among other things) to determine the patient's inner *diathesis* – which will then yield therapeutic indications[38] – and also with the followers of Erasistratus, who had different views on the correct interpretation of these causes. Galen firmly believes that causes are, or at least can be, relevant for the determination of the treatment, for it is quite possible that two cases of the same condition are brought about by different causes and that treatment has to be different accordingly.[39] Sometimes, the healer has to do research or even undertake provocative action in order to identify the cause (we shall see an example of this in a moment). On the other hand, Galen is also eager to point out that 'the Dogmatists' sometimes blindly rely on causal analysis, whereas such analysis is not always verifiable or plausible, and the results of that analysis are not always relevant to the treatment and can even be misleading.[40]

Once equipped with this theoretical knowledge and instruments, the healer can go about examining particular cases and determining the appropriate treatment. It is here that Galen's famous notion of *endeixis*, 'indication', comes in. Again, Galen was not the first to use the term; and like *methodos*, it was also used by his rivals, the Methodists.[41] But in his eagerness to distance himself from the Methodists, Galen gives the notion of *endeixis* his own peculiar meaning. There has recently been a fair amount of scholarly discussion of this term, partly inspired by the later history of the notion of 'indication' (and 'contra-indication', *antiendeuknunai*) in medical therapeutics, partly also by the more recent interest taken by students of ancient philosophy in medical accounts of methods of inferential reasoning.[42] Galen himself defines *endeixis* as 'the reflection of the consequence' (*emphasis tês akolouthias*).[43] This 'reflection' – or 'manifestation', 'appearance', 'imprint' – is provided by the body of the patient under examination, and the 'consequence' is either the causal connection between that bodily condition and the physical consequences of this, or the therapeutic procedure that follows from this condition. In other words, the body of the patient, or a particular part thereof, or its specific condition, 'indicates' (*endeiknusi*) what is wrong with it, and how it should be treated. Sometimes this indication is immediately and unmistakably obvious, e.g. in the way in which it is obvious that a condition of thirst indicates by its very nature that the remedy is to provide a drink: it is, so to speak, what the condition 'asks for'. Yet not always is the indication so straightforward or unambiguous, and in many cases it is clear only to the healer who knows how to identify and interpret correctly the signs given off by the body and to infer a therapeutic strategy from this; and in order to do this, one needs to know what signs to look for, and what signs are relevant. This knowledge is what Galen refers to as the knowledge of 'the actual nature' (or 'essence') 'of the matter'. This is, in his view, what inference by indication should be based on;[44] and this knowledge is in turn based on a combination of theory and earlier experience, which is brought to bear on the new situation the healer is confronted with.

Thus diagnosis, and the subsequent decision on treatment, are the medical response to the *endeixis* given by the body of the patient. But the adequacy of this response differs not only according to the complexity of the case one is confronted with, but also according to one's medical competence and background knowledge. And this is where Galen once again draws a sharp dividing line between his own method of healing and that of the Empiricists and the Methodists. The Empiricists do not take account of 'the actual nature of the matter'; their diagnostic procedures are either insufficiently specific (*adioristos*), based as they are on a superficial comparison of apparent similarities with earlier conditions, or based on the wrong sort of distinctions;[45] and their therapeutic practice is a matter of trial-and-error, uninformed by in-depth knowledge of the *krasis* of the patient, the nature of the condition and the appropriateness of the remedy. The Methodists likewise ignore the specific 'nature' or 'essence' of the condition and reduce it to one of their three 'generalities' (*koinotêtes*) such as a 'loose state', or a 'constricted state', or a 'mixed state', and thus fail to diagnose the condition at a sufficiently specific, detailed level – this in contrast to Galen's own distinction between 'primary' or 'common' *endeixeis*, which in a sense everyone knows, and the specific indications which show how to achieve the general 'aims' (*skopoi*) associated with the general ones.[46] Hence the Methodists' therapeutic strategy (such as the notorious *diatritos*) is likewise misguided.

The following passage from the *Therapeutics to Glaucon* provides an example of what Galen regards as good, proper use of *endeixis*:

For example, if someone has pains in the head, if he is nauseous and has heartburn and you order him to vomit, he will vomit either bile or phlegm or both. But if no noteworthy indication of affliction in the stomach is apparent, investigate whether there is a plethora or an obstruction or an inflammation of one of the parts in the head. First discover by questioning whether the pain stretches through the whole head or else is situated more vehemently in one of its parts. Discover next whether it occurs with heaviness or tension or a mordant sensation of throbbing. For heaviness indicates plethora; throbbing, inflammation. Tension, if without heaviness and throbbing from unconcocted and flatulent pneuma, indicates plethora; but if there is throbbing, an inflammation of membranous tissues; and if heaviness, an excess contained within the membranes. Accordingly, when you have determined (*dioristheiê*) all these factors, you must investigate each of their productive causes (*tên ergazomenên hekaston autôn aitian*), for this will show you the treatment (*ekeinê gar endeixetai soi tên therapeian*). For example, if an excess of vapours or humours happens to be contained there, see whether due to the intensity of the fever the humours have been liquefied, and boiling, so to speak, have attacked the head, thanks either to the weakness of that part or else to an excess throughout the body – since this would not be hard for someone to cure without purging the entire body. (I.16: XI 61–5, trans. Dickson)

The passage is particularly interesting because it shows how causes can be indicators of treatment, and at the same time how these causes themselves need to be identified first, either by physical examination or even by provocative action to bring them to the surface.

The most significant diagnostic 'indicators' according to Galen are the urine of the patient and the pulse. These are familiar diagnostic tools from earlier Greek medicine: urines received considerable discussion in the Hippocratic *Prognosticon* (esp. ch. 12), and pulse rhythms were recognized as diagnostic and prognostic indicators from Praxagoras and Herophilus onwards.[47] Urine and pulse are observable entities from which not-directly observable states or factors can be inferred if properly interpreted. This method of inference thus suits the pattern expressed in the classical formula *opsis adêlôn ta phainomena*, 'the appearances provide a view of what is obscure', which was attributed to Anaxagoras and Democritus and applied to the medical sphere by Diocles.[48] Galen adopts these ideas and elaborates on them, but in addition he mentions other factors that can serve as indicators, such as the difference between men and women, or the influence of weather and the environment. Yet as we have just seen in the passage cited above, he also mentions indicators that are not so easily observable, such as the 'mixture' or 'blending' (krasis) of the patient,[49] or the causes of the disease in question, or the critical days at which certain symptoms manifest themselves. With these factors, determining or identifying the indicator is itself not by any means a straightforward empirical process, since a patient's physiological temperament is not so easily recognizable; and as we have seen, the identification of the causes can itself also be a complicated procedure.

Even so, Galen is confident that to the expert physician meeting the requirements outlined above, the determination of the nature of the disease in question will indicate the treatment required (albeit perhaps without complete precision). In this determination of the nature of the disease, the healer will be guided by his/her background knowledge of the classification of diseases and symptoms. Here we enter Galen's pathology, as expounded in works such as *Causes of Diseases* (*Caus.Morb.*), *Causes of Symptoms* (*Symp.Caus.*), *Differences of Diseases* (*Morb.Diff.*), *Differences of Fevers* (*Diff.Feb.*), *On Plethora* (*Plen.*) and *On the Affected Parts*. It is a field far too extensive and complicated to cover here, and only some basic remarks must suffice. Briefly, Galen distinguishes three main types of disease: diseases consisting in physiological 'imbalances' (*duskrasiai*) affecting the homoeomerous parts of the body, diseases affecting the organic parts and diseases that consist in a breakdown of the body's overall coherence. Of the first type, Galen in turn distinguishes eight different types of 'imbalance'.[50] All these distinctions have implications for the treatment, and Galen organizes his discussion in the *Therapeutic Method* and the *Therapeutics to Glaucon* accordingly. Thus, in the former work, after devoting books 1 and 2 to theoretical issues of methodology and definition, he first treats ulcers and other lesions as well as sprains and fractures (books 3–6), followed by fevers (books 7–12) and by conditions requiring surgical intervention (books 13–14).[51] In the *Therapeutics to Glaucon*, Galen begins with a discussion of ephemeral fevers, and then moves on to discuss fevers caused by 'inflammation' (*phlegmonê*) and fevers caused by humours (*chumoi*), and in chapter 15, he discusses 'fevers accompanied by symptoms',[52] where he recognizes the difficulty of diagnosis where two diseases are present at the same time. In book 2, his approach is bodily-part-oriented, and the 'indications' here are provided by such criteria as 'mixture' (*krasis*), 'formation' (*diaplasis*), 'position' (*the-sis*) and 'power' (or 'faculty': *dunamis*). Within these categories he makes various further distinctions, which are all to be taken into account by the healer trying to decide on a proper mode of treatment (but which would take us too long to discuss here).

Once the nature of the disease has been identified, the healer has to determine 'the magnitude of the disease' (*to megethos tou nosēmatos*), the stage in which it is and whether it is curable or not.[53] Here, it is also possible that 'contra-indications' may occur, e.g. in cases where the patient's body is too weak to support the treatment normally required.[54] In such cases, the treatment needs to be adapted or replaced by an alternative, less vexing treatment.

These are, roughly speaking, the fundamental principles of Galen's therapeutics as applied to the treatment of diseases, although in the course of his discussions of specific diseases, specific modes of treatment or individual cases, Galen provides numerous further refinements and sub-distinctions, with ad hoc examples often serving as starting-points for more generalizing considerations. It is beyond the scope of this chapter to go through the large number and variety of remedies and substances that Galen recommends in his treatment of diseases.[55] One famous and influential medicine that may be mentioned here in particular is theriac, on which Galen wrote a separate treatise (*On Theriac to Piso* [*Ther.Pis.*]).[56] Another major therapeutic procedure is venesection, a remedy which had been in use in Greek medicine since the days of the Hippocratic Corpus (and probably earlier), although the extent to which writers like the Hippocratics, Diocles and others used the technique is difficult to assess.[57] In Galen's work, venesection is very prominent: he often recommends it in his own treatment of various diseases, and he devoted four separate works to the topic. The primary reason for the latter was that venesection had strongly been condemned as a useless and indeed quite dangerous method by the Hellenistic doctor Erasistratus, with whom Galen takes issue on a large number of points, possibly because the legacy of Erasistratus still exercised great influence in the second century CE. This was certainly the case for venesection, if we may believe Galen's own account of the views held by the Erasistrateans in Rome of his time. This no doubt explains the polemical tone of Galen's writings on venesection, of which *On Treatment by Bloodletting* (*Cur.Rat.Ven.Sec.*) is probably the most systematic. The basic principle underlying treatment by venesection was the need for evacuation, usually presented by *plêthos* or *plêthôra*, 'surplus' or 'excess', usually of blood but sometimes also of other substances in the body. Bloodletting was believed to redress the imbalance in the body caused by such excess. But there was also another purpose of bloodletting – so-called 'revulsive' bloodletting, which was meant to bring excessive blood-flow in one part of the body to a halt by subtracting blood from it at another part.[58] Again, Galen addresses the topic in his peculiar style, referring to a host of earlier authorities who advocated the technique, yet on the other hand giving the impression that he is the first to systematize it and to apply it with sufficient logical rigour and consideration of the need of the patient. Before even contemplating the use of venesection – clearly a technique not without risk – one needs to be clear on the question what states of the body require venesection and for what types of patients it is appropriate – and here he sums up a number of 'specifications' (*diorismoi*) that need to be taken into account such as age, season, nature of the disorder, or habit. One also needs to be able to determine which veins are most suitable for bloodletting, what quantity of blood one should withdraw and whether one should withdraw the required quantity slowly and steadily, or all at once. 'Indications' (*endeixeis*) here are the severity of the disease, the patient's age and the strength of the patient's faculties, the latter being indicated by the pulse. The quantity of blood to be withdrawn is indicated by other factors and is, as Galen concedes, very much a matter of 'conjecture' (*stochasmos*). But it is also possible that the state of the patient's body, or other factors taken into consideration, provide 'contra-indications', in which case bloodletting should be replaced by other, less aggressive means.[59]

PREVENTION OF DISEASE AND REGIMEN IN HEALTH

As said at the beginning of this chapter, Galen claims that the principal aim of medicine is the treatment of disease and the preservation of health. Most of our discussion so far has been concerned with the former, and it may be as well to conclude with some observations about the latter.

Regimen in health, *diaita hugieinê*, had been a major concern and constituent of Hippocratic medical activity; and preservation of health, prevention of disease and effective convalescence after treatment were considered at least as important as the cure of disease. *Therapeia* means 'care' as much as 'cure', and hence therapeutics was not concerned only with the sick body but also with the healthy body, and indeed not just with the body but also with the mind. These areas had often been discussed side by side in the same context, e.g. in the Hippocratic treatise *On Regimen* and in fourth- and third-century BCE medical writers such as Diocles of Carystus, Mnesitheus of Athens and Erasistratus of Ceos. While Hippocratic dietetics already comprised a wide range of measures and activities such as diet, exercise, sleeping patterns, bathing and hygiene, sexual activity and voice exercises, medical writers from the late fourth century BCE onwards became increasingly engaged in discussions of matters we would associate with life-style rather than medicine, such as cookery, cultivation of food and wine-tasting, gymnastics and fitness, and even with the upbringing of young children and the care for the elderly.

Galen poses no exception to this pattern. Indeed, in his view the *iatros* is by far the most competent expert to deal with these areas – rather than, say, gymnastics trainers (*paidotribai*). In another polemical work entitled *Thrasybulus* (*Thras.*), Galen addresses the question whether health belongs to the discipline of gymnastics or of medicine. Galen points out that the boundaries between therapeutics and hygiene are fluid, since the definition of health itself, too, is fluid. In his key work *On the Preservation of Health* (*San.Tu.*), he defines health as the state of right balance between elementary qualities such as hot, cold, dry and wet, within the homoeomerous parts of the body.[60] Yet this is a relative notion, for this balance is 'peculiar' (*oikeia*) not only to different species of animals but also to individual people – a point Galen elaborates on in books I and II of his important treatise *On Mixtures* (*Temp.*). Hence a mathematically exact definition of health cannot be given, there is always an element of specific or even individual variation; and there are differences and variations according to age or gender, climate and mode of life, which constitute and affect a person's health. This is not to say that there is no dividing line between health and illness, but it is up to the judgement of the competent *iatros* to determine this from one individual case to another – although, again, properly informed by the comprehensive, systematic and universal knowledge of medicine outlined above.

In the case of regimen in health, such systematicity is provided by Galen's distinction between 'bodies', 'signs' and 'causes'.[61] The 'bodies' (*sômata*) of individual people need to be examined and their generic and individual peculiarities need to be taken into account before determining the appropriate course of action; the 'signs' (*sêmeia*) are the diagnostic indicators that provide the relevant information; and the causes (*aitia*) are the factors that bring about health. They can in turn be subdivided into *prospheromena*, i.e. substances that are taken in by patients (e.g. food, wine, drugs, air etc.), *poioumena*, i.e. things that are done by or to patients (e.g. massage, walks, baths, sleep, sexual activity), *kenoumena*, i.e. things that need to be removed from the body, and *ta exôthen prospiptonta*, external influences brought about incidentally.

At the same time, in *San. Tu.* I 2 Galen distinguishes various causes of disturbance of health, which he divides in 'inevitable and innate forms of harm' (such as old age, gradual loss of bodily heat, etc.), and 'causes that are unnecessary and that do not arise from within ourselves', such as the influence of air and the environment.[62] It is the former which an effective strategy on health needs to address by a preventive or corrective regimen, by supplementing deficits or removing what is in excess; if necessary, even drugs or venesection may be used to achieve this. A major part of Galen's discussion (III 5–10, and the whole of book IV) is taken up by the phenomenon of 'fatigue' (*kopos*), a typically ambivalent condition on the borderline between health and sickness. He distinguishes several different kinds of fatigue, some of which – e.g. tiredness after exercise or sexual activity – are relatively harmless and easily addressed by what he calls 'apotherapy' (*apotherapeia*), a combination of massage, breathing exercises, etc. Other kinds of fatigue are more serious and in need of more extensive, long-term treatment, sometimes requiring the use of drugs and venesection in addition to dietetic measures.

To ensure the best possible physical condition (*aristê kataskeuê tou sômatos*), in particular the optimal bodily 'mixture' or 'blending' (*krasis*), the development of the body needs to be regulated right from the very beginning. Hence Galen devotes considerable attention to the role of regimen in health in the upbringing of children. This also includes moral and psychological guidance, since even moral dispositions and proneness to emotions (e.g. anger), unless properly directed, can have a detrimental effect on bodily health; and in his work *On Habits* (*Cons.*), Galen deals extensively with the role and management of emotions and affective states from a medical point of view. But Galen's theory of health is not restricted to the young and those in the prime of life: he devotes the whole of book 5 of *On the Preservation of Health* to the care of the elderly. Although ageing, Galen points out, is an inevitable process of wasting away (*marasmos*) brought about by cooling and drying and ultimately ending in death, this process can nevertheless be regulated and made as agreeable as possible by a range of dietary measures, such as food and exercise, again of course adapted to the physical peculiarities of the individual, thus enhancing people's quality of life and allowing some to reach a very advanced age.[63]

This brief account may give some idea of the extraordinary range and scope of Galen's therapeutics. Whether it was as successful in practical terms as Galen claims is another matter – and in this respect it would be very interesting to compare Galen's treatment of specific conditions to that proposed by the Methodist writer Caelius Aurelianus, who is equally insistent on the need to take the condition of the individual patient as point of departure, yet draws radically different conclusions from this for therapeutic practice. Whether such a comparison can be made at all – e.g. in the light of the problems of retrospective diagnosis – is a question I cannot address here. Yet however this may be, in its systematicity, its comprehensiveness, its theoretical and conceptual sophistication, and at the same time in its adaptability to practical, individual circumstances, and thus in its remarkable ability to link theory to practice, Galen's therapeutics certainly stands out as a most impressive achievement, from both a medical and from a philosophical point of view.

NOTES

1. E.g. *MM* II 3: X 92: 'the first and most particular concern of doctors, indeed the thing which is pretty well the defining feature of their business, is the removal of illnesses' (trans. Hankinson, 1991b, 46); see also *Cur.Rat.Ven.Sec.* 4: XI 259; *Thras.* 5: V 810.

2. This was the traditional tripartition of therapeutics which, according to Celsus (*On Medicine*, proem, 9) was established in the time of Diocles, Praxagoras and Herophilus (and possibly, depending on the interpretation of *iisdem temporibus*, as early as that of Hippocrates; see

the discussion of this passage in van der Eijk, 2005, 110–11). See also Galen, *Subf.Emp.* 5, p. 52,13–14 Deichgräber; *On the Parts of the Art of Medicine* 6.1–4, pp. 38–41 Lyons; and Sextus Empiricus, *Against the Mathematicians* 1.95. Subspecies were venesection, cautery, trepanation, etc.

3. Cf. Mani (1991, 27–9), who correctly stresses Galen's stance against specialization.

4. On the role of logic in Galen's therapeutics see Barnes (1991); Kudlien (1991); Hankinson (1991b, 99 ff.); Frede (1981); and see chs. 3 (Tieleman) and 6 (Hankinson) both in this volume.

5. For a collection of studies on this work see Kudlien and Durling (1991); for a translation and commentary of the first two books, and a general introduction to some of the theoretical issues in Galen's therapeutics, see Hankinson (1991b).

6. For an English translation of this work, and of Stephanus of Alexandria's commentary on it, see Dickson (1998).

7. For a translation of these works with introduction and essays see Brain (1986).

8. For a translation of this work see Green (1951).

9. This work has been translated into English by Grant (2000), and by Powell (2003).

10. On Galen as a 'raconteur' in therapeutics, and on the rhetorical and polemical aspects of *MM*, see Nutton (1991, 9–16).

11. For some examples see Nutton (1991, 18–19); Mani (1991); Brain (1986, 122 ff.).

12. The reader should be aware that the account offered in Galen's later summary *Ars Medica* (*Ars Med.*) differs in a number of ways from what is presented in *MM* and *MMG*. Within the restrictions of this volume, a detailed discussion of the relationship between the systematizing *Ars Med.* and the other works cannot be offered here; see, however, the useful discussion of *Ars Med.* in Boudon (2000, esp. 159–96).

13. Aristotle, *Nicomachean Ethics* 1.3 and 1.7, esp. 1098b1–8.

14. Similar points are made on induction in *Thras.* 5: V 812; *Sem.* 15: IV 581; *SMT* 2.4: XI 469–71.

15. E.g. at *MM* I 4: X 31: 'Thus attempting to discover something methodically is opposed to doing so by chance or spontaneously. The method follows a certain route in an orderly way, so that there is a first stage in the inquiry, a second, a third, a fourth, and so on through all of them in order until the investigator arrives at what was at issue at the outset. However, . . . experience is unsystematic and irrational, and requires good fortune to arrive at the discovery of what was sought' (trans. Hankinson, 1991b, 17).

16. E.g. *MM* XIII 20: X 927; *SI* 6: I 83.
17. In fact forty-eight hours; the ancients counted inclusively.
18. Cf. Nutton (1991, 17).
19. On the notion of *stochasmos* *[technikos]* see e.g. *Ars Med.* 19: I 353, and *Loc.Aff.* I 1: VIII 14: 'skill-based conjecture, which lies in the middle between exact knowledge and complete ignorance'.
20. *MMG* I 1: XI 3–4; cf. *MM* I 5: X 40. On division, see Barnes (1991, 65–7).
21. *MM* II 3: X 86.
22. *MM* I 8: X 65. Galen also wrote a special treatise *On Differences of Symptoms* (*Symp.Diff.*) (VII 42–84).
23. *MM* II 3: X 89–90.
24. *MM* II 6: X 121–2, with the comments by Hankinson (1991b, 199–200).
25. On the different kinds of fevers and their corresponding treatment see *MMG* I 5; Galen also wrote a special treatise *On Differences of Fevers* (*Diff.Feb.*) (VII 273–405); on different kinds of inflammations see *MMG* II 1.
26. On *diorismos* in Galen see van der Eijk (1997), and von Staden (1997).
27. For the difficulty of making such determinations see also *MM* III 3: X 181–2.
28. *MM* I 5: X 41.
29. *MM* I 8: X 63–67, and I 9: X 70.
30. *MM* II 1: X 80–1.
31. Cf. *MM* I 3: X 50; I 7: X 61–3.
32. *MM* I 7: X 50–2, 54–5, 57–61.
33. *MM* I 7: X 56.
34. E.g. inflammations (*phlegmonai*), of which Galen distinguishes several different kinds: cf. *MMG* II 1: XI 72.
35. *MM* X 7: X 49–50.
36. *MM* I 4: X 32 K.
37. See Hankinson (1998a, 23–7, 43–5); and see ch. 8 (Hankinson) in this volume, pp. 229–33.
38. *MM* IV 3: X 242–9.
39. *MMG* I 15: XI 47.
40. In this respect, Galen follows a criticism already voiced by Diocles, fr. 176,29–37 (van der Eijk, 2000).
41. For a discussion of Methodist use of *endeixis* see Pigeaud (1991, 15–18), and Gourevitch (1991).
42. See e.g. Kudlien (1991); Barnes (1991, 98–100); Hankinson (1991b, 202–6).
43. *MM* II 7: X 126 K.
44. See: *Inst.Log.* 1.11; *MM* II 34: X 102; II 5: X 104; III 1: X 157; VI 4: X 421–2; XIII 7: X 897ff.; *In Hipp.Epid.* VI I 2: XVIIA 814.

45. See *MM* III 3: X 181, 183–6; III 7: X 204–8.
46. *MM* III 1: X 157ff.; III 3: X 181–3; III 7: 205–8; VI 2: 387–9; XIII 15: X 909.
47. Praxagoras: frs. 26–8 Steckerl (1958); Herophilus: frs. 144–88 von Staden (1989).
48. Diocles, fr. 56 van der Eijk (2000), with the comments in van der Eijk (2001, 122–4). The idea, if not the slogan, is also present in the Hippocratic *de Arte*, chs. 9, 11.
49. Galen remarks that if he could determine the patient's individual *idiosunkrasia* exactly, he would be Asclepius: *MM* III.7: X 207, 209.
50. See *MM* II 6: X 121–2. These imbalances consist in an excess of the individual qualities hot, cold, dry, or wet, or in an excess of hot-and-wet, hot-and-dry, cold-and-wet, or cold-and-dry.
51. On the organization of *MM* see Nutton (1991, 6–8); it is important to note that in ancient medicine, fevers were generally considered to be diseases in their own right, possibly accompanying other diseases, rather than symptoms.
52. Or, as Daremberg (1856) translates, 'complications'.
53. *MMG* I 9: XI 65.
54. Cf. *Cur.Rat.Ven.Sec.* 13: XI 290; for more on contra-indication, cf. *MM* X 1: X 661–5.
55. For useful surveys of Galen's surgical therapies, see Mani (1991); on pharmacological treatment, see Harig (1974).
56. For discussions of this see Boudon (2002b). And see ch. 12 (Vogt) in this volume.
57. See Brain (1986); on venesection in Diocles see frs. 155–157 vdE and the comments in van der Eijk (2001, 292–5).
58. *Cur.Rat.Ven.Sec.* 12: XI 284; see the discussion by Brain (1986, 129–30).
59. *Cur.Rat.Ven.Sec.* 12: XI 285.
60. *San.Tu.* I.1: VI 2, and I.5: VI 13–15. See Wöhrle (1990, 217–19).
61. *San.Tu.* I 15: VI 78; cf. *Ars Med.* 1: I 308; see Wöhrle (1990, 227–8).
62. For a similar, though not quite identical division see *Ars Med.* 23: I 367.
63. Galen gives the example of a certain Antiochus, who was a doctor himself and who kept practising and visiting patients until well into his eighties. There is also the amusing anecdote in *On Marasmus* (*Marc.*) 2: VII 670–1 about the philosopher who claimed to have a cure for ageing; but when he ended up looking like the Hippocratic *facies*, contended that it would have worked if he had taken it early enough. It may be added that Galen himself, according to Nutton's revised biography, reached the age of at least eighty-one.

12 Drugs and pharmacology

PHARMACOLOGY, PHARMACY AND DRUG-LORE

'What drugs will not cure, the knife will; what the knife will not cure, the cautery will; what the cautery will not cure, must be considered incurable.' This final maxim of the Hippocratic *Aphorisms*[1] gives a good impression of the general attitude towards drugs in ancient medicine. Drug lore holds a middle position within the tripartite system of ancient therapeutics: dietetics, pharmacology and surgery (including cautery).[2] Dietetics is not mentioned in the aphorism, because it is regarded as a non-invasive method of preserving health rather than of curing disease, and is thus applied prophylactically, or only in mild cases of disease, while pharmacology and, especially, surgery are regarded as rather drastic 'intrusions' into the patient's organism – chosen in order to counteract the noxious impact of an illness or wound. Between the two of them, pharmacology has two advantages: it does not imply the additional risks of surgery, i.e. the possible complications by bleeding or infection of the surgical wound (a very real danger in times without asepsis and antisepsis!);[3] and it is more apt to stimulate the body's self-healing processes to restore its original balance – a holistic view of the human organism to which Galen was especially disposed. Therefore, in Galen's view 'the best physician was the one most capable of treating surgical conditions by means other than the knife, and particularly by diet and drugs'.[4]

I am immensely indebted to Jim Hankinson and Vivian Nutton for advice and comments on the first draft of this chapter, which greatly profited from their knowledge and competence. The remaining faults remain, of course, my own responsibility.

The word 'pharmacology', as we use it today, was unknown to
Galen and his contemporaries. It is a creation of modern medicine,
consisting of the scientific research into the question of how drugs
exert their effects on living organisms. It is thus distinct from modern
'pharmacy', the knowledge of how to prepare, dispense and employ
medication. The ancients' knowledge about drugs and medication
does not observe this modern distinction and is thus better characterized as 'drug-lore',[5] since both terms, of course, are derived from
the Greek word *pharmakon*, 'drug'. Nevertheless, while taking note
of the anachronism, it is quite correct in the current context to speak
of Galen's 'pharmacology', as his approach to drug-lore is among the
first attempts to not only collect remedies proven effective by experience, but to systematize the known *materia medica*, to understand
the interaction between body and drug, and especially to classify the
powers and effects of drugs. This theoretical approach, above all,
was held in highest regard for centuries: it was not before the mid-
nineteenth century that pharmacology finally abandoned Galen's
classifying system of qualities and degrees of intensity and started
anew on the entirely different scientific foundations of chemistry
and, in the twentieth century, cellular and molecular biology.

My aim in the present chapter is to outline Galen's pharmacology
and drug-lore. One striking feature that will arise in my discussion
of this branch of medicine in Galen is the contrast it exemplifies
between theory and practice: while he develops an elaborate theory of basic and derivative qualities involving their degrees of intensities, he is well aware of the fact that the practical applicability
of this theory is restricted to the so-called 'simple remedies' consisting in a single substance. Yet, in Galen's time and that of his
predecessors, pharmaceutical practice concentrated on the development of compound remedies, sometimes combining more than forty
separate substances, especially in the well-known and fashionable
'Mithridatium', 'theriac' and 'antidote' recipes (see pp. 312–14). Here,
Galen himself is very often at a loss to apply his own theory to the
remedies, though he can prove their efficacy by experience, both his
own and that of elder doctors, which he values highly and underpins with observations on practical use. Thus, the interrelation of
theory (*logos*) and experience (*empeiria*) deserves special consideration within the investigation of Galen's drug lore and pharmacology
(pp. 314–17).[6]

GALEN'S SYSTEMATIC APPROACH TO *PHARMAKA*

The Greek word *pharmakon* seems to have been known already in Mycenean Linear B.[7] It signifies, basically, any drug, without specifying whether it has a healing or noxious effect. From the Homeric epics onwards, and still in the time of Galen, this specification is usually given by additional adjectives, such as 'deadly' (*thanasimos*), 'noxious' (*dêlêtêrios*), 'man-slaying' (*androphonos*), or 'utterly destructive' (*diaphthartikos*) on the one hand, or 'soothing' (*êpion*) on the other. The important feature of the term, then, is not the particular quality of any drug's effect, but simply the more general, underlying fact that such effects occur when they are introduced into the human or animal organism. By their mode of administration (i.e. basically, feeding), drugs are closely related to food, and it is no surprise that the earliest extant definition uses the distinction between the two in order to explain the nature of *pharmaka*. This definition is found in a passage from the pseudo-Aristotelian *Problemata* (1.42, 864b 7–11), which presumably date from the mid-third century BC:[8]

healing drugs are the contrary to food. For what is by nature being concocted (i.e. digested), grows into the body and is called food. But what is not such as to be overpowered, goes into the blood-vessels and disturbs [them] through its excess of heat or coldness, and this is the nature of a drug.

Galen's definitions of drug and food run along the very same lines (e.g. *SMT* I.1: XI 380, quoted on p. 307); but he goes even further than that, and in *On Mixtures* (*Temp.*) III.2: I 656–7, = 92,13–93,2 Helmreich (1904) he distinguishes four different kinds of drugs:[9]

Now those substances which are assimilated are called foods; all others are called drugs. And there is a further distinction within drugs. There is one kind that remain as they are when taken, and transform and overpower the body, in the same manner that the body does foods; these drugs are of course deleterious and destructive to the animal's nature. The other kind takes the cause of its change from the body itself, then undergoes putrefaction and destruction, and in that process causes putrefaction and destruction to the body also. These too are clearly deleterious. In addition to these, a third kind heats the body reciprocally but does no harm; and a fourth both acts and is acted upon, so that they are gradually completely assimilated. This last kind, therefore, falls into the category of both drugs and food.

The decisive criterion here is the direction of the action: the body acts upon foodstuffs by metabolizing, i.e. assimilating them, but drugs act upon the body, and the impact with which they do this determines where they are to be placed on the long range from food-like drugs to deleterious poisons. As for the distinction between drug and poison, Galen's notion is different from that of his predecessor: In *Problemata* 2.47, 865a7–9, we encounter the notion that a drug can turn into poison when given in high dosage, whereas poison is defined as a substance that has a destructive effect even in small quantity. For Galen, however, poison is 'generically' (*tôi genei*) poisonous – i.e. by its nature, always and independent of dosage – but a sufficiently small quantity may go unnoticed, as does 'the hundredth part of a spark' which 'obviously still belongs to the category of fire, but not only would it not burn or heat us, it would not even make any impression on our perceptive faculties' (*Temp.* III.4: I 670, = 101,2–5 Helmreich).

The notion of a 'generic drug' makes sense only on the assumption that there are certain 'powers' innate to each single substance, and this assumption was indeed made in food and drug theory already by the Hippocratic doctors.[10] The powers in question are called *dunameis*: the properties, or capacities, of substances to have certain effects, independent of their quantity, and distinct from the different powers of other substances.[11] Galen incorporates this concept into his definition of drug in *SMT* I.1: XI 380:

Everything that has some power (*dunamis*) to alter our nature we call a *pharmakon*, in the same way, I believe, as [sc. we] also [sc. call everything] that has some power to increase its substance a foodstuff, and both of these terms are relative in regard to quantity . . . A *dunamis* is some active cause, whether in actuality or in prospect.

According to Galen, the *dunamis* of a particular substance in relation to a particular body or organ derives from the substance's innate elementary qualities. Basically speaking, a hot *pharmakon* will heat an organism and thus help curing diseases provoked by coldness (and similarly, *mutatis mutandis*, with the other qualities). Galen found the roots of this theory in his favourite sources, in the Hippocratic Corpus as well as in Aristotle. The core of the humoral theory is first established in a group of Hippocratic treatises written probably within roughly thirty years (around 420–390 BC),[12] above all in *De natura hominis* (ca. 400 BC), where the scheme of four elements correlated to humours is first developed.[13] A further source for Galen was Aristotle who, in his works on physics as well as on biology, is a strong advocate of the humoral theory which he uses in order to explain physical as well as physiological observations (though his system of humours is quite different from that in *De natura hominis*).[14]

Galen's adaptation of Hippocratic and Aristotelian humoral theory into his own humoral pathology is discussed elsewhere in this volume,[15] so it is sufficient here to sketch it in its special significance for his pharmacology. In this context, Galen carefully distinguishes between basic and derivative qualities.[16] The elementary or basic qualities (*taxeis* or *apostaseis*) of a substance are the same as the elementary qualities in Hippocratic medicine and Aristotelian physiology, constituting the very nature of a substance: hot and cold, dry and moist. According to Aristotle[17] and Galen, they fall into two sets of active (hot and cold) and passive (dry and moist) qualities, and each substance is a mixture (*krasis*) of one of the active qualities with one of the passive qualities.[18] The derivative qualities are the effects a substance can be observed to have on a body: heating and cooling, drying and moistening, but also mollifying, burning, purging, rotting, suppurating and the like.[19] These effects are not determinable in themselves, but only in relation to a body. So, for instance, seawater is essentially moist, but to the body its property is drying (*SMT* I 40: XI 455f.); pepper is cold to the touch but tastes hot and has a heating effect on the body (*SMT* I 11: XI 398f.).

This distinction goes back to Aristotle's definition of actuality and potentiality, and Galen explicitly refers to Aristotle; see for example *Temp.* III 3: I 666–7, = 98,23–99,13 Helmreich:

This, then, is among the many matters described correctly by Aristotle, who says that among bodies which are hot, cold, dry, and wet, some have these qualities in their very nature, others incidentally; water is in its own nature cold, but it will happen sometimes that it is hot incidentally. This acquired heat, however, is quickly lost, while the innate cold remains. And so just as hot water thrown on to a flame will extinguish it, so too opium, even if it is heated to a high degree before it is given, will cool the animal's internal heat, and endanger its life. All such drugs, then, when taken in small amounts and in conjunction with substances which are able to counteract the extreme nature of their cooling effect, may sometimes be of value to our bodies, as will be discussed in our works on drugs. Indeed, the drug extracted from the blister-beetle is of considerable benefit to dropsical patients, even though this beetle in general damages the bladder; if mixed with other substances which subdue it, and introduced to a body which contains a good deal of moisture, it has a voiding effect through the urine.

Consequently, it is not only the doctor's task to detect each drug's properties – he must also ascertain the individual strength of the substance. For, according to Galen, the properties of drugs are determined by four degrees of intensity (determined by their perceptibility): (i) weak, (ii) obvious, (iii) strong, (iv) massive:[20]

The variations of their individual effects are due to the drugs being to a certain degree warm or cold or wet or dry or having small or large particles . . . We have tried to describe this with exact definitions appropriate for the practical use of the art (sc. of medicine). We have shown that there is one kind of drug which arrives at a mixture (*krasis*) similar to that of our bodies, when it receives some impetus to change and alteration from their warmth, and that there is another kind of drug which becomes warmer than us. From this, it seems that four orders (*taxeis*) can be made: the first (i) obscure to the senses, so that it needs pure reason (*logos*) to discover it; a second (ii) which is manifest to the senses; a third (iii) which is moderately warming, but not to the point of burning; and finally a fourth (iv): caustic. Likewise also for the cooling drugs: the first order (i) of those [substances] requiring pure reason to make clear its cooling, the second (ii) of those that are perceptibly cooling, the third (iii) of the moderately cooling, and the fourth (iv) of those that cause necrosis. Analogous to these, [sc. there are four orders] in regard to the wetting and drying [sc. drugs]. (*SMT* VII.1: XII 2–4)

In choosing the healing drug, the doctor therefore must not only find the drug with a quality matching that of the patient's state of imbalance – taking into account the normal state of his individual mixture (*krasis*) – but he also has to ensure that the degree of intensity between the two of them is equal, otherwise there will be no healing effect in applying the drug.[21] Intensity, however, can be measured only relatively. The same bath can be hot for someone coming in from the cold outside, but cold for a feverish person. Therefore, the yardstick in relation to which a measurement is taken ought to be as neutral as possible regarding all the criteria. For Galen, this yardstick is the eucratic condition, one in which the body and sense organs are in the state of the best or intermediate mixture – in contrast to the dyscratic condition, when the mixture is out of balance (although not necessarily to the point of actual illness). Yet what a eucratic condition actually is can vary from person to person, as well as from age to age. Therefore, the doctor needs time to determine the individual's 'normal' condition first (cf. *Praen.* XIV 659, = *CMG* V 8,1, 126,28–128,10 and *ibid.* 606–7, = 76,1–8 specifically on the pulse rate). Normally, the doctor would take himself as the reference point for assessing a remedy, and thus needs to take into account his own remoteness from the eucratic condition (in age, temperament, daily constitution, etc.), as well as that of the patient. Furthermore, in order to determine the effect of a drug with most certainty, he ought to consider its effect on the – rather hypothetical – eucratic, dyscratic and ill person, and to compare the different results in each case. Thus, determining the intensity is a difficult calculation involving several rather vaguely determined factors.

GALEN'S WRITINGS ON SIMPLES AND COMPOUNDS

The system and theory of pharmacology sketched so far is most extensively explained in the tract *On Mixtures* (*Temp.*), which divides its attention between drugs and foodstuffs, and in the eleven books of *On the Powers [and Mixtures] of Simple Drugs* (*De Simplicium Medicamentorum [Temperamentis ac] Facultatibus*, [*SMT*] XI 379–892 and XII 1–377). The first five books of *SMT* outline Galen's theory of the four humours as applied to pharmacology, and the subdivisions according to the intensity and the distinction between basic and derivative qualities (see p. 308). Books VI–XI provide a catalogue of drugs and their healing properties, in large sections dealing with herbs and plants (books VI–VIII), earths (IX 1, 1–4), stones (IX 2, 1–21), '*metallika pharmaka*' (drugs which are mined; IX 3, 1–40) and finally animal products, ranging from blood, milk, excrements and entrails to the flesh of poisonous snakes, blister-beetles, cicadas and other insects (books X–XI) including a section on 'products of the sea useful in medicine' (ch. XI 2). In the four books of herbs and plants, the drugs are listed in alphabetical order but in the last three books the order seems to follow a more associative connection of the substances to one another.[22] In total, Galen lists some 440 different plants and some 250 other substances as remedies. For all of them he provides a wealth of detailed observations and of practical information as how to obtain, store, use and apply them. But only for about a third of them does he note their degree of intensity[23] – i.e. he classifies them according to the theoretic concepts he had developed most extensively in this very work. Thus, we find a significant difference between theory and its application in practice at the very core of Galen's pharmacological work (cf. pp. 313–18).

If it is difficult for him theoretically to explain the effect of each and every simple drug, this difficulty is naturally multiplied in discussing compound remedies. He covers them in two large complementary works: On the Composition of Drugs according to Places (De Compositione Medicamentorum secundum Locos [Comp.Med.Loc.], in eleven books: XII 378–1007 and XIII 1–361) and On the Composition of Drugs according to Kind (De Compositione Medicamentorum per Genera [Comp.Med.Gen.], seven books: XIII 362–1058). Both were written between AD 180 and 193, and in all probability simultaneously. Their introductory chapters partly repeat, and partly extend, the theory of humours, mixtures, degrees and intensities; but the bulk of the works consists of a more or less annotated compilation of the recipes both used and approved by Galen himself, but also transmitted from elder doctors. The books of Comp.Med.Loc. arrange the material according to the traditional order a capite ad calcem ('from head to foot'): starting with ailments of hair (book I), head (book II), ears and nose (book III), eyes (book IV), face and teeth (book V) and mouth (book VI), he continues going down the body through the respiratory tract (book VII), stomach and liver (book VIII), further inner organs and genitalia (book IX), kidney and bladder (book X 1), finally turning to sciatica (book X 2) and gout in the feet (book X 3). A different structure underlies the books of Comp.Med.Gen., namely one determined by the application methods of the remedies: four books on various plasters are followed by two books on multi-functional drugs (polychrêsta) and one book on emollients, laxative drugs and pain killers. It is in the nature of this two-fold compilation that several of the recipes are quoted in both works (e.g. a series of ten emollients taken from Andromachus in Comp.Med.Gen. XIII 976–988 which in Comp.Med.Loc. are quoted separately according to whether they are treatments for the stomach, liver, or pain in the loins).[24]

One of the classes of remedies treated in Comp.Med.Gen. is additionally dealt with in two separate and very brief treatises: On the

Power of Cleansing Drugs (De Purgantium Medicamentorum Fac-
ultate [Purg.Med.Fac.] XI 323–342) discusses purifying remedies and
their effects upon the bodily humours; complementary, the indications and counter-indications for such purgatives are treated in the
even shorter tract *Whom to Purge, With Which Cleansing Drugs,*
and When (Quos, Quibus Catharticis Medicamentis et Quando Pur-
gare Oporteat [Cath.Med.Purg.] XI 343–356), whose authenticity,
though, is doubtful. It has been called into question also for five
further works: The three volumes *On Remedies Easy to Prepare*
(De Remediis Parabilibus [Rem.]: XIV 311–581) might be genuine,
since there are genuine fragments of it in Syriac and Arabic. *On Sub-*
stitute Drugs (De Succedaneis [Suc.]: XIX 721–747) might or might
not be genuine. *On the Power of Centaura (De Virtute Centau-*
reae), which has been transmitted only in Latin, is most likely not
genuine.[25] Two further treatises have been transmitted under Galen's
name: *On Theriac, to Piso (De Theriaca ad Pisonem [Ther.Pis.]*
XIV 210–294) and *On Theriac to Pamphilianus (De Theriaca ad*
Pamphilianum [Ther.Pamph.] XIV 295–310), the latter most likely
not genuine, whereas the former was in all probability written by
Galen.[26]

ANTIDOTES, THERIAC AND MITHRIDATIUM

Their topic, theriac, is a special remedy in the larger group of so-
called 'antidotes' which were used to combat poisons and venoms
but also as a 'panacea' against all sorts of ailments.[27] On this subject –
which he had not sufficiently dealt with in the two extensive works
On Compounds (Comp.Med.Loc. and *Comp.Med.Gen.)*[28] – Galen
wrote the two books of *On Antidotes (De Antidotis [Ant.]:* XIV 1–
209). The remedy called theriac, according to Galen *(Ant.* I 1: XIV 2),
was created by Andromachus, the court physician of Nero, by adding
viper flesh to Mithridatium. This latter was allegedly invented by
Mithridates VI, Eupator Dionysos (132–63 BC), king of Pontus, who
was famous for his language skills and scientific interests, especially
in medicine, and who wrote treatises on the properties of *materia*
medica. He was said to have experimented with poisons and to have
immunized himself against them by daily drinking a quantity of both
remedies against poison and poison itself.[29] The story goes, as Galen
relates in *Ther.Pis.* 16: XIV 283f., that when he intended to commit
suicide after the defeat inflicted upon him by Pompey, he did not

die from the poison – though it worked to kill his daughters – and had instead to take to the sword.[30] The recipe for this remedy was brought to Rome by the victorious Pompey, and in the early imperial times gained a high reputation and became very fashionable among the Roman emperors, who used it both to protect themselves against poison and as a general tonic.[31]

The books of *On Antidotes* are a good test case for our assessment of Galen's discussion of compound remedies. The books are full of practical experience and advice and provide an intelligent evaluation of older doctors' recipes, based not only on their medical and pharmaceutic contents but also focusing on the precision (*akribeia*), clearness (*saphêneia*) and usefulness (*chrêsimon*) of their style.[32] A theoretical pharmacological evaluation, however, is absent. Galen elaborately comments on single ingredients, but separately. There is no statement on the interdependence of the separate substances. This is most apparent in the first five chapters of book I (*Ant.* I 1–5: XIV 1–32), where he concentrates on the best conditions for the water, wine and honey which make up the bulk of theriac (where to find them, when they are ripe for use, how to store them, etc.); in the following chapters, he also gives similar advice about other ingredients, but he unquestioningly accepts the transmitted and canonical forty-two ingredients of theriac, and above all he fails to explain why it has the desired effect in this and no other composition.

This failure is remarkable, for though Galen himself gives no concise explanation why antidotes have the faculties to heal and even to prevent illness, the general drift of the argument behind it could easily be deduced from his statements about simples, i.e. the separate substances of the composition, especially in *SMT*. Most of the ingredients of antidotes turn out to have heating and drying properties, albeit to different degrees.[33] Now, the noxious effect of poison is generally regarded as being due to its chilling the organism,[34] so that the resulting coldness is counter-balanced by the warming effect of the drugs, restoring a healthy balance (or prophylactically preventing its destruction). This allopathic concept is, in the case of theriac, combined with the notion of immunization: the main ingredient of theriac is the flesh of a viper, whose head and tail (which were believed to contain most of the viper's poison) are cut off. The consequent regular administration makes the organism grow accustomed to the remaining bits of snake poison, so that in case of a bite, the then much higher amount of poison does not harm the patient any more. Yet, instead of elaborating this theory, Galen prefers to refer to the long-standing tradition and, over the generations of doctors, constant improvement of the antidotes as sufficient proofs of their efficacy.

LOGOS AND EMPEIRIA

The evidence collected so far in this survey of Galen's pharmacology leads to a picture of a systematic theory regarding drug use (mostly of simple drugs) on the one hand, and of a large collection of recipes for compound remedies, mostly without proper explanations why they work, but approved of by older authorities or by Galen's own experience. This observation naturally leads to the question of the relation between theory and practice in Galen's pharmacology.

In general, the theoretical method applied to the compounds is derived from the pharmacological investigation of simples. Thus, in the introduction to book V of *Comp.Med.Gen.* (V 1: XIII 763–4), which focuses on multi-purpose drugs, Galen restates his basic theory and applies it to the compounds: first of all, the basic and derivative qualities of each single drug have to be investigated, for on only this basis can the qualities prevalent in a compound remedy be detected. But rather than continuing with a theoretical concept of how such a 'calculation' of prevalent qualities can be figured out, Galen turns the method around: 'It seems to me better to write down some two or three of the famous multi-purpose remedies, and then to expound the theory (*logos*) of their composition' (*Comp.Med.Gen.* V 1: XIII 764). But this 'theory of composition' remains, throughout the books on *Compounds*, a mere addition of theoretical statements on single ingredients, rather than a consistent theory of how their powers add up in a compound remedy to a new, 'compound' power. The discussion of the comparative values of these compounds remains focused on the experiences Galen had with them on the one hand, and on the qualities of the single ingredients on the other. Galen thus fails to apply his own method to remedies consisting of more than a single simple drug – and he even seems to be aware of this problem, but not to be disturbed by it. For Galen himself describes the aim of the pharmacological books on compounds as three-fold: (i) composition of remedies, (ii) assessment of transmitted remedies, and (iii) theoretical knowledge as a basis for making such an assessment (*Comp.Med.Gen.* II.1: XIII 459):[35]

For those who practise, it is important – as I say – in order to be able to compose efficient remedies and to criticize those prescribed by the doctors before us, to make apt use of all that has been written by them and of all that one might find himself according to the method (*methodos*) that is going to be taught here. But it is better to use those (remedies) that have been affirmed by experience (*peira*), and to learn the method of their use.

Such a statement implies that experience is to be valued more highly than theory, but this impression is corrected by such passages as the introduction to book VIII of *Comp.Med.Loc.* (VIII 1: XIII 116f.), where *logos* and *empeiria* are said both to be given as criteria by nature, but to contribute to medicine 'in some cases equally to the art, in other cases more the one than the other'. That the interrelation of both is strong is stressed elsewhere as well, e.g. in *Comp.Med.Gen.* VI 7: XIII 886f.:

It has often been demonstrated to you that some of the remedies are found by reason (*logos*) alone, some by experience (*peira*) without using reason, and that some need both working together. And further, that concerning those which have been detected by reason and experience together, a method of exploration is used for finding what is sought, and that those which are assumed by reason are confirmed by experience.

This theoretical balance between *logos* and *peira* is not specific to pharmacology, but can be seen throughout Galen's medicine.[36] What is rather specific, though, is that the powers of *logos* in Galen's pharmacology so very often seem to fail to explain the efficacy or otherwise of remedies.[37] This is not due to failures of the theoretical concept itself which, as we have seen, amounted to a coherent, concise and comprehensive system. Rather, the obstacles lie in the applicability of this system to practical usage and are largely due to the lack of technical means of measurement: intensities of degrees in the drug and in the patient could be judged by subjective and relative feeling only and, above all, the strength of the drug extract could normally not be judged precisely at all.[38] In consequence, empirical research and experience turn out to be better guides to the appropriate drugs than pure theory; but this experience, *pace* the Empiricists,[39] ought to involve a certain amount of rational support, which Galen calls 'qualified experience' and regards as opposed to theory as well as to unqualified experience:[40]

Galen's point seems to be that when trying to *discover* what the power of a particular foodstuff or drug is when it is administered to a patient, or when making a statement about the power a foodstuff or drug is supposed to have, the pharmacologist should not just rely on a small number of isolated empirical data related to the substance in question, collected at random without any underlying principle guiding his search. Moreover, when it comes to *judging* or *refuting* a theory or general statement about the supposed power of a particular foodstuff, the pharmacologist should not, according to Galen, believe that one counter-example is sufficient to discard the theory or statement in question. Both for heuristic and for critical purposes, Galen stresses, the pharmacologist's use of experience should not be *adioristôs*, i.e. 'unqualified', 'without distinction', or 'without proper definition'. It is here that Galen's concept of 'qualified experience' (*diôrismenê peira*) enters the discussion.[41]

On the basis of this epistemological doctrine, it becomes obvious why Galen in his pharmacological works collects such a huge amount of older doctors' recipes and remedies and why he so often shows off his own experiences of drugs during his career (sometimes in a rather anecdotal and frequently tediously self-praising manner).

The most important of the doctors from earlier generations whom he quotes are Apollonius the Herophilean, Heras of Cappadocia, Andromachus father and son, Servilius Damocrates, Asclepiades the Pharmacist and Statilius Crito; and there are a further twelve less frequently quoted authors of books of remedies. All these predecessors are known to us almost solely by way of what Galen's works preserve as quotations.[42] Most influential among those pharmacological works which have survived in their entirety is the *Materia Medica* of Dioscorides, whom Galen held in especially high esteem (cf. *SMT* VI praef.: XI 794f.). The principles of selection regarding the references to other doctors relate to the 'qualification' of their evaluation: Galen, for instance, explicitly states that he more often quotes younger pharmacologists than older ones (*Comp.Med.Gen.* II 5: XIII 502). The reason he gives is that tradition works like a process of selecting the best remedies. The longer a remedy could be tried out, the more secure is the evaluation of its quality, for the simple reason that there have been more experts who were able to experience it (cf. *Comp.Med.Loc.* VI 9: XII 988f. and VII 1: XIII 14). This notion of

validation by frequent experience is central to Galen's view on efficacy, and it also explains why he regards it as one of the three pillars
of pharmacology (as quoted above, p. 315, from *Comp.Med.Gen.* II 1:
XIII 459) to be qualified to assess other doctors' remedies. It also is
a sign that the balance between *logos* and *empeiria* in an area with
so few certainties necessarily has to favour *empeiria*, in the form of
the very Galenic concept of 'qualified experience'.

CONCLUSION

Taking all these different perspectives into account, it is no wonder that Galen's (surviving)[43] pharmacological writings come from
the latter part of his life. According to his own approach, drugs and
remedies have to be assessed by long experience – both that of the
individual doctor and that of a long tradition of doctors. In hardly
any other section of medicine does Galen rely so much on material
approved by tradition and experience. This is partly due to the fact
that his theoretical approach is applicable only to the basis of pharmacology, namely the simples. Even there, Galen himself does not
apply it wherever possible: in his expansive discussion of the best
honey and wine for compiling antidotes (*Ant.* I 2–5: XIV 11–31) all
mention of basic or derivative qualities or degrees of intensities is
notably absent. He was well aware that with drugs, the theoretical
basis is too weak. To a large extent, this is due to some methodical problems inherent in the system: the measurement of degrees of
intensities both in the drug and in the patient is unreliable if there is
no exact method to measure simple biological facts as temperature,
much less any biochemical analysis of how a substance can affect an
organism. As long as the sole yardstick is a 'neutral' eucratic body –
with all the difficulties of how to determine it that that entails (see
pp. 309f.) – from which the doctor has to estimate the relation to the
drug as well as to the dyscratic patient, there is no way to gain any
exactitude. Leave alone the problems of adding the exact measurable
faculties of more than one drug, which accumulate the uncertainties.

All things considered, in his using and prescribing of drugs, Galen
was very wise to rely on qualified experience rather than on his own
theory. The tradition after him continued to pursue both these different branches of his pharmacological work: it attempted to develop
his system of basic and derivative qualities and their degrees of

intensities on the one hand, while at the same time transmitting
certain remedies approved by him on the other,[44] disregarding any
theoretical basis but relying entirely on the high esteem of the name
of Galen.

NOTES

1. Hipp. *Aph.* VII 87. This aphorism is transmitted by most of the
   manuscript tradition, but not in an important tenth-century manuscript
   (Parisinus gr. 446 suppl.) and, more to the point, was probably unknown
   to Galen, for it does not appear in the commentaries on the *Aphorisms*
   by Galen and Theophilus. Cf. von Staden (1997, 61 n. 7). Yet the very
   same three stages (*gradus*) of medicine are paraphrased by Scribonius
   Largus in *Recipes* (*Compositiones*) Pref. 6 (written in AD 47 or 48), so
   that it is a sound assumption that the aphorism's message was common
   knowledge in Galen's times.
2. This canonical tripartition is found throughout ancient medicine, e.g.
   in the summary by Celsus, *On medicine* (*De medicina*), Prooem. 9:
   'In those times (sc. from Pythagoras and Hippocrates to Herophilus
   and Erasistratus), medicine was divided into three parts: one that cures
   with food, the other with medicaments, the third with the hand. The
   Greeks called the first *diaitêtikê*, the second *pharmakeutikê* and the
   third *cheirurgia*'; cf. ch. 11 (van der Eijk) in this volume, p. 284.
3. Throughout antiquity, 'surgical intervention was the treatment of last
   resort' (Nutton, 2004, 240), even for a doctor of such advanced skills
   and anatomical knowledge and of so large an experience in dissection as Galen. Surgery was largely confined to the treatment of war-
   wounds; cf. Salazar (2000), and generally for surgery (Nutton, 2004, 37f.:
   pre-Hippocratic healing of war-wounds; 179–86: Roman army medical
   service; 239f.: surgery in Galen) which indicate that both doctors and
   non-medical authors were quite aware of the life-threatening dangers of
   bleeding and post-operative infection.
4. Nutton (2004, 240), referring to Galen, *On Recognizing the Best Physician* [*Opt.Med.Cogn.*] 10,1: *CMG* Suppl. Or. IV, 116–117 Iskandar.
5. Dioscorides, praef. 5, comes closest to the modern term 'pharmacology'
   in using the phrase *ho peri tôn pharmakôn logos* 'the knowledge about
   pharmaka'; yet his work is basically a huge companion in pharmacy,
   collecting the descriptions, preparations and applications of more than
   1,000 substances (mostly plants), and focusing on a close observation of
   what they 'do' when given to a patient, but hardly ever discussing why
   or how they achieve their particular effect.

6. On Galen's views on the relation between *logos* and *empeiria*, see also chs. 3 (Tieleman, pp. 53–5), 6 (Hankinson, pp. 157–62), and 11 (van der Eijk, pp. 291–2) all in this volume.

7. Tablet Un 1314 from Pylos has in line 1 the word *pa-ma-ko*; tablets Ge 602–608 have a number of words 'which can be confidently identified with herbs and spices' (Ventris and Chadwick, 1973, 505 and 225).

8. Cf. Flashar (1962, 356–8).

9. This and the following translations from *Mixtures* are by Singer (1997, 271, 277).

10. On the beginnings of drug theory in the Hippocratic corpus, see Harig (1980).

11. In *The Faculties of the Soul Follow the Mixtures of the Body* (*QAM*) IV 769–70, Galen stresses that *dunamis* is a relational term: a power or activity arising in relation to the event caused in a certain object. Thus, one substance can have distinct powers in relation to different objects, such as aloe, which cleanses and strengthens the stomach, binds wounds, scars over grazes and dries moist eyes.

12. *De diaeta acut.*, *Epid. VI*, *De loc. in hom.*, *De ulc.*, *De morb. III*, *De aff.*, *De diaeta*.

13. Cf. Harig (1980). *Nat.Hom.* greatly influenced Galen, who wrote a commentary on it, and considered it to encapsulate the foundations of Hippocratic physics and physiology (see also *On the Elements according to Hippocrates* (*Hipp.Elem.*) I 413–508, = *CMG* V 1,2 [De Lacy, 1996]; and see ch. 8, Hankinson, in this volume). Though the Hippocratic doctors invented the theory behind all further pharmacology, they did not apply it to an assessment of the remedies and drugs used in their works. A number of recipes for remedies is scattered throughout the *Corpus Hippocraticum* (almost exclusively in the gynecological tracts), but they are not commented on and no attempt is made to classify them or explain the mechanisms behind them. It is a sad loss, that in the extant *Corpus Hippocraticum* no work solely on drug-lore has survived, though at least one might have existed, for the title *Pharmakitis* is reported: Hipp. *De aff.* 15 (6.224,8 L.) *et al.*, cf. Harig (1980, 225) and Goltz (1974, 139ff., 120ff.), who considers it to have been most probably been a collection of recipes without pharmacological theorizing.

14. See the general survey in Althoff (1992).

15. See ch. 10 (Debru) in this volume.

16. A distinction between basic and derivative qualities different from that in Galen was drawn by Aristotle, e.g. *Generation and Corruption* (*GC*) 2.1–3 329a24–331a6: only those which are active (hot and cold) or passive, i.e. acted upon (moist and dry) are basic qualities, all other tangible or perceptible contrarieties are secondary to them.

17. Cf. e.g. Aristotle *GC* 2.1–3 329a24–331a6 (summarized above in n. 16) and *Mete.* 4.1 328b10–26.

18. For a concise summary see *Comp.Med.Gen.* I 2: XIII 367–369 and *On His Own Opinions* (*Prop.Plac.*) 9,2f. Nutton (one of the few bits of the treatise to have survived in Greek): 'In my book *On the Properties of Simple Drugs* [i.e *SMT*] it was demonstrated that some (of them) act by heating or cooling or moistening or drying, and others by a joint action, by heating and moistening or by cooling and drying at the same time; but there is another group of drugs which work by the peculiar property of their entire substance. I showed that such (drugs) include the purgatives and the so-called destructive drugs, which differ from those simply called deadly in that destructive drugs never benefit us, unlike the deadly ones which are occasionally of some slight use when taken from time to time with an admixture of beneficial drugs. For example, we often make use of poppy juice in this way. Among beneficial drugs, some act through one or two qualities, others through the peculiarity of the whole of their substance.' An extensive discussion of the (slight) differences between Galen's view and that of his predecessors is to be found in book I of *SMT*.

19. At some places in his pharmacological works, as a further subdivision of derivative qualities Galen even distinguishes 'tertiary' qualities which determine the effect of a substance on a certain part of the body: sealing a wound, filling it with flesh and growing a scar (e.g. *Comp.Med.Gen.* VI 8: XIII 898); at other places these are subsumed under the heading of derivative qualities (e.g. *Comp.Med.Loc.* III 1: XII 612f.). Cf. Harig (1974, 111–13).

20. Cf. Scarborough (1984, 244f.).

21. Harig (1974, 31–3) demonstrates how the mistaken view that Galen combined the intensity of diseases and the intensity of *pharmaka* into a calculable system crept into a couple of histories of ancient medicine and pharmacology in the last decades of the nineteenth century.

22. This different mode of arrangement might reflect Dioscorides' warning in *De materia medica* (preface 3) against alphabetical ordering which destroys the context; instead he insists on arranging the material according to the correct internal conjunctions. He complains that 'Niger and the rest also made mistakes in organization of their material, some throwing together incompatible properties, others using an alphabetical arrangement which splits off genera and properties from what most resembles them. The result is almost impossible to memorize as a unit' (trans. Nutton and Scarborough, 1982, 196). Ironically, early on in its transmission Dioscorides' own work suffered rearrangement into alphabetical order (most notably in the oldest manuscript, the famous Vienna

Codex med. gr. 1 of 512 AD) which indicates that the users found their ways around his work more easily in this manner; cf. Nutton and Scarborough (1982, 212f.).

23. All substances concerned are listed in the appendix to Harig (1974, 205–16).

24. See the list in Fabricius (1972, 141f.).

25. I thank Vivian Nutton for these three assessments of authenticity.

26. Nutton (1997c) discusses the authenticity of both treatises and convincingly reaches the conclusion that *Ther.Pis.* is, and *Ther.Pamph.* is not, genuine.

27. Cf. Skoda (2001) and Totelin (2004).

28. Cross-references to a work 'On the theriac antidote' are made in *Comp.Med.Gen.* I 18: XIII 451 (cf. VII 10: XIII 909) in the future tense and in *Comp.Med.Loc.* III 3: XII 691 in the past tense. Assuming that this work 'On the theriac antidote' can be identified with *Ant.*, Jacques (1997, 103, n. 3) draws the conclusion that the three works were written in the order *Comp.Med.Gen.*, *Ant.* and *Comp.Med.Loc.* Nutton (1997c, 136, 148), however, convincingly argues that the cross-reference back in *Comp.Med.Loc.* 'looks exactly like the late cross-references detected by Bardong in other Galenic works, and, I would conclude, was added some time after the whole treatise had been finished. If I am right, Galen was contemplating a work on the theriac antidote while writing *De comp. med. sec. loc.*, but whether it became *De antidotis* [*Ant.*] or the *Ad Pisonem* [*Ther.Pis.*] is an open question' (Nutton, 1997, 148).

29. Cf. Pliny, *Nat. Hist.* XXV.3, 5–7. Cf. Totelin (2004, 3–6).

30. There are several other accounts of the death of Mithridates, some of them controversial. Cf. Watson (1966, 35). (It should be pointed out, though, that Watson's monograph on theriac and Mithridatium has rightly been criticized for superficiality and inadequate references, cf. Nutton (1979, 161, n. 2), Harig (1977, esp. 104f.) and Totelin (2004, 5f.), who rightly observes that Galen seems to have been suspicious about this story, and that the modern historian should be as well: 'If the King truly believed in the efficacy of his antidote, would he have chosen to die by drinking poison?' (Totelin, 2004, 6).)

31. On theriac in general, see Boudon (2002b). Galen himself was responsible for preparing and administering it to Marcus Aurelius, *Ant.* I.1: XIV 3–5. Galen's mentioning his measuring of opium for the emperor's theriac has led to the 'myth' of Marcus Aurelius having been addicted to opium. This is due to a misinterpretation of the sources, and has finally been proven false by Hadot (1984).

32. Cf. Vogt (2005).

33. Watson (1966: 73f.) collects the evidence from *SMT* for each of the main ingredients of antidotes.
34. Cf. the passage from *Temp.* III 2: I 656–7, quoted on p. 306.
35. Cf. a similar statement in *Comp.Med.Loc.* VIII 6: XIII 188.
36. Cf. Frede (1981); and ch. 3 (Tieleman), pp. 53–5 and ch. 6 (Hankinson), pp. 169–78 both in this volume.
37. Cf. von Staden (1997b).
38. This problem vitiates Galen's therapeutics in general, see Barnes (1991, 91f., esp. n. 125); and see Harig (1974).
39. On Galen's attitude to Empiricism, see ch. 3 (Tieleman) and ch. 6 (Hankinson) both in this volume.
40. The sources and consequences of the concept of 'qualified experience' in Galen's pharmacology are shown by van der Eijk (1997) and Von Staden (1997b).
41. Van der Eijk (1997, 36f.).
42. The material is collected in Fabricius (1972).
43. Galen had written an earlier work on the properties of drugs, which was destroyed in the fire at the Temple of Peace in AD 192: *Comp.Med.Gen.* XIII 362–3; cf. Nutton (2004, 244).
44. Cf. Nutton (2004, 244): 'Galen's so-called *Hiera*, a bitter purgative recommended for almost everything from headache to period pains, was far more familiar to doctors in early medieval Europe than any of his medical treatises.'

13 Commentary

In his biobibliographical treatise, *On My Own Books* (*Lib.Prop.*), Galen categorizes a significant segment of his vast written array according to the past authority (or authorities) with whose works, or wider thought, they are engaged. The names of Hippocrates, Erasistratus, Asclepiades (of Bithynia), Plato, Aristotle and Epicurus, as well as the collectivities of the Empiricists, Methodists and Stoics, all appear in chapter headings as having attracted Galen's dedicated literary attention.[1] Not all appear in the same light, however. Some – Erasistratus, the Empiricists, Methodists and Stoics – are critically identified, with Galen writing to differentiate himself from them; while the rest are referred to more neutrally, as having been written on, or about. The number, and type, of texts that come under each heading also varies considerably, and there are several cross-references to other categories in which the same treatise could (and sometimes does) also feature.

There is still more unevenness in terms of the survival of these texts, so that a distinctly (though revealingly) unrepresentative sample remains available for further study. It is worth, therefore, attempting to replace the extant portion of Galen's exegetical efforts within the wider patterns of his literary engagements with the works of others, before subjecting it to more detailed analysis; trying to get a sense of his interpretative project as a whole before focusing on its most historically successful products. Galen also found it impossible to catalogue his output without providing considerable background information about its composition – about his aims and methods in

My thanks to Jim Hankinson and Mike Trapp for their comments on earlier versions of this essay.

writing any given treatise, about how it related to his own situation at the time and the audience for which it was intended – and this is useful in understanding any aspect of his oeuvre. Though, of course, Galen's own narratives, self-serving and selective as they undoubtedly are, must always be treated with caution.

BIBLIOGRAPHY

In *On My Own Books*, the most extensive section organized by authority belongs, unsurprisingly, to Hippocrates, and the inclusion of the term *hypomnêmata* – 'commentaries' or 'notes' – in the chapter heading is also indicative of the type of text that predominates.[2] Now, *hypomnêma* is a far from straightforward word, as Galen emphasizes with his detailed autobiographical breakdown of this part of his output. In this case its origin lay in an exercise he undertook for himself, not the wider public, of collecting Hippocratic teachings by subject, clearly expressed and brought to completion in every way. Little or no reference was made in this undertaking to the works of previous Hippocratic exegetes, though Galen claims a familiarity with these 'phrase-by-phrase' (*kath' ekastên autou lexin*) interpretations. Nor was there much engagement with existing scholarship in a series of more specific commentaries subsequently composed at the request of friends, for his full library was inaccessible to him, and he was content with positive statements of his own views; though presumably some of his earlier notes were re-used and re-worked in this context. Only in the final stage of his exegetical activity did Galen, provoked by the popularity of a particularly crass and egregious reading of one of the Hippocratic *Aphorisms*, write for a general audience, not just the 'specific constitution', or perhaps 'situation', (*idian hexin*) of the immediate recipient.[3] This entailed a deeper involvement in detailed debates about alternative readings and meanings.

The later, and fuller, style of commentary was applied to the Hippocratic writings *Epidemics 2, 3* and *6, Humours, Nutriment, Prorrhetic, On the Nature of Man, In the Surgery* and *Airs, Waters, Places*, producing a total of thirty-five books. These followed the earlier twenty-seven books covering *Aphorisms, Fractures, Joints, Prognostic, Regimen in Acute Disease, Wounds, Wounds to the Head* and *Epidemics 1*. It is worth noting that this portion of Galen's literary output has, including texts preserved in Arabic, a very high survival rate.[4] Indeed, it has been claimed that Hippocratic commentaries by Galen which are not included in *On My Own Books* are transmitted in Arabic: for this catalogue was not his final act, and some other items are known to have slipped the net. In particular, the *Risâla* of the great ninth-century translator of Galen (and other Greek medical and philosophical writers), Hunain ibn Ishâq, lists a Galenic commentary on the Hippocratic *Oath* which he rendered into Syriac and two of his pupils then converted into Arabic.[5] Hunain does not question its authenticity, nor even remark that it was not included in *On My Own Books*, both points which he is usually quick to pick up on. Though no manuscript of the actual text of this commentary has been found, substantial extracts from it and other shorter citations are to be found in a range of medieval Arabic works.[6]

The despised Methodists, on the other hand, receive the least attention, and have no *hypomnêmata* dedicated to them; while the more neutrally referred to Asclepiades fares much the same.[7] Still, the hostile commentary does appear to be part of Galenic literary practice, with three books of (presumably) critical exegesis of the first book of Erasistratus' *On Fevers*, the third also forming the opening part of Galen's larger work *On Erasistratus' Therapeutic Reasoning*.[8] The oppositional tone of these texts is not explicit in their actual listing, but is certainly suggested by both the orientation of the chapter heading and the polemical character of the surviving treatises from this section, in particular the pair of treatises on venesection, one directed against Erasistratus and one against his followers at Rome.[9] The *hypomnêmata* dealing with the Empiricists are similarly presented, but raise a new set of questions concerning Galen's use of this word.

In the Hippocratic chapter the reference of *hypomnêma* stretched from informal and personal notes to elaborate and detailed commentaries composed for a wide audience; and, as Heinrich von Staden has demonstrated, in his oeuvre as a whole, Galen broadens its application still further.[10] Galen sometimes distinguishes clearly between *hypomnêmata* and other types of systematic writing (such as *sungrammata*), while at other times he seems to use the terms pretty interchangeably, or as ways of identifying parts and wholes, not different genres.[11] Still, the surviving corpus of Galen's Hippocratic commentaries demonstrates that even those he places at the looser, less developed, end of his output take what might be described as 'canonical' commentary form. They are 'phrase-by-phrase' interpretations, proceeding systematically through the whole work. There is a noticeable increase in the amount of engagement with the views of other exegetes in the later set, but the basic structure does not alter.[12] Moreover, most of these texts are referred to in a formulaic way within the catalogues of *On My Own Books*, the two key elements of the formula being 'commentary' (*hypomnêma*) 'on' (*eis*) whatever work it is. The expression is pretty clear, and it maps well onto the surviving evidence, so its repetition in relation to Erasistratus' *On Fevers* presumably places that exegetical triad of books in the same, or at least a similar, category. But Galen also uses *hypomnêma* more loosely in this chapter, and the clarity of the Hippocratic catalogues seriously breaks down in the section dealing with the Empiricists, as does the extant material; leaving the character of the *hypomnêmata* relating to the *Introduction* of the Empiricist Theodas, and to his colleague Menodotus' work *To Severus*, uncertain.[13] The text is problematic, and the passage confusingly contains two, non-identical, references to the latter, which may, therefore, have been either a looser work of critical exegesis or a formal commentary.[14]

Full commentaries *on* the writings of others reappear, however, in relation to the philosophy of Aristotle. Indeed much of the narrative surrounding the Hippocratic *hypomnêmata* is reprised in the transition to the philosophical portion of *On My Own Books*, though in a somewhat altered form. The story is a still more personal one, intimately bound up with Galen's early, and crucial, quest for sure knowledge, and secure methods of proof, as recounted in the extensive chapter on texts relating to logical demonstration (*apodeixis*) that effects the bibliographical passage from medicine to philosophy, and provides the philosophical underpinnings for his medical system.[15] Galen began this quest as a student of Stoic and Peripatetic logic but, after disillusionment verging on despair, discovered the path to truth lay instead in the mathematics, most especially the geometry, he had learned from his father (as he had learned from his father before him).[16] Thus he attained certainty for himself, a certainty he could explain and support, allowing him to adopt a didactic tone of his own – to become a teacher – as he did in his magnum opus *On demonstration*.

Along this path of discovery, and as Galen continued to explore and elaborate epistemological themes, his engagement with the ideas of others again took literary form, or forms, for the three-fold division into exegetical works composed as a personal exercise, exclusively for friends, and for friends but also with an eye to a wider audience, recurs in the chapter on apodeictic texts. The first, most personal, category is the largest in this case, and in it Galen places his youthful notes on Chrysippus' syllogistic and almost all his Peripatetic commentaries, the only exceptions being the books on Eudemus' *On Discourse*, written at the request of friends, and those on Aristotle's *Categories*, written with a wider pedagogic purpose. Not too wide, though: the friend who prompted Galen in this case is instructed to restrict its distribution to students of Aristotle who have either already read the *Categories* under the supervision of a teacher, or, if self-taught, have advanced as far as other commentaries, such as those of Adrastus and Aspasius.[17] Still, whatever their origins, all of these works did eventually emerge into the public domain in some way (Galen's Chrysippean notes were sold to an eager caller at his family home in Pergamum by a household slave, and then circulated further by those into whose possession they had thus passed); and they are, therefore, included in his bibliographic catalogue under the appropriate headings (which is, of course, to publicize them further).[18]

The chapters actually organized by philosophical authority, then, follow a section on ethical writings.[19] The first authority is Plato, this position of precedence reflecting his pre-eminent status within Galen's overall web of reference and deference, though Galen had paid scant attention to him as he strove to overcome his epistemological anxieties.[20] Still, his Platonic writings encompass books on Plato's logical theories, as well as a quartet of *hypomnêmata* dealing with medical statements in the *Timaeus*, eight summaries of Platonic dialogues and a range of other treatises, including the major work *On the Doctrines of Hippocrates and Plato* (*PHP*). Fragments of the commentary on the medical content of the *Timaeus* survive, and though not advertised as *hypomnêmata eis* (perhaps because they were not on the text as a whole), the most complete Greek fragments are in proper commentary form, with lemmata.[21]

Aristotle is next in Galen's philosophical ranking, and though the level of actual engagement with Peripatetic writing and thinking is, in some senses, higher than with Plato's, that is in part because it is more critical. The comprehensive list of substantial 'commentaries on' a range of Aristotelian texts included in this chapter serves to underline the point.[22] Most were mentioned in the section on works concerned with demonstration, in much the same terms, and with a rather disapproving edge: the three books on Aristotle's *On Interpretation*, along with the eight (in total) on the two books of *Prior Analytics* and eleven on the two of *Posterior Analytics*, four on the *Categories*, six on Theophrastus' *On Affirmation and Denial* and, finally, the three on Eudemus' *On Discourse*. Just before Eudemus in the catalogue come the only additional items, listed as 'on *In how many ways* (*eis to peri tou posachôs*) commentary in three books; on *The first mover is itself unmoved* (*eis to protôn kinoun akinêton* [*auto*])'. These are both works that take Aristotle's *Metaphysics* as their starting point, which may explain their previous omission from the apodeictic section of Galen's bibliography. According to Philippe Moraux, *Peri Posachôs* is just another way of referring to Aristotle's *Metaphysics* Δ, and the previous book ends with the statement that the 'first mover must itself be unmoved'.[23]

Despite the books of Peripatetic commentary adding up to an impressive total – thirty-eight compared to the sixty-two on Hippocratic texts – that they were important to Galen mainly in a developmental sense, as aids to clarifying his own ideas, as preparation for their articulation in *On demonstration*, is emphasized by their subsequent fate. Not only are all now lost, their disappearance seems to have been rapid and unremarked. While *On demonstration* is a relatively frequently cited text, Galen's Aristotelian commentaries are not, though they too can be located in a long and lively exegetical tradition.[24] This tradition stretched back beyond the two names Galen mentions in this respect – those of Adrastus and Aspasius (perhaps his older contemporaries) – to the first century BC, and was reinvigorated by Galen's younger contemporary Alexander of Aphrodisias, continuing right through antiquity and beyond.[25] None of Galen's exegetical efforts are mentioned, as such, by the Greek commentators, however; Galen appears in their works as a more broadly authoritative figure who had involved himself in a number of philosophical debates and disputes.[26] Still, at least one Galenic commentary made it into Arabic. Hunain's *Risâla* lists *On the First Mover* as having been rendered into Syriac and Arabic both by himself and several of his collaborators, and the work then goes on to have a complex Arabic afterlife.[27] The only other such commentary to appear in the *Risâla* is that *On Interpretation*, but Hunain records only finding an incomplete manuscript, not that he translated it.[28] None the less, this does go some way towards validating Galen's suspiciously flattering claims for the circulation of his more personal acts of exegesis.

The final philosophical pair around which Galen organizes his text are the Stoics and Epicurus.[29] The works relating to the teachings of the latter, and some of his followers, include no *hypomnêmata*, and, though the three books on Chrysippus' *First Syllogistic* and one on his *Second* are so described, it is without the crucial *'eis'* ('on'), moreover, Galen's previous allusions place them firmly in the category of notes rather than formal commentary. Galen's engagement with Stoic logic, serious and systematic as it was, proceeded rather differently from his involvement with Peripatetic ventures in the same field. In this also it seems that Galen was once again following precedent, or at least responding to an absence in that regard. For, in contrast to long-standing traditions not only of Hippocratic and Aristotelian, but also Platonic, commentary, the exegetical practices of both Stoics and Epicureans were rather slight.[30] Or, at least, neither Stoics nor Epicureans seem, by this time, to have produced full commentaries on their authoritative texts in the way that the other philosophical currents had; though both were interested in issues of general interpretation and specific doctrinal exposition.[31]

The first point to draw out from this overview is, therefore, the sense in which Galen can be located within existing and vibrant commentary traditions, both medical and philosophical; and to emphasize the centrality of these traditions within his intellectual and literary milieux. Established practices of extensive textual interpretation and exposition can, indeed, be found far beyond medicine and philosophy, in fields as diverse as astronomy and grammar (broadly construed), for instance; and this was an especially vital, and burgeoning, area of activity in the second century AD and beyond.[32] In many ways Galen and Alexander of Aphrodisias stand simply as the most successful representatives of much larger, and growing, hermeneutic communities, with one important area of contemporary growth being in the development of Christian commentary. Biblical exegesis takes, as it were, full classical form with Origen and Hippolytus as the second century draws to a close.[33]

In all these cases, textual exegesis enabled a direct relationship to be forged between exegete and ancient authorities and/or texts of particular pre-eminence. Whatever the precise nature, or content, of that relationship, it always staked some claim to a share in the prestige of the past authority and writing. For Galen, moreover, going straight back to the founding fathers themselves, unmediated by their current adherents, was especially crucial. It allowed him to rise above his contemporaries by asserting both his greater independence of judgement – he is no mindless follower of anyone or anything, but subjects all to stern scrutiny, to a rigorous assessment of their ideas and commitments – and his greater understanding of the works of the masters, sadly misconstrued as they often are, even by those who profess themselves most loyal.[34] Furthermore, these aims are achieved through both his formative and summative acts of exegesis. The mastery attained through his more personal interpretive writings is no less than that proclaimed in his more polished pieces, hence his enthusiastic reluctance in respect to their diffusion.

The second point to stress, though, is the way in which Galen appears to depart from, or at least re-figure and extend, established exegetical patterns. Given how much is known about Galen's activities in this area, in comparison to anyone else's, caution is clearly required in asserting his status as an innovator. Still, as things stand, several significant gaps emerge between Galen and his predecessors. His combination of medical and philosophical commentary (a very distinctive combination with its emphasis on the logical and demonstrative parts of philosophy) has no extant precedent. The relationship between medicine and philosophy was a close one in the ancient world, and a number of physicians are known to have had philosophical allegiances and involvements that might have encompassed commentary (certainly of the more informal varieties); but there is no actual evidence for prior activity of these kinds.[35] Galen also seems to be extending the exegetical remit within medicine, taking it beyond the confines of the Hippocratic Corpus to the work of another physician – Erasistratus.[36] Again, non-Hippocratic commentary could have arrived on the scene earlier. The sectarian divides that engendered 'agonal' commentary on Hippocratic texts, alongside sustained literary attacks on opponents' teachings and robust self-defence, might have led to a mixing of genres and purposes, but if so the results have disappeared without a trace.[37]

Linking his commentary on Erasistratus' *On Fevers* with his philosophical *hypomnêmata* is, of course, the sense in which both are external exegetical endeavours. Galen's position as a physician on the one hand, and as an anti-Erasistratean on the other, means that none of these interpretations are undertaken from the inside (the medical commentary on the 'divine' Plato's *Timaeus* perhaps comes closest in these respects). Galen's commentaries on the Peripatetics are avowedly critical, moreover, though certainly not matching his downright hostility to *On Fevers* or Chrysippus. This slant also seems distinctive, even if his greatest animosity is contained in his more privately composed and orientated texts. For, in general, commentary was an internal, and largely loyal, activity up to this point, undertaken within philosophical currents on their own authoritative texts, and within wider disciplines on works that played a similarly foundational role in their formation, such as the Hippocratic writings did for medicine.[38] Polemical tracts, composed from outside, might be detailed and specific in their attacks on particular treatises or authorities, as were, for example, Athenodorus the Stoic's work *Against Aristotle's Categories*, and Asclepiades of Bithynia's *Against Erasistratus* (or perhaps '*Refutations*'); but they did not take full commentary form.[39] Herophilus' more targeted book, 'against Hippocrates' *Prognostic*', demonstrates that criticism from inside, in the broader disciplinary sense, also occurred, though from a more general position of recognizing, and respecting, the founding father.[40] Asclepiades' Hippocratic commentaries (on *Aphorisms* and *In the Surgery*) can probably be placed in the same category, since, though the Bithynian certainly disagreed strongly with some Hippocratic doctrines (rejecting, for example, the important Hippocratic notion of 'critical days'), there is nothing in the few surviving references to his exegetical endeavours to suggest they were polemical in tone.[41]

In conclusion, then, it is probably safe to assert that here, as elsewhere, Galen does go further than his predecessors in various ways, though that is not to diminish their importance to him, nor indeed more generally. He builds on, but extends and exceeds, previous patterns. Still, it is in the more traditional areas that he had the most success: it is his internal, loyal, Hippocratic commentaries that have survived, and were to prove so immensely influential in shaping future understandings of Hippocratic thought. This is no accident, nor is the partial transmission of his commentary on the medical statements in Plato's *Timaeus*, which can also be placed in roughly the same category. It is important to remember, however, that the extant texts constitute less than half of Galen's exegetical efforts as catalogued in *On My Own Books*, and that they have a broader cultural, as well as Galenic, context.

CHRONOLOGY

Philosophical exegesis was largely an activity of Galen's youth, but his Hippocratic *hypomnêmata* were products of his full maturity. While his most direct and detailed engagement with a range of Peripatetic and Stoic texts occurred in a distinctly formative period of his career, in preparation for the full elaboration and presentation of his own theories in *On demonstration* (published around AD 150), almost the reverse process operated in relation to the Hippocratic Corpus. It was only after he had developed, and repeatedly proclaimed, his own medical system that various Hippocratic texts received a thorough interpretative treatment. Most scholars agree that the exegetical enterprise commenced around AD 175, well into Galen's second, permanent, stay at Rome, after his position there was well established, if never completely guaranteed.[42] This, too, is the most probable date for the commentary on the *Timaeus* which is promised in *On the Doctrines of Hippocrates and Plato* (*PHP*), itself completed by AD 176.[43]

As Galen tells it, moreover, this move was made only reluctantly. In an ideal world what he had already written should have sufficed. Thus, in his commentary on *Epidemics 3* he states:

Since I knew that I had always explicated Hippocrates' view in all the works I had written, and quoted his timeliest remarks, I thought it superfluous to write exegesis in commentaries, phrase by phrase, from beginning to end of all his works.[44]

But he eventually gave in to the begging of some of his companions (*hetairoi*) to be provided with these, too. Similarly in his commentary on *Prognostic*, though Galen claims that: 'all of the things useful for the medical art that one should learn from him [Hippocrates] have been recorded by me in many treatises', he then accedes again to demands from a group of his *hetairoi* who had found his oral expositions of Hippocratic teachings, particularly those less clearly articulated in the Corpus itself, to be much more satisfactory than any existing written commentary, and so committed his spoken words to papyrus.[45]

In the *Epidemics* 3 passage Galen proceeds to describe his exegetical career up to that point in some detail, providing a rough relative chronology for many of his commentaries, and still more specificity about their intended audience.[46] Having agreed to his companions' demands, he began with the 'most genuine and useful of Hippocrates' books', that is *Fractures, Joints, Ulcers, On Wounds in the Head, Aphorisms* and *Prognostic*. The commentary on *Regimen in Acute Diseases* was then produced, to meet a more specific friendly request, and that on *Humours* quickly followed, the speed being necessary 'on account of the impending journey of the man who asked me to write it'. All of these were, of course, very well received, and they reached well beyond Galen's immediate circle of *hetairoi* to many others, including physicians, who added their voices to the clamour that he should complete the set. So he launched on *In the Surgery*, and *Epidemics* 1 and 2, diverting at the urging of some friends to engage with *Prorrhetic*, before returning to *Epidemics* 3, the present work. A little over a decade had probably elapsed since he began his exegetical journey, and it was not over yet: commentaries on *Epidemics* 6, *Nutriment, Nature of Man* and *Airs, Waters, Places* were still to come. It is also worth noting that, though this account tallies, for the most part, with the listing in *On My Own Books*, there is some discrepancy. That listing makes no claims to be a sequence, rather a grouping of earlier, sparer, commentaries on the one hand, and their more elaborate successors on the other; but, while it would initially appear that the transition occurs with *Humours*, as those that follow come into the fuller category, *Epidemics* 1 is an exception, being classed, instead, with the earlier group in *On My Own Books*.[47]

The line that emerges clearly from all Galen's reflections on his more systematically interpretative compositions is, then, that the demands of an admiring public combined with the poor quality of existing Hippocratic commentary drove him down the exegetical path, with some additional impetus being provided by the admitted unclarity of some of the Hippocratic writings themselves. Galen himself had no particular desire to undertake this task, considering that his own works, consistent as they were with Hippocratic doctrine, incorporating, and sometimes explicating, Hippocratic statements, as they did, were sufficient. Wesley Smith has challenged this self-assessment, however, arguing that it is an internal rather than an external inadequacy which prompts Galen to take up the commentator's cudgels.[48] The problem is not with other people – with their bad commentaries or their need for Galen to spell things out for them, to provide, in writing, the understanding they lack – but with Galen himself; that is, with the mismatch between the claims he constantly makes to Hippocratic filiation, to be the true heir of the founding father of Greek medicine, and the rather slight nature of the actual support he offers for these claims. Eventually Galen comes to realize, or perhaps has it pointed out to him by his (numerous) opponents, that he must walk the walk as well as talk the talk. A more systematic engagement with the Hippocratic treatises themselves as well as with the exegetical tradition, with all its alternative readings and interpretations, is necessary if his Hippocratic heredity is to be convincingly established and maintained. Unfortunately (at least for a Hippocratic scholar such as Smith), it was too late by that time. Galen's system – a synthetic construction that drew most heavily on Hellenistic (and indeed more recent) medical developments – was already formed, and publicly formulated, its Hippocratism merely a legitimating cover; and Galen's exegetical turn would alter nothing.

All of Galen's statements about his aims and accomplishments, his projects and prestige, have, of course, to be approached somewhat gingerly. Self-promotion is always part of his agenda, and due allowance must be made for that fact. Still, it is not the only goal Galen pursues, his intellectual ambitions were as real as his desire to talk up the extent to which he had achieved them. So the truth is likely to lie somewhere between Galen's claims and Smith's countercharge. The turn to 'phrase-by-phrase' commentary cannot have been simply down to the demands of friends, there must have been something in it for Galen, too; but that is not to say that he himself did not believe in his own Hippocratism, that it was mere rhetorical gloss, or 'ideological patina', as Smith puts it.[49] He could have followed a different path to medical authority, one that acknowledged Hippocrates as the founding father of the medical art, but fell short of asserting actual paternity for his own vision of that art. Asclepiades of Bithynia, as already mentioned, adopted this more relaxed, and innovative, approach, as did the Methodists, more emphatically in some instances. There is nothing to suggest that Galen's choice was not born out of conviction, even if that was an easy conviction to come by in his world, rather than one needing to be fought for.

Indeed, the sense in which Galen is following established patterns, is participating in common practices, is worth stressing again here, too. Given what can be pieced together about the place of Hippocratic commentary in the medical culture of the second century AD, an activity apparently re-launched by the publication of the new 'editions' of the Hippocratic Corpus by Dioscurides and Artemidorus Capiton around the turn of that century, it would have been distinctly odd if Galen had not become an exegete at some time in his career.[50] Admittedly, the bulk of the evidence for this culture comes from Galen himself, but it is none the less notable that so many of the medical figures for whom he had any respect (and several for whom he had only scorn) have Hippocratic commentaries to their names. Many of these, moreover, are figures with whom Galen had personal, educational, links, and he was willing (at least prior to some of his own exegetical writing) to recommend their works to a wider audience.[51]

The two most authoritative exegetes are Sabinus and Rufus of Ephesus, representatives of an earlier generation; alongside whom can be placed Galen's teacher Pelops (and his teacher, Numisianus, though few of his writings survived).[52] The line from Sabinus to Galen is drawn by his fellow Pergamene, Stratonicus, student of the former and teacher of the latter. Galen also claims familiarity with the Hippocratic interpretations of the influential Quintus through the mediation of his most authentic exponent, Satyrus, who preceded Pelops on Galen's pedagogic register. It is knowledge he is asserting here, rather than admiration or affiliation – the knowledge requisite to master the field in general and to criticize the other students of Quintus, such as the Stoically inclined Aephicianus and the abhorrent Lycus (the 'Hippocratic bastard' as Galen calls him), for distortion of their master's message in particular.[53] The set is completed by the Empiricist pairing of Epicurus of Pergamum and Philip (the public interlocutor of Pelops), and assorted unnamed but respectable authors of Hippocratic commentaries in his father's and grandfather's generation. These latter (and, presumably, those of Rufus) Galen has just read, and made extracts from, while he announces (or implies) his direct interaction with the rest, which is crucial not only to establishing his pedagogic pedigree but also because their publications were limited. Hippocratic exegesis was very much a teaching tool, practised orally, circulated in written form among a select few, rarely reaching a wider audience and then incompletely. Galen's reach is wide, however, and he has harvested a full crop of previous interpretations.

Against this background, Galen was always going to compose 'phrase-by-phrase' commentaries on Hippocratic texts. Within the medical community that produced him, and of which he felt himself most a part, it was basically de rigueur. It was also a particularly integral facet of an aspect of Galen's persona and practice that has been rather obscured, both by a degree of Galenic coyness and by the absence of any surviving witnesses, but was clearly important none the less: his role as teacher. That this area of his activities should come more to the fore once his position and reputation had been safely established, that he should see the wider dissemination and fuller development of medical commentaries as helpful in the period of consolidation which followed the initial urgency of system building, is unsurprising. So too is his competitiveness in this as in all things: Galen's project to encompass and surpass past traditions, and so dominate the present and future, is clearly enacted here once more.

Still, the question remains whether (or to what extent) this order of things, the fact that his Hippocratic exegeses followed the construction of a medical system which grounded its claims to authority, in part, in a claim to conformity with Hippocratic doctrine, led to the kind of distortions that Smith alleges: to Galen creating a Hippocrates in his own image. It will be examined in more detail shortly. Before embarking on such an investigation it should be stressed, however, that this is what Hippocratic commentators had been doing since Hellenistic times, and that Aephicianus' Stoic Hippocrates, for example, demonstrates that the practice was alive and well among Galen's contemporaries. Galen does criticize Aephicianus in these very terms, though, and his claims to be the true heir of Hippocrates are not forgotten either. He also sets a number of more specific exegetical standards for himself against which his productions can be measured.

METHODOLOGY

Galen opens his first proper Hippocratic commentary, on Fractures, with a delineation of his exegetical principles.[54] The driving force behind his commentary is simple: 'that which is unclear (*asaphes*) in the text is to be made clear (*saphes*).' Something can be unclear in and of itself (*asaphes auto di'heauto*), or it can be rendered unclear by the inadequacies of the reader.[55] Poor preparation or education either in relation to specific topics and arguments or in general, as well as innate stupidity, can all produce unclarity. Demonstrating the truth or falsehood of what has been written, and defending it against sophistical misconstruals, is distinct from exegesis but has become pretty universal in commentary writing, and is allowed in moderation. A similar, if slightly differently weighted, formulation can be found in the prefatory remarks to the commentary on book 3 of *Aphorisms*.[56] In practice, moreover, Galen certainly gives as much space to demonstration as to clarification in his *hypomnêmata*, indeed the two are often inseparable.

Two other rough rules of interpretative writing emerge from Galen's commentaries, though not so straightforwardly. The first is the principle of utility, already cited (together with authenticity) as determining Galen's initial choice of Hippocratic works for systematic exegesis, which is then repeatedly evoked as a criterion for deciding both which passages within the selected texts deserve full elucidation, and the content of that elucidation. *Hypomnêmata* should be useful: they should attach themselves to worthy primary material, and treat that material in a functional rather than excessive or sophistical manner. The names of the patients in the *Epidemics* are not worth worrying about, for example, even where there are disputed readings, and a number of other matters of linguistic and historical detail are equally trifling.[57] Similarly (and connectedly), though Galen has the whole exegetical tradition at his command, he will be disciplined and focused in deploying it, otherwise his *hypomnêmata* will become overblown and unwieldy. In relation to existing interpretations, he will limit himself to refuting only the most dangerous of errors, and engaging more positively with the comments of the most famous, and those who have something really helpful to offer.[58] In relation to textual readings he will basically stick to the consensus he claims was forged by the first Hippocratic scholars, and avoid being drawn into discussions about recent (and reckless) deviations.[59]

Such formulations, however, serve to highlight Galen's dilemma. His commitment to the useful brings him into conflict with the competitive, display culture of which he is a part. His discipline might be mistaken for ignorance and inability, his omissions adjudged to be not from choice but necessity, and that would not do. Hence the parade of proclaimed learning and appeals to ancient consensus (both suspect) that accompany his insistent statements of method. Hence also the occasional breach of the rules he has laid down, so that his erudition can be exhibited. The most famous of these lapses is his digression on the obscure symbols that follow the case-histories in *Epidemics 3*, and excited much scholarly attention.[60] Galen condemns enquiries into their origins and meanings as useless, pursued by those physicians who consider historical knowledge and arcane information to be more valuable to their careers than a sound understanding of medicine; but none the less provides lengthy discussions of both. He is permitted such indulgence, he claims, on account of the great and useful services he has already rendered to the medical art, including in his Hippocratic commentaries: otherwise, 'I would be ashamed to be diverted to such nonsense'.[61] Elsewhere Galen makes a more serious attempt to square theory and practice by extending the remit of the useful. So, for example, Galen concludes a lengthy, and often poetical, discourse on the meaning of the word *pronoia* (literally 'forethought'), which appears in the opening line of the Hippocratic treatise *Prognostic*, with a claim to have provided a useful and apposite exegetical, if not medical, service.[62] This is quite different, he says, from the activities of those interpreters who spend time explicating the same line's qualifying 'I hold' or 'it seems to me' (*dokei moi*) phrase, an activity that is entirely superfluous and useless in all respects.[63]

Utility is a responsibility that relates to the audience of any interpretative writing, so Galen pairs it with a duty to the work being interpreted. In the extensive proem to the commentary on *Epidemics 1*, Quintus is criticized for lacking the two cardinal virtues of the exegete.[64] He neither expounds things that are 'useful' to the readers of his *hypomnēmata*, nor 'preserves' (*phulassein*) the 'meaning' or 'sense' (*gnōmē*) of the text (*sungramma*). What Galen means by the second part of this formula is rather less clear than might initially appear, as is illustrated by the example of Quintus' wickedness in this respect that he offers, in which the element of transgression against the text itself is rather under-developed.[65] Galen objects to his rival's apparently empiricist interpretation of a Hippocratic aphorism, not because it is incompatible with that aphorism itself, but because it is contradicted by a statement in *Airs, Waters, Places*. It would seem, therefore, that what is being preserved is not the meaning of the actual treatise but the consistency and integrity of Hippocratic doctrine more generally (indeed, of a particular understanding of that doctrine). This approach is more openly articulated in Galen's commentary on the introductory section of *Prognostic*, where there is an explicit switch of focus from text to author, to Hippocrates as author of a range of other works that are brought into play in exegesis.

In addition to *pronoia*, the other word that receives lengthy treatment here is *theion*, 'the divine element' that may be present in any disease and, the author of *Prognostic* asserts, needs to be considered alongside all the other possible factors in prognosticating.[66] This, too, was a matter of long-standing controversy, and Galen begins by outlining the view of various (anonymous) commentators that the reference is to the divine anger that can cause human illness, as shown in myth. He immediately objects, however, that:

> They do not show whether Hippocrates shared this opinion (*doxa*), which is the task of good exegetes. For we are enjoined not simply to state in our exegeses that which seems true to us, but also that which accords with the meaning (*gnômê*) of the author (*sungrapheus*), even if it is false.[67]

Moreover, Hippocrates definitely did not share this opinion, as *On Sacred Disease* demonstrates. Instead, with the assistance of selections from *Aphorisms* and *Epidemics*, the *theion* can be construed as nothing but the surrounding air (*aeros periechôn*).

This reading shows little respect for the integrity of *Prognostic* itself, rather, it is simply forced into line with an externally derived understanding of Hippocratic doctrine. The *gnômê* of the text has certainly been subordinated to that of its assumed author. Nor, indeed, has Galen actually confronted the possibility of non-alignment between his own opinion, that of Hippocrates and the truth. He has worked very hard to avoid that situation, and so flouted his own injunction. Still, as Galen describes the activities of others in the same field, as he refers to existing commentaries and commentators, it appears that all are playing the same games. Reading divine *anger* into the word '*theion*' is a more obvious move to make than taking it as synonymous with the surrounding air, but it still goes beyond the actual phrasing, which is more vague and open. Quintus' statement that an aphorism concerning the seasonality of diseases is 'known by experience alone' has no more support from what is written in *Aphorisms* than Galen's intertextual rejoinder already mentioned; and there are plenty of other examples where all parties to an argument seem to be adopting equally dubious exegetical strategies.[68]

There are, then, plenty of criticisms that can justly be levelled at Galen the exegete. Failures both in his own terms, and by more modern standards, are easy to point to. Indeed, even his desire for clarity itself can get him into trouble. Further on again in the commentary on *Prognostic*, Galen is unhappy at a second listing of dangerous (even deathly) symptoms, which he (very reasonably) finds hard to reconcile with an earlier version (ostensibly) of the same.[69] To elucidate the matter, and also protect the consistency (if not the *gnômê*) of the text, he suggests 'completely altering' (*metalabôn holên*) the wording of the lemma. By inserting an opening phrase making it clear that the second set of signs are later developments (to be looked for on the third day of an illness or after), then reworking its closing clauses to define more clearly their relationship with the previously enumerated indications of danger, the two lists can be made to collaborate, not conflict, removing any confusion in the process. It is not, however, that he is actually proposing a textual amendment here, though he does on other occasions, as did many of his predecessors, sometimes with quite dramatic effects on meaning.[70] It is just that he wants to clarify Hippocrates' thought (*dianoia*) in this respect, tidy things up.

Still, though the flaws in Galen's exegetical approach, and workings, are again apparent, this also emphasizes that (as yet at least), they fall short of substantiating the charge that he constructed Hippocrates in his own image, for there is nothing exclusive in his attitude or practice (rather the reverse). So far, Galen has merely helped to shore up the well-established, if contested, image of Hippocrates the Rationalist, with a naturalistic approach to the causes of disease, a Hippocrates particularly associated with a core set of treatises and ideas, with a coherent and extensive 'system' to his name. Certainly this, along with his various demonstrations of his competitive edge – in terms of method or learning, discipline or display – serves also to shore up his own position and status; but if specifically Galenic contributions are to be discovered then the medical content of his *hypomnêmata* needs to be examined in more detail.

LEMMATOLOGY

The prefaces, and other introductory passages, to Galen's commentaries have already been mentioned as places where he may reflect on the aims, audiences and methods of his interpretations. They may also deal with matters more specific to the treatise under scrutiny, such as its authenticity, title, style, subject matter and relation to other Hippocratic works: that is, all the preliminary points that need to be covered before the phrase-by-phrase exegesis begins; all the things that need to be said about the text as a whole, before its dissection, to provide some basic orientation and guidance to the readership.[71]

That the surgical works are genuine is not in any doubt, for example; but Galen notes that there is a question about whether *Fractures* and *Joints* were originally books one and two of a larger treatise, which obviously has a bearing on their reading.[72] Authentic texts may also be subject to interpolations, and more substantial accretions: a fate which Galen considers to have befallen, for instance, *On Wounds in the Head* as well as *Aphorisms*, *On Regimen in Acute Diseases*, and *Epidemics 2*, especially at the end of each, while the later interference with *On the Nature of Man* is a more complex matter.[73] Here two works now transmitted separately (*On Healthful Regimen* being the other) have been combined, with various unfortunate additions, mainly in between them but also spreading a bit further.[74] Galen is absolutely committed to the authenticity of the main section of *On the Nature of Man*, for it provides, 'the foundations for the whole art (*technê*) of Hippocrates', and, of course, acts similarly (if entirely implicitly at this juncture) for his own medical system.[75] He is reluctant even to consent to the common suggestion that the work was by Polybus (by now viewed as Hippocrates' pupil and successor, entirely faithful, so Galen claims, to his master's doctrines) rather than the great Hippocrates himself.[76] He is, on the other hand, content with the ascription of the good, majority, parts of *On Healthful Regimen* (those portions that are 'well-expressed and in accordance with Hippocratic *technê*') to Polybus.[77] The interpolated section, however, should be attributed to neither, but belongs to Hellenistic Alexandria: for not only is it inconsistent with both the phenomena themselves and *Epidemics 2*, but it also uses more recent language.[78]

Three categories of authenticity thus emerge, and are widely employed by Galen. Texts can be divided into those most genuinely by Hippocrates, the genuinely Hippocratic (such as those by such a close and loyal associate as Polybus) and the spurious, the *notha*, that contrast with both. The seven books of *Epidemics* can be used to illustrate the point.[79] Books One and Three come under the first heading. They are, by common consent, the only ones to have been written by Hippocrates 'for publication' (*pros ekdosin*). Books Two and Six had yet to reach that stage by the time of Hippocrates' death, but were revised and put into circulation by his son Thessalus; while book Four was either a particularly heavily revised example of this genre or the work of a grandson (also called Hippocrates). Books Five and Seven are still more distant productions, obviously *notha*, but it should also be stressed that spurious material has infiltrated all the other books too (to a greater or lesser extent). This serves to emphasize that the real contrast lies between this third, spurious, category and the other two. Indeed, Galen actually remarks that it makes no odds whether *Epidemics* 2 is by Hippocrates or Thessalus, and he is equally unconcerned about the authorship of *In the Surgery*.[80]

What does matter is that his audience is alerted to the difference in shape and style between books Two and Six of *Epidemics* and those Hippocrates wrote *pros ekdosin* before they embark on his *hypomnêmata* on the former.[81] The shared title should not mislead readers into expecting a well-crafted explanation and discussion of 'epidemic' diseases, as in Books One and Three, when what they will get is much more miscellaneous and aphoristic. Similarly, neither the title nor opening sequence of *In the Surgery* adequately prepare the readership for what is actually a more narrowly focused work than either would suggest (though still very useful for beginners).[82]

On the other hand, what is required as a preparatory preamble to *Epidemics 1* itself is rather different, and serves both to bring questions of Galenic specificity back to the fore and to move matters on the lemmata themselves. For the extensive proem to this treatise does its introductory work, essentially, by taking the title – *Epidêmiai* – as a lemma to be elucidated in full.[83] Galen asserts that Hippocrates used this word, which literally means 'visits', to refer to the visitations of disease in certain locations at certain times. He goes on to explain how whole communities (more or less) can simultaneously fall ill in this way. Living together in the same place means that the same factors will have shaped the bodily constitutions, the humoural mixtures (*krâseis*), of the inhabitants, having a homogenizing effect; and they will all be exposed to the same seasonal changes, and to any more erratic alterations in the surrounding air and environment. Galen refers to *Airs, Waters, Places, On the Nature of Man,* and *Aphorisms* to help support and clarify the points he makes, taking his swipe at Quintus as he does so. Indeed, Galen suggests that these three texts, and *Prognostic*, should be mastered before coming to *Epidemics*, a view he goes on to elaborate at considerable length, providing a mini-curriculum for Hippocratic study, beginning with *On the Nature of Man*. There is then some discussion of the orthography of the title, in which, incidentally, Galen enunciates for the first time (at least in extant medical writings) the distinction between epidemic and endemic diseases (*epidêma/epidêmia* and *endêma*, respectively) in roughly the modern manner. Finally he finds space to fit in some more explicit warnings against Empiricist readings of the *Epidemics* (in case his attack on Quintus was too subtle!), before eventually moving from such preliminary matters to the 'part-by-part' (*kata meros*) exegesis itself.

The individual interpretations that follow, in this commentary and all the others, replicate this basic pattern, with variations of emphasis and fullness. Elucidation of meaning may require paraphrase, or other linguistic clarification; but, more importantly, it entails explanation. How does this work? How does it fit into the wider Hippocratic system? Such an explication, moreover, functions simultaneously as demonstration, for if it does work, does fit well within the system, that implies its truth. The clarification of the Hippocratic lemma has served to show its consistency with the phenomena, and its contribution to the art of medicine. This is the main business of commentary, though Galen may also involve himself in further matters of language and history, engage in various exegetical debates, as his principles or inclinations dictate. Nor is his competition simply with other exegetes. Galen also has a tendency to fill in any gaps he feels have been left in any Hippocratic statement: to complete lists, add extra refinements to arguments, expand specific examples into general rules, and so show that his mastery really is total.

These points can easily be illustrated by Galen's commentary on one of the most famous Hippocratic pronouncements: the description in *Prognostic* of the most alarming appearance of a patient:

Nose sharp, eyes hollow, temples sunken, ears cold and contracted, and the lobes of the ears curled up, the skin of the forehead hard and taut and dry, and the colour of the whole face yellow (*chlôros*), or even black (*melan*).[84]

Galen's exegesis here also demonstrates the way in which his explanatory drive takes him, not just beyond any given lemma, but also beyond the boundaries of the Hippocratic Corpus, into the territory of Hellenistic, and indeed post-Hellenistic, medical developments. These, combined with the systematic humoralism of *On the Nature of Man*, are the main weapons in his explicatory armoury. Nor is any attempt made to conceal this fact. The point is rather to show, as von Staden puts it, 'the permanence of Hippocrates' truths'.[85] Or, perhaps more precisely, it is the permanence of medical truth itself that is on display. First expressed, albeit in somewhat compressed and embryonic manner, in Hippocratic texts; then elaborated and expanded by some (usually unnamed) Hellenistic physicians; and now brought to completion, fully realized, by Galen himself.

By the time he reaches this specific passage in his commentary on *Prognostic*, Galen has already established the basic principle that it is deviation from the normal, natural, healthy appearance which is really at issue here. So these are all observable (and, for each individual, roughly measurable) examples of dangerous divergence from that benchmark. Galen initially takes the 'sharp nose' as a separate lemma to refine that point, and also open discussion on the logical link between such signs (*sêmeia*) and the gloomy prognosis.[86] There is one, these matters are subject to rational enquiry, but Galen is keen to proceed *epilogistikôs*, by means of loose, practical, reflective reasoning in each case, rather than by means of anything more formal and deductive (*analogismos*). For the former course will command the greater and wider respect. He then puts the nose back into the rest of the face in offering a set of explanations for why these signs are so ominous.[87]

There are conditions which specifically involve the dissolution of the fleshy parts, but the more general explanation rests on the diminution of innate heat (*emphytos thermasia*) that is associated with much illness, particularly when serious. Heat is conserved in the innermost organs, but no longer reaches the extremities, and so also the supply of blood and *pneuma* to those outer zones dwindles dramatically. These processes of withdrawal are particularly apparent in the face, an external location that contains both bony and fleshy parts in close proximity. The stable, 'earthy' (geôdês), bones remain unchanged, while the moist flesh contracts around the bone of the nose (especially at the tip), and the eyes, normally hot and full of pneuma, 'grow hollow' even quicker; while the temples sink as the muscles they contain (called 'temporal/krotaphites') shrink away; and the ears contract with coldness. This contraction has a particular effect on the lobes, which are softer, less cartilaginous, than the rest of the ear. It causes them to curl back towards the source of the nerves that run to them. The skin becomes hard and taut as it dries out and stretches, and it is this drying also that produces the 'black' colour, that is the colour of dried blood. The yellow discoloration may be a stage on the way to black. Chlôros (also called ôchros by the ancients) is, for Galen, a very dark colour, darker than red (erythros) and caused by cold (as is black).

The combination of these features is so serious that the face may be described as 'deathly' (nekrôdês), though it is slightly less worrying in the context of a long drawn-out disease than if it appears suddenly at the beginning of an illness. Hippocrates will go on to discuss such a situation in the following passage, but Galen first wants to draw attention to something he overlooked. That is, as is mentioned in Aphorisms, that in cold lands and in winter, and in the case of those with cold constitutions and the elderly (who are both cold and dry in the Galenic schema), these signs are not so disastrous.[88]

Though possessing Hippocratic precursors, both the innate heat and pneuma are post-Aristotelian in their elaboration and integration into an overall somatic system. Similarly, precise references to nerves and cartilage, not to mention the naming of the muscles of the temples, derive from Hellenistic anatomy. Matters become more particularly Galenic in relation to two subsequent passages in Prognostic, both of which take Galen into discussions of the eyes. So, for example, he refers to things 'we have learnt from dissections' about the anatomy of the eye and its relationship to other structures and networks of and in the skull, in explaining how the whites of the eyes becoming red is another dangerous symptom.[89] Yet more bad signs are various movements of the hands – such as hunting for things in the air, or plucking at walls or bed-clothes – by those suffering from certain fevers, pneumonia and phrenitis.[90] The reason for both these motions, and the alarm they cause, resides, as Galen explains it, in the eyes and their workings.[91] In particular, when serious (phrenitis always being serious), these diseases affect the fluid between the crystalline body (the lens) and the pupil, as humours are vaporized in the head, making it cloudy. This fluid has a crucial role to play in Galen's theory of vision, as set out and as referred to in the commentary, in book thirteen of *On demonstration*, book seven of *On the Doctrines of Hippocrates and Plato*, and book ten of *On the Utility of the Parts*. It conveys the optical *pneuma* through the pupil to the external air, which is then aligned with the *pneuma* so as to act like a nerve, transmitting perceptions back to the brain. When clouded, however, the *pneuma* does not pass through cleanly, but is blocked in patches, creating dark images – sometimes resembling threads, or little gnats, or perhaps lentils – that float or fly across the sight, as if they were external objects. So people grab or pluck at them.

Plenty of other examples can be offered of references to other Hippocratic works, reliance on (often anonymous) Hellenistic endeavours and citation of Galen's own contributions to medical knowledge, all woven together in his explanatory and exegetical web.[92] It is, moreover, a seamless web, eliding differences between those who partake in the medical truth, while emphasizing (even creating) distinctions between them and the rest, those who have erred, have strayed from Hippocratic *gnômê* as Galen understands and promulgates it.

It also seems likely that, if the commentaries of, for example, Sabinus and Rufus of Ephesus, or even Lycus and Quintus, had survived, much the same pattern would be repeated. The figure of the main Hippocratic interlocutor and heir would obviously be altered, but little else. They would have conducted their exegetical business in roughly the same manner, including their construal of Hippocratic *gnômê*. This is easiest to judge in the case of Rufus, whose Hippocratic *hypomnêmata* Galen recommended as reading (at least before he completed his own), and who has a handful of extant treatises (though no commentaries) to his name, and certainly operated with a medical system also constructed from a synthesis of Hippocratic and Hellenistic teaching; but even Lycus and Quintus seem to have been working with many of the same concepts and assumptions.[93] In his surviving writings Rufus cuts a somewhat more modest figure than Galen (and, by all accounts, Lycus and Quintus, too), though he is not scared of an argument where necessary, and he seems less of a total system builder. He appears not to have become involved, for instance, in debates about elements, or theories of proof, and his references to philosophers such as Plato and Aristotle are more specifically medical and less general.

Still, these are all differences of degree, not dramatic rifts: divergences that would be expressed in the content, rather than form, or approach, of their commentaries. The point, once again, is that Galen was part of a medical community that held much in common. He built his system from the same constituents as others around, and before, him, but arranged them somewhat differently, and elaborated, and connected, them better, more fully and completely, than anyone else. Which is to say that the main difference between Galen and the rest lies in his success.

CONCLUSION

It is, then, not just that Galen's surviving commentaries form part of a larger exegetical project, one that encompassed significant sections of Peripatetic philosophy as well as Hippocratic medicine (and, indeed, other authorities, too); but that this project itself emerged out of, and participated in, a broader exegetical culture, both in general and particular. Textual commentary, in Galen's world, played a key role in the development of ideas and understanding, in their articulation and elaboration, and in their transmission and dispersal. It allowed the exegete to define himself and his doctrines in relation to what had gone before, to locate himself on an existing conceptual and ideological map, in an authoritative manner. The commentator was, after all, the student who had become the teacher. His commentary combined learning and teaching, announced his mastery of the subject, the sense in which he had absorbed, and could now contribute to, the tradition. Perhaps it was Galen's failure to actually pass that transitional point, to turn from student to teacher, in his philosophical commentaries (rather than in *On demonstration*), that consigned them to relative oblivion, as much as their external situation.

It is, moreover, the didactic role of Hippocratic commentary in Galen's most immediate medical community that comes across so clearly in his contributions to the genre. Whether that was the case in the distant past, in the world of the *palaioi*, the earliest commentators, is less clear. Galen's references are too partial (in all senses) to tell. However, his discussion of both his own role as (reluctant) public exegete and his relationship with his closest rivals is inextricably bound up with descriptions of, and allusions to, pedagogic lineages and practices. Elucidation of certain Hippocratic texts in a certain style was an intrinsic part of Galen's education, as of his colleagues', and competitors'. It was something each of his teachers engaged in, and which he readily received. Indeed, he went further in his quest for Hippocratic learning, so that his own teaching could lay claim to completeness in addition to all its other virtues.

Despite his rhetoric, there are undoubtedly omissions, elisions and distortions, in his works, but the richness of his commentaries is also obvious: presenting both opportunities and pitfalls for the scholar. One problem is that this portion of Galen's literary production is as resistant to summary as any other. Galen's efforts at systematization are continually undermined by his drive to encompass everything, to display his erudition as well as enact his methodological rigour. He himself recognizes this, as the assorted excuses and justifications he offers for his numerous breaches of his own exegetical principles show. Still, it is the dual ambition, the promised combination of both completeness and coherence, that there is a pattern into which everything will fit, that is also the mark of his success.

NOTES

1. The antiquity, if not originality, of these chapter headings is assured by their appearance in Hunain's Arabic translation of the text: see Boudon (2002a, 9–18).
2. *On My Own Books* (*Lib.Prop.*) (XIX 33–37, = B.-M. 159.9–162–11; I give rough equivalences between Véronique Boudon-Millot's *Bude'* edition and Kühn, as also for the *CMG* volumes (where possible), though it should be noted that the actual text is often not the same, and, where available, I have always used the post-Kühn editions.
3. The practice of writing private commentaries, for personal and pedagogic use, seems to have been a common one, see e.g. *On Hippocrates' 'Epidemics'* (*Hipp.Epid.*) VI 7 (*CMG* V 10,2,2, 412.15–413.30).
4. Indeed, Arabic translations of the handful now lost – the commentaries on *Humours*, *Nutriment*, *Wounds* and *Wounds in the Head* – may yet

be found, following the discoveries of the Arabic versions of those on *Airs, Waters, Places* (lost in Greek) and sections of *Epidemics* (some of the Greek text printed in Kühn, along with all that claiming to be commentary on *Humours* and *Nutriment*, is a Renaissance forgery: see instead *CMG* vols. V 10,1–10,2,4).

5. For an English summary of the *Risâla* see, e.g., Meyerhoff (1926): this commentary is no. 87; and for the Arabic text see Bergsträsser (1925).

6. Collected, in English translation, in Rosenthal (1956). Rosenthal remains uncommitted about the ascription to Galen.

7. *Lib.Prop.* 13 and 11 (XIX 38, = B.-M. 163.18–20 and 4–7).

8. *Lib.Prop.* 10.2 (XIX 37, = B.-M. 162.13–18).

9. *On Bloodletting against Erasistratus* (*Ven.Sect.Er.*) XI 147–186; and *On Bloodletting against the Erasistrateans at Rome* (*Ven.Sect.Er.Rom.*) XI 187–249; and see Brain (1986) for translation and discussion.

10. Von Staden (1998, esp. 72–3).

11. Distinctions are drawn at e.g. *On Hippocrates' 'Prorrhetics'* (*Hipp.Prorrh.*) 1.8 and 13, 3.53 (XVI 532, 543, and 811, = *CMG* V 9,2, 24,9–10; 29,20–23; 161,7–9); but the instances where that rule is breached are legion, see e.g. the examples in von Staden (1998, 72).

12. The level of Galen's engagement with the tradition is analysed in detail by Smith (1979, esp. 123–76); and see also the substantial study of Manetti and Roselli (1994). The other discussions I have found particularly useful are those relating to Galen and commentary in chapters 4 and 5 of Mansfeld (1994, 115–76).

13. *Lib.Prop.* 12 (XIX 38, = B.-M. 163.8–17).

14. See discussion at B.-M. 214–18, esp. notes 7 and 13.

15. *Lib.Prop.* 11 (XIX 39–45, = B.-M. 164.1–169.12).

16. See *introduction*, pp. 3–4; and chs. 3 and 5 (Tieleman, Morison) both in this volume.

·17. *Lib.Prop.* 14.15 (XIX 42–3, = B.-M. 166.22–167.6).

18. The story about his Chrysippean notes is recorded at *Lib.Prop.* 14.16 (XIX 43, = B.-M. 167.6–14).

19. The ethical chapter is *Lib.Prop.* 15 (XIX 45–6, = B.-M. 169.13–170.13).

20. *Lib.Prop.* 16 (XIX 46–7, = B.-M. 170.14–171.8); and see De Lacy (1972, 27–39). See further ch. 6 (Hankinson) in this volume.

21. See H. O. Schröder (ed.), *Galeni In Platonis Timaeum Commentarii Fragmenta* (*CMG Suppl.* 1, 1934). The material collected by Larrain (1992) does not add to our Galenic material, as argued by Nickel (2002, 73–8).

22. *Lib.Prop.* 17 (XIX 47, = B.-M. 171.6–172.2); for more on this, see ch. 4 (Morison) in this volume.

23. Moraux (1953, 73); Arist. *Metaph.* 1012b.

24. Citations of *On demonstration* are collected in von Mueller (1897); and see also Strohmeier (1998).

25. For an overview of the tradition see e.g. Sorabji (1990b); for Alexander more particularly see, e.g., Sharples (1987).

26. One quotation in Simplicius *In Phys.* (*CAG* X 1039,13–15) is generally assumed to be from Galen's commentary *On the First Mover*, though it is not explicitly labelled as such, and I would argue that it actually comes from *On demonstration* (also cited earlier in the same text, *CAG* IX 708,27–8). The argument is too complicated to go into here, however, and the basic point about Galen's invisibility *as a fellow commentator* remains either way. On his (rather dim) visibility as a medical authority see Todd (1977).

27. Bergsträsser (1925, 51.5–9) (Arabic). Most complexly, this work seems to have been refuted, in Arabic, probably by a member of the Aristotelian movement of Arab Baghdad with which al-Farabi was associated, who borrowed Alexander of Aphrodisias' name for the purpose: see Fazzo (2002, 109–45). This Arab text itself is published in Rescher and Marmura (1965), assuming the authenticity of the claimed authorship. Other references to Galen *On the Prime Mover* in Arabic are also collected in this book (1–4).

28. Bergsträsser (1925, 51.77–23) (Arabic).

29. *Lib.Prop.* 18 and 19 (XIX 47–8, = B.-M. 172.3–173.4).

30. On the development of Platonic commentary in relation to the practices of other philosophical schools see, e.g., Sedley (1997).

31. So, though Epicureans discussed specific textual/interpretative problems in Epicurus, they did not write commentaries (see, e.g., Puglia, 1988); and, while the Stoics had historical interests in literary criticism, and (in the Roman Empire, certainly) taught through oral exposition of key school texts (especially those of Chrysippus – see e.g. Arr. *Epict.* I.4.6–9 and 17.13–18), discounting Galen, the first known commentary on a Stoic text is from the sixth century AD – Simplicius' on Epictetus' *Enchiridion* (and Donini, 1994, 89–90, argues that the earlier silence is not accidental).

32. For discussion of Galen in relation to wider ancient 'scientific' commentary traditions such as astronomy see, e.g., von Staden (2002); and for Galen's relationships with exegetical practices within the discipline of grammar/rhetoric see, e.g., Sluiter (1995).

33. That is to say, Origen and Hippolytus composed systematic 'phrase-by-phrase' commentaries in the classical style (see e.g. Heine, 2004a, 2004b); though they clearly draw on existing Christian exegetical practices and Jewish interpretative traditions, as well as Hellenistic techniques: see e.g. Young (1997) for further discussion.

34. For his repeated claims not to follow any sect, and always decide for himself, see e.g. *On the Order of My Own Books* (*Ord.Lib.Prop.*) 1–2 (XIX 50–4, = B.-M. 88.13–92.7); and *The Passions of the Soul* (*Aff.Dig.*) 8 (V 42–3, = CMG V 4,1.1, 28,25–29,12).

35. Athenaeus of Attaleia, the founder of the pneumatist school of medicine, is, for example, described by Galen as a 'pupil' of Posidonius (*On Containing Causes* (*CC*) 2.1: *CMG Suppl. Or.* II 54,3–6 and 134,3–6); and, even if this statement (transmitted only in Arabic and Latin translations) is to be interpreted loosely, his Stoic commitments are plain (see e.g. Nutton, 2004, 202–5, for discussion). There is no indication that he (or any of his followers) wrote anything other than medical works, however.

36. And he composed epitomes of the anatomical writings of Marinus and Lycus (*Lib.Prop.* 4.9: XIX 25, = B.-M. 147.16–19).

37. On this 'agonal' exegetical tradition see, e.g., von Staden (1982).

38. This was, of course, changing, as philosophical authorities, texts and ideas became more common property in the Roman Empire (leading to the 'neo-Platonic' commentaries on Aristotle, for instance); and Homer obviously had a foundational role for classical culture more broadly, making Homeric exegesis a very open field.

39. Athenodorus: Simp. *In Cat.* 4 (*CAG* 8 62,25); this work engaged in sufficient detail with Aristotle's text for Athenodorus to be labelled 'exegete' at *CAG* 8 159,32, but there is no indication it was a commentary in the strict sense. Asclepiades: Caelius Aurelianus *On Acute Diseases* (*TP*) 5.51 and *On Chronic Diseases* (*CP*) 2.173.

40. Mentioned at Cael. Aur. *TP* 4.113, and see von Staden (1989) for discussion both of this passage in particular (74–5) and Herophilus' relationship with Hippocratic ideas and texts more generally (his humoral pathology could certainly be described as broadly 'Hippocratic', for example: 116, 242–7 and 301–5). There is, it should be stressed, no indication that Herophilus' book was a commentary.

41. For Asclepiades' denial of the existence of critical days see Cael. Aur. *CP* 1.108–9. His commentaries are referred to at *CP* 3.5 and Galen, *On Hippocrates' 'Surgery'* (*Hipp.Off.Med.*) XVIIIB 666, 715, 805 and 810; and see also Smith (1979, 222–6) for further discussion of his relations with Hippocrates.

42. The two fundamental works on Galenic chronology, as it relates to the commentaries, are Ilberg (1889, 229–38), and Bardong (1942). For more general biographical discussion see e.g. Nutton (2004, 216–29).

43. *PHP* VIII 5 (*CMG* V 4,1,2, 508,6–9 and 522,34–36, = V 682–3 and 702); for its dating see *CMG* V 4,1,1 46–8.

44. *Hipp.Epid.* 3 2 (*CMG* V 10,2,1, 60,11–15, = XVIIA 577).

45. On Hippocrates' 'Prognostic' (Hipp.Prog.) III 6 (CMG V 9,2, 328,11–22, = XVIIIB 230).

46. Hipp.Epid. 3 2 (CMG V 10,2,1, 60,15–62,2, = XVIIA 577–8).

47. Indeed it is, together with the commentary on Epidemics 3, a more minimal production than those on Epidemics 2 and 6, reflecting differences between the texts being interpreted. The developmental classification in the Lib.Prop. may, therefore, be a later spin on a rather more contingent process.

48. Smith (1979, esp. 122–4).

49. Smith (1979, 175).

50. On these 'editions' see Ilberg (1890).

51. The debt Galen as Hippocratic commentator owes to the medical community that produced him is emphasized and explored in Manetti and Roselli (1994, esp. 1580–1614). See also Smith (1979, esp. 62–77).

52. Galen's most concentrated coverage of his relationship with previous commentators comes in Ord.Lib.Prop. 3 (XIX 56–8, = B.-M. 98.3–99.9), and Hipp.Epid. 6 7 (CMG V 10,2,2, 412,15–413,30).

53. See e.g. Gal. Hipp.Epid. 3 1.4 (CMG V 10,2,1, 17,7–8, = XVIIA 507).

54. Gal. On Hippocrates' 'On Fractures' (Hipp.Fract.) pr. (XVIIIB 318–322).

55. Galen outlines this distinction briefly here, referring to a work On Exegesis for fuller treatment; but unless this is the same as his On clarity and unclarity (Peri saphêneias kai asapheias) listed at Lib.Prop. 20.2 (XIX 48, = B.-M. 173.13–14), this is otherwise unknown. He also generally tends towards blaming the reader for any Hippocratic 'unclarity', see Sluiter (1995).

56. On Hippocrates' 'Aphorisms' (Hipp.Aph.) 3 pr. (XVIIB 561–562).

57. See e.g. Hipp.Epid. 1 2.85 (CMG V 10,1, 99,22–100,2, = XVIIA 197–8); and on other invocations of utility see von Staden (2002, esp. 134–6).

58. See, e.g., Lib.Prop. 19.5 (XIX 34–5, = B.-M. 160.8–13); Hipp.Epid. 6 (CMG V 10,2,2, 412,15–413,9).

59. See e.g. Hipp.Off.Med. 1 pr. (XVIIIB 630–632).

60. Hipp.Epid. 3 2.4 and 5 (CMG V 10,2,1, 75,23–83,13, = XVIIA 600–613).

61. Hipp.Epid. 3 2.4 (CMG V 10,2,1 78,17, = XVIIA 604).

62. Hipp.Prog. 1.4 (CMG V 9,2 203,11–13, = XVIIIB 12), commenting on the line (2 110.1 L): 'I hold it to be an excellent thing for a physician to practise pronoia.' Galen had begun by assuming pronoia and prognosis to be synonyms, and indeed he sticks to that view.

63. Hipp.Prog. 1.4 (CMG V 9,2, 203,13–18, = XVIIIB 12).

64. Hipp.Epid. 1 pr. (CMG V 10,1, 6,16–19, = XVIIA 6).

65. Hipp.Epid. 1 pr. (CMG V 10,1, 6,6–16, = XVIIA).

66. Hipp.Prog. 1.4 (CMG V 9,2, 205,28–209,6, = XVIIIB 17–22), commenting on a phrase (2 112.4–6 L) omitted from the Teubner edition (and,

following that, the Loeb) despite its presence in all the manuscripts (not to mention the commentary tradition!).

67. *Hipp.Prog.* 1.4 (*CMG* V 9,2, 206,5–9, = XVIIIB 17–18).

68. For Quintus see, again, *Hipp.Epid.* *1* pr. (*CMG* V 10,1, 6,6–16, = XVIIA 6).

69. *Hipp.Prog.* 1.10 (*CMG* V 9,2, 223,17–225,6, = XVIIIB 49–51).

70. See, e.g., the lengthy discussion of a particularly vexed passage in *Epidemics 2* which *everyone* emended (*CMG* V 10,2,1, 230,4–234,7); and cf. *Hipp.Epid. 6* pr. (*CMG* V 10,2,2, 4,4–17, = XVIIA 794).

71. That this is his prefatory project is explicitly stated at e.g. *Hipp.Epid. 1* pr. (*CMG* V 10,1, 10,21–22, = XVIIA 13); and see also *Hipp.Epid. 6* pr. (*CMG* V 10,2,2, 5,2–3, = XVIIA 796), where more introductory material is required as the audience widens; and *Hipp.Off.Med.* pr. (XVIIIB 632). This issue is discussed by Mansfeld (1994, 117–47).

72. *On Hippocrates' 'On Joints'* (*Hipp.Art.*) pr. (XVIIIA 300–303).

73. All these are listed as such in *On Hippocrates' 'Regimen in Acute Diseases'* (*HVA*) 4 pr. (*CMG* V 9,1, 271,3–272,3, = XV 732–4), but there are references to interpolations in almost all his commentaries.

74. *On Hippocrates' 'Nature of Man'* (*HNH*) 1 pr. and 2 pr. (*CMG* V 9,1, 7,21–8,18 and 57,4–21, = XV 9–11 and 108–109).

75. *HNH* 1 pr. (*CMG* V 9,1, 8,19–20, = XV 11); the point is elaborated further in his work *On the Elements according to Hippocrates* ([*Hipp. Elem.*] *CMG* V 1,2); see also ch. 9 (Rocca) in this volume.

76. *HNH* 1 pr. (*CMG* V 9,1, 8,22–29, = XV 11–12). The ascription to Polybus goes back to Aristotle (*HA* 3.3), and the Peripatetic medical doxography used by Anonymus Londinensis (19.1–18), without any reference to his relationship with Hippocrates, his emergence as star pupil, successor and even son-in-law, may well be part of a later attempt to keep the Hippocratic Corpus within the family.

77. *HNH* 1 pr.; 2 pr. and 22; 3 pr. (*CMG* V 9,1, 8,14–19; 57,6–8 and 88,12–13; 89,14, = XV 11, 108, 173 and 175).

78. *HNH* 2.22 (*CMG* V 9,1, 87,15–88,11, = XV 171–3).

79. As set out at, e.g., *Hipp.Epid. 6* 1. pr. and 2 4.1 (*CMG* V 10,2,2, 5,3–11, = XVIIA 796, and *CMG* V 10,1, 310,23–30).

80. *Hipp.Epid. 2* 1 (*CMG* V 10,1, 155,31–33); *Hipp.Off.Med.* (XIIIB 666).

81. *Hipp.Epid. 6* 1 pr. and 2 4.1 (*CMG* V 10,2,2, 5,12–6,5, = XVIIA 796-7, and *CMG* V 10,1, 310,31–311,11).

82. *Hipp.Off.Med.* 1.pr. (XVIIIB 632 K).

83. *Hipp.Epid. 1* pr. (*CMG* V 10,1, 3,8–11,10, = Arabic-XVIIA 14).

84. Hippocrates, *Prog.* 2 (2 114.2–6 L): the so-called *'facies Hippocratica'*.

85. Von Staden (2002, 115). A similar attitude is taken (*mutatis mutandis*) in various philosophical commentaries, and is found, in a more extreme form, in the genre of the *De Evangelica Praeparatione*.

86. *Hipp.Prog.* 1.6 (*CMG* V 9,2, 211,1–17, = XVIIIB 25–6).
87. *Hipp.Prog.* 1.7 (*CMG* V 9,2, 211,18–214,14, = XVIIIB 26–32).
88. Galen closes his exegesis by quoting the relevant aphorism (2.34; 4 480.7–9 L).
89. *Hipp.Prog.* 1.10 (*CMG* V 9,2, 222,15–22, = XVIIIB 47); the implicit cross-references are to *On the Utility of the Parts* (*UP*) 10.2 and 8.9.
90. Hipp.*Prog.* 4 (2 122.5–10 L); cf. Galen, *On the Therapeutic Method* (*MM*) XIII 21 and *Loc.Aff.* IV 2 and V 4 (X 928–32, VIII 226–7 and 330–1).
91. Gal. *Hipp.Prog.* 1.23 (*CMG* V 9,2 235,18–238,8, = XVIIIB 71–5).
92. See, for instance, *Hipp.Aph.* V for intertwined references to Galen's works (e.g. *On Semen* [*Sem.*] at XVIIIA 840–841), Hellenistic reproductive anatomy (e.g. Praxagoras at XVIIIA 838) and other Hippocratic texts (e.g. *Nat.Puer.* at XVIIIA 828).
93. On Rufus see, e.g., Sideras (1994); for Quintus and Lycus in the general mix see e.g. Gal. *Hipp.Epid.* 6 5.14–15 (*CMG* V 10,2,2, 284,7–296,8, = XVIIA 269–277 + Arabic).

14 The fortunes of Galen

To describe the fortunes of Galen over the centuries is almost to write the history of medicine since his death.[1] Not only did his ideas constitute the basis of formal medicine in Europe at least until the seventeenth century, and arguably until the nineteenth, but as Yunani medicine (i.e. Greek medicine as consolidated and developed by Ibn Sina [Avicenna], d. 1037), they constitute a major medical tradition in the modern Muslim world. Galen's holistic approach can also be found among modern practitioners of complementary medicine, as well as in one branch of Tibetan medicine.[2] Galen's conception of Hippocrates and Hippocratic medicine not only dominated until recently historians' approaches to their medical past but, more subtly, continues to influence modern perceptions of what medicine is and how it should be practised. Galen's ideal of the learned, thinking practitioner still directs our preconceptions of what a doctor should be like, even if his demands for constant training in philosophy and in dissection can be fulfilled only with difficulty. Historians' knowledge of Galen continues to increase, not only because his writings have been studied more closely in the last thirty years than at any time since the seventeenth century, but also because there has been a steady accession of new discoveries, albeit principally in medieval translations rather than in his original Greek.[3] Indeed, modern scholars are more familiar with Galen's works than were their predecessors in Byzantium and all but a handful of experts in the Islamic world.

This paradoxical situation can be easily explained. Galen was so prolific that very few doctors in the age before printing could afford to have copies made of all his books, even if they could gain access to them, and over time many works became lost as a result either of chance or of deliberate selection. The process began even during Galen's lifetime, for the fire in Rome at the Temple of Peace in 192 destroyed much of his personal library. His semi-autobiographical treatise On Prognosis, for example, was among those that Galen believed had been lost, although a copy seems somehow to have survived elsewhere.[4] Most of his writings on grammar and on philosophy disappeared in Greek at a very early stage and, even when we know that copies survived, there is little evidence that they were ever read or cited. In the middle years of the ninth century, a Christian physician in Baghdad, Hunain ibn Ishaq (d. 873), composed a remarkable letter listing all the versions of 129 Galenic works that he had been able to locate and that had been translated either into Syriac, the language of most of the Christians in the Near East, or into Arabic, often by himself, his friends and family. Not only did Hunain explain his preferred principles of translation, and list the names of those who had sponsored these translations, usually doctors and courtiers, but he also commented on the difficulties he had encountered in his hunt for Greek manuscripts of Galen in Damascus, Alexandria and possibly also within the Byzantine Empire. Some treatises were common and had been often translated, particularly those that formed the standard syllabus of learned medicine, but others survived only in fragmentary copies or in defective translations. Even making allowance for exaggeration, and for the possibility that copies survived in regions of Byzantium inaccessible to him, Hunain's list is impressive. In a second tract, in addition to making some corrections, Hunain indicated which of these books had not been included by Galen himself in On My Own Books (Lib.Prop.) – some because they had been thought lost, some perhaps through inadvertence, and at least one, On His Own Opinions (Prop.Plac.), because it had not yet been written.[5]

A comparison with what survives today shows that almost all of the works translated into Arabic still exist in some form, even if only as scattered quotations. So, for example, new fragments of On demonstration have been recently recovered from the Doubts on Galen by al-Razi (Rhazes), d. 925/935, and approximately half of the Commentary on the Hippocratic Oath has been retrieved from a variety of later Arabic sources.[6] Galen's moral treatises were often ransacked for suitable quotations about love, grief, or how to profit from one's enemies.[7] Several Jewish writers, in particular, used

Galen's moral exhortations in their own treatises although, given their familiarity with Arabic, one need not assume that they always relied on an already existing Hebrew translation.[8] Galen, in short, retained authority for a long while as a writer on philosophical and moral topics in the Islamic world and among the Jewish communities in Southern Europe.

By contrast, very few of Galen's philosophical writings survived in their original Greek. Theological copyists were rarely interested in Galen's heretical views, and even manuscripts of his *Logic* seem to have been rare.[9] Increasingly, too, attention centred on Galen's writings of direct relevance to medical practice, and particularly those that said a great deal in a short space. It is hardly surprising that the final six books of Galen's major textbook of anatomy, *Anatomical procedures*, had disappeared in Greek by 1200, for its sheer size made it expensive to copy and it was hardly of use in a society where human dissection was effectively unknown.[10] Other texts were clearly regarded as superfluous to the everyday needs of the physician. This may explain why a group of little tracts, including two on causation, disappeared in the fourteenth or fifteenth century. They were certainly available in Greek in the early fourteenth century at Constantinople or in South Italy, for they were among those translated into Latin by Niccolò da Reggio (active 1304–50), a South Italian who was employed at the Angevin court of Naples as a doctor, diplomat and translator, but little trace of them remains in Greek.[11] Galen's *On His Own Opinions* survived entire in Greek in a single manuscript that was discovered only in 2005, and the earlier editor had to reconstruct it from two medieval Latin versions (one incomplete) and fragments in Greek and Hebrew.[12] With a few exceptions, then, it was this Byzantine Galen, less philosophical and less experimental than its Arabic equivalent, that passed into print in 1525, and that, with a few additions, formed the standard edition of Kühn of 1821–33. But discoveries since then, principally in Arabic, have now repaired some of the losses, restoring not only fragments but even whole treatises, some of them several books long. The most voluminous author to survive from Classical Antiquity has gained several hundred more pages over the last century and a half.

The stabilizing influence of print has also rendered the Galenic Corpus more accessible to potential readers. Whereas, in the Middle

Ages, it was only the very wealthy or the very committed who had access to what was thought to be a complete Galen, and most doctors owned copies of only a handful of standard tracts, anyone who wished and could afford it could buy an *Opera Omnia Galeni*, either in Greek or, more often, in a Latin translation (or could at least consult one).[13] Besides, a variety of printed finding aids, from summaries and indexes to a CD-ROM, has made consultation of particular passages or of particular topics easier today than it has ever been.[14] A scholar is now in a far better position to understand Galen, and Galen's opinions, than at any time since Galen's own day, to say nothing of the archaeological and inscriptional discoveries, not least at Pergamum itself, that have provided a material and social context in which to place his activities.[15]

Particularly striking is the unusually extensive and varied evidence for the respect in which he was held by others at the end of his life. Even if we regard with caution his claims that patients wrote to him for advice from Spain, Gaul, Asia Minor, Thrace and elsewhere, and assume that the writers of drug-books who included for centuries a 'Hiera of Galen' knew nothing of its origins, there can be little doubt that his influence was felt quickly throughout the Empire and for a variety of different reasons.[16] Athenaeus of Naucratis included him among his 'sophists at dinner' as a man who had produced more works on philosophy and medicine than any before him, although the opinions on wines and breads that are put into Galen's mouth are likely to be Athenaeus' own invention rather than citations from lost works of Galen.[17] The Aristotelian philosopher Alexander of Aphrodisias is said to have composed at least two treatises against him, and, although he thought little of him as a philosopher, he included Galen alongside Plato and Aristotle as examples of what it meant to be 'a man of repute'.[18] Around 210, a group of Christians in Rome led by Theodotus the shoemaker paid such respect to Galen's criticisms of their faith as ethically exemplary but philosophically naive that they modified their beliefs in ways that later Christians considered heretical.[19] Another theologian, the great Origen, writing around 240, seems to allude to Galen as an anatomist who could explain precisely why Providence had made each part of the body for its particular purpose.[20] The geographical spread of knowledge of Galen's writings is particularly noteworthy. Within a generation or so of his death, his *On the Doctrines of Hippocrates and Plato* (*PHP*) was being copied in Upper Egypt, and Gargilius Martialis, a retired army officer who died in 260 at Auzia (in modern Morocco), could cite him as an authority in thirteen chapters of his short Latin handbook on *Medicines from Vegetables and Fruits*.[21] Such swift success in so many different subjects and in so many different regions can be demonstrated for few other ancient authors, proof that Galen was not exaggerating unduly his own impact on his contemporaries.

His increasing authority can be easily seen from the way in which his theories and words came to dominate the Greek medical encyclopedias of Late Antiquity. Oribasius, writing at the end of the fourth century, included many substantial extracts from authors such as Antyllus, Sabinus and Rufus, predecessors of Galen within the Hippocratic tradition. Aetius, a century later, dispensed with many of these passages, while Paul of Aegina, in the seventh century, often subsumed what was left into a section consisting mainly of Galen's words. Although, as can be seen from the Arabic translations of the ninth century, many works of Rufus of Ephesus were still available then,[22] the situation was rapidly approaching in the Byzantine world when the only manuscripts of medicine that were copied bore the name of Galen or of his master Hippocrates, or filled in a few gaps that he had left – medical botany with Dioscorides, nosology with Aretaeus, gynaecology with Soranus and some surgery. Even Hippocrates came to be approached entirely through Galen. The favoured Hippocratic texts were those that he had recommended and were interpreted along lines he had laid down. Indeed, some of the Arabic translators of Hippocrates went so far as to construct their text of Hippocrates solely from the lemmata he had supplied in his commentary.[23] A medieval legend tells the story neatly. Galen, the apprentice of his uncle Hippocrates, became so successful that he took his uncle's patients away. Envious and angry at being supplanted, Hippocrates murdered Galen while he tended his herb garden. Galen did not go unmourned, and, on his deathbed, the penitent Hippocrates was forced to acknowledge that he had indeed been surpassed in every way by his brilliant nephew.[24]

Galen's authority was expressed in visual as well as written form. As early as 512, the artist of the Vienna Dioscorides could place Galen among the great pharmacologists, occupying the central place in the second illustration that had been occupied by Chiron the centaur in the first.[25] Other illuminators portrayed him as a monarch or a sage, in manuscripts and even in a window of Milan Cathedral.[26] In some Byzantine monastic frescoes he was painted alongside other worthies of Antiquity who foretold or acknowledged the truths of Christianity.[27] In a similar fresco in the crypt of the Italian cathedral at Anagni, Galen and Hippocrates discuss the divine basis of the cosmos.[28] No wonder, then, that a Byzantine hagiographer could include Galen as one of the 'philosophers of the cosmos' who had confirmed the purposefulness of the Creator, or that Muslim and Jewish philosophers, such as al-Razi or Maimonides (1138–1204), while accepting eagerly much of his teleology, should take pains to refute his, to them heretical, views on the eternity of creation or the nature of the soul.[29] Others, like the late-fourth-century bishop Nemesius of Emesa, or the fourteenth-century Jewish philosopher Ibn Falaquera, gladly quoted large sections of recherché tracts of Galen to support their own views of mankind or of morality.[30]

The most striking visual documentation of Galen's authority is to be found in the 116 miniatures in a Latin manuscript, Dresden, Db 92–93, that was produced in Flanders around 1460.[31] The first initial letter of each book in this massive collection of Galenic tracts is decorated with a beautiful scene suggested by the book's title or opening words. Throughout, Galen appears as the dominant figure, either working in his study surrounded by huge volumes or, more often, giving instructions to his students, patients or opponents. He speaks from a high throne, and it is his word that quells all dissension, to the obvious disgust of those arguing before him. In a nice touch, they are represented as foreigners, while Galen wears the fur-trimmed robe of a university doctor.

Galen's triumph was assisted by his own rhetoric. Time and again he had claimed that he had brought medicine to perfection himself, or that he was transmitting what Hippocrates had already completed. Hence it was easy to believe that Galen had provided all that was necessary for medicine, and the truth was already there in his many volumes, if one did but look closely. 'Hippocrates sowed the seed, Galen reaped the harvest', said one resigned author, with the implication that only unprofitable stubble remained.[32] A Renaissance poet and medical professor, Eobanus Hessus, expressed it neatly in a Latin epigram:

Dempseris Hippocratem, medicorum primus habebor
Debeo multa illi, debet et ille mihi.
Nam quae nota parum reliquis dedit, omnia feci
Mille libris claro lucidiora die
Hippocratem magnum breuis insula, me dedit ingens
Terra Asiae. plus nos scripsimus, ille minus.
Ille elementa dedit, nos inde extruximus arcem
Quam seruat medici praesul Apollo clari.

Remove Hippocrates; first then shall I be.
My debts to him are many; but so are his to me.
Things left undone, obscure, by him, I leave complete,
A thousand volumes, crystal clear and neat.

A tiny Island bore him, me the mighty land
Of Asia; he a few things, I a myriad penned.
He gave us building blocks, from which a citadel
I built for medicine; Apollo keeps it well.[33]

But the increasing authority of Galen also brought with it a major challenge – how to reduce to a manageable compass what he had written. Galen's prolixity presented a problem even to his admirers. 'You could have made a mattress out of a few threads', wrote a late-medieval annotator of a manuscript now in Cesena, and more than one weary Greek commentator lamented that Galen did not know how to rein in his pen.[34] The satirical author of the *Timarion* joked that Galen could not be present in court, because he was still engaged in adding yet one more qualification to his already enormous treatise on fevers.[35] Galen, everyone knew, was a wealthy man, with a huge library that allegedly contained books written on silk, and even a rare copy of the works of Anaxagoras, but not every doctor was as rich as he, certainly at the beginning of his career.[36] How then to secure the best of Galen's learning within a reasonable compass?

One early solution we have already encountered – the selection and subsequent rearrangement of Galenic passages within an encyclopedia – and similar medical mosaics can be found well into the Middle Ages. The medieval Latin authors Johannes de Sancto Amando (fl. 1261–98) and Petrus de Sancto Floro (fl. 1349–80), created their own medical dictionaries as a cento of Galenic passages.[37] Others, like the original compiler of the selection of Galenic information in Paris, BN gr. 2332, went carefully through a series of Galenic treatises extracting individual sentences, thus keeping both Galen's original wording and the original shape of each treatise. Even as late as the nineteenth century, such summaries of Galenic tracts were being composed for the benefit of students, following Galen's own example in his writings on anatomy, the pulse, venesection and general therapeutics.[38]

Another solution to this problem, first formulated in Late Antiquity, perhaps in Alexandria, and destined to play a crucial role in the future development of medicine, was the selection of a small number of Galen's writings for special comment. A similar procedure had already been adopted by the Hippocratics in teaching the Hippocratic Corpus, and Galen himself on more than one occasion had specified which of his own treatises he thought most important as well as the manner in which they were to be read.[39] But the Galenic syllabus as it existed in sixth-century Alexandria was more effective as pedagogy, surviving with slight modification for centuries. Although it was later called 'The Sixteen Books', it consisted of twenty-four treatises, some being regarded as constituents of larger works.[40] They were read in a specific order and were further explicated by means of lectures and commentaries. They began with first principles, as laid down in *On Sects for Beginners* (*SI*) and the *Art of Medicine* (*Ars Med.*). There followed brief guides to taking the pulse and therapeutics, before the student embarked on more extensive and advanced treatises. In modern terms, he was instructed in anatomy, physiology, pathology and therapeutics, ending possibly with dietetics and hygiene.[41] Although the student was encouraged to read other Galenic treatises, this syllabus itself provided an overall view of Galenic medicine that was enough for most purposes. It had the rare virtue of being both comprehensive and succinct. All that one might need to know could be found here, at least in outline.

The effectiveness of this syllabus can be judged by its remarkable longevity and geographical spread. By 550 it had been translated into Syriac by Sergius of Resaena, and lectures on it were being delivered in Latin at Ravenna, the centre of Byzantine administration in N. Italy.[42] By the tenth century it had been translated into Arabic, to become the basis for medical education throughout the Muslim world, including among the Christians and Jews. It was over time accompanied by the whole paraphernalia of education – certificates of attendance at lectures, examinations and aids to study, including, by 600 at the latest, abridgements for students, the so-called Alexandrian summaries.[43]

Its significance cannot be over-estimated. In the first place, it provided a definition of medicine in terms of books that required to be studied rather than of practices and techniques that needed to be mastered. From now on, one can talk of a division into 'formal' and 'informal', 'high' and 'low' medicine depending on academic book-learning. Increasingly, those in possession of this learning tried to restrict the appellation of doctor, or even the right to practice, to those like themselves who had read these books. Secondly, it gave added importance to an understanding of the basic theories behind medicine. Galen's insistence on the need for a doctor to understand philosophy came to be interpreted as a demand for a preparatory training in logic, as well as for a greater theoretical content in medical education. It is thus not surprising, or uncommon, to find in fifth- and sixth-century Alexandria the same man commenting on Aristotle as easily as on Hippocrates. Stephanus of Athens (ca. 550–630), for example, lectured on at least three works by Hippocrates and Galen and four by Aristotle, as well as writing on theology and astronomy.[44]

By 600 at the latest, Galen's ideas had turned into Galenism, one individual's opinions into an intellectual system that drove all before it. The Erasistrateans, Pneumatists, Empiricists and Methodists, familiar in Galen's own day, had disappeared before the early sixth century, and, save for the Methodists, perhaps long before then. The lively and wide-ranging medical debates of the Early Roman Empire were replaced by discussions about the proper interpretation of this or that passage in Galen. Galenism had triumphed – arguably to the detriment of Galen. His empiricism, his observational genius and his willingness to think on his feet found little place in Galenism, for its central texts were those that emphasized his conclusions rather than the means by which he had reached them. Anatomical dissection for the purposes of investigation, so much stressed by Galen, seems to have vanished almost entirely, although both the Byzantines and the Arabs were extremely proficient in surgery. A passing reference to the dissection of a foreign captive, an occasional new observation, and Ibn an-Nafis' conjecture of the circulation of the blood can hardly stand comparison with Galen's regular programme of anatomical research.[45] By contrast, Galen's ingenious suggestion that the properties of herbs might be correlated on a system of grades of intensity proved a stimulus to both observational and theoretical work on medical botany, particularly in the Muslim world.[46] Scholars like al-Biruni (973–1051) and Ibn al-Baitar (d. 1248) searched for plants from Spain to India, completing and extending what Galen had set out to do.[47]

But, increasingly, doctors sought to show their own mastery of logic and medicine by producing their own syntheses of Galen. At times, through bringing together passages drawn from the whole Galenic Corpus, they created an impression very different from that originally intended by Galen. One such conflation became a leading motif in later Galenist therapeutics: a passing sentence on the factors that altered the pulse was combined with a section from a commentary explaining Hippocrates' view of the determinants of health (diet, environment, exertion, sleep, excretions and mental activity) to form a programmatic statement of the aims of the whole art of medicine. From now on, Galenists generally organized their diagnoses – and, particularly, their treatments – at the bedside and in their writings, to take account of these 'six non-naturals', a technical term also produced by conflating several diverse Galenic discussions.[48]

Similar novelties emerged from a re-examination of passages where Galen appeared to contradict himself or to have failed to work out fully the implications of his statements. For example, although Galen had strongly believed in a Platonic tripartition based on the brain, heart and liver, each with its own system of vessels, he had not developed fully the parallelism between them. In particular, while he spoke frequently of a psychic *pneuma* produced in the brain, his references to a similar spirit generated in the heart are much fewer, and those to a spirit made in the liver almost non-existent.[49] At best this was a hypothesis, and it is not mentioned in Galen's own summary of his ideas, *On His Own Opinions*. But, particularly in later works like the *Canon* of Ibn Sina, a brilliant summary and logical restructuring of Galenic medicine, loose ends left by Galen were firmly tied: Galenism believed in a tripartite system of vessels in which each system paralleled the other two.[50] As with law and theology, there was agreement that the application of logic and learning to difficult or contradictory statements in medicine's base texts would lead to a reconciliation of any discrepancies.[51] Given the importance ascribed by Galenism to logic and learning, it is no surprise that it easily found a place in the European universities of the Late Middle Ages, and that medicine became one of the advanced subjects that were studied only after a first degree in arts, i.e. logic and philosophy.[52]

Its compatibility with the monotheism of the Christians, Muslims and Jews and with the predominant Aristotelianism that explained the natural world only added to its authority. Besides, the very fact of its longevity and of the survival and recovery of many patients treated according to Galenic principles reassured its adherents of its efficacy, even in the face of disastrous epidemics such as the Black Death and its subsequent recurrences.[53] While jokes and complaints about Galenic doctors were common at every period, there was rarely any sustained hostility to this formal medicine, save on the part of those who favoured religious healing exclusively. Debate centred more on the optimum degree of fidelity to Galen and Galenism. So, for example, the Greek doctor Alexander of Tralles, writing around 560, contrasted his own willingness to employ a variety of therapies with the reluctance of the book-bound, ineffective, and even murderous Galenist to depart from his master, even when commonsense demanded it. Alexander was no backwoodsman relying on a few books and herbal remedies, but a cosmopolitan Greek, the brother of both the emperor Justinian's legal adviser and the architect of Hagia Sophia, the greatest church of Byzantium. He had travelled widely, to North Africa, Italy and further West with the emperor's troops, and he had sought out remedies from peasants, *more galenico*, in Tuscany, Gaul, Spain and even Armenia. His knowledge of Galen is impressive, and he at times displays a similar spirit of inquiry, even if, as with his store of chants and charms, he claims to have been prevented from revealing all that he knows in his writings. How many others shared his independence and combativeness we cannot tell.[54]

There were others who argued that the fault lay more with Galenists than with Galen himself, and that the greater one's acquaintance with Galen's original writings, even if in translation, the better one's understanding of health and illness. The Egyptian doctor, Ibn Ridwan (998–1061/1068), who championed this point of view in his debate with the Syrian Ibn Butlan (d. 1066), is often characterized as a book-bound pedant (an opinion also held by his wife).[55] But his other writings show him to have been an acute observer and a vigorous critic of shoddy thinking, and his claims for Galen do point to a remarkable feature of Galen's influence.[56] Whether in the Muslim world or in Latin Europe, individual scholars who were exposed to some of Galen's original thoughts were often led to emulate him in their practices or in the theories that they promoted. Hunain's work on ophthalmology and the experiments on animals by al-Razi, for example, can easily be traced back to Galenic inspiration.

Of even greater significance was the arrival of Galenist 'physic' in Western Europe in the eleventh century, even if at first largely in an arabised form.[57] The increasing availability of translations of Galen from the middle of the thirteenth century, whether made from the Arabic or, increasingly, from the Greek, also directly influenced developments in university medicine. What Luis García Ballester has called the 'new Galen' challenged scholars in Spain and, particularly, at Montpellier to rethink their principles of diagnosis and therapy.[58] In Italy, many of the innovations introduced by Taddeo Alderotti and his pupils in the early fourteenth century can be similarly linked to the arrival of new translations.[59] The introduction of a formal dissection into university teaching by Mondino in Bologna around 1315 derives its inspiration in part from the new availability of Galenic anatomical writings, even if in a truncated form.[60] But there were limits to the effectiveness of Galen. Very few of the fifty-eight versions of Galen's works made in the first half of the fourteenth century by the brilliant translator, the Southern Italian Niccolò da Reggio, were widely copied, still less read, except by those who sought a 'tutto Galeno'.[61] Their impact on learned physicians was small, largely because they dealt with topics that were on the periphery of medical practice. The report that a volume of Niccolò's translations lay for decades rotting and neglected on top of a German cupboard warns against assuming that medieval doctors were always eager to read whatever their great predecessor from Pergamum had written.[62] Indeed, by 1450, his ideas had become so firmly embedded in modern medicine and so familiar, it seemed, to all practitioners that recourse to his original writings, with a few exceptions, was considered unnecessary or irrelevant for most purposes. After all, since the book in which he had himself laid down what all medical students needed to know, *Art of Medicine*, formed part of the *Articella*, the most popular medieval selection of basic medical texts, anyone who had studied medicine at university (and many who had not) had received a thorough grounding in the basic principles of Galen's own medicine.[63] If one had one's *Articella*, wrote one German physician to his student son, one had no need to bring in further books into the lecture room, for modern medicine was simply an extension of the older ideas contained therein.[64] Wolfgang Reichart was giving this advice in 1524, and looking back to his own student days in Italy. But by now new developments were taking place that were to lead to a very different Galenism.

The renaissance of Classical Antiquity in the fourteenth and fifteenth centuries, a renewed emphasis on the cultural and intellectual values of ancient authors and a corresponding reaction against medieval learning, had at first little impact on medicine.[65] The rediscovery of Celsus' *De Medicina* at Siena in 1426 provided a stylistic model for humanist medicine, and those who favoured the ancients could always use the medical books of Pliny's *Natural History* as a basis for their writings or lectures.[66] But this was Latin medicine, and until the 1450s Greek medical manuscripts were few and far between, even if there had been a large public eager and able to read them. The arrival of Byzantine exiles in Northern Italy, such as John Argyropoulos or Theodore Gaza, and the deliberate attempts by collectors, notably the Medici, Bessarion and, on a smaller scale, Giorgio Valla, to obtain a complete library of Greek medical and scientific manuscripts improved the accessibility of Galenic medicine – at least in theory. The spread of Greek in schools also widened the base of those who might take an interest in Galen.[67] By 1490, particularly in Northern Italy, humanists such as Politian in Florence or Urceus Codrus in Bologna, members of the Greek community in Venice and doctors, such as Alessandro Benedetti, who had spent some time in one of the Venetian colonies in the Aegean or in the former Byzantine world, were reading manuscripts of Galen and exchanging ideas and opinions about him.[68]

The central figure in this Galenic revival was Niccolò Leoniceno (1428–1524), who taught medicine, mathematics and philosophy at the University of Ferrara, a relatively recent creation that was at the very forefront of the new humanism.[69] Leoniceno taught also at Bologna, and had very close links with the Greek community in Venice and, not least, with Aldus Manutius and his circle there. A medical graduate of Padua, he was employed at the court of Ferrara as both a doctor and a translator of Greek texts, especially on history and moral themes. Above all, he succeeded in acquiring an amazing library of Greek medical and scientific manuscripts, more extensive than any other known before or since, and distinguished not only by its sheer size but also by the rarity of its contents.[70] The appearance in print in 1492 of his clarion call for Greek medicine, *De Plinii et plurimum aliorum Erroribus in Medicina*, marks a major turning-point in the history of Galen and Galenism.[71] It is true that our general ignorance of the first sixty years of his life may render this intervention even more striking than it appeared to contemporaries, but that was dramatic enough. Within a few pages, Leoniceno proved beyond any doubt that the Latin medical writings on which doctors had relied for centuries were filled with a variety of errors. Herbs were misrepresented or wrongly identified because, in the process of translation, scribes or scholars had wrongly copied, or scholars misunderstood, what they had read in their exemplars. Phantom diseases were created as a result of different Latin transcriptions of Arabic terms. This was not just the fault of the Arabs or their medieval interpreters for, in Leoniceno's eyes, the Roman Pliny was even more culpable in his reading of Dioscorides. Thus it was not enough to revert to Roman Antiquity to emend the errors of the Middle Ages: what was needed was a return to the Greeks.[72] In subsequent publications, Leoniceno continued his assault on medieval misunderstandings. He denounced medieval commentators who had discussed at great length the opening words of Galen's *Art of Medicine* in terms of competing methods of logic. Galen, he argued, was not talking about epistemology, but about three possible methods of academic exposition.[73] Furthermore, if one looked closely in the ancient Greek texts, one would find precedents, explanations and cures for many of the apparently new diseases, such as the French disease, that were now ravaging Europe.[74] A return to the Greek would thus purify medicine of error, while introducing new (or neglected) information for the modern doctor.

Leoniceno's arguments began a very vigorous debate that centred largely on Pliny's botanical information. Some of his opponents, such as Ermolao Barbaro, pointed out that many of Pliny's errors were not his, but the result of miscopying over the centuries; others, like Collenuccio, suggested that Leoniceno himself was often wrong in his identifications of plants and that philology by itself was not enough; but most were convinced by Leoniceno that it was

Galen and, above all, Dioscorides who provided the most accurate information on medical botany.[75] But there was a serious difficulty if Leoniceno's demands were to be generally met. It was not that most Italian physicians were unsympathetic to ancient medicine – after all, there had appeared almost simultaneously with Leoniceno's book the first printing of the collected works of Galen in Latin translation, brought together, claimed the publisher, after a diligent search through the libraries of the schools of Italy.[76] But any hopes they might have had of following Leoniceno foundered on the inaccessibility of the Greek originals and on the lack of any new translations based upon them.

The Aldine Press was the first to take up the challenge to print an ancient medical text in Greek with its edition of Dioscorides in 1499, and set in train plans for an edition of Galen. Leoniceno, who had already loaned Aldus at least one of his manuscripts, was known to be willing to sell some of his manuscripts, and copies were made of at least one other manuscript, from Florence.[77] The pseudo-Galenic *History of Philosophy* appeared in 1497–8 as part of the Aldine Aristotle, copied from a Florentine manuscript, but it was not Aldus but the rival firm of Callierges and Vlastos who published the first-ever printed text of a genuinely Galenic work, based on one of Leoniceno's manuscripts.[78] Their large and elegant folio, published at Venice in 1500, contained the *On the Therapeutic Method (MM)* and the smaller *Therapeutics to Glaucon (MMG)* in Greek alone. It was a commercial disaster. Although Callierges and Vlastos had certainly planned further volumes, none appeared, and they themselves ceased to publish for almost a decade. At the very least, it served as a warning of the hazards involved in printing so massive an author.[79]

For the moment, then, the new Hellenizers in medicine pursued other tacks. Both Alessandro Benedetti (1452–1512) and Giorgio Valla (1447–1500) responded to Leoniceno's challenge to remedy the confusion of medical terminology by publishing their own lists of anatomical terms, carefully collating what Galen had to say with standard medieval texts such as Mondino's *Anatomy*.[80] Benedetti's book bore as part of its title a Greek term, *Anatomice*, which clearly indicated his preferences in the ongoing debate.[81] Others, such as Giovanni Manardi, applied the same methodology to their studies of disease, attempting at one and the same time to reduce confusion and to restore a purer Greek-based Latin vocabulary to medicine.[82] The new hopes for medicine can be seen on the title page of Symphorien Champier's medico-philosophical treatise of 1516, which proclaimed the concord (*symphonia*) of Hippocrates, Plato, Aristotle and Galen.[83] The accompanying woodcut names only Galen, who is depicted clearly as the leader in this academic string quartet.

But even those who might be sympathetic to their cause grew irritated at the failure of the new Galenists to substantiate their claims. The Salzburg physician Leonhard Schmaus, as late as 1519, called for more Latin translations of these allegedly revolutionary works of the Greeks so that those without access to the Greek could judge for themselves. Schmaus had a point.[84] The early humanist translations from the Greek merely replaced the standard medieval versions in the *Articella*. They were more precise, but their overall contribution in terms of novelty was small. Indeed, of the translators active before 1525 only the Englishman Thomas Linacre, using manuscripts he had brought back from his long stay in Italy, and the French royal physician Guillaume Cop, translated into Latin works that were relatively unfamiliar.[85]

This situation changed dramatically in 1525–6, with the publication by the Aldine Press of a (nearly) complete Galen in Greek, followed in 1526 by a Hippocrates. Why this project had to wait for over a quarter of a century before being completed in an unseemly rush is unclear.[86] Certainly there was now a bigger market for a Greek publication than in 1500, and it now extended beyond Northern Italy. Indeed, the editorial team collected by Professor Opizzoni comprised three Englishmen, Thomas Lupset, Edward Rose and John Clement, the talented protégé of Sir Thomas More, and a German, Georg Agricola, later more famous for his work on mining and mineralogy.[87] A fortunate period of peace also meant that in Venice there was in 1525 a large supply of metal that might otherwise have been used in the Arsenal to make cannon but could be bought up and used for the type. Even if Bessarion's manuscripts in the Marciana were not yet fully accessible, there were other collections in the city and elsewhere that were drawn upon, as well as those acquired decades earlier by Aldus himself.[88]

Reactions to the publication of the Aldine Galen were lukewarm. It was a hasty and at times careless production – one passage was printed with a large gap, after a candle had been allowed to burn a hole in the manuscript that was being copied.[89] It was filled with errors of all kinds – Agricola was later reported to have filled several volumes with his own corrections – but it did make Galen available in Greek at last.[90] Although the editors may not have known it, they used some good manuscripts (although not the best) for their edition, and although subsequent editors, notably the Basle editors of 1538 and René Chartier a century later, made many corrections, and added occasional new discoveries, the Aldine remained the basis of all Galenic editing down to the mid-nineteenth century.[91] Even today, many Galenic works are available only in Kühn's slapdash edition of 1821–33, which adds very little, save error, to Chartier and which is, in many ways, merely a reprint of the Aldine.[92]

But the significance of the Aldine Galen lay less in its text than in the opportunity it now gave to translators around Europe to turn into Latin works previously unknown or neglected. Erasmus, one of the stiffest of critics of its Greek, was also alert to the main chance, publishing within a matter of months a Latin version of treatises of wider cultural interest, the *Exhortation to the Arts* (*Protr.*), *On the best Method of Teaching* (*Opt.Doct.*) and *The Best Doctor is also a Philosopher* (*Opt.Med.*).[93] He was followed by a whole phalanx of translators, from Spain to Poland, turning out versions in large numbers. The figures are impressive: between 1500 and 1525, an average of two or three editions was published a year, never exceeding seven in any one year. Between 1526 and 1560 the number jumps to an average of just over twelve, before sinking back to three for the rest of the century. Seventeen were published in 1528, twenty-one in both 1538 and 1547 and thirty-one in 1549.[94] Purified of medieval error, restored in part to light after centuries of oblivion, the new Galen offered new springs of learning to those who were prejudiced in favour of Antiquity – who were not always physicians. Its Greekness also gave it a certain social cachet – only the wealthiest of surgeons had studied Greek, and even fewer barbers and apothecaries – and it allowed the physician to reassert his claim to greater learning and to superiority over all other purveyors of healing. This humanist Galen was introduced wholesale into new universities such as Jena, and into older ones, such as Freiburg or Ingolstadt, when they updated their curricula.[95] Whether the statutes of the London College of Physicians imposing a tough examination in Galen and Hippocrates go back to its founder, Linacre, in 1518 or were brought in by a later president, Edward Wotton around 1542, or John Caius some twenty years later, is a moot point.[96] But the date is of less significance than the College's strongly Galenist tone, which lasted well into the eighteenth century and which was typical of the learned medical colleges around Europe.

The Aldine edition and the subsequent translations reintroduced works of Galen that had been unknown or neglected for centuries. For the first time it was possible, with the aid of treatises such as *On the Doctrines of Hippocrates and Plato*, to see clearly the ways in which Galen's philosophy and medicine interacted. Galen's dietetics, his pharmacology and his ideas on venesection or fevers were given a new precision. His commentaries on Hippocrates not only established further the authority of the Father of Medicine, but also helped to create a new model for the Renaissance physician.[97] Galen's injunctions and example changed learned preconceptions as to what the true doctor should do and how he should behave. Uroscopic diagnosis and medical astrology, which had been the badge of the learned physician in the fifteenth century, were by 1600 firmly associated with quackery, having been replaced by a full physical diagnosis and climatology.[98] The personal stories scattered throughout the Galenic Corpus, and particularly in *On Prognosis (Praen.)* and *On My Own Books*, became the basis for new biographies of Galen and for new histories of medicine. Catholics and Protestants disputed the extent and nature of Galen's Christian beliefs, distributing the events of his life according to the way in which they displayed the cardinal virtues, to the surprise of modern scholars unaccustomed to viewing Galen as an exemplum of charity and self-restraint.[99]

Supporters of Galen, like the young men who in the 1540s founded a 'Nova Academia Galenica' in Florence, emphasized two major advances: Galen's anatomy and his insistence on proper method.[100] The availability of Greek and of more accurate (or simply more stylish) versions had given greater precision to the details of many medical doctrines, e.g. on venesection. They had also revealed Galen's constant reiteration of the need to employ both logic and experience, both book-learning and practical skills, in a *method* of healing. To Galenists like the Englishman John Caius (1510–73), the German Crato von Crafftheim (1519–85), the Dutchman Pieter van Foreest (1522–97), or the Spaniard Luis Mercado (1520–86), Galen had not only laid down the general guidelines for proper medical practice, but had given in his voluminous writings innumerable indications of the proper method to be followed in specific cases. Both Caius and Crato had studied at Padua with Giambattista da Monte (1498–1551), who was the most influential spokesman for the true Galenic method of healing.[101] This demanded an enormous spread of learning in order to carry out a differential diagnosis that paid attention to all aspects of the individual patient. Da Monte, perhaps following earlier Paduan precedent, linked the theoretical and the practical in his teaching by going directly from the lecture room to visit the sick. Topics discussed in a lecture would then be further expounded at the bedside of a patient, where colleagues and students might be asked to comment on the specific features of the case. Galenic method, as taught in Padua, was thus an all-embracing system of medical thought that took into consideration all aspects of the individual patient, from environment to therapeutics.[102] Its defects were also clear – it was far from easy to reach a judgment swiftly among so many variables or when relevant passages had to be recalled, often from memory, from across the Galenic Corpus. (The first comprehensive index of topics, still valuable today, was that produced by Antonio Musa Brasavola in 1551 as part of the second Giuntine edition.)[103] Da Monte's own lectures neatly show the difficulty, for in commenting on the Galenic text he rarely managed to say all that he wanted to say, and both the course as a whole and individual lectures often end with apologies for failure to deal with everything in the set text.

But it was 'anatomy' more than 'method' that became the shibboleth of the Renaissance Galenism. The Latin Middle Ages had known relatively little about Galen's own anatomical writings, save for a far from accurate abridgement of *On the Utility of the Parts* (*UP*), *De Iuvamento Membrorum*, and they were in no position to appreciate the wider role of anatomy in Galen's thought. Neither the Byzantines nor the Arabs had practised dissection systematically. The introduction of a formal anatomy into university teaching by Mondino at Bologna around 1315, inspired by his acquaintance with the 'new Galen', marked an important step by introducing the visual evidence of a corpse into medical education. But the highly ritualized nature of this event, performed once a year, ensured that it was far more a visual demonstration of the truths already described in writing than an incitement to actual dissection by a physician. As carried out at the end of the fifteenth century, the cutting was done by a surgeon, while the duty of the professor of medicine was to explain to his students and to put into a wider context what might be visible in the body. Such university dissections, however, were far from common. Few universities outside Italy had an annual anatomy before 1500, and even where one was demanded by the statutes, local pressures and problems might prevent a dissection from taking place for years.[104]

Even before 1525 those who had access to Greek manuscripts were proclaiming the virtues of the new Galenic anatomy. Benedetti and Giorgio Valla, as has already been noted, produced their own syntheses of Greek anatomy, employing a more precise and a more consistent technical vocabulary. Medical teachers such as Matteo Corti (1475–1544), the best-paid of all Italian medical professors, were by 1520 demanding a return to Galenic anatomy.[105] The publication of the Aldine edition made clear why the new Galenists were so enthusiastic about anatomy. For the first time for centuries, physicians could read the first half of Galen's major manual of dissection *On Anatomical Procedures* (*AA*) (and rumours persisted that the missing books still survived somewhere). From *On the Utility of the Parts* and *On the Doctrines of Hippocrates and Plato*, they could gain not only medical information but a wider understanding of the contribution that could be made by dissection to wider, philosophical problems. They could also read Galen's introductory treatises on the anatomy of veins, arteries and nerves (and, from 1535, that on bones).[106] Above all, they saw a new side to Galen – the experimentalist, the dissector, for ever encouraging others to see for themselves and to practise dissection as regularly as he had done. To young physicians, members of a guild that had previously carefully distinguished their work from that of 'manual operators', this new material was exciting, if not revolutionary. Anatomy now stood at the very centre of the new medical curriculum.

Universities, like Oxford and Cambridge, where dissections had been unknown, now instituted anatomical teaching; where it had been sporadic, it was now carried out on a regular basis.[107] John Caius in the statutes of his refounded Cambridge College demanded a regular dissection for the medical students of the College (in addition to those provided by the University).[108] At Louvain, student pressure for the introduction of the new anatomy into the curriculum led to the dismissal of two senior professors who held firmly to an older Galenism.[109] At Protestant Wittenberg, Philip Melanchthon required all students, whatever their Faculty, to become acquainted with anatomy through attending lectures on Aristotle's *On the Soul*, whereby they would learn the majestic handiwork of the creator and the constraints of the earthly body that, temporarily, housed the human soul.[110] The same message could be found in a Catholic university like Ingolstadt just as much as in a Protestant one like Jena.[111]

Anatomy became fashionable – crowds flocked to see formal dissections, wherever they were held. In Paris in the late 1530s, Jacobus Sylvius (1478–1555) illustrated his lectures at the Collège de Tréguier on Galen's *On the Utility of the Parts* with specimens of animals he had recently dissected. The blood and smell did not deter his eager audience, who came from all over Europe and was not confined to medical students.[112] Old projects were revived. A Latin version of *Anatomical Procedures* prepared around 1500 by the Greek exile Demetrius Chalcondylas (ca. 1424–1511) was revised and published in 1529 by the professor of surgery at Bologna, Berengario da Carpi, although it was never to achieve the same impact as the version of Guinther von Andernach (1505–74) that appeared at Paris only two years later.[113] Emblematic is the frontispiece to the 1530 Paris reprint of Linacre's translation of the *Method of Healing* (*MM*), which displays a striking anatomical scene of Galen cutting up a human figure in front of an eager audience – even though the work itself has little to do with actual dissection.[114]

Galenic anatomy had apparently triumphed. The leading exponents of anatomy in Europe in the 1530s, like Sylvius and Matteo Corti at Bologna, were fervid Galenists, convinced that Galenic anatomy must underlie the effective practice of medicine. In short student guides to anatomy, Sylvius, Guinther, and another young Parisian teacher, Andreas Laguna (1499–1559), expounded Galenic methods and Galenic conclusions. Even if they themselves did not carry out the actual cutting, either because their manual dexterity was weak or because they believed that the teacher should concentrate on putting the discoveries of anatomy into a wider context, they stressed the need for everyone to have a detailed understanding of the human body.[115]

Yet following Galen's injunctions to dissect personally swiftly raised an unexpected problem. Not everything that Galen had said appeared to be confirmed by the evidence of observation. The so-called pre-Vesalian anatomists drew attention to anomalies they had discovered, although they found ways of explaining them and excusing Galen. It was well known, for instance, that Galen had himself carried out many of his dissections on animals, and the reason for the anomaly might lie with the corpse, not with the dissector.[116] It was the achievement of Andreas Vesalius (1514–64) to have seen that these anomalies were neither isolated nor accidental but the result of Galen's general reliance on animal, not human corpses.

Vesalius had been given a humanist education at Louvain before studying medicine in Paris, where he had already made a name for himself as an expert dissector.[117] In 1538 he was invited to take up the chair of surgery at Padua, the rival of Bologna as the greatest medical school in Europe. He was immediately involved in dissection and in matters Galenical, being called upon by Da Monte to revise the Latin translations of the anatomical works for the 1541–2 Giuntine edition of the *Opera Omnia*. In this, his methodology was typically Galenic, for he collated the earlier translations against Greek manuscripts supplied to him by Antonio Gadaldino.[118] Although when he began his Paduan teaching, Vesalius still accepted that Galen was largely working with human corpses, he became more and more convinced that this was not so. In a bitter argument with Corti at Bologna in 1540 he defended vigorously the evidence of human dissection against what Galen had himself said, and by 1542 at the very latest, when he began his great treatise on human anatomy, *De humani Corporis Fabrica*, his mind was made up.[119] Galen, he asserted over and over again, had got it wrong because he had never dissected a human corpse. In a neat appeal to ancient authority, he claimed in his preface to be reverting to a (lost) Alexandrian anatomy, that of Herophilus and Erasistratus, both famed for dissecting condemned criminals.[120]

The appearance of the *Fabrica* in 1543 produced very different reactions among Galenists. Some, like Gemusaeus, one of the editors of the 1538 Basle Galen, immediately acknowledged it as a masterpiece in every way.[121] Melanchthon, who swiftly read his own copy from cover to cover, eagerly adopted its conclusions for the second edition of his treatise *De Anima*. He accepted that Vesalius was working within the Galenic tradition, carrying out in practice a methodology that Galen himself had been able to suggest only in theory.[122] It was a view Melanchthon shared with other Galenists, like the physician–botanist Matthioli, who included Vesalius in his list of distinguished Galenic scholars of the age, alongside his teacher Sylvius.[123]

But many other Galenists were scandalized at what they saw as impiety towards their master, not least when large parts of the later books of the *Fabrica* were taken over directly from Galen's own writings – and without acknowledgment.[124] Besides, everyone knew that Galen had dissected animals, and had warned against relying utterly on the results of animal dissection in any description of the human body. But to accuse Galen of never seeing a human body and of deliberate misrepresentation was to go far beyond what the evidence warranted. Vesalius had simply swept aside all the instances where Galen specifically referred to an examination of the human body. His opponents accused Vesalius of ignorance and mistranslation: many of Galen's alleged errors were nothing more than misunderstandings by Vesalius.[125] The German translator and professor of medicine Janus Cornarius removed with ferocious strokes of the pen all reference to Vesalius' revised translations from his copy of the Latin Galen he was revising for the Basle publishers Froben and Episcopius.[126] Others argued that the fault lay further back, with ignorant copyists, and that a better Greek text, produced after a more careful search for manuscripts, would eliminate many of the errors signalled by Vesalius. John Caius filled the margins of his books with variant readings and with notes directed at the shortcomings of 'Wesalius'.[127] Others wondered whether it was not the human body that had changed over the centuries. After all, breeders of dogs were well aware that a hound could, over the generations, be bred with different characteristics: why should not the same be true of human breeding?[128]

Most of these objections to Vesalian anatomy were entirely valid. Vesalius had mistranslated and misunderstood Galen; he had often failed to give him credit for what he had seen; he had himself relied heavily upon Galen even as he protested against his errors; and Galen was very far from being a credulous believer in an easy transfer of animal data to humans. Galen had, on many occasions, seen inside a human body, and had criticized others for failing to make use of whatever opportunities chance had placed in their way.[129] But these objections to Vesalius did not alter the major point at issue: Galenic anatomy was animal anatomy, and, although Galen had had considerable experience of the body, not least as a surgeon to the gladiators, he had never dissected a human body as systematically as he had pigs and monkeys. Galenic anatomists continued to call down anathemas on Vesalius, but they were a fast diminishing minority, and by 1600 Galenic anatomy in its pure, pre-Vesalian form, was confined to the fringes of academia.[130]

A second and equally definitive assault on Galen represents the culmination of a long debate between Aristotelian believers in a unified soul, who predominated in the faculties of Arts and Theology, and the Galenist physicians who favoured tripartition. Strategies had long been devised on both sides to accommodate both views within an overall Christian framework; e.g. it was argued that the three systems of the body did not represent three parts of the soul, but three instruments by which the faculties of the soul controlled the body.[131] The publication in 1628 of William Harvey's anatomical demonstration of the circulation of the blood resolved the argument by combining Aristotelian notions of circularity and unity with Galenic experimentalism. Following his Paduan teacher, Fabricius of Aquapendente (1533–1619), Harvey (1578–1657) experimented with careful dissections of animals and man to show that Galen's venous and arterial systems formed a continuum (although visual proof of the existence of the linking capillaries had to wait until 1661). His arguments drew on both Aristotelian and Galenic precedents to establish a conclusion that, within a generation or so, effectively ended any appeal to Galen's anatomy and physiology.[132]

What it did not do was to put an end to Galenic medicine. Indeed, Galenic therapeutics, notably bloodletting and drugs, could be explained even better by Harveian than by Galenic physiology.[133] Harvey himself saw no reason whatsoever to change his methods of practice, even if, as his friend John Aubrey admitted, his therapeutic Galenism and his unwillingness to adopt new drugs and treatments, were as likely to harm his patients as to cure them.[134] But the chemical pharmacopoeia of the Paracelsians and, later, the mechanistic explanations of the iatromechanists, the advent of new drugs from America and the Indies, all combined to reduce Galenic influence still further. Galenism became the symbol of useless therapeutic conservatism, as expensive as it was ineffective, the subject of satire on stage and in literature.

Not that Galen entirely disappeared from medical schools. The vocabulary of medicine remained firmly Galenical, even if what was understood by such terms as 'temperament' and 'constitution' altered.[135] Medical semiotics long continued to follow Galen's ideas, and his views on hygiene, public health and general medicine were not neglected. Hippocrates was still the dominant figure of authority from the past, even if the extent to which that Hippocrates still represented Galen's vision of medicine remained undetected. At the end of the eighteenth century, there may even have been a return to Galen among the so-called eclectics, who sought within his many pages for therapies with a proven record of efficacy. That was one of the reasons why between 1821 and 1833 K. G. Kühn (1754–1840), professor of medicine at the most flourishing medical school in Germany, brought out his edition of Galen in twenty-two stubby volumes, almost 20,000 pages in length. Each page contained the Greek text and a Latin translation (sometimes a more accurate reflection of Galen's original than the Greek) for the benefit of those with little or no Greek. The main purpose of this now standard edition was medical, not philological: to provide a repository of potentially valuable therapies from the past, made accessible through the aid of a modified version of Brasavola's index.[136]

But within little more than a decade, even this limited aim was abandoned. New developments in medicine, the growth of clinical medicine, new discoveries in physiology, as well as a growing industrialization which left less space for the Galenic physician able to spend time investigating the individuality of the patient; all these combined to remove Galen and Galenic medicine from the purview of the average medical practitioner. Galen was now a classical text, to be interpreted by classical philologists or antiquarian doctors.[137]

The thirty years between 1884, when a Galenic text was first published in the Teubner series, and 1914, saw a massive renewal of interest in editing Galen, at least in Germany. From Bonn to Erlangen, from Greifswald to Ansbach, in *Festreden*, *Schulprogrämme* and dissertations, doctorands, school masters and even the occasional professor set their hand to editing an *opusculum* of Galen.[138] In 1901, prompted by the Dane J. L. Heiberg, the *Corpus Medicorum* was set up, under the auspices of the International Union of Academies, but with the direction firmly under the control of the Berlin Professors Hermann Diels and Ulrich von Wilamowitz-Moellendorff.[139] The first volume of the *CMG* Galen appeared in 1914, and a second, in part edited by Diels himself, soon followed.[140] The concern of these German editors was entirely philological, and their texts, and occasional commentaries, were left free of any medical matters. German physicians produced little to rival the French studies of Galenic physiology by Daremberg.[141] The important publication of the lost books of *On Anatomical Procedures*, in Arabic with German translation, by Max Simon in 1906, aroused very little interest among classicists, and little more among medics.[142] Galen was hardly worth studying as a doctor, for his medical ideas were long outmoded, and not much more as an ancient personality. Although Johannes Ilberg (1860–1930) in the 1880s and 1890s had effectively established the main outlines of the chronology of Galen's writings and in 1909 had published an extremely valuable essay on Galen's life in a journal aimed primarily at Gymnasium teachers, Wilamowitz-Moellendorf's own verdict on Galen as 'the great windbag' was damning.[143] He was to be edited because he wrote in Greek, and to be studied less for himself than as a source for something more valuable – the ideas of the Pre-Socratic philosophers, or of the elusive Stoic Posidonius. The decision to begin the *Corpus Medicorum* with Galen's commentaries on Hippocrates was no compliment to Galen himself. It was taken because it was the essential first stage in the editing of the far more valuable Hippocratic Corpus, and because it was thought (erroneously) that such an edition could be prepared without recourse to any Arabic intermediaries.[144]

The First World War, inflation and the decline of old-style classical philology put an end to this resurgence of German interest in editing Galen (it had never been strong elsewhere). Occasional volumes continued to appear in the *CMG* series in the 1920s and 1930s, most notably Wenkebach and Pfaff's edition of the commentaries on *On Hippocrates' Epidemics* (*Hipp.Epid.*), which introduced much new material in German translation from the Arabic.[145] The young men on whom Diels and Wilamowitz had pinned their hopes for the future of ancient medicine turned their attention to other things, and of the next generation of German classicists only Karl Deichgräber continued a strong interest in Galen, supervising several dissertations on ancient medicine during his last years in Göttingen.[146] In exile from the Nazis, Ludwig Edelstein (1902–65) and particularly Owsei Temkin (1902–2002) ensured that the German tradition of studies in ancient medicine was continued across the Atlantic in Baltimore, but they had few direct pupils.[147] An occasional translation or an article by an elderly physician was all that appeared from

Britain. After the Second World War, interest among Classicists or medics diminished further. The *Corpus Medicorum* struggled on in the face of both political and financial difficulties, although from the 1960s onwards it expanded its remit of its editions to include a modern translation and a commentary alongside its revised texts.[148]

If the outlook for Galenic studies in the 1960s looked bleak, this was the darkness before a new dawn. In particular, discoveries of Galenic texts in Arabic translation had already begun to be published in increasing number, notably by Richard Walzer, and both Manfred Ullmann and Fuat Sezgin had embarked on their own ambitious projects to catalogue Arabic manuscripts of medicine, including many containing versions of Galen by Hunain and his school.[149] Although classicists have perhaps paid less attention than they should have done to this abundance of new material, it has provided them with a remarkable accession of new information on Galen, ranging in length from a few lines to hundreds of pages. This flow of new treatises is also set to continue for a few years to come.

But the main impulse for a revival of Galenic studies came first from among the students of ancient philosophy, particularly in Britain and Italy. As first Hellenistic and then Roman philosophers began to be studied seriously for themselves, and not as repositories of earlier material, the merits of Galen as a logician and as an independent thinker of stature began to be realized for almost the first time since the twelfth century. A similar switch of interest among ancient historians towards the history and culture of the Greek world of the Roman Empire also drew attention to the importance of Galen and Galen's information for the history of his own time. Feminism has been less significant, for Galen had far less to say about women and women's conditions than Soranus or the Hippocratics, and a proper investigation into Galen's ideas on gender had to wait until 2000.[150] A cynic might also argue that, given the relatively circumscribed range of topics available for research in Classics, it was also inevitable that, as in the 1890s, seekers after thesis novelty should light on Galen *faute de mieux*.

The first international Galen conference, held in Cambridge in 1979, can be taken to mark the transition from the older tradition of mainly philological scholarship to the modern interest in Galen as a physician, philosopher and man of letters, whose influence stretched across the centuries. It brought together many younger scholars, from

Europe and America, and provided a catalyst for many new explorations, whether of individual treatises or of major themes.[151] Since then there has been a veritable explosion in Galenic studies. The *Corpus Medicorum*, having survived communism and, so far, capitalism, has re-established a steady series of editions by scholars from the USA, Britain, Italy and Germany, and now faces a competitor in the French Budé series.[152] Major treatises newly recovered include Galen's *On Recognizing the Best Physician* (*Opt.Med.Cogn.*) and his medico-philosophical testament *On His Own Opinions*, as well as the large commentary on *Airs, Waters, and Places*.[153] A large volume (and part of one other) in the survey of Roman Imperial history in *Aufstieg und Niedergang der römischen Welt* (*ANRW*) has been devoted to various aspects of Galen's life and thought.[154] Indeed, the task of compiling a Galenic bibliography, relatively easy a generation ago, is now immense, even with the aid of computers, and even the most diligent researcher may easily overlook important material now being produced all over the world.[155] It is a far cry from the discredited and neglected Galen of the 1950s to the modern recognition of Galen as not just a source for the ideas of others but a major scholar, philosopher, physician and scientist in his own right. It remains open to question whether his inclusion in 1997 as one of the World's Classics or the imaginative reconstruction of his memoirs by a leading novelist constitutes the higher accolade.[156]

NOTES

1. Nor can it compete with the magisterial survey of Temkin (1973).
2. In the 1990s, I was even introduced to a Galenist astrologer from Torquay. For Yunani medicine, see Hamarneh (1997); Attewell (2007).
3. Nutton (2002a, 2002b).
4. Galen, *In Hipp.Epid. VI comm. VIII*: CMG V 10,2,2, 495,2–12. It was not mentioned by him in the sections on prognosis and therapeutics in his own catalogue of his writings, *On My Own Books* (*Lib.Prop.*) XIX 30–33, = SM 2, 109,4–111,8.
5. See Bergsträsser (1925, 1932). A useful translation/summary of the first document was provided by Meyerhof (1926), repr., with identical pagination, as ch. 1 of Meyerhof (1984).
6. See Strohmaier (1998); Rosenthal (1956).
7. Meyerhof (1929); not all these 'sayings' are authentic: cf. Strohmaier (2002, 113–20).

8. Zonta (1995).
9. C. Larrain has recently discovered scraps of Galen (and ps. Galen) in Byzantine theological miscellanies (Larrain, 1993); see also Larrain (1992) (but note the severe review of D. Nickel, 2002).
10. See Garofalo (1986, vii–xii); French and Lloyd (1978) collect surviving citations of the lost books.
11. Galen, *De Causis Continentibus*, ed. K. Kalbfleisch., Diss., Marburg (1904); re-edition, including also the earlier Arabic translation, by M. C. Lyons, *CMG* Suppl. Or. II (1969); *De Causis Procatarcticis*, ed. K. Bardong, *CMG* Suppl. II (1937); re-edition, with translation and commentary, by Hankinson (1998). For Niccolò, see Thorndike (1946); McVaugh (2006).
12. Boudon-Millot and Pietrobelli (2005); Nutton (1999).
13. Pesenti (1998, 2001). Pesenti is preparing another study of collections with a 'tutto Galeno', e.g. Dresden, Db 92–93; Paris, *Académie Nationale de Médecine* 51–7.
14. The printed index to Galen by Gippert (1997), is less useful than appears at first sight, for, based on TLG, it indexes each form of the word separately, and gives no references at all for words with more than a dozen occurrences. The (partial) indexes to *CMG* offer better guidance to those without easy access to TLG.
15. Koester (1998).
16. *On Affected Parts (Loc.Aff.)* VIII 224–5. The *Advice to an Epileptic Boy (Puer.Epil.)*, XI 357–78 (tr. Temkin, 1934) is avowedly a letter to a patient he has never seen. For the *Hiera* of Galen, see *On the Preservation of Health (San.Tu.)* VI 429, = 188,19–27 Koch (1915); *On the Composition of Drugs according to Places (Comp.Med.Loc.)* XIII 129.
17. Athenaeus, *Sophists at Dinner* 1,1e;26c-27d;3,115c-116a. In general, see Braund and Wilkins (2000, 476–502).
18. See Todd (1977); Sharples (1982); Nutton (1984a); Tieleman (1997); Fazzo (2002).
19. Eusebius, *Ecclesiastical History* 5,28,13–14, with Gero (1990); Strohmaier (2006).
20. Origen, *Philokalia* fr. 2,2; see also Grant (1983).
21. Nutton (1984a, p. 316); Riddle (1984). Although the evidence for the identification of this writer with the Gargilius in the *Augustan History* is arguably worthless (*pace* Riddle, 1984, 411), and although a date in the fifth century might seem more appropriate for North African acquaintance with the Galenic Corpus, the agreement of data from within the work with information on two inscriptions from Auzia, *CIL* 8,9047 and 20751, leads me to accept Riddle's dating.
22. Ullmann (1992).

23. Weisser (1989).
24. Regenbogen (1961, 125–7); an illustration of the murder of Galen, from the frontispiece to the Augsburg 1497 edition of *Die Cyben Weisen Meister* is given by Jurina (1985, 163).
25. Dioscorides, Vienna, med. gr. 1, fol. 3v., illustrated in Collins (2000, 41), with a good discussion of the Ms., 39–50.
26. See Jacquart (1988); Belloni (1984).
27. See Nandris (1970); Taylor (1980–1); Duichev (1988, 90–1, 118–19).
28. See Smith (1965); Pressouyre (1966).
29. See Delehaye (1909, 219); Bürgel (1967).
30. See Telfer (1955); Zonta (1995).
31. The first half of this manuscript was badly damaged by water in 1945, but all the miniatures were reproduced in black and white (and some in colour) in E. C. van Leersum and W. Martin, *Miniaturen der lateinischen Galenos-Handschrift der Kgl. Oeffentl. Bibliothek in Dresden*, Leiden, 1910. Seventeen of the miniatures in the second half are given in colour in Nutton (1984b).
32. Palladius, *Commentary on Epidemics VI*, II,157 Dietz.
33. Eobanus Hessus, *Bonae Salutatis conservandae Praecepta*, Paris, S. De Colines, 1533, fol. 21v.
34. Nicolò de Leonardis (?), fl. 1430, in the margin of Cesena, Biblioteca Malatestiana S.V,4, fol. 132va: for verbosity, see Temkin (1973, p. 67f.).
35. *Timarion*, p. 75 Romano.
36. For the legends of his books, see Rosenthal (1975, 35).
37. Johannes de Sancto Amando, *Concordanciae*, ed. J. Pagel, Berlin, Reimer, 1894; Petrus de Sancto Floro, *Concordanciae, ibid.*, xxiv–lii; see also Pagel (1896). The differences between the two books reflect differences in the amount of Galen available before and after the versions of Niccolò, see Jacquart (1995, pp. 172–83); McVaugh (2006).
38. A. de Laguna, *Epitome omnium Galeni operum*, ed. 1, Venice, H. Scotus, 1539, which went through at least five printings in the sixteenth century, and two more in the next; J. R. Coxe, *The Writings of Hippocrates and Galen*, Philadelphia, Lindsay and Blakiston, 1846.
39. See Smith (1979); Kudlien (1989). Galen's *On My Own Books (Lib.Prop.)* and *The Order of My Own Books (Ord.lib. prop.)* XIX 1–48, 49–61 = SM II,80–124 are translated into English by Singer (1997, pp. 3–29).
40. See Temkin (1932); Beccaria (1971); Iskandar (1976); Lieber (1981); Palmieri (2001). A substantial bibliography of late-Antique Alexandrian medicine is given by Palmieri (2002).
41. The tracts were: *On Sects for Beginners (SI)*; *Art of Medicine (Ars Med.)*; *Synopsis on Pulses (Syn.Puls.)*; *Therapeutics to Glaucon (MMG)*; *Collection 1 (Anatomy for Beginners, sc. On Bones for Beginners (Oss.)*;

On Muscles (*Musc.*); *On the Anatomy of the Nerves* (*Nerv.Diss.*); *On the Anatomy of Veins and Arteries* (*Ven.Art.Diss.*); *On the Elements according to Hippocrates* (*Hipp.Elem.*); *On Temperaments* (*Temp.*); *On the Natural Faculties* (*Nat.Fac.*); *Collection 2* *On Causes and Symptoms*; *On Affected Parts* (*Loc.Aff.*); *Collection 3* *The sixteen Books on the pulse*; *On the Differences of Fevers* (*Diff.Feb.*); *On Crises* (*Cris.*); *On Critical Days* (*Di.Dec.*); *On the Therapeutic Method* (*Method of Healing*) (*MM*); *On the Preservation of Health* (*San.Tu.*). Three texts, *On Sects*, *Synopsis on the Pulse* and *On the Preservation of Health*, do not appear to have been translated into Syriac, and the last may not have formed part of the syllabus until the Muslim period.

42. For Greeks in Ravenna, cf. the sale document, dated 578, witnessed by the son of Leontius, 'doctor at the Greek *schola*'. For the Ravenna commentaries, see Palmieri (2001).

43. See Garofalo (1994); Gundert (1998); Savage-Smith (2002). For a possible summary of Galen's commentary *On Humours* [*Hum.*] see Boudon (2001).

44. See Wolska-Conus (1989); Westerinck (1964); Duffy (1964); Dickson (1998); Rouché (1999), offers important caveats.

45. There is only one historical example among those given by Bliquez and Kazhdan (1984), and by Browning (1985) (to which may be added Anastasius of Sinai, *Questions* 92). Most are reworkings of Galen. For Islam, see Savage-Smith (1995); for Ibn an-Nafis, see Meyerhof (1935a).

46. See Harig (1974).

47. See Hamarneh (1973); Meyerhof (1935a); cf. Levey and al-Khaledy (1967).

48. García-Ballester (1993).

49. Temkin (1977, 154–61).

50. Siraisi (1987), despite its subtitle, provides the best account in English of the *Canon*.

51. 'The Conciliator' was the title of one of the most famous Latin commentaries on Galen's *Art of Medicine* (*Ars Med.*).

52. See Siraisi (1990, 48–77); De Ridder-Symoens (1992).

53. Typical in justifying medicine from its past record even in the middle of a disastrous epidemic is S. Simoni, *Artificiosa curandae Pestis Methodus*, Leipzig: Voegel, 1576, sig. A 2r.: many thousands of plague sufferers have been cured by doctors, those who have died have done so because, on the whole, they refused to call in a doctor as soon as necessary.

54. See Temkin (1991, 231–5); Duffy (1964).

55. See Schacht and Meyerhof (1937).

56. See Dols (1984).

57. See Jordan (1990) (the whole issue is relevant); Burnett and Jacquart (1994).

58. García Ballester (1998).

59. Siraisi (1981).

60. *Ibid.*, 110–17; Giorgi and Pasini (1992). My forthcoming edition of Galen's *On problematical movements* will provide new details on the development of Western medieval academic Galenism.

61. Above, n. 11; Thorndike's list omits *De Crisibus* and *De Diebus Decretoriis*.

62. Stauber (1908, 249).

63. See O'Boyle (1998).

64. Ludwig (1999), *Ep.* 152, 265–9.

65. For a brief general survey of the context, see Nutton (1993).

66. See Baader (1982).

67. See Wilson (1993).

68. See Nutton (1987a).

69. See Mugnai Carrara (1979, 1991); Nutton (1997a).

70. Mugnai Carrara (1991); Fortuna (1992); cf. Heiberg (1896).

71. N. Leoniceno, *De Plinii et plurimum aliorum Erroribus in Medicina*, Ferrara: L. de Rubeis and A. de Grassis. Despite frequent references in modern literature to the subsequent controversy as 'The Pliny controversy', Pliny was only one of the objects of criticism.

72. Literature on the controversy is substantial; French (1986); Reeds (1991, 519–42); Mugnai Carrara (1991, 25–31); Godman (1998).

73. See Mugnai Carrara (1983).

74. N. Leoniceno, *De Morbo gallico*, Venice: Aldus, 1497; Arrizabalaga et al. (1997, 56–87).

75. Above, n. 71 .

76. Galen, *Opera Omnia*, ed. D. Bonardus, Venice: P. Pincius, 1490.

77. Plans were announced in 1497, and at least one scribe was actively copying: see Hoffmann (1985, 1986).

78. Leoniceno loaned Aldus his copy of Theophrastus' botanical writings for printing in the Aldine Aristotle: see Sicherl (1976, 42–50, 59–62).

79. See Nutton (1987a, 29).

80. See Landucci Ruffo (1981, 55–68).

81. G. Ferrari, ed., *Alessandro Benedetti, Historia Corporis humani sive Anatomice*, Florence: Giunti, 1998.

82. See Nutton (1997a, 8–11); Mugnai Carrara (1999).

83. S. Champier, *Symphonia Platonis cum Aristotele, et Galeni cum Hyppocrate*, Paris: J. Badius, 1516. See Temkin (1973, pl. 4); Copenhaver (1978, 67–80).

84. See Arbenz (1891, 248).

85. See Durling (1961). For Linacre, see Maddison *et al.* (1977, 76–106, 296–305). Leoniceno had certainly planned a complete translation of Galen.

86. Leoniceno's heirs in 1524 may have sold some of his manuscripts to the Aldine firm, but it is also clear that the process of making copies for the printer began earlier, perhaps around 1520, see Cataldi Palau (1998, 107, 460–3, 489–92, 540–6).

87. The bibliography of this edition is substantial: Nutton (1987a, 38–42); Béguin (1996, 31–42); Irigoin (1996, 207–16); Cataldi Palau (1998). Potter (1998) argues that vol. 5 of the Galen did not appear until 1526, after the Hippocrates.

88. Nutton (1987a, 41–8); Irigoin (1996).

89. Erasmus, *Epp.* 1594, 1698, 1707, 1713, 2049, 2216; G. Manardi, *Epistulae* XVIII,1; J. Caius, *De Libris Suis*, London: W. Seres, 1570, a story confirmed by the evidence of Vat. Reginensis 173.

90. P. Plateanus, pref. to G. Agricola, *Burmannus*, Basle: Froben, 1530, p. 5; Erasmus, *Ep.* 2216.

91. For the Basle edition, see Nutton (1987a, 43–4); for Chartier, see Kollesch (1967).

92. Nutton (2002c, 1–7).

93. D. Erasmus, trans., *Galeni Exhortatio ad bonas Artes . . . De optimo docendi Genere, Qualem oporteat esse Medicum*, Basle: Froben, 1526. For his views on the edition, *Epp.* 1707, 1713. See also Perilli (2005).

94. Figures based on Durling (1961). Recent discoveries and corrections to Durling have not changed the picture drastically.

95. See Rath (1960); K. Pielmeyer, *Statuten der deutschen Universitäten im Mittelalter*, MD Diss., Bonn, 1981.

96. See Clark (1966, vol. 1, 88–102).

97. See Wear (1981, 229–62).

98. See Nutton (1996).

99. See Nutton (forthcoming).

100. B. Landi, P. F. Paulus, L. Giacchinus, *Novae Academiae Florentinae Opuscula adversus Avicennam et Medicos neotericos qui Galeni Disciplina neglecta Barbaros colunt*, Venice: Giunta, 1533.

101. Wear (1981, 242–5); for his importance, O. Brunetto, *Lettere*, Venice, 1548, fol. 72v: 'Montano, cui dopo Hippocrate e Galeno piu che ad ogni altro deve la medicina'; J. Argenterius, *Opera varia de Re medica*, Florence: L. Torrentino, 1550, p. 8, says that he originally had few students and was derided for talking about Method, but quickly gained a huge audience.

102. See Bylebyl (1979).

103. A. M. Brasavola, *Index refertissimus in omnes Galeni Libros*, in *Galeni Opera omnia*, Venice: Giunta, 1550–1; it was begun at least in 1541.

104. French (1999, 34–67). Wellcome MS 5265, of 1464–5, shows how local circumstances might prevent formal dissections for years.

105. Nutton (1987b).

106. *On the Dissection of Muscles (for Beginners) (Musc.Diss.)* was not published until Kühn's edition in 1830, XVIIIB, 926–1026.

107. French (1999); Carlino (1999); Cunningham (1997, part I).

108. J. Venn, in E. S. Roberts, ed., *The Works of John Caius*, Cambridge: Cambridge University Press, 1912, p. 29.

109. O'Malley (1964, 65–70).

110. Nutton (1993b); Helm (2001a).

111. Helm (2001a, 2001b).

112. N. Du Fail, *Oeuvres facétieuses*, Paris: P. Daffis, 1874, vol. II, 145–6.

113. Fortuna (1999).

114. Maddison *et al.* (1997, pl. VI).

115. See Lind (1975).

116. Cunningham (1997, 57–79).

117. O'Malley (1964).

118. Caius, *De Libris Suis*, fol. 6a-b = p. 76 Roberts.

119. Cunningham (1997, 102–17).

120. A. Vesalius, *De humani Corporis Fabrica*, Basle: J. Oporinus, 1543, fols. 2r-4v: trans. in O'Malley (1964, 317–24). Cf. also Richardson (1998, pp. xlvii–lviii).

121. See Nutton (1997b).

122. See Nutton (1990a).

123. P. A. Matthioli, *Di Pedacio Dioscoride . . . Libri cinque*, Venice: N. de Bascarini, 1544, pref.; Augenio, *Varia Opera*, p. 8.

124. Cunningham (1997, 131–6).

125. Barcia Goyanes (1994), collects all the instances alleged by Vesalius' contemporaries for Vesalius' borrrowings and errors.

126. Cornarius' annotated copy of the 1542 Basle edition is now in the British Library, London, classmark 774 n. 13.

127. Nutton (1987a), based largely on Eton College, classmark Fc 2.6–8.

128. J. Sylvius, *In Hippocratis et Galeni Physiologia Partem anatomicam Isagoge*, Venice: V. Valgrisi, 1554, fol. 11r.

129. John Caius listed on the preliminary page of the Eton Basle edition all the references he knew to Galen seeing a human body.

130. Donzellini to Matthioli, in Matthioli, *Opera Omnia*, Frankfurt: N.Bassaei, 1598, p. 151; Argenterio, *Opera varia*, p. 8

131. Nutton (1990a).

132. French (1994, 1999, 232–5); Temkin (1977, 162–6).
133. W. Harvey, *De Motu Cordis et Sanguinis in Animalibus*, Frankfurt: G. Fitzer, 1628, chs. 12, 16.
134. J. Aubrey, *Brief Lives, William Harvey*, pp. 290–1 Penguin ed.
135. Maclean (2002); Temkin (1973).
136. Nutton (2002c).
137. Temkin (1973, 172–91), puts the historicizing of Galen as firmly in place by 1870.
138. A glance at the bibliography to the Corpus Galenicum assembled by Gerhard Fichtner, Tübingen: Institut für Geschichte der Medizin (1990), confirms the geographical spread of editors.
139. Kollesch (1968, 1992); Unte (1985).
140. Johannes Mewaldt, *In Hippocrates De natura hominis Commentarii*, Berlin and Leipzig: Teubner, 1914; Hermann Diels, *In Hippocratis Prorrheticum I Commentarii*, Berlin and Leipzig: Teubner, 1915. Diels had completed a first draft by 1910 (Braun *et al.*, 1995, 267–72). Diels claimed, *ibid.*, 230, to have read through the whole of Galen while ill (!).
141. C. Daremberg, *Exposition des Connaissances de Galien sur l'Anatomie, la Physiologie, et la Pathologie du Système nerveux*, MD thesis, Paris (1841). Still valuable is L. Israelson, *Die Materia medica des Klaudios Galenos*, Diss., Dorpat (1894), but Israelson was a pharmacologist, and Dorpat was not Germany.
142. M. Simon, ed., *Galen, Sieben Bücher Anatomie*, Leipzig: Teubner 1906.
143. Ilberg (1889–97, 1905). U. von Wilamowitz, *Philologische Untersuchungen* 9, 1886, 122, n. 12.
144. See the views of Wilamowitz, in Braun *et al.* (1995, 231).
145. E. Wenkebach, F. Pfaff, *Galeni In Hippocratis Epidemiarum Librum I et II Commentarii*, CMG V 10,1, 1934; *In Hippocratis Epidemiarum Librum III Commentarii*, CMG V 10,2,1, 1934; *In Hippocratis Epidemiarum Librum VI Commentarii*, CMG V 10,2,2, 1940; repr. 1956. For the discussion about the propriety of including Bergsträsser's edition of the (arabic) pseudo-Galenic commentary on Hippocrates' *On Sevens* in the Corpus Medicorum, see Braun *et al.* (1995, 283–4). Some background is provided by Temkin (1977, 7–10).
146. Deichgräber (1903–84) studied in Berlin with Jaeger before returning to his native Friesland to take his doctorate at Münster under Hermann Schöne. His thesis, *Die griechische Empirikerschule. Sammlung der Fragmente und Darstellung der Lehre* 1927; published, Berlin: Weidmann (1930); ed. 2, Berlin and Zurich, Weidmann (1965), is a model of its kind. He became Redakteur of the Corpus Medicorum, before obtaining chairs at Marburg (1935) and Göttingen (1938). For his somewhat

controversial career, see the obituary by Hans Gärtner in *Gnomon* 58, 1986, 475–80.

147. The only one to work directly on Galen was D. W. Peterson: *Galen's 'Therapeutics to Glaucon' and its early Commentaries*, Ph.D. Diss. Baltimore (1974); see also Peterson (1977).

148. Above, n. 139.

149. Details of translations, editions and fragments are best found in Ullmann (1970); Sezgin (1970). Strohmaier (2002), provides a good overview.

150. Flemming (2000).

151. Nutton (1981). The conference was organized by A. Z. Iskandar, G. E. R. Lloyd and V. Nutton.

152. Boudon-Millot (2000, 2007, with major introduction); Debru and Garofalo (2005).

153. Nutton (2002b, 165–8).

154. Vol. II 37,2, 1994; Galen's philosophy is also treated by contributors to Vol. II 36,5, 1992, which deals with Roman philosophy.

155. Cf. the bibliographies assembled by K. Schubring, in vol. XX of the 1965 reprint of Kühn's edition, pp. xvii–lxii; that by V. Nutton to the Oxford microform edition of Kühn (1976); that of Fichtner (1990); and that of Kollesch and Nickel, 'Bibliographia Galeniana', *ANRW* II 37,2, 1351–1420, 2063–70.

156. Singer (1997); Prantera (1991).

APPENDIX I   A GUIDE TO THE
EDITIONS AND ABBREVIATIONS
OF THE GALENIC CORPUS

"*" indicates that the text is spurious; "?" that it is of doubtful
authenticity.

SECTION I: TEXTS PRINTED IN KÜHN

Kühn ref.		Title	Abbreviation	Other edition(s)
I	1–39	Protrepticus	Protr.	SM 1; Kaibel (1913); CMG V 1,1; Boudon (2000a)
	40–52	De Optima Doctrina	Opt.Doct.	CMG V 1,1
	53–63	Quod Optimus Medicus sit quoque Philosophus	Opt.Med.	SM 2, Boudon-Millot (2007)
	64–105	De Sectis ad eos qui Introducuntur	Sect.Int.	SM 3
	106–223	*De Optima Secta	[Opt.Sect.]	
	224–304	De Constitutione Artis Medicae	CAM	CMG V 1,3
	305–412	Ars Medica	Ars Med.	Boudon (2000a)
	413–508	De Elementis ex Hippocrate	Hipp.Elem.	CMG V 1,2
	509–694	De Temperamentis	Temp.	Helmreich (1904)
II	1–204	De Naturalibus Facultatibus	Nat.Fac.	SM 3, Loeb
	205–731	De Anatomicis Administrationibus	AA	Garofalo (1986)
	732–778	De Ossibus ad Tirones	Oss.	Garofalo (2005)
	779–830	De Venarum Arteriarumque Dissectione	Ven.Art.Diss.	
	831–856	De Nervorum Dissectione	Nerv.Diss.	

(cont.)

391

(Cont.)

Kühn ref.		Title	Abbreviation	Other edition(s)
	857–886	De Instrumento Odoratus	Inst.Od.	CMG Suppl. V
	887–908	De Uteri Dissectione	Ut.Diss.	CMG V 2,1
III	1–933	De Usu Partium, I–XI	UP	Helmreich (1907–9)
IV	1–366	De Usu Partium, XII–XVII	UP	Helmreich (1907–9)
	367–464	De Motu Musculorum	Mot.Musc.	
	465–469	De Causis Respirationis	Caus.Resp.	Furley/Wilkie (1984)
	470–511	De Utilitate Respirationis	Ut.Resp.	Furley/Wilkie (1984)
	512–651	De Semine	Sem.	CMG V 3,1
	652–702	De Foetuum Formatione	Foet.Form.	CMG V 3,3
	703–736	An in Arteriis Sanguis Contineatur	Art.Sang.	Furley/Wilkie (1984)
	737–749	De Optima Corporis Nostri Constitutione	Opt.Corp.Const.	
	750–756	De Bono Habitu	Bon.Hab.	
	757–766	De Substantia Facultatum Naturalium	Sub.Nat.Fac.	CMG V 3.2
	767–822	Quod Animi Mores Corporis Temperamenta Sequuntur	QAM	SM 2
V	1–57	De Proprium Animi Cuiuslibet Affectuum Dignotione et Curatione	Aff.Dig.	CMG V 4,1,1; SM 1
	58–103	De Animi Cuiuslibet Peccatorum Dignotione et Curatione	Pecc.Dig.	CMG V 4,1,1; SM 1
	104–148	De Atra Bile	At.Bil.	CMG V 4,1,1
	149–180	De Usu Pulsuum	Us.Puls.	Furley/Wilkie (1984) Mueller (1874)
	181–805	De Placitis Hippocratis et Platonis	PHP	CMG V 4,1,2;
	806–898	Thrasybulus Sive Utrum Medicinae Sit an Gymnasticae Hygiene	Thras.	SM 3

Kühn ref.		Title	Abbreviation	Other edition(s)
	899–910	De Parvae Pilae Exercitio	Parv.Pil.	SM 1
	911–914	*De Venereis	[Ven.]	
VI	1–452	De Sanitate Tuenda	San.Tu.	CMG V 4,2
	453–748	De Alimentis Facultatibus	Alim.Fac.	CMG V 4,2
	749–815	De Bonis et Malis Alimentorum Sucis	Bon.Mal.Suc.	CMG V 4,2
	816–831	De Ptisana	Ptis.	CMG V 4,2
	832–835	De Dignotione ex Insomniis	Dig.Insomn.	
	836–880	De Morborum Differentiis	Morb.Diff.	
VII	1–41	De Causis Morborum	Caus.Morb.	
	42–84	De Symptomatum Differentiis	Symp.Diff.	
	85–272	De Symptomatum Causis	Caus.Symp.	
	273–405	De Febrium Differentiis	Diff.Feb.	
	406–439	De Morborum Temporibus	Morb.Temp.	
	440–462	De Totius Morbi Temporibus	Tot.Morb.Temp.	
	463–474	De Typis	Typ.	
	475–512	Adversus Eos qui de Typis Scripserunt	Adv.Typ.Scr.	
	513–583	De Plenitudine	Plen.	
	584–642	De Tremore, Palpitatione, Convulsione et Rigore	Trem.Palp.	
	643–665	De Comate Secundum Hippocrate	Com.Hipp.	CMG V 9,2
	666–704	De Marcore	Marc.	
	705–732	De Tumoribus Praeter Naturam	Tum.Pr.Nat.	
	733–752	De Inaequali Intemperie	Inaeq.Int.	
	753–960	De Difficultate Respirationis	Diff.Resp.	
VIII	1–452	De Locis Affectis	Loc.Aff.	
	453–492	De Pulsibus ad Tirones	Puls.	
	493–765	De Differentiis Pulsuum	Diff.Puls.	

(cont.)

(Cont.)

Kühn ref.		Title	Abbreviation	Other edition(s)
	766–961	De Dignoscendibus Pulsibus	Dig.Puls.	
IX	1–204	De Causis Pulsuum	Caus.Puls.	
	205–430	De Praesagitione ex Pulsibus	Praes.Puls.	
	431–549	?Synopsis de Pulsibus	Syn.Puls.	
	550–760	De Crisibus	Cris.	Alexanderson (1967)
	761–941	De Diebus Decretoriis	Di.Dec.	
X	1–1021	De Methodo Medendi	MM	
XI	1–146	Ad Glauconem de Methodo Medendi	MMG	
	147–186	De Venae Sectione adversus Erasistratum	Ven.Sect.Er.	
	187–249	De Venae Sectione adversus Erasistrateos Romae Degentes	Ven.Sect.Er.Rom.	
	250–316	De Curandi Ratione per Venae Sectionem	Cur.Rat.Ven.Sect.	
	317–322	De Hirundinibus, Revulsione, Cucurbitula Incisione et Scarificatione	HRCIS	
	323–342	De Purgantium Medicamentorum Facultate	Purg.Med.Fac.	
	343–356	*Quos, Quibus Catharticis Medicamentis et Quando Purgare Oporteat	[Cath.Med.Purg.]	
	357–368	Puero Epileptico Consilium	Puer.Epil.	
	369–892	De Simplicium Medicamentorum [Temperamentis Ac] Facultatibus, I–VI	SMT	
XII	1–377	De Simplicium Medicamentorum [Temperamentis Ac] Facultatibus, VII–XI	SMT	
	378–1003	De Compositione Medicamentorum secundum Locos, I–VI	Comp.Med.Loc.	

Kühn ref.		Title	Abbreviation	Other edition(s)
XIII	1–361	De Compositione Medicamentorum secundum Locos, VII–XI	Comp.Med.Loc.	
	362–1058	De Compositione Medicamentorum per Genera	Comp.Med.Gen.	
XIV	1–209	De Antidotis	Ant.	
	210–94	De Theriaca ad Pisonem	Ther.Pis.	
	295–310	*De Theriaca ad Pamphilianum	[Ther.Pamph.]	
	311–581	?De Remediis Parabilibus	Rem.	
	582–598	De Sophismatibus penes Dictionem	Soph.	Edlow (1977); Ebbesen (1981)
	599–673	De Praenotione ad Epigenem	Praen.	CMG V 8,1
	674–797	*Introductio seu Medicus	[Int.]	
XV	1–173	In Hippocratis de Natura Hominis	HNH	CMG V 9,1
	174–223	In Hippocratis de Salubri Victus Ratione	Hipp.Vict.	CMG V 9,1
	224–417	*In Hippocratis de Alimento	[Hipp.Alim.]	
	418–919	In Hippocratis de Acutorum Morborum Victu	HVA	CMG V 9,1
XVI	1–488	*In Hippocratis de Humoribus	[Hipp.Hum.]	
	489–840	In Hippocratis de Praedictionibus	Hipp.Prorrh.	CMG V 9,2
XVIIA	1–1009	In Hippocratis Epidemiarum Libri, I–VI	Hipp.Epid.	CMG V 10,1, V 10,2,1, V 10,2,2

(Comm. on *Epid.* II is spurious in Kühn; German trans. of Arabic version of genuine text in *CMG* V 10,1)

| XVIIB | 1–344 | In Hippocratis Epidemiarum Libri, I–VI | Hipp.Epid. | CMG V 10,2,2 |
| | 345–887 | In Hippocratis Aphorismi | Hipp.Aph. | |

(cont.)

(Cont.)

Kühn ref.		Title	Abbreviation	Other edition(s)
XVIIIA	1–195	In Hippocratis Aphorismi	Hipp.Aph.	
	196–245	Adversus Lycum	Adv.Lyc.	CMG V 10,3
	246–299	Adversus Julianum	Adv.Jul.	CMG V 10,3
	300–767	In Hippocratis De Articulis	Hipp.Art.	
	768–827	?De Fasciis	Fasc.	
	828–838	Ex Galeni Commentariis De Fasciis	Gal.Fasc.	
XVIIIB	1–317	In Hippocratis Prognosticum	Hipp.Prog.	CMG V 9,2
	318–628	In Hippocratis De Fracturis	Hipp.Fract.	
	629–925	In Hippocratis De Officina Medici	Hipp.Off.Med.	
	926–1026	De Musculorum Dissectione	Musc.Diss.	Debru/Garofalo (2005)
XIX	1–7	Quomodo Simulantes Morbum Deprehendendi	Sim.Morb.	
	8–48	De Libris Propriis	Lib.Prop.	SM 2, Boudon-Millot (2007)
	49–61	De Ordine Librorum Propriorum	Ord.Lib.Prop.	SM 2, Boudon-Millot (2007)
	62–157	?Glossarium	Gloss.	
	158–181	*An Animal Sit Quod in Utero Geritur	[An.Ut.]	
	182–221	*De Victus Ratione in Morbis Acutis ex Hippocratis Sententia	[Hipp.Vict.Morb. Ac.]	CMG V 9,1
	222–345	*Historia Philosopha	[Hist.Phil.]	
	346–462	*Definitiones Medicae	[Def.Med.]	
	463–484	Quod Qualitates Incorporeae Sint	Qual.Incorp.	
	485–496	*De Humoribus	[Hum.]	
	497–511	*De Praenotione	[Praes.]	
	512–518	*De Praesagitione Vera et Experta	[Praes.Ver.Exp.]	
	519–528	*De Venae Sectione	[Ven.Sect.]	
	529–573	*Prognostica de Decubitu ex Mathematica Scientia	[Prog.Dec.]	

Kühn ref.	Title	Abbreviation	Other edition(s)
574–601	*De Urinis	[Ur.]	
602–606	*De Urinis Compendium	[Ur.Comp.]	
607–628	*De Urinis ex Hippocrate, Galeno	[Ur.Hipp.Gal.]	
629–642	*De Pulsibus ad Antonium	[Puls.Ant.]	
643–698	*De Renum Affectibus	[Ren.Aff.]	
699–720	*De Melancholia	[Mel.]	
721–747	?De Succedaneis	Suc.	
748–781	*De Ponderibus et Mensuris	[Pond.Mens.]	

SECTION II: TEXTS NOT PRINTED IN KÜHN

Text	Abbreviation	Edition
De Anatomicis Administrationibus (books 9–14)	AA	Simon (1906) [Arabic]
De Causis Contentivis	CC	CMG Suppl. Or. II [Lat., Arab.]
De Causis Procatarcticis	CP	CMG Suppl. II [Latin]; Hankinson (1998)
De Consuetudine	Cons.	Dietz (1832); SM 2; CMG Suppl. III
De Diaeta Hippocratis in Morbis Acutis	Di.Hipp.Morb. Ac.	CMG Suppl. Or. II [genuine version in Arab.: cf.CMG V 9,1; XIX 182–221]
De Experientia Medica	Med.Exp.	Walzer (1944) [Arabic]
In Hippocratis de Officio Medici	Hipp.Off.Med.	CMG Suppl. Or. I [Arabic]
Institutio Logica	Inst.Log.	Kalbfleisch (1896)
De Nominibus Medicis	Med.Nam.	Meyerhof, Schacht (1931) [Arabic]
De Optimo Medico Cognoscendo	Opt.Med.Cogn.	CMG Suppl. Or. IV [Arabic]
De Partibus Artibus Medicativae	Part.Art.Med.	CMG Suppl. Or. II [Arabic, Latin]
De Partium Homoeomerum Differentiis	Part.Hom.Diff.	CMG Suppl. Or. III [Arabic]
In Platonis Timaeum	Plat.Tim.	CMG Suppl. I; Larrain (1992)
De Propriis Placitis	Prop.Plac.	CMG V 3,2 [Latin]
Subfiguratio Empirica	Subf.Emp.	Deichgräber (1930) [Latin]
De Victu Attenuante	Vict.At.	CMG V 4,2

APPENDIX 2 ENGLISH TITLES AND MODERN TRANSLATIONS

(This list is not complete: I have not included some of the obscurer opuscula and most of the spuria)

SECTION I:

Latin abbreviation	English title	Translations
Protr.	Exhortation to the Arts	Walsh (1930) (E); P. Singer (1997) (E); Barigazzi (1991) (I); Wenkebach (1935) (G); Daremberg (1854) (F); Boudon (2000a) (F)
Opt.Doct.	On the Best Method of Teaching	Barigazzi (1991) (I)
Opt.Med.	The Best Doctor is also a Philosopher	Brain (1977) (E); P.Singer (1997) (E); Daremberg (1854) (F) Boudon-Millot (2007) (F)
SI [*Opt.Sect.*]	On Sects for Beginners On the Best Sect	Frede (1985) (E); Daremberg (1854) (F)
CAM	On the Composition of the Art of Medicine	D.Dean-Jones (E: PhD Diss., University of Texas (1993); Fortuna (1997) (I)
Ars Med.	Art of Medicine	Malato (1972) (I); Lafout/Moreno (1947) (S); Singer (1997) (E); Boudon (2000a) (F)
Hipp.Elem.	On the Elements according to Hippocrates	De Lacy (1994) (E)
Temp.	On Mixtures	P.Singer (1997) (E)
Nat.Fac.	On the Natural Faculties	Brock (1916) (E); Daremberg (1854) (F)
AA	On Anatomical Procedures	C.Singer (1956) (E: books 1–9); Duckworth (1962) (E: books 9–15 from Arabic)
Oss.	On Bones for Beginners	C.Singer (1952) (E); Debru (2005) (F)
Ven.Art.Diss.	On the Anatomy of Veins and Arteries	Goss (1961) (E)

Latin abbreviation	English title	Translations
Nerv.Diss.	On the Anatomy of the Nerves	Goss (1966) (E)
Inst.Od.	On the Organ of Smell	Wright (1924) (E); Kollesch (1964) (G)
Ut.Diss.	On the Anatomy of the Uterus	Goss (1962) (E)
UP	On the Utility of the Parts	May (1967) (E); Daremberg (1854) (F)
Mot.Musc.	On the Movement of Muscles	Daremberg (1854) (F); Goss (1968) (E)
Caus.Resp.	On the Causes of Breathing	Furley/Wilkie (1984) (E)
Ut.Resp.	On the Use of Breathing	Furley/Wilkie (1984) (E)
Sem.	On Semen	De Lacy (1992) (E)
Foet.Form.	On the Formation of the Foetus	P. Singer (1997) (E); Nickel (2002) (G)
Art.Sang.	On whether Blood is Naturally Contained in the Arteries	Furley/Wilkie (1984) (E)
Opt.Corp.Const.	The Best Constitution of our Bodies	Penella/Hall (1973) (E); P.Singer (1997) (E)
Bon.Hab.	Good Condition	P.Singer (1997) (E)
Sub.Nat.Fac.	On the Substance of the Natural Powers	Nutton (1999) (E) (as part of *Prop.Plac.*)
QAM	The Faculties of the Soul Follow the Mixtures of the Body	P.Singer (1997) (E); Vegetti/Menghi (1984) (I); García Ballester (1972) (S); Daremberg (1854) (F)
Aff.Dig.	The Passions of the Soul	Harkins (1963) (E); Vegetti/Menghi (1984) (I); P.Singer (1997) (E)
Pecc.Dig.	On the Diagnosis and cure of the Errors of the Soul	Harkins (1963) (E); P.Singer (1997) (E) Vegetti/Menghi (1984) (I)
At.Bil.	On Black Bile	Grant (2000) (E)
Us.Puls.	On the Function of the Pulse	Furley/Wilkie (1984) (E)
PHP	On the Doctrines of Hippocrates and Plato	De Lacy (1978) (E)
Thras.	Thrasybulus	P.Singer (1997) (E)
Parv.Pil.	Exercise with the Small Ball	P.Singer (1997) (E)
San.Tu.	On the Preservation of Health	Green (1951) (E)
Alim.Fac.	On the Properties of Foodstuffs	Grant (2000) (E); Powell (2003) (E)
Ptis.	On Barley Soup	Grant (2000) (E)
Morb.Diff.	Differences of Diseases	Johnston (2006) (E)
Caus.Morb.	Causes of Diseases	Grant (2000) (E); Johnston (2006) (E)
Symp.Diff.	Differences of Symptoms	Johnston (2006) (E)

(cont.)

(Cont.)

Latin abbreviation	English title	Translations
Symp.Caus.	Causes of Symptoms	Johnston (2006) (E)
Diff.Feb.	On the differences of Fevers	
Morb.Temp.	Opportune Moments in Diseases	
Tot.Morb.Temp.	Opportune Moments in Diseases as a Whole	
Plen.	On Plethora	
Trem.Palp.	On Tremor, Palpitation, Spasm and Rigor	Sider/McVaugh (1979) (E)
Marc.	On Marasmus	Theoharides (1971) (E)
Tum.Pr.Nat.	On Abnormal Swellings	Reedy (1975) (E); Lytton/Resuhr (1978) (E)
Inaeq.Int.	On Uneven Distemper	Grant (2000) (E)
Diff.Resp.	Difficulties in Breathing	
Loc.Aff.	On Affected Parts	Siegel (1975) (E); Aparicio (1997) (S); Daremberg (1854) (F)
Puls.	On the Pulse for Beginnners	P.Singer (1997) (E)
Diff.Puls.	Differences of Pulses	
Dig.Puls.	Diagnosis by Pulses	
Caus.Puls.	Causes of Pulses	
Praes.Puls.	Prognosis by Pulses	
Syn.Puls.	Synopsis on Pulses	
Cris.	On Crises	
Di.Dec.	On Critical Days	
MM	On the Therapeutic Method	Hankinson (1991) (E) (Bks 1–2)
MMG	Therapeutics to Glaucon	Daremberg (1854) (F)
Ven.Sect.Er.	On Bloodletting against Erasistratus	Brain (1986) (E)
Ven.Sect.Er.Rom.	On Bloodletting against the Erasistrateans at Rome	Brain (1986) (E)
Cur.Rat.Ven.Sect.	On Treatment by Bloodletting	Brain (1986) (E)
Purg.Med.Fac.	On the Power of Cleansing Drugs	
[Cath.Med.Purg.]	Whom to Purge, With Which Cleansing Drugs, and When	
Puer.Epil.	Advice to an Epileptic Boy	Temkin (1934) (E)
SMT	On the Powers [and Mixtures] of Simple Drugs	
Comp.Med.Loc.	On the Composition of Drugs according to Places	

Latin abbreviation	English title	Translations
Comp.Med.Gen.	On the Composition of Drugs according to Kind	
Ant.	On Antidotes	
Ther.Pis.	On Theriac to Piso	
[*Ther.Pamph.*]	On Theriac to Pamphilianus	
Soph.	On Linguistic Sophisms	Edlow (1977) (E); Schiaparelli (2002) (I)
Praen.	On Prognosis	Nutton (1979) (E)
[*Int.*]	Introduction	
HNH	On Hippocrates' 'Nature of Man'	
HVA	On Hippocrates' 'Regimen in Acute Diseases'	
Hipp.Prorrh.	On Hippocrates' 'Prorrhetics'	
Hipp.Epid.	On Hippocrates' 'Epidemics'	Pfaff (1935) (1956) (G) (Comm. on parts of books 2, 6: from Arabic)
Hipp.Aph.	On Hippocrates' 'Aphorisms'	
Adv.Lyc.	Against Lycus	
Adv.Jul.	Against Julian	Tecusan (2004) (E)
Hipp.Art.	On Hippocrates' 'On Joints'	
Hipp.Prog.	On Hippocrates' 'Prognostic'	
Hipp.Fract.	On Hippocrates' 'Fractures'	
Hipp.Off.Med.	On Hippocrates' 'Surgery'	
Musc.Diss.	On the dissection of Muscles (for Beginners)	Debru (2005) (F)
Sim.Morb.	How to Detect Malingerers	Brock (1929) (E)
Lib.Prop.	On My Own Books	P.Singer (1997) (E); Boudon-Millot (2007) (F)
Ord.Lib.Prop.	The Order of My Own Books	P.Singer (1997) (E); Boudon-Millot (2007) (F)
Gloss.	Glossary of Hippocratic Terms	
[*Hist.Phil.*]	History of Philosophy	
[*Def.Med.*]	Medical Definitions	Lafout/Moreno (1947) (S)
[*Hum.*]	On Humours	Grant (2000) (E)

SECTION II:

Latin abbreviation	English title	Translations
CC	On Containing Causes	Lyons (1969) (E: from Arabic)
CP	On Antecedent Causes	Hankinson (1998) (E: from Latin)
Cons.	On Habits	Brock (1929) (E)
Inst.Log.	Introduction to Logic	Kieffer (1964) (E)
Med.Nam.	On Medical Names	Meyerhof/Schacht (1931) (G: from Arabic)
Med.Exp.	On Medical Experience	Frede/Walzer (1985) (E: from Arabic)
Mor.	On Moral Character (epitome)	Mattock (1972) (E: from Arabic)
Opt.Med.Cogn.	On Recognizing the Best Physician	Iskandar (1988) (E: from Arabic)
Part.Art.Med.	On the Parts of the Art of Medicine	Lyons (1969) (E: from Arabic)
Part.Hom.Diff.	On the Differences of Uniform Parts	Strohmaier (1970) (G: from Arabic)
Plat.Tim.	On Plato's 'Timaeus'	
Prop.Plac.	On His Own Opinions	Nutton (1999) (E: from Latin, Greek, Hebrew and Arabic)
Subf.Emp.	Outline of Empiricism	Frede (1985) (E: from Latin)
Vict.Att.	On the Thinning Diet	P.Singer (1997) (E)

BIBLIOGRAPHY

This bibliography is divided into three sections. In Section A are listed all of the editions of Galen referred to in the text, as well as others of importance. Section B collects all important translations of works of Galen into English, as well as a selection of those rendered into other modern languages (in particular in cases where no English version exists). Finally, section C lists all of the secondary material referred to in the text, plus a representative sample of other important works of secondary literature which are not. The items listed are predominantly in English; but since much important work on Galen his been done in other languages, items in French, German, Italian and Spanish have also been included. Several works appear in more than one section, a few in all three (when they contain text, translation, as well as critical material). It is to be hoped that this reduplication will assist readers in navigating the bibliography. They should also consult the two appendices, which relate English and Latin names and abbreviations of the treatises with their location in Kühn and other editions, and with translations into modern languages where applicable.

A: TEXTS

Alexanderson, B. (1967) *Galeni de Crisibus (Cris.)* Studia Graeca et Latina Gothoburgensia, 23

Bardong, K. (1937) *Galeni de Causis Procatarcticis (CP)*: CMG Suppl. II [Lat.] (Berlin)

Barigazzi, A. (1991) *Galeni de Optimo Docendi Genere, Exhortatio ad Medicinam (Protrepticus) (Opt.Doct., Protr.)* (ed., trans. [Italian]): CMG V 1,1 (Berlin)

Boudon, V. (2000a) *Galien, Exhortation à la Médecine. Art médical (Protr., Ars Med.)*(ed., trans. [French]) (Paris)

Boudon-Millot, V. (2007) *Galien: Sur l'ordre de ses Propres Livres; Sur ses Propres Livers; Que l' Excellent Médecin est aussi Philosophe (Ord.Lib. Prop.; Lib.Prop.; Opt.Med.)* (ed., trans. [French]) (Paris)

Boudon-Millot, V. and Pietrobelli, A. (2005) 'Galien ressuscité: édition princeps du texte grec du *De propriis placitis'* (*Prop.Plac.: Gr.*), *Revue des Études Grecques* 118, 168–71

De Boer, W. (1937) *Galeni de Animi Affectuum et Peccatorum Dignotione et Curatione; de Atra Bile (Aff.Dig., Pecc.Dig., At.Bil.)*: *CMG* V 4,1,1, (Berlin)

Debru, A. and Garofalo, I. (2005) *Galien: Les Os pour les Débutants; L'Anatomie des Muscles (Oss., Musc.Diss.)* (ed., trans. [French]) (Paris)

Deichgräber, K. (1965²) *Die griechische Empirikerschule: Sammlung der Fragmente und Darstellung der Lehre* (Berlin and Zurich) (1st edn., 1930) (contains *Outline of Empiricism* [*Subf.Emp.*])

De Lacy, P. H. (1978–84) *Galen: On the Doctrines of Hippocrates and Plato (PHP)* (3 vols., ed., trans. and comm.): *CMG* V 4,1,2 (Berlin)

(1992) *Galen: On Semen (Sem.)* (ed., trans. and comm.): *CMG* V 3,1 (Berlin)

(1996) *Galen: On the Elements according to Hippocrates (Hipp.Elem.)* (ed., trans. and comm.): *CMG* V 1,2 (Berlin)

Diels, H. (1915) *Galeni in Hippocratis de Praedictionibus (Hipp.Prorrh.)*: *CMG* V 9,2 (Berlin)

Ebbesen, S. (1981) *Commentators and Commentaries on Aristotle's Sophistici Elenchi*, 3 vols. *(Soph.)* (Leiden)

Edlow, R. B. (1977) *Galen on Language and Ambiguity (Soph.)*(ed., trans. and comm.) (Leiden)

Fortuna, S. (1997) *Galeni de Constitutione Artis Medicae ad Patrophilum (CAM)* (ed., trans. [Italian]): *CMG* V 1,3 (Berlin)

Furley, D. J. and Wilkie, J. S. (1984) *Galen On Respiration and the Arteries (Ut.Resp., Art.Sang., Us.Puls., Caus.Resp.)* (ed., trans. and comm.) (Princeton, N.J.)

Garofalo, I. (1986) *Galenus: Anatomicarum administrationum libri qui supersunt novem. Earundem interpretatio arabica Hunaino Isaaci filio ascripta;* vol. 1, libri I–IV *(AA)* (Naples)

(2000) *Galenus – Anatomicarum administrationum libri qui supersunt novem, Earundem interpretatio arabica Hunaino Isaaci filio ascripta;* vol. II, libri V–IX (Naples)

Hankinson, R. J. (1998) *Galen: On Antecedent Causes (CP)* (ed., trans. and comm.) Cambridge Classical Texts and Commentaries (Cambridge)

Heeg, J. (1925) *Galeni in Hippocratis Prognosticum (Hipp.Prog.)*: *CMG* V 9,2 (Berlin)

Helmreich, G. (1893) *Galeni Pergameni Scripta Minora*, vol. 3 (Leipzig) (= *SM* 3)

(1904) *De Temperamentis (Temp.)* (Leipzig) (repr. Stuttgart, 1969)

(1907/1909) *De Usu Partium (UP)*, 2 vols. (Leipzig) (repr. Amsterdam, 1968)

Ilberg, J. (1927) *Sorani Gynaecia: CMG* IV (Leipzig/Berlin)

Iskandar, A. Z. (1988) *Galeni de Optimo Medico Cognoscendo (Opt.Med.Cogn.)* (ed., trans. and comm.: from Arabic): *CMG* Suppl. Or. IV (Berlin)

Kalbfleisch, K. (1896) *Galeni Institutio Logica (Inst.Log.)* (Leipzig) (1904) *Galeni de Causis Contentivis (CC): CMG* Suppl. I (Berlin)

Koch, K., Helmreich, G., Kalbfleisch, K. and Hartlich, O. (1923) *Galeni de Sanitate Tuenda* [Koch]; *de Alimentorum Facultatibus* [Helmreich]; *de Bonis et Malis Alimentorum Sucis* [Helmreich]; *de Victu Attenuante* [Kalbfleisch]; *de Ptisana* [Hartlich], *(San.Tu., Alim.Fac., Bon.Mal.Suc., Vict.At., Ptis.]: CMG* V 4,2 (Berlin)

Kollesch, J. (1964) *De Instrumento Odoratus (Inst.Od.)* (ed., trans. and comm. [German]): *CMG* Suppl. V (Berlin)

Kollesch, J., Nickel, D. and Strohmaier, G. (1969) *Galeni de Partibus Artibus Medicativae, de Causis Contentivis (Part.Art.Med., CC)* (ed. from Latin): *CMG* Suppl. Or. I (Berlin)

Kühn, C. G. (1819–33) *Galeni Opera Omnia* (20 vols. in 22) Leipzig (re-issued 1965, Hildesheim)

Lyons, M. C. (1963) *Galeni in Hippocratis de Officio Medici (Hipp.Off.Med.)* (ed., trans. from Arabic): *CMG* Suppl. Or. I (Berlin)

(1969) *Galeni de Partibus Artibus Medicativae, de Causis Contentivis, de Diaeta in Morbis Acutis Secundum Hippocratem (Part.Art.Med., CC, Di.Hipp.Morb.Ac.)* (ed., trans. from Arabic): *CMG* Suppl. Or. II (Berlin)

Marquardt, J. (1884) *Galeni Pergameni Scripta Minora*, vol. 1 (Leipzig) (= *SM* 1)

Marx, F. (1915) *Cornelii Celsi De Medicina, CML* 1 (Leipzig/Berlin)

Mewaldt, J., Helmreich, G. and Westenberger, J. (1914) *Galeni: In Hippocratis de Natura Hominis* [Mewaldt]; *In Hippocratis de Acutorum Morborum Victu* [Helmreich]; *De Diaeta Hippocratis in Morbis Acutis* [Westenberger], *(HNH, HVA, [Hipp.Vict.Morb.Ac.]): CMG* V 9,1 (Berlin)

Meyerhof, M. and Schacht, J. (1931) *Galen über die medizinischen Namen (Med.Nam.)* (ed., trans. from Arabic) *Abhandlungen der Preussischen Akademie der Wissenschaften Phil.-hist.* Kl. 3 (Berlin)

Müller, I. von (1897) 'Über Galens Werk vom wissenschaftlichen Beweis', *Abhandlung der Königlichen Bayerischen Akademie der Wissenschaften* 20, 1895,2 (contains fragments of Galen's *De Demonstratione* [*Dem.*])

Müller, J. (1891) *Galeni Pergameni Scripta Minora*, vol. 2 (Leipzig) (= *SM* 2)

Mynas, M. (1844) *Galênou Eisagôgê Dialektikê (Inst.Log.)*(Paris)

Nickel, D. (2001) *Galeni de Foetuum Formatione* (ed., trans. and comm. [German]) (*Foet. Form.*): *CMG* V 3,3 (Berlin)

Nutton, V. (1979) *Galen: On Prognosis* (ed., trans. and comm.) (*Praen.*): *CMG* V 8,1 (Berlin)

(1999) *Galen: On my own Opinions* (ed., trans. and comm.) (*Prop. Plac.*): *CMG* V 3.2 (Berlin)

Schiaparelli, A. (2002) *Galeno e le Fallacie Linguistiche. Il 'de Captionibus in dictione' (Soph.*, ed., trans. and comm. [Italian]), Istituto Veneto di Scienze, Lettere e Arti. (Memorie, Classe di scienze morali, lettere ed arti) 101

Schmutte, J. M. (1941) *Galeni de Consuetudinibus: CMG* Suppl. III (Berlin)

Schröder, H. O. (1934) *Galeni In Platonis Timaeum Commentarii Fragmenta: CMG* Suppl. 1

Simon, M. (1906) *Galen, Sieben Bücher Anatomie* (edn. of Arabic text of *AA* XI.6–XV) (Leipzig)

Strohmaier, G. (1970) *Galeni de Partium Homoeomerum Differentiis* (ed., trans. [German] from Arabic) (*Part.Hom.Diff.*): *CMG* Suppl. Or. III (Berlin)

Walzer, R. (1944) *Galen on Medical Experience: Arabic Text with an English Translation* (Oxford)

Wasserstein, A. (1982) *Galen's Commentary on the Treatise 'Airs, Waters, Places' in the Hebrew Translation of Solomon ha-Me'ati'* (ed., trans. and comm.) (Jerusalem)

Wenkebach, E. and Pfaff, F. (1934) *In Hippocratis Epidemiarum Librum I comm. III* [Wenkebach]; *In Hippocratis Epidemiarum Librum II comm. V* [Pfaff: Arabic] (*Hipp.Epi.d.*): *CMG* V 10,1 (Berlin)

B: TRANSLATIONS

Barigazzi, A. (1991) *Galeni de Optimo Docendi Genere, Exhortatio ad Medicinam (Protrepticus)* (*Opt.Doct.*, *Protr.*: Italian): *CMG* V 1,1 (Berlin)

Boudon, V. (2000a) *Galien, Exhortation à la Médecine. Art médical* (*Protr.*, *Ars Med.*: French) (Paris)

Brain, P. (1977) 'Galen on the ideal of the physician' (*Opt.Med.*), *South African Medical Journal* 52

(1986) *Galen on Bloodletting* (*Ven.Sect.Er.*, *Ven.Sect.Er.Rom. Cur.Rat.Ven. Sect.*) (Cambridge)

Brock, A. J. (1916) *Galen on the Natural Faculties, Loeb Classical Library* (*Nat.Fac.*) (London)

(1929) *Greek Medicine* (selections from *SI*, *Nat.Fac.*, *UP*, *AA*, *Aff.Dig.*, *Lib.Prop.*, *Cons.*, *SMT*, *Ant.*, *Praen.*, *Loc.Aff.*, *Sim.Morb.*)

Daremberg, C. (1854/1856) *Œuvres anatomiques, physiologiques, et médicales de Galien*, 2 vols. (*Opt.Med., Protr., QAM, Cons., UP, Nat.Fac., Mot.Musc., SI, Loc.Aff., MMG*: French) (Paris)

Debru, A. and Garofalo, I. (2005) *Galien: Les Os pour les Débutants; L'Anatomie des Muscles* (*Oss., Mot.Musc.*: French) (Paris)

De Lacy, P. H. (1978) *Galen: On the Doctrines of Hippocrates and Plato (PHP)*: CMG V.4.1.2 (Berlin)

(1992) *Galen: On Semen (Sem.)*: CMG V 3,1 (Berlin)

(1996) *Galen: On the Elements according to Hippocrates (Hipp.Elem.)*: CMG V 1,2 (Berlin)

Duckworth, W. L.H, Lyons, M. C. and Towers, B. (1962) *Galen on Anatomical Procedures: The Later Books* (*AA* IX.6–XV, from Arabic) (Cambridge)

Edlow, R. B. (1977) *Galen on Language and Ambiguity (Soph.)* (Leiden)

Frede, M. (1985) *Galen: Three Treatises on the Nature of Science* (*SI, Subf.Emp.* [from Latin], with repr. of Walzer's 1944 trans. of *Med.Exp.*, with Greek fragments translated into English by M. Frede) (Indianapolis, Ind.)

Fortuna, S. (1997) *Galeni de Constitutione Artis Medicae ad Patrophilum* (*CAM*: Italian): CMG V 1,3 (Berlin)

Furley, D. J. and Wilkie, J. S. (1984) *Galen On Respiration and the Arteries* (*Ut.Resp., Art.Sang., Us.Puls., Caus.Resp.*) (Princeton, N.J.)

García Ballester, L. (1972a) *Alma y Enfermedad en la Obra de Galeno* (*QAM*: Spanish) (Valencia)

Goss, C. M. (1961) 'On the anatomy of veins and arteries' *(Ven.Art.Diss.)*, *Anatomical Record* 141

(1962) 'On the anatomy of the uterus' (*Ut.Diss.*), *Anatomical Record* 144

(1966) 'On the anatomy of the nerves' *(Nerv.Diss.)*, *American Journal of Anatomy* 118

(1968) 'On the movement of the muscles' (*Mot.Musc.*), *American Journal of Anatomy* 123

Grant, M. (2000) *Galen on Food and Diet ([Hum.], At.Bil., Inaeq.Int., Caus.Morb., Ptis., Alim.Fac.)* (London)

Green, R. M. (1951) *Galen's Hygiene (San.Tu.)* (Springfield, Ill.)

Hankinson, R. J. (1991) *Galen: On the Therapeutic Method, Books I and II (MM I–II)* (Oxford)

(1998) *Galen On Antecedent Causes (CP)* Cambridge Classical Texts and Commentaries (Cambridge)

Harkins, P. W. (1963) *Galen on the Passions and Errors of the Soul (Aff.Dig., Pecc.Dig.)* (Columbus, OH)

Iskandar, A. Z. (1988) *Galeni de Optimo Medico Cognoscendo* (*Opt.Med.Cogn.*, from Arabic): CMG Suppl. Or. IV (Berlin)

Johnston, I. (2006) *Galen on Diseases and Symptoms* (*Morb.D.H.*, *Caus.Morb.*, *Supp.Diff.*, *Caus.Symp.*) (Cambridge)

Kieffer, J. S. (1964) *Galen's Institutio Logica (Inst.Log.)* (Baltimore, Md.)

Kollesch, J. (1964) *Galeni de Instrumento Odoratus* (*Inst.Od.*: German): *CMG* Suppl. V (Berlin)

Lafout, J. B. and Moreno, A. R. (1947) *Obras de Galeno* (*Ars Med.*, *[Def.Med.]*: Spanish) (La Plata)

Lyons, M. C. (1963) *Galeni in Hippocratis Officina Medici (Hipp.Off.Med.)*: *CMG* Suppl. Or. I (Berlin)
(1969) *Galeni de Hippocratis in Victu Morborum Acutorum, de Causis Contentivis, de Partibus Artis Medicative* (*Hipp.Vict.Morb.Ac.* [genuine version], *CC*, *Part.Art.Med.*, from Arabic): *CMG* Suppl. Or. II (Berlin)

Lytton, D. C. and Resuhr, L. M. (1978) 'Galen on abnormal swellings' (*Tum.Pr.Nat.*), *Journal of the History of Medicine and Allied Sciences* 33

Malato, M. I. (1972) *L'arte medica* (*Ars Med.*: Italian) (Rome)

Mattock, J. N. (1972) 'A translation of the Arabic epitome of Galen's book "*peri êthôn*"' (*Mor.*), in Stern *et al.* (1972)

May, M. T. (1967) *Galen on the Usefulness of the Parts of the Body*, 2 vols. (*UP*) (Baltimore, Md.)

Menghi, M. and Vegetti, M. (1984) *Galeno: Le Passioni e gli Errori dell'Anima* (*Aff.Dig.*, *Pecc.Dig.*, *QAM*: Italian) (Venice)

Meyerhof, M. and Schacht, J. (1931) *Galen über die medizinischen Namen* (*Med.Nom.*: German, from Arabic) *Abhandlungen der Preussischen Akademie der Wissenschaften Phil.-hist. Kl.* 3 (Berlin)

Nickel, D. (2001) *Galeni de Foetuum Formatione: CMG* V 3,3 (*Foet.Form.*: German) (Berlin)

Nutton, V. (1979) *Galen on Prognosis: CMG* V 8,1 (*Prae.*) (Berlin)
(1999) *Galen on My Own Opinions: CMG* V 3,2 (*Prop.Plac.*, from Greek, Latin and Hebrew) (Berlin)

Penella, R. J. and Hall, T. S. (1973) 'Galen's "On the Best Constitution of Our Body"' (*Opt.Corp.Const.*), *Bulletin of the History of Medicine* 47

Pfaff, E. (1934) *Galens Kommentare zu dem II. Buche der Epidemien des Hippokrates* (*Hipp.Epid. II*: German from Arabic): *CMG* V 10,1 (Berlin)
(1956) *Galens Kommentare zu dem VI. Buche der Epidemien des Hippokrates Buch VI 6.5-VIII* (*Hipp.Epid. VI*: VI–VIII: German from Arabic): *CMG* V 10,2,2 (Berlin)

Powell, O. (2003) *Galen: On the Properties of Foodstuffs (Alim.Fac.)* (Cambridge)

Reedy, J. (1975) 'Galen on cancer and related diseases', *Clio Medica* 10, 229–38

Sider, D., McVaugh, M. (1979) 'Galen on tremor, palpitation, spasm and rigor' (*Trem.Palp.*), *Transactions and Studies of the College of Physicians of Philadelphia* n.s. 3

Siegel, R. E. (1975) *Galen on the Affected Parts (Loc.Aff.)* (Basle)

Simon, M. (1906) *Galen, Sieben Bücher Anatomie* (German from Arabic of *AA* XI.6-XV) (Leipzig)

Singer, C. (1952) 'Galen's elementary course on bones' (*Oss.*), *Proceedings of the Royal Society for Medicine* 45

(1956) *Galen on Anatomical Procedures (AA I–IX.6)* (London)

Singer, P. (1997) *Galen: Selected Works (Lib.Prop., Ord.Lib.Prop., Opt.Med., Protr., Thras., Aff.Dig., Pecc.Dig., QAM, Foet.Form., Temp., Opt.Corp.Const., Bon.Hab., Parv.Pil., Vict.Att., Puls., Ars Med.)* (Oxford)

Strohmeier, G. (1970) *Galeni de Partium Homoeomerum Differentiis* (German from Arabic of *Part.Hom.Diff.*): CMG Suppl. Or. III (Berlin)

Temkin, O. (1934) 'Galen's advice for an epileptic boy' (*Puer.Epil.*), *Bulletin of the History of Medicine* 2

Theoharides, T. C. (1971) 'Galen on marasmus' (*Marc.*), *Journal of the History of Medicine and Allied Sciences* 26

Walsh, J. (1930) 'Galen's exhortation to study the arts, especially medicine' (*Protr.*), *Medical Life* 37

Walzer, R. (1944) *Galen on Medical Experience (Med.Exp.,* from Arabic) (Oxford) (repr. in Frede, 1985)

Wasserstein, A. (1982) *Galen's Commentary on the Treatise 'Airs, Waters, Places' in the Hebrew Translation of Solomon ha-Me'ati'* (ed., trans. and comm.) (Jerusalem)

Wright, J. (1924) 'Galen on the organ of smell' (*Inst.Od.*), *Laryngoscope* 34

C: GENERAL

Accattino, P. (1994) 'Galeno e la riproduzione animale: analisi del "De Semine"', *ANRW* II 37.2, 1856–86

Ackerknecht, E. H. (1982) 'Diathesis: the word and the concept in medical history', *Bulletin of the History of Medicine* 56, 317–25

Allen, J. (1994) 'Failure and expertise in the ancient conception of an art', in T. Horowitz and A. Janis (eds.) *Scientific Failure* (Lanham, Md), 83–110

(2001) *Inference from Signs* (Oxford)

(2005) 'The Stoics on the origin of language and the foundations of etymology', in Frede and Inwood (2005)

Althoff, J. (1992) *Warm, kalt, flüssig und fest bei Aristoteles. Die Elementarqualitäten in den zoologischen Schriften* [Hermes Einzelschriften 57] (Stuttgart)

Amacher, M.P (1964) 'Galen's experiment on the arterial pulse and the experiment repeated', *Sudhoffs Archiv* 48, 177–80

Annas, J. (1980) 'Truth and knowledge', in Barnes *et al.* (1980), 84–104

(1990) 'Stoic epistemology', in Everson (1990), 184–203

Arbenz, E. (1891) *Die Vadianische Briefsammlung der Stadtbibliothek St. Gallen, II, Mitteilungen zur vaterländischen Geschichte* 25, 2

Arrizabalaga, J., Henderson, J. and French, R. (1997) *The Great Pox: The French Disease in Renaissance Europe* (New Haven, Conn./London)

Attewell, G. (2007) *Refiguring Unani Tibb. Plural Healing in late Colonial India* (New Delhi)

Baader, G. (1982) 'Mittelalterliche Medizin im italienischen Frühhumanismus', in G. Keil, P. Assion and W. F. Daems (eds.) *Fachprosa-Studien* (Berlin), 204–54

Ballester, L. G. (1972a) *Alma y Enfermedad en la Obra de Galeno (QAM: Sp.)*(Valencia)

(1972b) *Galeno* (Madrid)

(1981) 'Galen as a medical practitioner: problems in diagnosis', in Nutton (1981), 13–46

Barcia Goyanes, J. J. (1994) *El Mito de Vesalio* (Valencia)

Bardong, K. (1942) 'Beiträge zur Hippokrates-und Galenforschung', *Nachr. Akad. Göttingen, phil.-hist. Kl.* 7, 603–40

Barnes, J. (1991) 'Galen on logic and therapy', in Durling and Kudlien (1991), 50–102

(1993a) '"A third sort of syllogism": Galen and the logic of relations', in R. W. Sharples (ed.), *Modern Thinkers and Ancient Thinkers* (London), 172–94

(1993b) 'Galen and the utility of logic', in Kollesch and Nickel (1993), 33–52

(1997) '*Logique et pharmacologie:* à propos de quelques remarques d'ordre linguistique dans le *De Simplicium Medicamentorum Temperamentis ac Facultatibus* de Galien', in Debru (1997), 3–33

(2003) 'Proofs and syllogisms in Galen', in Barnes and Jouanna (2003), 1–24

Barnes, J., Brunschwig, J., Burnyeat, M. F. and Schofield, M. (eds.) (1982) *Science and Speculation* (Cambridge)

Barnes, J., Burnyeat, M. F. and Schofield, M. (eds.) (1980) *Doubt and Dogmatism* (Oxford)

Barnes, J., and Jouanna, J. (eds.) (2003) *Galien et la Philosophie. Entretiens sur l'antiquité classique* XLIX (Vandoeuvres-Genève)

Beccaria, A. (1971) 'Sulle tracce di un antico commento latino e greco di Ippocrate e Galeno', *Italia medioevale e umanistica* 14, 1–24

Béguin, D. (1996) 'Sur la méthode de travail suivie dans la préparation de l'édition aldine des Opera Omnia de Galien (1525)', in Garzya (1996)

Belloni, L. (1984) 'Die Zunft der Mailänder Apotheker und das Glasfenster vom heiligen Johannes dem Damaszener im Dom von Mailand', in O. Baur and O. Glandien (eds.) Zusammenhang. Festschrift für Marielene Putscher (Cologne), 177–88, Abb. 1 and 3

Bergsträsser, G. (1925) 'Hunain ibn Ishaq, Über die syrischen und arabischen Galen-Übersetzungen', Abhandlungen für die Kunde des Morgenlandes 17.2

(1932) 'Neue Materialien zu Hunain Ibn Ishaq's Galen-bibliographie', ibid. 19.2

Biesterfeldt, H. H. (1983) Galens Traktat Dass die Kräfte der Seele den Mischungen des Körpers folgen, Abhandlungen für die Kunde des Morgenlandes xl.4 (Wiesbaden) (edition of the Arabic translation of QAM)

Bliquez, L. and Kazhdan, A. (1984) 'Four testimonia to dissection in Byzantine times', Bulletin of the History of Medicine 58, 554–7

Bobzien, S. (2004) 'Peripatetic Hypothetical Syllogistic in Galen', Rhizai 2, 57–102

Boudon, V. (1994) 'Les oeuvres de Galien pour les débutants', ANRW II 37.2 (Berlin) 1421–67

(1996) 'L'Ars medica de Galien, est-il un traité authentique?', Revue des Etudes Grecques 109, 111–56

(2000a) Galien, Exhortation à la Médecine. Art médical (Paris)

(2000b) 'Galien par lui-même', in Manetti (2000)

(2001) 'Deux manuscrits médicaux arabes de Meshed (Rida tibb 5223 et 80): nouvelles découvertes sur le texte de Galien', Comptes rendus de l'Académie des Inscriptions et Belles Lettres, 197–220

(2002a) 'Galen's On my own Books: new material from Meshed, Rida, tibb. 5223', in Nutton (2002b, 9–18)

(2002b) 'La thériaque selon Galien: poison salutaire ou remède empoisonné?', in F. Collard and E. Samama (eds.), Le corps à l'épreuve. Poisons, remèdes et chirurgie: aspects des pratiques médicales dans l'Antiquité et au Moyen Âge (Langres), 45–56

(2003a) 'Aux marges de la médecine rationnelle: médecins et charlatans à Rome au temps de Galien (IIe s. de notre ère)', Révue des Etudes Grecques 116, 109–31

(2003b) 'Art, science et conjecture chez Galien', in Barnes and Jouanna (2003)

Boudon-Millot, V. (2007) Galien, Introduction Générale; Sur l'Ordre des ses Propres Livres; Sur ses Propres Livres; Que l'Excellent Médicin est aussi Philosophe (Paris)

Boudon-Millot, V. and Pietrobelli, A. (2005) 'Galien ressuscité: édition *princeps* du texte grec du *De propriis placitis*', *Revue des Etudes Grecques* 118, 168–71

Brain, P. (1986) *Galen on Bloodletting* (Cambridge)

Braund, D. C. and Wilkins, J. (eds.) (2000) *Athenaeus and his World: Reading Greek Culture in the Roman Empire* (Exeter)

Brock, A. J. (1916) *Galen on the Natural Faculties, Loeb Classical Library* (London)

Browning, R. (1985) 'A further testimony to human dissection in the Byzantine world', *Bulletin of the History of Medicine* 59, 518–20

Brunschwig, J. (1986) 'The cradle argument', in Schofield and Striker (1985), 113–44

Brunt, P. A. (1994) 'The bubble of the Second Sophistic', *Bulletin of the Institute of Classical Studies* 31, 25–52

Bürgel, J. C. (1967) 'Averroes "contra Galenum"', *Nachrichten der Akademie der Wissenschaften in Göttingen, philologisch-historische Klasse* 9, 265–340

Burnett, C. and Jacquart, D. (eds.) (1994) *Constantine the African and 'Ali ibn al-Abbas al-Magusi. The Pantegni and Related Texts* (Leiden)

Bylebyl, J. J. (1979) 'Padua and humanistic medicine', in C. Webster (ed.), *Health, Medicine and Mortality in the Sixteenth Century* (Cambridge), 335–70

Carlino, A. (1999) *Books of the Body: Anatomical Ritual and Renaissance Learning* (Chicago, Ill.)

Caston, V. (1997) 'Epiphenomenalisms, ancient and modern', *Philosophical Review* 106.3, 309–63

Cataldi Palau, A. (1998) *Gian Francesco Asola e la Tipografia Aldina* (Genoa)

Clark, G. N. (1964) *A History of the Royal College of Physicians of London* (Oxford)

Collins, M. (2000) *Medieval Herbals: The Illustrative Tradition* (London)

Copenhaver, B. (1978) *Symphorien Champier and the Reception of the Occultist Tradition in Renaissance France* (The Hague)

Cunningham, A. (1997) *The Anatomical Renaissance: The Resurrection of the Anatomical Projects of the Ancients* (Aldershot)

Dalrymple, W. (1993) *City of Djinns* (London)

Daremberg, C. (1841) *Exposition des Connaissances de Galien sur l'Anatomie, la Physiologie, et la Pathologie du Système nerveux*, MD thesis, Paris

(1854/1856) *Galien. Oeuvres*, 2 vols. (Paris)

Davies, J. (1860) *The Fables of Babrius, in Two Parts, Translated into English Verse from the Text of Sir G. C. Lewis* (London)

Debru, A. (1991) 'Expérience, plausibilité et certitude chez Galien', in López Férez (1991), 31–40

(1994) 'L'expérimentation chez Galien', *ANRW* II 37.2, 1718–56

(1995) 'Les démonstrations médicales à Rome au temps de Galien', in van der Eijk *et al.* (1995), 69–81

(1996) *Le Corps Respirant* (Leiden)

(ed.) (1997) *Galen on Pharmacology: Philosophy, History, and Medicine*, Studies in Ancient Medicine 16 (Leiden)

Debru, A. and Garofalo, I. (2005) *Galien: Les Os pour les Débutants; L'Anatomie des Muscles* (Paris)

Deichgräber, K. (1957) 'Parabasenverse aus Thesmophoriazusen II bei Galen', *Sitzungsberichte der deutschen Akademie der Wissenschaften zu Berlin, Klasse für Sprachen, Literatur und Kunst* 1956. 2 (Berlin)

De Lacy, P. H. (1972) 'Galen's Platonism', *American Journal of Philology* 93, 27–3

(1988) 'The third part of the soul', in Manuli and Vegetti (1988), 43–64

(1991) 'Galen's response to skepticism', *Illinois Classical Studies* 16, 283–306

Delehaye, H. (1909) *Les Légendes grecques des Saints militaires* (Paris)

De Ridder-Symoens, H. (1992) *A History of the University in Europe*, vol. 1 (Cambridge)

Dickson, K. (1998) *Stephanus the Philosopher and Physician: Commentary on Galen's Therapeutics to Glaucon* (Leiden)

Dillon, J. (1977) *The Middle Platonists* (London/Ithaca, N.Y.)

(1993) *Alcinous: The Handbook of Platonism*, Clarendon Later Ancient Philosophers (Oxford)

Dols, M. W. (1984) *Medieval Islamic Medicine: Ibn Ridwan's Treatise 'On the Prevention of Bodily Ills in Egypt'* (Berkeley, Calif.)

Donini, P. L. (1974) *Tre Studi sull'Aristotelismo nel II secolo d.C.* (Turin)

(1980) 'Motivi filosofici in Galeno', *La Parola del Passato* 194, 333–70

(1988) 'Tipologia degli errori e loro correzione secondo Galeno', in Manuli and Vegetti (1988), 65–116

(1992) 'Galeno e la filosofia', *ANRW* II 36.5, 3484–3504

(1994) 'Testi e commenti, manuali e insegnamento: la forma sistemica e i metodi della filosofia in età postellenistica', *ANRW* II 36.7, 5027–5100

(1995) 'Struttura delle passioni e del vizio e del loro cura in Crisippo', *Elenchos* 16, 305–30

(2007) 'Seneca e Galeno sulla Struttura biproposizionale delle passioni', in Crisippo, *Revista di storia della filosofia* 62, 431–52

Dorandi, T. (2000) *Le style et la tablette. Dans le secret des auteurs antiques* (Paris)

Drabkin, I. A. (1950) *Caelius Aurelianus On Acute and On Chronic Diseases* (Baltimore, MD)

Duckworth, W. L.H, Lyons, M. C. and Towers, B. (1962) *Galen on Anatomical Procedures: The Later Books* (Cambridge)

Duffy, J. M. (1984) 'Byzantine medicine in the sixth and seventh centuries: aspects of teaching and practice', *Dumbarton Oaks Papers* 38, 21–7

Duichev, I. (1988) *Antike heidnische Dichter und Denker in der alten bulgarischen Malerei* (Sofia)

Durling, R. J. (1961) 'A chronological census of Renaissance editions and translations of Galen', *Journal of the Warburg and Courtauld Institutes* 24, 230–305

(1991) 'Endeixis as a scientific term: (B) Endeixis in authors other than Galen and its medieval Latin equivalents', in Durling and Kudlien (1991), 112–13

Durling, R. J. and Kudlien, F. (eds.) (1991) *Galen's Method of Healing* (Leiden)

Ebbesen, S. (1981) *Commentators and Commentaries on Aristotle's Sophistici Elenchi*, 3 vols. (Leiden)

Ebert, T. (2005) 'La théorie du signe entre la médecine et la philosophie', in Kany-Turpin (2005), 51–63

Edelstein, L. (1967a) 'The Methodists', in Edelstein (1967c), 173–91

(1967b) 'Empiricism and skepticism in the teaching of the Greek Empiricist school', in Edelstein (1967c), 195–203

(1967c) *Ancient Medicine* (Baltimore, MD)

Edlow, R. B. (1977) *Galen on Language and Ambiguity* (Leiden)

Eijk, P. J. van der (1997) 'Galen's use of the concept of "qualified experience" in his dietetic and pharmacological works', in Debru (1997), 35–57 (reprinted as, and cited by way of, ch. 10 in van der Eijk, 2005, 279–98)

(1999a) 'The methodism of Caelius Aurelianus: some epistemological issues', in P. Mudry (ed.), *Le traité des Maladies aiguës et des Maladies chroniques de Caelius Aurelianus. nouvelles approches* (Nantes), 47–83 (reprinted as ch.11 in van der Eijk, 2005, 299–327)

(ed.) (1999b) *Ancient Histories of Medicine* (Leiden)

(2000–1) *Diocles of Carystus*, 2 vols. (Leiden)

(2005) *Medicine and Philosophy in Classical Antiquity* (Cambridge)

Eijk, P. J. van der, Horstmanshoff, H. F. J. and Schrijvers, P.H. (eds.) (1995) *Ancient Medicine in its Socio-Cultural Context*, 2 vols. (Amsterdam)

Everson, S. (ed.) (1990) *Epistemology*, Cambridge Companions to Ancient Thought 1 (Cambridge)

(ed.) (1991) *Psychology*, Cambridge Companions to Ancient Thought 2 (Cambridge)

(ed.) (1994) *Language*, Cambridge Companions to Ancient Thought 3 (Cambridge)

Fabricius, C. (1972) *Galens Exzerpte aus älteren Pharmakologen* [Ars medica. Texte und Untersuchungen zur Quellenkunde der Alten Medizin, II. Abteilung, Bd. 2] (Berlin/New York)

Fazzo, S. (2002) 'Alexandre d'Aphrodise contre Galien: la naissance d'une légende', *Philosophie Antique* 2, 109–45

Ferrari, G. (ed.) (1998) *Alessandro Benedetti, Historia Corporis humani sive Anatomice* (Florence)

Fischer, K. D., Nickel, D. and Potter, P. (eds.) (1998) *Text and Tradition: Studies in Ancient Medicine and its Transmission presented to Jutta Kollesch* (Leiden)

Flashar, H. (1962) *Aristoteles: Problemata Physica. Übersetzt und erläutert* (Berlin)

Flemming, R. (2000) *Medicine and the Making of Roman Women* (Oxford)

Fortuna, S. (1992) 'A proposito dei manoscritti di Galeno nella biblioteca di Nicolò Leoniceno', *Italia medioevale e umanistica* 35, 431–8

(1999) 'I procedimenti anatomici di Galeno e la traduzione latina di Demetrio Calcondila', *Medicina nei Secoli* 11, 9–28

Frede, D. and Inwood, B. (eds.) *Language and Learning: Philosophy of Language in the Hellenistic Age* (Cambridge)

Frede, M. (1981) 'On Galen's epistemology', in Nutton (1981), 65–86 (repr. in Frede, 1987a, 279–98)

(1982) 'On the method of the so-called Methodical school of medicine', in Barnes *et al.* (1982), 1–23 (repr. in Frede, 1987a, 261–78)

(1983) 'Stoics and skeptics on clear and distinct impressions', in M. F. Burnyeat (ed.), *The Skeptical Tradition* (California), 65–93 (repr. in Frede, 1987a, 151–76)

(1985) *Galen: Three Treatises on the Nature of Science* (Indianapolis, Ind.)

(1987a) *Essays in Ancient Philosophy* (Oxford)

(1987b) 'The ancient Empiricists', in Frede (1987a), 243–60

(1988) 'The Empiricist attitude towards reason and theory', in Hankinson (1988c), 79–97

(1990) 'An Empiricist view of knowledge: memorism', in Everson (1990), 225–50

(1999) 'Stoic epistemology', in K. Algra *et al.* (eds.), *The Cambridge History of Hellenistic Philosophy* (Cambridge), 295–322

(2003) 'Galen's theology', in Barnes and Jouanna (2003), 74–129

French, R. K. (1986) 'Pliny and Renaissance medicine', in R. K. French and F. Greenaway (eds.), *Science in the Early Roman Empire: Pliny the Elder, his Sources and his Influence* (London), 252–81

(1994) *William Harvey's Natural Philosophy* (Cambridge)

(1999) *Dissection and Vivisection in the European Renaissance* (Aldershot)

French, R. K. and Lloyd, G. E. R. (1978) 'Greek fragments of the lost books of Galen's Anatomical Procedures', *Sudhoffs Archiv* 62, 236–49

Furley, D. J. and Wilkie, J. S. (1984) *Galen on Respiration and the Arteries* (Princeton, N.J.)

García Ballester, L. (1972a) *Alma y Enfermedad en la Obra de Galeno* (Valencia)

   (1972b) *Galeno en la sociedad e la ciencia de su tiempo* (Madrid)

   (1981) 'Galen as a medical practitioner: problems in diagnosis', in Nutton (1981), 13–46

   (1988) 'Soul and body: disease of the soul and disease of the body in Galen's medical thought', in Manuli and Vegetti (1988), 117–52

   (1993) 'On the origins of the "six non-natural things" in Galen', in Kollesch and Nickel (1993), 105–15

   (1994) 'Galen as a clinician: his methods in diagnosis', *ANRW* II 37.2, 1636–72

   (1998) 'The new Galen: a challenge to Latin Galenism in thirteenth-century Montpellier', in Fischer *et al.* (1998), 55–83

Garofalo, I. (1986) *Galenus – Anatomicarum Administrationum Libri qui supersunt novem*, vol. I Libri I–IV (Naples)

   (1991) *Galeno, Procedamenti anatomici*, 3 vols. (Milan)

   (1994) 'La traduzione araba dei compendi alessandrini delle opere del canone di Galeno', *Medicina nei Secoli* 6, 329–48

   (2000) *Galenus – Anatomicarum Administrationum Libri qui supersunt novem*, vol. II Libri V–IX (Naples)

Garzya, A. (ed.) (1996) *Storia e Ecdotica dei testi medici greci* (Naples)

Giorgi, P. P. and Pasini, G. F. (1992) *Mondino de' Liuzzi, Anothomia* (Bologna)

Gill, C. (1998) 'Did Galen understand Platonic and Stoic thought on the emotions?', in J. Sihvola and T. Enjberg. Pederson (eds.), *The Emotions in Hellenistic Philosophy* (Dordrecht), 113–48

Gippert, J. (1997) *Index Galenicus* (Dettelbach)

Godman, P. (1998) *From Poliziano to Machiavelli: Florentine Humanism in the High Renaissance* (Princeton, N.J.)

Goltz, D. (1974) *Studien zur altorientalischen und griechischen Heilkunde. Therapie – Arzneibereitung – Rezeptstruktur* [*Sudhoffs Archiv*, Beiheft 16] (Wiesbaden)

Gottschalk, H. B. (1987) 'Aristotelian philosophy in the Roman world from the time of Cicero to the end of the second century AD', *ANRW* II 36.2, 1079–1174

Gourevitch, D. (1991) 'La pratique Méthodique: définition de la maladie, indication et traitement', in Mudry and Pigeaud (1991), 57–81

Grant, M. (2000) *Galen on Food and Diet* (London/New York)

Grant, R. M. (1983) 'Paul, Galen, and Origen', *Journal of Theological Studies* n.s. 34, 533–6

Green, R. M. (1951) *Galen's Hygiene (De Sanitate Tuenda)* (Springfield, Ill.)

Greenhill, W. A. (1854) 'Galen', in *Smith's Dictionary of Greek and Roman Biography* II (London) 207–17

Grice, H. P. (1989) *Studies in the Way of Words* (Cambridge, Mass.)

Grmek, M. D. and Gourevitch, D. (1994), 'Aux sources de la doctrine médicale de Galien: l'enseignement de Marinus, Quintus et Numisianus', *ANRW* II, 37.2, 1491–1528

Gundert, B. (1998) 'Die Tabulae Vindobonenses als Zeugnis alexandrinischer Lehrtätigkeit um 600 n. Chr.', in Fischer *et al.* (1998), 91–144

Hadot, P. (1984) 'Marc Aurèle était-il opiomane?', in E.Lucchesi and H. D. Saffrey (eds.), *Mémorial André-Jean Festugière. Antiquité païenne et chrétienne*, Cahiers d'orientalisme X (Geneva), 33–50

Hamarneh, S. K. (ed.) (1973) *Al-Biruni's Book on Pharmacy and Materia Medica* (Karachi)

(1997) *Yunani (Unani), Arabic and Islamic Medicine and Pharmacy* (Karachi)

Hankinson, R. J. (1987a) 'Evidence, externality and antecedence', *Phronesis* 32.1, 80–10

(1987b) 'Causes and empiricism', *Phronesis* 32.3, 329–48

(1988a) 'Galen explains the elephant', in M. Matthen and B. Linsky (eds.), *Philosophy and Biology, Canadian Journal of Philosophy* Suppl.Vol. 14, 135–57

(1988b) 'Galien: la médecine et la philosophie antisceptique', *Revue de philosophie ancienne* 2, 227–67

(ed.) (1988c) *Method, Medicine and Metaphysics. Apeiron* Suppl. Vol. 22.1

(1989) 'Galen and the best of all possible worlds', *Classical Quarterly* n.s. 39.1, 206–27

(1991a) 'Galen on the foundations of science', in López Férez (1991), 15–29

(1991b) *Galen: On the Therapeutic Method* Books I and II, Clarendon Later Ancient Philosophers (Oxford)

(1991c) 'Galen's anatomy of the soul', *Phronesis* 36.3, 197–233

(1991d) 'Greek medical models of mind', in Everson (1991), 194–217

(1992a) 'A purely verbal dispute? Galen on Stoic and Academic epistemology', in A.-J.Voelke (ed.), *Le Stoïcisme: Revue internationale de philosophie* 45.3, 267–300

(1992b) 'Galen's philosophical eclecticism', *ANRW* II, 36.5, 3504–22

(1993) 'Actions and passions: affection, emotion, and moral self-management in Galen's philosophical psychology', in J. Brunschwig and M. Nussbaum (eds.), *Passions & Perceptions: Studies in Hellenistic Philosophy of Mind* (Cambridge), 184–222

(1994a) 'Usage and abusage: Galen on language', in Everson (1994), 166–87

(1994b) 'Galen and the logic of relations' in Schrenk (1994), 57–75

(1994c) 'Galen's theory of causation', *ANRW* II, 37.2, 1757–74

(1994d) 'Galen's concept of scientific progress', *ANRW* II, 37.2, 1775–89

(1994e) 'Galen's anatomical procedures', *ANRW* II 37.2, 1834–55

(1995a) 'The growth of medical empiricism', in D. Bates (ed.), *Knowledge and the Scholarly Medical Traditions* (Cambridge), 60–83

(1995b) *The Sceptics* (London)

(1997a) 'Natural criteria and the transparency of judgement: Philo, Antiochus and Galen on epistemological justification', in B. Inwood and J. Mansfeld (eds.), *Assent and Argument: Studies in Cicero's Academic Books* (Leiden), 161–216

(1997b) 'Le phénomène et l'obscur: Galien et les animaux', in B. Cassin and J.-L. Labarrière (eds.), *L'animal dans l'antiquité* (Paris), 75–93

(1998a) *Galen on Antecedent Causes* (Cambridge)

(1998b) *Cause and Explanation in Ancient Greek Thought* (Oxford).

(2003a) 'Causation in Galen', in Barnes and Jouanna (2003), 31–72

(2003b) 'Epistemology', in B. Inwood (ed.), *Cambridge Companion to the Stoics* (Cambridge), 69–84

(2003c) 'Academics and Pyrrhonists', in C. Shields (ed.), *Blackwell Guide to Hellenistic Thought* (Oxford), 268–99

(2005) 'Prédiction, prophétie, prognostic: la gnoséologie de l'avenir dans la divination et la médicine antique', in Kany-Turpin (2005), 147–62

(2006) 'Body and soul in Galen', in R. A. H. King (ed.), *Common to Body and Soul* (Berlin), 231–57

(forthcoming (1)) 'Galen on the limitations of knowledge', in C. Gill, J. Wilkins and T. Whitmarsh (eds.), *Galen and the World of Knowledge* (Exeter)

(forthcoming (2)) 'Medicine and the science of the soul', in F. Wallis (ed.), *Medicine and the Soul of Science* (Montreal)

(forthcoming (3)) 'Teleology and necessity in Greek embryology'

Harig, G. (1974) *Bestimmung der Intensität im medizinischen System Galens* (Berlin)

(1976) 'Der Begriff der lauen Wärme in der theoretischen Pharmakologie Galens. Beziehungen zwischen Medizin und Mathematik in der Antike,' *NTM. Schriftenreihe für Geschichte der Naturwissenschaften, Technik und Medizin* 13, 70–6

(1977) 'Die antike Auffassung vom Gift und Tod des Mithridates', *NTM. Schriftenreihe für Geschichte der Naturwissenschaften, Technik und Medizin* 14, 104–12

(1980) 'Anfänge der theoretischen Pharmakologie im Corpus Hippocraticum', in M. D. Grmek (ed.), *Hippocratica. Actes du Colloque hippocratique de Paris (4–9 septembre 1978)* (Paris), 223–45

Harrison, S. J. (2000) *Apuleius: A Latin Sophist* (Oxford)

Heiberg, J. L. (1896) *Beiträge zur Geschichte Georg Valla's und seiner Bibliothek* (Leipzig)

Heine, R. (2004a) 'The Alexandrians', in Young *et al.* (2004), 117–30

(2004b) 'Hippolytus, Ps.-Hippolytus and the early canons', in Young *et al.* (2004), 142–51

Helm, J. (2001a) 'Religion and medicine: anatomical education at Wittenberg and Ingolstadt', in J. Helm and A. Winkelmanns (eds.), *Religious Confessions and the Sciences in the Sixteenth Century* (Leiden), 51–68

(2001b) 'Protestant and Catholic medicine in the sixteenth century? The case of Ingolstadt anatomy', *Medical History* 45, 83–96

Herbst, W. (1911) *Galeni Pergameni de Atticissantium studiis testimonia collecta atque examinata* (Diss., Leipzig)

Hintikka, J. and Remes, U. (1974) *The Method of Analysis* (Dordrecht)

Hoffmann, P. (1985) 'Un mystérieux collaborateur d'Alde Manuce: l'Anonymus Harvardianus', *Mélanges de l'Ecole Française de Rome* 97, 45–153

(1986) 'Autres données relatives à un mystérieux collaborateur d'Alde Manuce: l'Anonymus Harvardianus', *Mélanges de l'Ecole Française de Rome* 98, 673–708

Horstmanshoff, H. F. J. (1995) 'Galen and his patients', in van der Eijk *et al.* (1995), 448–59

Ierodiakonou, K. (1995) 'Alexander of Aphrodisias on medicine as a stochastic art', in van der Eijk *et al.* (1995), 473–86

(2002) 'Zeno's arguments', in T. Scaltsas and A. Mason (eds.), *The Philosophy of Zeno* (Larnaka), 81–112

Ilberg, J. (1889–97) 'Über die Schriftstellerei des Klaudios Galenos', *Rheinisches Museum* 44 (1889), 207–39; 47 (1892), 489–514; 51 (1896), 165–96; 52 (1897), 591–623

(1890) 'Die Hippokratesausgaben des Artemidorus Kapiton und Dioskurides', *Rheinisches Museum* 45, 111–37

(1905) 'Aus Galens Praxis', *Neue Jahrbücher für das klassische Altertum* 15, 276–312

Ioppolo, A. M. (1986) *Opinione e Scienza* (Naples)

(1993) 'The Academic position of Favorinus of Arelate', *Phronesis* 38 2, 183–213

Irigoin, J. (1996) 'Autour des sources manuscrits de l'éditio princeps de Galien', in Garzya (1996)

Iskandar, A. Z. (1976) 'An attempted reconstruction of the Late Alexandrian medical curriculum', *Medical History* 20, 235–58

(1988) *Galeni de Optimo Medico Cognoscendo*: *CMG* Suppl. Or. IV (Berlin)

Israelson, L. (1894) *Die Materia medica des Klaudios Galenos* (Diss., Dorpat)

Jackson, S. W. (1969) 'Galen – on mental disorders', *Journal of the History of Behavioral Sciences*, 365–84
    (1986) *Melancholia and Depression from Hippocratic Times to Modern Times* (New Haven, Conn.)
Jacquart, D. (1988) 'Représentations de Galien dans la peinture médiévale', *Dossiers Histoire et Archéologie* 123, 22–9
    (1995) 'Les "Concordances" de Pierre de Saint-Flour et l'enseignement de la médecine à Paris dans la seconde moitié du XIVe siècle', in O. Weijers (ed.), *Vocabulary of Teaching and Research between Middle Ages and Renaissance* (Turnhout)
Jacques, J. M. (1997) 'La méthode de Galien pharmacologue dans les deux traités sur les médicaments composés (*Peri suntheseôs pharmarkôn*)', in Debru (1997), 103–29
Johnston, I. (2006) *Galen on Diseases and Symptoms* (Cambridge)
Jordan, M. (1990) 'The construction of a philosophical medicine: exegesis and argument in Salernitan teaching on the soul', *Osiris*, ser. 2,6, 42–61
Jouanna, J. (2003) 'La notion de nature chez Galien', in Barnes and Jouanna (2003)
Jurina, K. (1985) *Vom Quacksalber zum Doctor Medicina* (Cologne)
Kany-Turpin, J. (ed.) *Signe et Prédiction dans l'Antiquité* (St Etienne)
Koester, H. (ed.) (1998) *Pergamon, Citadel of the Gods* (Harrisburg, Penn.)
Kollesch, J. (1967) 'René Chartier – Herausgeber und Fälscher der Werke Galens', *Klio* 48, 183–98
    (1968) 'Das Corpus Medicorum Graecorum – Konzeption und Durchführung,' *Medizinhistorisches Journal* 3, 68–73
    (1981) 'Galen und die zweite Sophistik', in Nutton (1981), 1–11
    (1988) 'Anschauungen von den *Arkhai* in der *Ars Medica* und die Seelenlehre Galens', in Manuli and Vegetti (1988), 215–19
    (1992) 'Das Berliner Corpus der antiken Ärzte: Zur Konzeption und zum Stand der Arbeiten,' in Garzya (1992), 347–50
Kollesch, J. and Nickel, D. (1992) 'Bibliographia Galeniana', *ANRW* II 37,2, 1351–1420, 63–70
    (eds.) (1993) *Galen und das Hellenistiche Erbe* (Stuttgart)
Kudlien, F. (1981) 'Galen's religious belief', in Nutton (1981), 117–30
    (1991) '*Endeixis* as a scientific term: (A) Galen's usage of the word (in medicine and logic)', in Durling and Kudlien (1991), 103–11
Landucci Ruffo, P. (1981) 'Le fonti della medicina nell'enciclopedia di Giorgio Valla', in V. Branca (ed.), *Giorgio Valla tra Scienza e Sapienza* (Florence)
Larrain, C. (1992) *Galens Kommentar zu Platons Timaios, Beiträge zur Altertumskunde* (Stuttgart)
    (1993) 'Ein bislang unbekanntes griechisches Fragment der Galen zugeschriebenen Schrift De motibus dubiis', *Philologus* 137, 265–73

Levey, M. and al-Khaledy, N. (1967) *The Medical Formulary of Al-Samarqandi and the Relation of Early Arabic Simples to those Found in the Indigenous Medicine of the Near East and India* (Philadelphia, Penn.)

Lewis, Sir G. C. (1859) *Babrii Fabulæ Aesopeœ* (London)

Lieber, E. (1981) 'Galen in Hebrew: the transmission of Galen's works in the medieval Islamic world', in Nutton (1981), 167–86

Lind, L. R. (1975) *Studies in Pre-Vesalian Anatomy* (Philadelphia, Penn.)

Lloyd, G. E.R (1966) *Polarity and Analogy* (Cambridge)

(1979) *Magic, Reason and Experience* (Cambridge)

(1981) 'Science and Mathematics', in *The Legacy of Greece: A New Appraisal*, ed. M. I. Finley (Oxford), 256–300

(1983) *Science, Folklore and Ideology* (Cambridge)

(1987) *The Revolutions of Wisdom* (Berkeley)

(1988) 'Scholarship, authority and argument in Galen's *Quod animi mores*', in Manuli and Vegetti (1988), 11–22

(1991a) 'Galen on Hellenistics and Hippocrateans: contemporary battles and past authorities', in Lloyd (1991b); repr. in Kollesch and Nickel (1992), 125–43

(1991b) *Methods and Problems in Greek Science* (Cambridge)

(1996a) 'Theories and Practices of Demonstration in Galen', in M. Frede and G. Striker, *Rationality in Greek Thought* (Oxford), 255–77

(1996b) *Aristotelian Explorations* (Cambridge)

(2005) 'Mathematics as a model of method in Galen', in R.W. Sharples (ed.), *Philosophy and the Sciences in Antiquity* (London), 110–30

Long, A. A. (1988) 'Ptolemy on the Criterion: an epistemology for the practising scientist', in J. Dillon and A. A. Long. (eds.), *The Question of 'Eclecticism'* (California), 176–207; repr. in P. M. Huby and G. Neal (eds.), *The Criterion of Truth* (Liverpool, 1989), 151–78

(2005) 'Stoic linguistics, Plato's Cratylus, and Augustine's De dialectica', in D. Frede and B. Inwood (eds.), *Language and Learning: Philosophy of Language in the Hellenistic Age* (Cambridge), 36–55

Long, A. A. and Sedley, D. N. (1987) *The Hellenistic Philosophers*, 2 vols. (Cambridge) (= LS)

Lonie, I. M. (1964) 'Erasistratus, the Erasistrateans and Aristotle', *Bulletin of the History of Medicine* 38: 426–43

López Férez, J. A. (ed.) (1991) *Galeno: obra, pensamiento y influencia* (Madrid)

Ludwig, W. (1999) *Vater und Sohn im 16. Jahrhundert: der Briefwechsel von Wolfgang Reichart, genannt Rychardus, mit seinem Sohn Zenon (1520–43)* (Hildesheim)

Lukasiewicz, J. (1951) *Aristotle's Syllogistic from the Standpoint of Modern Logic* (Oxford)

Maclean, I. (2002) *Logic, Signs and Nature in the Renaissance: The Case of Learned Medicine* (Cambridge)

Maddison, F., Pelling, M. and Webster, C. (eds.) (1997) *Linacre Studies: Essays on the Life and Work of Thomas Linacre c.1460–1524* (Oxford)

Manetti, D. (ed.) (2000) *Studi su Galeno. Scienza, filosofia, retorica e filologia* (Florence)

Manetti, D. and Roselli, A. (1994) 'Galeno commentatore di Ippocrate', *ANRW* II 37.2, 1529–1635

Mani, N. (1991) 'Die wissenschaftlichen Grundlagen der Chirurgie bei Galen (mit besonderer Berücksichtigung der MM)', in Durling and Kudlien (1991), 26–49

Mansfeld, J. (1990) 'Doxography and dialectic: the *Sitz im Leben* of the *Placita*', *ANRW* I 36,4, 3056–3229

(1991) 'The idea of the will in Chrysippus, Posidonius and Galen', in *Proceedings of the Boston area Colloquium in Ancient Philosophy* VII, 107–57

(1994) *Prolegomena: Questions to be Settled before the Study of an Author or a Text*, Philosophia Antiqua 61 (Leiden)

Manuli, P. (1993) 'Galen and Stoicism', in Kollesch and Nickel (1992), 53–61

Manuli, P. and Vegetti, M. (eds.) (1988) *Le Opere Psicologiche di Galeno* (Naples)

Mates, B. (1953) *Stoic Logic* (Berkeley, Calif.)

Matthen, M. (1988) 'Empiricism and ontology in ancient medicine', in Hankinson (1988c), 99–121

Mattock, J. N. (1972) 'A translation of the Arabic epitome of Galen's book "*peri êthôn*"', in Stern *et al.* (1972), 235–60

May, M. T. (1968) *Galen on the Usefulness of the Part of the Body*, 2 vols. (Baltimore, MD)

Menghi, M. and Vegetti, M. (1984) *Galeno: Le Passioni e gli Errori dell'Anima* (Venice)

Meyerhof, M. (1926) 'New light on Hunain ibn Ishaq and his period', *Isis* 8, 685–724

(1929) 'Autobiographische Bruchstücke Galens aus arabischen Quellen', *Sudhoffs Archiv* 22, 72–86

(1935a) 'Ibn an-Nafis (XIIIth century) and his theory of the lesser circulation', *Isis* 23, 100–20

(1935b) 'Esquisse d'histoire de la pharmacologie chez les Musulmans d'Espagne', *Al-Andalus* 3, 1–41

(1984) *Studies in Medieval Arabic Medicine* (London)

Moraux, P. (1953) *Les listes anciennes des ouvrages d'Aristote* (Louvain)

(1981) 'Galien comme philosophe', in Nutton (1981), 87–116

(1984) *Der Aristotelismus bei den Griechen*. 2. Bd. Der Aristotelismus im I. und II. Jh. n. Chr. (Berlin/New York)

(1985) 'Galen and Aristotle's *de Partibus Animalium*', in A. Gotthelf (ed.), *Aristotle on Nature and Living Things* (Bristol, N.J.), 327–44

Mudry, P. and Pigeaud, J. (eds.) (1991) *Les écoles médicales à Rome* (Geneva)

Mueller, I. von (1897) 'Über Galens Werk vom wissenschaftlichen Beweis', *Abhandlung der Königlichen Bayerischen Akademie der Wissenschaften* 20, 1895, 2

(1898) 'Über die dem Galen zuschriebene Abhandlung *Peri tês aristês haireseôs*', *Sitzungsberichte der philosophisch-philologischen Klasse der Königlichen Bayerischen Akademie der Wissenschaften* 23, 53–162

Mugnai Carrara, D. (1979) 'Profilo di Nicolò Leoniceno', *Interpres* 2, 169–212

(1983) 'Una polemica umanistico-scolastica circa l'interpretazione delle tre dottrine ordinate di Galeno', *Annali dell'Istituto e Museo di Storia della Scienza di Firenze* 8, 31–57

(1991) *La Biblioteca di Nicolò Leoniceno* (Florence)

(1999) 'Epistemological problems in Giovanni Mainardi's commentary on Galen's *Ars Parva*', in A. Grafton and N. Siraisi (eds.), *Natural Particulars: Nature and the Disciplines in Renaissance Europe* (Cambridge, Mass.), 251–74

Mynas, M. (1844) *Galênou Eisagôgê Dialektikê* (Paris)

Nandris, G. (1970) *Christian Humanism in the Neo-Byzantine Mural Painting of Eastern Europe* (Wiesbaden), 24–44

Neugebauer, O. (1949) 'Astronomical fragments in Galen's treatise On Seven-Month Children', *Rivista degli Studi Orientali* 24, 92–4

Nickel, D. (1989) *Untersuchungen zur Embryologie Galens, Schriften zur Geschichte und Kultur der Antike* 27 (Berlin)

(2001) *Galeni de Foetuum Formatione* (ed., trans. and comm. [German]): CMG V 3,3 (Berlin)

(2002) 'On the authenticity of an "excerpt" from Galen's Commentary on the Timaeus', in Nutton (2002b), 73–8

Nutton, V. (1972a) 'Galen and medical autobiography', *Proceedings of the Cambridge Philological Society* n.s. 18, 50–62

(1972b) 'Ammianus and Alexandria', *Clio Medica* 3 (1972) 165–76

(1973) 'The chronology of Galen's early career', *Classical Quarterly* n.s. 23, 158–71

(1976) *C. G.Kühn's Edition of Galen* (Oxford)

(1979) *Galen On Prognosis* (ed., trans. and comm.): CMG V 8,1 (Berlin)

(ed.) (1981) *Galen: Problems and Prospects* (London)

(1984a) 'Galen in the eyes of his contemporaries', *Bulletin of the History of Medicine* 38, 319–23 (reprinted as ch. III in Nutton, 1988)

(1984b) 'Galeno salvato dalle acque', *Kos* 1, 2, 33–50

(1987a) 'John Caius and the Manuscripts of Galen', *Cambridge Philosophical Society*, 19–33

(1987b) '"Qui magni Galeni doctrinam in re medica primus revocavit". Matteo Corti und der Galenismus im medizinischen Unterricht der Renaissance', in G. Keil, B. Moeller and W. Trusen (eds.), *Der Humanismus und die oberen Fakultäten* (Weinheim), 173–84

(1987c) 'Numisianus and Galen', *Sudhoffs Archiv* 71, 235–9

(1987d) 'Galen's philosophical testament', in P. Moraux (ed.), *Aristoteles – Werk und Wirkung* 2: *Kommentierung, Überlieferung, Nachleben* (Berlin)

(1988) *From Democedes to Harvey* (London)

(1990a) 'The anatomy of the soul in early Renaissance medicine', in G. Dunstan (ed.), *The Human Embryo: Aristotle and the Arabic and European Traditions* (Exeter), 145–52

(1990b) 'The patient's choice: a new treatise by Galen', *Classical Quarterly* 40, 236–57

(1991) 'Style and content in the *Method of Healing*', in Durling and Kudlien (1991), 1–25

(1993a) 'Greek science in the sixteenth-century Renaissance', in J. V. Field and F. A. J. L. James (eds.), *Renaissance and Revolution: Humanists, Scholars, Craftsmen and Natural Philosophers in Early Modern Europe* (Cambridge), 15–28

(1993b) 'Wittenberg anatomy', in O. P. Grell and A. Cunningham (eds.), *Medicine and the Reformation* (London), 11–32

(1993c) 'Galen and Egypt', in Kollesch and Nickel (1993), 11–31

(1995) 'Galen *ad multos annos*', *Dynamis* 15, 25–40

(1996) '"Idle old trots, coblers and costardmongers"; Pieter van Foreest on quackery', in H. A. Bosman-Jelgersma (ed.), *Petrus Forestus medicus* (Amsterdam) (1996), 243–56

(1997a) 'The rise of medical humanism; Ferrara, 1464–1555', *Renaissance Studies* 11, 2–19

(1997b) 'An early reader of Vesalius' Fabrica', *Vesalius* 3, 73–4

(1997c) 'Galen on theriac: problems of authenticity', in Debru (1997), 133–51

(1999) *Galen On My Own Opinions: CMG* V,3,2 (Berlin)

(2002a) 'Asclepius transformed', in Tuplin and Rihll (2002), 242–55

(ed.) (2002b) *The Unknown Galen, Bulletin of the Institute of Classical Studies*, Supplement 77

(2002c) 'In defence of Kühn', in Nutton (2002b)

(2004) *Ancient Medicine* (London)

(forthcoming) 'Biographical accounts of Galen, 1340–1660', in T. Rütten (ed.), *Geschichte der Medizingeschichtsschreibung* (Wolfenbüttel)

Nutton, V. and Scarborough, J. (1982) 'The Preface of Dioscorides' Materia Medica: introduction, translation, and commentary', *Transactions and Studies of the College of Physicians at Philadelphia*, ser. 5, vol. 4, 187–227

O'Boyle, C. (1998) *The Art of Medicine: Medical Teaching at the University of Paris 1250–1400* (Leiden)

O'Malley, C. D. (1964) *Andreas Vesalius of Brussels, 1514–1564* (London/Berkeley, Calif.)

Ormos, I. (1993) 'Bemerkungen zur editorischen Bearbeitung der Galenschrift *Über die Sektion toter Lebewesen*', in Kollesch and Nickel (1992), 165–72

Pagel, J. (1896) *Neue literarische Beiträge zur mittelalterlichen Medizin* (Berlin)

Palmieri, N. (2001) 'Nouvelles remarques sur les commentaires à Galien de l'école médicale de Ravenne', in A. Debru and N. Palmieri (eds.), *Docente Natura. Mélanges de Médecine ancienne et médiévale offerts à Jean Sabbah* (St Etienne), 209–46

(2002) 'La médecine alexandrine et son rayonnement occidental (VIe–VIIe s. ap. J.-Ch.)', *Lettre d'Informations du Centre Jean Palerne. Médecine antique et médiévale*, n.s. 1, 5–23

Pellegrin, P. (2005) 'Scepticisme et sémiologie médicale', in Kany-Turpin (2005), 65–82

Perilli, L. (2005) 'Cronaca di un'avventura editoriale: il "Galeno" di Aldo Manuzio e l'ombra di Erasmo', *Giornale critico della Filosofia italiana* 84, 424–32

Pesenti, T. (1998) 'I libri di medicina di Giovanni di Marco da Rimini (c. 1400–1474)', *Il Bibliotecario*, n.s. 2, 93–109

(2002) 'The libri Galieni in Italian universities in the fourteenth century', *Italia medioevale e umanistica* 42: 119–47

Peterson, D. W. (1974) *Galen's 'Therapeutics to Glaucon' and its early Commentaries*, Ph.D. diss., Baltimore, Md.

(1977) 'Observations on the chronology of the Galenic Corpus', *Bulletin of the History of Medicine* 51, 484–95

Pigeaud, J. (1988) 'Le psychopathologie de Galien', in Manuli and Vegetti (1988), 153–84

(1991) 'Les fondements du Méthodisme', in Mudry and Pigeaud (1991), 7–50

Pleket, H. W. (1995) 'The social status of physicians in the Graeco-Roman world', in van der Eijk et al. (1995), 27–34

Potter, P. (1998) 'The Editiones principes of Galen and Hippocrates and their relationship', in Fischer *et al.* (1998), 243–61

Powell, O. (2003) *Galen: On the Properties of Foodstuffs (De alimentorum facultatibus)* (Cambridge)

Prantera, A. (1991) *The Side of the Moon* (London)

Pressouyre, L. (1966) 'Le cosmos platonicien de la Cathédrale d'Anagni', *Mélanges d'Archéologie et d'Histoire* 78, 551–93

Puglia, E. (1988) *Demetrio Lacone, aporie testuali ed esegetici in Epicuro* (Naples)

Rath, G. (1960) 'Medical education in the S. German universities in the fifteenth and sixteenth centuries', *Journal of Medical Education* 35, 511–17

Reeds, K. M. (1991) *Botany in Medieval and Renaissance Universities* (New York/London)

Regenbogen, O. (1961) *Kleine Schriften* (Munich)

Rescher, N. (1966) *Galen and the Syllogism* (Pittsburgh)
    (1967) *Temporal Modalities in Arabic Logic* (Dordrecht)

Richardson, W. F. (trans.) (1998) *Andreas Vesalius, On the Fabric of the Human Body*, vol. 1 (San Francisco, Calif.)

Riddle, J. M. (1984) 'Gargilius Martialis as a medical writer', *Journal of the History of Medicine and Allied Sciences* 39, 408–29
    (1985) *Dioscorides on Pharmacy and Medicine* (Austin, Tex.)

Robinson, R. (1969a) *Essays in Ancient Philosophy* (Oxford)
    (1969b) 'Analysis in Greek geometry', in Robinson (1969a), 1–15 (originally published in *Mind*, 1936)

Rocca, J. (2002) 'The brain beyond Kühn: reflections on *Anatomical Procedures*, book IX', in Nutton (2002b), 87–100
    (2003) *Galen on the Brain: Anatomical Knowledge and Physiological Speculation in the Second Century AD* (Leiden)
    (2004) 'Galen and the artful symmetry of the brain', in Rose (2004), 77–88
    (forthcoming) 'Teachers and tradition: Galen and a history of anatomy'

Rose F. C. (ed.) (2004) *Neurology of the Arts* (London)

Roselli, A. (1999) 'Notes on the DOXAI of doctors in Galen's Commentaries on Hippocrates', in van der Eijk (1999b), 359–81

Rosenthal, F. (1956) 'An ancient Commentary on the Hippocratic Oath', *Bulletin of the History of Medicine* 30, 52–87
    (1975) *The Classical Heritage in Islam* (London)

Rouché, M. (1999) 'Did medical students study philosophy at Alexandria?', *Bulletin of the Institute of Classical Studies* 43, 153–69

Salazar, C. F. (2000) *The Treatment of War Wounds in Graeco-Roman Antiquity* (Leiden/New York)

Sandbach, F. H. (1930) 'Ennoia and prolêpsis in the Stoic theory of knowledge', Classical Quarterly 24, 44–51

Savage-Smith, E. (1955) 'Attitudes to dissection in medieval Islam', Journal of the History of Medicine 50, 67–110

(2002) 'Galen's lost ophthalmology and the Summaria Alexandrinorum', in Nutton (2002b), 121–38

Scarborough, J. (1969) Roman Medicine (London)

(1971) 'Galen and the gladiators', Episteme 5, 98–111

(1983) 'Theoretical assumptions in Hippocratic pharmacology', in F. Lasserre and P. Mudry (eds.), Formes de pensée dans la collection hippocratique: actes du IVe Colloque international hippocratique (Lausanne 1981) (Geneva), 307–25

(1984) 'Early Byzantine pharmacology', Symposium on Byzantine Medicine, ed. John Scarborough [Dumbarton Oaks Papers 38] (Washington, D.C.), 213–32

Schacht, J. and Meyerhof, M. (1937) The Medico-philosophical Controversy between Ibn Butlan of Baghdad and Ibn Ridwan of Cairo: A Contribution to the History of Greek Learning among the Arabs (Cairo)

Schiaparelli, A. (2002) Galeno e le Fallacie Linguistiche. Il 'de Captionibus in dictione', Istituto Veneto di Scienze, Lettere e Arti (Memorie, Classe di scienze morali, lettere ed arti), 101

Schofield, M. and Striker, G. (eds.) (1985) The Norms of Nature (Cambridge)

Schrenk, L. (ed.) (1994) Aristotle and Later Antiquity (Washington, D.C.)

Sedley, D. N. (1982) 'On signs', in Barnes et al. (1982), 239–72

(1997) 'Plato's auctoritas and the rebirth of the commentary tradition', in J. Barnes and M. Griffin (eds.), Philosophia Togata II (Oxford), 110–29

Sezgin, F. (1970) Geschichte des arabischen Schrifttums, vol. 3 (Leiden)

Sharples, R. B. (1982) 'Alexander of Aphrodisias, On Time', Phronesis 27, 72–8

(1987) 'Alexander of Aphrodisias: scholasticism and innovation', ANRW II 36.2, 1176–243

Sicherl, M. (1976) Handschriftliche Vorlagen der Editio princeps des Aristoteles (Wiesbaden)

Sideras, A. (1994) 'Rufus von Ephesos und sein Werk im Rahmen der antiken Medizin', ANRW II 37.2, 1077–1253

Siegel, R. E. (1968) Galen's System of Physiology and Medicine (Basle/New York)

(1970) Galen on Sense-Perception (Basle/New York)

Simon, M. (1906) Galen, Sieben Bücher Anatomie (Leipzig)

Singer, P. (1991) 'Aspects of Galen's Platonism', in López Férez (1991), 41–55

(1997) Galen: Selected Works (Oxford)

Siraisi, N. G. (1981) *Taddeo Alderotti and his Pupils: Two Generations of Italian Medical Learning* (Princeton, N.J.)

(1987) *Avicenna in Renaissance Italy: The Canon and Medical Teaching in Italian Universities after 1500* (Princeton, N.J.)

(1990) *Medieval and Early Renaissance Medicine* (Chicago, Ill.)

Skoda, F. (2001) 'Désignations de l'antidote en grec ancien', in A. Debru and N. Palmieri (eds.), *Docente natura. Mélanges de médecine ancienne et médiévale offerts à Guy Sabbah*, Saint-Etienne: Publications de l'Université de Saint-Etienne, 273–329

Sluiter, I. (1995) 'The embarrassment of imperfection: Galen's assessment of Hippocrates' linguistic merits', in van der Eijk *et al.* (1995), 519–35

Smith, M. Q. (1965) 'Anagni: an example of medieval typological decoration', *Papers of the British School at Rome* 33, 1–47

Smith, W. D. (1979) *The Hippocratic Tradition* (Ithaca, NY/London)

Sorabji R. R. K. (ed.) (1990a) *Aristotle Transformed* (London)

(1990b) 'The ancient commentators on Aristotle', in Sorabji (1990a), 1–30

(2000) *Emotion and Peace of Mind: From Stoic Agitation to Christian Temptation* (Oxford)

Staden, H. von (1982) 'Hairesis and heresy: the case of the haireseis iatrikai', in B. Meyer and E. Sanders (eds.), *Jewish and Christian Self-Definition* III (London), 76–100 (+199–206)

(1989) *Herophilus: The Art of Medicine in Early Alexandria* (Cambridge)

(1991) 'Galen as historian: his use of sources on the Herophileans', in López Férez (1991), 205–22

(1995a) 'Anatomy as rhetoric: Galen on dissection and persuasion', *Journal of the History of Medicine* 50, 47–66

(1995b) 'Science as text, science as history: Galen on metaphor', in van der Eijk *et al.* (1995), 499–518

(1997a) 'Galen and the "Second Sophistic"', in R. Sorabji (ed.), *Aristotle and After, Bulletin of the Institute of Classical Studies* Suppl. 68 (London: Institute for Classical Studies), 33–55

(1997b) 'Inefficacy, error, and failure: Galen on *dokima pharmaka eprakta*', in Debru (1997), 59–83

(1998) 'Gattungen und Gedächtnis: Galen über Wahrheit und Lehrdichtung', in W. Kullmann, J. Althoff and M. Asper (eds.), *Gattungen wissenschaftlicher Literatur in der Antike* (Tübingen)

(2000) 'Body, soul and nerves: Epicurus, Herophilus, Erasistratus, the Stoics, and Galen', in J. P. Wright and P. Potter (eds.), *Psyche and Soma* (Oxford)

(2002) '"A woman does not become ambidextrous": Galen and the culture of scientific commentary', in R. Gibson and C. Kraus (eds.), *The Classical Commentary* (Leiden), 109–39

Stauber, R. (1908) *Die Schedelsche Bibliothek* (Freiberg)

Steckerl, F. (1958) *The Fragments of Praxagoras and his School* (Leiden)

Stein, M. (1997) 'La thériaque chez Galien: sa préparation et son usage thérapeutique', in Debru (1997), 199–209

Stern, S. M., Hourani, A. and Brown, V. (eds.) (1972) *Islamic Philosophy and the Classical Tradition* (Oxford)

Striker, G. (1985) 'Antipater: or the art of living', in Schofield and Striker (1985), 185–204

Strohmaier, G. (1981) 'Galen in Arabic: problems and prospects', in Nutton (1981), 187–96

(1998) 'Bekannte und unbekannte Zitate in den Zweifeln an Galen des Rhazes', in Fischer *et al.* (1988)

(2002) 'The uses of Galen in Arabic literature', in Nutton (2002b)

(2003) 'Die Ethik Galens und ihre Rezeption in der Welt des Islams', in Jouanna and Barnes (2003)

(2006) 'Galen in den Schulen der Juden und Christen', *Judaica. Beiträge zum Verstehen des Judentums* 62, 140–56.

(forthcoming) 'La longévité de Galien et les deux places de son tombeau', in V. Boudon-Millot, A. Guardasole and C. Magdelaine (eds.), *La science médicale antique: nouveaux regards*, Études en l'honneur de J. Jouanna (Paris)

Swain, S. (1996) *Hellenism and Empire: Language, Classicism, and Power in the Greek World AD 50–250* (Oxford)

Taylor, M. D. (1980–1) 'A historiated Tree of Jesse', *Dumbarton Oaks Papers* 34–5, 125–76

Tecusan, M.-M. (2004) *The Fragments of the Methodists*, vol. 1 (Leiden)

Telfer, W. (1955) *Nemesius of Emesa, On the Nature of Man* (London)

Temkin, O. (1932) 'Geschichte des Hippokratismus im ausgehenden Altertum', *Kyklos* 4, 1932, 1–80

(1934) 'Galen's advice for an epileptic boy', *Bulletin of the History of Medicine* 2, 179–89

(1956) *Soranus' Gynecology* (Baltimore, MD)

(1973) *Galenism: Rise and Decline of a Medical Philosophy* (Ithaca, N.Y.)

(1977) *The Double Face of Janus* (Baltimore, MD)

(1991) *Hippocrates in a World of Pagans and Christians* (Baltimore, MD)

Thorndike, L. (1946) 'Translations of works from the Greek by Niccolò da Reggio (c. 1308–1345)', *Byzantina-Metabyzantina* 1, 213–35

Tieleman, T. (1996) *Galen and Chrysippus On the Soul. Argument and Refutation in the De Placitis Books II–III* (Leiden)

(1997) 'The hunt for Galen's shadow: Alexander of Aphrodisias, De anima 94,7–100', in K. A. Algra, *et al.* (eds.), *Polyhistor: Studies in the History and Historiography of Ancient Philosophy* (Leiden), 256–83

(2002) 'Galen on the seat of the intellect: anatomical experiment and philosophical tradition', in Tuplin and Rihll (2002), 254–73

(2003a) 'Galen's psychology', in Barnes and Jouanna (2003)

(2003b) *Chrysippus on Affections* (Leiden)

Todd, R. B. (1976) *Alexander of Aphrodisias on Stoic Physics* (Leiden)

(1977) 'Greek medical ideas in the Aristotelian Commentators', *Symbolae Osloenses* 52, 117–34

Totelin, L. M. V. (2004) 'Mithradates' antidote – a pharmacological ghost', *Early Science and Medicine* 9.1, 1–19

Touwaide, A. (1994) 'Galien et la toxicologie', *ANRW* II 37.2, 1887–1986

Tuplin, C. J. and Rihll, T. (eds.) (2002) *Science and Mathematics in Ancient Greek Culture* (Oxford)

Ullmann, M. (1970) *Die Medizin im Islam* (Leiden)

(1992) 'Die arabische Überlieferung der Schriften des Rufus von Ephesos', *ANRW* II 37,2, 1293–1313

Unte, W. (1985) 'Wilamowitz als wissenschaftlicher Organisator,' in W. M. Calder, III, H. Flashar and T. Lindkem (eds.), *Wilamowitz nach 50 Jahren* (Darmstadt), 720–70

Vallance, J. (1990) *The Lost Theory of Asclepiades of Bithynia* (Oxford)

Vegetti, M. (1981) 'Modelli dei medicina in Galeno', in Nutton (1981), 47–64

(1990) 'I nervi dell'anima', *Biologica* 4, 11–26

(1994) 'L'immagine del medico e lo statuto epistemologico della medicina in Galeno', *ANRW* II 37.2, 1672–1717

(1999a) 'Tradition and truth: forms of philosophical–scientific historiography in Galen's *De placitis*', in van der Eijk (1999b), 333–57

(1999b) 'Historiographical strategies in Galen's physiology (*De usu partium, De naturalibus facultatibus*)', in van der Eijk (1999b), 383–95

(2001) 'Il confronto degli antichi e dei moderni in Galeno', in G. Cajani and D. Lanza (eds.), *L'Antico degli antichi* (Palermo), 87–100

Veith, I. (1959) 'Galen, the first medical autobiographer', *Modern Medicine* 27, 232–45

Ventris, M. and Chadwick, J. (1973[2]) *Documents in Mycenean Greek* (Cambridge)

Vogt, S. (2005), '" . . . er schrieb in Versen, und er tat recht daran." Lehrdichtung im Urteil Galens', in T. Foegen (ed.), *Antike Fachtexte/Ancient Technical Texts* (Berlin/New York), 51–78

Walsh, J. (1926) 'Galen's discovery and promulgation of the function of the recurrent laryngeal nerve', *Annals of Medical History* 8, 176–84

(1927) 'Galen's studies at the Alexandrian school', *Annals of Medical History* 9, 132–43

(1931) 'Refutation of the charges of cowardice made against Galen', *Annals of Medical History* n.s. 3, 195–208

Walzer, R. (1944) *Galen on Medical Experience: Arabic Text with an English Translation* (Oxford)

(1949a) *Galen on Jews and Christians* (Oxford)

(1949b) 'New light on Galen's moral philosophy, from a recently discovered Arabic source', *Classical Quarterly* 43, 82–96 (repr. in Walzer, 1962)

(1954) 'A diatribe of Galen', *Harvard Theological Review* 47, 243–54 (repr. in Walzer, 1962)

(1962) *Greek into Arabic: Essays on Islamic Philosophy* (Oxford)

Wasserstein, A. (1982) *Galen's Commentary on the Treatise 'Airs, Waters, Places' in the Hebrew Translation of Solomon ha-Me'ati'* (ed., trans. and comm.) (Jerusalem)

Watson, G. (1966) *Theriac and Mithridatium: A Study in Therapeutics* (London)

Wear, A. (1981) 'Galen in the Renaissance', in Nutton (1981)

Weisser, U. (1989) 'Das Corpus Hippocraticum in der arabischen Medizin', in G. Baader and R. Winau (eds.), *Die hippokratischen Epidemien* (Stuttgart), 387–408

Westerink, L. G. (1964) 'Philosophy and medicine in Late Antiquity', *Janus* 51, 169–177

Whittaker, J. (1987) 'Platonic philosophy in the early centuries of the Empire', *ANRW* II 36.1, 81–123

Williams, B. A. O. (1994) 'Cratylus' theory of names and its refutation', in Everson (1994), 28–36

Wilson, N. G. (1987) 'Aspects of the transmission of Galen', in G. Cavallo (ed.), *Le strade del testo: Studi e Commenti* 5 (Bari), 45–64

(1993) *From Byzantium to Italy: Greek Studies in the Renaissance* (London)

Wöhrle, G. (1990) *Studien zur Theorie der antiken Gesundheitslehre* (Stuttgart)

Wolska-Conus, W. (1989) 'Stéphanos d'Athènes et Stéphanos d'Alexandrie. Essai d'identification et de biographie', *Revue des Etudes Byzantines* 47, 5–89

Young, F. (1997) *Biblical Exegesis and the Formation of Christian Culture* (Cambridge)

Young, F., Ayres, L. and Louth, A. (eds.) (2004) *The Cambridge History of Early Christian Literature* (Cambridge)

Zonta, M. (1995) *Un Interprete ebreo della Filosofia di Galeno: gli Scritti filosofici di Galeno nell' Opera di Shem Tob ibn Falaquera* (Turin)

INDEX

Note: Works by or debatably by Galen are indexed by title in the form most commonly used in the text (usually English), and only where there is substantive comment or extended quotation (not for every citation). Latin titles and standard abbreviations are to be found in the Appendixes on pp. 391–403.

Other authors' works are indexed under the author's name.

Academics *see* Carneades, Academy of
actuality/potentiality, Aristotelian
  theory of 308–9
Adrastus 52, 327, 328
Aephicianus 335, 336
Aetius 359
agnosticism, as Galen's philosophical
  stance 178–9
  on the nature of the soul 185–6, 196,
    198–9, 211, 233, 280
  on physiology 280–1
  on theology 233
Agricola, Georg 370
al-Biruni 364
al-Farabi 350
al-Razi (Rhazes) 356, 360, 366
Albinus of Smyrna 4
Alcinous 206
  Didaskalikos 115
Alderotti, Taddeo 366
Aldus Manutius/Aldine Press 367,
  369–72, 386, 387
Alexander of Aphrodisias 24–5, 29, 93,
  107–8, 202, 203–4, 328, 329, 350,
  358
Alexander of Damascus 12, 29, 44, 48,
  180
Alexander of Tralles 365

Alexandria, as centre of medical studies
  243–4, 259, 263, 268, 341
  sixth-century Galenic syllabus 362–3,
    384–5
alphabetical ordering, arguments
  for/against 320–1
Ammonius 88–9, 147
anatomy
  'adventitious' 246, 259
  central role in medical study 242–3,
    257, 276, 281
  Galen's training/predecessors 242,
    243–4, 257
  Galen's writings on 36, 41, 258
  historical development 256–7, 258,
    262
  Renaissance interest in 372, 373–8
  value denied by medical schools
    246
Anaxagoras 158–9, 294
ancient world, revivals of interest in
  381
'ancients,' Galen's respect for 159,
  180–1, 204
  role in commentaries 330
Andromachus (court physician to Nero)
  312, 316
Andromachus (son of the above) 316

435

animals
  butchery 249
  extent of awareness 181
  false analogies with human
    physiology 254
  functions (of different species)
    238
  and humour theory 220–1
  processes of genesis/growth 233–4
  see also dissection; instinct;
    vivisection
Annia Faustina 15–16, 30
Anonymus Londinensis 353
antidotes 312–14
  reasons for functioning 313–14
Antiochus 303
Antipater 80, 115
Antisthenes 154
apepsia (bad/no digestion), correct
    use/etymology 133, 140–1
Apollo (God), significance of name 122,
    125
Apollonius the Herophilean 316
appearance (of patient), described by
    Hippocrates/elucidated by Galen
    343–6
Apuleius Platonicus, L., De
    interpretatione 83, 114
aqueduct (in brain) 248
Arabic, translations/commentaries of
    Galen xv, 1, 3, 86, 182, 324–5,
    328–9, 348–9, 350, 356–7, 362
Archigenes 41, 47, 64–5
Archimedes xvii
Aretaeus 359
arguments (in logic)
  indemonstrable see indemonstrables
  validity 79–83
Argyropoulos, John 367
Aristophanes 145–7
Aristotle/Aristotelian philosophy xvii,
    2, 51–3, 59, 64, 83
  coining of term 'Empiricism' 171–2
  doctrine of the soul 186–7, 189, 193,
    197–8, 200, 201, 202, 203,
    234
  and element/humour theory 211–12,
    214–15, 217, 236, 237, 238, 307–9,
    319; influence on Galen 215–16,
    218, 219–20, 221

Galen's commentaries on 43, 44, 48,
    64–5, 116, 180–1, 323, 326, 327–9;
    listed 67–8
  medical theory 56, 58, 61–3, 285,
    287; of reproduction 278
  philosophical method 168, 257, 264
  physiology 263, 265–6
  Renaissance followers 378
  teleology 225–6, 227, 229, 239
  theory of logic 73, 85–91, 94; Galen's
    dissatisfaction with 106–8
  use of language 133–4
  works (wrongly) attributed to see
    Problemata
  Categories 327
  see also actuality; categories; ethics
Arria (Platonist) 2
Ars Medica 22–3, 301
  authenticity 237
  influence xv
Artemidorus Capiton 335
arteries, operation/function 239
Articella (medieval medical selection)
    366–7
Asclepiades of Bithynia 223–4, 226,
    227, 238, 316, 351
  Against Erasistratus 331
  Galen's commentaries on 323, 325
Aspasius 27, 52, 327, 328
asplanchnos (lacking in sensibility),
    correct use/etymology 127–8
Athenaeus of Attaleia 215–16, 230, 236,
    237, 240, 351
Athenaeus of Naucratis 358
Athenodorus the Stoic 351
  Against Aristotle's Categories 331
atomism 212–13, 237, 266
Attalus, King of Pergamum 32
Attalus (Methodist doctor) see Statilius
    Attalus
Attic usage
  Galen's preference for 144–5
  move towards ('atticization') 144–5
'attraction of the specific property' 271
Aubrey, John 378
Augustine of Hippo, St 42
Averroes (Ibn Rushd) 86
Avicenna (Ibn Sina) 86, 355
  Canon 364
axioms 71–2, 79, 110–12, 115, 166, 181

Barbaro, Ermolao 368
Barnes, Jonathan 105, 113, 115, 131,
    146–7
Benedetti, Alessandro 367, 369, 374
Berengario da Carpi 375
Bessarion, Johannes 367, 370
The Best Doctor Is Also a Philosopher
    (Opt.Med.) 42–3
blood, medical theories relating to 104,
    219, 237, 238, 274–5
    experimental investigation 270
    see also arteries; menstrual blood;
    veins
bloodletting xvi, 296–7
    purpose 296–7
    specifications for use 297
    see also cupping-glass
Bobzien, Susanne 98–9, 115
Boethus, Flavius
    patronage of Galen 8, 11–13, 25
    philosophical stance 44, 48
    wife cured by Galen 2, 13–14, 23
Boudon, Véronique 1
brain
    analogy with other body parts 254–56
    etymology 133–5
    experimental investigation 247,
    249–53, 272
    medical theories relating to 46–7,
    56–8, 74, 75–83, 114, 187–8, 191,
    242–3, 260, 268–70, 277
    observation (in humans) 252
    vascular structures 253–6
    see also aqueduct; choroid plexus;
    retiform plexus; ventricles
Brasavola, Antonio Musa 373
breathing
    Galen's works on 29, 149–50, 156,
    264–5
    and nutrition 275–8
    purpose 277–8
    as voluntary activity 275–7
Brock, Arthur xvi

Caelius Aurelianus 300
Caius, John 372–3, 374, 377, 388
Callierges and Vlastos (publishing firm)
    369
Callistus 22
Caracalla, Emperor 20

Carneades, Academy of 161, 163,
    202
carotid artery
    ligature, effect of 269
    naming of 121, 135–6
categories, Aristotelian theory of 85,
    105, 107–8
cause(s)
    antecedent/preceding 230, 240, 291–2
    containing 229, 239
    distinguished from bodies/signs 299
    external 172–3, 229–30
    final 239, 266
    identification of, as
        medical/philosophical principle
        60–1, 65
    instrumental 239
    interaction 241
    role in therapeutics 291–2
    types 226–7, 266
    see also faculties; teleology
celestial bodies, as evidence of design
    234–5, 241
Celsus 35, 246, 300–1, 367
Chalcondylas, Demetrius 375
Champier, Symphorien 370
Chartier, René 371
Chaucer, Goeffrey xvi
children
    formation of character 197, 207–8
    health care 299–300
    and humour theory 221
    see also newborns
chitôn (tunic/pericardium),
    etymology/correct use 129
choroid plexus 253
chreia (need/purpose/function), of body
    parts 228–9
Christians/Christianity, influence of
    Galen on 358
Chrysippus 43, 76, 161, 236
    Galen's commentaries on 327,
    331
    theories of the soul, critiqued by
        Galen 189, 190, 192, 195–6, 207,
        268
    use/theories of language, critiqued by
        Galen 118, 123–6, 127, 128–9, 132,
        147, 148–9
Cicero, M. Tullius 163

clarity
  importance to communication 145–7
  obstacles to 147–52
  as principle of commentary 336–7,
    352
Clement, John 370
coction, processes of 254–5
Codrus, Urceus 367
Collenuccio, Pandolfo 368
colour 237
commentaries (by Galen)
  bibliography 323–32
  categories 325–6, 327
  chronology 332–6
  cited by other commentators 350
  didactic purpose 347–8
  duty to subject of commentary 338–9
  exegetical method 336–40, 343–4
  failings 339–40, 348
  influence of existing traditions
    329–30, 335–6, 349, 352
  intended audience 324
  introduction of
    post-Hippocratic/Hellenistic theory
    344–6
  lemmatology 341–7
  originality 330–2
  prefaces/introductions 341–3
  reasons for writing 333–5, 336, 337
  see also Aristotle; Hippocrates; Plato
Commentary on the Hippocratic Oath
  356
Commodus, Prince/Emperor
  Galen's medical care of xv, 15–16, 19
  personality/reign 19
  referenced in Galen's works 20–1, 32
communication
  as function of language 138–43
  Galen's regrets of need for words 140
  importance of audience 142
  threats to 152
  see also clarity
composition, as logical category 85
conflict, states of (in logic) 96–9
  incomplete 101–2
contemporaries (doctors/medical
  theorists/philosophers), Galen's
  dealings with 8–9, 13, 34–5
  Galen's criticisms of methods 23–4,
    39–42, 149–50, 155–6, 165, 291

hostility towards Galen 36, 39–40
  see also names of
    medical/philosophical schools
Cop, Guillaume 370
Cornarius, Janus 377
correctness of names 118–43, 155
  debate on existence 126, 129
  external/internal 127–9, 130, 153–4,
    155
  importance of issue 137–43
  (lack of) medical relevance 129–32,
    137–8, 155
  role of common understanding 121,
    145
  typology 120–1, 152
  see also misnomers
Corti, Matteo 374, 375, 376
Crafftheim, Crato von 372–73
cupping-glass 173, 183
Cynic philosophy 14, 30
  see also Diogenes the Cynic

da Monte, Giambattista 373, 376, 387
Dante (Alighieri) xv–xvi
Daremberg, Charles 380
de Boer, Wilko xx
de Lacy, Phillip xx–xxi, 77, 205
Debru, Arnelle 178, 223
definition, role in diagnostic method
  59–60, 167–8
Deichgräber, Karl 380, 389–90
Demiurge, Galen's notion of 218,
  227–8, 233–4, 239, 266
Democritus 263, 294
demonstration(s) 69–75
  defining features 70–4
  Galen's works on 66–7, 116
  importance in medicine 165–9, 264
  importance in study of logic 91,
    100–5, 158
  ingredients for success 79–83
  see also public demonstrations
Descartes, René xvi
diaeresis see division
diagnosis
  Galen's (descriptions of) successes
    5–11, 15–19
  Galen's methods 16–17, 59–62
diatritos see three-day fast
Didius Julianus, Emperor 20

Diels, Hermann 379
dietetics 304
Dieuches 236
digestive system 273–5
    processes 133
    regulation of nourishment 274–5
Diocles of Carystus 236, 285, 294, 296, 298
Diogenes of Babylon (the Stoic) 76–7
Diogenes the Cynic 3
diorismos (qualification/specification), role in therapeutics 289–90
Dioscorides 335, 359, 368–9
    Materia Medica 316, 320–1
disease(s)
    defined 230–1, 240, 290
    degree of severity 175, 296
    four-point diagnosis 290–1
    prevention see health
    remedies 296–7
    types 238, 295
'dispositions', and disease 230–1
dissection (as practised by Galen)
    12–13, 38, 162, 190–1, 249–52, 263–4
    abandonment by Galenists 363
    of the brain, described 250–2
    faulty (by others) 135
    function 56
    importance to medical knowledge 247, 263
    introduction into medieval syllabus 366
    pride in own skill 248
    problems of 376–8
    Renaissance practice 373–5
    see also vivisection
division, logical method 59–60, 170
    applied to medicine 168, 289
doctors see contemporaries, Galen's dealings with; medicine
'Dogmatists,' Galen's criticisms of 291–2
    see also Rationalist school
dreams, significance in Roman culture 30
drugs
    ancient/literary usage 306, 319
    attitudes towards 304

catalogued 310–11
compound 173, 176, 305, 311–12, 313–14; theory of composition 314–15
    defined 306–8
    elementary qualities 307–9
    Galen's writings on 310–12; chronology 317–18; influence of earlier doctors 316–17
    intensity 309, 320
    problems of Galen's system 314–15, 317
    properties/powers 307–12, 319, 320; determination 177–8, 222, 316
    theory vs. practice 305, 314–17
    types 306–7
    see also pharmacology; purgatives
'dummy' names, Galen's use of 142
dunameis (capacities/powers) see drugs; powers; faculties; soul: parts

Eastern Mediterranean, Galen's travels in 4–5, 14, 15, 27
Edelstein, Ludwig 380
education
    see also Galen, biography; Galen, works; universities
education, role of language in 142–4
egô, etymology 123–6
elementary qualities 61
elements/element theory 211–17, 218, 225
    affectibility 213–14
    blending 217
    composition of substances 216
    defined 212
    and disease cures 237
    Galen's development of 215–17
    misconceptions 220
    opponents, critiqued 215–16
    reasons for number/selection 216–17
    relationship with humours 219
    single-element theory 212–14
    see also humours/humour theory
embryology 278–80
    formation of foetus 237
    limitations of knowledge 280
Empedocles 211, 263
empirical approach see peira; practical experience

Empiricist school (of medicine) 26,
    53–4, 315–16
  foundations of theory 170–3, 246
  Galen's affinities with 27, 62–3
  Galen's criticisms of 41–2, 164–5,
    285, 287–8, 291–2, 293, 323, 325
  limitations of approach 166, 175, 176,
    177–8
  moderate vs. hard-line 173
  objections to anatomy, critiqued by
    Galen 61, 246, 257
endeixis (indication), Galen's notion of
    292–4
enkephalos see brain
Eobanus Hessus 360–1
ephemeral fevers 136–7
Epictetus 154, 202, 350
Epicurus/Epicurean philosophy 65, 179,
    181, 224, 350
  Galen's commentaries on 323,
    329
Epicurus of Pergamum (Empiricist
    doctor) 335
epidemics see Hippocrates: Epidemics
Erasistratus of Ceos 10, 36, 263, 270,
    271, 285, 298
  anatomical studies 54, 243–4, 247,
    248, 257, 276
  Galen's criticisms of 40–1, 223–4,
    227, 230, 249, 266, 275, 292, 296,
    323
  On Fevers, Galen's commentary on
    325, 326, 330–1
Erasmus, Desiderius 371
essence (of medical case), as central to
    endeixis 293
ethics, Aristotelian theory of 287
etymology
  faulty/misleading 123–7, 132–7
  (limited) usefulness of study 131–2,
    152
Euclid 109–10
  Elements of Geometry 106–8
eucratic condition 309–10
Eudemus (Peripatetic philosopher) 6,
    7–9, 38–9, 44, 86
  On Discourse 327, 328
Eudemus the Herophilean (anatomist)
    244
Euripides, Medea 128, 206

evident truths 159
evil, origins of 208
excretory products 77
exercise, correct use of terms for
    141–2
eye, anatomy of 345–6
  see also optic nerve

Fabricius of Aquapendente 378
faculties 223–5
  as causes 224–5
  fundamental nature 223–4
  natural 266–7, 270–1
  psychic (of the soul) 206–7, 266
  taxonomy 266–7
The Faculties of the Soul Follow the
    Mixture of the Body (QAM) 184–5,
    196–202, 208
  polemical aim 201–2
  theoretical basis 200–1
fasting period see three-day fast
fatigue 299
Favorinus 162
fevers 302, 303
  see also ephemeral fever; Erasistratus,
    On Fevers; quartan fever
Fichtner, Gerhard 389
First World War xvi
foetus see embryology; newborn
foodstuffs, naming of 146–7
Foreest, Pieter van 372–3
'fourth figure' (in logic) 85–91, 114
  Galen's (alleged) discovery of 85–6;
    alternative theories 88–91;
    evidence against 86–8
Frede, Michael 50, 209, 211, 240

Gadaldino, Antonio 376
Galen of Pergamum
  artistic depictions 359–60, 370, 375,
    384
  biography/personality: date of death
    25; early life 1–2; education 3–4,
    157–8 (see also under
    logic/philosophy); later years 22–5,
    358–9; moral outlook 21, 23–5, 32;
    personal character 23–5; response
    to adversity 22
  contemporary reputation 358–9;   .
  geographical extent 358–9

medical career xv, 4–23, 26–7;
Imperial service 14, 321; as
physician to gladiatorial school 4,
244–5; training 3–4, 243–4, 263 (see
also contemporaries, Galen's
dealings with; diagnosis; public
demonstrations/debates)
medical theory, overoptimism of
178–80
posthumous influence/reputation
xv–xvii, 355–82; decline 375–9;
defenders' response to criticisms
377–8; in Eastern medicine 31; in
European universities 46; in
late-Antique Europe 359–66; in
medieval Europe 322, 366–7;
misconceptions in 320; modern
revivals 379–80, 381–2;
Renaissance revival 367–78 (see
also Galenism)
works: Alexandrian Syllabus (sixth
century) 362–3, 384–5;
autobiographical style/self-
presentation 6–7, 9, 14, 19, 24, 316,
334–5, 360–1; composition 16, 19,
20, 22–3; dedications 11;
destruction by fire 21–2, 322, 356;
division between technical and
polemical 34–6; medieval/
Renaissance translations 366–7,
369–72; order of composition 321;
pedagogic function 35–6, 140, 326,
347–8; published selections from
361–2; recommended order of
reading 119, 154; size of output
355–6, 361 (see also specific
titles/topics)
'Galenism'
criticisms 365–6
decline 378–9
departures from Galen's own
principles 363–5
domination of medical theory 363,
365
medieval spread 366
Galilieo Galilei xvi
García Ballester, Luis 25, 366
Gargilius Martialis, Medicines from
Vegetables and Fruits 359,
383

Gaza, Theodore 367
Gemusaeus, Hieronymus 376
geometry
importance in Galen's thought 47–8,
51–2, 158, 169, 326
presentation of proofs 106–8
relationship with medicine 54–5, 62,
166–7
Germany, Galen studies in 379–81
Gibbon, Edward 20
Gippert, J. 383
Glaucon 5–6, 286
God
as craftsman 237
Galen's view of 233–5
see also Demiurge
grammar/oratory, Galen's works on
116–17
Greek language
correctness of usage 138–9, 143–52,
167–8
limitations 140–2
reasons for use 145–52
surviving manuscripts in 357
see also Attic
Greek peoples, Galen's identification
with/writing for 20
Grice, H.P. 99
Guinther von Andernach 375

Hadrian, Emperor 243
Hankinson, R.J. 130–1
Harvey, William xvi, 257, 378
head
injuries 252, 277
pains, causes of 294
headless creatures 133–4
health (preservation of) 297–300
causes of disturbance 299
as doctor's preserve 298
heart, medical theories relating to 56–7,
74, 75–83, 128–9, 135–6, 187–8, 267,
269–70
see also pericardium
Heiberg, J.L. 379
Helmreich, Georg xx
Heraclitus 211
Heras of Cappadocia 316
herbs, investigations into 363–4
see also foodstuffs

Herophilus of Alexandria 16, 41, 257,
    261, 285, 294, 351
anatomical studies 54, 243-4, 247,
    248, 253-4, 263
on observable phenomena 58-9
Against Hippocrates' Prognostic 331
Hippocrates/Hippocratic doctrine xvi,
    xvii, 16, 20, 117, 278
on anatomy 258, 263
authenticity of works 341-2
and element/humour theory 210,
    211-14, 217, 236-7, 307-8
Galen's commentaries on 37, 43, 55,
    176-7, 180-1, 284, 323, 324-6, 330,
    332-6, 337-48, 355; reinterpreta-
    tions/misrepresentations in 40,
    334-5, 336, 339-40
Galen's (professed) reverence for 52-3
influence on Galen's beliefs/medical
    theory 162, 167, 176
late-Antique/medieval reputation
    (compared with Galen's) 359-61
other commentaries on 335-6, 346-7
pharmacology 319
(alleged) physiological theory 273,
    319
Renaissance study 379, 380
on the soul 185, 186-90, 193, 200
therapeutics 285, 289, 296, 297-8
use of language 116, 135, 143-4, 146,
    150, 155-6
Aphorisms 288, 304, 318, 324
Epidemics 342-3, 352
On Sacred Disease 204
Prognosticon 294, 338-40, 343-6
see also *On the Doctrines of
    Hippocrates and Plato*
Hippocrates (grandson of the above)
    342
Hippolytus (Biblical commentator) 329,
    350
homeostatic systems 232-3
Homer, *Iliad/Odyssey* 306, 351
homosexuality 2
hormê, significance/translation
    205
human nature
deficiencies, medical remedies for
    199-200
Galen's view of 157, 287

Hume, David, *Dialogues Concerning
    Natural Religion* 242
humours/humour theory 214, 217-23,
    237
defined 219
imbalance 219-21
misapplication of theory 219-21
natural *vs.* acquired properties 222
and pharmacology 308-9, 310
problems of theory 237
purging 218-19
Hunain ibn Ishâq 325, 328-9, 348, 356,
    366, 381
hypomnêmata (privately circulated
    commentaries) 51-2, 63, 324-6
Galen's account of production 326-7
use of term 325-6, 349
useful purpose 337

Ibn al-Baitar 364
Ibn al-Salah 86, 88
Ibn an-Nafis 363
Ibn Butlan 365
Ibn Falaquera 360
Ibn Ridwan 365
Ibn Rushd see Averroes
Ibn Sina see Avicenna
'if', in conditional statements 95-6,
    97-8
Ilberg, Johannes 23
imbalance, as distinguishing feature of
    disease 295, 303
treatment with drugs 309
see also humours
inconsistency, as feature of Galen's
    commentaries
on drug use 314-15
ironed out by later commentators
    364-5
on logic 104
on the nature of the soul 184, 194,
    196-201, 202
on therapeutics 301
on use of language 138, 152-4
indemonstrables (in Stoic theory of
    logic) 92-3, 94-8, 100
first indemonstrable 95-7, 112
see also third indemonstrable
India (modern), medical methods 31
indication see *endeixis*

individual cases, need for individual
    judgment 288–91
induction, (limitations as) diagnostic
    method 168–9
inference, modes of 183
innate heat, theories of 271, 273, 275,
    277, 344–5
instinct, Galen's commentaries on 162
intensity, measurement 309–10
    see also disease; drugs
Introduction to Logic (Inst.Log.) 70,
    83–5
    corruption of text 105, 112, 115
    treatment of relational syllogisms
        105–13
    'irrational,' double/false meaning 148–9

Jewish citations/commentaries on
    Galen 356–7
Johannes de Sancto Amando 361, 384
Judaeo-Christian theology 228
Julian 37
Julian (contemporary doctor) 174
Justinian, Emperor 365
Justus, wife of 10, 28

knowledge, human capacity for
    attaining 158–62
Kühn, Karl Gottlob xvi, xix–xx, 83–4,
    371, 379

lacunae (in Galen's texts) 1
Laguna, Andreas 375
language
    ambiguity 140–2, 156
    function 138–43
    Galen's philosophy of 117–54
    Galen's pride in correct use 138
    importance of correct view 119–20
    limitations 140–3
    list of Galen's works on 116–17
    misuse 119–20 (see also solecisms)
    see also correctness of names; names
Larrain, C. 383
law, demonstrations in 101
Leibniz, Gottfried Wilhelm 83
Leoniceno, Niccolò 367–9, 386, 387
letters, significance of 121, 124,
    155
Linacre, Thomas 370, 371, 375

liver
    disease, diagnosis of 5–6
    and embryology 279
    medical theories relating to 57, 64,
        127–8, 187–8, 193, 268, 269–70,
        274–5
Lloyd, G.E.R. 209
logic 66–113
    ancient, Galen's criticisms of 74–5
    application to medicine 69–70, 73,
        74–5, 291
    Galen's stature in study of 105, 113
    Galen's training in 68, 105–6, 157–8
    hypothetical 91–105, 112
    importance in Galen's thought 68–70
    list of Galen's works on 66–8
    relationship with language 117–18
Lonie, I.M. 40
Lucian, Lexiphanes 145
Lucius Verus, Emperor 14–15
lungs, anatomy/physiology 254–5,
    275
Lupset, Thomas 370
Lycus the Macedonian 37–8, 243, 257,
    259, 335, 346, 351

magnetism 224
Maimonides, Moses 360
malaria see quartan fever
malformations 240
mammary gland, analogy with brain
    254
man, naming of 120, 121
Manardi, Giovanni 369–70
Marcus Aurelius, Emperor xv, 14, 21,
    321
    death 19
    illness 17–19, 31
    praise/patronage of Galen 18–19
Marinus 257
    Galen's commentaries on 41, 47, 244,
        351
Marquardt, Joachim xx
Martialius, confrontations with Galen
    11, 29, 36, 37
Mates, Benson 98
mathematics 158
    see also geometry
Matthioli, Pietro Andrea 377
Medici family 367

medicine
  agreed starting points 167–9
  contemporary methods, critiqued by
    Galen *see* contemporaries
  lack of precision 175–6
  linguisticians' neglect of 131–2
  naming of parts/concepts 126–7,
    129–43
  schools of thought *see* sects
  as stochastic art 175, 238
  theoretical foundations, need for
    empirical confirmation 170 (*see
    also* practical experience)
  theory, history/branches of 40–2
  training in *see* Galen, medical career;
    universities
  tripartite division 304, 318
medieval period/culture *see* Galen,
  posthumous reputation; Galen,
  works; universities
Melanchthon, Philip 375, 376–7
Menodotus, *To Severus* 326
menstrual blood, role in formation of
  human/animal body 218
Mercado, Luis 372–3
method, as basis of Galen's approach
  287–8, 301
  Renaissance interest in 372–3
Methodist school (of medicine) 26, 246
  Galen's criticisms of 14, 27, 40, 41–2,
    53, 59, 173–5, 176, 183, 257, 285,
    287–8, 291–2, 293, 323, 325
  medical principles 246
  treatment methods (contrasted with
    Galen's) 15–16, 30, 300
methodology 49–63
  intellectual background 50–3
  medical 55–9
mind, definition/location 76–7, 81–3,
  114
misnomers 129, 155
  see also solecisms
Mithridates VI of Pontus 312–13, 321
Mnesitheus of Athens 168, 236, 289,
  298
monism 212–14
Moore, George 163
Moraux, Philippe 328
More, Thomas 370
motion, transmission of 235

The Movement of the Chest and Lungs
  12
Mueller, Ivan xx, 63, 326
muscles, and voluntary activities
  276–7, 280–1
Mynas, Minoïdes 84, 86

names, appropriateness of 120–37, 155
  see also correctness of names;
    misnomers
nasal passages 248
'natural criteria' 162–5, 181
nature, as Artist 234
Nemesius of Emesa 360
neologisms 142–3
Neoplatonism 239
Nero, Emperor 312
nerves, Galen's study of 12–13, 55–8,
  272
  see also optic nerve
newborn babies, instincts 162
Niccolò da Reggio 357, 366
Nicon of Pergamum (father of Galen) 2,
  3–4, 6, 30, 51, 68
Numisianus 4, 26, 39, 243, 244, 335
Nutton, Vivian 22, 23, 25, 202–3, 208

oil, properties 238
old age/people
  health care 300, 303
  and humour theory 221
On Affected Parts (Loc.Aff.) 5–6, 23
On Anatomical Procedures (AA) 19,
  357
On Ancient Medicine 35
On Antecedent Causes (CP) 182
On Antidotes (Ant.) 22, 312, 321
On Bones for Beginners (Oss.) 36
On Containing Causes (CC) 229
On Demonstration (Dem.) 49, 69–70,
  74, 190–1, 328, 356
On Hippocrates' 'Epidemics'
  (Hipp.Epid.) 35, 342–3, 352
On Hippocrates' 'Prognostic'
  (Hipp.Prog.) 338–40, 343–6
On His Own Opinions (Prop.Plac.) 23,
  24–5, 183, 196, 199, 202–3
  surviving manuscripts 357
On Medical Experience (Med.Exp.) 171,
  182

On Mixtures (Temp.) 298, 310
On My Own Books (Lib.Prop.) 1, 35,
    50-1, 323-33
On Prognosis (Praen.) 6-11, 356
    publication 19
On Propositions Missed out in the
    Expression of Demonstrations 79
On Propositions With the Same
    Meaning 93-4
On Remedies Easy to Prepare (Rem.)
    312
On Sects for Beginners (SI) 35
On Slander 7, 19
On Substitute Drugs (Suc.) 312
On the Art 35
On the Composition of Drugs according
    to Kind (Comp.Med.Gen.) 311,
    314-15, 321
On the Composition of Drugs according
    to Places (Comp.Med.Loc.) 311,
    321
On the Correctness of Names 118-20,
    123-7, 138, 154
On the Doctrines of Hippocrates and
    Plato (PHP) 264, 268-70, 332
    composition/publication 19
    on language 123-7
    on methodology 49, 55-8
    on the soul 184-98, 204-5
    structure/theoretical aims 188-90
On the Elements according to
    Hippocrates (Hipp.Elem.) 211
On the Movement of the Thorax and
    Lungs 258
On the Natural Faculties (Nat.Fac.)
    264, 270-1
On the Nature of Man (HNH) 35
On the Power of Centaura 312
On the Power of Cleansing Drugs
    (Purg.Med.Fac.) 311-12
On the Powers and Mixtures of Simple
    Drugs (SMT) 169-70, 310-11
On the Preservation of Health (San.Tu.)
    284-5, 298, 300
On the Properties of Foodstuffs
    (Alim.Fac.) 284-5
On the Pulse for Beginners (Puls.) 35-6
On the Therapeutic Method (MM)
    22-3, 284, 286, 288-93, 295
    composition 19

influence xvi
    on methodology 49-50, 59-62
    philosophical commentary 159
On the Utility of the Parts (UP) 184-5,
    226, 264, 267
    composition/publication 19
On Theriac to Pamphilianus 321
On Theriac to Piso (Ther.Pis.) 22, 296,
    312
    authenticity 321
On Things Said in Many Ways 118
opium, natural qualities 222
Opizzoni, Professor 370
Opportune Moments in Diseases
    (Morb.Temp.) 153
opposites, as principle of cure 61
optic nerve 235, 247-8, 272
The Order of My Own Books
    (Ord.Lib.Prop.) 1
organisms, functional unity 267
organs, bodily
    formation (in embryo) 278-80
    functions 265-6
    shared function 269
Oribasius xv, 359
Origen 329, 350, 358

pain, causes of 212-13
paradisjunctions 98
paroxysm, defined 31
passion(s)
    debates on 194-6
    Galen's discussion of 193-7, 206-7
The Passions of the Soul (Aff.Dig.)
    22-3
Paul of Aegina 359
peira (empirical testing), role in medical
    theory/practice 176-8, 315-16
Peitholaus (tutor of Commodus) 16
Pelops 4, 39, 171, 243, 335
penis, construction of 2-3
Perennis 21, 32
Pergamum 1-2, 4, 13-14, 32, 244-5
    archaeological discoveries 358
    gladiatorial school see under Galen:
        medical career
    natives of, presence in Rome 27
    population 25
pericardium, medical theories/naming
    129-30

Peripatetic philosophical school 10–11,
    70–1, 179, 227
  Galen's commentaries on 327, 328,
    331
  Galen's early studies/disenchantment
    with 51–2, 326
  logic 108, 115, 157–8
  theories of the soul 194, 197–8
Pertinax, Emperor 19–20
Peterson, D.W. 390
Petrus de Sancto Floro 361, 384
Pfaff, Franz 380
pharmacology, development of
    term/methods 305, 318
  see also drugs
'Philip the Empiricist' 171, 335
philosophy/philosophers 6–7, 48
  contrasted with medicine 199–200
  disputes between 51–2, 157–8, 179,
    181, 183
  Galen's attitudes to 43–5, 209
  Galen's commentaries on 50–3,
    158–62, 327–9
  Galen's training in 3–4, 62–3, 68,
    157–8
  linguisticians' neglect of 131–2
  linked with medicine 27–8, 42–5,
    210–11
  unanswerable questions 178–9
  see also logic; names of individual
    philosophers/schools
physics 210–36
  Galen's, basic principles 214–15,
    235–6
  importance to medical practice 176,
    210–11
  scope 236
physiology
  central concepts 265–7
  Galen's works on 264–5
  organizing principles 268–71
  philosophical preoccupation with
    263–4
  unresolved questions 280–1
Piso, L. Calpurnius 22
Plato xvii, 59, 155
  doctrine of the soul 185, 186–90,
    191–2, 193–4, 197–8, 200, 201;
    Galen's divergences from 198–9
  and element theory 214, 238

Galen's commentaries on 43, 47,
    52–3, 55–6, 67, 180–1, 323, 327, 331
  logical theory 90–1, 115
  medical theory 62–3, 64, 285, 289
  philosophical method 168
  physiology 263, 268, 273
  teleology 229, 239
  theology 228, 237
  vocabulary 148, 186–7
  Cratylus (on language) 120–3, 124,
    127, 133, 138, 139, 155, 156
  Republic 110–11
  see also Neoplatonism; On the
    Doctrines of Hippocrates and Plato
plêthôra (excess), as cause of disease
    296–7
Pliny the Elder (C. Plinius Secundus)
    367, 368–9, 386
pneuma, theories of 235, 239, 247–8,
    249–50, 252–3, 254–6, 260–1, 271–2,
    274–5, 344–6
  and respiratory system 275, 277–8
  and the soul 185–6, 201, 252
Pneumatism 230, 237, 291
poisons 307
  operation 235
polemic, role in Galen's works 34–7,
    43–4
Politian 367
Polybus 341, 342, 353
Pompey (Cn. Pompeius Magnus) 312–13
Posidonius the Stoic 32, 186–7, 189,
    195, 197, 200, 207, 351, 380
potentiality see actuality
practical experience
  as foundation of Empiricist system
    171–2
  Galen's overestimation of value
    178–80
  importance in Galen's medical theory
    14–16, 54–5, 64, 165–78, 179–80,
    317–18
  limitations 173
  see also peira
Prantl, Carl 86
Praxagoras 294
premises
  ambiguous 76–8, 81–3
  choice of (in investigation of the soul)
    190–1

correct formulation 75, 92–4, 118
dialectical 72, 78, 80–1
general 109–10, 111–12
inappropriate 124–6
missing 78–81, 109–10, 111–12
rhetorical 72, 124–6
role in logical demonstration 71–4
scientific 72
self-evident 72–3
single, validity of arguments based on
    115
sophistical 72, 76–7
true/false 103
types of 72–3, 124
see also axioms
principles, elements distinguished from
    214–15
print, impact on availability of works
    357–8, 369–72
Problemata (pseudo-Aristotle) 306, 307
pronoia (forethought), commentary on
    meaning 338, 352
proof(s), presentation of 106
psychological disorders 9–10, 28
Ptolemy xvii
public demonstrations/debates, Galen's
    involvement in 11–12, 19, 26–7, 36,
    37–9, 242, 244–6, 259
    termination 29, 37
    see also dissection; vivisection
Public Pronouncements in the Presence
    of Pertinax 20
pulse
    causes 224
    changes in 231–3
    correct terminology 138, 142–4,
    150–2
    as diagnostic tool 294–5
    Galen's studies of 16–18, 41, 265
    method of taking 164–5
purgatives 218–19
purpose, as causal explanation 227
Pyrrhonian scepticism
    Galen's early tendencies towards 51,
    158
    Galen's objections to 12, 158–9,
    163–4, 180

quartan fever 8–9, 28
Quintus 41, 45, 243, 335, 346

criticised in Galen's commentaries
    338, 343

Rationalist (Dogmatist) school (of
    medicine) 26, 170–3, 175, 178
    foundations of theory 172
    Galen's affinities with 26, 58, 61–3,
    69–70, 172
    Galen's criticisms of 41–2, 53–4, 176,
    217, 223
reason, human faculty of 170–8
'reasonable' propositions 261–62
Reichart, Wolfgang 367
relational syllogisms 91, 93, 105–13
    examples 109–11
    practical usefulness 105–6
    problems of definition 108, 112–13
remedies see diseases; drugs
reproduction 265, 278–80
    analogical approach 279–80
respiration see breathing
retiform plexus 253–6, 261
    physiological importance 254
Rome, Galen's relocation to/activities in
    4–14, 245–6
Rose, Edward 370
Rufus of Ephesus 39, 136, 335, 346–7,
    359

Sabinus 335, 346
Sarton, George 25
Satyrus (teacher of medicine) 4, 243,
    335
Sceptic philosophy 43
    Galen's objections to 157, 162–5, 180
    see also Carneades, Academy of;
    Pyrrhonian scepticism
Schmaus, Leonhard 370
Second Sophistic movement 144–5,
    245–6
sects, medical 26, 46, 49–50, 53–5
    debates between 170–4, 179–80
    Galen's critiques of 35, 178
    Galen's rejection of all 41–2, 350–1
    see also Empiricist; Methodist;
    Rationalist
semen 237, 278
sensory perception, evidence based in
    159–60, 182
Septimius Severus, Emperor 20, 21

Sergius of Rasaena 362
Sergius Paulus 8
Servilius Damocrates 316
sex, Galen's attitudes to 2–3
Sextus Empiricus 146, 147
    Outlines of Pyrrhonism 163, 229
Sextus Quintilius 15
Sezgin, Fuat 381
signs, diagnostic 31
similar things, distinguishing between
    159–62, 170
Simon, Max 380
Simoni, S., Artificiosa curandae Pestis
    Methodus 385
Simplicius 350
'six non-naturals' 364
sklêron, meaning/etymology 121
slaves, fortitude under torture 21, 32
smell, sense of see nasal passages
Smith, Wesley 334, 336
Socrates 120–1, 154, 239
solecisms 148–53
Sophism, Galen's criticisms of 160,
    168–70, 285
    see also Second Sophistic
Soranus 359, 381
sorcery, associated with medicine 27–8,
    45
soul
    dependence on body/temperament
        184–5, 196–8, 199–200, 201–2, 207,
        208, 209
    desiderative part 186, 193, 198
    existence 184
    Galen's vocabulary of 205, 206, 208
    natural endowment 197
    nature 184–202, 378
    parts/capacities 185–7, 188, 203,
        268–70
    physical location 187–96
    rational part 186, 198
    seat of ruling part 75–83, 123–6,
        135–6, 204–5, 250
    spirited part 186, 191–3, 194, 198
    see also agnosticism; faculties
spinal cord 248–9, 260
    experimental investigation 270
spleen, function 227
spontaneous generation, doctrine of 241
statements

causal 99–100
conditional 95–8
conjunctive 97–8
disjunctive 97–8, 102
universal 113
states of affairs
    relations between 96–100
    unrelated 103, 115
Statilius Attalus 30, 174
Statilius Crito 316
Stephanus of Athens 363
Stesichorus 128
Stoic philosophy 70–1, 179, 181
    and element theory 216, 217, 237
    Galen's commentaries on 32, 43, 68,
        323, 329
    Galen's early studies/disenchantment
        with 51–2, 326
    linguistics, critiqued by Galen 147
    logic, critiqued by Galen 70, 73, 74,
        75–83, 92–3, 94–8, 103–4, 106–8,
        112, 157–8 (see also
        indemonstrables)
    other commentaries on 350
    teleology 229, 291
    terminological disputes, critiqued by
        Galen 161
    theories of the soul 187, 189, 190–3,
        194–6, 234, 268; critiqued by Galen
        190–3, 202, 276
    see also names of individual
        philosophers, e.g. Chrysippus,
        Posidonius
Stratonicus 335
students, works aimed at see Galen,
    works: pedagogic function
stupor, induction of 252
    see also carotid
surgery, attitudes towards 304, 318
syllogisms
    'compound' 88–91
    construction 87–8
    quasi-disjunctive 91
    relational see relational syllogisms
    see also Aristotle, theory of logic;
        fourth figure; logic
Sylvius, Jacobus 375, 377
symptoms, defined 240
synonyms, (pointless) distinctions
    between 147–8

teleology 225–9, 240
  non-Aristotelian/Platonic 229–33
  and respiration 277–8
Temkin, Owsei 380
temperament
  causes of 209
  relationship with soul *see under* soul
Temple of Peace, fire in 21–2, 38
terminological disputes/niceties,
  Galen's disdain for 160–1
terra sigillata 15
testes, analogy with brain 254, 255–6
Theagenes the Cynic 30
theion (divine element), commentary on
  meaning 339–40
Theocritus 150
Theodas, *Introduction* 326
Theodotus the Shoemaker 358
theology *see* Demiurge; God
Theophrastus 52, 86, 204, 238, 386
  On Affirmation and Denial 328
therapeutics
  commentaries on Galen's approach
    283–6
  concern with preservation of health
    298
  correct starting points 167, 291
  fundamental principles 288–97
  Galen's relationship with older
    authorities 285–6
  Galen's writings on 284–6
  originality of Galen's approach
    285
  range of Galen's approach 300
  relationship between theory and
    practice 285, 286–7 (*see also*
    individual cases)
  role in Galen's career/self-image
    283–4
  tripartition 300–1
  underlying rationale 286
Therapeutics to Glaucon (MMG) 284,
  286, 293–4, 295–6
theriac 8, 28, 39, 46, 296, 312–13
  composition 313–14
  Galen's works on *see On Antidotes;*
    On Theriac to Pamphilianus; On
    Theriac to Piso
Thessalus (founder of Methodism) 24,
  53, 59, 174, 288

Thessalus (son of Hippocrates) 342
things (not words), as focus of study
  91–2, 93, 97, 126–7, 132–3, 137,
  138–43, 156
third indemonstrable (in logic) 100–5
  limitations on usefulness 101–4
  standard form 100–1
Thrasybulus 298
three-day fast, recommended by
  Methodist school 30, 288, 302
To those who criticise linguistic
  solecisms 153
touch, role in diagnosis 164
  and humour theory 221, 238
twentieth century, studies/influence of
  Galen xvi–xvii
Tyrtaeus 128

ulcers, treatment of 174–5
Ullmann, Manfred 381
universities, medical studies in 366–7,
  371–5
urine
  as diagnostic tool 294–5
  functioning of system 223–4, 271
utility, as principle of commentary
  337–8

Valla, Giorgio 367, 369, 374
veins, action of 274
venesection *see* bloodletting
ventricles (of brain)
  damage to, impact on organism
    252–3
  linked with eye 251–2
  role in motor/sensory activities
    251–2
  structure 247–56
Vesalius (von Wesel), Andreas xvi, 257,
  376–8, 388
vision, Galen's theory of 346
vivisection, Galen's use of 57, 205,
  244–5, 247, 249–52, 263, 269–70,
  276
voice, production 206, 276–7
  experimental investigation 270
voluntary *vs.* involuntary movements
  see breathing; muscles
von Staden, Heinrich 41, 325,
  344

Wallies, Maximilian 88–9
Walzer, Richard 381
Wenkebach, Ernst
    380
Whom to Purge, with what Cleansing
    Drugs and When (Cath.Med.Purg.)
    311–12
Wilamowitz-Moellendorff, Ulrich von
    379–80
Williams, Bernard 120
Willis, Thomas 257
windpipe, medical/logical theories
    relating to 75–83, 104

wine
    natural qualities 222
    peppered, use in treatments 18
Wittgenstein, Ludwig 42
women
    Galen's attitudes to 2–3, 381
    as inferior sex 2, 25
words see correctness of names; names;
    solecisms; synonyms; things
Wotton, Edward 372
wounds, hollow vs. simple 174–5

Zeno of Citium 76–7, 81–3

Made in the USA
San Bernardino, CA
28 November 2018